Travel Around the World

TRAVEL AROUND THE WORLD, by Arnie Weissmann

Director of Project Development/Project Editor—Kevin Gillespie
Editorial Director—David Gunderson
Cartographer—Richard Milk
Desktop Publisher—Kevin Callahan
International Editor—Carol Flake
North America Editor—Jeff Hill
Cruise Editor—Barbara Redding
Electronic Products Group Consultant—Magdala Poon
Testing Program—Bette Birnbaum, Bill Johnson

Travel Around the World was very much a team effort. In addition to those mentioned above, hundreds of correspondents around the world contributed to the development of the textbook. They provided the author with invaluable insights into what travelers will encounter wherever they go.

Weissmann Travel Reports also gratefully acknowledges the many educators who contributed to the development of the Travel Around the World program, including:

Debbie Adams	Kingwood College, Kingwood, Texas
Paul Ancel	Grant MacEwan Community College, Edmonton, Alberta
Bill Berg	Carlson Travel Academies
Linda Capron	American Express Travel School, Phoenix, Arizona
Jim Fraser	Holland College, Charlottetown, Prince Edward Island
Larkin Franks	Mt. Hood Community College, Gresham, Oregon
Robert Gandolfo	MTI College, Orange, California
Sonya Garwood	Cloud County Community College, Concordia, Kansas
Greg Green	Suomi College, Hancock, Michigan
Cathy Griffith-Mills	Seneca College, North York, Ontario
Patricia Harris	Van Dyck Institute of Tourism, St. Petersburg, Florida
Maeva Hofmann	Sarasota Travel School, Sarasota, Florida
Dixie Keyser	CompuCollege, Burnaby, British Columbia
Nick Marks	Central Piedmont Community College, Charlotte, North Carolina
Maria McConnell	Lorain County Community College, Elyria, Ohio
John Oatham	Empire College, Santa Rosa, California
Sonya Philpitt	Carmel Unified School District, Carmel, California
Marie Rennie	Niagara College, Niagara Falls, Ontario
Nancy Roop	Lincoln College School of Travel, Normal, Illinois
Janice Santovasi	Morse School of Business, Hartford, Connecticut
Bob Simons	Fox Valley Travel School, Fond du Lac, Wisconsin
Paul Smith	West London College/Avon House, London, United Kingdom
Sue Spatuk	Southern Alberta Institute of Technology, Calgary, Alberta
Marion Spicer	Bryan Career College, Springfield, Missouri
Sondra Stock	Pinellas Tech, St. Petersburg, Florida
Tammy Taylor	Sullivan College, Lexington, Kentucky
William Verrinder	CCI Travel and Tourism School, Memphis, Tennessee
Mary Beth Walsh	Moraine Valley Community College, Palos Hills, Illinois
David Wright	Seneca College, North York, Ontario
Tom Zitzmann	Carlson Travel Academy, Minneapolis, Minnesota

ISBN: 0-945305-45-1

Published by Weissmann Travel Reports, P.O. Box 49279, Austin, TX 78765, 800/776-0720, ext 102. (Weissmann Travel Reports is a division of Reed Travel Group.)

Printed in the United States of America. 6 5 4 3 2

Travel Around the World

A complete program for learning about geography, destinations and *selling* travel

Arnie Weissmann

Travel Around the World

Contents

List of Maps in *Travel Around the World*

Introduction

AFTER YOU HAVE BECOME A TRAVEL COUNSELOR, you will be asked to give advice about destinations you have never visited. Your clients may have been saving up for their vacation for years, and they may not get time off again for another 12 months. They are placing their trust in you to help them spend their time and money wisely.

It's a lot of responsibility. To handle that responsibility you must develop a capacity for problem solving and critical thinking. While it's impossible to "memorize the world," you can develop the skills you need to analyze any destination and determine if clients will be happy there. This textbook will help you develop those skills.

Every chapter in this book follows the same format and contains the same type of information:

♦ Clients who are looking at a particular destination will need to know **what to do there**. Does the destination match their interests and expectations? There are, for example, tremendous differences among Caribbean islands, just as there are among European cities or Asian countries. You must be absolutely positive that what your clients want to see and do is available in a destination before you send them there. Museum goers or history buffs will be disappointed if the only thing to do there is lie on a beach.

♦ It's very important to pace a vacation carefully. When you construct an **itinerary** for your clients, you'll have to allow enough time for them to get from one area to another and, equally important, allow enough time for them to see what they've traveled to see.

♦ Make it your business to determine the **climate** in a given destination and **when to go** there. You'll have to find out if the time of year your clients have available is the best time to go. Odds are they won't be as happy if you send them to a destination during a season that is too cold, too hot or too rainy.

♦ Arranging **transportation** — both to a destination and within a locale — is critical. Knowing when to put clients on a tour, a train or in a rental car can spell the difference between a terrific experience and a disaster.

♦ **Accommodations**, too, can make or break a vacation. Few vacationers will want to stay in a motel if there's a castle in the neighborhood for not much more. Nor will they be happy if their hotel is too far from the water during a beach holiday.

♦ For the majority of countries in the world, a travel agent should provide **health advisories** concerning local sanitation and medical standards. All too often travelers spend time lying sick in bed when they should be stretched out on a beach blanket.

♦ A lot of people love to shop (in fact, for some people, it's the main reason to travel). So knowing **what to buy** allows them to budget properly for souvenirs and to check prices on similar items at home to determine whether they're spending their money wisely on vacation.

♦ Knowing before departure **what there is to eat** at a destination can be very comforting to clients, especially if there are concerns about sanitation and hygiene in a particular locale. Clients should know before they leave if the range of food available includes the type of food they enjoy. They should also know about unique

A bagpiper in Scotland

Favorite destinations: A quiet beach

national and regional specialties they'll be able to sample.

♦ Two other sections in each chapter will help you prepare your clients for encounters with the people and cultures of the countries they'll visit: **Travel Tips** gives you pointers you can give to clients on what to do and not do (so they'll feel more comfortable in strange situations) and **Fascinating Facts** provides you with interesting details about customs and culture that make a destination come to life.

Taking all this information into account, you'll have to make the hardest decision of all: Will a particular destination make your clients the happiest? You may discover during your research that although your clients think they want to go to country X, your judgment tells you they really would be happier in country Y. For instance, a couple may come into your office and tell you that they want to go to the Cayman Islands because they've always wanted to go snorkeling on a lush, tropical island. During your research, you discover that there's excellent snorkeling in the Caymans, but not much in the way of lush scenery. Further research shows you that St. John in the U.S. Virgin Islands has both lush terrain and fine snorkeling. If St. John can also satisfy their other desires, it shouldn't be difficult to persuade your clients to alter their plans, especially if they sense you're acting in their best interests. When they return

from their trip happy, you will have earned their repeat business—and possibly referrals to new clients.

Three Objectives

Studying about destinations is an important part of the curriculum for any student training for employment in the travel industry. *Travel Around the World* was created specifically to serve as the key geography component in that curriculum. It is guided by three objectives:

♦ To develop a student's ability to research and assess destinations.
♦ To provide a student with the critical skills needed to determine a client's needs, interests and expectations.
♦ To improve a student's ability to sell travel by familiarizing the student with popular destinations and geographic principles. A student who learns to sell travel well will be able to satisfy future employers, too.

How this Book Is Organized

The contents of *Travel Around the World* were carefully crafted to reflect the priorities of the industry and of educators and are based on current and developing travel patterns of business and leisure travelers.

This book is divided into 50 chapters organized in eight units. The first unit introduces geography terms and concepts a travel counselor must understand to be able to match clients and destinations and to sell travel. The second unit includes five chapters covering the United States and two on Canada. In the remaining six units, we examine what draws tourists to countries in the rest of North America and other continents. More than 60 countries are covered in depth; the tourism appeal of all other countries is summarized in Geofile chapters, organized by continent at the end of the units.

Following each chapter are two pages of review and application exercises. These pages include review questions, a map skills exercise and an exercise that requires students to apply their geography knowledge to selling travel. Following each unit there are additional review exercises, including a crossword puzzle — an enjoyable way to review important concepts and facts.

(The information in this textbook was abridged from the travel counselor's editions of Weissmann Travel Reports *International Profiles*, *North America Profiles*, *City Profiles* and *Ports of Call* — subscription services that provide travel information to travel agents on thousands of destinations worldwide.)

Geography
for the Travel and Tourism Student

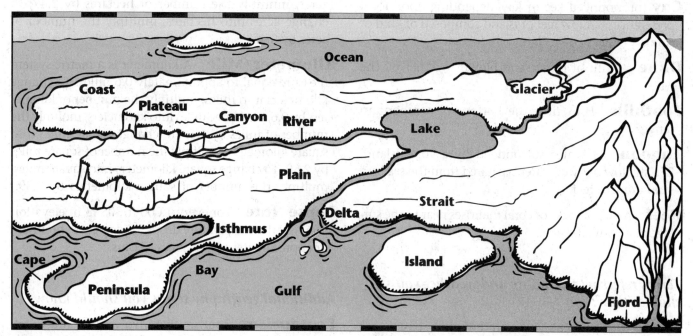

WELCOME TO THE WORLD OF PHYSICAL GEOGRAPHY! You don't need a strong background in science to understand it. Because you live with the rules of physical geography every day, you've probably already heard all the terms and concepts used in this chapter. We've kept this section short because, even though physical geography can include many fields of scientific study (oceanography, climatology, cartography, etc.), we're only concerned with the aspects of each of these that will help you as a travel counselor.

When you understand the contents of this chapter, your confidence will greatly increase. You'll soon be able to answer clients' questions such as "What's the water temperature like?" or "Is the scenery going to be lush and green, or are you sending me to a desert island?"

The Language of Geography

The following terms appear throughout this textbook and in other references you'll be using as a travel counselor. It's useful to learn the meanings of those you don't already know. First, let's look at terms that refer to some major land and water forms above. Read the definition of the term, then locate the form on the drawing above.

Bay   A body of water partly surrounded by land, with a wide opening to an ocean.

Canyon   A narrow valley with steep sides, often with a stream or river flowing through it.

Cape   A landform projecting into a sea or ocean, generally smaller than a peninsula.

Coast   The land along an ocean or sea.

Delta   Land built up by silt that has overflowed from rivers as they meet large bodies of water. Deltas are usually triangular in shape.

Fjord (fee-YORD)   A long, narrow arm of a sea bordered by high, rocky cliffs.

Glacier   Large mass of ice moving slowly down a slope. Glaciers are usually formed at heights where snow cannot melt and run off down streams.

Gulf   Part of an ocean or sea that juts into the land.

Isthmus (ISS-mus)   A narrow landform connecting larger landforms across a body of water.

Peninsula   A landform almost surrounded by water.

Plain   Large area of mostly flat, treeless land.

Plateau (pla-TOE)   An extended, flat area of land higher than land surrounding it.

Strait   A narrow passage of water connecting two larger bodies of water.

Other land and water terms you should know:

Archipelago (ar-keh-PEL-ah-go)   An island group.

Atoll   Small ring or horseshoe-shaped island formed from the remains of coral animals.

Cay (pronounced kee or kay, depending upon local preference)   A low reef or island composed of sand or coral.

Dune   A hill of loose sand blown together by the wind.

Foothills   Hills near the bottom of a mountain range.

Lagoon   1) Water surrounded by a coral island; 2) a shallow body of water separated from the sea by a sand dune or reef.

Reef   A line of rocks or coral that rises near to the surface of a body of water.

Terms referring to climate and weather you should know:

Climate   An area's year-round weather, based on a comparison of several years. Generally speaking, climate refers to a large geographical region.

Cyclone   The general name for a low-pressure, circular, violent storm system characterized by very strong winds and rains. Known as hurricanes if they materialize in the West Indies (Caribbean) and typhoons when occurring in the China Sea or western Pacific.

Monsoons   Winds found in Southeast Asia that bring rains in the summer and cool (but not necessarily cold) and dry weather in the winter.

Weather   Atmospheric condition at any given moment in a specific, fairly small location: raining, sunny, snowing, etc.

Terms referring to measurement of distance, area or temperature you should know:

Celsius (SELL-see-us)   The preferred term used when referring to Centigrade temperature. Say "18 degrees Celsius," not "18 degrees Centigrade."

Centigrade/Fahrenheit   Centigrade is a metric-system measure for determining temperature. A rough but close way to convert it to Fahrenheit (the temperature scale commonly used in the United States) is to take Centigrade temperature, double it and add 32 (approximate). To find Centigrade from Fahrenheit, reverse the process.

Hectare/Acre   A hectare is a metric-system measure of area equal to 2.47 acres. To change hectares into acres, multiply the number of hectares by 2.47; to change acres into hectares, multiply the number of acres by 0.4.

Kilometer/Mile   A kilometer is a metric-system measure equal to approximately 0.6 miles. To change kilometers into miles, multiply the number of kilometers by 0.6; to change miles into kilometers, multiply the number of miles by 1.6. (To change square miles into square kilometers, multiply the number of square miles by 2.59. To change square kilometers into square miles, multiply the number of square kilometers by 0.39.)

Lapse Rate   For every 1,000 ft/305 m in elevation you rise, the temperature drops 3.5 degrees Fahrenheit, or approximately 1.5 degrees Celsius.

Additional geography terms you should know:

Ecotourism—Tourism that involves traveling to relatively undisturbed or uncontaminated natural areas with the specific objective of admiring, studying and enjoying the area's scenery and its wild plants and animals as well as cultural features.

International Date Line   An imaginary line through the Pacific Ocean that basically follows the 180-degree longitude line (on the opposite side of the world from Greenwich Mean Time, or GMT, also called Universal Time Coordinated, or UTC), where the hours gained going east are balanced by those lost going west. If you cross it while traveling west from North or South America, you add a calendar day; if traveling east toward the Americas, you subtract a day.

Latitude   Imaginary lines circling the globe in an east/west direction (parallel to the Equator). A geographic feature's latitude is expressed by the number of degrees that it is north or south of the Equator. The climate is usually similar at latitudes that are an equal distance north or south of the Equator.

Leeward   The side of a mountain or other geographical feature that is sheltered from the wind. In the case of a mountain, the leeward side is generally drier than the windward side. The Caribbean Leeward Islands (northern part of the Lesser Antilles) are generally flatter and drier than the Windward Islands.

Longitude Imaginary lines going in a north/south (pole-to-pole) direction, perpendicular to the Equator, at intervals of 15 degrees. A geographic feature's longitude is expressed by the number of degrees it is east or west of the prime meridian, which runs through Greenwich, England. The geographic feature's exact location on a map or globe can be determined by knowing its longitude and latitude. Fifteen degrees in either direction from any longitudinal line represents a time zone change of one hour.

Time Zones For every 15 degrees longitude away from Greenwich, England, add (if going east) or subtract (if going west) one hour. Because individual countries can choose to set their clocks however they want, there are numerous exceptions to this rule.

Tropics The area bordered on the north by the Tropic of Cancer (23 1/2 degrees above the Equator) and on the south by the Tropic of Capricorn (23 1/2 degrees below the Equator). The average temperatures at sea level in the tropics are warmer than temperatures at sea level outside the tropics.

Windward The side of a mountain or other geographical feature that the wind hits. It's generally wetter and greener than the leeward side of a mountain. The Caribbean Windward Islands (southern part of the Lesser Antilles) are generally greener and more mountainous than the Caribbean Leeward Islands.

Continents

The major landmasses of the world are its continents. Islands are generally thought to be associated with the nearest continent, although islands in the Pacific Ocean not associated with a continent are collectively referred to as "Oceania" (the continent of Australia is often also included in Oceania).

Europe The landmass west of the Ural Mountains in Russia and west of the Bosporus Strait in Turkey, extending west to the Atlantic Ocean. Also includes the islands/nations of the United Kingdom, Ireland, Iceland and Malta.

Asia The landmass east of the Bosporus Strait in Turkey, east of the Ural Mountains in Russia and east of the Suez Canal in Egypt, continuing east to the Pacific Ocean.

Also includes the islands/nations of Cyprus, Sri Lanka, the Maldives, Japan, Taiwan, Indonesia and the Philippines.

Note: Because Europe and Asia are connected at the Ural Mountains, some people consider the entire landmass to be one continent, Eurasia.

Africa The landmass bordered by the Atlantic Ocean on the west, the Indian Ocean on the east, the Red Sea and Suez Canal on the northeast and the Mediterranean Sea on the north. It includes the islands/nations of the Seychelles, Comoros, Mauritius, Reunion, Sao Tome and Principe, Madagascar and Cape Verde, as well as the Canary Islands (a Spanish possession).

North America The landmass bordered by the Atlantic Ocean on the east, the Pacific Ocean on the west, the Arctic Ocean on the north and the nation of Colombia on the south. It includes Greenland, Bermuda, the Bahamas and the islands of the Caribbean Sea.

South America The landmass bordered by the Pacific Ocean on the west, the Atlantic Ocean on the east and the nation of Panama on the north. It includes the Galapagos Islands and the Falkland Islands.

Antarctica The southernmost landmass, almost entirely south of the Antarctic Circle; it's bordered on the north by the Pacific, Atlantic and Indian Oceans.

Australia The landmass bordered by the Indian Ocean to the west, south and northwest; the Timor Sea, the Arafura Sea and the Gulf of Carpenteria to the north; the Coral Sea to the east and northeast; and the Tasman Sea to the southeast.

Antarctica

Major Mountain Ranges

Major mountain ranges affect weather and climate patterns, influencing where and how populations live. For the traveler, they offer a wealth of scenic and recreational opportunities: Skiing, hiking, trekking, spectacular vistas, resorts (both rustic and deluxe) and wildlife watching are just some of the attractions.

Rockies North American range running north/south from Alaska to Mexico. The Sierra Nevada range between California and Nevada is actually part of the Rockies.

Sierra Madre (Occidental) Continuation of the Rockies chain in Mexico, running in a north/south direction.

Andes Continuation of the Rockies/Sierra Madre in South America, running in a north/south direction (primarily in Ecuador, Bolivia, Peru, Chile and Argentina).

Alps European chain running in an east/west direction (primarily in Germany, Austria, Switzerland, France, Italy and Slovenia).

Himalaya (the plural is also Himalaya, not Himalayas) Asian chain running in an east/west direction, primarily in China (Tibet), Bhutan, Nepal, India and Pakistan.

Water/Oceans

Though our planet is called Earth, it's water that covers 71 percent of its surface! The heating and cooling of oceans are major influences on climate and weather patterns. As with mountain ranges, a city's proximity to an ocean, river or lake has a profound influence on its culture and prosperity. Water and oceans provide major travel and recreation opportunities — the desire of a traveler to be near freshwater or saltwater is often the determining factor in making destination choices.

Ocean Names (descending in order of size)
1. Pacific (nearly as large as the other three combined).
2. Atlantic.
3. Indian.
4. Arctic.

Note: There is no Antarctic Ocean.

Direction of Movement
1. Oceans in the Northern Hemisphere circulate generally clockwise.
2. Oceans in the Southern Hemisphere circulate generally counterclockwise.

Major Ocean Currents
1. **Gulf Stream** Warm North Atlantic current originating in the Caribbean that helps to moderate temperatures as far north as Great Britain and Norway.
2. **Japan Current** A warm current going from the Equator past Japan, it moderates Alaska's coastal temperatures.
3. **Humboldt** Cold water along the Peruvian and Chilean coastline.
4. **California** A cold current flowing southward along the Pacific coast of North America that causes land temperatures to be fairly constant.
5. **Benguela** Cold Antarctic current along the southwest African coast.

A question commonly asked of travel agents is "What is the water temperature at the beach?" Assuming that your client will be traveling in the appropriate season to visit the beach, the relative water temperature can be determined if you as the agent understand the nature of water currents. Water currents move in a generally clockwise direction in the Northern Hemisphere and a generally counterclockwise direction in the Southern Hemisphere (see Fig. 1). The currents in the Northern and Southern hemispheres come together at the Equator along the western coasts of South America and Africa (in the Pacific and Atlantic oceans, respectively), and then have a chance to really warm up as they move westward along the Equator for the width of their respective oceans. When these currents hit a landmass again, however, they must diverge; in the Northern Hemisphere, the current follows the coastline north, and in the Southern Hemisphere, the current follows the coastline south. When the currents reach the poles, the water cools drastically.

To see how this affects beach water temperatures, let's look at the northern Pacific. Remember, the water will be moving in a clockwise direction along the Equator and has a chance to get warm as it travels from the western coast of South America to the eastern coast of Asia. When it reaches the islands and landmass of eastern Asia, it will flow north along the coast, bringing warm water to the shores of the Philippines, Hong Kong and Japan. It really won't begin to get drastically colder until it reaches the ice

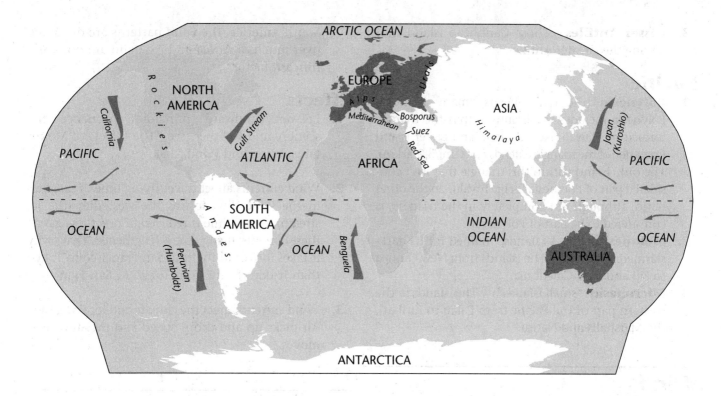

and glaciers around the northern parts of Russia and Alaska. After passing by the polar region, it begins to head south again, along the west coast of Alaska and Canada. That colder water won't warm up much until it gets back toward the Equator; in fact, the water is much colder in Los Angeles than at the southern tip of Japan, even though both places are at the same approximate latitude.

In the north Atlantic Ocean, the Caribbean Sea and the eastern coast of the United States get the benefit of the warm water (this flow of water is called the Gulf Stream). Europe's Atlantic beaches at the same latitude are much cooler.

In the Southern Hemisphere, a similar principle, but with opposite results, holds true. There, the water moves along the Equator in a counterclockwise direction. Consequently, the water along the east coast of South America, Africa and Australia is warmer than the water along the west coast of these continents (the west-coast water was cooled as it flowed by Antarctica). In smaller bodies of water, such as the Mediterranean, Caribbean, Gulf of Mexico, South China Sea, etc., there are similar, smaller currents moving in the same direction as other water in the hemisphere, but because of their smaller size, there is generally little change in water temperature. For reasons that will be discussed later, it's also important to know that oceans tend to make temperatures more moderate and air more humid along their coasts.

Island Groups

Islands, especially those in warm climates, are among the most popular destinations — the combination of sun, sand and surf appeals to just about everyone. Snorkeling, swimming, fishing, diving, sailing and the relaxing sense of getting away from it all are the main reasons people visit islands. The more frequently traveled islands offer extensive resort facilities, ranging from budget guest houses to the most luxurious accommodations anywhere. While many vacationers travel to islands as part of a visit to a mainland country (Greece and the Greek islands, for example), some islands are destinations in themselves. The most popular of these are in the Caribbean Sea and the Pacific Ocean.

Caribbean   These are islands that border (or are in) the Caribbean Sea. The Bahamas are very near the Caribbean Sea but do not technically touch it, and so are not Caribbean islands. Bermuda is far north of the Caribbean Sea and is not a Caribbean island.

1. **Antilles**   Another name for the Caribbean islands.
2. **Greater Antilles**   The largest of the Caribbean islands: Cuba, Hispaniola (the home of the countries of Haiti and the Dominican Republic), Jamaica and Puerto Rico.

Geography for the Travel and Tourism Student   5

3. **Lesser Antilles**   Those Caribbean islands not among the Greater Antilles.

Pacific

1. **Polynesia** (the term means "many islands") Polynesia includes the islands within the triangle formed by Hawaii, New Zealand and Easter Island (each side of the triangle extends 5,000 mi/3,200 km). The only island within this triangle that isn't considered part of Polynesia is Fiji. Tuvalu, on the other hand, although not completely in the triangle, is considered to be part of Polynesia.
2. **Melanesia** ("black islands," named for its dark-skinned residents)   The islands from New Guinea to Fiji and New Caledonia.
3. **Micronesia** ("small islands")   The islands in the western part of the Pacific from Palau to Kiribati, the Marshalls and Nauru.

Winds

Direction

1. Wind currents generally move west to east both above the tropics in the Northern Hemisphere and below the tropics in the Southern Hemisphere. The upper-air currents are particularly strong in these regions and are known as "westerlies," or the "jet stream."
2. Wind currents in the tropics generally move from east to west (slightly northeast above the Equator, and slightly southeast below). These steady humid winds are known as "trade winds." While they are quite noticeable on islands and in northern Australia and tropical Central and

Fiji

South America, the wind patterns are disrupted over much of Africa and Asia and are not a significant factor.

Effects

1. Leeward/windward principles influence the scenery and weather (see "The Effects of Mountains, Water and Wind," below.)

2. Wind currents affect travel/flying time. If one flies in the same direction as the westerlies (the jet stream), flying time is reduced; if one flies against these currents, flying time is lengthened. That's why it takes longer to fly from San Francisco to Tokyo than it does to fly from Tokyo to San Francisco.

3. Wind currents affect the climate and local weather. Air picks up and drops speed and moisture as it moves.

The Effects of Mountains, Water and Wind

Three major factors determine the weather, water temperature and physical conditions (arid, lush, etc.) of a destination: mountains, water currents and wind. If you understand the influences these factors have on each other, you can determine a great deal about a geographic region's characteristics.

To understand the principles, let's apply what we learned from the paragraphs above to the northern Pacific Ocean and the west coast of North America. The ocean has made the air along the coast damp. This moist air blows inland (heading east) and up against the Canadian Rockies/Sierra Nevada/Sierra Madre Mountains (which run north/south). Refer to the term "Lapse Rate" in the glossary, and you'll see that for every 1,000 ft/ 305 m in elevation, the air temperature cools 3.5 degrees F/ 1.5 degrees C. As the air cools, it drops moisture in the form of rain/snow. Moisture is important for plant life, so the western slope of the mountains becomes very green and lush. The western slope is the windward side (that's the side the wind hits); a green, lush look is typical of windward slopes in general. The opposite side of the mountain is the leeward side; the leeward slope of a mountain and the land below it tend to be dry because little moisture actually makes it over the top of tall mountains. In the case of the Sierra Nevadas, for example, the Lake Tahoe/Yosemite

National Park area in California, on the windward side, is much greener than Reno in Nevada, which is on the leeward side. This same effect occurs wherever moist air hits a mountain.

However, other factors, such as wind patterns over landmasses, must be taken into consideration. In Europe, prevailing winds and the Alps mountain range determine the terrain and climate for much of the continent. The Alps run in an east-west direction. A moist westerly wind comes from the Atlantic Ocean across Great Britain and the west coast of continental Europe and then runs smack into the sharply rising Alps. The wind begins to climb the Alps, but because of the mountains' height and conflicting air currents from northern Europe, the moist air slows and backs up onto itself. That's why fog, dampness and (often) mugginess are so common from Ireland to the Alps (and that's also why the area is so green).

In contrast, to the south of the Alps (in Albania, Greece and southern portions of Italy and the states of the former Yugoslavia), conditions are very dry — little of the moisture has made it over the mountains. Although these countries have a coast along the Mediterranean, that body of water is relatively small and doesn't produce enough moisture to have much effect on areas inland.

Trade winds affect tropical islands in a similar way. Because the winds move from the east (slightly northeast in the Northern Hemisphere, slightly southeast in the Southern Hemisphere), the east (windward) side of a mountainous island will have a greener, more lush look. But it will also be subject to more rainy weather, since the mountains have caused the air to drop moisture on that side. The west (leeward) side will be drier and look more arid. This is important to take into consideration when you book clients onto islands that are mountainous in nature; if clients are interested in lush scenery and don't mind the possibility of a fair amount of rain, book them on the east side. But if they're interested in sun, beaches or golf, most of these activities will be taking place on the western side of that island.

Taking all this knowledge into account — the direction of the water and wind, elevation (mountains), location (Northern or Southern Hemisphere, east or west side of continent, etc.) — you have a basis for advising

Utah

a client not only about the water temperature, but also about the proper clothing to take, the likelihood of rain and a little bit about the nature of the terrain.

Note: While these general patterns of air and water currents hold true in most cases and are useful as rules of thumb, there are numerous other influences (the seasons, conflicting currents, terrain, localized temperatures) that can cause exceptions to these rules.

Great Circle/Polar Routes

Travelers going from North America to other points in the Northern Hemisphere will likely fly very far north. For instance, Newfoundland (Canada), Greenland and Iceland are often flown over by carriers going between North America and Europe. On a flat map, this "polar routing" seems to make no sense — it looks as if the pilot is making the flight longer than it needs to be. But actually, these routes, known as "great circle" routes, are the shortest, and it's important for you as a travel counselor to understand this so that you can route passengers intelligently. (Great circle routes are not limited to those flying over the polar regions. The term refers to any route connecting two points on Earth that uses the shortest navigational path.)

On most flat maps, it seems that a flight originating in Los Angeles that flew to Moscow via New York and Paris would be traveling in a fairly straight line, moving

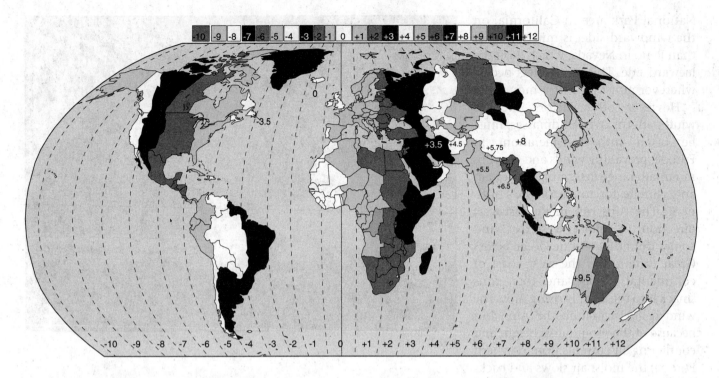

steadily east-northeast. And, on most flat maps, it seems that if the same plane flew to Moscow via Helsinki, Finland, it would be going too far out of its way to the north. But in fact, a flight via New York and Paris would spend almost 15 hours in the air, while the flight with a stop in Helsinki would take just a little over 12 hours of flying time.

To demonstrate this, take a piece of string and, on a globe (not a map), put one end on Los Angeles, then string it out to New York, then Paris, then Moscow. Cut the string to the exact length, then take that same string and, starting in Los Angeles, straighten it first to Helsinki, then Moscow. You'll see that you have some string left over.

Time Zones

If clients are traveling a great distance in an easterly or westerly direction, they'll cross one or more time zones, or possibly even the International Date Line. Crossing time zones can be very confusing to clients; they often want to know how many actual hours it will take to fly from one place to another, but if they subtract their departure time from their arrival time, they may come up with a nonsensical number. For instance, it's possible, if crossing the International Date Line heading east, to arrive in North America at a clock/date time that is earlier than the clock/date time of departure!

As you'll recall from the definitions in the glossary, a time zone change occurs every time a traveler moves 15 degrees longitude in either direction away from Greenwich, England (which, by agreement among nations, is the "starting point" of time). To determine what time it is anywhere else in the world, add one hour to the time in Greenwich for every 15 degrees east or subtract one hour for every 15 degrees west of Greenwich that you travel (*see map above*). The time in Greenwich is called Greenwich Mean Time (GMT); North America's Eastern Standard Time (EST) zone is 75 degrees west of Greenwich, which means EST is five hours earlier than GMT (75 divided by 15 = 5). Therefore, EST's time designation is -5 GMT.

There are numerous exceptions to the 15-degree rule. For instance, all of China sets its clocks to the time in its capital, Beijing. India sets its clocks one-half hour off from most of its neighbors, and Nepal decided to be ten minutes off from India! And just to make it more complicated, daylight saving time, when clocks are adjusted by one hour for summer, is observed in some areas but not in others.

In the Pacific, exactly halfway (180 degrees) around the world from Greenwich, is an imaginary longitudinal line (that zigs and zags around certain islands and landmasses) that is both 12 hours ahead of and 12 hours behind GMT. This line is called the International Date Line. If you cross it while traveling west from North or South America, you continue to subtract an hour, but you add a day to the date. If you're traveling east toward the Americas, you add an hour but subtract a day from the date.

So, to calculate the time in the air — the elapsed flying time — one would need to take into account the number of time zones crossed between the departure city and arrival city, the difference between the published departure and arrival times, the exceptions to the normal progression of time zones and the crossing of the International Date Line! Even with the help of world time charts, which are available in various travel industry references, this can be very tricky. Fortunately, a travel agent's computer reservation system (CRS) lists the elapsed flying time of published flights, and if a CRS is not available, you can always call an airline's reservation agent for the elapsed flying time of any of its flights.

It's also important for you to be aware that, when travelers take long trips and cross many time zones, it takes a while for their bodies to adjust their "internal clock" to the clock time of the arrival city. This "jet lag" can have an exhausting effect, upsetting sleeping patterns and mental alertness for several days.

Reading Maps in this Book

In each chapter of this textbook, you'll encouter maps. An understanding of the information presented in the maps will strengthen your knowledge of travel and tourism.

The map of England and Wales above is typical of the maps in this book. In the top right-hand corner is the map key. It tells you what the symbols stand for on the map. For example, the symbol for capital city is ✪. (The capital city in this case is London.) The ■ symbol identifies the location of other cities, such as York and Liverpool. Locate them on the map. Now look for the symbol ▲. It stands for national park. There is one national park identified on the map. Can you find it? (Answers to questions asked in this section on reading maps are at the end of the section.) A castle 🏰 and a ruin ∴ are also identified. What are their names?

The heavy black line identifies the political boundaries between countries, states or provinces. Regions within countries are indicated by terms in all caps, and the dotted line shows the course of rivers. What is the

name of the river shown on the map? The direction north on the maps is always toward the top of the page.

At times, you may also want to use the map scale to find distances between tourist sites. Using the scale, you'll see that the distance between London and Cambridge is about 50 miles/80 kilometers. Now find the distance between London and Birmingham.

(**Answers:** *Park*—Lake District National Park; *Castle* — Windsor; *Ruin* — Stonehenge; *River* — Thames; *Distance* — a little greater than 100 miles/161 kilometers.)

Geography for the Travel and Tourism Student

Part A

Match the definitions in Column A with the correct terms from Column B.

Column A

_____ **1.** Land built up by silt that has overflowed from rivers as they meet large bodies of water.

_____ **2.** A narrow landform connecting larger landforms across a body of water.

_____ **3.** A low reef or island composed of sand or coral.

_____ **4.** Large mass of ice moving slowly down a slope.

_____ **5.** The general name for a low-pressure, circular, violent storm system characterized by very strong winds and rains.

_____ **6.** Imaginary lines circling the globe in an east/west direction (parallel to the Equator).

_____ **7.** A long, narrow arm of a sea bordered by high, rocky cliffs.

_____ **8.** A narrow passage of water connecting two larger bodies of water.

_____ **9.** The side of a mountain or other geographical feature that is sheltered from the wind.

_____ **10.** A narrow valley with steep sides, often with a stream or river flowing through it.

Column B

canyon
cape
delta
monsoon
glacier
isthmus
windward
plateau
strait
archipelago
cay
dune
lagoon
longitude
cyclone
typhoon
fjord
hectare
latitude
leeward

Part B

1. If a Caribbean island is mountainous, is it likely to have lush areas? Why or why not?

2. If it's 2 pm in New York City (-5 GMT), what time is it in Paris, France (+1 GMT)? in Sydney, Australia (+10)?

3. Would the water be warmer for swimming along the New Jersey coast or near Los Angeles? Why?

4. How many degrees (Fahrenheit and Celsius) does the temperature drop for every 1,000 feet of elevation?

5. If the daytime average temperature during the month your clients arrive at their destination is 32 degrees Celsius, what kind of clothing would you suggest that they bring? If it's 32 degrees Fahrenheit, would you change your advice? In what way?

Part C

Refer to the map of Belize to answer these questions.

1. What is the capital of Belize?

2. What national park is shown on the map?

3. What ruin is located north of Belize City?

4. What country borders Belize on the south?

5. About how far is it (in miles and in kilometers) from Dangriga to Xunantunich?

Arctic Ocean

Alaska
(U.S.A.)

GREENLAND

CANADA

Ottawa

PACIFIC OCEAN

UNITED STATES

Washington, D.C.

ATLANTIC OCEAN

MEXICO

Gulf
of
Mexico

Caribbean Sea

Hawaii (U.S.A.)

The United States, Canada and Greenland

✪ Capital

━━━ International Boundary

─── State or Provincial Boundary

Km 0 150 300   600

Mi 0   150   300   600

Copyright Weissmann Travel Reports

United States, Canada
and Greenland

THE NUMBER AND VARIETY OF TOURIST attractions in the United States and Canada could fill a lifetime of vacations. From the Native peoples' totem poles in British Columbia to the high-tech entertainment machine that is Disney World, the creations of man are well represented. And from the bottom of Death Valley in California to the towering peaks in Jasper National Park in Alberta, the wonders of nature, too, find full expression. Majestic mountain ranges, sprawling deserts, thousands of miles of coastline, scores of dynamic cities, world-class museums and a unique blend of the world's cultures make these two countries vacation destinations with endless appeal.

A nation of more than 260 million people, the United States is spread across the width of North America and also includes the states of Alaska and Hawaii. The United States is made of up several regions. In this unit, we look at the country in five chapters, each covering a different region. The United States offers tourists countless attractions from great cities like New York and San Francisco, to fabulous resorts such as Disney World in Orlando and the MGM Grand Hotel/Casino in Las Vegas, to beautiful national parks, among them Yosemite and Yellowstone.

Canada is larger than the United States in area, but has a population of only 29 million. Most Canadians live in the southern part of the country, which has a warmer climate. Each of its 10 provinces and 2 territories has its own personality: Beautiful British Columbia has cities with a Victorian charm, while French-Canadian culture blossoms in the province of Quebec. The Yukon Territory is filled with reminders of Gold Rush days, while the Atlantic Coast provinces have some of the most charming fishing villages in North America.

Just east of northern Canada is the world's largest island, Greenland. This huge, icy wilderness is governed by Denmark.

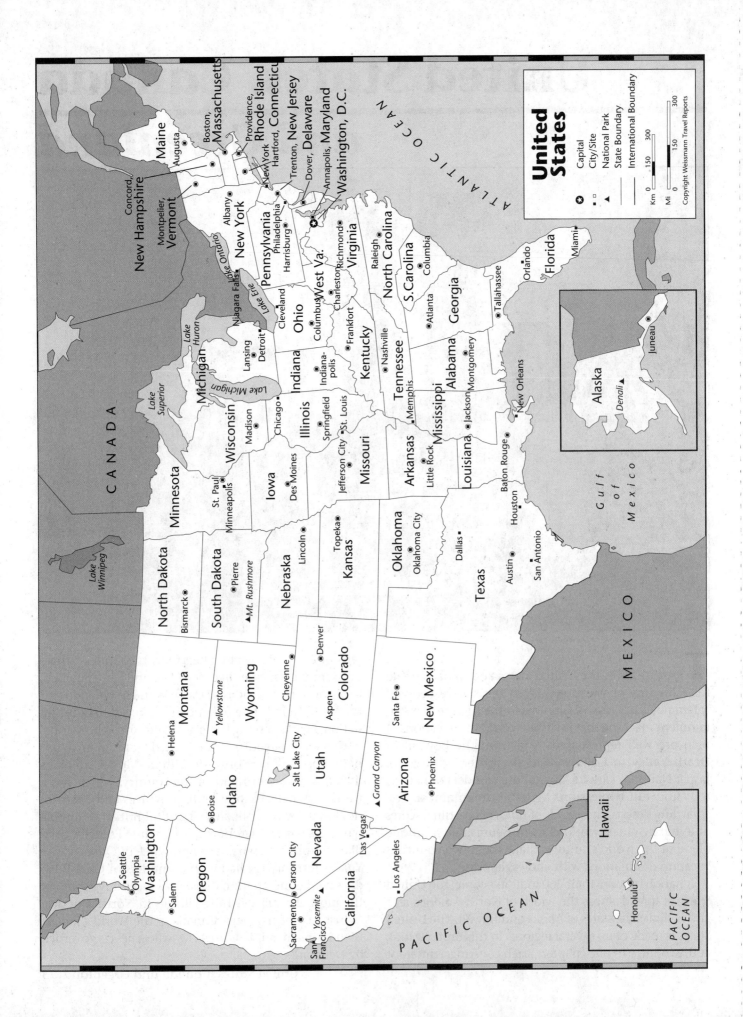

United States

- ✪ Capital
- ■ City/Site
- ▲ National Park
- — State Boundary
- ━ International Boundary

Km 0   150   300
Mi 0   150   300

Copyright Weissmann Travel Reports

CANADA

ATLANTIC OCEAN

Maine
Augusta ■

New Hampshire
Concord ■
Montpelier ■ Vermont

Boston, Massachusetts
Providence, Rhode Island
Hartford, Connecticut
New York
Trenton, New Jersey
Dover, Delaware
Annapolis, Maryland
Washington, D.C.

Albany ■
New York

Lake Ontario
Lake Erie
Niagara Falls

Pennsylvania
Harrisburg ■ Philadelphia ■

West Va.
Charleston ■
Richmond ■ Virginia
Raleigh ■
North Carolina
Columbia ■ S. Carolina

Florida
Orlando ■
Miami ■

Cleveland ■
Ohio
Columbus ■ Frankfort ■
Kentucky
Nashville ■
Tennessee

Georgia
Atlanta ■
Tallahassee ■

Alabama
Montgomery ■

Lake Huron
Lake Superior

Michigan
Lansing ■ Detroit ■
Lake Michigan

Indiana
Indiana-polis ■

Illinois
Springfield ■ St. Louis ■

Wisconsin
Madison ■
Chicago ■

Minnesota
St. Paul ■
Minneapolis ■

Iowa
Des Moines ■

Missouri
Jefferson City ■

Arkansas
Little Rock ■

Mississippi
Jackson ■

Louisiana
Baton Rouge ■
New Orleans ■

Memphis ■

North Dakota
Bismarck ■

South Dakota
Pierre ■
▲ Mt. Rushmore

Nebraska
Lincoln ■

Kansas
Topeka ■

Oklahoma
Oklahoma City ■

Texas
Dallas ■
Austin ■
San Antonio ■
Houston ■

Lake Winnipeg

Montana
Helena ■

Wyoming
Cheyenne ■
▲ Yellowstone

Colorado
Denver ■
Aspen ■

New Mexico
Santa Fe ■

Idaho
Boise ■

Utah
Salt Lake City ■
▲ Grand Canyon

Arizona
Phoenix ■

Nevada
Carson City ■
Las Vegas ■

Washington
Seattle ■
Olympia ■

Oregon
Salem ■

California
Sacramento ■
San Francisco ■
▲ Yosemite
Los Angeles ■

Gulf of Mexico

MEXICO

Alaska
Juneau ■
Denali ▲

Hawaii
Honolulu ■

PACIFIC OCEAN

PACIFIC OCEAN

New England

New England is famous for its natural beauty and its place in colonial history. Yellow and orange foliage splashes the hills of the region every fall, drawing thousands of people from all over the world. Revolutionary War monuments and artifacts make the region a kind of walk-in, live-in history book. On every trip to Boston, it seems, we end up visiting at least one of the stops on the Freedom Trail.

But our real fascination with the region is the people, who are aware of the history around them but are truly living in a contemporary world. Many of them can trace their families back to the hardy colonists who first settled the area — and will be glad to spin yarns about them. But many other residents have been drawn from around the nation and the world by the area's renowned schools, its high-tech industries and its reputation as a wonderful place to live. This mix of people, in fact, is what has made Boston one of the most cosmopolitan, sophisticated cities in the world.

Travelers can easily find enough to see and do — and enough people to meet — to spend two weeks in the region.

What to Do There

Connecticut

Connecticut is a small yet diverse state, combining urban life with pastoral serenity. It will appeal to a broad spectrum of travelers and offers activities ranging from hikes in the foothills of the Berkshire Mountains to deep-sea fishing off its coastline to pre-Broadway theater runs. Among the state's many attractions are the P. T. Barnum Museum in Bridgeport (everything about the circus), outstanding historic homes (including fine examples of colonial architecture in Litchfield) and the country's oldest statehouse in Hartford.

Mystic There's plenty for kids of all ages to see at the Mystic Seaport Museum (a re-created seaside village with ships, artisans and cruises), Olde Mistick Village (shops and restaurants), Memory Lane Doll and Toy Museum and Mystic Marinelife Aquarium (where you can see the penguins being fed). Not to be missed is the Old Lighthouse Museum (with a view of Long Island Sound and three states from the top of the circular staircase).

Selling Points

Boston, fall foliage, colonial history, lobster, skiing, antiques, Acadia National Park, arts and cultural events, maple syrup, beautiful coastline and covered bridges are among New England's main attractions.

Travelers interested in U.S. history, quaint towns, scenic beauty and outdoor recreation will be happy almost anywhere in New England. But for those who need the stimulation of the big city, there's really only one place to go: Boston.

Fascinating Facts About New England

Puffin-watching (it's a penguin-like seabird) has become a major pastime in Maine, especially in June and July at their breeding grounds . . . Portsmouth, Rhode Island, has a memorial to the U.S.'s first African-American regiment, which fought in the battle of Rhode Island in 1778 . . . The Haskell Free Library and Opera House in Derby Line, Vermont, is the only theater in the world where the stage is in one country (Canada) and the seats are in another (the U.S.). . . .

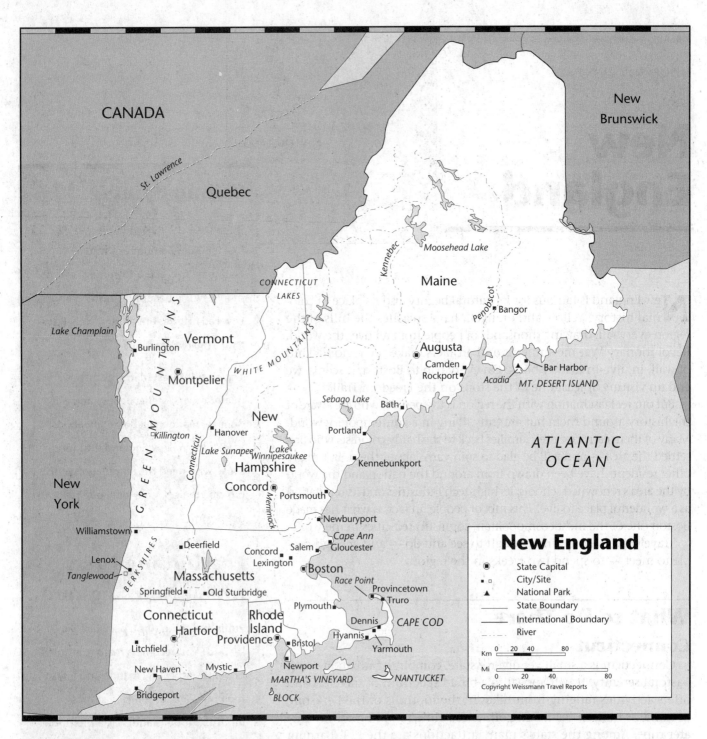

New England

State Capital
City/Site
National Park
State Boundary
International Boundary
River

Km 0 20 40 80

Mi 0 20 40 80

Copyright Weissmann Travel Reports

New Haven Most people associate this city with Yale University — and if you stick to the university area, you'll enjoy the city. The campus has two important museums: The Center for British Art houses an impressive collection in many media (the building is special, too — it has translucent marble walls) and the University Gallery (it has as an enormous and wide-ranging collection). During your visit also try to see the excellent Peabody Museum of Natural History.

While the days of the pre-Broadway show have changed, the area has several important theaters: the Yale Repertory Theatre and the Long Wharf in New Haven, the Hartford Stage Company in Hartford and the Goodspeed Opera House (specializing in musicals — both new and revivals) in East Hadda.

Maine

The unspoiled beauty of Maine usually makes visitors think that time has slowed down. The state will surely appeal to anyone who seeks a break from the hustle and hassles of big-city life. But don't be surprised if you run into a slew of other escape artists in the state's tourist centers (Portland, Bar Harbor, Kennebunkport). Maine's popularity as a vacation spot is growing every year.

Even if the pace seems relaxed, there's plenty to do: downhill and cross-country skiing (in winter months) as well as hiking, hunting, canoeing, fishing (including deep-sea), river rafting and sailing almost year-round. The fall foliage is spectacular.

Acadia National Park   Acadia is the second most popular national park in the United States. That can sometimes mean big crowds in the summer. But we think it's worth it. This spellbinding preserve is a combination of spruce forests, rocky coasts (with cliffs), placid bays and intriguing little islands.

Portland   What makes a stroll along the cobblestone streets of Portland's restored waterfront so pleasant is that it doesn't have that gussied-up-for-the-tourists feeling that sinks so many historic towns. The atmosphere is authentic — the shops and restaurants may survive in large part on tourist dollars, but the fishing boats tied up in the harbor go out each morning and return with a full load.

Of special interest to us is the Children's Museum of Portland—it shouldn't be missed. Among its features is a camera obscura, a periscopelike device that gives visitors a panoramic view of Portland. (Adults may be as awestruck by the camera as the kids!)

Massachusetts

Sometimes we think something historically significant happened on every square inch of Massachusetts. A hotbed of revolution against the British in the late 1700s, it was the state where the Minutemen first organized for the battles of Lexington and Concord and local residents dressed up for the Boston Tea Party. The state has a wide selection of historic sites, including 18th- and 19th-century buildings that have been meticulously preserved as Historic Deerfield (in the western part of the state) and Old Sturbridge, a reconstructed 19th-century living history village. Nearby is Springfield — birthplace of the American automobile, the motorcycle, the gas pump and the basketball (one of its museums houses the Basketball Hall of Fame). Plymouth Rock, where the Pilgrims landed in 1620, is on the Atlantic coast. (Be warned that the rock's size is dwarfed by its importance.) In Plymouth you can also tour the *Mayflower II,* a replica of the ship that brought the Pilgrims to the New World, as well as the Plimoth Plantation (a 1620-style Pilgrim village).

Take the children to the Whale Discovery Center. Or,

Portland Head Lighthouse, Maine

even better, take them on a whale-watching expedition (from many places along the coast, mid-April through mid-October). The last time we went we saw seven whales and schools of dolphins.

In the northeastern part of the state, travelers should stop in Salem, where the Puritans conducted witch trials in the 17th century. There's even a Salem Witch Museum. Also in the area is Newburyport, a town filled with boatyards, taverns and magnificent Federal-style mansions.

The Berkshires   For more than a century, the tranquil beauty of these hills in the far-west region of the state has attracted artists and visitors. The hills, forests, ponds and sparkling lakes have been augmented with charming inns, intimate bed-and-breakfasts, health spas, fine restaurants and ski resorts. Add a summer-long festival of the arts with music, theater, dance, painting and sculpture and you have an unparalleled combination. Tanglewood, one of the country's premier outdoor music sites, is the summer home of the Boston Symphony.

Cape Cod   This long, fishhook-shaped stretch of land in the Atlantic Ocean is primarily a summer resort area, offering miles of beaches, including the Cape Cod National Seashore. The Cape can be reached by car (traffic is slow!), bus, plane or train. Sand dunes, cottages weathered by salt air and excellent seafood only hint at the cape's attractions. Many of the small towns have classic village greens and 18th-century houses with salt-spray roses tumbling over trellises and gates. If you like beaches warm and cozy, the mid-Cape towns of Hyannis, Yarmouth and Dennis are recommended (they're good for families, with many oceanfront restaurants,

Faneuil Hall Marketplace, Boston

summer theaters and fishing charters). Truro, farther north on the Cape, is set among heaths and moors like those of Scotland. At the north end of the Cape is Provincetown ("P-town"), which has the hubbub atmosphere of an artists colony and is very hospitable to gays and lesbians. (It can seem excessively trendy.) We find it eerily wonderful to stop at the lighthouse at Race Point (at the very tip of the Cape) and watch the sun get lost in the fog.

If you really want to get away from it all, consider two islands off the coast — Nantucket and Martha's Vineyard, both easily reached by ferry. They were originally settled by missionaries and whalers, but today they are primarily resorts (somewhat exclusive), offering soft, sandy beaches, cliffs and forests, as well as opportunities for sailing, biking, hiking and shopping.

Boston   Founded in 1630, Boston is one of the oldest cities in the United States. It has been dubbed the "Cradle of Liberty" for leading the American colonies in their struggle for independence. It has also been called the "Hub of the Universe" because of its citizens' intellectual and cultural achievements. The city and its surrounding area are home to many leading colleges and universities, including Harvard University and the Massachusetts Institute of Technology (MIT). Equally enticing are its abundance of restaurants (many of special interest to seafood lovers), shopping areas and professional sports teams. Check to see if the Boston Red Sox are playing at historic Fenway Park.

Many of Boston's points of interest are conveniently located within walking distance of one another or along the route of the city's excellent transit system. For a quick history lesson and some exercise, set out along Freedom Trail, a red line painted along the sidewalks of downtown. Highlights along the route include the Old State House, Paul Revere's house, Granary Burying Ground (burial place of Samuel Adams, John Hancock and other patriots), and the Old North Church (the city's oldest house of worship and the point from which Paul Revere was signaled that the British were coming).

The downtown area is bordered by the Boston Common and Public Garden, where swan boats glide in the summer and ice-skaters glide in the winter. For a bird's-eye view of Boston, go to the John Hancock Observatory on the 60th floor of New England's tallest building.

Within walking distance of the Common is the Beacon Hill neighborhood, known for its narrow but elegant town houses and hidden gardens. Beacon Hill's north slope is the location of the Black Heritage Trail. Also near downtown is Faneuil Hall Marketplace, a restored historic district with dozens of popular shops and restaurants (it's where a lot of Bostonians eat lunch).

Boston has many theaters, the Boston Symphony, the Boston Pops Orchestra and the Boston Ballet. It has the New England Aquarium (one of our favorites), the *USS Constitution* ("Old Ironsides"), and the John F. Kennedy Library and Museum, a memorial to the 35th president. Finally, we recommend two arts museums: the Museum of Fine Arts, which has an outstanding collection of impressionists (more Monets than any museum outside Paris) and one of the leading Egyptian collections in the Western world; and the Isabella Stewart Gardner home, a Venetian-style palazzo with flowering courtyard, antique furniture and paintings.

New Hampshire

We tend to think of New Hampshire as a pocket-size New England. Its small space contains a great deal of beauty. The pristine countryside is dotted with colonial villages (note the many white church spires) and lakes. More than half the covered bridges in New England are in the state, including the longest in the country — a 460-ft/140-m span crossing the Connecticut River. White Mountain National Forest and the Connecticut

Lakes country (a densely wooded area at the border with Canada) top the list of places to see fall foliage or to go fishing, hiking and camping. There's good salmon and trout fishing on Lake Sunapee.

The state has several interesting museums (including the New Hampshire Historical Museum and Library in Concord and the Hood Museum of Art — a fine collection ranging from centuries-old art from Asia to the works of Frank Stella — on the Dartmouth College campus in Hanover) and historic homes (Strawbery Banke in Portsmouth has 37 structures dating from 1695 to 1945, some with resident craftsmen demonstrating their talents).

White Mountains
Several of the U.S. Northeast's highest peaks lie in White Mountain National Forest, a region of hiking trails, lakes, waterfalls, fishing streams and wildlife that spreads across northern New Hampshire into Maine. The area also hosts some of New England's finest ski resorts, including Mount Washington Valley and Bretton Woods ski areas. The Flume (open from May to November) is an impressive natural gorge in the White Mountains.

Rhode Island
Rhode Island has long had a reputation for attracting an exclusive clientele. The nation's first industrialists and traders built their very first vacation homes, in Newport, as early as the 1830s. Today, you needn't be rich to visit Rhode Island — just curious about how the well-to-do live.

The state is very popular in New England as a destination for long holiday weekends. One of the best getaway-from-it-alls is Block Island, off the coast. You reach it by ferry, but you don't completely leave civilization behind. Block Island has resisted the kind of rampant overdevelopment that can turn a pleasant hideaway into something closer to a theme park. It's a good place to walk or rent bicycles. We rate it very high on our list of vacation spots.

For water sport lovers, Rhode Island offers yachting, fishing, scuba diving or just plain swimming and relaxing along its beautiful beaches. For a change of pace, travelers can explore antique shops in Gloucester, the Herreshoff Marine Museum and Monument in Bristol and Little Compton (a typical New England village).

Newport
This beautiful seaport is noted for its enchanting coastline, tennis tournament and jazz festival. But the most famous places in town, by far, are the summer homes built there by industrialists and robber barons in the 1800s. These grand summer mansions — called "cottages" by their owners! — are perched along the oceanfront; tours are sometimes conducted by guides dressed as butlers and maids. One of the most famous is The Breakers, designed as a palace for Cornelius Vanderbilt II, but we find the Marble House to be the big daddy of extravagance — where the Gilded Age went over the top (don't miss the heavily ornamented fireplace).

Vermont
In winter, Vermont's charming towns and rugged countryside become a fairyland for snowboarders, downhill skiers, ice-skaters, ice anglers and snow sculptors. When the snow melts, the state is just as lovely—spring is when the Green Mountain State truly lives up to its name. Pleasant summer temperatures make Vermont one of the most comfortable places in the country to go camping, enjoy outdoor recreation (the state has 65 state parks) or attend cultural festivals. And the state's colorful fall foliage is legendary (even residents of other New England states head for Vermont in the autumn). Given the chance, we'd see Vermont any time of year.

Burlington
Vermont's largest city sits on the shores of Lake Champlain. A good way to view it is to take a cruise along the shore. The city maintains two public beaches. Among the historical attractions are the

Geostats

State	Capital	Population	Land Area	
			Sq. miles	Sq. Kilometers
Connecticut	Hartford	3,275,251	4,845	12,548
Maine	Augusta	1,240,209	30,865	79,937
Massachusetts	Boston	6,041,123	7,838	20,3001
New Hampshire	Concord	1,136,820	8,969	23,229
Rhode Island	Providence	996,757	1,045	2,706
Vermont	Montpelier	580,209	9,249	23,954

Skiing in New England

restored farmhouse of Revolutionary War hero Ethan Allen; the Pearl Street District (beautiful 18th-century homes); the College Street/Main District (19th-century architecture); and the South Willard Street District for its impressive mansions.

Ski Areas Vermont has 12 ski areas, with 175 lifts and more than 900 miles of trails. New England's most extensive ski resort is Killington in the Green Mountains. It has six different peaks connected by 19 chair lifts and one of the longest gondolas in North America. Its trails are evenly distributed between beginner, intermediate and expert levels. Families may want to participate in the Killington Ski School, famous for its method of instruction, which, it claims, can get beginners on the slopes in two hours. Lodges, chalets, condominiums and hotels, as well as an assortment of restaurants, pubs, shops and other apres-ski amenities are nearby.

Itineraries

We suggest two different itineraries, each eight days long. Both start and end in Boston; both are based on travel by rental car. One is a summer itinerary, the other an autumn adventure.

Boston and Cape Cod

Day 1 — Arrive Boston.

Days 2–3 — Tour Boston.

Day 4 — Leave Boston for Cape Cod.

Day 5 — Go to the beach, or go on a whale-watching expedition, or both. Drive to Provincetown for dinner.

Day 6 — Drive west along the coastline toward Newport, Rhode Island.

Day 7 — Tour the famous "cottages" of the rich and famous in Newport.

Day 8 — Drive north toward Boston, stopping at sites along the way. Depart Boston in the evening.

If you have additional days, you may want to add a trip to Martha's Vineyard, Nantucket or Block Island.

Boston and Fall Foliage

Days 1–3 — See the other itinerary.

Day 4 — Leave Boston and drive to Lexington and Concord. Visit Revolutionary War sights. Then head toward the White Mountains in New Hampshire.

Day 5 — The White Mountains.

Day 6 — In the morning, drive to Maine. After lunch, continue on toward Acadia National Park, on the coast.

Day 7 — Acadia National Park.

Day 8 — Drive to Portsmouth, New Hampshire, and spend a few hours at Strawbery Banke. Continue on to Boston for evening departure from New England.

Climate/When to Go

New England has four distinct seasons, each of which has its attractions. Fall is, for thousands of travelers every year, the most beautiful: During the last week of September and the first two weeks of October in much of the region, the fall foliage is at its peak of color. The temperature during the day settles in the high 60s F/20 C and at night drops to the cool, crisp 40s F/4 C. Winter offers wonderful skiing conditions in the mountainous areas of Vermont and New Hampshire — areas that have the coolest temperatures during the summer. Ocean breezes tend to make coastal towns warmer during the winter and cooler in summer. Beach weather can be glorious in July and August, but travelers who like to swim should be aware that the water never really gets that warm.

Transportation

Major airlines and their affiliated regional carriers and regional airlines serve the major airports of New England. The area has a excellent network of interstate highways and is served by Amtrak trains and Greyhound bus lines, too. Our recommendation, for visitors who want to tour the entire region, is to fly into Logan International Airport (BOS) in Boston and either rent a car or take an escorted bus tour. It's the only way to wander the back roads, where New England's charm and character are most evident.

Accommodations

Visitors to New England can select from a full range of accommodations — from budget lodgings to first-class country inns and deluxe hotels. We think no trip to the region would be complete without a stop at one of the many charming bed-and-breakfast inns. Most of them are restored colonial mansions and Victorian homes. For some high-quality pampering, you may want to choose one of New England's famous deluxe hotels (such as the Ritz-Carlton or the Copley Plaza in Boston) or one of the region's historic treasures (such as Mt. Washington Hotel in Bretton Woods, New Hampshire).

What to Buy

Shop for arts and crafts at the region's many craft "villages" and craft fairs. Handcrafted items include wood carvings, furniture, pottery, glass, Native American baskets, woven clothing and rugs. Two places where you'll find large selections of handicrafts are Strawbery Banke in Portsmouth, New Hampshire, and Deerfield, Massachusetts (which holds the Old Deerfield Crafts Fair twice a year — summer and fall).

Antique dealers are everywhere in New England, but we've found some of the largest concentrations of them in Boston and Essex, Massachusetts, and Stamford, Woodbury and Mystic, Connecticut. Don't expect to find bargains everywhere, though. Auctions — held throughout the area throughout the year — and flea markets (we like the one held weekends in Mashpee on Cape Cod) may offer better buys and excitement at the same time. Food "souvenirs" are plentiful, too — look for maple syrup in Vermont and New Hampshire.

What to Eat

You can find nearly every kind of cuisine in New England, but it's hard to find a restaurant that doesn't serve seafood. We like Maine lobster at a "lobster shack," a bare-bones, no-frills eatery along the coast. We also like clams (especially at a clam bake on the beach), fish chowder and scrod, an ordinary but tasty fish. Ordering blueberry pie would be a good decision in Maine (the leading U.S. producer of blueberries) or Massachusetts. Other regional fruits include cranberries, apples (for cider) and grapes (for wine). You'll probably find Vermont's maple syrup on the breakfast table and, when in Boston, eat baked beans the way the Bostonians do.

Travel Tips for the Client

Do be respectful of wildlife (bears, moose and other animals of the forest) while driving along the back roads. And remember that the region is not a petting zoo. Take pictures, not chances . . . Do take warm clothing to New England during the summer months—nights can be chilly . . . Do be prepared for aggressive drivers, especially in Boston . . . Do be prepared for winter driving. Carry emergency supplies (water, blankets, food, sand or kitty litter for traction, a shovel, tire chains and a distress flag for the radio antenna . . . Don't go hiking in the mountains of Vermont and New Hampshire without first checking with park rangers on weather conditions—they are known to change suddenly. . . .

New England

Review Questions

1. In what city is the Faneuil Hall Marketplace? Describe it. What are some of the important collections in that city's Museum of Fine Arts?

2. To what towns on Cape Cod would you send families that are looking to enjoy warm and cozy beaches, oceanfront restaurants, summer theaters and fishing charters?

3. What is New England's most extensive ski resort? In what mountains and state is it?

4. What kind of structure does New Hampshire have more of than any other New England state?

5. Where in New England would visitors most likely go to see lavish 19th-century mansions of wealthy industrialists?

6. What would a tourist see if he or she followed a red line painted on a sidewalk of downtown Boston? What is the name of this route?

7. In what state would you visit Block Island? What kind of place is it? What might you do there?

8. What is Tanglewood? In what hills and state would you find it?

9. In what state is Acadia National Park? What might a tourist see there?

10. What might a tourist visit in Mystic, Connecticut?

New England

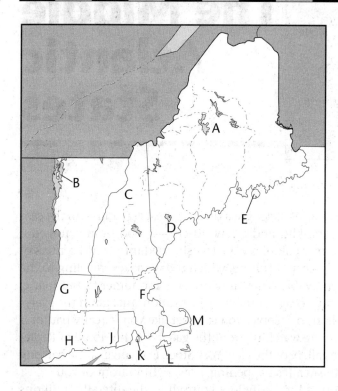

Map Skills Exercise

Match the tourist destination listed below with the corresponding letter on the map. You can use each letter only once.

1. _____ Boston
2. _____ Acadia National Park
3. _____ Cape Cod
4. _____ Newport
5. _____ Mystic
6. _____ Lake Champlain
7. _____ White Mountains
8. _____ Portland
9. _____ Martha's Vineyard
10. _____ Berkshires

Selling Exercise

In helping clients plan a trip, you'll often work with them to create an itinerary, or daily plan. On page 20 of your textbook, you'll find two itineraries that we've created for visiting New England. One is a summer itinerary, the other for the fall. Look over both. Which cities and towns would a traveler visit on the first itinerary? What is probably the main purpose of the autumn itinerary? If a client has two additional days to spend in New England, what might you suggest adding to the autumn itinerary?

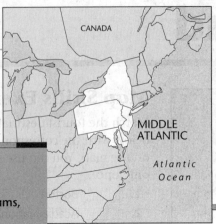

CANADA

MIDDLE
ATLANTIC

Atlantic
Ocean

The Middle Atlantic States

In the Middle Atlantic states great dreams, great zeal and — in the case of Benjamin Franklin and a few others — good humor forged a nation. These farmer colonies were transformed into world centers of government, finance and culture, which today makes traveling to the region ever so enjoyable. They are not static monuments, but living, breathing and (quite often) competing institutions that affect the everyday lives of millions of people. You can feel like you're really part of it all — whether you're watching from the gallery of the House of Representatives or the gallery of the New York Stock Exchange or the balcony of a Broadway theater. It's happening, now, right in front of you.

Of course, you can as easily lose yourself in the (literally) millions of square feet of space in the region's great museums, or find solace at a memorial to heroic sacrifice. You can search for the latest fashions in New York City or the freshest crab cake on Maryland's Eastern Shore (maybe cheesesteak on the streets of Philadelphia). If nothing else delights you, surely the natural beauty of the region will. Climb high into the gorgeous Adirondacks. Drop a line into the ocean off Montauk Point. Stick your toes in Chesapeake Bay.

What to Do There
Delaware

Delaware is an attractive state that can easily be seen on an itinerary that includes Washington, D.C., Baltimore, Philadelphia or southern New Jersey. (A ferry from Cape May in southern New Jersey runs to Lewes in central Delaware.) Delaware has quiet beach resorts such as Bethany Beach and Rehoboth Beach on the Atlantic Ocean, historic sites and the Winterthur Museum.

Brandywine Valley   Spread over northern Delaware and part of Pennsylvania, this scenic and historic valley is a must for any visitor to Delaware's largest city, Wilmington. The top draw is the Winterthur Museum, a nine-story mansion that was once the home of Henry Francis du Pont and now contains one of the top collections of American antiques and decorative arts in the United States.

Middle Atlantic

- ✪ National Capital
- ◉ State Capital
- ■ □ City/Site
- ▲ Park or Preserve
- _ . . _ River

CANADA

St. Lawrence

THOUSAND ISLANDS

ADIRONDACKS

Lake Ontario

New York

Niagara Falls

Rochester

Buffalo

Saratoga Springs

Cooperstown

FINGER LAKES

Albany

CATSKILLS

Hudson

Lake Erie

Allegheny

Pennsylvania

POCONOS

Montauk Point

Newark

New York

West Hampton

LONG ISLAND

Pittsburgh

A L L E G H E N I E S

Harrisburg

Hershey

Princeton

Trenton

Lancaster

Valley Forge

Spring Lake

Philadelphia

Delaware

PINE BARRENS

Gettysburg

Brandywine Valley

Wilmington

Maryland

New Jersey

Baltimore

Atlantic City

Washington

Annapolis

Dover

Arlington

D.C.

Delaware

Cape May

Chesapeake Bay

Lewes

Rehoboth Beach

Bethany Beach

A T L A N T I C   O C E A N

Potomac

Km 0   25   50

Mi 0   25   50

Copyright Weissmann Travel Reports

Maryland

Maryland's location makes it an excellent stop-off point or side trip en route to/from Washington, D.C. But it's a worthy destination by itself, too. The Eastern Shore of Chesapeake Bay is popular for sailing and yachting. Historic homes and villages, the U.S. Naval Academy (at Annapolis), horse racing and deep-sea fishing are among its other major attractions. And Baltimore is one of the best rejuvenated cities in the country. But our very

favorite thing to do in this state is to eat — the state's seafood, to be specific. If you can, visit during crabbing season, April to October.

Baltimore This city's Inner Harbor, a glittering warehouse-district-turned-marketplace, has made Baltimore a model of urban renaissance. It's *the* place to go in this city. In fact, the Inner Harbor is a good place to start your visit. We suggest picking up tickets at the

Niagara Falls

National Aquarium first thing, before the lines get too long. (You'll go back later at the time indicated on the tickets.) For an overview of the city, take a quick ride to the observation level of the World Trade Center. Then browse through the colorful shops in Harborplace before returning to the aquarium. One of the best facilities of its kind anywhere, the National Aquarium has seven levels of exhibits, including a stunning re-creation of a tropical rain forest (look for the sloth named Rapunzel hanging in the trees). Don't miss the Atlantic coral reef and the dolphins in the Marine Mammal Pavilion.

If you like historical ships, you can find several specimens at the Baltimore Maritime Museum nearby. Also in the Inner Harbor are the Maryland Science Center (with an IMAX theater, a planetarium and lots of hands-on exhibits) and Columbus Center, a new US$160 million marine-research facility designed to offer hands-on displays.

Diehard baseball fans will want to head a few blocks west of the Inner Harbor to the home of the Orioles, Camden Yards (baseball on real grass!). Just a fly ball away from the stadium are Babe Ruth's Birthplace and the Baltimore Orioles Museum, which feature exhibits about the Babe, the Orioles and Maryland's baseball heritage. The new Ruth Baseball Center uses the latest computer and laser technology to give visitors the full baseball experience.

Baltimore has dozens of historical sites worth visiting. Two that stand out are the restored Ft. McHenry (the scene of the 1814 battle that inspired the words to *The Star-Spangled Banner*) and Edgar Allan Poe's grave site at Westminster Presbyterian Church Cemetery (a spooky place with tilted tombstones — look for the frightful black raven on Poe's tombstone).

New Jersey

This small state is home to industrial cities (Newark), pastoral horse farms, beach resorts (Cape May and Spring Lake), pristine wilderness (in the Pine Barrens) and densely populated suburbs (adjacent to Philadelphia and New York City). The state's varied terrain — from flat coastal and farming areas to low mountains — offers travelers an array of activities ranging from golfing to fishing and bird-watching. Send clients who like surf-kissed beaches, boardwalks, gambling (Atlantic City), horse racing, American history (Princeton and Monmouth battlefields), Victoriana and the great outdoors.

Atlantic City   Most visitors to this New Jersey coastal city congregate around the blackjack tables and slot machines — turning their backs on the city itself and its once famous oceanfront. And for good reason: Outside of the 12 ritzy casinos that line the water, there hasn't been much else to see or do. In our opinion, gambling is the only reason to visit Atlantic City. If you are so inclined, we recommend two nights.

New York

New York State really has it all: one of the most vibrant cities in the world and an abundance of mind-calming natural beauty. The combination is unbeatable. New York City has superior restaurants, shopping and hotels and an almost endless variety of entertainment and attractions. In Upstate New York (which is virtually everything outside New York City and Long Island) you'll find an abundance of prime vacation areas: the Catskill and Adirondack Mountains, the relaxing Finger Lakes region, Cooperstown's Baseball Hall of Fame, the therapeutic springs of Saratoga, the charming Thousand Islands in the St. Lawrence River and the beautiful Hudson River Valley. The only clients who may want to think twice about visiting New York are those who can't afford it — it can be a fairly expensive place to vacation.

The Adirondacks   When New Yorkers talk about the beauty of Upstate, they're often thinking about the Adirondack Mountains region. Much of this huge highlands area is still unspoiled wilderness — not as rugged as the Rockies, but not without dramatic vistas. The region is most beautiful in autumn, when the leaves turn color. The range's 46 peaks guarantee that there's plenty of snow for skiing in the winter.

Niagara Falls   One of the world's first and most famous tourist sights, these impressive 180-ft-/55-m-high falls on the border of the U.S. and Canada offer the same combination of natural wonder and commercial tackiness that has inspired visitors since the 19th century. Even if you're not on your honeymoon, they're well worth seeing. Niagara Falls can be seen in a day, but we recommend an overnight to view the falls and rapids under different lighting conditions. And be sure to see the falls from both sides of the border — the views are different.

New York City This vibrant metropolis has something for everyone every hour of the day. There are enough activities and attractions to keep you busy for as much time as you have available.

New York City is divided into five parts (they're known as boroughs). Most visitors (especially newcomers to the city) will spend all their time in the borough of Manhattan, an island 13 miles/21 km long. Manhattan teems with such diversity and electricity that even its irritations are fascinating. It's among a handful of urban areas — London and Paris are two others — whose neighborhoods, buildings and street names are familiar even to those who never go there. When most people think about New York City — Times Square, Wall Street, Central Park, Fifth Avenue, Greenwich Village — they're thinking about Manhattan. We recommend seeing most of Manhattan on foot; that way, you'll take in the sights, smells and sounds that make up the city's pageant.

We'd suggest you start your visit at Battery Park at the southern tip of Manhattan Island and work your way northward. Don't be satisfied viewing one of the most important monuments in the world — the Statue of Liberty — from the skyscrapers or the shore: Buy tickets at the historic Castle Clinton for the ferry out to the statue, walk around it and climb up inside it to the crown. (You can also sail past the statue on the Staten Island Ferry. At 50 cents over and back to Staten Island, it's still one of the best bargains in town.) Ellis Island is another important stop in the harbor. It was the gateway for millions seeking a new life in the U.S. The Museum of Immigration there is a tribute to America's immigrant heritage.

On your return to Manhattan, head east to the Financial District for a visit to Wall Street and the New York Stock Exchange, where you can view the trading action from a public gallery. Then head directly to the nearby refurbished South Street Seaport area, with its sailing ships, outdoor concerts and shops. To the northeast of the seaport is the famous and beautiful Brooklyn Bridge and north of that, Chinatown. Head north again to Little Italy. Northwest of Little Italy is Soho with lots of galleries, cafes and boutiques. And the famous bohemian-enclave-gone-upscale, Greenwich Village, is just north of that.

After spending a couple of days exploring the area

The Statue of Liberty

known as Lower Manhattan, you'll want to move on to Midtown and Uptown. The Empire State Building stands at the corner of 34th and Fifth Avenue. (Definitely take the elevator to the observation deck, especially at night, when the skyscape of New York is absolutely spellbinding.) Twelve or so blocks to the northeast is the Chrysler Building, a stunning example of art-deco architecture. From the Chrysler Building, you may want to head east to the United Nations or head back to Fifth Avenue, where you can experience firsthand upscale shopping. Keep walking until you get to Rockefeller Center (home to restaurants and, in the winter, an ice-skating rink and the city's gigantic Christmas tree) and Radio City Music Hall. At the heart of midtown are the theater district and Times Square (the corner of 42nd Street and Broadway). We think it's practically a crime to visit New York without seeing at least one star-studded theatrical extravaganza. (Not too distant from this area are Carnegie Hall — where all performers hope one day to play — and Lincoln Center, home to the Metropolitan Opera House, the New York Philharmonic and the American Ballet Theater.) Reinforce your worldly sophistication at the Museum of Modern Art (extraordinary collection of 20th-century painting, sculpture and design) and your serenity at St. Patrick's Cathedral, with its impressive Gothic dimensions.

You'll need yet another few days to see the New York

that lies north of 59th Street. Central Park splits the area pretty much down the middle, and you'll at least want to make a swing through this large park in the heart of the city during the day. Don't forget to stop in at some of the world's greatest museums bordering the park: the American Museum of Natural History, the Guggenheim (the building was designed by Frank Lloyd Wright) and the Metropolitan Museum of Art, which ranks with the Louvre in Paris and the Hermitage in St. Petersburg. Farther north is the African-American community of Harlem, rich in history and culture.

If you're looking for entertainment in the evening, New York City has some of the trendiest clubs and discos in the nation. And they can be notoriously hard to get into — doormen select carefully only those who have the look their club is trying to promote.

Don't hesitate to venture off Manhattan Island. Other parts of the city have some interesting things to see and do. In Brooklyn, for instance, stop in Brooklyn Heights, a lovely neighborhood just across from Manhattan. If you're there in the evening, walk along the promenade and look back at the towering "peaks" of lower Manhattan. Other places to see in Brooklyn include Prospect Park, one of New York's most beautiful parks, and adjacent to the park, the Brooklyn Botanic Gardens and the Brooklyn Museum. The museum has a wonderful collection of American, Egyptian, Asian and European art. In the Bronx you'll find Yankee Stadium, the world-famous Bronx Zoo and the magnificent New York Botanical Gardens.

If you're looking for a beach on your visit to New York City, then consider taking a trip out to Long Island. This large island stretches from Manhattan out into the Atlantic Ocean for more than 100 miles. A day trip is Jones Beach, one of the most popular recreation areas on the east coast. Further out on the island is a group of small towns collectively referred to as the Hamptons (Southampton, East Hampton, etc.). In the Hamptons, summer homes of the rich and famous line the shore. At the very easternmost tip of the island you'll find one of the most beautiful spots in the United States: Montauk Point. Waves crash against a rocky shore there (one of the nation's oldest lighthouses still stands there, too).

Pennsylvania

In addition to offering lovely rolling farmland, the Allegheny Mountains, and distinctive cultural groups, Pennsylvania is rich in historic landmarks. Pennsylvania was the site of the adoption of the Declaration of Independence in 1776 and the U.S. Constitution in 1787. Many crucial battles and events of the American Revolution took place there. But, while keeping an eye on the past, the state is firmly footed in the future. Major cities (Pittsburgh and Philadelphia) offer a wealth of historic sites juxtaposed with vibrant downtowns and ultramodern transportation systems. Ski and summer resorts abound in the Pocono Mountains — just a few hours' drive from New York City, Philadelphia and Washington, D.C.

Amish Country/Pennsylvania Dutch
Centered on the city of Lancaster, this pretty rural area of rolling hills is home to three religious communities: the Amish, the Moravians and the Mennonites, all of which practice a theology of prayerful devotion through unadorned living. The very religious Amish lifestyle forgoes modern conveniences (electricity, automobiles) in favor of a simple, formal lifestyle (hand tools, horse and carriage, simple black clothing). Many visitors to the area stay in small local hotels and eat the simple home cooking of the region. The Amish make beautiful quilts, which are often sold along the road or in private homes.

Gettysburg   Probably no other U.S. city can conjure such powerful ghosts of blue and gray uniforms from the U.S. Civil War, smoke and battle, loss and death as Gettysburg can. It's home to the country's largest battlefield shrine. Tour the excellent Gettysburg Museum of the Civil War. It has an impressive collection, including uniforms and weaponry used during the war. Be sure to see the Gettysburg National Cemetery, where President Abraham Lincoln delivered his Gettysburg Address.

Hershey   Hershey is the town that chocolate built. Milton Hershey created the town to house and entertain Hershey employees. It's rather thematic: The street lamps, for instance, are shaped like Hershey's Kisses. It's great fun to tour Hershey Chocolate World, a simulation of the actual chocolate factory; the Hershey Museum of American Life (excellent Native American exhibits); and HERSHEYPARK (a theme park).

Philadelphia   Dazzling new skyscrapers, clean downtown streets — could this be the same Philadelphia we used to know? It's hard to believe, but it's true. The place that was once called Filthydelphia has undeniably cleaned up its act. New hotels have been built. Roadways and public transportation have been improved. Philly has even been voted friendliest U.S. city by a major magazine. All this rejuvenation makes it easier to enjoy the attractions that this tradition-bound city has always offered: great restaurants and museums; excellent classical, jazz and folk music; and its stock in trade: historic sites.

We think every U.S. citizen and visitor to the country

should make the trip to Independence National Historical Park, which is often called "the nation's most historic square mile." Two of the country's most treasured monuments, Independence Hall and the Liberty Bell, are there, as are several other places of historic importance. Other important sites include Graff House (where Thomas Jefferson composed the Declaration of Independence), Congress Hall (where the U.S. Congress met until 1800), and the Betsy Ross House (home of the seamstress who reputedly made the first U.S. flag).

One of the brightest stars in Philadelphia's firmament is the Franklin Institute. The institute is part of the city's cultural hub along the Benjamin Franklin Parkway, which is lined by such world-renowned institutions as the Philadelphia Museum of Art (Asian, American and European art from ancient to ultramodern), the Rodin Museum and the Academy of Natural Sciences Museum (the country's oldest natural-history museum, with a great dinosaur exhibit).

Along the waterfront, visit the Independence Seaport Museum. Several historic ships are docked at the museum, including the *USS Olympia,* Admiral Dewey's flagship during the Spanish-American War.

Not far away is the new ferry that takes passengers across the Delaware River to the New Jersey State Aquarium in Camden. Other sights in Philadelphia include the Barnes Foundation Gallery, world famous for its collection of French impressionist works, and Fairmount Park, the largest city park in the world. And excursions can be taken from town to Valley Forge, where the Continental Army spent a winter of extreme hardship during the Revolutionary War.

Pittsburgh   Don't go to Pittsburgh looking for soot. That Pittsburgh — the steel town of lore — got scrubbed some time ago. Go instead to find a good-natured, energetic city with a dazzling skyline (lots of mirrored glass reflects the hills and the three rivers — the Allegheny and the Monongahela flow together to form the Ohio right downtown). Go instead to see the

Penguins play on home ice; to see the dinosaurs (there are 10 of them — complete — at the Museum of Natural History); or to take on the Warhols — there are more pieces of art by native son Andy Warhol in Pittsburgh than anywhere else. (Check out the Andy Warhol Museum on the city's north side.). Other attractions in this town include Point State Park (at the confluence of the three rivers and site of the largest fountain in the U.S.) and Three Rivers Stadium (home to the baseball Pirates and the football Steelers).

Washington, D.C.

Washington, D.C. is a treasure trove of tourist attractions. We could spend weeks in the Smithsonian Institution's museums alone. Then there's the White House, the Capitol, the Washington Monument, the Lincoln Memorial, the National Gallery of Art . . . our list goes on and on. Washington is the place to learn about the workings of the U.S. government and the art, history and culture that have shaped the country. It's a sophisticated, world-class city with top-notch entertainment and fine restaurants.

Arlington National Cemetery (Virginia)   More than 60,000 U.S. war casualties and veterans are buried in Arlington National Cemetery across the Potomac River from Washington. Though a solemn destination, it's also an inspiring place to visit. Most people will want to stop at the grave site of President John F. Kennedy (where the eternal flame burns). Be sure to watch the changing of the guard at the Tombs of The Unknowns, which honors veterans of both World Wars and the Korea and Vietnam wars. Nearby is the famous Marine Corps Memorial, a statue of Marines raising the American flag at Iwo Jima during World War II.

Jefferson Memorial   This elegant, understated dome and colonnaded white-marble rotunda honors America's third president and primary architect of U.S. political philosophy. Its statue of Jefferson gazes out across the Tidal Basin.

Geostats

State	Capital	Population	Land Area	
			Sq. Miles	Sq. Kilometers
Delaware	Dover	706,351	1,955	5,063
Maryland	Annapolis	5,006,265	9,775	25,316
New Jersey	Trenton	7,903,925	7,419	19,214
New York	Albany	18,169,051	47,224	122,305
Pennsylvania	Harrisburg	12,052,367	44,820	116,079
Washington, D.C.	——	570,175	61	158

John F. Kennedy Center for the Performing Arts
We think everyone who visits Washington should take in a performance of some kind at this center, and there's plenty to choose from: The city's — and the nation's — cultural showplace offers theater, dance, music and film in its six theaters almost every day.

Lincoln Memorial   One inside wall of the memorial is engraved with the Gettysburg Address, the other with Lincoln's second inaugural address. And, of course, there is the unforgettable sculpture of a seated Lincoln. Sit on the steps of the memorial and gaze out over the Reflecting Pool.

National Gallery of Art   We remember sitting at the National Gallery — one of the world's premier art museums — surrounded by Rembrandts. We can't remember if there were six portraits or seven, but we do remember being inspired. That was on our first visit to the old part of the museum (it houses the Old Masters). We had to go back again to see the East Wing, which is all angles and skylights, designed by I. M. Pei in the 1970s.

Smithsonian Institution   Affectionately referred to as "America's attic" for its apparently infinite trove of artifacts, relics and memorabilia, the Smithsonian is truly among the world's great museums. It is actually many museums — each devoted to a different area of interest or study. Most are located on the National Mall just west of the Capitol, but others can be found elsewhere in D.C. If, however, your stay in Washington is limited, you may need to pare down the list — try to see at least the National Museum of Natural History, the National Museum of American History and the National Air and Space Museum.

Even Washington has dinosaurs. They're some of the bigger specimens among the 81 million or so housed in the National Museum of Natural History. There you feel like you've entered a 3-D encyclopedia about the study of plants, fossils, minerals and man. A good place to be a child.

The National Museum of American History is really the nation's closet, only neater. It offers a truly engrossing and complete look at U.S. history, from the flag that inspired *The Star-Spangled Banner* to Archie Bunker's easy chair. One of the most popular exhibits is the collection of First Ladies' inaugural ball gowns.

With more than 8 million visitors a year, the Air and Space branch of the Smithsonian is the world's most popular museum. You'll find exhibits, many of them interactive, on the history of aviation and space exploration. You can look into one of the first space capsules or up at Lindbergh's *Spirit of St. Louis*.

U.S. Capitol   Pause to admire the towering rotunda, the Statuary Hall and the famous reception room of the Senate. If you want to see how the real work of Congress gets done, though, you probably have to sit in on a congressional hearing, most of which are open to the public.

U.S. Holocaust Memorial Museum   This museum tells a story of man-made horror — the systematic slaughter of millions of people in Nazi concentration camps. The artifacts speak clearly and movingly: the boxcar that took prisoners to the death camps, the actual barracks from Auschwitz, the videotaped testimony of witnesses.

Vietnam Veterans Memorial   The black-granite walls of the Vietnam Veterans Memorial gradually descend into the earth, taking you down into an incredibly quiet place. It's overwhelming to see the names inscribed on the walls — 58,191 men and women killed in Vietnam or missing. The new Korean War Memorial is nearby.

Washington Monument   This 555-ft/169-m white-marble obelisk is popular for the view it provides of the city.

White House   You can take a brief, free public tour of the White House, the home and office of the president of the U.S. But don't expect to see the Oval Office or the presidential living quarters — they are always off limits to the uninvited public.

Itinerary

This 12-day itinerary covers the main cities of the region and throws in a few interesting side trips, too. Fly in to New York City and fly out of Washington, D.C. Use Amtrak and/or rental cars to travel between points.

Day 1 — Arrive New York City.

Days 2–3 — Tour New York City.

Day 4 — Take Amtrak or rent a car and travel to Philadelphia.

Day 5 — Tour Philadelphia.

Day 6 — Day trip to Atlantic City and return to Philadelphia.

Day 7 — Day trip to Amish Country and return to Philadelphia.

Day 8 — In the morning, take Amtrak or your car to Baltimore. Tour the harbor area. Overnight in Baltimore.

Day 9 — Travel to Washington, D.C.

Days 10–11 — Tour Washington, D.C.

Day 12 — Fly out of Washington, D.C.

Climate/When to Go

In general, the Middle Atlantic States have relatively warm summers and cold winters, with moderate temperatures in the fall and spring. Fall is the prettiest season, when the foliage is in its colorful glory. If you go in the summer, be prepared for hot, humid weather in much of the region. Expect cool temperature and some snow in the winter. But along the Great Lakes, the amount of snow during winter can be awesome. Spring and fall are probably the best times to visit the region, unless you're going to the beach and then you'll want to be there during the summer.

Transportation

Major international airports in the region include: three serving the New York City area (John F. Kennedy Airport — JFK, LaGuardia Airport — LGA and, in northern New Jersey, Newark International Airport — EWR); Philadelphia International Airport (PHL); and three serving Washington, D.C. (Dulles International Airport — IAD, Baltimore-Washington International Airport — BWI, and close to Washington, National Airport — DCA).

Amtrak provides rail service throughout the region and to points beyond. A major Amtrak line connects New York City, Philadelphia, Baltimore and Washington, D.C., Greyhound provides coach service connecting the major cities in the region. New York City and Washington, D.C., have extensive subway systems for easy travel to most parts of town. Major highways crisscross the Middle Atlantic States. To go to points on Long Island, consider taking Long Island Railroad trains.

Accommodations

Visitors will find every kind of accommodation available from bare-bones budget lodging to inns and B-and-Bs (bed-and-breakfasts) to the most sumptuous deluxe hotels and resorts. Hotels can be very expensive in Washington, D.C., and especially in New York City. New York City abounds with legendary hotels, including the Waldorf-Astoria and the Plaza. The newest major hotel there is the Four Seasons, designed by renowned architect I. M. Pei. In Atlantic City, try to stay at one of the 12 casino/hotels.

What to Buy

New York City is the shopping capital of the world — you can buy almost anything and almost at any price there. The city has a long-standing tradition of having the world's greatest department stores (Macy's, Bloomingdale's, Saks Fifth Avenue, Bergdorf Goodman, among others). Bibliophiles will be no less pleased with the number and variety of excellent bookstores in Manhattan. Two to consider visiting: the Strand (for millions of used books) and Barnes and Noble (good prices on new books and remainders in this huge store). In Washington, D.C., the various museum shops are a must. In Amish Country in Pennsylvania, you'll want to check out the quilts, wooden toys, "hex" signs and other handiwork.

What to Eat

Like Paris, New York City is a world-class culinary experience. The city offers a wide variety of restaurants and some them are among the best in the world. Washington, D.C., too, is a food-lover's paradise.

Look for regional cuisine. In Amish Country sample "Pennsylvania Dutch" cooking, such as shoofly pie (rich brown sugar or molasses pie) or scrapple (seasoned ground meat and cornmeal, molded and fried). In Maryland every visitor should try the seafood, especially the steamed blue crabs in season (May–October). In New York City sample ethnic cuisine — head for Chinatown and Little Italy — and don't forget to have lunch in a Jewish deli.

Travel Tips for the Client

In summer, don't miss the beaches of Delaware, New Jersey or New York State . . . Don't photograph the people of Amish Country as it's considered disrespectful of their religion . . . Consider taking a snack to eat if you choose to stand in line for the White House tour — the wait may be long . . . Do tip the croupiers if you win in Atlantic City, as they depend on tips for the bulk of their salaries . . . Do walk as much as possible in New York City — the passing parade of people and architecture is undoubtedly the city's greatest attraction. . . .

The Middle Atlantic States

Review Questions

1. Most visitors to New York City spend all of their time in just one of the five boroughs. Which borough is that? What is the best way to visit most of its sights?

2. Major tourist attractions in Washington, D.C., include four that are named for presidents. What are they?

3. Why would you recommend a tourist visit the area around Lancaster, Pennsylvania?

4. What city should a tourist interested in gambling be sure not to miss? In what state is it?

5. What two treasured monuments are in Independence National Historical Park? What city would tourists visit to see them?

6. What district in Baltimore is *the* place to go?

7. What natural wonder in New York State should a tourist also see from Canada?

8. What is the world's most popular museum? What institution is it part of?

9. In New York City, what three of the world's greatest museums border Central Park?

10. Where would a visitor see the country's largest battlefield shrine?

The Middle Atlantic States

Map Skills Exercise

Match the tourist destination listed below with the corresponding letter on the map. You can use each letter only once.

1. _____ New York City
2. _____ Washington, D.C.
3. _____ Chesapeake Bay
4. _____ Adirondack Mountains
5. _____ Pittsburgh
6. _____ Philadelphia
7. _____ Niagara Falls
8. _____ Baltimore
9. _____ Atlantic City
10. _____ Amish country

Selling Exercise

A computer firm wants to hold a series of seminars for its clients from the United States, Canada and Europe. They have selected New York City as the site for the meetings. The business manager of the firm calls you and asks you some questions about New York: What airports serve the city? What are some of the ways visitors can get around? What should visitors know about hotels in New York? When is the best time to schedule meetings there? What kind of entertainment might the clients enjoy in the evenings? Provide answers for her questions.

The South

Selling Points

The beaches and resorts along the Atlantic and Gulf of Mexico coasts, country music and blues, historical sites (including battlefields), Orlando and the Disney theme parks, Southern culture and cooking, antebellum mansions, mountains (the Appalachians and the Ozarks) and Mardi Gras in New Orleans are among the South's main attractions.

Almost everyone will find some fun and something of interest in the South. There are exciting cities to visit such as Miami, Atlanta and Nashville. The region offers visitors a host of outdoor recreational opportunities and wonderful scenery, from the Great Smoky Mountains in North Carolina to Big Bend National Park, more than 1,000 miles away in western Texas. Do make your clients aware that summers in much of the region can be very hot and humid.

Fascinating Facts About the South

The 333-ft-/101-m-tall George Washington Masonic National Memorial in Alexandria, Virginia, was patterned after the famous ancient lighthouse in Alexandria, Egypt . . . The first child born of English parents in America was Virginia Dare, who opened her eyes on Roanoke Island in 1587. . . .

The South stretches the imagination. You can start in Richmond, Virginia — once the capital of a breakaway nation, the Confederate States of America — and travel all the way to Texas, once a republic in its own right. You can follow the trail from slavery to Civil War to the civil rights struggle to space exploration to the Magic Kingdom. You will hear many accents: some quick, some drawled, many singing praises. The South will stretch you from breakfast grits to the last iced tea — and make you argue about the barbecue in between. (Should it be pork? Should it be beef? How 'bout some chicken? Only a Southerner knows for sure.)

What never seems to get stretched, though, is the hospitality. There's always something to celebrate, always time to sit a spell and listen to a story.

What to Do There

◆ The Southeast

Florida

The Sunshine State is one of the top tourist destinations in the United States. And it's not just sunshine that's the draw. The state is practically a tourist's paradise: hundreds of miles of gorgeous beaches line its seemingly endless coastline, theme parks draw millions of visitors from around the world and others fly in to pulsate to the rhythms of its most exciting city, Miami. Other leading attractions include the Everglades, baseball's spring training camps, the Keys (an arc of islands, some resort, extending far into the Gulf of Mexico) and the Kennedy Space Center.

Miami   A truly international city, Miami has benefited from rapid growth and an ethnic diversity that is evident in its myriad styles, cuisine and music. Experience the city by visiting Bayside Marketplace, lunching in Little Havana (complete with sidewalk vendors, restaurants and lots of atmosphere in the Cuban-American sector), shopping in Coconut Grove and betting on the world's fastest action game, jai-alai. The best way to get around Miami is on the high-tech

Metromover, part of the Metrorail system circling the city. After you've covered the city of Miami, take a causeway to the city of Miami Beach for more good food, the Art Deco District (one of the hottest restaurant/club strips in the U.S.) and, of course, the beach.

Orlando   Orlando is the No. 1 tourist destination in the world. The city is most closely associated with Walt Disney World: The Magic Kingdom, Disney-MGM Studios Theme Park and EPCOT Center. The Magic Kingdom — Disney's best-known theme park — is modeled after the original Disneyland in Southern California and it's especially appealing to families with children. Beloved characters such as Mickey Mouse, Goofy and Donald Duck come alive along the streets of Main Street U.S.A., Tomorrowland, Fantasyland, Frontierland, Liberty Square, Adventureland and Mickey's Starland. Recently, however, Disney has made an effort to appeal to "older" crowds. The latest attraction, the ExtraTERRORestrial Alien Encounter, subjects visitors to a good dose of fear when their futuristic teletransport system fails and they come face to face with a frightening alien. The other new attraction, Transportarium, is a journey through time in a theater- in-the-round.

Disney-MGM Studios is a combination film and television production studio and theme park. The newest addition to the park is Sunset Boulevard, a district lined with shops that culminates at the Twilight Zone Tower of Terror.

EPCOT   The EPCOT complex at is divided into two parts: Future World and World Showcase. The exhibits at Future World present educational displays of the 21st century through amazing interactive, high-tech, audio-visual experiences. For example, we found that once we were inside the giant geosphere in the Spaceship Earth exhibit, the view of Earth from space and the trip through the stars seemed startlingly realistic.

The other main section of EPCOT, World Showcase, celebrates cultures and peoples from around the world. Pavilions of 11 nations display architectural structures, exhibits and entertainment unique to each culture. You can meander through educational exhibits and shops selling goods from the country and sample a variety of ethnic foods. Our favorite eatery was the beautifully tiled Moroccan restaurant, which served excellent couscous.

Universal Studios Florida   Disney doesn't have a monopoly on fun in Orlando. Do visit Universal Studios. It's both a full-fledged production studio and a thrill-packed theme park. The thrills include the new

Dynamite Nights Stuntacular Lagoon Show (your boat jumps through a three-story inferno) and JAWS, a three-ton killer "shark" that will attempt to devour you.

Other attractions in Orlando include Sea World (featuring performing aquatic animals such as Shamu, the killer whale) and Splendid China (a park that takes visitors through 5,000 years of Chinese history and culture).

Everglades National Park   This huge national park is covered by tropical mangrove, freshwater

The Atlanta skyline

Gulf Coast, popular resort areas include Ft. Myers, (a pretty beach community), Sarasota (a beautiful resort city that's home to the Ringling Museum of Art, which includes a circus collection) and Tampa-St. Petersburg (a fast-growing major metropolitan area).

Georgia

Georgia has moved wholeheartedly into the 1990s without giving up the gentility and warmth of antebellum (pre-Civil War) days. Travelers who enjoy the sophistication of a big city (Atlanta) or time down on the plantation can enjoy the state. Visitors will find good food, excellent shopping and an opportunity to take in sights from American history. During the summer and early fall, beach fans will love the coast.

Atlanta   What Atlanta is known for — besides Scarlett O'Hara, Martin Luther King, Jr., and Ted Turner — is its energy and determination. It rebuilt itself from the ashes of the Civil War. It made progress — not headlines — during the civil rights movement in the 1960s. And it has become the regional business center and the transportation hub of the U.S. southeast.

There's a lot happening in this city. For the 1996 Summer Olympics, Atlanta built four major sport facilities including a natatorium (for swimming) and a velodrome (for bike racing). In addition to these Olympic treasures, Atlanta has built a new aquarium, opening in 1997, and Gone With the Wind Country, a theme park with replicas of Tara and Twelve Oaks.

It's great to explore places that are not brand new, too. Among our favorites is the Atlanta Zoo, one of the best in the United States. We also recommend a tour of Underground Atlanta, in the heart of the old city. Check out nearby World of Coca-Cola, a high-tech shrine to that holy sugar water whose corporate headquarters is in Atlanta.

Another must-see is the Martin Luther King, Jr. Historic District. Within a few blocks, you can visit Dr. King's birthplace, the Ebenezer Baptist Church where he preached, the MLK Center for Nonviolent Social Change and his gravesite. In the new museum dedicated to Dr. King's memory, you'll see his Nobel Peace Prize.

Just outside Atlanta there are a number of places to visit. Foremost among these is Stone Mountain Park. The park offers plenty of opportunities for outdoor recreation. Stone Mountain itself is the world's largest granite monolith. Into the side of this giant rock, sculptors have carved huge reliefs of Confederate heroes — Robert E. Lee, Stonewall Jackson and Jefferson Davis — atop their steeds.

marshes and forest and is home to alligators, manatees, beautiful birds and a wide variety of wetland flora. Stroll some of the boardwalks over the swamps and take the trails through dense woodlands. If you've got time, take one of the canoe tours or go on a "swamp tromp" (wear old clothes for these ranger-led hikes through the marsh). You can camp overnight, stay at the Flamingo Lodge or stay in cities near the entrances.

Kennedy Space Center   The space center has been the site of all U.S. manned space flights since 1964. Spaceport USA, which is adjacent, is a visitors center, museum and starting point for the bus tours of the launch sites. Be sure to see the rocket displays, look at a piece of moon rock and watch the various films.

Other Popular Coastal Cities   On the Atlantic Coast you'll find Ft. Lauderdale (a lovely Riviera community, north of Miami, with lots of private yachts and popular with college students on spring break), St. Augustine (founded by the Spanish in 1565) and Daytona Beach (site of the Daytona 500 auto race). On the

Savannah   Beautiful homes and a series of wonderful town squares are the main features of charming Savannah, Georgia's oldest city. Take a tour of the old homes and architecture of the city and make sure you see the Owens-Thomas House while you're there. Day trips can be made to the nearby beaches and golf courses of Hilton Head Island off the mainland of South Carolina.

North Carolina

North Carolina has many riches for the traveler. Its beautiful eastern shores are washed by the sometimes treacherous waters of the Atlantic Ocean, while the state's western mountain ranges climb into the mist. In between are gentle hills, bustling cities like Charlotte and Winston-Salem, and history — including battlefields of the American Revolution.

Asheville   Asheville, in western North Carolina, is well situated near the Great Smoky Mountains and Pisgah National Forest (stunning mountain landscapes). If you're interested in man-made splendor, you must see the Biltmore Estate, built by philanthropist George W. Vanderbilt in the 1890s. The 250-room mansion, modeled after a French chateau, is open to the public.

Cape Hatteras and Cape Lookout National Seashores   This long, thin stretch of island and peninsula beach sits out in the Atlantic, defending the coast from Atlantic Ocean storms. Stay in Nags Head or Atlantic Beach, two of the region's most popular resorts. The unspoiled beaches are open for swimming, surfing and horseback riding. If you have time, try one of the guided nature walks through the marsh and sand dunes.

Great Smoky Mountains National Park

This national park is the single most heavily trafficked in the United States. That's because of its proximity to the high-population areas on the East Coast and the sheer beauty of its mountains enshrouded in mist.

South Carolina

You know you have reached the Deep South when you enter a state with festivals honoring sweet potatoes, catfish and collards. The land slopes down from the Blue Ridge Mountains, through national forests and a green lowland dotted with lakes to miles and miles of beach.

Charleston   The heart of this beautiful city is the Historic District. The past is everywhere — look up and you'll find that church spires, not skyscrapers, are the tallest structures (just as they were 300 years ago). Shops are small and located near rows of brick and wood homes decorated with ornate cast-iron and gingerbread trim. Several of the major historic homes are open to the public. After a walk through the district, we like to take the tour boat to Fort Sumter, the island where the Civil War began.

The Beach Resorts   South Carolina's coastline is well developed for tourism. Hilton Head Island, for instance, draws about a million visitors every year. it's a year-round destination, with beaches, windsurfing, sailing, surf-fishing, golf, tennis and luxury accommodations. Up the coast is Myrtle Beach, a party-on, family-fun destination with plenty of diversion (such as miniature golf and water slides). It's also gaining a reputation as the coastal country-music capital, with five country-music theaters.

Virginia

We're hard pressed to name another state whose love of history surpasses Virginia's. Where else but Virginia was Thomas Jefferson's 250th birthday a statewide obsession? Virginia takes its role seriously as the state where much of American history has been played out. There

Geostats

State	Capital	Population	Land Area	
			Sq. Miles	Sq. Kilometers
Florida	Tallahassee	13,952,714	53,937	139,691
Georgia	Atlanta	7,055,336	57,919	150,004
North Carolina	Raleigh	7,069,836	48,718	126,174
South Carolina	Columbia	3,663,984	30,111	77,894
Virginia	Richmond	6,551,522	39,598	102,554
West Virginia	Charleston	1,828,140	24,087	62,383

you'll find Colonial Williamsburg; the sites of many battles in the American Revolution and Civil War; Arlington National Cemetery; and Richmond, capital of Virginia and former capital of the Confederacy.

Blue Ridge Parkway   Located in the western portion of the state, this wonderful 470-mi/752-km drive begins in Virginia at the southern end of the Shenandoah National Park and ends at Great Smoky Mountains National Park at the North Carolina/Tennessee border. The drive basically stays in the Blue Ridge Mountains. It's been called "America's Most Scenic Highway." Along the way visitors find beautiful scenery, quaint inns and restaurants, historic sites and independent "mountain" people. The most popular time to visit is in May–October when most of the accommodations and visitors facilities are open, although we prefer it in the fall (for the foliage) and in April (for the wildflowers).

Williamsburg, Jamestown and Yorktown   The Colonial Parkway links these sites in a historic triangle. Williamsburg was once the colonial capital of Virginia and the attractions depicting colonial times are truly fascinating. Walk leisurely through the streets, listening to the sound of the blacksmith's hammer, eating in a quaint inn or visiting an apothecary, a jail or the governor's palace.

Jamestown is a must visit for anyone interested in U.S. history. Be sure to see the old church and the glassblower's shop, then stroll along the banks of the James River to see re-created 17th-century sailing vessels. You can also visit a Powhatan Indian village as it would have been in the 1600s and James Fort, the home of the first English settlers. The third point on the historic triangle is Yorktown. Here you can visit the site of the decisive battle of the American Revolution where Lord Cornwallis surrendered to General Washington.

West Virginia

White-water rafters rank West Virginia's rivers up there with the best in the world. They award the rivers points for challenge, variety and surrounding beauty, as well as for the sheer number of accessible waterways. More cautious types need not shy away from the waters, though, for river guides also lead gentler float trips through the gorgeous Appalachian Mountain scenery. The state has several superior resorts and spas, as well as the biggest downhill skiing drops east of the Mississippi River.

Though the mountains play a key role in most of the state's lore, true mountain culture is disappearing. The visitor will have to work more than a little to uncover the handicrafts and music of that culture — finding it, with any luck, in the cities or at festivals.

New River Gorge National River   This park, which follows 53mi/85km of the free-flowing New River, is one of the best-kept secrets in the eastern U.S. Besides thrilling raft trips, it offers rock climbing, wildlife viewing, camping, fishing and hiking.

◆ The South-Central States and Texas

Alabama

You'll know that you're in the heart of Dixie when you visit Alabama. A visitor may very well encounter a horse-drawn carriage pulling up in front of a white-columned antebellum mansion, statues honoring Confederate heroes and landmarks commemorating the civil rights movement.

Birmingham and Montgomery   The best introduction to Birmingham, Alabama's largest city, is to see it from the observation deck of the cast-iron statue of the Roman god Vulcan atop Red Mountain. The statue is a tribute to the importance of iron and steel manufacturing in this industrial city's history. Birmingham was founded after the Civil War so don't expect to see many antebellum mansions. Montgomery is the older of the two cities and was the first capital of the Confederacy. There's plenty to see in the city's historic downtown. Be sure to visit the first White House of the Confederacy and the Dexter Avenue Baptist Church where Martin Luther King., Jr., preached.

Huntsville   This city has played an important role in the nation's space program. It is home to many sites connected with the space program. Among the latest attractions is "Journey to Jupiter" a motion simulator that allows visitors to imagine they're traveling to that faraway planet.

Gulf Coast Beaches   This coastal strip has beautiful, snow-white beaches that rival Florida's. Side trips from beach resorts include visits to historic Civil War forts and to Mobile, Alabama's only seaport. Enjoy the gentility of Southern living in this port city.

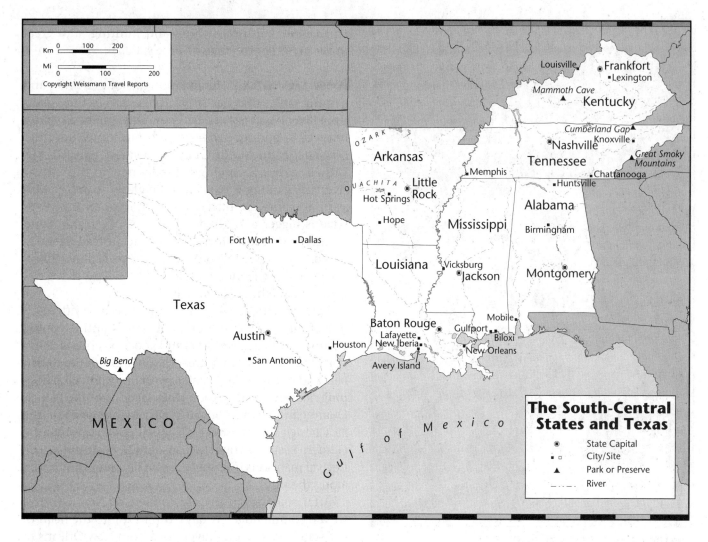

Km 0 100 200
Mi 0 100 200
Copyright Weissmann Travel Reports

O Z A R K

Arkansas

O U A C H I T A

Little Rock

Hot Springs

Hope

Memphis

Tennessee

Nashville

Knoxville

Chattanooga

Huntsville

Alabama

Birmingham

Mississippi

Fort Worth

Dallas

Louisiana

Vicksburg

Jackson

Montgomery

Texas

Austin

San Antonio

Houston

Baton Rouge

Lafayette

New Iberia

Avery Island

Gulfport

Biloxi

New Orleans

Mobile

Big Bend

M E X I C O

Gulf of Mexico

Louisville

Frankfort

Lexington

Mammoth Cave

Kentucky

Cumberland Gap

Great Smoky
Mountains

**The South-Central
States and Texas**

◉ State Capital
▪ □ City/Site
▲ Park or Preserve
— ·· — River

Arkansas

Tradition paints Arkansas as home to hot springs and hillbillies. Travelers who enjoy the simple pleasures of life in an unhurried atmosphere will have a great time in this state. Since the presidential election of 1992, tourists now also visit towns connected with Bill Clinton's life, including Hope, where he was born, and Hot Springs, where he grew up.

Little Rock and Hot Springs   Sites to see and things to do in Little Rock are really rather typical of medium-sized state capitals. So a morning's tour around this pleasant town may be enough for most visitors. An hour's drive southwest of Little Rock lies the spa town of Hot Springs and Hot Springs National Park. At the turn of the century, the region was a popular playground for rich northerners. A massive effort has rejuvenated much of the area.

Ouachita and Ozark Mountains   The great outdoors is one of Arkansas' main attractions, and many outdoor places to visit are in these mountains in the western part of the state. These heavily forested regions offer some of the best scenery in mid-America.

Kentucky

Almost all of Kentucky is hilly or mountainous, and its untamed natural beauty includes more miles of navigable water than any state other than Alaska (plus, 48 percent of Kentucky is covered by forests). Awe-inspiring mountain scenery, horse racing (including the Kentucky Derby at Churchill Downs in Louisville), horse farms carpeted with lovely bluegrass (especially around Lexington), bourbon distilleries and Southern cooking are among Kentucky's main attractions. Send clients who are interested in beautiful scenery, outdoor activities, arts and crafts and the history of the American South.

Mammoth Cave National Park   Mammoth Cave is one of the most amazing cave systems anywhere. Like Niagara Falls, it's a classic U.S. tourist site — and remains one of the country's most popular attractions.

Bourbon Street, New Orleans

and Creole cultures, fishing and hunting, and great music are other top draws to the state.

New Orleans   The invasion of slot machines and gaming tables that has swept the length of the Mississippi River has at last reached New Orleans, the city once reserved — and revered — for jazz musicians, unorthodox chefs and Mardi Gras, the wildest party in the United States. Gambling is hardly new to this city — riverboat gaming was a colorful part of life on the Mississippi before the turn of the century. Gaming 1990s style is bigger and glitzier, however. We recommend against getting stuck to a slot machine. Instead, spend as much time as possible prowling the streets of neighborhoods like the French Quarter or the sleepy, faded elegance that is the Mansion District.

The French Quarter (Vieux Carre) is a wonder — a mix of clubs, souvenir shops, restaurants, antique stores, beautiful homes, seedy bars and voodoo vendors. Bourbon Street and its cross streets house most of the tourist bars and music clubs. Spend at least one night club hopping. During the day, tour other sections of the French Quarter and surrounding areas. Try to take a ride on the St. Charles Avenue streetcar, which passes through the Garden District. You'll see absolutely beautiful Greek Revival mansions interspersed with boutiques and shops along the way.

After soaking up the atmosphere of New Orleans, we'd recommend a few days' trip west into the heart of the state. Travel along River Road from New Orleans to Baton Rouge. Some of the most impressive and oft-photographed antebellum houses in the United States are along this route. Next go on to Lafayette in the center of Cajun country. The Cajuns are descendants of French settlers from Nova Scotia who were forced to leave that territory by the British in 1755. Lafayette has great seafood and Cajun cooking. Head south to New Iberia in bayou country. Bayous are swampy regions covering much of southern Louisiana. Nearby you can visit Avery Island. Look for alligators and visit the island's Jungle Gardens and Bird Sanctuary.

There are a number of ways to see Mammoth Cave, the world's longest cave system, each one suited to particular interests and physical stamina (remember — it is way underground and involves some real walking). The scenic tours range from a little over an hour to 6.5 hours, depending on the areas visited. There are special tours for the disabled.

Louisiana

For decades — even centuries — the people of Louisiana have found one excuse after another to throw a party or have a parade. The advent of casino riverboats chugging up and down the Mississippi has added another dimension to the state's emphasis on enjoyment. The focus of that enjoyment, of course, is Louisiana's party town, New Orleans. A place to visit all year round, except maybe in the sweltering summer, New Orleans especially shines during Mardi Gras. Cajun

Mississippi

The neon and noise of dockside gambling are quickly overshadowing traditional images of Mississippi as the land of magnolias and moss. Since gaming was legalized in 1992 in this Deep South state, more than 25 casinos have opened, bringing roulette wheels, slot machines, traffic jams and flashy billboards to the state's once tranquil waterways. In addition, the casinos are spawning new resort developments on the Gulf of Mexico coast. The towns of Biloxi and Gulfport are at the center of the transformation.

Even if gambling is what takes you to the state, allow time to take a cruise on the Mississippi River, stroll along the sandy coastal beaches and tour the famous antebellum homes. Don't miss the McRaven Home in Vicksburg and Beauvoir in Biloxi, last home of Confederate President Jefferson Davis, with its beautiful view of the Gulf of Mexico. If you're interested in the history of the Civil War, be sure also to visit the Vicksburg National Military Park.

Tennessee

When hearing the name Tennessee, you might think of the frenzied foot-stomping at the Grand Ole Opry in Nashville or the blue mist rising off the Smoky Mountains. Certainly many people will think of Graceland, home of Elvis Presley — surely it's unique in the universe. We heartily recommend a visit to this beautiful state.

Memphis   On the one hand, Memphis is a genteel place where folks sip iced tea under magnolia trees as the Mississippi River flows by. On the other, it's a vibrant and downright earthy sort of town that gave birth to both the blues and rock 'n' roll. The music scene is as big a draw as — if not bigger than — the traditional Old South attractions. Music lovers will want to tour the Beale Street district, downtown near the river. After a tour there, it's time to head to Graceland. Tacky yet terrific. The mansion is the centerpiece of one of the nation's biggest tourist draws.

Eastern Tennessee   The scenery in Great Smoky Mountains National Park, extending into North Carolina, is both relaxing and striking. In spring, beautiful flowers decorate the roadsides in the park. The park is prettiest in autumn, around mid-October, when the fall foliage is at its most brilliant. To the north, Cumberland Gap National Historic Park is a wonderful place to visit for its scenic as well as its historic importance. Pioneers crossed through the Cumberland Gap in the 18th century on their way west to settle Kentucky and Tennessee.

Nashville   Going to Nashville is a kind of pilgrimage for country-music lovers. Where else can fans see so many stars — and not a few legends — perform?

The first thought on the mind of many tourists is to attend a concert at the Grand Ole Opry, the granddaddy of country-music palaces. The Opry is now the heart of the Opryland USA theme park on the outskirts of the city. It has restaurants, shops, amusement rides, museums and a dozen live shows featuring gospel, bluegrass and Broadway-style productions. A visit to the Minnie Pearl Museum is a real hoot. You'll see personal items and photographs of the country-music comedienne that will make you chuckle.

Opryland isn't the only place for music lovers in Nashville. Downtown has been recently spruced up. Ryman Auditorium, the best-known place, has been refurbished to accommodate live music once again. And don't miss the Country Music Hall of Fame and Museum. (If you have extra time, take a tour of the Hermitage, Andrew Jackson's grand home.)

Texas

Texas has so many alluring destinations that you may be tempted to see it all in a single trip. Don't. The state is so huge — the sky stretches 800 mi/1,300 km across it — that your memories will be a big blur. Instead, explore a region, spending at least a week there and returning later to see what you missed.

Geostats

State	Capital	Population	Land Area	
			Sq. Miles	Sq. Kilometers
Alabama	Montgomery	4,218,792	50,750	131,537
Arkansas	Little Rock	2,452,671	52,075	134,869
Kentucky	Frankfort	3,826,794	39,732	102,902
Louisiana	Baton Rouge	4,315,085	43,566	112,832
Mississippi	Jackson	2,669,111	46,914	121,503
Tennessee	Nashville	5,175,240	41,219	106,753
Texas	Austin	18,378,185	261,914	678,331

Dallas/Fort Worth   Dallas is a business center for insurance, oil, merchandising, tourism and high tech, and the third-largest fashion and film industry center in the U.S. The Big D's big-business profile — combined with its Southwest location — has given the city a unique blend of the urbane, the genteel and the rowdy. Its sister city, Fort Worth (30 mi/50 km away by freeway) is rodeos, Western wear and cattlemen — a "cowtown" proud of its past. Its stockyards are a tourist attraction — but so is the Kimbell Art Museum, considered one of the best small museums in the world.

Houston   Few cities are as forward-thinking and as modern-looking as Houston. Located in flat, marshy terrain, the fourth-largest city in the U.S. has a recognizable skyline of densely packed mirrored-glass-and-steel skyscrapers. It's easy to get the impression that the city sprang whole from money raked in during the oil boom. But a closer look reveals a rich, if not always revered, history that's visible in the old buildings of Market Square and in the Victorian homes of the quaint Heights neighborhood. The city is also the cultural capital of the region, recognized in opera, theater and dance. (Be warned that the traffic can be nightmarish.)

San Antonio   Hispanic culture dominates in San Antonio — the city's ties to Mexico are so strong a visit seems almost like a trip across the border. But other groups have contributed significantly to its development, too — the German immigrants of the 19th century, for instance. Their impact can be seen in everything from architectural styles to breweries. Two things not to miss: the River Walk (a major tourist attraction with restored historic buildings, shops, hotels, restaurants/cafes and nightclubs) and the Alamo. It's legendary as the place where Davy Crockett and a handful of others resisted 5,000 Mexican troops in the Texas War of Independence.

Big Bend National Park   This giant park isn't easy to get to, but it's worth the effort. The three ecosystems that converge there — river, mountain and desert — have been laced together by paved and unpaved scenic roads. Wildlife abounds — mountain lions and bears (seldom seen), bobcats, deer, javelina, road runners, foxes, snakes (including rattlesnakes), tarantulas and more varieties of birds than have been sighted in any other national park.

Itinerary

The South is such a large area, you just wouldn't be able to see it in one trip. Instead, we suggest you consider several trips there, each covering a single state or region.

Florida   On this 10-day itinerary, you would land in Tampa, on Florida's west coast. Tour the area and then drive south, toward the Everglades. (After visiting the Everglades you may want to take a trip out to the Florida Keys.) Heading north again, you'd drive along Florida's east coast to Miami. See the city and nearby Miami Beach. Then continue north through Ft. Lauderdale to Cape Canaveral to visit the Kennedy Space Center. Head inland to Orlando and Disney World. Depart Orlando.

Historic America (The Southern Colonies/ The U.S. Civil War)   This trip would take you from Virginia to Georgia. You would begin in Washington, D.C. After visiting historical sites in northern Virginia — including Civil War battlefields — you'd travel to Richmond, once capital of the Confederate States of America. Also, in Virginia you'd visit Williamsburg, Jamestown and Yorktown. Then on into North Carolina, stopping at Raleigh, the capital. Next you'd tour beautiful Charleston in South Carolina, followed by lovely Savannah in Georgia. After seeing the homes and squares in Savannah, head northwest to Atlanta, Georgia's historic capital and site of the 1996 Olympics. Depart Atlanta.

Other itineraries in the South we'd suggest: the cities of eastern and central Texas (Houston, San Antonio, Austin, Dallas and Ft. Worth); music towns (Nashville, Memphis, Branson in Missouri and, perhaps, add the Ozark Mountains); Gulf Coast (Mobile, Biloxi, New Orleans and Cajun Country).

Climate/When to Go

Almost all parts of the South experience four seasons. We believe that temperatures make late spring and early fall the best times to visit (summers can get very hot, with temperatures at or above 100 F/37 C and with very high humidity). Winters are generally mild, especially in the far south, though the temperature does drop to freezing or below in most parts of the region at least a few days every year. Spring and fall produce temperatures that range from daytime highs in the 70s and low 80s/21–27 C to nighttime lows in the 50s and 60s F/12–17 C. Spring weather can be quite unsettled, with some intense thunderstorms (even spawning tornadoes). Tropical storms, including hurricanes, can strike coastal areas, most often in late summer and fall. Southern Florida has a tropical climate and winter is the prime tourist season there.

Transportation

The major airports in the region include Dallas/Ft. Worth International Airport (DFW — the second-busiest airport in the nation), Hartsfield International Airport (ATL) in Atlanta (the third busiest), Houston Intercontinental Airport (IAH), Miami International Airport (MIA), Nashville International Airport (BNA), and Orlando International Airport (MCO). To reach northern Virginia, you may want to fly in to an airport that serves Washington, D.C. — Washington Dulles International Airport (IAD) or Washington National Airport (DCA). Because the South is such a huge region, we suggest flying in to one city, renting a car to sightsee, and then flying out of another city. Major car-rental companies have branches at most large airports.

Major interstate highways crisscross the region and many cities are served by Amtrak. Among the Amtrak routes that serve the South are those running from New York to Florida, from Chicago to New Orleans, from Chicago to Houston and from Los Angeles to Florida. Greyhound/Trailways provides bus service between major cities.

If you choose to relive the days of Huck Finn and Tom Sawyer, you'll want to float through the center of the region, down the Mississippi River in style on such classic riverboats as the Mississippi Queen.

Accommodations

The South has it all — five-star resorts, spas, luxury oceanfront hotels, restored mansion inns, B-and-Bs, lodges, motels and campgrounds. In Orlando, visitors can choose from more than a dozen hotels or theme resorts near Disney World — some are owned and operated by Disney. The Disney attention to detail creates a fantasy atmosphere in the Polynesian, Caribbean Beach, Fort Wilderness and other resorts. Miami has deluxe beach- or bay-front hotels and resorts and a number of appealing properties in its Art Deco District. In Nashville, you may want to consider staying at the deluxe all-suites Hermitage (in a historic structure from 1910) or at the enormous Opryland

Hotel. (The hotel is too massive for our tastes.) Tourist-oriented New Orleans has scores of hotels and guest houses. Be aware that French Quarter lodgings can be quite noisy, since the streets are full of activity nearly 24 hours a day.

What to Buy

Look for colonial-era antiques, Civil War memorabilia and Western wear. In south Florida you'll find tropical fruits (both fresh and in the form of preserves) which can be shipped directly home or to friends. Other treats which are eats include peanuts and pecans. The South is also a good place to buy country-music paraphernalia and crafts made by Southerners, such as pottery and quilts. There are also outlet centers and malls all over the South.

What to Eat

The South is famous for its down-home Southern cooking as well as regional cuisines like Cajun and Creole food in Louisiana, Tex-Mex and barbecue fare in Texas and Caribbean and Cuban cuisine in south Florida. If you're near the coasts, look for seafood, including oysters, shrimp, grouper and po'boys (kind of a seafood sandwich).

Don't be surprised if that down-home Southern cooking you're hankering for involves a lot of good ol' frying. Southern dishes you'll want to consider include fried shrimp, catfish, Southern barbecue, many recipes for chicken (from fried to fricasseed), collard and mustard greens and black-eyed peas. New Orleans is world famous for its Cajun and Creole food. Sample Oysters Rockefeller (originated in New Orleans), crawdads, bisque, scampi and gumbo there. If you're in Texas, try the chili (it's the state dish), chicken-fried steak and fajitas.

Travel Tips for the Client

Do dress comfortably in summer or you'll swelter in the heat and humidity . . . Don't ignore hurricane warnings along the coast (hurricane season is July–October) . . . Do take a swamp tour to get an appreciation of the marshlands and bayous of Louisiana, but don't forget to take insect repellent! . . . Don't expect to see flamingos everywhere in Florida . . . Do drive along Monument Avenue in Richmond, one of the South's most beautiful city streets. . . .

The South

Review Questions

1. What is the world's No. 1 tourist destination? What state is it in?

2. What are two sights not to miss in San Antonio?

3. What area of New Orleans is the major attraction for tourists?

4. What two places in Memphis, Tennessee, would be most likely to attract music lovers?

5. Why would you recommend late spring or early fall for a visit to most places in the South? What weather warnings should visitors to coastal areas watch out for in summer or fall?

6. What is the world's longest cave system? What state is it in?

7. In what two cities would a tourist find important places associated with Martin Luther King, Jr.? What sights in these two cities might you recommend to a tourist interested in Dr. King?

8. What two places would you suggest to a tourist interested in South Carolina beach resorts?

9. In Virginia, three historic sites are linked by the Colonial Parkway. What are those sites?

10. What national park in Florida consists of swamp and woodland? What animals might a visitor see there?

The South

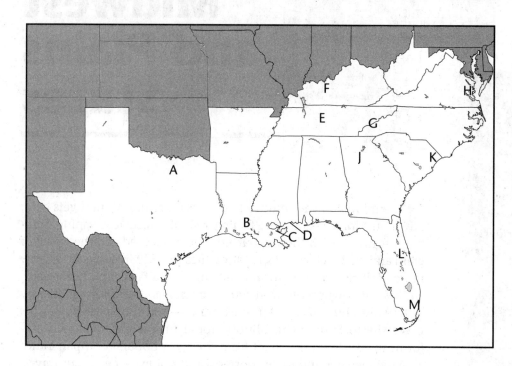

Map Skills Exercise

Match the tourist destination listed below with the corresponding letter on the map. You can use each letter only once.

1. _____ Second-busiest airport in the U.S.
2. _____ New Orleans
3. _____ Mammoth Cave
4. _____ Nashville
5. _____ Walt Disney World
6. _____ Miami
7. _____ Williamsburg
8. _____ Cajun Country
9. _____ Myrtle Beach
10. _____ Biloxi

Selling Exercise

A family plans to spend three full days in Orlando. What would you suggest they see and do there? (Select activities or sights for each of the three days.)

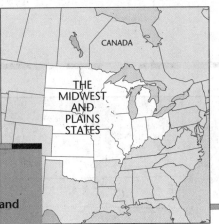

CANADA

THE
MIDWEST
AND
PLAINS
STATES

The Midwest and Plains States

The middle of the country knows its extremes. Winter gets cold, a time for ice skating, ice fishing and (of course) ice scraping. Summer turns hot, with the sun burning the berries red and the waves of grain amber. Big cities — especially Chicago and Minneapolis — grow more high-rises and highways and cultivate a faster and faster pace, while small towns try to work with the seasons. There is grand history — Lincoln's huge face at Mt. Rushmore — and simple history — his grave site in Springfield, Illinois. You'll find world-renowned performing arts down the street from the most popular oompah band.

What we've found to be constant, and not extreme, in our travels through the Midwest and the Plains are the values of the people who live there: hard work, faith, philanthropy, civic pride. Most everywhere you go, you're bound to find someone who, over a cup of coffee, will want to get to know you, too.

What to Do There

◆ The Midwest

Illinois

Chicago's big-city boisterousness seems far removed from the farmland and college towns of the rest of Illinois — and certainly the Windy City will forever attract more visitors than the low-key countryside. But visitors will find an energizing strain running through both town and country, as well as a shared Midwestern sense of work's importance.

In the state's interior, vast tracts of flat prairie (now covered by corn and soybean fields) have served as inspiration for artists ranging from poet Carl Sandburg to architect Frank Lloyd Wright. The state immortalizes Abraham Lincoln (in Springfield) with museums and historic sites while it honors its Native American ancestry at Cahokia Mounds State Park and the Dickson Mounds State Museum. Illinois has carefully preserved its historic districts (Nauvoo, Galena, Quincy), while boasting some of America's best 19th- and 20th-century architecture.

The state is drawing on the past to fund the future, as well: Riverboat gambling is attracting visitors from around the country.

Chicago

Architecture and art are often thought of as defining elements of Chicago. Some visitors go for its world-class museums, good shopping (check out the downtown Loop area) and a thriving theater scene. But what looms as large in our memories of Chicago is: water. Where else in the country's heartland can you find sandy beaches that are within walking distance of the world's tallest buildings?

Once you've taken in the views of Lake Michigan, proceed directly to the city's world-famous museums: the Art Institute of Chicago (it has one of the best collections of impressionist paintings outside the Louvre in

Paris); the Museum of Science and Industry (don't miss the coal mine, the submarine tour and the train engines); and the Field Museum of Natural History, the Adler Planetarium and the Shedd Aquarium and Oceanarium (the last three are all within sight of each other). Each ranks among the best of its kind.

Chicago's theater/club scene is acknowledged as being one of the most creative in the nation. If you enjoy Broadway-style productions, the Shubert Theater features touring shows. The Chicago Symphony is one of the finest in the world. Outdoor concerts are popular in the summer. The legendary Second City style of comedy improvisation (in the section of the city called Old Town) nurtured emerging talents John Belushi, George Wendt, Bill Murray. Also in Old Town, you'll find Zanies comedy club, where Jay Leno and Jerry Seinfeld, among others,

performed their early routines. Additionally, the city is deeply rooted in blues and folk-music clubs. Sports fans will want to see a Cubs baseball game at Wrigley Field or watch the White Sox play at the new Comiskey Park.

The city's architecture is world renowned. Chicago is where the skyscraper was born and also took the art to (literally) new heights: It boasts some of the tallest buildings in the world — the Sears Tower was the tallest (a new building in Malaysia has now won that title), and several others are in the top 10 (all have observation decks). Many other downtown buildings were also designed by the foremost architects in the U.S. Huge sculptures by Chagall, Miro and Picasso stand in the city's plazas, while dozens of homes designed by Frank Lloyd Wright (tours of the homes and his studio are available) are concentrated in the suburb of Oak Park. Sophistication blended with the unpretentious nature of Midwesterners makes Chicago one of the most pleasant cities in the U.S. to visit.

Indiana

Indiana is rich in historic sites that recount the nation's growth (battlefields, forts and historic homes) as well as arresting geography (sand dunes, caves and fossil beds). If you're visiting the state you might consider stopping at Mounds State Park near Anderson to see prehistoric Indian mounds dating back some 2,000 years. Near Lafayette, you can tour the Tippecanoe Battlefield State Memorial where General William Henry Harrison defeated a coalition of Indian tribes trying to stem the westward expansion of whites. One of our favorite outdoor experiences in the state is a visit Indiana Dunes State Park, where you can climb huge sand dunes along the shores of Lake Michigan. A trip to the park is a plus for visitors to nearby Chicago who are looking for an outdoor experience.

Indianapolis is the state's major city and the home of the Indianapolis 500 auto race, run every Memorial Day weekend. The city is a sporting town and has several professional sports teams and many excellent sports facilities. Indianapolis has many non-sports attractions too, including museums, a zoo and theaters.

Iowa

Tucked into vast acres of rolling farmland are such diverse wonders and amusements as the world's longest underground boat tour (Spook Cave near Marquette), the Bellevue "butterfly garden" (featuring hundreds of live butterflies) and Lake Okoboji, one of the world's three blue-water lakes. You can also find a Trappist abbey (near Dubuque), prehistoric Native American burial mounds (Effigy Mounds), an Amish community (Kalona) and the Amana Colonies (a religious group that manufactures household appliances). Divide remaining time among scenic railroad rides, cave exploration, winter skiing and Mississippi riverboat rides.

Michigan

Michigan is, at the same time, the center of the huge American automobile industry and a heavily forested state. Geographically, it consists of the Upper and Lower Peninsulas, both extending out into the Great Lakes.

The season of a visit will largely determine which attractions (and pretty scenes) are best for the traveler. The roadside fruit and vegetable stands, selling peaches, apple cider and cherries, set up shop from May to October. Summer is a great time to stroll along the hundreds of miles of shoreline along the four Great Lakes almost surrounding the state. We're referring to Lakes Superior, Huron, Michigan and Erie. Those who love brilliant foliage will want to visit sometime during September or October. Skiers will find snow by Thanksgiving. The best times to visit Detroit are between April and November when temperatures are most pleasant.

Detroit   Economic hard times have taken their toll on the Motor City. Much of it is run-down and crime is a problem. The best place to visit is probably along the waterfront where you'll discover convention halls, hotels, restaurants, night spots and sports facilities. We suggest starting your trip at the Renaissance Center, seven circular buildings on the waterfront connected by walkways. You'll find an observation deck atop the tallest, the 70-story Westin Hotel where you can observe Detroit as the birds do.

Just east of the Renaissance Center lies Belle Isle, one of the best city parks in the United States. The park is home to the Anne Scrips Whitcombe Conservatory displaying flowers and plants, many from desert or tropical environments.

One must-see in town is the Motown Museum housing memorabilia of the many wonderful artists who have recorded under the company's labels. You might want to drive across the Ambassador Bridge and check out another country — Canada. Windsor in Ontario is just across the bridge from Detroit.

Minnesota

Escape civilization and venture to Boundary Waters Canoe Area in far northern Minnesota. About all you'll see is dense forest, rocky shores, crystalline lakes and streams and an immense moose or two tramping about. When your body aches from paddling and escaping bears, you can head for the Twin Cities (Minneapolis and St. Paul) for a rendezvous with culture. The combination of a vast unspoiled wilderness and urban sophistication makes Minnesota a great destination. Anyone who dreads cold weather should avoid the state in winter.

Minneapolis/St. Paul What residents strive for and offer visitors is big-city activities and amenities (old and new) without an excess of big-city problems. Of the two, Minneapolis is the more rushed. Both cities highly prize the arts. The Guthrie Theater in Minneapolis is one of the nation's best; its world-renowned repertory company produces Broadway-quality — or better — theater year round. In St. Paul, the Ordway Music Theatre is home to opera and orchestra.

The Mall of America

Of course, there's also the Mall of America in suburban Bloomington. It's the biggest mall in the United States and a major draw for visitors. One of the most interesting corners of the mall is Lego Imagination Center, where everything is made of Lego blocks. Kids love it.

Missouri

Mark Twain country boasts rolling hills, farmland, the Mississippi River and the lovely Ozark Mountains, two major U.S. cities (St. Louis and Kansas City) and a bustling music town, Branson. Visitors will find steamboat excursions (and riverboat gambling), theme parks, sites related to Mark Twain (Hannibal) and Harry S Truman (Independence) as well as more than 5,000 caves. Great steaks, statues, fountains and boulevards characterize Kansas City on the Missouri River. Send clients who are interested in 19th-century architecture, theme parks, outdoor recreation and pleasant Midwestern scenery.

Branson Move over, Nashville. The little upstart, Branson, Missouri, is stealing the show. So many music stars — particularly country-and-western singers — visit Branson that some people now call it the Music Show Capital of the U.S. (almost 6 million visitors turn up each year to clap and tap along). The shows themselves often resemble Las Vegas-style variety acts and are generally offered twice a day (at midday and at night).

St. Louis The revitalized city of St. Louis has seen a great deal of change in recent years. The city's rebirth has brought about the transformations of both Laclede's Landing (a restored warehouse district now full of shops, restaurants and clubs) and the St. Louis Union Station (now a shopping and dining complex with an adjoining hotel). St. Louis embraces change, but the "Gateway to the West" is carefully maintaining existing attractions. Among its steadfast draws are the Gateway Arch (you can ride up the 630 ft/192 m for great views), the Anheuser-Busch Brewery and Grant's Farm (where the Budweiser Clydesdales live).

Ohio

Don't underestimate Ohio. It has a lot to offer any visitor. You can cruise the Ohio River on an old-fashioned paddle-wheeler in Cincinnati. Sip a fresh brew in Columbus' historic German Village. And watch hippopotamuses swim in Toledo in the world's only Hippoquarium. In between the state's many large (Cleveland, Cincinnati and Columbus) and medium-sized cities (Dayton, Toledo and Akron) are vast fields of corn and grain, wildlife refuge areas and classic American small towns.

Columbus This capital is the largest city in the world named after the famous explorer, Christopher Columbus. You can visit a full-sized replica of his flagship, the *Santa Maria*, permanently moored downtown. Other attractions include the Franklin Park Conservatory — inspired by London's Crystal Palace — where you'll find an exhibit showcasing seven of the world's ecosystems; and German Village, a historic district known for its 19th-century-style restaurants, shops, homes and beer gardens.

Cincinnati Ride a paddle-wheeler along the Ohio River past Cincinnati. It's the best way to appreciate this river city. You'll be amazed by the neighborhoods built on steep hills — the houses seem in danger of tumbling into the river. And you'll get a flavor of the city's past as the boat rides by red-brick warehouses and barge docks. There's almost a European charm to Cincinnati, traceable to its German heritage.

Visitors are intrigued by this lovely town and by its good restaurants and nightlife. Key to keeping the downtown alive was the decision to build the new baseball and football stadium there instead of in the suburbs. When the Reds and Bengals are playing, the downtown is packed. If you have time, cross the river to Covington on the Kentucky side. Visit Covington Landing, said to be the largest floating entertainment complex in the U.S.

Cleveland Cleveland reminds us a lot of a boxer who has a penchant for classical music. There's a rough, brawny side to this port on the Great Lakes — born in its noisy loading docks and its smoky steel mills. But it also has a refined side visible in the theaters and spacious museums in lovely University Circle. Must-sees are the Museum of Art and the Museum of Natural History, where the reconstructed skeleton of Lucy, one of the most important anthropological finds dug up in East Africa, is on display.

New in town is the Rock and Roll Hall of Fame. It has received rave reviews — for style (I.M. Pei's geometric shapes include a cantilevered glass "tent" that seems to rise straight out of the water) and substance (its interactive exhibits chronicle the evolution of rock).

Wisconsin

Wisconsin is one of the country's most attractive states. That's why so many Midwesterners don't bother to leave the region for vacations — they head to Door County or the Wisconsin Dells. Unlike its neighbors to the south, Wisconsin, nicknamed "America's Dairyland," is hilly with pastures of alfalfa and clover rolling right up to the red barns on its many farms. The picture-book farm landscapes are complemented by pleasant wooded stretches. In addition to its natural attractiveness, the state offers the big-city draw of Milwaukee.

Door County, in the northern part of the state, is a beautiful recreational area that juts out into Lake Michigan. It's a great place to rent a cabin and fish, water-ski, go boating or just take it easy. Wisconsin Dells is in the south central region of the state. If you want pure scenic beauty here, you'll find it on one of the boat tours through the towering sandstone cliffs along the Wisconsin River. On land, there's no shortage of entertainment, including a greyhound track and a Native American-run bingo and casino palace. The city of Milwaukee revels in its rich ethnic heritage. Immigrants from Poland, Scandinavia, Ireland, Italy and Germany came to the city at the turn of the century in large numbers to work in its meat-packing plants and breweries. The Germans were the biggest immigrant group of all and consequently beer has played a major part in the city's history. Don't forget to tour one of the big breweries.

◆ The Plains States

Kansas

It may come as a surprise that Kansas, a state of wheat and cattle, is in many ways the heart of what people think of as the Old West. There, you can trace the paths of the thundering herds of cattle drives, the westward trek (by wagon and rail) of the pioneers (the Chisholm and Santa Fe trails; the towns of Atchison and Topeka),

Geostats — The Midwest

State	Capital	Population	Land Area Sq. Miles	Sq. Kilometers
Illinois	Springfield	11,751,774	55,593	143,980
Indiana	Indianapolis	5,752,073	35,870	92,900
Iowa	Des Moines	2,829,252	55,875	144,711
Michigan	Lansing	9,496,147	56,809	147,130
Minnesota	St. Paul	4,567,267	79,617	206,200
Missouri	Jefferson City	5,277,640	68,898	178,439
Ohio	Columbus	11,102,198	40,953	106,064
Wisconsin	Madison	5,081,658	54,314	140,668

the famous lawmen and notorious outlaws (the Dalton Gang Hideout is in Meade, southwest of Dodge City). In Dodge City itself, visit historic Front Street, the re-created main street lined with museums, saloons, Boot Hill Cemetery and Hangman's Tree. You can also take a 36-hour wagon-train ride through the tall grass prairie of the Flint Hills. Send clients interested in cowboys and the history of the American West and those who prefer a leisurely, uncrowded atmosphere.

Nebraska

Once a hotbed of cattle drives, westward expansion and warring between homesteaders and Native American tribes, Nebraska is where the Midwest becomes the West. Its colorful past is recounted in a number of museums, national monuments and historic sites (among them Fort Robinson, Fort Kearny and Fort McPherson National Cemetery). Wildlife refuges (including a bison herd at Fort Niobrara National Wildlife Refuge) and national grasslands acknowledge the value of retaining Nebraska's prairies and unusual geologic formations (Scotts Bluff National Monument, Chimney Rock National Historic Site). Nebraska easily fits into a tour of the West that includes Colorado and Wyoming. Send clients who want an atypical vacation in a less well-known part of the U.S. and who are interested in the history of the American West.

North Dakota

North Dakota, a land of sweeping vistas and abundant wildlife, offers a more authentic view of the West than other more popular destinations. Teddy Roosevelt loved the state so much he bought a ranch there (part of which is now within Theodore Roosevelt National Park). Native American culture and legalized gambling (slots, blackjack and horse racing) are two of the state's other leading attractions. The International Peace Garden straddles the border with Canada. Send clients looking for an open area to hunt, fish, camp or watch wildlife or who are interested in the history of the American West. (Of note, North Dakota is the least visited state in the U.S. No doubt geography is partly to blame — it has no major cross-country highways passing through it and no large cities to attract tourists.)

Oklahoma

If you're fascinated by Native American and cowboy history and culture then you may love a trip to Oklahoma. Soak up Native American culture with a visit to Anadarko, 70 miles/113 km southwest of the state capital, Oklahoma City. Anadarko is a rich source of Native

Cowtown, Wichita, Kansas

American history, artifacts and crafts. Each August, local tribes sponsor the week-long American Indian Exposition featuring powwows, arts and crafts exhibits and the National War Dance Championship. Lovers of Cowboy America may want to visit Guthrie, the state's first capital, and its many attractions depicting the life of the early European settlers in the late 1800s. The state's two largest cities, Oklahoma City and Tulsa, also have sites associated with western history. Oklahoma City is home to the National Cowboy Hall of Fame and Western Heritage Center.

In Oklahoma City, the site of the most devastating terrorist attack in American history, the Federal Building, is also likely to become a major tourist draw.

South Dakota

While most of South Dakota consists of high plains and rolling hills, the Black Hills (in the southwest corner) are characterized by impressive mountains, rivers and lakes. Mount Rushmore is its biggest attraction, but the state also features impressive caves (Jewel Cave National Monument, Wind Cave National Park) and the beautiful, winding Needles Highway (Highway 87) that cuts through granite spires, around hairpin turns and through tunnels. Nearby is the mysterious landscape of the Badlands National Park. Deadwood is once again a thriving gambling town (book far ahead for accommodations), reviving the pastime that got Wild Bill Hickock killed holding aces and eights. Send clients who love outdoor activities, impressive mountain scenery, wildlife watching (managed bison herds and several national wildlife refuges) and spectacular national monuments. (Anyone traveling to Yellowstone or Grand Teton National Park in Wyoming should consider including

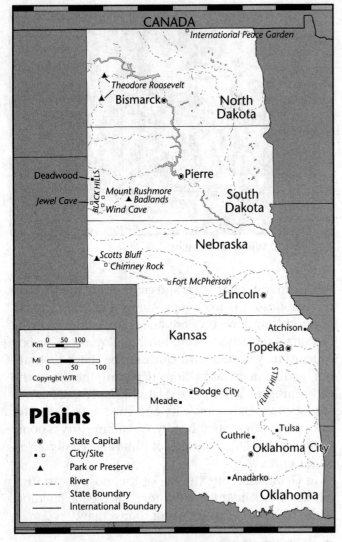

CANADA
International Peace Garden

Theodore Roosevelt
Bismarck●

North
Dakota

Deadwood

BLACK HILLS

Jewel Cave
Mount Rushmore
▲ Badlands
Wind Cave

●Pierre

South
Dakota

Nebraska

▲Scotts Bluff
□ Chimney Rock

□ Fort McPherson

Lincoln ●

Atchison ■

Kansas

Topeka●

FLINT HILLS

■Dodge City
Meade ■

● Tulsa
Guthrie ■

Oklahoma City

■ Anadarko
Oklahoma

Km 0   50   100

Mi 0   50   100
Copyright WTR

Plains

● State Capital
■ □ City/Site
▲ Park or Preserve
–·–·– River
——— State Boundary
——— International Boundary

take you to parts of the area rather than one sweeping trip covering all 13 states. Here's an itinerary that will take you to the major cities and a wonderful resort along the Great Lakes.

Day 1 — Arrive Chicago.

Day 2 — Chicago.

Day 3 — Depart Chicago for Milwaukee. Tour that city and overnight there.

Day 4 — Travel north along Lake Michigan through Door County and overnight in the city of Green Bay.

Day 5 — Cross into the state of Michigan and arrive at Mackinac Island, a beautiful resort island between Michigan's peninsulas.

Day 6 — Enjoy some relaxation on Mackinac Island.

Day 7 — Travel through the lower peninsula of Michigan to Detroit.

Day 8 — Detroit.

Day 9 — Depart Detroit for Cleveland. Overnight there.

Day 10 — Tour Cleveland and depart for home in the evening.

You also might want to consider a "heartland tour" that would take you to the medium-sized cities of the area (Des Moines, Omaha, Sioux Falls, Oklahoma City) coupled with key tourist attractions outside these cities (for example, Mt. Rushmore, Branson or Scotts Bluff National Monument).

Climate/When to Go

The region has four distinct seasons, ranging from cold winters to hot, somewhat humid summers. By far, the best time to visit is May–October, even though some summer days will be unpleasant. In spring, be prepared for occasional heavy rain and possible tornadoes. There can be plenty of snow in winter, especially in the snow belts along the Great Lakes. The foliage is beautiful during the fall when the leaves turn colors.

western South Dakota — the Black Hills, Mt. Rushmore and Badlands National Park — in the itinerary.)

Mount Rushmore National Memorial

Located in the Black Hills, Mt. Rushmore is one of the most famous landmarks in the U.S. The likenesses of four U.S. presidents — Washington, Jefferson, Lincoln and Theodore Roosevelt (each 60 ft/18 m tall) — have been carved into this mountain. We recommend that you see Mount Rushmore in three ways — from the ground looking up, face to face from a helicopter and at night, when the lighting is particularly dramatic. Be sure to visit the museum, which details how the monument came to be.

Itinerary

Like the U.S. South, the Midwest and Plains region is huge. We suggest that you consider itineraries that will

Transportation

The major airports in the region include O'Hare International Airport (ORD) serving Chicago; Detroit International Airport (DTW); Minneapolis-St. Paul International Airport (MSP); Hopkins International Airport (CLE) serving Cleveland; Cincinnati-Northern Kentucky International Airport (CVG); Lambert-St. Louis International Airport (STL) and Kansas City International Airport (MCI). The airports mentioned above serving Chicago, Minneapolis, Detroit and St. Louis are ranked among the top 25 busiest in the United States. O'Hare International Airport serving Chicago is, in fact, the busiest airport in the entire world.

Major interstate highways crisscross the region and many cities are served by Amtrak. (There is no Amtrak service in Oklahoma or South Dakota.) Greyhound provides bus service between cities and parts outside the region. Chicago is well served by suburban trains and the El, an elevated train/subway system.

One unique way to travel in the region is by riverboat. The Delta Queen and the Mississippi Queen sail up the Mississippi River from the South a few times each year.

Accommodations

Accommodations range from deluxe hotels to bed-and-breakfasts, motels, campgrounds and resorts. In Chicago, you can choose from among the well-kept older hotels, such as the Drake, on or just off Michigan Avenue or one of the new hotels, such as the Sheraton Chicago. Luxury condos and cottages are available along the shores of the Great Lakes. If you decide to travel to beautiful Mackinac Island between the two peninsulas of Michigan, consider staying at the Grand Hotel and enjoying the sweeping views from its veranda.

What to Buy

Shopping in Chicago is a real treat. The Magnificent Mile along Michigan Avenue is one of the world's great cosmopolitan shopping areas, featuring department stores, boutiques, specialty stores and a multistory shopping mall. Also, go downtown to State Street to visit Marshall Field and other stores.

Items to look for in individual states include ceramics (Michigan), maple syrup and glass products (Ohio); cold-weather gear (Minnesota); Black Hills gold jewelry (South Dakota); and Native American arts and crafts and Western gear (Plains states).

What to Eat

Literally every type of food is available in the region. In the big cities, look especially for ethnic foods, including German, Polish, Czech, Swedish, Italian, French, Kosher, Indian, Thai and Chinese. If you go for McDonald's, visit the original one in the Chicago suburb of Des Plaines. In the upper Midwest (dairy country), try the cheeses. Ohio is known for maple-sugar products (watch for roadside stands). Try the home-style cooking in the Plains states and in the countryside in the Midwest states.

Travel Tips for the Client

Don't pass up the opportunity to hear some authentic Chicago blues. It's a powerhouse style unique to the city . . . Do visit one of the 104 lighthouses along the Great Lakes . . . Don't drive across the region in winter without checking road conditions first. And carry emergency supplies . . . Be careful not to get too close to buffalo. These scruffy, massive creatures are fast and unpredictable. . . .

Geostats — The Plains States

State	Capital	Population	Land Area Sq. Miles	Land Area Sq. Kilometers
Kansas	Topeka	2,554,047	81,823	211,913
Nebraska	Lincoln	1,622,858	76,878	199,106
North Dakota	Bismarck	637,988	68,994	178,688
Oklahoma	Oklahoma City	3,258,069	68,679	177,872
South Dakota	Pierre	721,164	75,896	196,563

The Midwest and Plains States

Review Questions

1. What is the world's busiest airport? What city does it serve?

2. In which state can visitors enjoy the shorelines of four Great Lakes? Which lakes are they?

3. Why might you recommend a family visiting Minneapolis/St. Paul go to the suburb of Bloomington?

4. Where in Missouri would you most likely send a country-and-western music lover?

5. Why might you recommend that a rock music fan visit Cleveland?

6. What do the main attractions of Anadarko all have in common? In what state is it?

7. Where in Detroit can a visitor get a bird's-eye view of the city? What seven-building center is it part of?

8. In what two scenic areas of Wisconsin do Midwesterners often vacation?

9. What three ways might you recommend a tourist see Mount Rushmore?

10. What is Chicago's Magnificent Mile?

The Midwest and Plains States

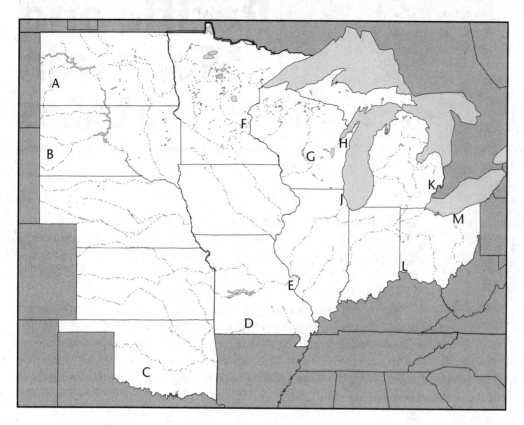

Map Skills Exercise

Match the tourist destination listed below with the corresponding letter on the map. You can use each letter only once.

1. _____ Mt. Rushmore
2. _____ Chicago
3. _____ Branson
4. _____ Wisconsin Dells
5. _____ Detroit
6. _____ Rock and Roll Hall of Fame
7. _____ Gateway Arch
8. _____ Mall of America
9. _____ Theodore Roosevelt National Park
10. _____ Anadarko

Selling Exercise

You work for an auto club. Three friends who want to take a driving tour of the Plains states come to you for advice. They are particularly interested in Native American and cowboy history, but they have time to visit only four sites. Plot on a map a driving tour for them. (Use outline map #5 for this exercise.) List at least one attraction on the map for each site you select for them.

The Pacific and Mountain States

The picture is — as they still say in California — awesome. From searing desert to crushing glacier, from the soaring majesty of the Rockies to the gaping maw of the Grand Canyon, the United States at its most beautiful lies in the Pacific and Mountain States. Hawaii, way out in the ocean, can even be called paradise.

The region has always been a magnet for adventurers, and today's attractions are no exception: the made-up world of Hollywood movies; spiritual fulfillment in New Mexico's empty desert; the perfect wave off Oahu's northern shore. The region can be choked with pollution and trends — for the worst examples, go to L.A. — or a breath of fresh air in the forests of Idaho. It has a rainbow of cultures — for the best examples, go to L.A. or San Francisco. There's even the take-a-chance frontier of Las Vegas, where millions gamble for millions. Fool's gold? Maybe not.

What to Do There

◆ The Pacific States
Alaska

Alaska today offers visitors something more precious than gold: the chance to see mountains, fjords, forests and valleys almost untouched by human hands. But that's changing. More and more people seem to be discovering the state (cruise ships, in particular, are now bringing hundreds of thousands of people each year.) Remember, Alaska isn't cheap — per-day expenses are comparable with those in New York City.

Anchorage   The city of Anchorage itself, Alaska's largest, looks a lot like other major cities in the U.S.. This may disappoint many visitors. Not to worry. Glaciers, hiking trails, mountains and white-water rivers are just minutes away.

You can get a good introduction to the state at the Anchorage Museum of History and Art, which has exhibits showing how Alaskans have lived, from the first Alaskans who crossed the Bering Land Bridge from Asia to the boom-time workers of the 20th century. Be sure to drop by Earthquake Park, which commemorates the 1964 quake that ravaged the city.

Anchorage is an excellent base for many of the more popular excursions to Alaska's abundant nature areas. Consider taking day trips to the Kenai Peninsula for its outdoor activities, Denali National Park, or Valdez to see the massive Columbia Glacier. It's awe inspiring to watch great chunks of the glacier drop off into the ocean.

Cruising to Alaska

A great way to see Alaska is to take a cruise along the Inside Passage. There are a number of ways to see this spectacular seaway. Many people choose to ride one of the 23 cruise ships that ply Alaskan waters (embarkation is usually from Vancouver in British Columbia.) An inexpensive way is to take one of the ferries that make two- to four-day runs up to Alaska from Washington State or British Columbia. The ferries stop at Ketchikan, Juneau and Sitka, among other ports. Juneau, Alaska's capital, is a narrow little city with a beautiful harbor surrounded by spectacular mountains. If you stop in Sitka, check out the architecture from the time it was the capital of Russian America. As you sail along the rugged coast of the state, you'll see some of the most beautiful scenery in the world: cloud-capped mountains, glaciers, coniferous forests, moose, whales and many other animals.

Denali National Park

This huge national park lies between Anchorage and Fairbanks, Alaska's second-largest city. It's a truly spectacular area, featuring the majestic 20,320-ft/6,194-m Mt. McKinley, the highest peak in North America. A good time to visit is from mid-May to mid-September, when temperatures are most pleasant. Denali offers excellent guided hiking and sightseeing tours, some going deep into the park.

California

From the fast-lane glitz of Los Angeles to the strong traditions of San Francisco's Chinatown, and from the barren wasteland of Death Valley to the overwhelming visual poetry of Yosemite, the state covers all types of terrain, both physical and cultural. California is host to a wealth of outstanding attractions: sequoia and redwood forests, beaches, cultural offerings, nightlife, historic sites and terrific food. The northern portion of the state is famed for the Wine Country of Napa and Sonoma valleys. It's also home to Marin County, San Francisco, Lake Tahoe, Mount Shasta and Yosemite. The popular destinations of Hollywood, Disneyland, Palm Springs, San Diego and Death Valley can be found in the southern half of the state.

Los Angeles

This gigantic Southern California metropolis is a mix of glamour, urban sprawl, oceanfront playground and sheer unshackled energy. People used to

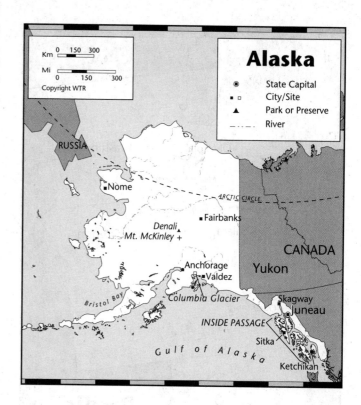

criticize it as the capital of kitsch or lowbrow taste, the world's garden of glitz. But that judgment has given way to the realization that Los Angeles' culture is rich, and the creativity of its citizens is boundless.

In your wanderings around the city, don't miss those landmarks — well-known and some less-known — that make Los Angeles L.A. There's the famous Hollywood sign telegraphing its address from the hills. There are the Watts Towers, one man's magnificent assemblage of discarded steel, cement, tile and whatever else came along. There's the Coca Cola Bottling Plant, built to look like an ocean liner, and the Capitol Records office tower, resembling a stack of records. With all its ethnic diversity, L.A. is no melting pot — it's the whole kitchen, what with Chinatown, Little Tokyo, Koreatown, the Jewish traditions of Fairfax, South Central (the heart of the city's African-American culture) and the Latino flavor of Olvera Street and the Old Plaza. With so much to see and do in the area, you'll want to divide your time among the five areas of the city described below.

The Coast

Places to stop along the coast include Malibu for great surfing and secluded beaches, as well as fine ocean views from the hillside, and the town itself, home to many movie stars. Be sure to allow time to see the J. Paul Getty Museum. Known as "the richest museum in the world," the Getty houses its collection of antiquities in an ostentatious mansion. In Santa Monica check out the Pier, a well-preserved amusement complex that will

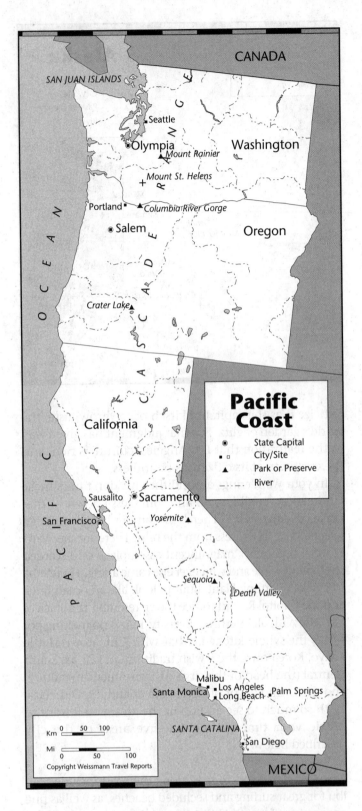

Pacific Coast

- ◉ / ◎ State Capital
- ■ / □ City/Site
- ▲ Park or Preserve
- ‒‒‒ River

Copyright Weissmann Travel Reports

bladers, bodybuilders and street performers of almost every stripe. The atmosphere is definitely funky. Then in Long Beach, you can see the classic ocean liner, the *Queen Mary*. From Long Beach head for very beautiful and unusual Santa Catalina Island for the beach, tennis, golf, horseback riding and fishing (there's even a herd of buffalo in the center of the island).

Westside   There you'll find Beverly Hills, known to all in story and song ("swimming pools, movie stars"). Even if you're not a pro-ranked shopper, you can't miss a stroll past the exclusive boutiques on Rodeo (ro-DAY-oh) Drive — we rate it among the top ten shopping experiences in the world. You can also buy maps — of dubious reliability — locating movie stars' homes.

Hollywood   See the Hollywood Walk of Fame (almost 2,000 star-shaped plaques with famous and not-so-famous stars' names embedded in the sidewalk). Stars also left lasting impressions (handprints, even nose prints) in the cement in front of Mann's (formerly Grauman's) Chinese Theater. If you are interested in natural history, the George C. Page Museum of La Brea Discoveries is the site of real primeval tar pits into which all kinds of creatures fell and died — their fossils are on display. The biggest draw in Hollywood these days has to be Universal Studios. On the tour there, you can meet prehistoric celebrities on the set of *The Flintstones,* battle Klingons, confront King Kong and Bruce the Shark (from *Jaws*) and ride through Jurassic Park.

Downtown   In Downtown you'll find museums, theaters, stores and restaurants. Start your own tour at the sensational Museum of Contemporary Art: The collection of international works (from the 1940s to the present) is housed in a stunning Arata Isozaki-designed building, a work of modern art itself. You may also want to visit ethnic areas: Little Tokyo, Chinatown and Olvera Street, which showcases L.A.'s Mexican heritage, with lots of little boutiques, eateries and outdoor market stalls.

Anaheim   The primary attraction of this suburb is Disneyland. Even the adults will enjoy this theme park, and there's now an element of nostalgia for many parents — they first went there when they were children. If you have time, consider stopping in at Knott's Berry Farm (a long-standing theme park with an Old West setting).

take you back to the days of fedoras and flappers. Santa Monica is also a haven for shoppers and cafe society — lots of upscale boutiques and restaurants. From Santa Monica, ease over to Venice Beach with its carnival-like atmosphere on weekends with roller-skaters, roller-

San Diego   It's easy to see why San Diego has long been on the lists of most-livable U.S. cities: It's weather is almost perfect. And its classic California attractions — particularly the Spanish missions and the rugged coastline — are awesome. Additionally, San Diego has some great cultural offerings.

One place you will want to visit for sure is Balboa Park, which has long been at the top of our list of best parks in the world. The park is a huge expanse with theaters and wonderful museums hidden in lush vegetation straight out of a Dr. Seuss book. But the park is best known for its superlative San Diego Zoo, one of the world's greatest.

San Diego's downtown, once deteriorating, is a big attraction now, too. There, you'll want to walk through the Gaslamp Quarter — a 16-block National Historic District with beautifully restored Victorian buildings and restaurants. The area also has one of the finest collection, of upscale shops anywhere, Paladion San Diego. The picturesque waterfront area known as the Embarcadero includes the lovely Martin Luther King Jr. Promenade, a park along Harbor Drive.

Other attractions in San Diego include the San Diego de Alcala Mission, Sea World, harbor cruises, Wild Animal Park (where you can get up close and personal with the animals) and historic Old Town. Day trips can be taken to Tijuana, Mexico, on a shiny red trolley that runs from downtown San Diego (bring proof of citizenship).

Sea World, San Diego

San Francisco   San Francisco is one of our favorite cities in the world. It's physically beautiful, it's culturally and historically stimulating — and it has great restaurants! The city itself is relatively small. When planning your visit, think of it as a group of neighborhoods or commercial areas, many of which are practically right in a row (downtown, Chinatown, North Beach and Fisherman's Wharf, for instance).

Chinatown   A remarkable city within a city. Great Chinese restaurants abound there. You also find tourist-oriented shops and attractions as well as streets lined with markets and shops where Chinese-American citizens buy meat, produce and pastries. Among the many sights in this community are the Buddha's Universal Church, the largest Buddhist temple in America, and the Chinatown Wax Museum (illustrating the role of Chinese immigrants in American history). Nearby is the elegant 19th-century neighborhood of Nob Hill and the TransAmerica Pyramid, the pylon-shaped office building that has become an unlikely symbol for the city.

Downtown   Start your visit there just outside downtown in the Mission District. Linger awhile in this fascinating Latino community, with its bakeries, bars and little shops. You may also want to walk over to Castro Street, a few blocks to the west. It's the heart of the gay community. Lots of restaurants, bars and shops there. Plan on a stop at the Japan Center to the north (cultural and commercial attractions). Visit the Civic Center, the towering complex that's the center of city government. Nearby is the Performing Arts Center. Cross the street to the Moscone Convention Center. The convention center is part of the Yerba Buena Gardens, the largest urban cultural complex built in the U.S. during the last 20 years. It includes a stunning waterfall memorial to Martin Luther King, Jr., and the Center for the Arts, which city officials hope will be San Francisco's equivalent of New York's Lincoln Center. And just across the street from the center is the San Francisco Museum of Modern Art. You'll also want to stop at Union Square — one of the places to shop in San Francisco — or the Embarcadero Center, a huge shopping and restaurant complex (near the waterfront).

Fisherman's Wharf Every type of seafood is available, in both sit-down restaurants and stand-up food stalls (some sell take-along crab-salad sandwiches made on sourdough bread). Nearby is Ghirardelli Square, a former chocolate factory turned into a shopping center. You can take a ferry from Fisherman's Wharf out in the bay to Alcatraz, once an impregnable-fortress-style federal prison. Now, it's a very popular tourist attraction.

Golden Gate Bridge More than anything else, this graceful, almost delicate-looking bridge leading to Marin County has come to symbolize San Francisco (it has the tallest supporting towers ever built). Drive across the bridge to Sausalito, a very nice town of waterfront shops and restaurants.

Golden Gate Park This is a green oasis in the midst of a city where lawns are considered a luxury. It has a dozen artificial lakes, an amazing assortment of trees and plants from around the world, Dutch windmills, an equestrian center, a trotting track, tennis courts, a golf course and more. Inside the park you'll find excellent museums, including the Steinhart Aquarium and the Natural History Museum. One of the park's loveliest sights is the Japanese Tea Garden — a teahouse, a Moon Bridge and a colorful pagoda.

North Beach/Washington Square This is where you get to ride San Francisco's famous cable cars. There's plenty of nightlife and, especially around the Washington Square — Little Italy — area, some of the best Italian restaurants in the U.S. Steep, winding Lombard Street is there. It's reputed to be the "Crookedest Street in the World." Climb Telegraph Hill and stand in the shadow of Coit Tower for an excellent view of the city.

Additional cultural attractions include the San Francisco Opera, one of the finest opera companies in the world, and the San Francisco Ballet, acclaimed for its dancers and also for its choreographic achievements in classical ballet and new work.

Yosemite National Park Yosemite still is one of the most majestically beautiful places in the United States. It is, unfortunately, extremely overcrowded, and it's often frustrating to visit this park. Once there, look for such familiar formations in the valleys as Half Dome, Cathedral Spires and El Capitan. The largest pure-granite outcropping in the world, El Capitan has absolutely sheer walls. Yosemite's waterfalls are most impressive in the spring. Sequoia National Park is relatively close by.

Hawaii

When potential travelers daydream of resort vacations, they dream most often of Hawaii, according to pollsters. We don't doubt the dreams, and we think Hawaii delivers: The islands can seem touristy in spots, and they are not inexpensive, but we'd bet that even the most cynical visitor will, at some point, use the word paradise.

Hawaii's islands vary greatly in flavor, weather, population and natural wonders. They can please lovestruck honeymooners as well as outdoors lovers in search of an active volcano — provided travelers are matched with the island that suits their tastes. Our recommendation is to settle first on the Hawaii you're dreaming of — whether you want beaches or rare orchids, luaus or hikes in the rain forest — and then plan your itinerary accordingly. The four principal islands are Hawaii, Kauai, Maui and Oahu.

Hawaii Hawaii, known as the Big Island, is peaceful; some accommodations lie in very rural areas, and the topography runs to extremes — deserts, volcanoes and rain forests.

Visitors determined to see an active volcano will find one of the best bets is on the Big Island: The world's most active volcano, Kilauea, has been erupting steadily for the past 10 years. You'll also find colorful beaches — golden, green (olivine), gray, black and white. The deep-sea fishing and snorkeling are both great and during at least a few months in winter, you can snow ski, though only for the novelty of it.

Hawaii boasts Mauna Kea (the world's tallest mountain, if you count the portion below the surface of the sea); four huge cattle and horse ranches (Parker's is actually the second-largest cattle ranch in the U.S.); and more gorgeous flowers than you can imagine — most of the orchids for the leis made in the state are grown there. All of this peace and nature means, of course, that nightlife and shopping are limited.

Hilo The largest city on the island is a must for garden enthusiasts. Among the gardens to visit there are Orchids of Hawaii and Liliuokalani (one of the largest formal Asian gardens in the world). The most expensive resort ever built is also on this island, the Hilton Waikoloa Village in Kohala.

Kauai We think Kauai is Hawaii's most beautiful, most tropical and most romantic island. Known as the "Garden Isle," it has many public and private gardens. The principal city, Lihue, has a small but excellent museum, the Kauai Museum, with exhibits on local culture.

The north shore of the island is one of the most magnificent spots in the state. Among the attractions there are Wailua Falls and the 3-mi/5-km Wailua River Trip (to beautiful Fern Grotto, site of many weddings). Not far from Wailua River is the Holoholoku Heiau, one of Kauai's oldest temples (human sacrifices were once offered there).

On the south shore, don't miss Prince Kuhio's birthplace, Menehune Gardens and Fishponds, Captain Cook's first landing point (in 1778) and the view of Waimea Canyon. Drive along the canyon rim to Kokee State Park, where you can get great views of the Kalalau Valley. Then head on to Kalalau Lookout for spectacular views of the Na Pali Coast.

We consider it mandatory to take a helicopter ride around the island (they often go through Waimea Canyon and along the Na Pali Coast). Another aerial tour is to areas where the movie *Jurassic Park* was filmed.

Maui   This is the island that puts a California edge on laid-back Hawaii style. A little trendy, a little artsy and full of deluxe resort hotels, it's been years since Maui could claim it was off the beaten trail. It's the second most popular of the islands — and the most expensive. Golfers will be in heaven, as will tennis players and divers and other water-sports enthusiasts. Visitors will find good restaurants, but rather limited nightlife and shopping.

Maui is beautiful, with rolling hills and valleys filled with sugarcane fields and two mountainous regions running through it. You can hike through the rain forest, and the whale-watching (November-March) is great, too.

Key tourist attractions on the island include Mt. Haleakala in Haleakala National Park, the Hana Highway, Waimoku Falls and the towns of Hana and Lahaina. Catch the sunrise from the summit of Mt. Haleakala. The morning view from this volcano inspired Mark Twain to say it was one of the loveliest he'd ever seen. After touring the park in the morning, take a drive along the Hana Highway through the lushest foliage on Maui and passing roadside waterfalls and dramatic coastal scenery. Spend some time in the fairly sleepy town of Hana (one of our favorites in Hawaii). Then, take the road beyond Hana to one of Maui's top attractions: Waimoku Falls and the pools of 'Ohe'o, the so-called Seven Sacred Pools. Also, visit the town of Lahaina, once a whaling village and before that, home to Hawaii's kings.

Oahu   This island has Honolulu (meaning urban freeways and bustle) and Waikiki (equated with development and crowds) and Diamond Head (an extinct volcano that tends to show up on picture postcards).

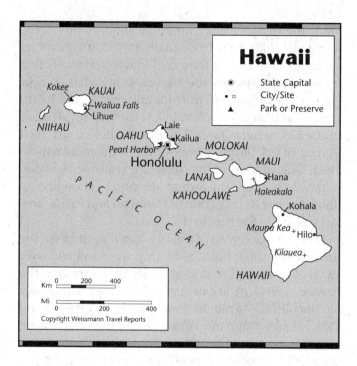

Oahu is the island for nightlife, surfing, restaurants, deep-sea fishing, hiking, golf, shopping and history. It also has the best beaches of all the Hawaiian islands, and many are surprisingly uncrowded. The notable exception is highly developed Waikiki, which has wall-to-wall people year-round. The best beach on the island is Kailua. (Year after year it's voted one of the top three in the nation.) Major water-related attractions include swimming with dolphins at Kaena Point, and the Blow Hole (just past Diamond Head where the ocean rushes through crevices in the coral, sending plumes of water high into the air).

You'll want to spend a whole day at the Polynesian Cultural Center in Laie. You can visit its fascinating replicas of Polynesian and Melanesian villages, see demonstrations of dances and crafts and stay for the buffet dinner and South Pacific review in the evening. (It's one of the state's top tourist attractions and is run by the Mormon Church.)

On the southern coast of the island is Honolulu, Hawaii's capital. To the west of downtown are Pearl Harbor and the airport; to the east are Waikiki Beach and Diamond Head. In Honolulu, you'll want to visit the new waterfront Aloha Tower Marketplace. Its 100 shops and restaurants are not particularly special, but we enjoyed the great harbor views and the constant activity of leisure and commercial boats at the working piers. Nearby is the Hawaii Maritime Center (now part of the renowned Bishop Museum), which has exhibits on whaling, underwater archaeology and Pacific canoes, plus a children's section. Don't leave without seeing the

Maritime Center's two impressive ships — one is the world's last fully rigged four-masted ship, and the other, a replica of the kind of watercraft in which Hawaii's first inhabitants sailed to the islands from what is now French Polynesia. Also in Honolulu, you'll find Iolani Palace National Historic Landmark, the only royal palace in the U.S., where Queen Liliuokalani held court until a group of U.S. businessmen overthrew the monarchy in 1893. Guided tours of the palace are available. And definitely do not miss the Bishop Museum — allow several hours to view its collection of Hawaiian and Pacific artifacts, possibly the best in the world.

Pearl Harbor is west of the city. You'll want to see the *Arizona* Memorial there. (The ship was sunk and over 1,000 of its crew killed during the Japanese attack on the harbor in 1941.) You can conclude the day with a visit to Punchbowl — a national war cemetery with sweeping views of Honolulu and Waikiki that's the final resting place for more than 20,000 servicepeople. The national cemetery has become Hawaii's most popular attraction.

Waikiki   East of the city and only 2 mi/3 km long and not quite that wide — has hundreds of hotels/condos, restaurants, nightclubs and shops. It's a great place to revel in being a tourist, but the beach is fairly crowded. Diamond Head can be seen from the beach. You might think about hiking up it.

Other Major Islands   The other two large islands, Lanai and Molokai, are not as popular among tourists as the big four. Lanai, the smallest island open to visitors, is changing fairly rapidly. It now has two 18-hole golf courses! But it's still uncrowded and quiet. The Garden of the Gods there is well worth seeing; it's a multicolored, barren volcanic area that looks a bit like Arizona's Painted Desert in miniature. Most visitors see Lanai on a one-day boat/snorkeling trip from Maui.

The island of Molokai (between Oahu and Maui) is for those who want to unwind solo. It's a great place — if you like long isolated beaches, deep-sea fishing or history and if relaxing and hiking sound like enough. Sights to see include Kalaupapa, the leper colony with an infamous past, and Papohaku Beach (longest white-sand beach in the state).

Oregon

The ragged coastline and forested mountains of Oregon strike us as more dependably impressive than those of other Pacific coast states — and fewer tourists visit them. Oregon is an ideal destination for the reflective traveler who wants to go beach-combing and rock hunting, or who is content to plunk down in a dramatic setting and absorb what's all around.

The western third of the state is the prettiest, stretching from the rugged, mountainous Pacific coast to the rivers and breathtaking waterfalls of the Cascade Mountains. Visit Crater Lake National Park in this region. Thousands of years ago a tremendous explosion blew up a mountain and left this volcanic caldera. The lake in the caldera is incredibly deep, 1,962 ft/598 m. You'll be bowled over by the rich blue color of the water.

Oregon is the perfect destination for those travelers who love the outdoors, rural towns, and year-round pleasant temperatures. But keep in mind, those who feel their vacation will be ruined if it rains should look elsewhere. While you're touring the state, don't forget to visit Portland, the state's sophisticated largest city. Preserving the natural environment was a major consideration in the development of this beautiful town. One city park, for example, is six times the size of Central Park in New York City; and it teems with wildlife.

Washington

Washington State was meant to be savored, from its seashores to its volcanic peaks and from its lovely largest city, Seattle, to its charming coastal villages.

Geostats — The Pacific States

State	Capital	Population	Land Area Sq. Miles	Sq. Kilometers
Alaska	Juneau	606,276	570,374	1,477,212
California	Sacramento	31,430,697	155,973	403,954
Hawaii	Honolulu	1,178,564	6,423	16,634
Oregon	Salem	3,086,188	96,002	248,636
Washington	Olympia	5,343,090	66,581	172,438

Seattle Its contributions to popular culture in recent years (from that sleepless movie to that flannel-shirt-and-baggy-pants look) have crowned Seattle king of the lifestyle cities. It's where those in search of laid-back-but-cultured living are flocking.

Start your visit at Seattle Center. On a clear day, the view from the Space Needle at the Center (605 ft/184 m high) is wonderful. Then head back down the Needle to the Pacific Science Center, one of our favorite science museums. Another must-see attraction is Pike Place Market, a restored 1907 market not far from the waterfront. Hike down the hill from the market to the waterfront. Slow down and enjoy the great views of the harbor or enjoy one of the many attractions near the water, among them the Seattle Aquarium and Pioneer Square, a restored historic district.

One of the things we like most about Seattle is that it has such a rich cultural life. The city has some of the best local theater products in the country. Several Tony- and Pulitzer-winning plays have debuted on its stages. Seattle also has many dance clubs. The fashion-and-music nonmovement known as grunge can be traced to Seattle's dance clubs. The Pioneer Square District is the hottest area for these clubs.

Visitors should also consider making day trips to the beautiful areas surrounding Seattle. We recommend taking a ferry to the San Juan Islands, where you can relax and enjoy the beautiful scenery in a world rolled back in time 100 years. You can also make several wonderful car trips from Seattle, among which we include Mt. Rainier National Park, home of the majestic peak and beautiful forests.

Columbia River Gorge/Mt. St. Helens If you're visiting Portland, Oregon, or southwestern Washington, you might want to consider a trip to these areas. The Columbia River Gorge is spectacular. The best way to see it is via a drive on the Columbia River Scenic Highway or from a riverboat. If you're adventurous you'll want to hike down into the gorge. Located 50 miles north of the Gorge is Mt. St. Helens, the site of a staggering volcanic eruption in 1980. Today, you can see the awe-inspiring aftereffects of the explosion, including the enormous log-jam at Spirit Lake and, of course, the hulking crag of Mt. St. Helens itself.

◆ The Mountain States

Arizona

Many classic American images of the United States comes to life on a visit to Arizona: the OK Corral, saguaro

Portland, Oregon

cactus and the most beautiful hole in the ground anywhere, the Grand Canyon. It's a great destination for resort vacations, too, whether you want the full spa treatment, a horseback safari, a work-stint at a dude ranch or just a round of golf. Scenic Lake Powell, the largest man-made lake in the country, is a popular spot for water sports and fishing. Spanish missions, the Arizona-Sonora Desert Museum (near Tucson) and the living-history town of Tombstone (Boot Hill) all shed light onto Arizona's rugged character. Visitors to Arizona can also tour several Indian reservations

Grand Canyon National Park This natural treasure, cut by the Colorado River, measures 277 mi/446 km in length and averages 1 mi/1.6 km in depth. Light plays magical tricks on the tiers of rocks that form the canyon, altering their color and texture right before your eyes. What you see at sunrise, for example, may look dramatically different when viewed at sunset. The canyon is best appreciated from below the rim. But bear in mind that any hike below the rim is an arduous undertaking and is recommended only for those in good

Mountain States

◉ State Capital
■ □ City/Site
▲ Park or Preserve
--- River

Glacier ▲

R O C K I E S

MONTANA

Helena ◉

Little Bighorn Battlefield □

Hells Canyon ▲

Yellowstone ▲

WYOMING

Boise ◉   ■ Sun Valley   Grand Teton ▲
                            ■ Jackson
                Snake

IDAHO

Cheyenne ◉

Great Salt Lake   Salt Lake City ◉
                   ■ Alta   Dinosaur ▲ Steamboat ■
                                         Springs   Rocky Mountain ▲
UTAH   Vail ■   ◉ Denver
Reno ■   ■ Breckenridge
Lake Tahoe ◉ Carson City   Aspen ■
                        Arches ▲   ■ Colorado Springs
        NEVADA
                        Canyonlands ▲
                                                   COLORADO
                        Bryce Canyon ▲
                Zion ▲
M O J A V E   Lake Powell
                                        Colorado
D E S E R T   Lake Mead   M O U N T A I N S
        Las Vegas ■   Red River ■
                   Grand Canyon ▲   Chaco Culture ▲   ■ Taos
        Hoover Dam   Espanola ■
                                                   Santa Fe ◉
                Petrified Forest ▲
                                        NEW
        Arizona   MEXICO   Albuquerque ■

        Phoenix ◉
            S O N O R A   White Sands ▲
            D E S E R T   Tucson ■   Las Cruces ■
MEXICO   Carlsbad Caverns □
                    Tombstone ■

Km 0 50 100
Mi 0 50 100
Copyright WTR

physical condition. We think the best way to go below the rim is to take an overnight trip with an experienced guide. Mules, rafts, steam trains and helicopters/light planes provide alternative means to explore the canyon. The park is drawing nearly five million visitors a year.

Phoenix   The Phoenix metropolitan area is one of the fastest growing in the United States. With more than 140 golf courses, 1,000 tennis courts and dozens of resorts, it's a magnet not only for individual leisure travelers, but also for conventions and conferences. After a round of golf, you might want to visit the Desert Botanical Garden

(a huge desert garden) or the Heard Museum (largest Native American museum in the Southwest).

Tucson   Tucson is a compact, pleasant and laid-back city. Visitors often come to rejuvenate at a spa or play golf in the sunniest city in the U.S. It also makes an ideal base for exploring the beautiful Sonora Desert.

Colorado

It's hard to top the treasures that Mother Nature has bestowed on Colorado. But those determined Coloradans keep trying. Lately, they've added gambling in several mountain towns, major league baseball (the Colorado Rockies) and a huge new international airport outside Denver.

Ski Resorts   In the contiguous United States, nothing quite compares to the Rocky Mountains for skiing. The dry snow is dreamy, the alpine vistas are beautiful and the above-treeline skiing is some of the best in the world. Skiers and vacationers the world over know that Colorado has many top-quality resorts — at least 10 are of the highest rank. Among these are Vail, Breckenridge, Aspen and Steamboat Springs. Vail and Breckenridge are both within 100 mi/161 km of Denver. Aspen is further from Denver, about 200 mi/322 km west of the city. To get from Denver to Aspen, you can take a plane to the resort area's small airport or ride Amtrak. The train trip takes all day and gives you an exciting panorama of Colorado sights. Allow time for celebrity-watching. Aspen is a haven for the rich and famous. Steamboat Springs is in remote northwestern Colorado. It's extremely popular among families attracted to the kids-stay-and-ski-free program.

Rocky Mountain National Park   This park, northwest of Denver, is an area of magnificent peaks, valleys and nature trails. The park is often ranked among the top five national parks in the U.S., and deservedly so. The scenic drive along Trail Ridge Road is a must, taking you through stunning landscapes.

Denver   Start your visit to this city downtown at the gold-domed state capitol — that's real gold leaf. Nearby is one of our favorite Denver attractions — the U.S. Mint, which produces five billion coins each year. Also in the vicinity is the Molly Brown House Museum, displaying the collections of the rags-to-riches heroine of the *Titanic* ocean liner disaster.

From these attractions, it's a short walk to Larimer Square. The 10-block area has gas lamps, arcades, carriage rides and fine Victorian architecture. Take time as well to stroll through the nearby 16th Street Mall, a mile-long, car-free zone lined with trees, shops and sidewalk cafes.

The advent of gambling in the nearby towns of Central City and Black Hawk has created more excitement than this city has seen since the gold Rush of the 1850s. The casinos, in re-fitted Victorian buildings, are loud and gaudy, with such colorful names as Bullwacker's and Annie Oakley's. The gambling is low stakes. (The maximum bet is $5; slots, blackjack and poker only.)

Colorado Springs   This pleasant city, Colorado's second largest, is near beautiful Pike's Peak. The Air Force

Academy is located here and has an appealing mountain setting. In addition, the U.S. Olympic Training Center with its 20 sports complexes is worth seeing. The surrounding area is very beautiful. Consider touring Cave of the Winds, named for the breezes that whisk through the caverns, and the Garden of the Gods, slabs of unusual sandstone that have been tilted and sculptured into fascinating shapes.

Idaho

Some of the wildest rivers and loftiest peaks in all of North America are in Idaho. It has forests — perfect for tramping through — that are largely unmarred by human presence. Summer visitors can camp and fish; winter visitors will find some of the best skiing in the West. Unlike some of the neighboring states, Idaho isn't inundated with tourists.

Among the state's best-known tourist sites is Sun Valley. This famous ski resort is one of the oldest and most elegant in the United States and attracts the rich and famous.

Another scenic place to visit is Hells Canyon National Recreation Area. Hells Canyon is the deepest gorge in North America with walls rising almost 8,000 feet/2,500 m above the canyon floor. The truly impressive views of the canyon are not from the mountains but from the river itself.

Montana

One can get lost in the wonders of nature in Montana. Visitors come to stroll through the wildflowers along mountain trails, fish for trout and salmon in rushing rivers and gaze at the big sky over the vast plains of the eastern part of the state. The western portion is mountainous (the Rocky Mountains). Although the state borders Yellowstone National Park, few park visitors venture north to see Montana. Thus with small crowds and minimal commercialism, Montana is a quiet vacation state.

Top tourist draws to the state include Glacier National Park on the Canadian border, where a visitor can see a spectacular array of glaciers and lakes, wildlife and wildflowers; and the Little Big Horn Battlefield National Monument, site of Custer's last stand against the Sioux Indians in the 1870s.

Nevada

Most of Nevada is either desert or farmland interrupted by several north-south mountain ranges. The mammoth tourist industry drives the economy. Las Vegas in the south and Reno in the north are the two centers of the tourist industry.

Las Vegas Casino owners are acutely aware that they now have competition because legalized gambling has been approved in many states. To broaden the city's appeal, they're adding attractions to amuse kids of all ages. Besides spectacular gambling opportunities, you'll find spill-your-guts amusement-park rides, virtual reality shows and Disney-style entertainment.

The new Stratosphere Tower is probably the showiest attraction — or at least the most visible: At 1,149 feet, it is the nation's tallest observation tower. But there's also a roller coaster at the top, a ride that lets you free-fall 160 ft/49 m, and a King Kong replica that climbs part of the tower (you can go for a ride in his belt!).

The green glass towers of the MGM Grand are more than visible — they're symbolic of the hotel's Old Hollywood theme. Inside the casino is a three-story replica of the Emerald City of *Wizard of Oz* fame, surrounded by a yellow brick road and fields of poppies. (This theme park/mega-resort is huge: With 5,005 rooms, the Grand is the largest hotel in the world.)

New York New York Hotel and Casino will make you think of Manhattan with its replicas of the Empire State Building (only 48 stories, alas) and a more petite Statue of Liberty. The Monte Carlo, with its 3,000 rooms, will bring you back to the Victorian age. And Luxor tries to remind you of Egypt: We enjoyed King Tut's Tomb — it's an amazing replica of the tomb originally uncovered in 1922. The jewelry, pottery and other items have been painstakingly reproduced.

The splashiest entertainment on The Strip (Las Vegas Boulevard, where you'll find many of the biggest hotels) has to be the sea battle at the Treasure Island Hotel. In a 15-minute war waged in front of the hotel in a 75-ft/23-m deep lagoon, an English frigate is sunk by a pirate ship. This spectacle is probably the most popular freebie on The Strip.

Other hotel/casinos on The Strip worth visiting include Caesar's Palace, undoubtedly the most upscale casino; Excalibur, a castle-shaped medieval fantasy world; and the Mirage with its live volcano, indoor shark tanks and big show featuring Siegfried and Roy and their white tigers.

After you've tramped along The Strip, visit downtown Las Vegas on Fremont Street, also known as Glitter Gulch. The hotels are older there and you can stroll along the pedestrian mall linking the street's casinos, cafes and shops. Don't forget to visit the famous Hoover Dam, southwest of the city, which creates Lake Mead.

Reno Not as big or splashy as Vegas, Reno combines urban living with Old West charm. For visitors interested in gambling or nightlife, numerous casinos and club facilities (with big-name entertainment) beckon. Several new additions are in the works or have just been completed, including a huge casino/resort modeled after a 16th-century Spanish seaport. Proximity to Lake Tahoe offers Reno visitors a chance to enjoy outdoor and sporting activities while staying in a sophisticated urban setting.

New Mexico

From the sophistication of Santa Fe to the deep recesses of Carlsbad Caverns, it's with good reason that New Mexico is known as the "Land of Enchantment." Most of the state is a wonderful combination of mountains, rolling hills, deserts, plains and farmland. Its peaks draw crowds each year to ski at the resorts in Taos, Angel Fire and Red River. New Mexico's remarkable cultural texture stems from the crossing of Native

Geostats — The Mountain States

State	Capital	Population	Land Area Sq. Miles	Land Area Sq. Kilometers
Arizona	Phoenix	4,075,052	113,642	294,321
Colorado	Denver	3,655,647	103,729	268,648
Idaho	Boise	1,133,034	82,751	214,317
Montana	Helena	856,047	145,556	376,975
Nevada	Carson City	1,457,028	109,806	284,387
New Mexico	Santa Fe	1,653,521	121,364	314,321
Utah	Salt Lake City	1,907,936	82,168	212,807
Wyoming	Cheyenne	475,981	97,105	251,492

American, Hispanic and Anglo cultures. Adobe architecture, Native American pueblos (near Espanola and Acoma) and ancient ruins (Chaco Culture National Historical Park) make New Mexico a unique destination. There are scores of festivals celebrating everything from hot-air balloons (in Albuquerque) to the chile harvest (Las Cruces Whole Enchilada Festival). Visitors can also find horse racing and relics of the Wild West along the Santa Fe Trail (Cimarron).

Albuquerque This fast-growing city in the foothills of the New Mexico mountains has come into its own. Start your visit with a walk through Old Town, the city's historic district. Be sure to see the Museum of Natural History (with full-size dinosaur models and a simulated volcano). At the Indian Pueblo Cultural Center, pueblo history is kept alive in a museum that was built to resemble Pueblo Bonito in Chaco Canyon. Outdoors, head for one of the tranquil places down by the Rio Grande River, which flows through the city. Then, go up to Sandia Peak, where you can have dinner and enjoy spectacular mountain views.

Carlsbad Caverns National Park Though it's far off the beaten track, Carlsbad is one of the most impressive series of limestone caves in the world. This three-level cavern (830 ft/253 m below the earth's surface) contains a cathedral-like chamber which is the largest known underground room in the world.

Santa Fe Santa Fe was founded by the Spanish in 1610 and has been a seat of government ever since. (It's New Mexico's capital, today.) Everywhere you go in town you'll find variations on adobe style, with thick, earth-tone stucco walls and hand-hewn wood beams. (We love the way the vegetation drapes over the walls.) That architecture is part of what has come to be known as "Santa Fe style" — a unique mix of Native American, Spanish and Anglo cultures.

We suggest starting a visit at the plaza, the heart of the city. It's a good place to stroll and get a feel for the place — for its special attitude and pace. You'll see several paintings with Southwestern motifs by Georgia O'Keeffe in the Museum of Fine Arts there. After the plaza we suggest walking about to see adobe buildings and stopping at some of the churches, art galleries and other museums. Among the city's annual events, there is none bigger than the annual Santa Fe Opera, held every July and August. Do get out in the surrounding Sangre de Cristo Mountains for the views and mountain air. (Be aware that Santa Fe may seem too commercial to many visitors.)

Utah

Utah is home to some of the most magnificent scenery and best skiing (Snowbird, Alta) in North America. One of the nation's most popular recreation spots, rugged Utah is filled with stark landscapes (Monument Valley), fascinating geological formations (Arches, Bryce Canyon/Zion and Canyonlands national parks), lakes (Great Salt Lake, Lake Powell) and fossils (Dinosaur National Monument). This beautiful state is also rich in the history of the American West, from the Pony Express to the founding of Salt Lake City by Mormons.

Bryce Canyon/Zion National Parks Not a true canyon but a large natural amphitheater, Bryce's surreal landscape was sculpted by weather and time. The park is centered around formations known as hoodoos, thousands of pillars that tower above the amphitheater floor. Bryce should be viewed both from the rim — to see the big picture — and from one of the many trails — for a more intimate look. Just 70 m/113 km away is Zion National Park. This park is set in a deep canyon. It has towering monoliths, beautifully colored rocks, great hiking, abundant wildlife and unique geological shapes. A highlight of a trip there is a walk through the Narrows, where the walls of Zion Canyon come close together. Very close. At one point, the walls are only 20 ft/60 m apart — and they tower 2,000 ft/610 m!

Salt Lake City Located at the base of the beautiful Wasatch Mountain Range, Salt Lake City is the heart of "Mormon Country." The city's foremost attraction is the Temple Square and Tabernacle, the center of activity for the Church of Jesus Christ of Latter-Day Saints. The Tabernacle is home to the Mormon Tabernacle Choir, which performs most Thursday evenings (dress rehearsal for Sundays). You may also want to visit the Family History Library, a vast genealogical archive used by Mormons and non-Mormons alike to trace family history. Be sure to make a thorough tour of the countryside as well. Visit the Great Salt Lake, drive through the Wasatch Range and see This Is the Place Monument (commemorating the spot where Mormon pioneers first viewed the valley). There is excellent world-class downhill and cross-country skiing nearby, as well as the Bonneville Salt Flats (where automobile speed tests are conducted).

Wyoming

Tourists go to Wyoming to experience Yellowstone National Park. Many also tour nearby Grand Teton National Park. We recommend seeing both if you can.

Yellowstone National Park What makes this park one of the most popular in the United Sates are its mountain views, abundant animal life and unusual thermal attractions. Don't miss the steaming paint pots, hot springs and more than 200 geysers, of which Old Faithful is the most famous.

For information, start your visit at one of the National Park Service's visitor centers. While you're driving through the park, take time to stretch and enjoy many of the famous scenic wonders. Here are a few of the most popular and accessible attractions for you to consider.

Yellowstone Lake This large lake in the center of the park is approximately 20 mi/32 km long and 14 mi/ 23 km wide. Lake Yellowstone Hotel on its shores is a classic hostelry from the golden age of touring. The hotel has been beautifully restored to the look it had in its heyday in the 1920s.

Grand Canyon of the Yellowstone In shades of yellow, orange, red and brown, this picturesque canyon formed by the Yellowstone River is home to two of the park's most beautiful waterfalls: the Upper Falls and the Lower Falls.

Hayden Valley This valley is home to an abundance of wildlife. Nature photographers, in particular, will want to linger for the perfect picture of the area's waterfowl, moose, bears, elk, bison and deer.

Mammoth Hot Springs Here you'll find the park headquarters and the site of Ft. Yellowstone, built by the Army a century ago. The self-guiding trails and boardwalks in this region will help you witness geology in action. Watch as hundreds of gallons of water bring tons of limestone to the surface each day from the Mammoth Terraces.

Old Faithful The world's best-known geyser, Old Faithful erupts 18 to 22 times a day to an average height of 130 ft/40 m. Nearby is Old Faithful Inn, one of the largest log buildings in the world. Make your reservations several months early if you want to stay there.

Grand Teton National Park A visit to Grand Teton, just south of Yellowstone National Park, shouldn't be rushed. Allow time to hike, float the Snake River and breathe in the crisp air. Grand Teton, the mountain that gave the park its name, is one of the most impressive peaks in North America. Rising 13,000 ft/3,962 m, it can be seen from most parts of the park.

Jackson This town is in Jackson Hole, a lush valley just south of Grand Teton National Park. The town still retains the flavor of its Wild West past. It still has wooden sidewalks and places like the Million Dollar Cowboy Bar where seats are saddles. Take time to ride the stagecoach around town and watch the shoot-out scheduled every evening (except Sundays) during summer vacation times. Nearby are three excellent ski resorts. The ski area on Rendezvous Mountain has the biggest lift-served vertical drop in the U.S.— 4,139 ft/1,262 m.

Itineraries

You would never plan an itinerary covering this entire vast region, unless you had at least one year to spend. Here's several itineraries we suggest covering parts of the region.

California Coast Visit California's three big, exciting coastal cities — San Francisco, Los Angeles and San Diego, with possible inland side trips to Yosemite, Death Valley and/or the desert resort of Palm Springs.

Desert Southwest Start the trip in Phoenix and travel to the Grand Canyon, Bryce Canyon and Zion National Park. End your trip with a stay in Las Vegas.

Alaska Fly in to Anchorage. See that city as well as Denali National Park and Fairbanks before heading south to Skagway (through Canada's Yukon) at the northern end of the Inside Passage. Board a cruise ship there for the trip south to Vancouver.

Hawaii Fly in to Honolulu. Spend a few days there and tour Oahu. Add visits to one or more of the other major islands (Hawaii, Maui and Kauai) to your trip before departing from Honolulu.

Other itineraries can be created to cover individual states. There's plenty to do and see in most of them. For instance, tour Colorado, arriving and departing Denver.

Climate/When to Go

The climate varies tremendously in this huge area. Hawaii has a tropical climate. The best times to visit are in late spring and early autumn, when the temperatures are most pleasant. The climate in central and northern Alaska is severe. The coastal areas have a milder climate.

The best time to see Anchorage or take a cruise along the coast is from mid-May to mid-September. Summer daytime highs in Juneau or Anchorage average 60–70 F/ 15–25 C. The best time to visit the mountain states (Colorado, Montana, etc.) is generally late spring to early fall. Ski enthusiasts will, of course, want to go there in winter. You may want to visit the desert southwest in the cooler months. Summers there can be very hot with temperatures exceeding 100 F/38 C on many, many days.

Transportation

The major airports in this region include Los Angeles International Airport (LAX); San Francisco International Airport (SFO); Denver International Airport (DEN); Phoenix Sky Harbor International Airport (PHX); McCarran International Airport in Las Vegas (LAS); Seattle-Tacoma International Airport (SEA); and Honolulu International Airport (HNL).

Major interstate highways crisscross the continental U.S. states (the lower 48 states) in this region and Amtrak serves the area, too. Los Angeles is the western terminus for many Amtrak lines. Lines from there connect to New Orleans, Chicago and Seattle. Greyhound serves the continental states of the region and has bus service to Alaska, too.

Alaska is also connected to the lower 48 states by highway and ferry. Cruise ships sail up the west coast to Alaska, principally from Vancouver in British Columbia. In Hawaii, American Hawaii Cruise lines offers two weekly cruises visiting major islands. Hawaiian Airlines and commuter airlines connect places within the islands.

Accommodations

Accommodations range from deluxe hotels to bed-and-breakfasts, wilderness lodges, condominiums, campgrounds and resorts. Las Vegas has more hotel rooms (more than 85,000) than any other city in the United States (Orlando is second). Despite the immense number of rooms, Vegas can still sell out at times because of an influx of conventioneers, so make reservations early. You might want to consider staying at a dude ranch in western states such as Colorado or Arizona. Arizona also has several resorts and spas that rank among the best in the United States. In downtown Los Angeles, consider staying at the Biltmore, the class European palace hotel.

What to Buy

Throughout the region, shop for Native American (or in Hawaii, Native Hawaiian) arts and crafts, Western wear, Western art and outdoor gear. Also, in Hawaii look for Hawaiian shirts, macadamia nuts and wood products. Intricately carved and painted kachina dolls made by the Hopi are popular in Arizona. The big cities such as Los Angeles, San Francisco and Seattle have a full range of department stores, boutiques, etc.

What to Eat

Every type of cuisine is available in the big cities. When you're in California or Washington, try the locally produced wines. In Alaska, you'll want to sample wild game and seafood (especially truly fresh Alaskan king crab). Don't forget to eat salmon in Alaska, Washington and Oregon and trout — along with a baked potato — in Idaho. Do not leave Hawaii without attending a luau with all the delicious Hawaiian delicacies. In Nevada, many casinos offer bargain-priced meals in order to attract customers to the slot machines and gambling tables. Take advantage of these low prices. Throughout the Southwest, you'll find many fine Mexican restaurants.

Travel Tips for the Client

Don't be surprised if you're affected by the high altitudes in the Mountain States . . . If you're indoors during an earthquake, stand in a strong doorway or get underneath a sturdy desk or table . . . Do expect to pay dearly for most things in Alaska. The state ranks as the most expensive place to travel in the United States . . . Do pay extra for a fresh flower lei upon arrival in Hawaii, as it really starts the trip off right . . . Do set a limit to lose in the casinos in Nevada (and don't keep betting once you've reached it). . . .

The Pacific and Mountain States

Review Questions

1. What is the main attraction in the Los Angeles suburb of Anaheim? What is another attraction in this suburb?

2. In what national park would a visitor see Old Faithful and Mammoth Hot Springs?

3. What are the major attractions in Hollywood?

4. What waterfront area in San Francisco is noted for its seafood restaurants? To where might you take a ferry from this area?

5. Which Hawaiian island has the most bustle and the best beaches? Which island has the world's most active volcano, Kilauea? To which island would you send a client who wanted to see Kalaupapa, the leper colony?

6. Mount McKinley, the highest peak in the U.S., is in what national park? In what state?

7. What are some of the ways you might explore the Grand Canyon?

8. Which resort hotel/casino in Las Vegas has the Emerald City? a reproduction of the tomb of King Tut? a sea battle? a volcano?

9. Where would a tourist see the largest known underground chamber in the world? In what state? What city in that state has given its name to a style of architecture?

10. Describe Bryce Canyon and Zion National Park. In what state are they?

The Pacific and Mountain States

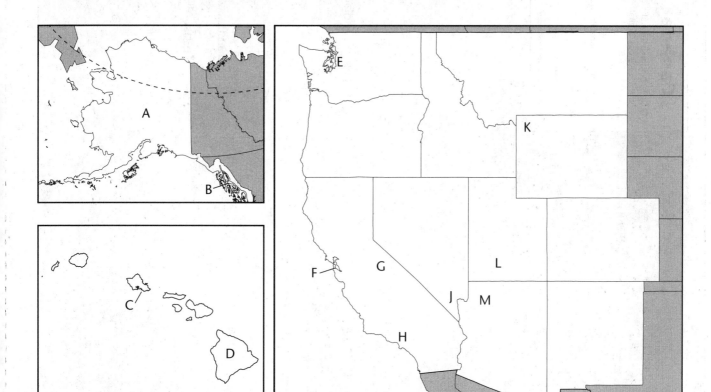

Map Skills Exercise

Match the tourist destination listed below with the corresponding letter on the map.
You can use each letter only once.

1. _____ Grand Canyon National Park
2. _____ Yosemite National Park
3. _____ Yellowstone National Park
4. _____ Denali National Park
5. _____ Bryce Canyon National Park

6. _____ Las Vegas
7. _____ San Francisco
8. _____ Honolulu
9. _____ Seattle
10. _____ Inside Passage

Selling Exercise

One of your clients has two friends in Germany planning to visit the United States. They want to tour the Pacific and Mountain region, because they've heard it's the most beautiful part of the country. They have time to tour just five sites and would like to include the three most exciting cities in the region and the two most captivating national parks. Which cities and parks would you suggest they see? Why?

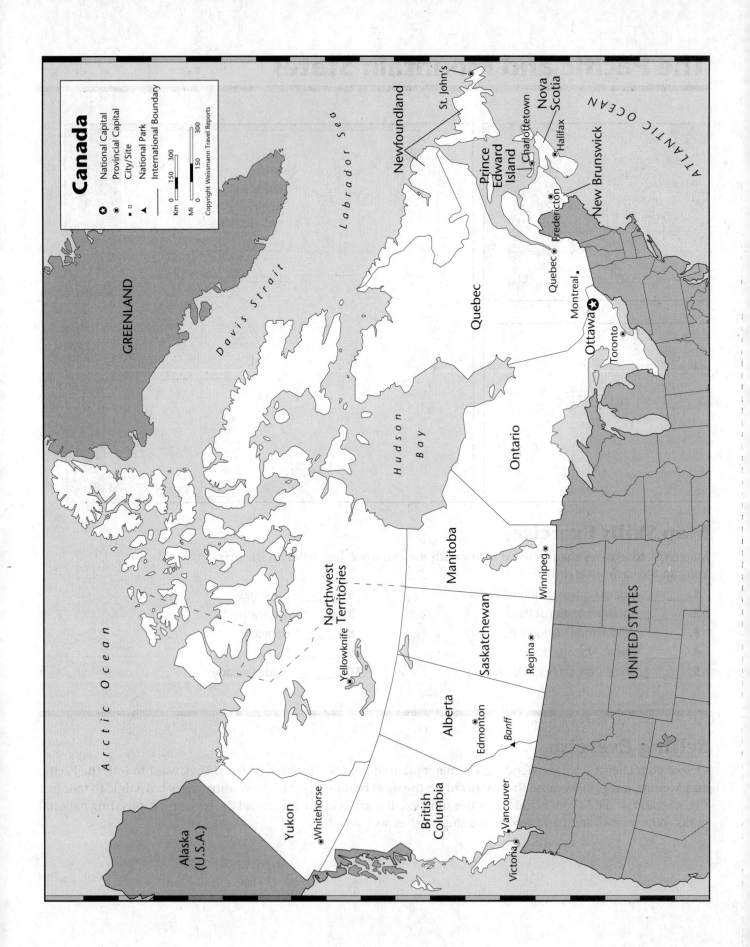

Canada

- ★ National Capital
- ◉ Provincial Capital
- ▫ City/Site
- ▲ National Park
- — International Boundary

Km 0 150 300
Mi 0 150 300

Copyright Weissmann Travel Reports

GREENLAND

Arctic Ocean

Davis Strait

Labrador Sea

Hudson Bay

ATLANTIC OCEAN

Newfoundland

St. John's

Prince Edward Island

Charlottetown

Nova Scotia

Halifax

New Brunswick

Fredericton

Quebec

Quebec

Montreal

Ottawa ★

Toronto

Ontario

Manitoba

Winnipeg ◉

Northwest Territories

Yellowknife ◉

Saskatchewan

Regina ◉

Alberta

Edmonton ◉

Banff ▲

Yukon

Whitehorse ◉

British Columbia

Vancouver ▫

Victoria ◉

Alaska (U.S.A.)

UNITED STATES

Eastern Canada

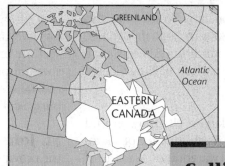

In Eastern Canada, heritage counts. So do the rivers, the lakes and the sea. In fact, it's the combination of all these that makes the region so truly delightful.

The history is readily apparent in the old maritime villages along the Atlantic coast. The fishing business there may have changed over the generations, but the lore is still evident in anyone who drops a net or a one-liner. The history is fascinating, too, along the St. Lawrence Seaway and the Great Lakes, where you'll find towns and cities that grew up and, in some cases, grew rich as ports for Canada's agricultural and industrial products.

What washes over the heritage that humans have brought to the place — the forts, the brightly painted churches, the cobblestones of old Montreal, the broad clean boulevards of Toronto — is the astounding natural beauty of the region: the pine and birch forests of New Brunswick, the foggy cliffs of Newfoundland, the roar at Niagara Falls, the waves pounding Nova Scotia. Take plenty of film.

What to Do There

New Brunswick

New Brunswick is often seen in a trip that includes other Maritime Provinces. This beautiful province is not as crowded with tourists as neighboring Nova Scotia, since the scenery in Nova Scotia is even more dramatic. Besides scenery, the province's appeal includes viewing some of the highest tides in the world in the Bay of Fundy and experiencing Acadian culture.

Caraquet This is the oldest French settlement in New Brunswick, established by Acadians in 1758. It's worth visiting primarily for the Acadian Historical Village, more than 40 restored buildings re-creating an 18th-century Acadian settlement. Be sure to have a lunch of authentic Acadian food at the village's restaurant.

Fredericton Fredericton is one of the most beautiful cities in Atlantic Canada. The city is full of attractions that connect it to its British heritage. Visit Christ Church Cathedral and you'll see a Bible

Selling Points

History; outdoor recreation and sports; islands; fall foliage; wildlife (including moose, caribou and whales); lighthouses; fresh seafood; small, pretty towns and big cities (Toronto and Montreal) are among Eastern Canada's main attractions.

Practically every traveler will find something of interest in Eastern Canada. It's got scenic beauty as well as big cities. Plus it's home to unique cultures, such as those in Quebec and in the Maritime provinces. Do remember its cool or cold in much of the region throughout the year.

Fascinating Facts About Eastern Canada

Toronto is a $1 billion a year film production center — the third largest after New York and Los Angeles . . . Jumbo, the famous circus elephant, was struck and killed by a train in St. Thomas, Ontario, in 1885. The town erected a statue in honor of Jumbo . . . In 1917, two ships collided in Halifax Harbour. One of them was a French munitions ship, and the resulting explosion was the largest man-made detonation in history (until the atomic bomb was dropped on Hiroshima in World War II). It killed 2,000 people and injured another 9,000. . . .

signed by numerous English monarchs. To see what military life was like in the mid-1800s in English Canada, tour the British Military Compound. In the Legislative Assembly Building you'll find a portrait of King George III by Joshua Reynolds.

St. John   New Brunswick's largest city may remind visitors of a small Boston, with its abundance of Victorian and Georgian buildings and warehouses — many of which have been turned into shops. You'll want to see the Reversing Falls here, which occur when the tide rolls into the St. John River from the Bay of Fundy, causing the river to literally flow backward.

Newfoundland

Newfoundland is a throwback to earlier times in North America, when families were close-knit and passed the time in conversation — not in front of the television. And there are other reasons that a visit to this province may feel like a trip to another era. The natives speak with a strong accent and in a dialect of English that's long since disappeared elsewhere. The province has two major parts, an island (Newfoundland) and a section on the mainland (Labrador). You'll want to spend most of your time on the island with its rugged coastal scenery and mountainous interior, often resembling Scotland or Scandinavia.

St. John's   To get a good feel for this city, capital of the province, head straight for the waterfront. You'll find seagoing vessels of all ages and heritages, from weathered fishing boats to glitzy cruise ships. The city surrounding the waterfront is just as enchanting, with its hilly streets (great for exercise) and parti-colored houses. Immerse yourself in the local culture by taking part in a "screech-in" at a pub or restaurant. Pucker up your lips and get ready to kiss a codfish. It's part of inducting newcomers to St. John's.

St. John's is a natural base to visit other parts of the island. We recommend seeing Cape Spear National Historic Park with its old lighthouse and the Ocean Science Center, a research institute devoted to oceanography.

Peggy's Cove, Nova Scotia

St. Anthony   This is the largest town on the Great Northern Peninsula of the island, known to travelers mainly for L'Anse Aux Meadows National Historic Park. In the park, you'll get to see the remains of an 11th-century Viking area consisting of several houses, a sauna and cooking pits. The site is thought by some to be the oldest European settlement in the Americas.

Nova Scotia

If there were a contest for most photogenic place on Earth, Nova Scotia would be high on our list of nominees. This eastern Canadian province has many a stunning landscape, and more — fishing villages with brightly painted clapboard houses; valleys covered with apple blossoms; the constant, invigorating presence of the sea. Combined with fascinating cultures, the postcard-perfect terrain of Nova Scotia makes it one of Canada's most popular tourist destinations.

Halifax   Halifax's most interesting sights reflect its strong maritime influence. The centerpiece of the renovated waterfront district is Historic Properties, a collection of refurbished warehouses that now house promenades, restaurants, pubs, art galleries and offices. Nearby, the schooner *Bluenose II* is moored (cruises on the harbor July–September).

Halifax's British influence is still strong as well. In July and August, visitors to the city are invited to join the mayor of Halifax for Afternoon Tea (3:30–4:30 pm) at City Hall. Be sure to see the city's many historic landmarks, including Province House (Nova Scotia's seat of government) and the Halifax Citadel National Historic Park. The latter is a remarkable star-shaped fortress dating

from 1828 — guards in period dress (kilts) re-create the atmosphere of a 19th-century military fortification.

Museums you might want to visit include the Maritime Museum of the Atlantic (features nautical and marine history of Atlantic Canada, including relics of the *Titanic* and an exhibit of the gigantic Halifax explosion of 1917). After taking in museums, catch a breath of fresh air at the Halifax Public Gardens (exotic imported flowers and trees in one of Canada's finest Victorian gardens).

Touring Trails   The best way to see Nova Scotia is by driving along one of a number of designated touring trails that meander through the province. The Cabot Trail on Cape Breton Island richly deserves its reputation as one of the most beautiful sightseeing routes in North America. We consider the trail an absolute must-see for any visitor to Nova Scotia. It begins near the town of Baddeck. Visit the Alexander Graham Bell National Historic Park, which displays some of the memorabilia and inventions (including the first iron lung) of the great scientist. As you head up the western half of the trail, you'll find tartans galore at the Museum of Cape Breton Heritage and salmon aplenty in the Margaree Valley. Also stop at Cheticamp to see the Acadian Museum. Then take a long while to see the absolutely beautiful Cape Breton Highlands National Park, with its mountainous shoreline overlooking a tempestuous sea. As you head around the cape and back down to Baddeck, stop in South Gut St. Ann's for a visit to Gaelic College. The college's Great Hall of the Clans recounts the history of Scotland and the cape's Scottish settlers. (While you're on Cape Breton you may want to visit the Fortress of Louisbourg in the eastern part of the island. It has a fascinating history. Built by the French in the 18th century, this massive bastion was destroyed by the British and then restored by the Canadian government. Louisbourg is today a living museum to life in the old days.) Another of the best driving trails is the Lighthouse

Route along the south shore of Nova Scotia. It starts at Yarmouth and ends in Halifax — after passing some 30 lighthouses. One pleasant stop along the way is Lunenburg, a major fishing port, which is home of the Fishermen's Museum. Not far from Lunenburg is Ovens Natural Park, a photogenic coastal area complete with rugged cliffs and blowholes. Chester is one of the province's prettiest seaside villages along the trail (it's popular with yachters). And as you head up the coastline to Halifax, make a stop in Peggy's Cove, which is probably the world's most photographed fishing village. The houses are painted in pastels, the sea crashes wildly on the rocky coast, there's an old lighthouse on a granite cliff, and the fishing boats congregate at the old wharves.

Ontario

Most of the people in Ontario live along its southern edge, where waterways and weather have made commerce profitable. That profit has turned the province into Canada's richest, and with the riches have come bright lights and big cities: Ottawa, the nation's capital, and Toronto, the ever-clean and lively city that has become a center of finance, theater, media and filmmaking.

But Ontario's riches extend far beyond the densely populated southern corridor, past parks developed along scenic lakes and into areas of untouched forest and tundra. Here and there you'll find moose and polar bears, historic outposts, living museums, even amusement parks (which don't come close, of course, to nature's own water park, Niagara Falls).

Niagara Falls   One of the world's first and most famous tourist sights, these impressive 180-ft-/55-m-high falls offer the same combination of natural wonder and commercial tackiness that has drawn visitors since the mid-19th century. They can be seen in a day, but we

Geostats

Province	Capital	Population	Land Area	
			Sq. Mile	Sq. Kilometer
New Brunswick	Fredericton	759,000	28,355	73,437
Newfoundland	St. John's	582,000	156,649	405,705
Nova Scotia	Halifax	937,000	21,425	55,489
Ontario	Toronto	10,928,000	412,581	1,068,544
Prince Edward Island	Charlottetown	134,000	2,185	5,659
Quebec	Quebec City	7,281,000	594,860	1,540,628

recommend an overnight so you can view the falls under different lighting conditions. There are lots of things to do related to the falls, such as taking the Maid of the Mist boat into the heart of the falls and viewing the falls via helicopter. From April through October, the nearby town of Niagara-on-the-Lake is home to the George Bernard Shaw Festival, one of the best theater festivals anywhere.

Ottawa

Ottawa has so much to offer year round that even confirmed sun worshipers could be tempted to bundle up for a cold-weather visit to the capital city of Canada. Ottawa knows how to make snow and ice enjoyable. It's great fun to watch the downtown spectacle of Ottawans ice-skating on the Rideau Canal or cross-country skiing on the Greenbelt around the city. Plus, one of the city's best festivals is winter carnival — Winterlude — featuring ice carving, snow sculpture and canoe races on ice. For those who want to get out of the cold, there are plenty of indoor sights to see, from museums to the historic government buildings on Parliament Hill.

One of the first things you'll notice about Ottawa is how dedicated the city is to preserving and celebrating culture. You can see it in the exciting architecture of the National Gallery, built of native pink granite and glass. And there's the Canadian Museum of Civilization, a sleek waterfront building. (This grand museum is actually in Hull, just across the river in Quebec province). There's also the National Museum of Science and Technology (with great hands-on displays) and the Canadian Museum of Nature.

Of course, you can't see Ottawa without including a visit to Parliament Hill, the center of national government, with its impressive neo-Gothic buildings. You could also spend the better part of a day at Byward Market, a wonderful combination of open-air market and indoor shops and restaurants in the middle of the city.

Ottawa boasts an active nightlife, with a variety of clubs, bars and performance venues for every taste, from denim to demitasse.

St. Lawrence River/Lake Ontario

If you have the time to drive between Ottawa and Toronto, this trip will take you past some lovely scenery and through some historic towns, as it skirts the St. Lawrence Seaway, the Thousand Islands and Lake Ontario. The Thousand Islands is an unusual mix of commercial seaway and thousands (yes, really thousands) of charming little islands — the area has scores of parks and major resort complexes.

Another stop is Kingston, a lovely city with an old-fashioned charm built where Lake Ontario empties into the St. Lawrence River. Its major attraction is Old Fort Henry, which was erected by the British during the War of 1812.

Toronto

We suggest a stay in Toronto of at least three nights —enough time to sample the theater (almost on par with New York's and London's) or take in a professional sports game (the Blue Jays took the World Series two years in a row) and still explore at least a few of the neighborhoods.

But first, peer down on those neighborhoods (and straight down into the SkyDome next door) from the top of the CN Tower (at 1,815 ft/553 m, the world's tallest freestanding structure). On a stormy day, you could see lightning strike below you. Of course, on a clear day, you could see the mist of Niagara Falls, 50 mi/80 km away. The tower has attractions from top to bottom. You can dine at the revolving restaurant on the top, or take the motion-simulated ride at Mind-Warp Theatre.

Then start strolling — Toronto is a pedestrian-oriented city. You'll notice that street signs are often in English and the language of the neighborhood. You'll find this especially true in the Chinatowns, of which Toronto has three: the one most people refer to is downtown on Dundas Street. We also had a memorable time in the Greek neighborhood called Danforth. It's lively at night, the stores are eclectic, and now more and more cafes line the sidewalks.

Sidewalk cafes are also a familiar fixture in the Italian community called Corso Italia. There's also Yorkville, the onetime-bohemian-district-turned-chic-shopping-and-dining-district. A new park has put the icing on the cake — and being Yorkville, a simple lawn wouldn't do: The new park has 13 zones, with examples of Southern Ontario flora, a marsh, a small wooded area and a forest of pines that get misted every evening. The Beaches, a two-mile strip near Lake Ontario with both stately and California beach-style homes, is another favorite for people watching, with a funky cafe and ice-cream-shop scene. Other ethnic neighborhoods include Polish, Korean, Jewish and West Indian. The artsy crowd will want to head for Queen Street West, between University and Spadina. It's a former warehouse district transformed into a funky-club-and-shop place: a center for the artistic young to congregate. The Underground is Canada's largest underground city for shopping and eating. Also consider strolling through Cabbagetown (in-again Victorian neighborhood); the Annex (tree-lined streets with eccentric architecture); and the Church/Wellesley area (gay village).

For shopping, go to Harbourfront or visit Ontario Place. The lakefront park, open May–September, has a marina, a retired Canadian warship, children's villages, an IMAX theater, restaurants, miniature golf, shops and lots more.

Depending on the sporting season, fans will want to head to the SkyDome to catch the Blue Jays playing baseball, the Argonauts playing football or — until they get their own downtown arena — the Raptors playing basketball. Toronto's Hockey Hall of Fame and Museum is no sedate shrine, and all hockey fans must make the pilgrimage. (They must also get to a Maple Leaf game during the season.)

Toronto is a theater city. Try to attend at least one performance at one of the city's magnificent old venues that have been lovingly restored — the Royal Alexandra Theatre (dating back to 1907); the Pantages Theatre; or the Elgin and Winter Garden complex.

The Ontario Science Centre, with 650 exhibits, is in an absolutely stunning building; visitors of every age will enjoy trekking through the steamy tropical rain forest or watching as a chrysanthemum, frozen in liquid nitrogen, is shattered into thousands of icy shards.

Rest up for a visit to the sprawling Royal Ontario Museum. Canada's largest museum has five floors of fine multidisciplined collections of culture, science and history — its ancient Egyptian and Nubian galleries and Chinese antiquities are especially impressive. But everyone must stroll through the Bat Cave, a realistic model of an actual cave in Jamaica that's home to millions of bats, spiders and snakes and other creepy crawly things.

The Art Gallery of Ontario (downtown near Chinatown) is also huge and has an eclectic collection — from Rubens to Oldenburg to 893 pieces by Henry Moore (the world's largest public collection of his work). If the weather's nice, take a relaxing boat cruise or a sailboat ride on Lake Ontario.

If you're in Toronto in August or September, check out the Canadian National Exhibition (entertainment, competition, agricultural show and a midway). If you're a Shakespeare fan and are in Toronto during the months of May through October, consider traveling west of town to the Shakespearean Festival at Stratford. The plays are put on by one of the best Shakespearean companies in the world.

Prince Edward Island

To get to this island province, fly or take a ferry from nearby New Brunswick or Nova Scotia. You'll probably want to start your visit in Charlottetown, the province's lovely capital and only large city. The city dates back to the 18th century. Some of the historic sites can be seen on a walk through the old part of town (shops, restaurants and quaint stores). Be sure to visit Province House, including the Confederation Room, where in 1864 the idea of uniting Canada (then just the provinces of Ontario and Quebec) with the coastal provinces was discussed.

To really experience the province, consider taking one of the three scenic driving trails that meander around the island. These drives will take you through some of the most interesting coastal towns and give you plenty of opportunities to head off on some of the many little side roads. Kings Byway is the driving trail that goes through the eastern part of the island. You'll travel from Charlottetown to many interesting sites. Consider stopping at Pinette to join the local citizens in a little clam dig at low tide. Near Gladstone you can visit Fantasyland with its sculptures of fairy-tale characters. In Buffaloland, you can view the herd of bison.

On the north side of the island, 16 mi/26 km from Charlottetown, is Prince Edward Island National Park. (Take Blue Heron Drive to get there.) Although it's small, this park is one of Canada's most popular national parks. The park is home to beautiful fields, long sandy beaches and steep cliffs. The town of Cavendish is actually located within the park. The town is the site of the Green Gables House, the setting for L.M. Montgomery's *Anne of Green Gables*. If you grew up a fan of the childhood odyssey, you'll be enchanted by how true the house and garden are to the book.

Quebec

For many visitors, Quebec's French culture makes it the most fascinating province in Canada. Despite its cultural difference, Quebec is not without similarities to the rest of Canada, of course. It has many of the same recreational opportunities that draw visitors to the western "great outdoors" provinces: mountains for skiing, lakes for boating, extensive shoreline — good for whale-watching and sportfishing. It has wonderful parks for hiking and camping. But it's the French heritage that makes Quebec unique.

Montreal Montreal is the most cosmopolitan city in Canada. Built on islands in the St. Lawrence River, the city offer travelers a wealth of rich history, a beautiful setting, cultural events and shopping for high-quality items.

Spend a day just exploring the city. Stroll through Vieux Montreal and Vieux Port. You'll want to wander the refurbished old waterfront area of Vieux Montreal, snooping in the shops and getting a bite to eat at selected restau-

Place Royale and Chateau Frontenac, Quebec City

rants. Try to include a climb to the top of Mt. Royal, 772 ft/232 m high, to view the city and its island from on high. Before returning to your hotel, head for the heart of downtown — the Ste. Catherine Street area. Veteran shoppers and window-shoppers will want to soak up the atmosphere, and perhaps make purchases, in the major department stores and elegant boutiques of this district.

On a second day, journey to the Pointe a Calliere Museum, where an ongoing dig sets the stage for a restoration of the original French site. Then fast-forward into the state-of-the-art Biodome. In the Biodome you can explore four totally different habitats including a tropical forest and a polar wilderness. The Biodome is in one of the buildings left over from the 1976 Olympics. It's right next door to the 70,000-seat Olympic Stadium and the Olympic Tower. Seen head-on, the stadium and its tall tower look positively sphinxlike.

Across the Rue Sherbrooke from the Olympic complex is the highly regarded Jardin Botanique, the world's second-largest botanical gardens. This green paradise includes 30 gardens with thousands of species of plants and animals. Among the 30 is a re-created Ming Dynasty garden, created by designers and gardeners from China.

Before leaving the city, consider a visit to Parc des Iles on another island in the St. Lawrence River. The island was the site of the 1967 World's Fair. You'll find the newest attraction in the former French pavilion: the glitzy European-style Casino de Montreal.

Quebec City Quebec City is a captivating Old World destination — the kind of place you'd expect to find in the south of France. Poised on and around a cliff over the St. Lawrence River, the capital of Quebec province offers sweeping views of the river and the mountains. Its historical and cultural offerings — not to mention its food and accommodations — are first-rate. It's hard to visit Quebec City without falling in love with it.

Start your visit with a tour of Vieux-Quebec, the old walled city around which modern Quebec has grown. (It's the only walled city in the Americas north of Mexico.) The old city is easily seen on a walking tour. Take your time, for there's plenty to view along these worn streets: some of the oldest buildings in Canada and some of the trendiest bistros and boutiques, too.

We also urge you to see Place Royale — where Samuel de Champlain began the first permanent settlement of

New France — and the Parc des Champs-de-Bataille, which includes the Plains of Abraham where the British won a decisive victory over the French in 1759.

St. Lawrence River Region The natural wonders of Quebec are as important as the cosmopolitan attractions of the province's major cities. Much of this beauty is along or not far from the banks of the St. Lawrence River. The shores of the river offer splendid driving tours. Just east of Quebec City is Montmorency Falls. The huge waterfall is one of the most impressive in North America — even more so in winter when the water freezes and forms an enormous cone of ice. Further east is the Charlevoix region. This lovely area of peaks and valleys has resorts, lots of history and scenic views, including whale-watching in season. One stop you might consider in the area is at Cote-de-Beaupre, home of Ste. Anne de Beaupre, the most important Roman Catholic shrine in Canada. The waters of the fountain of the basilica, some say, have miraculous healing powers.

If you drive all the way east on the southern shore of the river, you'll come to the Gaspe Peninsula, bathed in the waters of the Gulf of St. Lawrence. Explore the tiny fishing villages, shop for antiques and stroll on the beaches of this beautiful part of Quebec.

Skiing One of the best places to ski in the province is in the Laurentian Mountains, 80 mi/120 km from Montreal. The primary attraction of this ski region is the charm of its French Canadian villages. Another good ski area is the Big Four Ski East, south of Montreal near the Vermont border. The Appalachian Mountains extend north into this area and skiing is comparable to that at any resort in Vermont.

Itinerary

The region is so large, you'll want to make several trips there, covering different sections and provinces. Here's an itinerary that will take you along the banks of the St. Lawrence River, to the shores of the Great Lakes, and to the big cities of eastern Canada.

Days 1–2 — Arrive and tour Quebec City.

Day 3 — Tour surrounding area, including the shrine of Ste. Anne de Beaupre.

Day 4 — Drive to Montreal, stopping at Montmorency Falls along the way.

Days 5–6 — Montreal.

Day 6 — Drive to Ottawa.

Days 7–8 — Tour Ottawa/Hull and surrounding region.

Day 9 — Drive to Toronto, visiting the Thousand Islands along the way.

Days 10–11 — Toronto

Day 12 — Drive to Niagara Falls. Overnight there.

Day 13 — Return to Toronto.

Day 14 — Depart Toronto.

Another itinerary to consider is one to the Maritime provinces. Here's an itinerary covering Nova Scotia. Prince Edward Island and New Brunswick. Start and end the trip in Halifax. In between visit Peggy's Cove, the Cabot Trail and the Fortress of Louisbourg in Nova Scotia; Charlottetown, Cavendish and the National Park on Prince Edward Island; and St. John, Fredericton and Caraquet in New Brunswick. If you have time, consider adding a ferry trip to St. John's in Newfoundland.

Climate/When to Go

The huge provinces of Ontario and Quebec have a wide range of climates. Generally, in the south, where most visitors go, summers are warm and humid and winters, stormy with plenty of snow. The best time to visit is May to mid-October.

The ocean moderates the climate in much of the Atlantic provinces. The summer is the best time to visit there, but you may also want to consider early autumn when the leaves change colors.

Transportation

International airports in the region include those at Ottawa (MacDonald/Cartier International Airport — YOW), Toronto (Lester B. Pearson International Airport — YYZ), Halifax (YHZ) and two at Montreal (Mirabel International Airport — YMX) and Dorval International Airport — YUL). Mirabel is served primarily by international carriers and Dorval by North American airlines.

There are also many other airports serving the region, including airports in provinces with small total populations such as Newfoundland and Prince Edward Island.

Despite Canadian government cutbacks, VIA Rail provides considerable rail service in Eastern Canada and connections to Amtrak trains to the United States through Toronto and Montreal. There is no passenger rail service on Prince Edward Island or on the island of Newfoundland. Greyhound and other bus companies provide coach service between cities in the region and to points beyond. The Trans Canada Highway connects the Atlantic provinces to central and western Canada. Several major highways connect the eastern provinces to the United States.

Ferry service connects the Atlantic coast provinces to each other and to the United States. Many visitors travel to Nova Scotia by car ferry from Maine. Ferries are an important means of transportation connecting Prince Edward Island with New Brunswick and Nova Scotia. Maine Atlantic provides car ferry service between Nova Scotia and the island of Newfoundland.

Accommodations

Visitors will find a full range of accommodations in this region, from deluxe hotels to budget lodgings to cabins in remote areas. Lodgings at guest farms are popular in some areas. Niagara Falls in Ontario offers visitors honeymoon hotels with heart-shaped bathtubs. The grand old King Edward Hotel in Toronto still serves English high tea in the afternoons. In Quebec city, stay at Le Chateau Frontenac, a 100-year-old hotel that captures Quebec's Gallic spirit.

What to Buy

Devotees of crafts will find many galleries offering fine work by Inuit (Eskimo) natives and other Canadian artists. Toronto has several distinct shopping districts, including Bloor-Yorkville (upscale boutiques); Yonge Street (large downtown department stores); Kensington Market (raucous, multilingual, ethnic market for foods furniture, clothing, jewelry — great fun); and Eaton Centre, the splashy focal point for upscale shopping with more than 300 stores. Antique lovers and those looking for the rare find in high-quality junk will enjoy the region's large open markets.

Tax Refund: Visitors to Canada may claim a refund of general sales tax (value-added tax) on short-term accommodations and on all purchases exported.

What to Eat

Eastern Canada is home to a number of restaurants serving traditional English fare: Roast beef and Yorkshire pudding turn up on a lot of menus. In the Atlantic provinces definitely dine in the seafood restaurants (try lobster and fish chowder). The big cities — especially Toronto and Montreal — are very cosmopolitan and that means there's a wide variety of ethnic cuisine: Italian, Asian and many others. In Quebec, try the different French Canadian dishes — in particular, *cipaille* (a pie containing wild fowl, game or beef and vegetables), *pot-en-pot* (a seafood-and-potato dish) and *trempette* (bread soused with maple syrup and topped with creme fraiches or whipped cream).

Travel Tips for the Client

Do take a ride in a rickshaw in downtown Ottawa . . . Do note that not all Quebecois speak English, so don't behave as though you think they should . . . In New Brunswick, don't pronounce Saint John as if there were an S at the end (that city is in Newfoundland) . . . Do watch out for moose on the roads at night . . . Don't forget to take a sweater — even in summer . . . Do take insect repellent along in summer (the mosquitoes and black flies can be murderous in some areas) . . . Both Canadian and U.S. residents need proof of citizenship to cross the border — a passport or birth certificate is recommended. . . .

Eastern Canada

Review Questions

1. What is a major natural attraction at St. John? Describe it.

2. What are some of the attractions at Cape Spear National Historic Park and at L'Anse Aux Meadows National Historic Park?

3. What is the best way to see Nova Scotia?

4. What is Winterlude? What are some of the activities that take place during the celebration?

5. What structure would a tourist seek out for a very high view of Toronto and the surrounding area? What else can you do in this structure?

6. What is the Underground in Toronto?

7. What happens in SkyDome?

8. Why might a tourist want to visit the town of Cavendish? In what province would you find it?

9. Where is the heart of downtown Montreal? Why might a tourist want to visit there?

10. Within what modern city is the only walled city in the Americas north of Mexico? What important historical event happened at the Place Royale in that city?

Eastern Canada

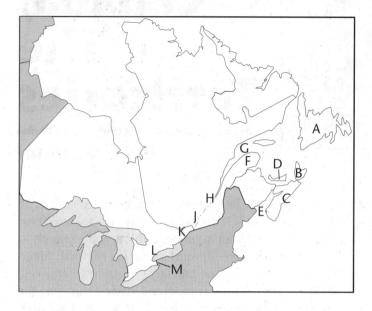

Map Skills Exercise

Match the tourist destination listed below with the corresponding letter on the map. You can use each letter only once.

1. _____ Toronto
2. _____ Halifax
3. _____ Montreal
4. _____ Prince Edward Island
5. _____ Niagara Falls
6. _____ Cabot Trail
7. _____ Gaspe Peninsula
8. _____ Ottawa
9. _____ Bay of Fundy
10. _____ Quebec City

Selling Exercise

To better serve your clients, you'll often want to create travel profiles of them. To do this you'll need to interview them, asking questions such as: What would you like to do and see on your next vacation? Where have you traveled before? What did you enjoy on those trips? What didn't you like? What time of year do you plan to travel on your next trip?

Role play with a fellow student. One of you acts as travel agent, the other as client. The student who is playing the role of agent prepares a travel profile of the client. Then reverse roles so that the other student can develop a profile. Use the profile you've developed to plan a one-week itinerary for your classmate through Eastern Canada.

Western Canada, The Territories
and Greenland

Western Canada is a little bit frontier, a little bit polished, but all beautiful. The plains, which stretch out in miles of golden wheat — interrupted now and then by an occasional onion-dome church — run up to the Rockies, which tower upward into some of North America's most breathtaking vistas. The mountains are sometimes interrupted, too — by placid Lake Louise, for instance, or the glaciers that feed the lake. In the far west is lively Vancouver, where nature's assets have been treated well: Its tall buildings have not been allowed to detract from the lovely harbor, the wide-open parkland or the backdrop of snowy peaks.

This part of Canada has great rodeos, important dinosaur bones and the largest mall in the world. It has room for salmon as well as skiers, bears as well as ballet. For years people have gone there to seek fortune or to find a new home. The latest wave of immigration — especially from Asia — suggests that many still see the place that way: a multicultural haven with the potential for quality life.

What to Do There

◆ The Provinces
Alberta

For sheer natural beauty, no other place in North America can equal Alberta and its two most wonderful national parks, Banff and Jasper. The parks' snowcapped Rockies are truly awesome, their lakes like perfect mirrors reflecting intensely blue skies. (You may simply fall in love with Lake Louise.) Consider Alberta if you love the great outdoors, magnificent scenery and cooler climates. You'll also find plenty to do in the province's major cities, Calgary and Edmonton, but don't expect them to be urban centers comparable to Toronto or Montreal.

Calgary Down-home festivals, rodeos, ranch resorts — sometimes Calgary likes to hide its city polish. But we enjoy Calgary the most when we take advantage of both its worlds: boot-scooting bars and a museum tour followed by fine dining.

Selling Points

Magnificent scenery, the Calgary Stampede, skiing, totem poles, gold-rush historic sites, the Royal Canadian Mounted Police Museum, Vancouver, mountains and wilderness, Arctic adventures and polar bears are some of the attractions in the western provinces and the territories.

Send clients to this region of Canada who love the great outdoors, spectacular scenery and cooler climates. If the client wants to include just one beautiful and fascinating city on the trip, then make it Vancouver.

Fascinating Facts About the Western Provinces and the Territories

Above the Arctic Circle, the sun never sets on June 21 and never rises on December 21 . . . The world's largest population of red-sided garter snakes lives north of Narcisse, Manitoba. The best time to see them is mid-April to mid-May when tens of thousands emerge from their sinkholes to mate in giant writhing masses . . . Alberta was named for Princess Louise C. Alberta, daughter of Queen Victoria . . . British Columbia has at least 11 major waterfalls higher than Niagara's. . . .

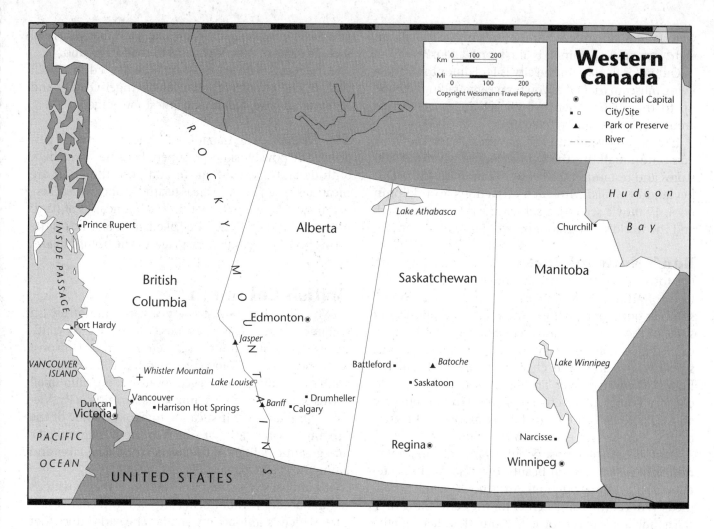

Western Canada

- ◉ Provincial Capital
- ▪ □ City/Site
- ▲ Park or Preserve
- — · · — River

Km 0 100 200
Mi 0 100 200
Copyright Weissmann Travel Reports

ROCKY MOUNTAINS

Hudson Bay

INSIDE PASSAGE

Prince Rupert

Alberta

Lake Athabasca

Churchill

British Columbia

Saskatchewan

Manitoba

Edmonton ◉

Port Hardy

▲ Jasper

Battleford ▪

▲ Batoche

Lake Winnipeg

VANCOUVER ISLAND

Whistler Mountain +

▪ Saskatoon

Lake Louise

Vancouver ▪ ▪ Drumheller
Duncan ▪ ▪ Banff ▪ Calgary
Victoria ▪ ▪ Harrison Hot Springs

Narcisse ▪

PACIFIC OCEAN

Regina ◉

Winnipeg ◉

UNITED STATES

A great starting place for a visit for both adults and children — note that the city has proclaimed itself child friendly — is the Glenbow Museum. It's filled with paintings, sculptures, artifacts and photography from a host of Native American cultures, prehistoric to the present. We found a recent exhibit on tattoos, body piercing and body painting to be especially engrossing. Then, get a splendid perspective on Calgary and the surrounding countryside with an elevator ride to the top of the nearby Calgary Tower, one of the highest man-made structures in the Western Hemisphere.

Another important stop is the Calgary Chinese Cultural Center. Its structure is a masterpiece: The six-story Great Cultural hall within it was modeled after the Temple of Heaven in Beijing, China. It's breathtaking, as is the permanent collection of Chinese artifacts on display.

Undoubtedly the most important entertainment in this city is the annual Calgary Exhibition and Stampede. The mammoth rodeo rules the city for 10 days every July. Everyone wears Western dress, appropriate for square dancing and country-and-western music. And while

you're in Calgary, do see the Saddledome, home of the Flames hockey team. The Saddledome has the world's largest concrete suspended roof (it looks rather like a saddle), top-flight acoustics and amazing sight lines.

For a day trip from Calgary consider a drive to Drumheller to see dinosaur attractions. Some of the greatest dinosaur finds have been made in Alberta. In Drumheller's Royal Tyrell Museum of Paleontology you'll see one of the world's largest fossil collections. From town, you can drive the Dinosaur Trail, a 30-mi/ 48-km scenic and educational route.

Edmonton   What most people quickly discover about Edmonton is that it is a vibrant, modern metropolis with a lovely skyline, plenty of museums and historic attractions and some of the best shopping in the world. The city is home to the largest shopping mall on Earth.

Begin your tour of the city in the downtown area. Architecture buffs should pay particular attention to the Alberta Legislature Building and its distinctive dome. Then take a look at the Citadel, an ultra-contemporary structure that contains five full theaters, a beautiful waterfall and a garden. Edmonton's new city hall, an eight-story glass pyramid, is also worth a look.

Our favorite place in the city is Ft. Edmonton Park, a living museum that takes you from early trading post life up to the 1920s. There, you'll get a chance to ride around in an antique vehicle too.

If shopping is an interest, save a day for the West Edmonton Mall. It's the world's largest with over 800 stores and restaurants. The West Edmonton is the Disneyland of malls, with such attractions as a dolphin pool, 19 movie screens, a submarine ride, a water park and the world's first indoor bungee jump.

Banff National Park
This national park and the town of Banff are wonderful, year-round, destinations offering terrific skiing in the winter and lots of summer outdoor activities. And it all takes place amid some of the most beautiful scenery in the world. Snow-capped mountains in every direction, evergreen forests, streams, lakes and rivers characterize the park. Hiking, horseback riding, river rafting, rock climbing, cross-country skiing, interpretive programs and camping are all available. Wildlife — including moose and grizzly bears — can be seen even from the main roads.

Banff is Canada's most popular national park, noted not only for its natural beauty but also for its recreational and cultural offerings. Attractions include scheduled events at the Banff Center for the Performing Arts, the gondola ride to the top of Sulphur Mountain and the Luxton Museum, which depicts the life of Plains Indians. The classic Banff Springs Hotel is the place to stay — it merits a visit even if you're not overnighting there. If you stay, insist on a room with a view. It costs more but it's worth it. If you're in Banff in the summer, make sure you get to the Banff Festival of the Arts (opera, drama, concerts, art exhibits and dance). It's one of the better art festivals in North America.

Lake Louise
Near Banff is beautiful Lake Louise. It's a small but stunningly blue lake fed directly by the dramatic glaciers at one end. On the opposite shore from the glaciers is Chateau Lake Louise, a deluxe resort. If you stay there, be sure to get a room overlooking the lake. Be aware that ice may be covering the lake through April and possibly even May. In that case you won't be able to enjoy the beautiful blue water.

Jasper National Park
This national park northwest of Banff also offers towering mountains, splendid lakes, forests, ice fields, waterfalls and hot springs. However, it is less alpine than Banff. The farther north you travel into Jasper, the more likely it is that vistas will include some of Alberta's plains in the foreground.

Attractions within Jasper include Mt. Edith Cavell (one of the park's highest peaks), Angel Glacier and Maligne Canyon, a dramatic limestone gorge.

Ski Areas   The Canadian Rockies are a skier's paradise. The powder skiing is superb because of the high altitude and dry, cold air. In addition, the vistas are breathtaking and the ski areas relatively uncrowded. Several major ski resorts lie within the boundaries of Banff National Park. Of these, the Lake Louise Ski Area is the most spectacular and offers a view of the beautiful lake.

British Columbia
We think that almost every square mile of British Columbia is drop-dead gorgeous. Vancouver, its beautiful big city, bustles around a glistening harbor. Hop on a ferry and you're on Vancouver Island, which has an irresistible combination of rugged countryside, quaint small towns and Canada's most unabashedly British city, Victoria. Or paddle off in a canoe to explore some of the province's wilderness. Or search for trout, salmon, pike and gigantic halibut in the rivers and glacial lakes and along the Pacific coast.

It's almost impossible to experience the province's natural beauty without being affected by its native culture, which is unique in Canada. The early tribes that lived in western British Columbia had unquestionably the most elaborate nonagricultural society in North America. Abundant fish and other resources allowed them plenty of time for artistic and social development. Above all else they were masters at woodworking and the decorative arts: Timbered houses, totem poles, finely carved wooden utensils and oceangoing canoes were among the many items they built from local timber.

Because the province lies on the Pacific, it has large communities of Chinese and other Asians living among the descendants of people from the British Isles. Send clients here who love the outdoors. But we also think just about everyone will enjoy Vancouver, one of the loveliest and most progressives cities in North America.

Inside Passage
No visit to British Columbia is complete without a cruise along the Inside Passage, which stretches along the coast from Washington state to Alaska. Most visitors board one of the many cruise ships that depart from Vancouver throughout the summer. A much less expensive alternative is to take the ferries; they allow you to get off and stay at various ports as

long as you like. Ferries depart Port Hardy on Vancouver Island and head to Prince Rupert (a 15-hour daylight cruise). At Prince Rupert, ferry passengers can transfer to the ferry that continues north to Alaska.

As you sail along, you'll see some of the most beautiful scenery in the world — snow- and cloud-capped mountains, glaciers, fjords, and islands covered with coniferous trees — as well as birds, whales, bears, moose and other animals.

Burrard Inlet, Vancouver

Ski Areas British Columbia's rugged forested mountains are dotted with a variety of ski resorts. Some are isolated and sleepy, while others are world class. All of them, however, tend to be uncrowded, relatively inexpensive and refreshingly pristine.

Located side-by-side just 70 mi/115 km north of Vancouver are Whistler/Blackcomb Ski Mountains. Coupled with abundant snowfall (more than 30 ft/9 m a year), the geography provides for some mighty fine skiing. The mountains have different terrains: Whistler has lots of tight tree runs, steep chutes and mogul fields, while Blackcomb offers vast wide-open terrain with incredibly long runs and glacier skiing. In the same class as Whistler/Blackcomb is Panorama, often considered one of the top five Canadian resorts. Other skiing areas include Grouse Mountain and Cypress Bowl, both fairly close to Vancouver.

Vancouver Nature bestowed a treasure trove of gifts on Vancouver — from the chilly green waters that lap the city's ragged shores to the frosted peaks that dwarf its tall buildings. But you have to give city leaders some credit, too. They have worked hard to enhance the city's natural beauty — not muck it up. The result, we think, is one of the most captivating cities in North America. If you're starting your visit in the downtown area, head first to Gastown, where Vancouver was born and then reborn: Its three blocks contain buildings that have been restored to their turn-of-the-century splendor and now house restaurants, boutiques and galleries. Nearby is Canada Place. Built for Expo '86, this waterfront landmark looks like a ship. Inside are the Vancouver Trade and Convention Center and an Imax theater. Just minutes from downtown is Stanley Park, which has

more than 1,000 acres/400 hectares of peaceful woodlands, trails and gardens. This gorgeous greenery is among our favorite 10 city parks in the world. Within the park is one of North America's biggest and best aquatic zoos.

Museum buffs will have a field day in Vancouver. Be sure to visit Science World in the Expo Centre for its entertaining hands-on science exhibits and domed-screen Omnimax Theatre. Also visit the H.R. MacMillan Planetarium and the Maritime Museum (for an introduction to the seafarer's life).

As a gateway to Asia, Vancouver's multicultural mix has grown steadily richer in the last century. You'll find East Indian, Japanese, Italian, Greek and especially Chinese cultural influences contributing to the city's British and Pacific Northwest heritage.

If you're adventurous, be sure to walk across the Capilano Suspension Bridge (230 ft/70 m above the river), just north of the city. It really sways and can make you dizzy, but it's fabulous — worth the fright. The bridge is close to Grouse Mountain — there's a wonderful panoramic view of Vancouver from the top.

If you enjoy spas, you may want to visit Harrison Hot Springs, the nearest major hot spring to Vancouver, 90 m/144 km east. This spa features hot mineral springs as well as a recreational lake.

Vancouver Island This huge island off the southwest coast is simply beautiful. It's a favorite with anglers year-round (steelhead in the cold weather, several varieties of salmon April–October, trout all summer and bass in June) — almost any stream or lake has possibilities. (Campbell River claims to be the salmon capital of the world.) Among the important sights on the island are Fisgard Lighthouse, Strathcona Provincial Park Colwood's Hatley Castle, Long Beach and Fort Rodd Hill National Historic Park. The British Columbia Forest Museum is in Duncan ("The City of Totems"). If you're there from May to October, take the 15-hour ferry ride from Port Hardy to Prince Rupert (on the mainland) up the Inside Passage: It's a spectacular trip and fairly reasonably priced.

At the southern end of the island is Victoria, British Columbia's capital. Victoria enjoys a spectacular setting: a busy harbor with snow-capped mountains as a backdrop. It has a large number of British-born residents, so congenial pubs, afternoon tea and cricket are an integral part of life. (We enjoyed having tea at the Empress Hotel.) Daily round-trip cruises connect Victoria and Seattle on a very scenic voyage.

There are two must-sees in the Victoria area: the world-renowned Butchart Gardens and the Royal British Columbia Museum. The gardens, created in 1904, include a Japanese garden and an English rose garden. The Royal British Columbia Museum's dioramas and exhibits on deep-sea exploration, British Columbia's natural habitats and native peoples are some of the most ambitious and spectacular you'll see anywhere.

Manitoba

Travelers seeking a vacation off the beaten path or a wilderness adventure will have a good time in Manitoba. One exciting adventure you might consider is a trip to Churchill, in the far northeastern part of the province on chilly Hudson Bay. The town is accessible only by air or a two-day train trip from Winnipeg, the provincial capital. Churchill is world famous as the planet's polar bear capital. Once there, take a ride in a tundra buggy to see the bears.

A less adventurous way to visit the province is to drive across its southern part on a trip from Ontario to Saskatchewan or vice versa. You'll pass through many of the larger cities and towns and have a chance to visit some provincial parks and huge lakes like Lake Winnipeg and Lake Manitoba.

In contrast to Churchill, Winnipeg is a fairly cosmopolitan city. It's home to the Winnipeg Symphony Orchestra and the world-renowned Royal Winnipeg Ballet. Another leading attraction is the Crystal Casino, a European-style casino in the Hotel Fort Garry, built to resemble a French chateau. This is an upscale casino. There are more modest casinos in town, too, offering blackjack and bingo.

Tourists interested in Canadian history and culture will also find lots to see in Winnipeg. Check out the Ukrainian Cultural and Education Center to learn about the contributions of the province's largest ethnic group and then lunch in nearby Chinatown. At the Riel House National Historic Site you'll learn about the Northwest Rebellion of the 1880s. Also visit the Manitoba Museum of Man and Nature, which covers the natural and cultural history of province. Allow several hours for your visit to do it justice.

Saskatchewan

This huge, flat territory grows more wheat than any other Canadian province and more than any U.S. state. It's also famous as the headquarters of the Royal Canadian Mounted Police. In fact, the popular image of the Mounties in their red coats riding across the prairie probably originated in Saskatchewan.

The history of the Canadian prairie unfolds in a visit to the province's two major cities, Saskatoon and Regina. Saskatoon is the largest city and business center. The first decades of this century come alive in a visit to Boomtown here, a living museum recreating the shops and life of that period. The Ukrainian Museum of Canada, also in town, does a nice job of displaying the ornate crafts of immigrants from Ukraine who played a major part in the settlement of the province. History enthusiasts will also

Geostats — The Western Provinces

Province	Capital	Population	Land Area Sq. Miles	Sq. Kilometers
Alberta	Edmonton	2,716,000	255,287	661,168
British Columbia	Victoria	3,668,000	365,948	947,769
Manitoba	Winnipeg	1,131,000	250,947	649,928
Saskatchewan	Regina	1,016,000	251,866	652,308

want to visit the Diefenbaker Centre at the University of Saskatchewan, dedicated to the life and times of this former prime minister. When you get to Regina, the provincial capital, be sure to tour the Royal Canadian Mounted Police Museum with exhibits, regalia and memorabilia of these bulwarks of law and order on the prairie.

Other historic places to visit in the province include Battleford, the original seat of government for the old North West Territories, and Batoche National Historic Park, site of the final battle, in 1885, of the Northwest Rebellion.

Don't send clients to Saskatchewan who are seeking dramatic scenery or the energy of the big city. It's a better place for those interested in Canadian history or seeking wide open spaces.

◆ The Territories
Northwest Territories

This huge region — nearly half the size of the continental United States — is primarily tundra, arctic and sub-arctic treeless plain. In some areas, however, you'll find forests and mountains. Wildlife — including musk-ox and caribou — is plentiful and varied, adding to the region's fascination. Many large islands in the Arctic Ocean, among them Baffin and Ellesmere, are also parts of the Territories. Travel options for visitors include flying in to remote lodges for hunting and fishing trips in the wilderness, trekking across the tundra in search of nesting birds and wildflowers, exploring remote Inuit communities or even taking a plane to the North Pole and camping nearby. We recommend that first-time visitors sign on to an established tour with experienced guides.

You can also drive into the Northwest Territories. If you're in the upper part of Alberta you may want to head north and visit Wood Buffalo National Park, Great Slave Lake and Yellowknife, the territorial capital. All three are not far above the Alberta border and much of the park is actually in northern Alberta. In the unlikely case you're in the northern Yukon, you can drive across the territorial border and tour the delta region of the mighty MacKenzie River as it empties into the Arctic Ocean.

A trip to the Northwest Territories is a once-in-a-lifetime experience for adventurous travelers. (Note that the eastern part of the Northwest Territories has been ceded to the Inuit and will become a separate territory called Nunavut.)

The Yukon

The Yukon is a rough, isolated land — mysterious, beautiful, untouched — inland from Alaska and northwest of British Columbia. Clear blue lakes, mountains, glaciers and silence stretch for miles and miles. Both caribou and black bears outnumber people. Most visitors just pass through this territory as they travel from British Columbia or the Alaskan panhandle to the heartland of Alaska. These visitors miss a chance to see some great scenery and relive the rugged life of the gold rush of the 1890s. The Yukon will appeal mostly to those who seek an exotic, occasionally rugged adventure in a remote, mountainous sub-Arctic location.

Dawson   This town still preserves much of the atmosphere of the great gold rush. Exhibits at the Dawson City Museum tell the story of the gold mania. English majors will want to visit the home of Jack London and explore Eldorado, a structure designed to resemble the hotel in London's *The Call of the Wild*. If you like old-style casinos, stop by Diamond Tooth Gertie's Gambling Hall to see the cancan girls and hear the honky-tonk music.

Kluane National Park   Located in the southwestern corner of the territory, this park is an immense wilderness. Stop by on your way to Alaska and check out the glaciers and Canada's highest peak, Mt. Logan, 19,550 ft/5,960 m.

Whitehorse   Whitehorse is the Yukon's capital and biggest town. Among the attractions you'll want to visit is the MacBride Museum to view Native American displays and a gallery of wonderful old photos. At night, take in the Frantic Follies, an 1890s revue with comedy skits and dancing girls — definitely the best show in town.

Geostats — The Territories

Territory	Capital	Population	Land Area	
			Sq. Miles	Sq. Kilometers
Northwest Territories	Yellowknife	64,000	1,322,910	3,426,205
Yukon	Whitehorse	30,000	186,661	483,433

Itinerary

This region is vast. A first trip to the region might cover key destinations in Alberta and British Columbia. Here's a 15-day itinerary to that area.

Day 1 — Arrive Vancouver.

Days 2–3 — Vancouver.

Day 4 — Day trip to Victoria and Vancouver Island.

Day 5 — Leave Vancouver for Alberta. Overnight in Kamloops or other spot in central British Columbia.

Day 6 — Arrive Lake Louise.

Day 7 — Lake Louise.

Days 8–9 — Jasper National Park.

Day 10 — Drive from Jasper to Banff.

Days 11–12 — Banff.

Days 13–14 — Calgary.

Day 15 — Depart Calgary.

Climate/When to Go

In British Columbia, the climate in the southwest, where most tourists go, is mild and wet with cool summers. In the prairie provinces, summers are moderately warm and winters, very cold. Winters in the Territories are extremely cold and dark, since they're at a high latitude. If you're not planning a ski trip, then summer is probably the best time to visit the region.

Transportation

International airports in the region include those at Vancouver (YVR), Edmonton (YEG) and Calgary (YYC). Airports also serve smaller cities and towns, including those in the Territories. Canada's VIA Rail provides train service across the prairie provinces and British Columbia. Trains head east and west three times a week. Grey-

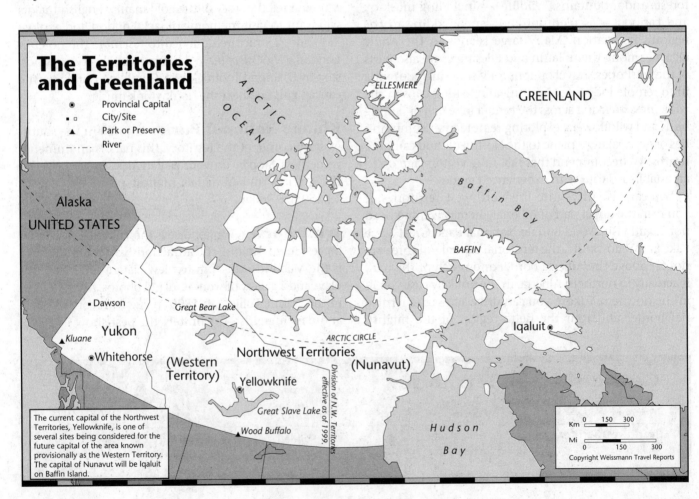

The Territories and Greenland

◉ Provincial Capital
■ □ City/Site
▲ Park or Preserve
-·-·- River

The current capital of the Northwest Territories, Yellowknife, is one of several sites being considered for the future capital of the area known provisionally as the Western Territory. The capital of Nunavut will be Iqaluit on Baffin Island.

ARCTIC OCEAN

ELLESMERE

GREENLAND

Baffin Bay

BAFFIN

Alaska
UNITED STATES

Dawson

Great Bear Lake

ARCTIC CIRCLE

Kluane

Yukon

Whitehorse

(Western Territory)

Northwest Territories

(Nunavut)

Iqaluit

Yellowknife

Division of N.W. Territories effective as of 1999.

Great Slave Lake

Wood Buffalo

Hudson Bay

Km 0 150 300
Mi 0 150 300

Copyright Weissmann Travel Reports

hound and other motorcoach companies operate in the region, including in the Territories. Major east-west highways — Highway #1 (the Trans Canada Highway) and Highway #16 (the Yellowhand Highway) run from eastern Canada to the Pacific coast. (If you're on the Trans Canada Highway in British Columbia, you'll come across the spectacular Hell's Gate, a deep gorge along the Fraser River where a fish ladder had to built so that salmon could swim upriver. For an awesome view of the gorge, take the tramway that descends 500 ft/150 m from the highway to the viewing area.)

Visitors coming from the United States can choose among several highways entering western Canada. Some of the highways in the Territories are fashioned of gravel, making dirt and flying stones common. Ferries ply the waters among cities and towns along the British Columbia coast.

Accommodations

Visitors will find a full range of accommodations in this region, from deluxe hotels and resorts to fly-in lodges and cabins in remote regions. The world-famous European-style village at year-round Whistler Resort in British Columbia offers hotels, lodges, pensions and condominiums. In Alberta, we rank the Banff Springs Hotel at the top of our list. Other top resorts in the province include Chateau Lake Louise and Jasper Park Lodge. In the Territories, expect a selection of lodging only in major centers like Dawson or Yellowknife.

What to Buy

Regional arts and crafts (native Indian, Ukrainian and other) are a favorite purchase. Search for wood carvings and jewelry made using local minerals. If you're looking for top-grade Western wear, try Western Outfitters or Alberta Boots in Calgary. In the Territories try finding moose-hair tufting, porcupine quillwork and soapstone sculptures.

What to Eat

You can find cuisines from all over the world in British Columbia and Alberta. In Vancouver, visit Chinatown (the second-largest in North America, after San Francisco) for a great selection of restaurants — dim sum is served at most for lunch. Seafood and freshwater fish are also plentiful in these two provinces, although beef is still king in Alberta. Try ethnic foods (Ukrainian, French Canadian and others) in the prairie provinces. Wild game (moose, caribou, musk ox) is a must in the Territories.

Travel Tips for the Client

Be as noisy as possible when you're in bear country — the most dangerous situations occur when you startle them . . . Don't forget that only Canadian postage stamps will move mail in Canada . . . Don't drive too long across the vast prairies. It can be hypnotic and you might have an accident . . . Do bring insect repellent in summer (the mosquitos and black flies can be infuriating in many areas) . . . Do try regional specialties such as king crab and reindeer sausage. . . .

Greenland

This Danish possession may be cold — it's sheathed in snow and ice much of the year — but it's heating up as an ecotourism destination. More and more people want to take in its stark, pristine beauty, to boat among the icebergs and to experience its culture — before the rest of the world tampers with it excessively. People who enjoy, say, Alaska or Canada's Northwest Territories will be attracted to Greenland. It is the largest island in the world. More than half of it is north of the Arctic Circle; 84% is covered year-round with a layer of ice up to 11,000 ft/3,355 m thick. Greenland has a fascinating natural environment, with rugged mountains, fjords, icebergs and islands. Vegetation is sparse, with low, dense shrubbery and ephemeral flowers. But there is a vast array of land and sea animals and birds. About 90% of the people live in small villages and towns on the west coast.

Geostats — Greenland

Capital	Population	Land Area	
		Sq. Miles	Sq. Kilometers
Nuuk	57,611	840,000	2,175,516

Western Canada, the Territories and Greenland

Review Questions

1. What is the most important entertainment in Calgary every July? Describe what takes place there.

2. Where would you drive from Calgary to see dinosaur attractions? What is the name of the museum there?

3. What is the name of the world's largest shopping mall? How many stores and restaurants will you find there?

4. What is Canada's most popular national park?

5. What is the Inside Passage?

6. In what city would you find Gastown and Stanley Park? Describe them.

7. What are the two must-sees in the Victoria area?

8. What town is famous as the planet's polar bear capital? In what province will you find it?

9. In what city can you visit the Royal Canadian Mounted Police Museum? In what province is the city located?

10. To whom would a trip to the Yukon most likely appeal?

Western Canada, the Territories and Greenland

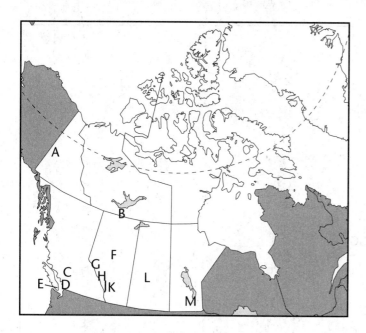

Map Skills Exercise

Match the tourist destination listed below with the corresponding letter on the map. You can use each letter only once.

1. _____ Vancouver
2. _____ Calgary
3. _____ Lake Louise
4. _____ Saskatoon
5. _____ Victoria
6. _____ Edmonton
7. _____ Dawson
8. _____ Banff National Park
9. _____ Jasper National Park
10. _____ Winnipeg

Selling Exercise

Your job is to promote tourism to one of Canada's western provinces or territories. In an interview with a reporter from a U.S. television station, you're asked why people might want to visit your province or territory. How would you respond? (Your answer to the question should be at least a paragraph long.)

Unit Review United States, Canada and Greenland

Map Skills Exercise

Match the tourist destination listed below with the corresponding letter on the map. You can use each letter only once.

1. _____ Miami Beach
2. _____ Branson
3. _____ Rock and Roll Hall of Fame
4. _____ Cape Cod
5. _____ the French Quarter
6. _____ Banff National Park
7. _____ Denali National Park
8. _____ Universal Studios and Knott's Berry Farm
9. _____ Cabot Trail
10. _____ El Capitan and Half Dome
11. _____ Royal Ontario Museum
12. _____ Kilauea volcano
13. _____ Graceland
14. _____ Grand Canyon National Park
15. _____ Amish Country
16. _____ Walt Disney World
17. _____ Aspen
18. _____ Gastown and Canada Place
19. _____ Niagara Falls
20. _____ Myrtle Beach
21. _____ Martin Luther King, Jr. Historic District
22. _____ Mall of America
23. _____ Mt. Rushmore

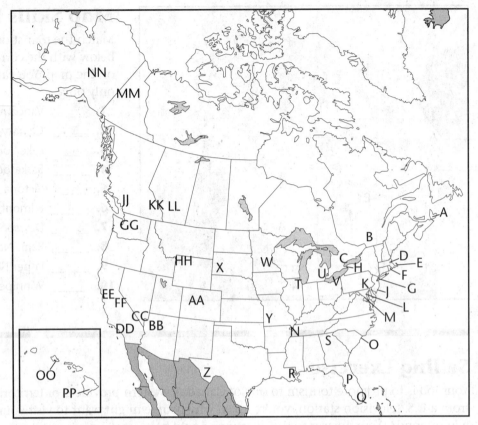

24. _____ Big Bend National Park
25. _____ The Breakers
26. _____ The Saddledome
27. _____ Pike Place Market and Pioneer Square
28. _____ Atlantic City
29. _____ Renaissance Center
30. _____ Yellowstone National Park
31. _____ Field Museum of Natural History
32. _____ Fremont Street and The Strip
33. _____ Mt. Royal

34. _____ Golden Gate Park
35. _____ Honolulu
36. _____ New England Aquarium
37. _____ National Aquarium (U.S.)
38. _____ Dawson
39. _____ John F. Kennedy Center for the Performing Arts
40. _____ Lincoln Center and Ellis Island

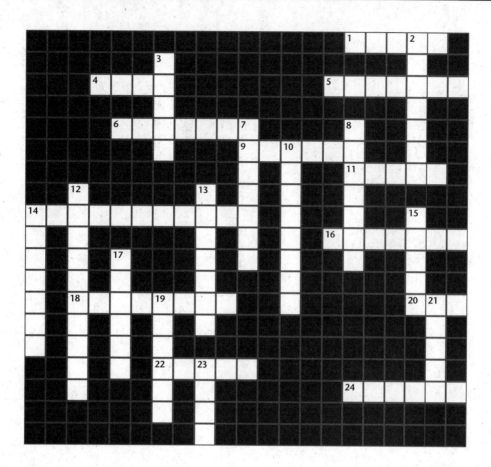

Content Review Crossword Puzzle

Across

1. _____ Hills in South Dakota
4. Gateway _____ in St. Louis
5. Oahu beach
6. Home of SkyDome and CN Tower
9. Mounted Police Museum is there
11. Mega-resort in Las Vegas
14. Washington, D.C., tourist attraction
16. _____ Exhibition and Stampede
18. California national park
20. Do this at Killington
22. It's part of Disney World
24. Connecticut town with ships

Down

2. City renowned for its architecture
3. Fisherman's _____
7. No. 1 tourist city in the world
8. City with star-shaped fortress with guards in kilts
10. It's now big in Mississippi
12. It's in Anaheim
13. Philadelphia's got this bell
14. Park in Vancouver
15. Montmorency _____.
17. Follow the Freedom Trail there
19. The Guggenheim in New York City is one
21. The "Garden Isle"
23. Mammoth _____

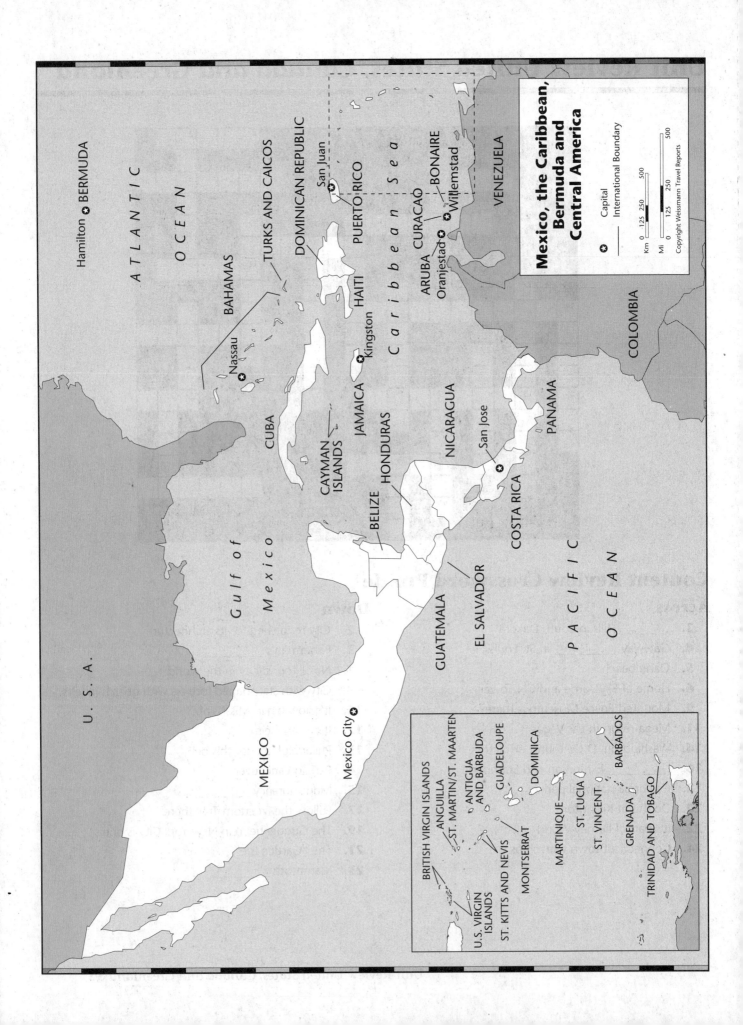

Mexico, the Caribbean, Bermuda and Central America

⊗ Capital
— International Boundary

Km 0 125 250   500
Mi 0 125 250   500

Copyright Weissmann Travel Reports

BERMUDA
⊗ Hamilton

ATLANTIC

OCEAN

BAHAMAS

Nassau ⊗

TURKS AND CAICOS

DOMINICAN REPUBLIC

San Juan ⊗
PUERTO RICO

HAITI

CUBA

CAYMAN
ISLANDS

JAMAICA
Kingston ⊗

Caribbean Sea

BONAIRE

CURACAO
⊗ Willemstad

ARUBA
Oranjestad ⊗

VENEZUELA

COLOMBIA

U.S.A.

Gulf of

Mexico

MEXICO

Mexico City ⊗

BELIZE

HONDURAS

GUATEMALA

EL SALVADOR

NICARAGUA

San Jose ⊗

COSTA RICA

PANAMA

PACIFIC

OCEAN

U. S. A.

BRITISH VIRGIN ISLANDS
ANGUILLA
ST. MARTIN/ST. MAARTEN
ANTIGUA
AND BARBUDA
GUADELOUPE
DOMINICA
MARTINIQUE
ST. LUCIA
ST. VINCENT
GRENADA
BARBADOS
TRINIDAD AND TOBAGO

U.S. VIRGIN
ISLANDS
ST. KITTS AND NEVIS
MONTSERRAT

Mexico, the Caribbean,

Bermuda and Central America

Latin America begins at the Rio Grande. In the southern part of North America, the language spoken by most people is Spanish and the climate tends to be much warmer. Mexico is the largest nation in this region, in area and population. Mexico is a land of vast deserts, jungles, mountains, volcanoes and some very big cities. Fabulous beach resorts that attract tourists from around the world are sprinkled along Mexico's Gulf, Caribbean and Pacific coastlines. It's also home to wondrous ruins from ancient civilizations, Maya and Aztec among them.

Just south of Mexico is Central America, a region that is divided into seven countries. Most share cultural similarities with Mexico: They're Spanish speaking and Roman Catholic in religion, and they have a significant Indian heritage. The region is primarily hot and humid (except at high altitudes) and very green. Ecotourism is popular there, especially in the countries of Costa Rica and Belize.

To the east of Mexico and Central America in the Caribbean Sea lie numerous islands, some small and some very large. We cannot overemphasize the fact that not all of them are lush and mountainous, nor do they all have great beaches. Those that are generally green

and fit the expectations of most clients' idea of a Caribbean vacation include Jamaica (north shore), many of the British Virgin Islands, St. John in the U.S. Virgin Islands, Montserrat, Guadeloupe, Dominica, Martinique, Grenada, St. Lucia, St. Vincent and Tobago. Most of the others range from dead-level flat to low hills, with fairly dry climates and scrublike foliage. The basic rule of thumb is that if the island has mountains, some of it is probably green. However, just because an island isn't physically beautiful doesn't mean certain clients won't love it. Bonaire and the Cayman Islands, for instance, offer better snorkeling and diving than many islands that are much prettier.

The Caribbean islands were colonized by European powers beginning in about AD 1500. The European nations had a strong influence on the cultures that developed, and today, enjoying these cultures is part of any trip to the region. European nations that have had the most lasting influence on the region are Great Britain, France, the Netherlands and Spain. The Bahamas and Bermuda, though not in the Caribbean, are also covered in this unit.

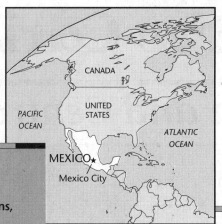

Mexico

There are many reasons people go to Mexico. Some want to experience a foreign culture at budget prices, while others set out to explore mountains or deserts, or city streets lined with outstanding Spanish colonial architecture. Some go to fish, others for the pleasure of enjoying those fish on a plate (Mexico truly has one of the world's most delightful cuisines). But if there's one image that captures Mexico's magic for us, it's the Mayan ruins of Tulum set against an emerald sea. No other country in the Western Hemisphere can come close to Mexico's combination of truly spectacular historical sites and dazzling beaches. It draws us again and again.

In the past few years, those assets have been polished up a bit. More of the Mayan and Aztec ruins have been restored, and venerable resorts such as Acapulco have received much-needed facelifts. The Mexican government has been working hard to promote the country's other riches, too — the colonial cities, sportsfishing, diving, health spas. New toll roads have been paved, and new resorts have gone up in sleepy beach communities.

A Land of Contradictions

It's no wonder, then, that even as Mexico struggles with serious internal crises — a dramatic devaluation of the peso, political assassinations, a peasant and Indian uprising in the southern state of Chiapas — tourism is still going strong. We're compelled, of course, to remind would-be visitors of Mexico's unevenness. It remains a land of baffling contradictions. Just down the street from a five-star resort families camp in ramshackle buildings without plumbing. Burros, with rough-hewn carts in tow, amble alongside express highways. Mexico has colorful fiestas, but it also grapples with serious pollution and corruption and the drug cartels.

Mexico is a large country with diverse landscapes: mountains with near alpine conditions, volcanic regions, arid coastal plains, enchanting white-sand beaches and the Yucatan's thick tropical jungle with high heat and humidity. Although no one knows Mexico City's population with certainty, it is by all estimates the most populous city in the world.

What to Do There

◆ East Coast Resorts/Yucatan Peninsula

Cancun   There's a reason that Cancun does not sound or smell or look like Old Mexico: It's not. Before the 1970s, not one hotel stood on this long strip of land. In fact, developers even designed and constructed the beach. The look is, for the most part, high-tech, and some visitors who love Mexico will simply never find Cancun spontaneous or messy enough. But those who want no mess can revel in its ease as a getaway, with ultramodern hotels, terrific beaches, good deep-sea diving and nearby Mayan ruins to explore. Today, Cancun is Mexico's leading tourist destination.

While technically an island, shaped like the number 7, Cancun does not feel like one. It has calm, shallow waters off the shorter side, wilder Caribbean seas off the longer and a vast freshwater lagoon between the island and the mainland. (There is a "downtown"Cancun, the original town on the mainland — a short bus or taxi ride away. It has its tourist restaurants and shops, too, but a bit more flavor.) Activities in the resort area of Cancun center around the water. You can simply lie on the beach, or you can scuba dive and snorkel — the reefs offshore attract myriad neon-colored sea creatures. Fishing is popular as well. Go on a leisure cruise (the most recent variation is aboard a semisubmersible, which offers underwater views of the coral and the lagoon).

The "sights" in Cancun, amazingly enough, are the hotels on "Hotel Row." We recommend stopping at several of them to have a margarita and marvel at the architecture — it's a pleasant diversion from sand, sun and surf. Though most are techie with a Mayan twist, architectural styles have taken a Las Vegas turn lately: Middle Eastern spires and purely fantastical designs are taking over. Then there are the shopping places — plenty of upscale malls to browse through, as well as boutiques and public markets where souvenirs and crafts are sold. Entertainment possibilities include the Ballet Folklorico and Magico Mexico, a theme park with historical fantasies played out by legions of actors. Discos and nightclubs abound (including Fat Tuesday and Planet Hollywood).

Chichen Itza   The older parts of this large, impressive site are classic Maya; later additions were made by the more warlike Toltecs. The stone carvings, even on walls, are very well preserved, and there's color left on some of the art that's been shaded from the sun. The most dramatic structure is the pyramid-shaped Castle of Kukulkan. The climb to the top is a dizzying experience, but not to be missed for the views and the opportunity to descend into the heart of the pyramid.

Other buildings include the Temple of the Warriors, the Ball Court (where death was an integral part of sports) and the Cenote Sagrado, or Sacred Well (the site of human-sacrifice ceremonies where the deep waters now look exceedingly murky). The astronomical tower, a natural observatory that was partially destroyed by an earthquake, has a variety of holes that point to different celestial groupings.

Although it covers a vast area, with hundreds of structures still unexcavated, Chichen Itza nevertheless gets very crowded with tourists, especially 11 am–3 pm. Plan a minimum of four hours. (You may want to stay for the good sound-and-light show in the evening.) Most people get to Chichen Itza by rented car or on a tour from either Merida or Cancun.

Cozumel   Cozumel, just 40 mi/65 km south of Cancun, has long been subjected to comparisons with its near neighbor. We like Cozumel better. It's still more laid-back and has superior snorkeling, diving (especially around Palancar Reef) and fishing. However, two or three cruise ships are docked there at any one time, and it, thus, has had the attendant development you'd expect to find in any popular resort area.

In addition to water-related activities, you can take excursions to see Mayan ruins. Shops, restaurants and nightlife are concentrated in the only town on the island, San Miguel. It's a lively place built around a pedestrian-zone central square. Most visitors rent scooters, mopeds or Jeeps to explore the island.

Isla Mujeres   Isla Mujeres is a sleepy island off the Yucatan Peninsula that's been a haven for divers and anglers for years. It can be visited as a snorkeling day trip or as a destination in its own right; divers could spend four nights there and see Cancun and Mayan ruins on a day trip. Nondivers be forewarned, however: Isla Mujeres is really quiet at night. Experienced divers can go with a guide to "The Cave of the Sleeping Sharks," where the brave (or foolish) actually pet nurse sharks in the cave — the mixture of salt and fresh water there makes sharks groggy and slow. (Go at your own risk — no wild animal's behavior is 100% predictable.)

Merida   The capital of the Yucatan, Merida is a charming colonial city, one of the first strongholds of the Spanish in New Spain. It has good shopping, fine restaurants and hotels, a couple of nice squares and markets, and

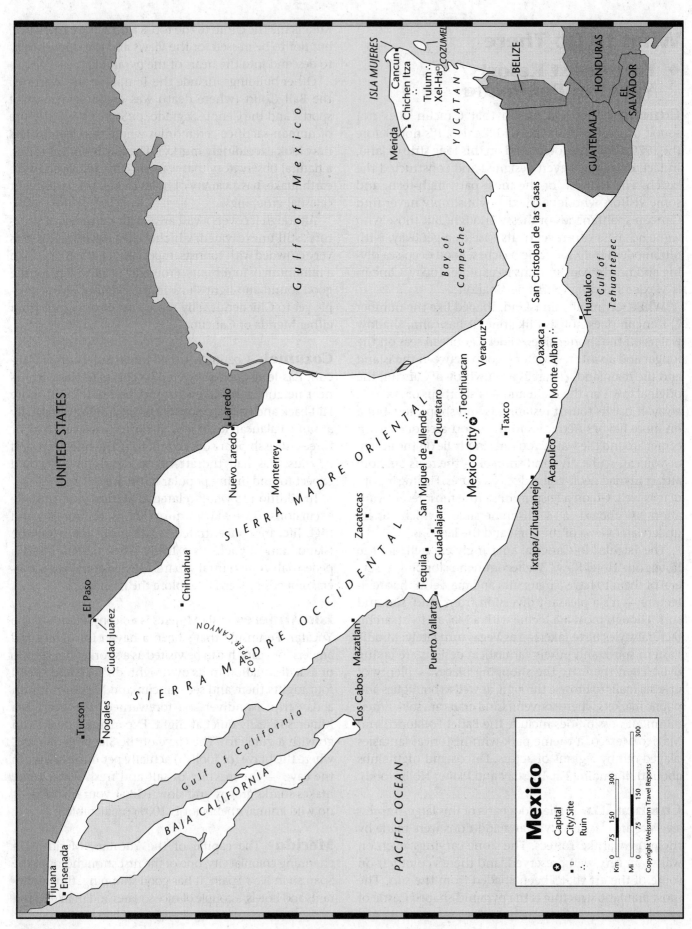

UNITED STATES

Tucson
Nogales
Tijuana
Ensenada
El Paso
Ciudad Juarez

PACIFIC OCEAN

BAJA CALIFORNIA

Gulf of California

Los Cabos

SIERRA MADRE OCCIDENTAL

COPPER CANYON

Chihuahua

Mazatlan

Puerto Vallarta

Tequila

Guadalajara

Zacatecas

San Miguel de Allende

Queretaro

SIERRA MADRE ORIENTAL

Monterrey

Nuevo Laredo
Laredo

Mexico City

Taxco

Acapulco

Ixtapa/Zihuatanejo

∴Teotihuacan

Veracruz

Oaxaca
Monte Alban ∴

Huatulco

Gulf of Tehuantepec

San Cristobal de las Casas

Bay of Campeche

Gulf of Mexico

Merida

Cancun
Chichen Itza
∴
ISLA MUJERES
Tulum∴
Xel-Ha□ COZUMEL

YUCATAN

BELIZE

GUATEMALA

HONDURAS

EL SALVADOR

Mexico

⊛ Capital
■ City/Site
∴ Ruin

Km 0   75   150   300
Mi 0   75   150   300

Copyright Weissmann Travel Reports

friendly people. There are two main reasons to see this city: 1) to try Yucatecan dishes such as *huevos motulenos* (eggs baked on tortillas with sauce), stuffed cheese balls, *poc-chuc* (pork tacos) and black beans, and 2) to use it as a base to see Chichen Itza and other Mayan ruins. The city is also the shopping center of the Yucatan (hammocks are a major local product).

Tulum and Xel-Ha   Plan a two-hour stay at Tulum to explore the ruins of the only seaside Mayan city enclosed by a fortress wall. Splendid beaches and water are nearby, so bring your swimsuit. You may want to stop at Xel-Ha (pronounced SHELL-ha) Lagoon, too, where you can snorkel and swim through underground tunnels. (This is not for the claustrophobic.) Xel-ha can be crowded on weekends, when tour groups arrive en masse.

◆ West Coast Resorts and Oaxaca

Acapulco   Acapulco became a household word in the '50s, when the jet set brought out the lounge chairs and the photographers. Almost instantly the Mexican Riviera became a glamorous destination, a world of movie stars and cliff divers. But in the following years the city faded from fame, partly because the jet set aged and its successors, the beautiful people, found their photographers in other places. Mexico also developed some new resorts — notably Cancun — that captured the public imagination.

Now Acapulco is trying to regain its status as a world-class playground. After spending some US$300 million, it has a cleaner ocean, the high-rise hotel area is getting spruced up and its beaches are no longer overrun with vendors. A new toll road from Mexico City has cut the drive time to about four hours. Although it's still less popular than it once was, today hundreds of thousands of visitors from around the world go to Acapulco to enjoy its setting (on a large, beautiful bay backed by gorgeous mountains), long beaches, fantastic restaurants, excellent shopping and wild nightlife.

No visit to Acapulco would be complete without seeing the famous cliff divers at La Quebrada, who have been leaping from the rocks (80–145 ft/25–45 m up) into a small crevasse of ocean since 1934. You can watch from a nearby restaurant or from the landing.

Huatulco   This area has nine bays with beautiful beaches (among the cleanest, safest and least crowded on the west coast) and big waves (great for bodysurfing). Huatulco is targeted for development as a major tourist destination —

along the lines of Cancun — but with an eye to environmental protection, too. There are now several major resort hotels up and running, with more scheduled.

Ixtapa/Zihuatanejo   Ixtapa is an international beach resort that, like Cancun, is sometimes criticized because it has little Mexican flavor. The building frenzy continues, from new highways to a new marina. We like snorkeling around the little islands while looking at the mountains in the background. Ixtapa is also known for its great fishing. Serious fishermen will also want to head just 3 mi/5 km south to Zihuatanejo. It has sheltered beaches, small hotels, a villagelike ambience, cobblestone streets and fine restaurants.

Los Cabos   Today, this area at the southern tip of Baja California is developing faster than you can say "Jack Nicklaus." Los Cabos is blooming with megaresorts and championship golf courses. "Build it and they will come" seems to be the thinking, and hordes of golfers, sportfishing enthusiasts and tequila-guzzling college students continue to answer the call.

Collectively known as Los Cabos, Cabo San Lucas and San Jose del Cabo (plus the 18 mi/29 km of beach between them) aren't typically Mexican — they're less colorful than most of the nation and laid-back in a way that reminds one more of Southern California. In fact, the combination of heavy tourism and the location gives Los Cabos a sense of being only peripherally a part of Mexico — signs are in English and prices are often quoted in U.S. dollars, for instance.

What Los Cabos has to offer — in addition to being one of the five top fishing spots in the world — are long stretches of golden sand and secluded coves of clear blue water where visitors can snorkel, surf, sailboard and sail. Activities at the resorts that now dot the area range from golf, tennis and horseback riding to party-boat cruises.

Where the Pacific and the Sea of Cortes actually lap towering granite monoliths create the most dramatic setting in Los Cabos. The Arch is the best known, and as the name implies, it's a sea arch carved out of rock by the water. Whales often can be spotted nearby, too.

Mazatlan   After enjoying Mazatlan's beaches or deep-sea fishing or golfing, you can leave the tourist zone and immerse yourself in a real Mexican city there. We liked wandering down Mazatlan's cobblestone streets, poking in shops in colonial buildings or just people watching in the almost-century-old market. Prices have endeared Mazatlan to *norteamericanos* — this is especially evident in the spring, when thousands of U.S. college students swell its population during their annual break from classes. But travelers go to Mazatlan for many other reasons, too. The deep-sea fishing, for instance, is famous. Then there are the beaches: They seem endless and include nearly every type of surf-and-sand experience — there are romantic, secluded coves as well as umbrella-packed expanses.

We found several attractions worth visiting. The Mazatlan Aquarium has more than 200 species of fish (including piranhas, marlins and sharks) and the Public Market is a sensory feast, but it's not for the squeamish: Be prepared for the sight of the skinned heads of cattle, eyes fixed open.

Geostats

Official Name: United Mexican States.

Visa Info: U.S. and Canadian citizens need proof of citizenship (other than voter's registration for Canadians) and photo ID to obtain a tourist card (if going beyond border towns). For visitors from the U.S. not bringing in a vehicle: A tourist card, good for up to 180 days, is issued free. It requires proof of U.S. citizenship, photo ID. Tourist cards may also be obtained in advance from Mexican consulates and airlines serving Mexico. Tourists taking their car into Mexico should check with the Mexican consulate before departure to find out the latest regulations.

Health Certificates: Yellow-fever certificate needed if arriving from infected area.

Capital: Mexico City.

Population: 93,986,000.

Size: 764,000 sq mi/1,978,000 sq km. About three times the size of Texas.

Language: Spanish.

Climate: Varies from tropical to desert.

Economy: Industry, agriculture, tourism.

Government: Federal republic.

Religion: Roman Catholic.

Currency: Nuevo peso (MXN). 100 centavos = 1 MXN. Traveler's checks and credit cards are accepted at most tourist locations. AE, DC, MC, VI.

Time Zone: 1 to 3 hours behind eastern standard time; 6 to 8 hours behind Greenwich mean time.

Electricity: 120 volts.

One of our favorite things to do in Mazatlan is to stroll along the promenade in Olas Altas, where the city's first beachfront hotels were built. A number of structures remain from the 19th and early 20th centuries, when Olas Altas was the city's center. Today the area is home to artisans, galleries and cafes.

There's a lot to do in Mazatlan at night, and the city is relatively low-crime. Discos are plentiful at the hotels. The highlight of Mazatlan's calendar is Carnival — with parades, coronation parties, street dances, floats, fireworks and costumed merrymakers.

Oaxaca   The loveliest state capital in Mexico, Oaxaca has the country's largest Indian market, ancient ruins, colonial architecture, good food and friendly people. The church of Santo Domingo is spectacular — white interior, beautifully painted dome and gold leaf everywhere. We also enjoyed the Regional Museum (spectacular jewelry from ancient tombs nearby). The Saturday Indian market is a riot of color and activity. Little Spanish is heard — most vendors and buyers speak Mixtec and Zapotec. Be sure to get out of town and visit the ruins of Monte Alban, a city built around 300 BC and set on a hilltop.

Puerto Vallarta   Puerto Vallarta is one of Mexico's most picturesque resort cities — its cobblestone streets and white adobe buildings with red tile roofs are nestled between the green palm tree-covered mountains and the deep blue ocean. All this stunning scenery has made Puerto Vallarta one of the most popular — and touristy — resorts in Mexico. This once quaint coastal village is now home to dozens of large, luxury resorts, fancy restaurants and trendy boutiques.

Puerto Vallarta is best known for having the best variety of beaches in Mexico, but it also has a lively nightlife and established U.S. and Canadian communities. The fishing is fabulous. City tours are available, as are tours of some of the casas in Gringo Gulch (yes, the tour includes old pads of Elizabeth Taylor and Richard Burton).

◆ Mexico City and Central Mexico

Mexico City   Mexico city sprawls, it's crowded — some 20 million people strain its resources every day — and millions of its residents live in a poverty that can't be overlooked. But it's a lively place, the cultural center of the country. It has world-class art and food, great music and, perhaps most important, some of the finest antiquities anywhere. To best understand Mexico City, start at its heart: the Zocalo, or central square. The Metropolitan Cathedral, on the north side, is a must-see. The cathedral and the city around it were built on top of the Aztec capital city, razed by the Spaniards in the 1500s. The Aztec ruins were first uncovered in 1978, when public workers dug up an eight-ton stone disc. It had been part of the holiest Aztec shrine, the Templo Mayor. A museum not far from the cathedral, El Museo del Templo Mayor, houses artifacts from the dig. On the east side of the Zocalo is the National Palace. The main reason to make a stop there is to see the stunning murals by Diego Rivera.

The area surrounding the Zocalo is known as the Historic Center —it's almost a "museum" of colonial architecture, covering more than 500 blocks. After touring there, head west to Alameda Central. This park, an oasis of green, is loaded with fountains and statuary and surrounded by museums. One of them is the Palace of Fine Arts where the Ballet Folklorico performs.

Southwest of Alameda Central is an area known as la Zona Rosa (literal translation: the pink zone). It is the trendy, cosmopolitan, well-to-do section with fine hotels, restaurants and nightlife: a nice area of the city in which to stay. Farther west is another must-see: sprawling Chapultepec Park.

But if you have time to see only one attraction, make it the Museum of Anthropology. What you see will be awe-inspiring: the Aztec Calendar Stone, giant stone Olmec heads from the jungles of the east coast, treasures recovered from a sacred Mayan well, a replica of a Mayan ruler's tomb. In our estimation, it is the best of its kind in the Americas.

A word of caution: We strongly recommend that travelers with respiratory, heart or blood-pressure ailments consult their doctors before visiting the city because of the very polluted air and the altitude.

Coyoacan

Once a city in its own right, Coyoacan has been engulfed by Mexico City's urban sprawl. It was home to Diego Rivera, Frida Kahlo and Leon Trotsky. Kahlo's home is now a museum/gallery. Her tragic life and haunting self-portraits have earned her cult status. Leon Trotsky's home has been turned into a museum, too — actually, it's more of a memorial. In the nearby suburb of San Angel you'll find the two-story home/studio-turned-museum of Diego Riviera. It's filled with personal items and paintings. A few minutes southwest of Coyoacan is University City, home of the University of Mexico. The university is the country's architectural showpiece. Be sure to see the O'Gorman mosaics on the library's facade and the Rivera mosaic over the main entrance to the Olympic Stadium.

Guadalajara

Mexico's second-largest city is a feast: colonial architecture, museums, open plazas, intriguing gardens, good shopping, nightlife. At the heart of the city is the twin-towered Cathedral, which is where any tour of Guadalajara should begin. The Cathedral is surrounded by four main plazas. In and around these plazas you'll find most of Guadalajara's cultural attractions. Just east of the downtown plazas is Guadalajara's largest market, the Mercado Libertad. (Remember to haggle!)

On the northern edge of town is the Guadalajara Zoo, one of the largest in Latin America. The artisan district of Tlaquepaque is in the southeast corner of town. There are shops and galleries galore that specialize in ceramics, papier-mache, glass and bronze.

Several interesting day trips are possible from Guadalajara, including tours and tastings at tequila distilleries — where else but in Tequila.

San Miguel de Allende

Now an artists and writers colony and a U.S. retirement community, San Miguel de Allende (100 mi/160 km northwest of Mexico City) was founded in 1542 when silver was discovered in the area. The entire town has since been declared a national monument — it's great to walk the narrow, winding cobblestone streets. It's gotten to be sort of touristy, and the atmosphere reminds us of Santa Fe, New Mexico, with similarly splendid buildings, art galleries and shops. Nearby is the 18th-century city of Queretaro, where Emperor Maximilian was executed; it has an interesting regional museum, churches and plazas.

Taxco

A beautiful village with white stucco buildings and geraniums, known for its silver work and fine cathedral, Taxco was forgotten until a U.S. citizen/resident began boosting the town as a tourist destination. He succeeded all too well: Mexicans joke that they, too, would vacation in Taxco, if only they spoke English. Buy silver and sightsee a bit there. Taxco is frequently seen as a long day excursion from Mexico City. Plan a few hours' stop there if you're driving between Mexico City and Acapulco.

Teotihuacan

Teotihuacan (32 mi/51 km northeast of Mexico City) is one of the most interesting and accessible archaeological attractions in the country. Already ancient and deserted when the Aztecs first saw

Pyramid of the Sun, Teotihuacan

it centuries ago, its exact origins remain unclear. At one time an advanced Indian civilization thrived there (it had up to 200,000 residents around AD 400). Most visitors go to see two very impressive structures: the Pyramid of the Sun and Pyramid of the Moon. A court and other buildings also remain. We recommend arranging a guided tour (English available) — most will give good information and will still allow visitors plenty of time to explore on their own.

Veracruz   Veracruz is a good place to go for pleasant atmosphere and, according to many Mexicans, the best seafood in the country. The beach is not the draw there — the sand is gray and there is little surf. But ask any Mexican his favorite city, and odds are it will be Veracruz. It's full of the lilt of the Caribbean, and marimba music echoes through the streets all night long. Its *zocalo*, or main square, is the most animated and raucous of any in the country. Veracruz exhibits some of that banana-port decadence of the tropics, but set amid architecture dating back to the Spanish Conquest.

Zacatecas   This silver-mining town founded in 1546 was a major city of Spain's New World empire. Wealth from its silver gave Zacatecas its delightful colonial architecture. The pink sandstone cathedral and its intricate carved-stone facade are outstanding examples of *cantera* architecture, and its six museums include the exceptional Pedro Coronel Museum, which houses works by Chagall, Picasso and Goya and — surprisingly — Tibetan art. After a day of museums, drop by the Hotel Quinta Real. It's built around the beautifully paved and restored Plaza de Toros San Pedro, among the oldest

bullfighting arenas in the Americas. Other activities, besides strolling, include a cable-car ride across the city, ending at La Bufa, a peak outside of town (nice view of the city).

◆ Border Towns and Northern Mexico

Border Towns   More often than not, border towns give a distorted view of how the rest of Mexico lives, but if you bear that in mind, they can be interesting. The towns are most often visited for their shopping — a mix of junk souvenirs and quality handicrafts, rustic furniture, cheap liquor, etc. Prices are often second only to those at the point of origin (sometimes cheaper!). Other major reasons to visit are to attend a bullfight or horse race, or to say you've been in Mexico. Some of the most important border towns are Ciudad Juarez (across from El Paso, Texas), Nuevo Laredo (across from Laredo, Texas), Nogales (south of Tucson) and Tijuana (south of San Diego).

Ciudad Juarez, an industrial city of 1 million, has become our favorite border town. It has two centers of interest: the area around the central market and the ProNaF area. The central market area goes on for blocks in every direction, with both stalls and stores specializing in everything from bulk candy to potions for magical cures. The more recently built ProNaF area has an art museum and an excellent arts/crafts center, where high-quality crafts from throughout Mexico can be purchased at reasonable prices. Juarez also has a dog racetrack.

Tijuana is the largest border town. It has two bullrings and a jai alai palace, a convention center, all categories of hotels and good nightlife. The Tijuana Cultural Center, a multimillion-dollar showcase displaying exhibits about Mexico's people, events and culture, is well worth a visit, as is the Mexitlan, a city block's worth of scale reproductions of edifices — sculptures, temples, monuments and other buildings — that reflect 1,500 years of Mexican history. Families can spend some time at the Mundo Divertido, an amusement park.

Ensenada   This major port and tourist town can be reached on excellent toll roads (passing through splendid mountain and coastal scenery). Ensenada attracts college students, sport fishing enthusiasts and anyone who enjoys lying around on nice beaches. Gamblers find it a popular place for offtrack betting via satellite. Considering how large it is and how close it is to the U.S. border (60 miles/100 km), Ensenada's really a very nice, laid-back destination.

Copper Canyon   A train trip through the Copper Canyon is a great way to see a beautiful slice of Mexico — it begins in the desert, cuts through the mountains and ends up at the sea. This can be done independently or on a tour, but we highly recommend a tour. The trains not only pass through eye-catching scenery; they also stop near undeveloped Indian villages. Some tours offer camping and rafting as well. While you can make the trip in an all-day excursion, the best way to enjoy it is to stop at one or more points on the way and spend a night or two. The canyon lies about 300 mi/485 km south-southwest of El Paso, Texas.

Itineraries

Mexico is so diverse and large, yet so nearby for other North Americans, that it's better to see it over the course of several trips. We suggest seeing one region for every week of vacation available.

First Itinerary: Cancun, Cozumel and nearby Mayan ruins.

Day 1 — Arrive Cancun.

Day 2 — Cancun.

Day 3 — Day trip to Chichen Itza. Overnight Cancun (or Chichen Itza).

Day 4 — Day trip to Tulum.

Day 5 — Drive/ferry or fly to Cozumel from Cancun.

Day 6 — Cozumel.

Day 7 — Depart Cozumel.

Second Itinerary: Mexico City and a West Coast Resort

Day 1 — Arrive Mexico City.

Days 2–3 — Mexico City.

Day 4 — Day trip to San Miguel de Allende.

Day 5 — Drive to Acapulco with stop in Taxco.

Days 6–7 — Acapulco.

Day 8 — Depart Mexico.

Another possible 7–10 day itinerary would be a tour of the Copper Canyon area, combined with a visit to Mazatlan and Puerto Vallarta.

Climate/When to Go

The best time to visit Mexico is mid-September to mid-May. Mexico City, due to its high elevation, is cold during the winter. Be prepared for higher humidity in coastal areas and at the inland archaeological sites in the Yucatan peninsula where temperatures in summer can hover at the 100 F/38 C range with near 100% humidity. The average coastal day temperatures year-round are in the 70s–80s F/23–32 C, with nights in the 60s–70s F/15–27 C.

Transportation

Mexicana, Aeromexico, LACSA, TAESA, American, Continental, Delta, Northwest and United offer frequent nonstop flights from several U.S. cities, and Canadian Airlines, Iberia and Japan Airlines fly nonstop from Canada. Mexicana, Aeromexico and several smaller regional carriers offer frequent flights within the country. Benito Juarez Airport (MEX) is 4 mi/6 km from Mexico City. Rail service from the U.S. and within Mexico has deteriorated in the past few years. We don't recommend any of the long-distance trains, except to the adventurous. The only exception is to see the Copper Canyon area. Some U.S. bus companies have been given permission to operate within Mexico, and they now take visitors from several U.S. border towns into the interior of Mexico. In addition, Mexican buses provide first-class service between cities — some vehicles are air-conditioned, show U.S. movies and have hostesses.

About 1.5 million North American visitors drive into Mexico each year. Everyone driving a car in Mexico must have a tourist permit, and Mexican insurance is required, even for one-day border crossings. If you're in a resort area such as Cancun, Merida or Puerto Vallarta, you may find a car convenient, but in big cities such as Acapulco, Mexico City and Guadalajara, take taxis — the driving is nerve-racking. Mexico City's subway is clean, efficient and quiet — outside of rush hour — but its route is still limited. However, it goes near many tourist attractions.

Accommodations

Accommodations range from deluxe resorts to a few scattered B-and-Bs, historic inns, spas, motels and very basic local hotels. For sanitation, comfort and to minimize potential hassles, stay away from the bottom end, but make certain that even costly properties are well located (some "beach resorts" aren't very close to the water). In most cases, first-time visitors or inexperienced travelers should stay in better hotels — or a hotel that is part of a U.S. chain.

Health Advisories

The one thing most people know about travel in Mexico is that they will get an upset stomach or diarrhea. Methods to consider in preventing such problems are: Wash your hands frequently; avoid food from street stands; don't drink tap water or anything with ice; don't eat dairy products — difficult in a country where cheese is so important to the cuisine.

Medical facilities in the larger cities are good. However, sanitary conditions in most restaurants are not up to Western standards. Avoid foods that are difficult to clean, such as lettuce. Make sure meat is cooked thoroughly. Stick with prepackaged or boiled drinks.

Although there have been several cases of cholera in Mexico over the past few years, it's more or less under control. Malaria and dengue fever are endemic in the lowlands and along the coast. Air pollution is extreme in Mexico City, especially from December through May, and may cause problems for people with respiratory diseases.

Crafts store in Mexico

What to Buy

The operative law for shopping in Mexico is *caveat emptor* — let the buyer beware. With that in mind, shop for almost anything you fancy. Mexico has everything from stuffed frogs (in various poses and costumes) to high-quality silver work. Handicrafts, clothing (hats, serapes, sweaters) and folk art vary regionally in style; pottery, woven fabrics, hammocks and baskets are often good buys. Folk art from Oaxaca and Michoacan remains our favorite. High-grade silver is stamped ".925" (by law) — but learn how to double-check for plated silver anyway.

What to Eat

Mexican cuisine — depending on the region — can share similarities with Caribbean, Spanish and even East Indian cooking. In the coastal states — Yucatan, Merida, Campeche and Veracruz, for example — the emphasis is on fresh seafood. Yucatan boasts wonderful *sopa de lima* (tortillas, chicken and a lime-like fruit) and *pollo pibil* (chicken cooked in a pit in banana leaves). Oaxaca

boasts seven different moles (sauces made with such unusual ingredients as chocolate, raisins, peanuts and pumpkin seeds). In many other places, poultry, beef and pork dishes are featured. The basic *bolillos* (crispy bread rolls) and tortillas are magnificent, because they're usually prepared fresh daily. Be sure to try *chiles rellenos* (poblano peppers stuffed with cheese or meat, then fried in egg batter) covered in walnut-and-cream sauce.

Travel Tips for the Client

Do expect business lunches to start around 2 pm. And don't call your host by first name unless you have been asked to do so — relations tend to be rather formal and dress is definitely conservative . . . Do not wear T-shirts and shorts in the big cities unless you want to advertise that you are a tourist . . . Do carry a copy of your tourist card with you at all times . . . If the top of your bottled water doesn't "pop" when you open it, someone may have filled the bottle with tap water and resealed it. Don't drink it . . . Don't be misled by the prices on items in shops. The $ indicates pesos, not dollars . . . Tip 10–15% in restaurants.

Mexico

Review Questions

1. What is the leading tourist destination in Mexico? What are the attractions there?

2. What are the two main reasons for a tourist to see Merida?

3. What kinds of visitors does Los Cabos attract?

4. What has been done in and around Acapulco in an effort to regain its status as a world-class playground?

5. How does Cozumel compare with Cancun?

6. What awe-inspiring antiquities will a visitor see in Mexico City's Museum of Anthropology?

7. What do most visitors go to Teotihuacan to see?

8. What do visitors shop for in border towns? How would you generally describe the prices?

9. What methods can a tourist in Mexico use to prevent stomach problems?

10. How would you describe the Saturday Indian market in Oaxaca?

Mexico

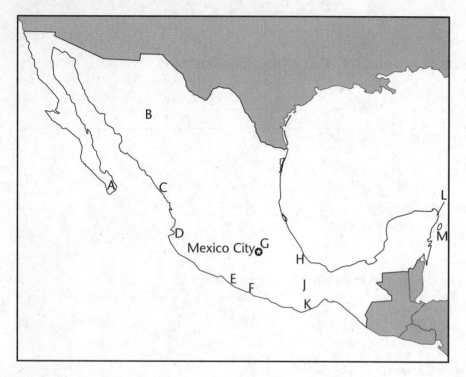

Map Skills Exercise

Match the tourist destination listed below with the corresponding letter on the map. You can use each letter only once.

1. _____ Cancun
2. _____ Acapulco
3. _____ Ixtapa
4. _____ Cozumel
5. _____ Los Cabos
6. _____ Veracruz
7. _____ Teotihuacan
8. _____ Puerto Vallarta
9. _____ Oaxaca
10. _____ Copper Canyon

Selling Exercise

A civic organization in your area has a travel club and the members want to visit Mexico. You are asked to give a presentation to them in which you will discuss the appeal of key Mexican destinations. Create a chart for your presentation that will indicate the appeal of five Mexican destinations.

Bermuda

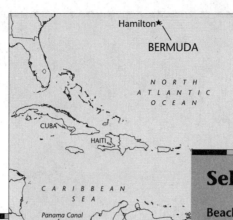

Bermuda is an isolated bit of paradise in the Atlantic Ocean, less than a two-hour flight southeast of New York City. Early residents (including pirates) had its beautiful bays, beaches and clear waters to themselves — the first tourists didn't arrive until 1863. Those same bays now offer excellent fishing, scuba diving, sailing, sunning and swimming.

Immaculate and very friendly, the country has a wide variety of accommodations, excellent shopping (especially for goods from Great Britain and Europe), great entertainment and superb restaurants. It is a bit more formal than the islands of the Caribbean.

Settling the Islands

Bermuda was discovered by Spanish explorer Juan Bermudez in 1503, but it remained uninhabited until the British arrived in 1609. Today, 20 islands are inhabited — out of the 150 mostly very small ones that make up Bermuda (the country is shaped like a fishhook). The water ranges from turquoise to blue and the sand from white to pink. Palm trees and flowers dot the landscape.

What to Do There

Hamilton Hamilton, the capital (pop. 1,617), is fairly small (it can be toured on foot). Orient yourself from Front Street, which has block after block of shops and restaurants across from the harbor. Sights in town include City Hall, Cathedral of the Most Holy Trinity (look for the needlepoint prayer cushions), Sessions House (Parliament building) and the Cabinet Building (ask to see the Senate chamber). Ft. Hamilton, a restored 19th-century fort with superb views, lies just outside of town. Southeast of town is the botanical garden (including Camden House, the official residence of Bermuda's premier). Cruise and harbor-tour boats, ferries and buses to other parts of the island are all boarded in Hamilton.

Selling Points

Beaches, golf, tennis, deep-sea fishing, scuba diving, cricket, sailing, surfing, food, shopping and relaxation are Bermuda's foremost attractions.

Send those who will enjoy a clean, formal, semitropical destination with small but beautiful beaches. Don't send anyone who can't afford it or who is mistaking it for a Caribbean destination (it's neither as tropical nor as informal as the islands farther south in the Caribbean).

Fascinating Facts About Bermuda

During summer, outdoor concerts are held in Hamilton's Victoria Park. Every visitor gets a listing of special events on arrival . . . Bermuda hosts a "College Week" during spring break that includes free and subsidized activities for students . . . Bermuda is both formal and informal. It's a beach destination, yet its residents have a certain reserve. Many restaurants require a coat and tie after 6 pm . . . Several hundred residents emigrate from Bermuda each year because of expensive housing costs. . . .

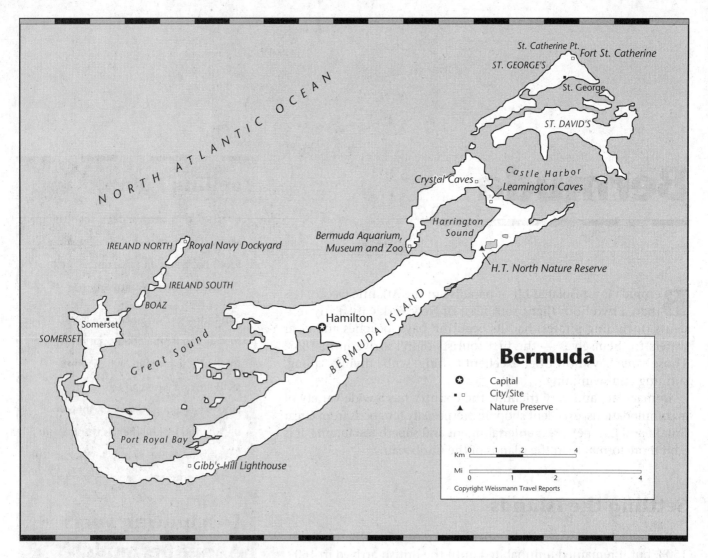

St. Catherine Pt.
Fort St. Catherine
ST. GEORGE'S
St. George
ST. DAVID'S
Castle Harbor
Crystal Caves
Leamington Caves
Harrington Sound
Bermuda Aquarium,
Museum and Zoo
H.T. North Nature Reserve
NORTH ATLANTIC OCEAN
IRELAND NORTH
Royal Navy Dockyard
IRELAND SOUTH
BOAZ
Somerset
SOMERSET
Great Sound
Hamilton
BERMUDA ISLAND
Port Royal Bay
Gibb's Hill Lighthouse

Bermuda

- ⊛ Capital
- ■ □ City/Site
- ▲ Nature Preserve

Km 0 1 2 4
Mi 0 1 2 4
Copyright Weissmann Travel Reports

Harrington Sound

The area around Harrington Sound in east-central Bermuda has several attractions. Among them are an aquarium/museum/zoo complex, the Crystal and Leamington caves, the H. T. North Nature Reserve, Verdmont (a restored 18th-century mansion) and the Blue Grotto Dolphin Show. Plan a half day in the area (more, if you're visiting the nature reserve).

St. George

About 30 minutes north of Hamilton by car, St. George (pop. 1,647), Bermuda's first capital (founded in 1612), is the oldest continuously inhabited English settlement outside of England. It's quiet, but because of its age, it has more character than other villages. Take the self-guided walking tour (the tourist office in King's Square has maps). It takes you by the State House (the oldest building on the island), St. Peter's Church (check out the cemetery behind it), the restored Somers Wharf area (a shopping/restaurant complex), the reproduction of the *Deliverance* (a boat built by those first shipwrecked on the island) and the

Confederate Museum (artifacts from the U.S. Civil War). Be sure to look for the "Old Church Ruins," the shell of what was to be a magnificent cathedral (it was never completed). Just outside town is Ft. St. Catherine, which is really worth a visit. The village also has some fairly good beaches.

Somerset/Ireland Islands

It will take the better part of a day to see these two islands, which are connected by short bridges to the main island (about 30 minutes by road from Hamilton). Somerset is quaint but sleepy. Stop and have a meal or some homemade ice cream from the fountain at Simmons Ice Cream Factory. On Ireland Island you'll find the Maritime Museum (housed in an old Victorian fort) and the Royal Navy Dockyard. The museum has everything from sunken treasure to an exhibit about how scuba equipment evolved (allow 2 hours). Nearby you'll find boutiques, galleries and a theater showing a multimedia presentation of "The Attack on Washington (D.C.)" — it recounts

Bermuda's participation in the War of 1812. Gibb's Hill Lighthouse, a white cast-iron structure that offers excellent views of the entire island, is usually seen on the way between Hamilton and Somerset Island.

Itinerary

Because the island is so small and logistics are no problem, the days on our itinerary can be reshuffled into any order. We suggest renting a motorbike and exploring, stopping anywhere that strikes your fancy.

Day 1 — Arrive Bermuda.

Day 2 — Explore hotel/resort grounds, visit beach.

Day 3 — Half-day tour of Hamilton, harbor tour, beach visit.

Day 4 — Tour St. George and the surrounding area (if time permits, spread this out over two days).

Day 5 — At least half-day tour of Somerset and Ireland islands, perhaps half-day enjoying the water.

Day 6 — Half-day shopping in Hamilton, half-day enjoying the water.

Day 7 — See anything that you haven't gotten to yet or spend more time on the beach.

Day 8 — Depart Bermuda.

Climate/When to Go

Bermuda is a year-round travel destination. Winters and summers are more clearly defined there than in the Caribbean. The highs in summer (May–November) usually hover around the 70s–80s F/23–27 C. December, March and April are in the 60s F/15–22 C, often accompanied by rain and wind. We find January/February too chilly for lying on the beach (golf and tennis are still good, though). Bring a sweater for evenings year-round.

Transportation

Several U.S. and European airlines and Air Canada fly direct to Bermuda from North America and Europe. The airport lies 12 mi/19 km from Hamilton (up to a half-hour trip, depending on traffic). To get around the

Church Beach

island, rent bicycles and motorbikes or take buses (stops are white poles with green stripes — tokens or correct change required), ferry boats (between Hamilton and most ports — you can take motorbikes onto ferries) and taxis (fares go up 25% after midnight). There are no rental cars, and you must be at least 16 to rent a motorbike. Driving is on the left, with a 20-mph/32-kph speed limit. You may also charter a yacht or take a full- or half-day cruise.

Accommodations

Accommodations range from deluxe international beach resorts to cozy bed-and-breakfasts and quaint inns. There's a good selection of immaculate, well-located properties, so the choice will probably be based on other considerations (golf, tennis, restaurants, beach).

More Fascinating Facts About Bermuda

A rail line once ran through the island. Its right-of-way is now a walking path (ask for a copy of the Bermuda Railway Trail Guide at the tourist office) . . . The country is divided into administrative zones called parishes . . . Off-season rates can be 40% less than those during high season . . . To reduce traffic jams, Bermudians are allowed only one car per family . . . Appleby Walking Club hosts sunset and sunrise "strides" in Hamilton and Horseshoe Bay . . . Note the "white-icing" effect on the roofs of most homes. . . .

Geostats

Official Name: Bermuda.

Visa Info: For a tourist visit of up to 6 months, U.S. and Canadian citizens need proof of citizenship (passport or photo ID and birth certificate/voter registration card) and return/onward passage.

Health Certificates: None required currently, but check with local health authorities for latest info.

Capital: Hamilton.

Population: 59,212.

Size: 20.6 sq mi/53.3 sq km.

Language: English.

Climate: Mild.

Economy: Tourism.

Government: Parliamentary British colony.

Religions: Protestant, Roman Catholic.

Currency: Bermudian dollar (BED). 100 cents = 1 BED.

Time Zone: 1 hour ahead of EST. 4 hours behind GMT.

Health Advisories

Few health hazards threaten on Bermuda. The food and water are safe, and medication is available. There are excellent medical and dental facilities in Hamilton and other major towns.

What to Buy

Goods from Great Britain offer the best value —Wedgwood china, cashmere, English antiques and imported clothes. Wood carvings, items salvaged from shipwrecks, copper enamel, pottery and tiles are also available. Among local products that make nice gifts are Royall Lyme Toiletries (factory outlet in West End), Original Horton's Bermuda Black Rum Cake, Gosling's Black Seal Rum, Bermuda Gold (loquat liqueur) and Outerbridge's Original Sherry Pepper Sauce.

What to Eat

If there's a lousy restaurant on Bermuda, we haven't found it. Many of them offer Continental, American or British cuisine, as well as seafood and steaks. Unique local dishes include hoppin' John (black-eyed peas, rice and salt pork) and Bermuda fish chowder (traditionally served with black rum and sherry peppers). Try *syllabub* (a cream-and-cider drink). Many hotels have excellent dinner menus. Hamilton has a few sandwich shops and fast-food places.

Travel Tips for the Client

Don't go expecting this to be the Caribbean—it isn't. It's much more formal and clean, and there's no obvious poverty, no reggae music and none of the culture one normally associates with the Caribbean . . . Do bring plenty of money — you'll need it . . . Do look both ways before crossing streets. Many tourists have never driven a motorbike before, let alone on the left side of the road. . . Do follow Bermuda's dress code: no beach attire in public . . . Don't think the weather is always going to be warm and balmy. When we visited one April, it was considerably warmer at our offices in Austin, Texas, than in Hamilton . . . Do ask the caretaker at St. George's Confederate Museum to make an impression of the Confederate seal for you, using the original press of the U.S. Confederacy . . . Don't even think about taking illicit drugs, spear guns or firearms in or out. Prohibitions are strictly enforced . . . Do note that Bermuda has more golf courses per square mile (or per square kilometer) than any other country in the world. Six of the country's eight golf courses are public and two are private. Professional, invitational and amateur golf tournaments take place year-round — most during November and March. . . .

Tipping: Do tip 15% if it has not already been added to restaurant or hotel bills.

Bermuda

Bermuda

Review Questions

1. How long does it take to fly from New York City to Bermuda?

2. What are Bermuda's foremost attractions for tourists?

3. What is the capital of Bermuda?

4. Which one of the following could a tourist visit in Bermuda's capital city: Blue Grotto Dolphin Show, Simmons Ice Cream Factory, Ft. St. Catherine or Cathedral of the Most Holy Trinity?

5. In what town would you find the State House, St. Peter's Church and Somers Wharf?

6. How much time should a tourist allot to see Somerset and Ireland islands?

7. How might you advise a tourist to get around Bermuda?

8. Why would you recommend that a visitor to Bermuda buy Wedgwood china, cashmere and English antiques?

9. What is *syllabub*?

10. What might the caretaker at St. George's Confederate Museum do for you, if asked?

Bermuda

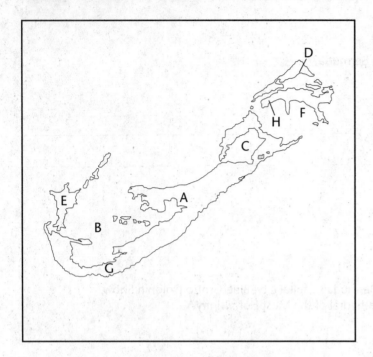

Map Skills Exercise

Match the tourist destination listed below with the corresponding letter on the map. You can use each letter only once.

1. _____ Hamilton
2. _____ Harrington Sound
3. _____ Somerset Island
4. _____ St. George
5. _____ Gibb's Hill Lighthouse

Selling Exercise

A group of friends is considering taking a golfing vacation in the Caribbean islands, the Bahamas or Bermuda. What would you say to persuade them that Bermuda would be an excellent choice for their vacation?

Bahamas

There's a fair amount of variety in the Bahamas. In the touristy towns of Nassau and Freeport, you can gamble, see Las Vegas-style revues, shop in ritzy boutiques and stay in whitewashed waterfront resorts. Yet in the Out Islands, it's still possible to find utter solitude on a pink- or white-sand beach. The scuba diving, snorkeling, fishing and sailing are good to excellent around this 700-island country, which stretches 500 mi/800 km, from near Haiti to within 50 mi/ 80 km of Florida. Don't expect much diversity in the scenery, though; the islands are as flat as the Florida mainland. And, because of the country's proximity to the U.S., you are certain to run into plenty of vacationers, especially in the areas developed for tourism.

Although island culture has been heavily influenced by the U.S., it is still very British. The Bahamas gained its independence from Great Britain in 1973. The main islands are New Providence and Grand Bahama island — 75% of the 255,000 people live on one or the other. Tourism accounts for half of the economic activity of the country.

What to Do There

Abaco   This chain of islands was settled by American Torics after the Revolution; hence, towns have names like New Plymouth. The very slow-paced islands (some don't have cars or televisions) are known for their shipbuilding, diving, fishing and great sailing waters.

There are three primary tourist areas: Green Turtle Cay (peace, relaxation, deep-sea fishing and great diving — good offshore coral gardens), Walker's Cay (a very posh but fairly informal resort island that offers good diving, water sports and deep-sea fishing — adventurous divers will want to see the sleeping sharks in underwater caverns off Walker's Cay) and Great Abaco Island. By far the largest of the Abacos, Great Abaco's attractions include blue holes (deep underwater pools created when the tops of subterranean limestone caves collapsed), orchids, a bird sanctuary, caves and great shelling at Seven Mile Beach. The largest town, Marsh Harbour, is fairly hilly and has plenty to do and see. From there, visit Man-o-War Cay (to see shipbuilding as it has been done for centuries and to shop).

Selling Points

Sunny beaches, golf, boating, fishing, snorkeling/scuba diving, historical sites, gambling, nightlife, shopping, restaurants, investment opportunities and boat cruises over coral reefs are the islands' main attractions.

Visitors who haven't traveled the Caribbean very much or who only want to snorkel, dive, fish, go boating, gamble and/or shop will enjoy the Bahamas.

Fascinating Facts About the Bahamas

Expect to see plenty of flamingos wading in the waters around the islands — the flamingo is the national bird . . . The Bahamian government has a "Director of Sunshine," who is responsible for spreading sunshine and ensuring perfect weather for visitors to the Bahamas. We trust it's a largely ceremonial position . . . Nassau is a popular destination for U.S. college students during spring break . . . For centuries, San Salvador island in the Bahamas was thought to be where Columbus first spotted land in the New World. In 1986, evidence was found that questioned this claim. . . .

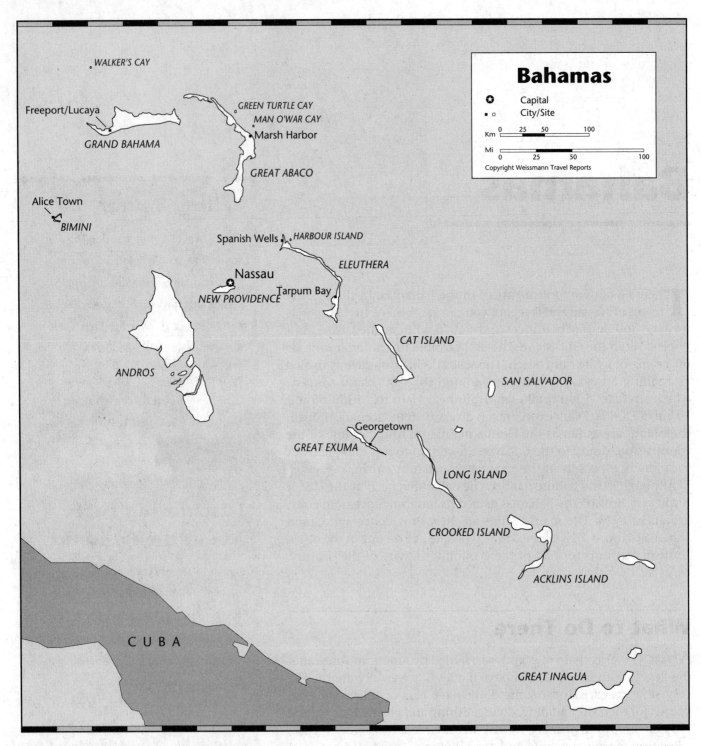

Divers will want to explore Pelican Cay National Park, an underwater preserve offering day and night dives.

Andros

Andros is the largest of the Bahama islands, but it's sparsely populated. It offers excellent wall diving (among the best in the world), great sailing, fishing (bonefish), hunting (duck, quail, pigeon and partridge), beaches and isolation. The forest and mangrove swamp in the south support many species of native wildlife.

Bimini

Ernest Hemingway loved Bimini, as will almost any fishing enthusiast — marlin, sailfish and bluefin tuna are abundant. More than 40 fishing tournaments are held on the island each year. The main village, Alice Town, can be seen in less than an hour (several bars/hotels display Hemingway memorabilia, and there's a colorful church — that's about it). Another attraction is the alleged site (on South Bimini) of Ponce de Leon's "Fountain of Youth."

Eleuthera   This island group was settled more than 300 years ago by the English, who formed the New World's first democracy. While waves pound the east side of the main island (Eleuthera), the sea on the west side is often as smooth as a pond. Eleuthera's attractions are fishing, golf (an 18-hole course), diving (superb) and beaches. At Tan Bay Beach, 2 mi/3 km north of Savanna Sound, you can wade 400 ft/122 m out into the ocean at low tide and the waves will still be below your knees.

When you're on the north end of the main island, stay on one of the two small islands nearby, Harbour Island or Spanish Wells. Harbour Island is our favorite. Its Dunmore Town is one of the oldest and most beautiful towns in the Bahamas.

When traveling to the south end of the main island, ask the driver to stop at the Blow Hole (water shoots straight up through eroded rock, when conditions are right). On the south end of Eleuthera are the Ocean Blue Hole (in Rock Sound — go there to feed the fish), Tarpum Bay (a small artists colony, where fishermen come in every afternoon at 3 pm to sell their fish) and many resorts (including Windermere Island Club and Club Med).

Exumas   Most visitors arrive in (and tour) the Exumas by yacht. The 365 islands, 35 mi/56 km southeast of Nassau, are sparsely populated, with terrain ranging from flat desert to lush, rolling hills. Visitors usually stay on the largest, Great Exuma. The biggest village, George Town, which has an airport, is a great place to rent a boat to explore the other Exumas. Rent a car and follow the Slave Route running the length of the island, the scenery is very interesting. Beautiful Stocking Island lies about 1 mi/1.6 km offshore (good snorkeling). There's outstanding scuba diving at the Exuma National Land and Sea Park. Divers at Ocean Rock in the park will see an underwater valley filled with caves of black coral.

Grand Bahama Island/Freeport

About two-thirds of this island's visitors are cruise-ship passengers or gamblers who don't even spend the night, which is ironic because Grand Bahama has some of the finest accommodations in the islands. Its main tourist areas, the town of Freeport and the Lucaya Beach complex, are about 5 mi/8 km apart. Note that Freeport hotels don't have beaches, apart from the only all-inclusive property, the Italian-owned Club Fortuna Beach Resort. (Make sure your hotel provides free bus service to a beach). The entire area has been developed in the past 30 years, yielding wide boulevards ("dual carriageways") and sprawling, modern resorts. It offers excellent offshore diving and shipwreck-viewing, six great golf

Golf course in the Bahamas

courses, two casinos and better shopping than in Nassau. One Port Lucaya attraction that shouldn't be missed: swimming in scuba gear with dolphins at the Underwater Explorers Society (UNEXSO) facility. They are booked for weeks in advance in high season, so reserve a space as early as possible. At the Rand Memorial Nature Centre, see flamingos and other native birds and learn about the local flora. The best beaches on the island — by far — lie on the east end. Plan a day trip east.

Nassau/New Providence Island   The

rich-in-history capital of the Bahamas, Nassau (pop. 135,000) is on the island of New Providence. Its compact central area can be seen on foot — begin your walk at the visitor's center, near where the cruise ships dock. Visitors will want to see the pink-and-white Parliament buildings and the statues — Columbus on the steps below Government House, Queen Victoria in front of the House of Assembly — and climb the Queen's Steps.

History buffs will want to visit Ft. Charlotte (moat, dungeon, panoramic harbor view from the top) and, perhaps, Ft. Montagu — captured by the U.S. forces at one point during the Revolutionary War. Other attractions in or near town include Coral World underwater observatory; the Seaquarium (sea lions, dolphins, living coral reefs and other marine life); the Emancipation Museum in 18th-century Vendue House, which has exhibits on Bahamian slaves and their quest for freedom; and the shops on Bay Street (there's a market that sells mainly straw items). The top of the water tower affords great views. Rawson Square is where the Nassau locals meet — you'll see them relaxing in the shade of fig trees. Horse-drawn carriages for tourists depart from the square. New on the Nassau waterfront is the Junkanoo Expo, a museum that showcases the colorful costumes, paintings and handicrafts of past Junkanoos (carnival-like festivals based loosely on African customs). Nassau has quite a few hotels, but its beaches are generally not as good as Cable Beach or those on Paradise Island.

Cable Beach, 7 mi/11 km from downtown Nassau, has a concentration of hotels as well as beaches, a casino and restaurants; in addition, limestone caves lie beyond the resort area.

Paradise Island, reached from Nassau via a bridge (or a "bum boat" from Nassau docks), has wonderful beaches, hotels, gambling and restaurants. Paradise Lagoon spotlights trained porpoises.

Elsewhere on New Providence Island is St. Augustine's Monastery. Travel there via jitney (round trip from Nassau) to get a good tour of rich and poor, old and new neighborhoods on the east end of the island and Blackbeard's Tower — reputedly the pirate's lookout. Adelaide Village, on the south side of the island, is perhaps the last remaining area on New Providence barely touched by tourism. (Villagers lives in stone cottages with thatched roofs.) From Nassau's port, the Blue Lagoon Cruise and similar excursions sail to private islands for beaches, food and fun.

Out Islands   The islands other than New Providence and Grand Bahama are referred to as the Out Islands. Life on these islands is more leisurely than on the more touristy and commercial islands of New Providence and Grand Bahama. Among the more frequently visited minor islands are Acklins and Crooked Islands (bonefishing, scenic beaches, snorkeling, history); the Berry Islands (underwater rock formations, an offshore shipwreck and the Stirrup Cay Lighthouse); Chub Cay, a private fishing/diving resort (isolation, diving/snorkeling and great wall and drop-off diving in very clear water); and Long Island, which offers diving (underwater wrecks and shark feeding), limestone caves and a resort complex. While the major islands have their own airports, the smaller islands can be reached only by chartered boat or seaplane.

Itinerary

We suggest that first-time visitors spend the first three nights on New Providence (Nassau, Paradise Island or Cable Beach), transferring on Day 4 to Freeport and spending the next three nights in Freeport or Lucaya. From there, go to another island(s) of choice, generally staying three nights at each destination. The exception to the above rule is for those coming exclusively for scuba diving, golf or deep-sea fishing. They'll most likely want to go straight to an island featuring their favorite activity and not budge for a week.

Climate/When to Go

Because of the Gulf Stream, winters in the Bahamas are fairly mild, about 10 degrees F/5 C warmer than in nearby Florida. The summers can be humid, rainy and warm (day temperatures reaching into the low 90s F/ 30s C), but moderated by trade winds. High season is from November to March, when the weather is generally good. Hurricane season is from July to October. Average day temperatures in fall and spring are in the 70s–80s F/23–32 C, with nights in the 60s F/15–22 C; winter temperatures can be about 10 degrees F/5 C cooler.

Transportation

Bahamasair, Airways International and Trinity Air Bahamas fly nonstop from the U.S. (Florida cities) to Nassau and Freeport; Paradise Island Airlines flies nonstop to Freeport only. Most major American carriers and their affiliates as well as several small regional airlines offer direct flights from Florida cities. Charter flights are also available. Air Canada flies nonstop to Nassau and Freeport. Nassau's International Airport (NAS) is 12 mi/19 km from town. Freeport's International Airport (FPO) is just 5 mi/8 km from the tourist area. Cruise lines visit Nassau, Freeport and private islands (often owned by the line) on various itineraries. There is daily JetFoil service from Ft. Lauderdale, Florida, to Freeport. For travel between islands, Bahamasair offers frequent service, and boats can be rented. Passage can also be booked on mail boats for travel between various islands and Nassau.

Taxis are the main form of transport on most islands, making it sometimes expensive to get around. There are private mini-van "jitneys" on New Providence and in Freeport/Lucaya (to get from Freeport to Lucaya costs about US$0.75 by jitney; a taxi costs US$7). Riding in a surrey with fringe on top is the most interesting way to see Nassau. Car, motorbike and bicycle rentals are also available on some islands (driving is on the left).

Accommodations

Accommodations range from deluxe resorts to locally owned B-and-Bs, hotels and inns. On New Providence, even budget travelers will want to avoid the cheapest accommodations (far below standard). On the Out Islands, quaint accommodations are often the most fun. Make sure that properties far from the Freeport airport on Grand Bahama provide shuttle service, as taxi fares can quickly add up.

Health Advisories

You can drink the water, though it may taste a bit mineral-laden; on some islands (including New Providence),

the taste is bad enough that most people stick with bottled drinks. Be aware that some large predatory fish may contain neurotoxins that can cause diarrhea, headaches and other symptoms. To be on the safe side, avoid eating the local grouper, varieties of jack and barracuda. Medical facilities are good; there are hospitals in Nassau and Freeport and clinics on most populated islands.

What to Buy

Many items sold in the Bahamas are duty-free. The islands have a good selection of jewelry from around the world (including Colombian emeralds) as well as imported woolens, Swiss watches, china from England and other foreign luxury items. Local goods include liquor, Androsia batiks, handicrafts, shell and coral jewelry and art. Straw markets in Nassau, in Freeport's International Bazaar and on several islands sell assorted goods woven from straw, from hats to dolls.

What to Eat

The main tourist areas offer a variety of restaurants and foods, including seafood, steaks, international (Continental, Chinese, Japanese, Polynesian) cuisine, English-style pubs, American fast-food joints, and small places serving local cuisine, including conch fritters, chowders, salads, pea soup with dumplings and fried fish with johnnycake (sweeter than on some Caribbean islands). The "lobster," a variety of giant crawfish, is delicious. Try the guava duff or soursop ice cream for dessert. The various nonalcoholic malt drinks are also good. Among the excellent tropical fruits are sugar apples, a lychee-like fruit called kinip, wild "sea grapes," mangos and dilly.

Travel Tips for the Client

Do bring plugs for your ears if you plan to ride the buses on New Providence. The younger drivers play their music very loud . . . Do fly a yellow flag until you are cleared by customs, if arriving by private boat . . . Do attend one of the local folk performances in Nassau's Dundas Performing Arts Center . . . Do inquire about the Bahamas Discovery Card if booking a package through a tour operator or airline. The free card offers savings of up to 50% at participating hotels, island attractions and restaurants. . . .

Bahamas

Review Questions

1. What are the main islands of the Bahamas? What percentage of Bahamians lives on them?

2. What are the blue holes on Great Abaco island?

3. Why will a fishing enthusiast love Bimini?

4. Where should a visitor on the north end of Eleuthera stay?

5. What should a visitor note about most hotels in Freeport? What should a visitor be sure his or her hotel provides?

6. How do the Out Islands compare with New Providence and Grand Bahama?

7. What kind of people make up about two-thirds of the visitors to Grand Bahama Island? Why is this ironic?

8. During which months of the year is high season in the Bahamas? Why?

9. From what city are both Cable Beach and Paradise Island easily accessible? What do Cable Beach and Paradise Island offer tourists?

10. Why should you avoid eating local grouper and varieties of jack and barracuda in the Bahamas?

Bahamas

Map Skills Exercise

Match the tourist destination listed below with the corresponding letter on the map. You can use each letter only once.

1. _____ Andros Island
2. _____ Nassau
3. _____ Freeport
4. _____ Bimini
5. _____ Eleuthera
6. _____ Great Abaco

Selling Exercise

You are working for an advertising agency and are asked to create a slogan. The slogan will be part of an ad campaign designed to promote travel to the Bahamas. Write a 3- to 10-word slogan that will capture the essence of the Bahamas and help interest tourists in traveling there.

Puerto Rico

Selling Points

Deep-sea fishing, gambling, historical attractions, nightlife, horse racing, culture, beaches, rain forests, shopping, golfing, tennis, caves, hiking, horseback riding, world-class surfing and water sports (including snorkeling and scuba diving) are among Puerto Rico's main attractions.

Travelers who want to get away from it all in comfort (there are some lovely luxury resorts) and those who enjoy exploring (the island is so large it offers a variety of things to see and do) will like Puerto Rico.

Fascinating Facts About Puerto Rico

In San Juan, Casa Blanca, the house of Ponce de Leon, the explorer who searched for the mythical Fountain of Youth, was lived in by his family or his descendants for more than 250 years. It is now a museum . . . Although Puerto Ricans are U.S. citizens, they pay no federal income tax (but neither can they vote in presidential elections) . . . If you're interested in surfing, try the beach at Rincon . . . In San Juan, at midnight on 25 June (St. John the Baptist Day), people walk backward into the sea or a pool three times. This ritual is performed to wash away the year's sins and ensure good luck for the following year. . . .

Puerto Rico has both Old World charm — some of the best Spanish colonial architecture in the Caribbean — and New World pleasures — scuba diving, snorkeling, gambling, a championship golf course and, of course, beaches for lounging. It has diverse cultures (U.S., Spanish, French, African and native), varied topography (rain forest, mountains, desert and plains) and the region's largest city (San Juan). In short, Puerto Rico is a good choice for travelers who like the Caribbean on a scale a little different from what most islands can offer.

But being the hub of the Caribbean and a self-governing commonwealth of the U.S. has its disadvantages, too. Crime and pollution trouble parts of San Juan, just as they do other large North American cities. In addition, the heavy influx of airline and cruise-ship passengers into San Juan, particularly in the winter months, can mean traffic jams and long lines at popular historic sites and restaurants. And while most tourist facilities are geared to the needs and wants of U.S. visitors, Puerto Rico is not the United States — service, infrastructure and customs differ. (English is widely spoken, for instance, but the language of the island is most definitely Spanish.)

The best advice we can give is: Don't limit your stay to San Juan. As much as we enjoy wandering its cobblestone streets, we take equal pleasure in the small towns and scenic roads of the interior and the coast.

What to Do There

Camuy Caves These 16 caves, accessible via a guided tram/walking tour, offer a chance to see the world's third-largest underground river. (Those with proper equipment are allowed to explore on their own.) Don't miss the Tres Pueblos Sinkhole (65 ft/ 20 m in diameter, 400 ft/122 m deep). If you're planning to visit the area, read *Discovery at Rio Camuy* by Russell and Jeanne Gurnee (Crown Publishers).

El Yunque El Yunque Caribbean National Forest is a mountain surrounded by a 28,000-acre/11,332-hectare bird sanctuary and rain forest. The only tropical rain forest in the U.S. National Forest system took a beating in 1988, when Hurricane Hugo downed about a third of its trees. Many of the locals, who have always attributed almost magical powers to this forest, believe that it saved them from the worst of the hurricane. Even if there are no magical powers, the forest has a fairy-tale atmosphere. Be sure to go atop the observation tower for an excellent view of the area. The waterfall, especially during or at the end of the rainy season, is quite nice, but twice when we were there it was barely a trickle. Bring sturdy nonslick shoes to hike on one of the many trails. El Yunque is 25 mi/40 km east of San Juan.

Phosphorescent Bay

On the southwestern part of the island (west of Ponce), Phosphorescent Bay must be seen at night by boat. It's an eerie experience, particularly on a moonless night; the water and schools of fish actually glow when they have been disturbed. The night boat tours usually last about an hour. Divers and snorkelers may enjoy getting into the water.

Ponce

Puerto Rico's second-largest city, Ponce (pop. 300,000) sits on the Caribbean (south) side of the island, about a two-hour drive from San Juan. The town is fairly compact, so it doesn't take long to see. Points of interest include the main square (Plaza Las Delicias, with graceful fountains); the market; Casa Paoli (it houses the Puerto Rico Center for Folkloric Research and is the venue of many cultural activities); the Museum of Puerto Rican Music, where memorabilia of famous musicians and displays recount the rich musical history of the island; and Serralles Castle Museum, a fine 1930s mansion that belonged to the island's oldest rum-making family — you take the scenic drive up El Vigia Hill. For a pleasant outing, head to the Hacienda Buena Vista, a restored 19th-century coffee plantation and grain mill where visitors can learn about the old methods used to process coffee and grain.

Carnival, which is celebrated the six days before Ash Wednesday, means a series of parades and special events in Ponce that often center on the figure of King Momo, once the village idiot and now the unchallenged sovereign of these pre-Lenten festivities.

San Juan

The capital city is an intriguing mixture of old and new. Start your tour in charming Old San Juan, which is perched atop a hill on a small peninsula facing the Atlantic Ocean. This walled city — seven square blocks of which are now a designated historic landmark — was founded in 1510; today it is a showcase for four centuries of architectural treasures and the heart of the island's unique cultural identity.

Take time to stroll along the narrow, blue-grey cobblestone streets and investigate the pastel-colored buildings, restaurants, boutiques, museums, mansions and

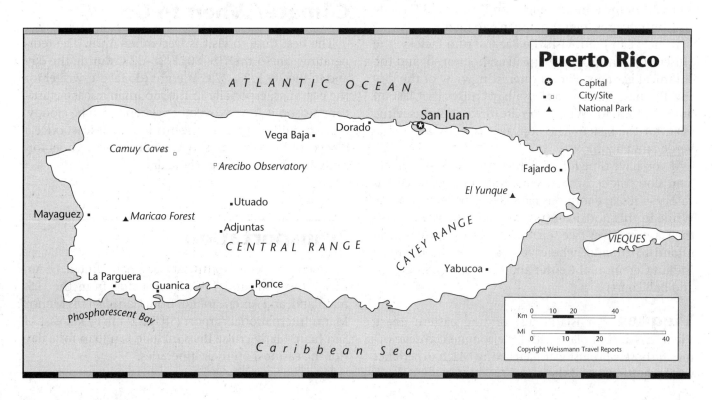

La Fortaleza, San Juan

We suggest a first-time visitor stay seven nights:

Day 1 — Arrive San Juan.

Day 2 — Tour Old San Juan.

Day 3 — Tour New San Juan.

Day 4 — Drive to Ponce to explore the Plaza Las Delicias and the beaches.

Day 5 — Spend part of the day on the beach, but leave plenty of time to get to Phosphorescent Bay for a night tour.

Day 6 — Drive to Arecibo to see the Camuy Caves. It takes about 2 hours to drive back to San Juan.

Day 7 — San Juan, with a possible excursion to El Yunque or a day spent shopping and relaxing.

Day 8 — Depart San Juan.

Climate/When to Go

The best time to visit is December–April. The temperatures are in the 70s–80s F/23–32 C during the day and in the 70s F/23–27 C at night (do take a sweater for the evenings, especially in the mountain areas). Hurricane season is June–November, when it can be cloudy, more humid and rainy. It seems to rain at least once a day year-round, but most of the rain comes in brief torrents and doesn't ruin a whole day.

Transportation

American, Delta, Northwest (seasonal), United, USAir, Kiwi, Tower Air and TWA fly nonstop from the U.S. mainland, and American flies from Canada. Luis Munoz Marin International Airport (SJU) is 9 mi/14 km east of San Juan. Many cruise lines include San Juan for a day (for the casinos) on their itineraries.

nightclubs. The Paseo de la Princesa, a promenade that follows the waterfront, and the Paseo de la Muralla, which winds along the city walls, are particularly lovely. And save some energy and time for the three trademark forts that have resisted attacks by foreign invaders as well as by the city's developers: El Morro, San Cristobal and San Jeronimo. Another must-see is La Fortaleza, which was built in 1540 and is the oldest governor's mansion still in use in the Americas. Other sights include the Pablo Casals Museum (a collection of music and photographs of the famous cellist-conductor) and Casa de los Contrafuertes (oldest house in San Juan).

In new San Juan, visit the Bacardi rum factory, the Museum of Anthropology (plan an hour or so) and the botanical gardens. For an interesting view of the city and the harbor, there are also bay cruises that last an hour and a half. When you are tired of sightseeing, head for the beach. The best near the city are at Isla Verde and Luquillo.

If you have time for a day trip, drive west out of San Juan along the coast to Arecibo. Tour the Arecibo Observatory — it's an enormous radio telescope set in a crater. While in this north-central stretch of the island, visit the Camuy Caves (see separate paragraph), then head inland to Utuado, where you can visit the Caguana Indian Ceremonial Center and Museum (petroglyphs and ball courts).

Vieques An island just off the eastern coast, Vieques is a quiet place with little commercial development; those who just want a relaxing beach experience will be quite satisfied there.

Accommodations

Accommodations range from luxurious first-class resort properties to comfortable mid-range hotels, locally owned B-and-Bs, hotels, paradores (small guest houses that are located at scenic or historical sites) and campgrounds. Pay particular attention to a hotel's location as some are miles from interesting cities or beaches. Many fine old private residences have been converted into guest houses. Some are beautiful beach cottages, others plantation homes or former Spanish haciendas.

Health Advisories

You'll find modern medical facilities throughout the island, with hospitals in major towns and clinics with registered nurses in the villages. There is a slight risk of contracting bilharzia (a parasitic disease), so avoid entering freshwater ponds or slow-moving streams.

What to Buy

Shop for locally produced fabrics, lace, straw and wood products, colorful masks (made of papier-mache or coconut shells), ceramics and tiles, *cuatros* (handmade guitars), santos (small carved-wood religious figures), cigars, local rum, embroidered goods and hammocks (locally claimed to be a Puerto Rican invention, found in many different styles, materials and colors). Puerto Rico is not a duty-free port.

What to Eat

The cuisine is a mixture of Spanish, Indian and Creole, with plenty of American, Oriental and European thrown in. The local food is highly seasoned, unique and quite good. Try the *empanadillas* (meat- or seafood-filled turnovers), paella and seafood. Other good local dishes include black bean soup, *lechon asado* (roast suckling pig), *bacalaitos* (salted cod fritters), *mofongo* (mashed plantain with garlic), *sancocho* (beef stew with vegetable roots) and *tostones* (fried cakes made of green plantains). *Comida criolla* refers to island cuisine.

Geostats

Official Name: Commonwealth of Puerto Rico.

Visa Info: Proof of citizenship recommended but not required for U.S. citizens coming from the U.S. mainland or the U.S. Virgin Islands. U.S. citizens who travel via another country and all Canadians must bring proof of citizenship.

Health Certificates: No vaccinations are required.

Capital: San Juan.

Population: 3,523,000.

Size: 3,453 sq mi/8,860 sq km.

Languages: Spanish, English.

Climate: Tropical.

Economy: Manufacturing, agriculture.

Government: Commonwealth of the U.S.

Religions: Roman Catholic, Protestant.

Currency: U.S. dollar. 100 cents = 1 dollar. Traveler's checks and credit cards are widely accepted.

Time Zone: Eastern (1 hour ahead in winter); 4 hours behind GMT.

Electricity: 120 volts.

Travel Tips for the Client

Do enjoy and dance to some of the local music. Some clubs even give patrons dancing lessons . . . Don't expect quick service in all restaurants. Service is more leisurely than many people from Canada and the mainland U.S. are used to . . . Do speak Spanish if you know any. It will be much appreciated. . . .

Puerto Rico

Review Questions

1. What do Camuy Caves offer visitors a chance to see?

2. What is the name of the only tropical rain forest in the U.S. National Forest system? What happened there in 1988?

3. Why is Phosphorescent Bay an eerie experience, particularly on a moonless night?

4. What will a visitor find in the Museum of Puerto Rican Music in Ponce?

5. For what is walled Old San Juan a showcase? What will a visitor see while strolling through Old San Juan?

6. What kind of visitors will Vieques satisfy?

7. What seems to happen at least once a day year-round on Puerto Rico? Does it ruin a whole day?

8. Why should an agent pay particular attention to the location of hotels he or she books on Puerto Rico?

9. Who was Ponce de Leon? In what city can a tourist visit his house, Casa Blanca, which is now a museum?

10. What would a tourist shopping for *cuatros* and santos be looking to buy?

Puerto Rico

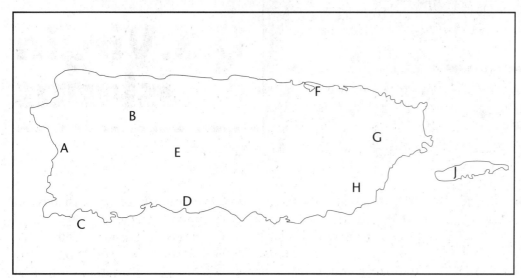

Map Skills Exercise

Match the tourist destination listed below with the corresponding letter on the map. You can use each letter only once.

1. _____ San Juan

2. _____ El Yunque

3. _____ Ponce

4. _____ Vieques

5. _____ Camuy Caves

6. _____ Phosphorescent Bay

Selling Exercise

One morning, your boss informs all agents that the next person to book travel to Puerto Rico will receive double commission. That afternoon, a couple comes in to your office and asks your advice on which island to visit in the Caribbean. They mention to you that they're interested in beaches, nightlife and historical sites. What would you say to them to interest them in visiting Puerto Rico?

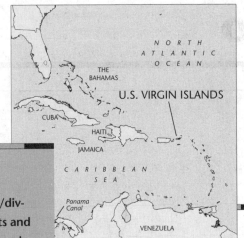

U.S. Virgin Islands

Puerto Rico

Wrapped in the familiarity of American culture, these islands can provide a smooth introduction to the tropics.

Of the three main islands, St. Thomas is the most crowded, with a bustling cruise port, some of the best duty-free shopping in the Caribbean and plenty of first-class U.S.-style hotels and Continental restaurants. St. John, the smallest island, appeals to nature lovers with its lush forests and secluded beaches. (It is sparsely developed, thanks to a national park that covers a huge chunk of the island.) St. Croix, the largest island, is the most interesting from a historical point of view, with many wonderful old forts and buildings, as well as shops and restaurants in a more relaxed atmosphere than that of St. Thomas. Repeat visitors usually develop a fondness for one island's style; first-timers might want to sample all three.

Fearful of German expansion, the U.S. bought the islands from Denmark in 1917, during World War I, for $25 million.

What to Do There

St. Croix   There are two main towns on St. Croix, the largest island: Christiansted and Frederiksted, both named after Danish kings. Christiansted is larger, yet the whole town can be seen in about three hours (including a half hour at the 18th-century Ft. Christiansvaern and a half hour at Government House). Get a map and a Walking Tour Guide from the tourist office (in the Old Scale House) and explore whatever sounds appealing. The whole area from the wharf to the fort is a National Historic Site (it includes the house where Alexander Hamilton lived). The outdoor market on Company Street is bustling Wednesday and Saturday and is great for sampling local fruits and vegetables. The shopping in general is less hectic than on St. Thomas, though many of the shops are branches of St. Thomas stores. Frederiksted can be seen in two hours: Stroll down Strand Street (shops and cafes) and visit the museum. The city's harbor is spectacular for picture-taking; a walking tour there would include Ft. Frederick (which includes a museum and an art gallery with a rotating exhibit of local art) and the Market Place. Don't miss the little St. Croix Aquarium, which showcases local marine life. Though Frederiksted can be quite sleepy, it is very busy when cruise ships arrive.

Also on St. Croix are the Cruzan Rum Pavilion (tours and tastings), the Estate Whim Plantation Museum (with sugar mill ruins and a restored 19th-century village) and the St. George Village Botanical Gardens, which are set in the ruins of a 19th-century sugarcane plantation.

Outside of the main towns are some wonderful beaches. We recommend Cane Bay for snorkeling/diving, Davis Beach for bodysurfing, Rainbow Beach for shelling and Reef Beach for windsurfing.

There are also a number of wildlife refuges on the island: Green Cay National Wildlife Refuge, east of Christiansted; Sandy Point National Wildlife Refuge, south of Frederiksted, which has a turtle-nesting site and a large salt pond that's excellent for bird-watching; and Salt River Bay, northwest of Christiansted (good bird-watching and an underwater canyon for divers). On the eastern part of the island are Fairleigh Dickinson Park and Cramer Park (hiking and snorkeling). Anglers will enjoy the excellent kingfishing at Lang Bank. Also, Buck Island is usually seen as a day trip from St. Croix. Attractions there include beautiful, unspoiled beaches and diving and snorkeling.

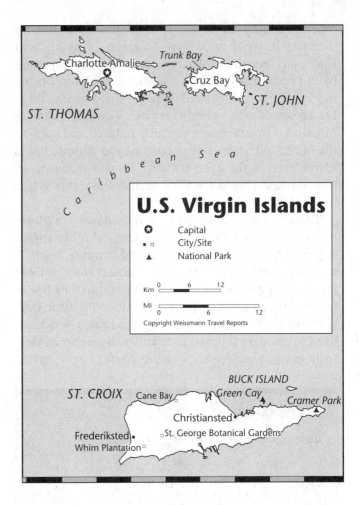

St. John

St. John is the most scenic and the most unspoiled of the U.S. Virgins. Like St. Thomas, it's volcanic in origin, with mountains reaching 1,277 ft/389 m; two-thirds of it is set aside as national parkland. The main reason to stay on St. John is to relax and immerse yourself in the scenery. (The ruins of the Annaberg Plantation are about the only nonnature-related attraction.) People who want nightlife will want to go just for the day. Ferries (leaving on the half hour) run between the only real town on St. John, Cruz Bay, and St. Thomas.

Many visitors go to St. John for a day of sunning, snorkeling and swimming and a taxi tour of the island. Once you've arrived, head for the park headquarters at the National Park Service dock for trail and hiking maps and to check the schedule of events for park-sponsored tours, organized walks, slide shows and evening programs. Allow some time for snorkeling — everyone should at least put on a mask and peek underwater. There are millions of tiny, brightly colored fish. Shallow reefs surround the island, and you can easily swim out to most of the reefs from lovely, sandy bays.

Trunk Bay, one of the most beautiful in the Caribbean, has long been discovered by day-trippers, so we advise visitors to arrive early or head to another beach instead. The underwater snorkeling trail is still a good trip for beginning snorkelers, but much of the coral is dead — the result of damage from sediment stirred up by hordes of fin-flappers. From roads at higher elevations, the views are quite extraordinary (many of the islands seen are in the British Virgin Islands). To get a different and quite lovely perspective, take one of the boat trips around the island or go on a sunset cruise.

St. Thomas

St. Thomas, the most developed island, has a volcanic background. Its principal town, Charlotte Amalie, is the capital of the U.S.V.I. It's also a model that other Caribbean cities are attempting to duplicate — or to avoid. It is small enough (pop. 12,331) to be seen on foot, but that means it can also be a madhouse of shopping-crazed tourists on days when many cruise ships are in the harbor. Indeed, this is the place to go for some of the best duty-free shopping in the Caribbean.

Most visitors spend at least half a day shopping, but there are plenty of other things to see and do in town. Ft. Christian, near King's Wharf on the harbor, is the oldest building in town. It now houses a history museum in what once were dungeons. Government House has some interesting art, including two paintings by impressionist Camille Pissarro (he was born on the island). You can take the 99 Steps up Blackbeard's Hill to Blackbeard's Castle — and a very nice view. Seven Arches Museum, a private home carefully restored and open to the public, offers the rare opportunity to glimpse life as it was lived in the 19th century. We also recommend that you take time to visit the second-oldest synagogue in the Western Hemisphere.

There are plenty of attractions outside Charlotte Amalie, too. The views are excellent from Mountain Top (the highest viewing point) and Paradise Point. A visit to Coral World, an undersea observatory at Coki Point, will give you a look at what life is like 14 ft/4 m below the sea's surface (the 50,000-gallon Predator Tank is stocked with sharks, barracudas and rays). A ride on the 48-passenger submarine *Atlantis* will give you a view from even lower depths — some 90 ft/27 m — day or night. If you're interested in game fishing, the North Drop and the Saddle are good spots (20 mi/32 km off Red Hook).

Of course, the most beautiful attractions on the island are the beaches. In fact, most visitors stay at full-service resorts outside of the capital.

Itinerary

St. Croix will appeal to those who think they'd like a less-hectic version of St. Thomas combined with lots of interesting historic buildings (though it, too, can get a bit crowded on days that cruise ships dock). St. John will appeal to those who truly want to get away. First-time visitors who want to check everything out might want to split their time between St. Thomas (four days) and St. Croix (three days) with a day trip from St. Thomas to St. John.

Day 1 — Arrive St. Thomas.

Day 2 — St. Thomas.

Day 3 — St. Thomas.

Day 4 — Day trip to St. John.

Day 5 — Arrive St. Croix.

Day 6 — St. Croix.

Day 7 — St. Croix.

Day 8 — Depart the U.S. Virgin Islands.

Climate/When to Go

The weather is both beautiful and beautifully consistent year-round. Temperatures are generally in the 80s F/27–33 C during the day and in the 70s F/21–26 C at night. The winter months are slightly cooler and windier than the summer months. There is more rain in the fall (meaning more frequent short showers). June–November is hurricane season.

Transportation

American, Continental, Delta and USAir fly nonstop from the U.S. mainland to both St. Thomas and St. Croix, and various local and regional carriers fly from

Geostats

Official Name: U.S. Virgin Islands.

Visa Info: Proof of citizenship required for U.S. and Canadian citizens (passport recommended).

Health Certificates: No vaccinations are required for U.S. and Canadian citizens.

Capital: Charlotte Amalie, St. Thomas.

Population: 101,809.

Size: 133 sq mi/344 sq km.

Languages: English, Spanish.

Climate: Tropical.

Economy: Tourism.

Government: Unincorporated Territory of the U.S.

Religions: Roman Catholic, Protestant.

Currency: U.S. dollar (USD). 100 cents = 1 USD. Traveler's checks and credit cards are widely accepted. AE, DC, MC, VI.

Time Zone: Atlantic standard time; 1 hour ahead of Eastern standard time; 4 hours behind Greenwich mean time.

Electricity: 120 volts.

other Caribbean islands. While there is no direct service from Canada, American offers single-carrier service via Miami to St. Thomas and St. Croix. Cyril E. King Airport (STT) is located just 2 mi/3 km from Charlotte Amalie on St. Thomas. The Alexander Hamilton Airport (STX) on St. Croix is 8 mi/12 km from Christiansted. Many cruise lines include Charlotte Amalie and St. Croix on their itineraries. Getting to St. John usually requires flying into St. Thomas, taxiing to Red Hook or Charlotte Amalie and then taking the ferry. Ferries leave St. Thomas for the British Virgin Islands.

Beach scene, U.S. Virgin Islands

Accommodations

Accommodations range from deluxe resorts to campgrounds, B-and-Bs, condominiums, inns and local hotels. The deluxe hotels are generally quite beautifully landscaped and have excellent service and amenities, but be careful when making a selection — some are not as close to the beach as less-expensive properties.

Health Advisories

There are hospitals on St. Thomas and St. Croix and a clinic on St. John. We've heard conflicting reports about the potability of the water; ask locally, and if at all in doubt, stick with bottled water, prepackaged drinks and boiled beverages. Take insect repellent — many beaches have sand fleas and no-see-ums (very tiny flies that pack a big bite).

What to Buy

Shop for local handicrafts (clothing, art, gemstones and other jewelry), liquor (especially rum), calypso and steel-band records, leather goods and pottery from there and other Caribbean islands. There's also excellent duty-free shopping (jewelry, gemstones, cameras, watches, perfumes, crystal, linens, designer clothes, liquor, etc.). The U.S. duty-free limit for U.S. citizens — US$1,200 per person — is twice that of any other port, but remember that just because something's duty-free doesn't mean it's cheaper than in your hometown. Be aware that cruise lines that recommend particular shops are often paid by those shops.

What to Eat

The U.S. Virgin Islands offer a wide variety of local, U.S. and international cuisines. There's excellent lobster, tuna, red snapper, grouper, yellowtail, wahoo, veal, steak and much more. The varied West Indies cuisine is exceptionally good, based primarily on seafood, vegetables and fruit. Try pates and conch fritters from the snack kiosks. We also like the soursop ice cream, fungi, bullfoot soup and the nonalcoholic malt drinks. Goat water is a tasty stew, and callaloo is made from spinach, okra, goat, fish, crab and West Indian spices. The light Cruzan rum is the choice drink of most locals.

Travel Tips for the Client

Do conserve water — it is a precious resource on the islands . . . Don't expect anything to be inexpensive: The U.S.V.I. have one of the highest costs of living in the U.S. . . . Do snorkel in Francis Bay on St. John if you want to see sea turtles . . . Do bring at least a sports coat with you; a few restaurants require them after 6 pm. . . .

U.S. Virgin Islands

Review Questions

1. Why is St. John so sparsely developed?

2. From what country did the United States purchase the Virgin Islands? Why and when did the United States buy the islands from that country?

3. Compare and contrast St. Thomas and St. Croix.

4. On what days of the week is St. Croix's outdoor market on Company Street bustling? For what is the market great?

5. What is the main reason to stay on St. John?

6. What might you advise tourists not to go to Trunk Bay?

7. When is Charlotte Amalie a madhouse of shopping-crazed tourists?

8. For what activities should you probably recommend each of these beaches on St. Croix: Cane Bay, Davis Beach, Rainbow Beach, Reef Beach?

9. What is Coral World? What will a visitor see in the Predator Tank?

10. How do travelers coming by air to the Virgin Islands usually get to St. John?

U.S. Virgin Islands

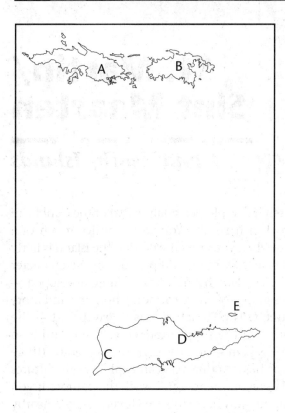

Map Skills Exercise

Match the tourist destination listed below with the corresponding letter on the map. You can use each letter only once.

1. _____ St. John

2. _____ St. Thomas

3. _____ Buck Island

4. _____ Frederiksted

5. _____ Christiansted

Selling Exercise

A couple wants to honeymoon in the U.S. Virgin Islands. They're particularly interested in snorkeling opportunities. What would you say to the couple about snorkeling in the Virgin Islands to get them to book their honeymoon through you?

St. Martin/ Sint Maarten

and Nearby Islands

St. Martin/Sint Maarten has a split personality: Part of the Caribbean island is French, part of it Dutch. You won't notice much of a change in the geography when you cross the border (the island is fairly hilly, with many good beaches), but you'll pick up on the character differences immediately. The Dutch side is much more developed — there are more buildings going up, more car horns honking and more people clogging the streets. The French side is slower paced — the resorts are more elegant and the shops more chic. The island is so small — only 37 sq mi/96 sq km — and the division so friendly (there are no border or customs hassles) that you can explore both cultures from the same hotel. We recommend a full week there, more if you intend to use it as a hopping off place to three lovely islands nearby — Saba, St. Eustatius and St. Barthelemy.

What to Do There

St. Martin (French side)   The northern, French side of the island has begun to embrace development. The run-down, informal town of Marigot has begun to evolve into a coastal resort, which makes the ever-increasing numbers of French and American tourists feel right at home. The food in Marigot is wonderful, and there's an interesting central marina. Climb the trail that goes up from the center of town to the old fort. The fort offers great views of Marigot and the ocean. Along Marigot's waterfront, you will find excellent restaurants, duty-free shops and boutiques specializing in the latest Italian and French clothing. The town and beach at Grand Case (on the northern end of the island) is much quieter than Marigot and has a row of some of St. Martin's finest (and most expensive) restaurants. The north and east coasts are fairly isolated, although several hotels have been built there recently. There's a strong Mediterranean ambience to the French side — open markets, outdoor cafes and nude- and topless-bathing beaches. Everyone speaks French, but service people usually know some English, and even those who don't are eager to help.

Sint Maarten (Dutch Side)

The Dutch side of the island is much more developed for tourism than the French side, with big hotels and time-share developments. Philipsburg, the capital of Sint Maarten, is built around two main streets (Front and Back) along the port area. Brick walkways have been added and store fronts have been renovated recently on Front Street, making the city's main tourist area a more attractive place to walk and shop. Traffic and pedestrian congestion remain a problem, however, particularly on days that cruise ships disgorge their passengers. You might want to change your plans and opt for the beach if you see several cruise ships in the port that day. Several casinos, restaurants and recently restored Ft. Amsterdam offer a variety of distractions for visitors. If the kids are along, visit the Sint Maarten Zoo, one of only a few zoos in the Caribbean. The rest of the island is fairly flat and sandy (ideal for motorbikes).

Nearby Islands

Saba This Dutch island (pronounced SAY-ba), is usually seen as a day trip from Sint Maarten, but divers and travelers in search of tranquillity prefer to stay there at least two nights. Saba is basically a mountain rising out of the sea, with almost no flat land or real beaches. Consequently, it is definitely not for those seeking the typical Caribbean beach vacation. For a great view of the island visitors can climb the 1,064 steps to Mt. Scenery's crater. While you're in the town of Windwardside, purchase some of the beautiful lace made by local women and visit the Harry L. Johnson Memorial Museum, decorated in the motif of an 1880s ship captain's house. The diving on Saba is among the best in the Caribbean. The island itself is lush and green with beautiful flora (including wild ferns and orchids). Follow some of the old hiking trails that wind throughout the island.

St. Barthelemy "St. Barts" is a French island just southeast of St. Martin that has become popular among the rich and famous. The island's major town, Gustavia, is a charming collection of red-roofed buildings that wrap around a small harbor. The town can be toured on foot (stop and rest in one of the bistros or patisseries). To see the rest of this island, rent a car or motorbike. St. Barts has miles of excellent uncrowded beaches, several snorkeling reefs and top-drawer French restaurants. Be sure to visit Colombier to see the residents, who still dress in a manner befitting their 17th-century Norman French heritage. Most visitors only make a day trip to St. Barts from St. Martin, but if you are primarily inter-

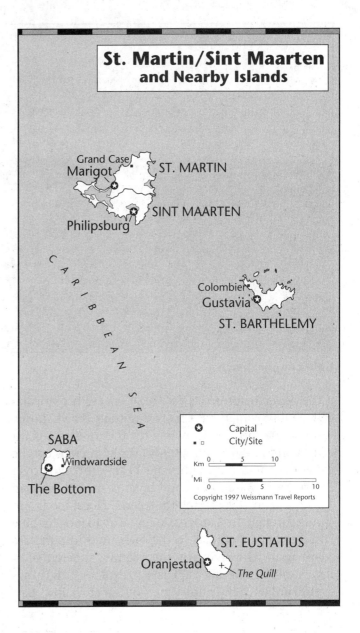

ested in peaceful, beautiful beaches, a stay of 3 or 4 nights is about right.

St. Eustatius Like Saba, "Statia" is less developed than Sint Maarten, and therein lies the attraction. Upon arrival, follow the route of the Walking Tour (obtain a map from the St. Eustatius Historical Foundation). Sights in Oranjestad, the capital (and only town), include Fort Oranje (with bronze cannons and a plaque from Franklin Roosevelt commemorating it as the first foreign country to recognize the U.S.) and the yellow house where the British admiral stayed after defeating the islanders. Other sights are Honen Dalim (one of the New World's oldest synagogues), a Jewish cemetery and a Dutch Reformed church built in 1775 (it has an impressive view from its tower). On the southern end of Statia

Baie Longue Beach

is the perfectly formed, 1,800-ft/549-m extinct volcano called Quill, which has fine hiking trails. The half-day walk to the top is worthwhile for the forests of giant cedars and rare hummingbirds (at night, crabs can be caught in the crater). Other musts are snorkeling over the ruins of warehouses and taverns sunk during an earthquake in 1690, trying the splendid local foods and sifting through the sands of Gallows Bay to look for blue "trading beads" similar to the ones used to purchase Manhattan. The diving on this island is superlative — divers should stay at least 3 days to explore such things as the sunken 18th-century man-of-war at Gallows Bay.

Itinerary

Don't go to St. Martin/Sint Maarten and stay the entire week on the main island. When you're so close to Saba, Statia and St. Barts, you should consider day trips. Below is a bare-bones 7-day stay.

Day 1 — Arrive in Sint Maarten.

Day 2 — Tour Sint Maarten, then go to the beach.

Day 3 — Tour St. Martin, then head for another beach.

Day 4 — Take a day trip to another island.

Day 5 — Go shopping, then head for the beach.

Day 6 — Day trip to another island or return to your favorite beach. Overnight on St. Martin/Sint Maarten.

Day 7 — Depart.

Climate/When to Go

Just about any time is good to travel to the island, but the chance of clouds is greater from July to October — intense but very brief showers are possible then, too. Hurricanes are possible in late summer and fall. The days are usually in the 80s F/28–32 C, with nights in the 60–70s F/15–27 C. Trade winds seem to be blowing all the time, so bring a sweater for evenings.

Transportation

BWIA International, American Airlines and Continental fly nonstop from the U.S. to Sint Maarten. There is no direct service from Canada. Princess Juliana Airport (SXM), the international airport for the island, is about 7 mi/11 km west of Philipsburg. Many smaller Caribbean air carriers include Sint Maarten on their schedules, and many cruise ships stop in Philipsburg for a day. St. Barts can be reached by catamaran (departing from Sint Maarten 11 times a day, except Sunday) or by air on Windward Islands Airways from Sint Maarten. Saba is reached by a short flight (Winair has three daily flights from Sint Maarten), motor yacht or catamaran from Sint Maarten. Statia is a 15-minute flight from Sint Maarten (there are five daily round-trips) or a day's sailboat excursion. Rental cars are available, except on Saba. Motorbikes and taxis are also used for touring.

Accommodations

It's difficult to say which side of St. Martin/Sint Maarten to choose. It used to be a rule of thumb that if travelers were more formal than informal, they would stay on the Dutch side, and if the opposite were true, they would stay on the French side. Lately, the French side has been moving upscale, and the Dutch have let things slide a bit. The French side is still very French, while the Dutch side is more cosmopolitan and crowded but poses fewer language barriers to English-speaking visitors. On Saba, there are no deluxe resort hotels, just inns and small guest houses (that's part of its charm). Likewise, on Statia, we stayed at the Old Gin House Hotel, built from the ruins of a century-old cotton gin — and had a great time. On St. Barts, you can choose between a simple guest house and a luxurious and expensive resort.

Health Advisories

Western sanitation and food-preparation standards are followed on the islands. There are hospitals on St. Martin/Sint Maarten, and clinics and doctors on Saba, Statia and St. Barts.

What to Buy

St. Martin/Sint Maarten is a great place for duty-free shopping, with everything from jewelry and watches to china and crystal to stereos and cameras. As with any place in the world that labels itself "duty-free," make sure you have a good idea of what things cost at home before buying. Duty-free doesn't mean profit-free.

What to Eat

There's a fine choice of good food, ranging from Continental to island cuisine and including Creole, Dutch, French, Italian and other international foods. Seafood (great lobster) and fish are most prominent.

Travel Tips for the Client

Don't be surprised by nudity on some beaches. There is even a clothing-optional hotel (although on our last trip to Orient Beach, the gapers and oglers outnumbered the total tanners) . . . Don't go only for water activities and gambling — see some of the historical sites that make the islands unique . . . Do plan some time to stroll along the beaches. . . .

Geostats

Official Names: St. Martin, Sint Maarten.

Visa Info: Passport needed by Canadians; U.S. citizens need photo ID and proof of citizenship. Both require onward ticket.

Health Certificates: Yellow-fever certificate needed if coming from an infected area.

Capitals: Marigot (St. Martin), Philipsburg (Sint Maarten).

Population: 28,000 (St. Martin), 32,000 (Sint Maarten).

Size: 37 sq mi/96 sq km.

Languages: Official: Dutch, French; in Sint Maarten English is almost universally spoken, and almost everyone on the French side can speak some English.

Climate: Tropical.

Economy: Agriculture, tourism.

Government: St. Martin is a sub-prefecture of Guadeloupe, which is an Overseas Region of France. Sint Maarten is an Autonomous Part of the Kingdom of Netherlands.

Religions: Roman Catholic, Protestant.

Currency: St. Martin: French franc (FFR). 100 centimes = 1 FFR. Sint Maarten: Netherlands Antilles florin (NAF). 100 cents = 1 NAF. Credit cards and traveler's checks accepted in most areas. MC and VI.

Time Zone: 1 hour ahead of EST; 4 hours behind GMT.

Electricity: 110 V, Dutch side; 220 V, French side.

Departure Tax: NAF 9.

St. Martin/Sint Maarten and Nearby Islands

Review Questions

1. How do the French and Dutch sides of St. Martin/Sint Maarten differ?

2. What can be found along Marigot's waterfront?

3. What is a problem in Philipsburg, particularly on days when cruise ships are in port?

4. For what sort of travelers is Saba a good place to stay for at least two nights?

5. With whom has "St. Barts" become popular? How would you describe Gustavia, its major town?

6. Who presented the plaque found at Fort Oranje on St. Eustatius? What does the plaque commemorate?

7. What can be seen on the half-day walk to the top of the Quill?

8. Lately, how have the Dutch and French sides of St. Martin changed?

9. What features on the French side of St. Martin contribute to its Mediterranean ambience?

10. How do the town and beach of Grand Case compare with Marigot? What does Grand Case offer tourists?

St. Martin/Sint Maarten and Nearby Islands

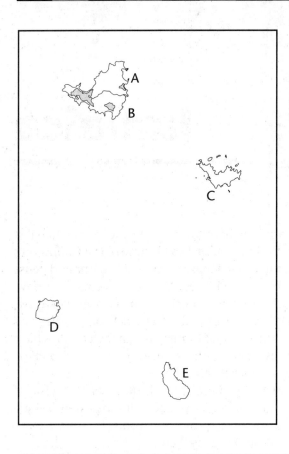

Map Skills Exercise

Match the tourist destination listed below with the corresponding letter on the map. You can use each letter only once.

1. _____ Saba

2. _____ St. Martin

3. _____ Sint Maarten

4. _____ St. Barthelemy

5. _____ St. Eustatius

Selling Exercise

A trade show is being held in your city on travel to the Caribbean. You have been asked to make a brief presentation on travel to St. Martin/Sint Maarten at the show. Your presentation will be part of a series on travel to various Caribbean islands. Prepare a five minute talk on St. Martin/Sint Maarten that will distinguish it from other Caribbean islands in the minds of travelers. Your presentation should also inform listeners about the attractions on the island.

Jamaica

Selling Points

Swimming, sunning, diving, partying, horseback riding, Red Stripe beer, beaches, mountains, Kingston, world-class resorts, rafting, hiking, tennis, golf, polo, reggae, fishing, great food and coffee, caves, beautiful scenery and historical sites are Jamaica's foremost attractions.

Travelers who appreciate water, scenery, music/dance and food will enjoy Jamaica. But the island isn't for those interested in great shopping or immaculate surroundings. Poverty is widespread and highly visible.

Fascinating Facts About Jamaica

If you want to get a taste of reggae music, listen to the music of Bob Marley's son, Ziggy, or Third World, a legendary band out of Kingston. . . Though not generally touted, scuba diving and snorkeling can be excellent in Jamaica (most resorts offer the sports). . . The tomb of reggae singer Bob Marley is in the small village of Nine Miles (just west of Ocho Rios) . . . Reggae Sunsplash in August is Jamaica's main summer event. Top musicians and performers from all over the world go to the island. . . .

Unlike its smaller island-neighbors, Jamaica is much more than just a beach. It does indeed have stretches of some of the Caribbean's loveliest white sand, but it also showcases steep mountains and dense jungles, big cities and charming villages. All of these attractions have contributed to the sprawl of resorts (many of them all-inclusive) whose affordable hotel-air packages have turned Jamaica into one of the most visited vacation spots in the region. Montego Bay and Ocho Rios have also become popular stops for cruise ships, whose passengers flood the cities when ships make their brief calls in port.

As hard as it is to argue with success, we think parts of the island have become too devoted to the tourist trade and lost their unique ambience. The increase in tourism has also brought a worrisome uptick in crime; visitors should exercise caution.

Jamaica is the third-largest island in the Caribbean (144 mi/232 km long and 52 mi/84 km wide). A wealth of resources — bauxite, alumina, sugarcane, bananas, citrus, rum, allspice and coffee — have contributed to its prosperity. But tourism has brought the greatest influx of foreign currency in recent years.

What to Do There

Kingston   Kingston (pop. 850,000) is trying hard to overcome its old image as a commercial and business destination, riddled with large pockets of poverty and crime. Though not a tourist/vacation mecca like Montego Bay or Ocho Rios, Kingston is worth seeing because it is the cultural and musical center of the country (disco and reggae keep Kingston hopping). But visitors should be prepared to find a large chaotic city with its share of problems.

Any visit to Kingston should include the Devon House (restored home and showplace of local arts and crafts), Hope Botanical Gardens (quite good) and the Institute of Jamaica (to see the Shark Papers — documents found in the belly of a shark that helped solve a notorious maritime case in the 1800s). Although an earthquake in 1907 destroyed much of the city, a few old buildings remain, including the

Gordon House (home of the national legislature) and the Parish Church at St. Andrew (1700s church).

For those interested in the performing arts, the National Dance Theatre Company is in Kingston. Jam World, the new venue for Reggae Sunsplash (the island's annual reggae festival) and other events, recently opened in Kingston. A must-see is the Bob Marley Museum, which displays items relating to the famous reggae singer in his former recording studio in Kingston.

Note: The crime rate in Kingston is serious enough to warrant that precautions be taken. Wear a money belt, don't flaunt jewelry or expensive watches, and don't walk by yourself after dark or ride public transportation at night (except licensed taxis). Pickpockets and purse snatchers frequently hit bus riders. It is best to stay in one of the larger hotels in the center of the city, if possible.

Montego Bay

"Mo' bay," as the locals call this town, vies with Ocho Rios as the island's most visited resort town. We recommend Mo' Bay for its restaurants, nightlife, shopping and leisure activities. The beaches of the town itself are not the best on the island; water sports and fishing in the area are limited. And the city is rather dirty. But the area does have several fine resorts and golf courses. Its port is a major stop for many cruise ships — so don't come here expecting an isolated town or secluded beaches. Sights in the area include Greenwood Great House (built by Elizabeth Barrett Browning's ancestors) and the Rocklands Feeding Station, where visitors can hand-feed hummingbirds. We were fascinated by the Craft Market (Harbour Street) and spooked by Rose Hall (its beautiful mistress, Annie Palmer, was thought to be a voodoo witch who killed her husbands and lovers — the tour is quite interesting). The shopping in Mo' Bay is good; we particularly enjoyed the Gallery of West Indian Art, a store full of colorful wood carvings made by local artists.

Negril

With the best (and, in some parts, least crowded) beaches in Jamaica, Negril is absolute fun. Wide white-sand beaches stretch along Long Bay and Bloody Bay, making both great places to relax, sunbathe, swim and watch spectacular sunsets. Negril has a very informal, laid-back feel. Topless and clothing-optional beaches exist, usually at resorts; inquire locally. For a particularly scenic view visit the Negril Lighthouse, perched on high cliffs just west of town. Beneath it, snorkelers and divers can explore caves. Nature lovers will want to visit Great Morass swamplands to see birds and plants.

Statue of Bob Marley

Ocho Rios

A major port of call for cruise ships, Ocho Rios offers the island's best shopping, a variety of nightlife and fairly good (though often crowded) beaches. Our only regret is that, as Ocho Rios continues to develop, it is losing the charm that made it so popular in the first place. Ocho Rios' setting — on the edge of the jungle in a sheltered bay with a mountainous backdrop — is lovely. After you've wandered around town and spent time at the beach, visit Dunn's River Falls. We enjoyed getting drenched as we climbed to the top of the 600-ft/183-m falls.

Port Antonio

Port Antonio has a lovely mountain setting, plus golfing, deep-sea fishing, barbecues and swimming in the Blue Hole Lagoon or at Boston Beach. Tours are available to the nearby Caves of Nonsuch, Athenry Gardens and Crystal Springs in Buff Bay. Crystal Springs is a must-see for nature lovers; it has more than 15,000 varieties of plants and a vast number of orchids. Port Antonio is often seen as a day trip from Ocho Rios.

Itinerary

As is true with most Caribbean islands, Jamaica is best seen on one's own (not with an escorted tour) or on a

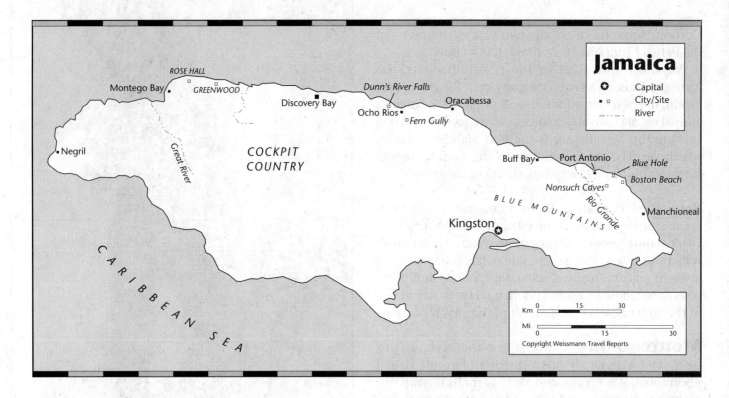

Club Med-type package. Jamaica has developed a deservedly strong reputation for its wide range of "all-inclusive" resorts. Be aware, though, that many of these resorts do not offer sightseeing as part of their packages — excursions are extra. We suggest staying in Negril or Ocho Rios; that way, you can see Montego Bay on the drive between the two. Scheduling Negril first will allow you to unwind.

Day 1 — Arrive Montego Bay and drive to Negril.

Day 2 — Negril.

Day 3 — Negril.

Day 4 — Go to Ocho Rios and, if possible, see Montego Bay on the way.

Day 5 — Ocho Rios.

Day 6 — Ocho Rios.

Day 7 — Ocho Rios.

Day 8 — Depart.

Climate/When to Go

Our favorite time to go there (and everyone else's) is November–April — Jamaica can be very crowded then. The temperature is fairly stable year-round, so it's really pleasant anytime. Winter coastal-area day temperatures are in the 70s–80s F/23–32 C. June–September is usually in the 80s–90s F/30–35 C. Nights tend to be 5–10 F/3–5 C degrees cooler everywhere, and the temperatures in the hills are usually cooler than on the coasts by 5–10 F/3–5 C degrees.

Transportation

Air Jamaica, several U.S. carriers and a number of charters offer nonstop flights from various U.S. cities. Air Canada flies from Canada. Trans-Jamaica Airlines offers daily flights between major Jamaican cities. Montego Bay's Sir Donald Sangster International Airport (MBJ) is just 2 mi/3 km from downtown. Norman Manley International Airport (KIN) is 11 mi/18 km from Kingston. Many cruise lines schedule Ocho Rios, Mo' Bay and Port Antonio stops on their itineraries.

The main roads are excellent, but be forewarned that Jamaicans drive on the left side of the road — and they drive like maniacs. Local buses are not recommended except to the budget-minded or well-seasoned traveler, but escorted half- and full-day tours, bicycles, rental cars and taxis are enjoyable ways of getting around.

Accommodations

Accommodations range from deluxe, 5-star sophisticated properties, quaint B-and-Bs and inns to dives. It's particularly important on Jamaica to be very selective because many places that sound good aren't. If you find somewhere that makes you happy, keep going there. Many resorts offer all-inclusive packages (including all meals and drinks).

Health Advisories

Three limited outbreaks of typhoid have occurred in recent years in western Jamaica. Don't forget insect repellent (the mosquitos can be vicious, but they don't carry malaria).

You'll find hospital facilities in each major Jamaican town; doctors are available 24 hours a day in Kingston and the principal resort areas; and doctors or registered nurses may be found in some of the smaller towns.

You can drink the tap water in cities. The food in the resorts, restaurants and hotels that cater to tourists is as safe as on mainland North America. Local restaurant and/or market food is generally safe if it's freshly prepared and served hot.

What to Buy

Among the items available are rum, Blue Mountain coffee, gemstone jewelry, shells, native musical instruments, hand-carved mahogany items, local trinkets and handicrafts, local art (there's everything — from neo-expressionist to primitive), colorful clothing and fabric, woven straw baskets, embroidery, leather goods, striking local art and reggae music cassettes. Duty-free shopping is available at the Kingston and Montego Bay airports and in select stores in Ocho Rios and Montego Bay.

What to Eat

For true Jamaican taste, try red pea soup, pepperpot soup (hot and spicy), jerk chicken or pork, callaloo (a spinachlike vegetable), grilled lobster and roasted breadfruit (tastes a lot more like bread than fruit!). Also nice are the curried goat, beef patties and various seafood dishes. For drinks, try Red Stripe beer and the locally produced liqueur Tia Maria. Do try the local restaurants, even if you're staying at an all-inclusive property where all meals are included.

Travel Tips for the Client

Do try jerk chicken or pork, but have a cold Red Stripe beer ready to wash it down — it's very spicy . . . Don't leave your belongings untended on the beach or even in a locked car. . . Don't be surprised to see very persistent Jamaican peddlers outside every hotel . . . Do try to attend a performance of the Jamaican Dance Troupe; it's excellent . . . Even though buying marijuana on the island might seem a common, casual act, it is nonetheless a potentially dangerous undertaking, with buyers risking physical harm and possible jail terms . . . Do have the name and address of the place you are staying your first night. This information is required by immigration upon your arrival . . . Do take a coat and tie; many of the restaurants require at least a coat after 6 pm. . . .

Geostats

Official Name: Jamaica.

Visa Info: U.S. and Canadian citizens need photo ID and proof of citizenship, sufficient funds and return ticket. A tourist card is issued upon arrival for visits of up to six months. Visitors on business need a visa.

Health Certificates: Yellow-fever certificate needed if visitor is arriving from an infected area.

Capital: Kingston.

Population: 2,562,000.

Size: 4,411 sq mi/11,424 sq km. A bit smaller than Connecticut.

Languages: English, Jamaican patois.

Climate: Tropical.

Economy: Tourism, mining, agriculture.

Government: Parliamentary democracy.

Religions: Protestant, Roman Catholic.

Currency: Jamaican dollar (JAD). 100 cents = 1 JAD. Currency should only be exchanged at banks or official exchange bureaus.

Time Zone: Eastern; 5 hours behind GMT.

Electricity: 110 volts, but 220-volt systems exist in some larger properties.

Jamaica

Review Questions

1. What kind of travelers will appreciate Jamaica? What kind of travelers won't care for it?

2. Though not a tourist/vacation mecca, why is Kingston worth seeing?

3. What are the Shark Papers? Where can they be seen?

4. What precautions against crime should a visitor in Kingston take?

5. For what attractions would you recommend Mo'Bay to a client?

6. How would you describe the feel of Negril? Along which bays are its wide beaches?

7. Why is Crystal Springs, near Port Antonio, a must for nature lovers?

8. Of what should a traveler be aware about many all-inclusive resorts?

9. Why should a traveler have the name and address of the place he or she is staying the first night on Jamaica?

10. What is the lovely setting for Ocho Rios?

Jamaica

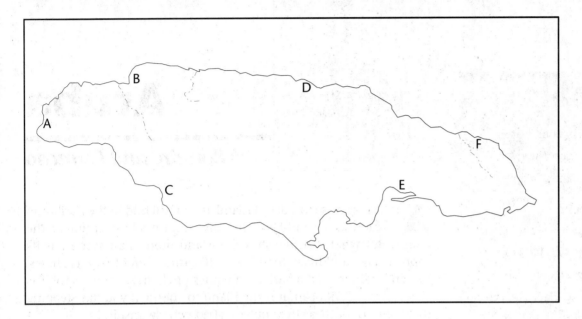

Map Skills Exercise

Match the tourist destination listed below with the corresponding letter on the map. You can use each letter only once.

1. _____ Kingston   **4.** _____ Port Antonio

2. _____ Ocho Rios   **5.** _____ Negril

3. _____ Montego Bay

Selling Exercise

You are a photographer on assignment in Jamaica. You've been asked by a travel magazine to photograph major tourist sites and attractions in the country. In a fax sent to the magazine, you described the five most outstanding photos you took. What did you say in the fax?

Aruba

Bonaire and Curacao

Aruba is as close to a desert island as you will find in the Caribbean — cacti and wind-bent divi divi trees easily outnumber the palms. But what distinguishes the island more than scenery is its sophisticated and lively nightlife — 10 casinos offer first-rate shows, top entertainers and a variety of games of chance. Aruba is the Las Vegas of the Caribbean; it is the island to choose if you like stepping into evening clothes after you've doffed your swimsuit.

Its proximity to Bonaire and Curacao, the other traditional members of the Dutch Antilles, leads many people to lump them all together. Actually, all three islands have been influenced as much by Venezuela (only 15 mi/24 km away from Aruba) as by the Netherlands.

The number of tourists has nearly doubled in the past five years — Aruba is one of the most popular destinations in the Caribbean. More than two dozen resort hotels now dot the beaches.

What to Do There

Oranjestad   This capital city features lots of Dutch colonial architecture, good restaurants and quaint shops (selling everything from china to watches). Be sure to see the Protestant church and 18th-century Ft. Zoutman with its William III Tower. The Cas di Culture (Cultural Center) has very good exhibits, as well as concerts. While you're downtown, visit the waterfront fruit and fish market and numismatic and archaeological museums. We liked the nice gardens in Wilhelmina Park. There's plenty of nightlife around Oranjestad — nearly all of the island's 10 casinos are within a few minutes of the city. The casinos offer a variety of games as well as first-class entertainment and restaurants. (Book your dinner-show reservations early, particularly during high season.)

Other Island Attractions   Though sand and surf are the main draws, there are other things to see. Begin with an overview of Aruba from Yamanota Hill, the island's highest point (617 ft/188 m). Then set out to explore the island's manmade attractions. Among them: the 100-year-old hand-carved oak altar of St. Ann Church (in Noord) and the gold smelter and mine ruins of Bushiribana and Balashi. Natural wonders include the Natural Bridge, sculpted out of coral rock by centuries of raging wind and sea (this is considered one of the island's most romantic spots) and the Boca Prins Sand Dunes (try the local sport of dune sliding, but wear long pants and shoes). The many caves include Guadirikiri (a large bat cave) and Fontein (a must — it features impressive Arawak Indian petroglyphs). Arikok National Park, though small, offers Mt. Arikok (577 ft/176 m) and rock petroglyphs. Bicycle and hiking tours are available, as well as special tours for those interested in botany and birds.

Water Sports and Beaches

All the beaches are public and free. The water is a wonderful blue-green color most everywhere. Snorkelers should seek out the two shallow-water shipwrecks: the *Pedernales*, a World War II oil tanker torpedoed by the Germans, and the *Antilla*, a German sub-supply ship sunk by the Allies (near Malmok, on the northwestern end of the island). Scuba divers should also be on the lookout for older shipwrecks, located farther offshore. Though overshadowed by Bonaire's world-renowned diving, Aruba is becoming better known with the underwater crowd. Experienced divers will particularly enjoy the Mangel Halto Reef, with 100-degree slopes, and diving at Natural Bridge, which has beautiful black and soft coral as well as giant barrel sponges.

Landlubbers who would like to experience the joys of scuba diving without getting wet can take a trip on the submarine *Atlantis* down to the Barcadera Reef (46 passengers at a time). The constant trade winds have made the island one of the world's top windsurfing spots; it's a popular place to learn the sport. Another option for the non-wet crowd is to rent three-wheeled sailcarts at Druif Beach.

Itinerary

Because the island is only 19 mi/30 km long and 6 mi/10 km wide, logistics present no problems when planning an itinerary. You can see all the sights in two days, using Oranjestad as a base (we'd stay no less than five days, total). If your schedule permits, visit the Netherlands Antilles islands as well — we suggest three days on Bonaire (more for avid divers) and two (maximum) on Curacao. Venezuela is also a very popular destination — it's close as well as convenient.

Climate/When to Go

Aruba's temperatures vary little year-round and the humidity is very low. The average day temperatures are in the 70s–80s F/23–32 C, with nights in the 60s–70s F/15–27 C. Aruba is outside the hurricane belt; therefore, it's one of the best islands to visit during July–October, when the rest of the Caribbean is threatened (even so, our favorite time to visit Aruba is January–June). It's rainy November–February, but the rain seldom lasts longer than half an hour. The island's constant breezes are refreshing year-round, but you'll have to hang onto your hat at the beach.

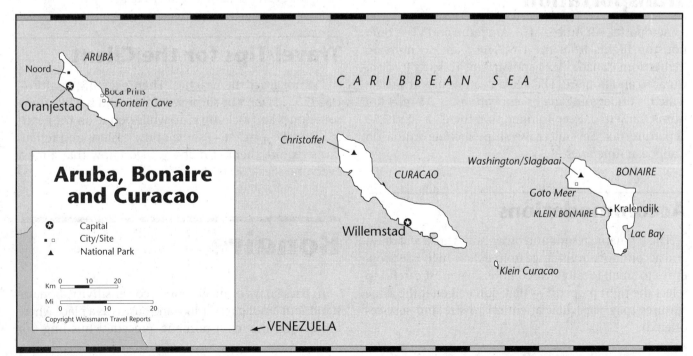

Aruba, Bonaire and Curacao

⊕ Capital
■ □ City/Site
▲ National Park

Km 0 10 20
Mi 0 10 20
Copyright Weissmann Travel Reports

Geostats

Official Name: Aruba.

Visa Info: No visa needed by U.S. and Canadian citizens.

Health Certificates: Yellow-fever certificate required of visitors coming from an infected area.

Capital: Oranjestad.

Population: 67,000

Size: 69 sq mi/179 sq km.

Languages: Papiamento, Dutch, English, Spanish.

Climate: Tropical, hot and dry.

Economy: Tourism.

Government: Parliamentary democracy.

Religions: Protestant, Roman Catholic.

Currency: Aruba florin. 100 cents = 1 Aruba florin. Credit cards and traveler's checks accepted in most areas. MC, VI.

Time Zone: 1 hour ahead of Eastern; 4 hours behind GMT.

Electricity: 110 Volts.

Departure Tax: US$11.

Transportation

Aeropostal, Air Aruba, ALM, American and Viasa offer nonstop flights from the U.S. There are no nonstop flights from Canada. ALM and Air Aruba also fly to/from Curacao and Bonaire. The Reina Beatrix Airport (AUA), which is undergoing major renovations, is 2.5 mi/4 km from Oranjestad. Keep in mind that there's a US$12.50 departure tax. Several cruise ships include Aruba on Caribbean itineraries.

Accommodations

The big-name resorts and other hotels are a real draw, and accommodations range from deluxe high-rise properties to small locally owned hotels. Be most careful to select the right property — they don't all offer the same features (pay particular attention to size and services offered).

Health Advisories

The sun can be intense, so use sunscreen, moisturizing lotion, sunglasses and wear a hat. There's a fine hospital in Oranjestad. You can eat the food and drink the water in Aruba.

What to Buy

Though not a duty-free port, the duty on most items is so low that shoppers often find bargains on all sorts of high-quality goods, including Madeira embroidery, jewelry, watches, porcelain, Delft ceramics, liquor, Italian wood carvings, china, linens, crystal and perfumes from both South America and Europe. For an out-of-the-ordinary shopping experience, head for Schooner Harbor, where you can browse through shops and craft stalls aboard ships and sloops.

What to Eat

Aruba has a tremendous variety of restaurants, including Oriental, Indonesian, Dutch, French and Italian. Excellent local food can be found at many of Aruba's cafes. Island staples are meat and seafood and a variety of vegetables and fruits. Among the local specialties, try shrimp *en coco* (a delicacy made with brandy and coconut), fried fish breaded with *funchi* (cornmeal) and lamb with *pan bati* (a pancake). Be sure to go to a restaurant offering a rijstafel, an Indonesian buffet that could feed an army.

Travel Tips for the Client

Do not litter the beaches. There's a stiff penalty — US$275 . . . Don't be surprised if the wind is a bit strong sometimes and kicks up sand while you're on the beach . . . Do take a jacket — some of the casinos and restaurants require them at night . . . Do know that almost everyone speaks English. . . .

Bonaire

In these days of heightened eco-sensitivity, Bonaire stands out among its Caribbean cousins as a place where protecting the environment precedes hustling for tourists. As a result, travelers to the second of the so-called "ABC Islands" (Aruba-Bonaire-Curacao) won't find hotels crowding the beaches, neon-topped restaurants and bumper-to-bumper traffic. Instead, you'll discover the Caribbean's first — and one of its biggest — national parks, aflutter with 190 different species of birds, including a flock of flamingos that nearly outnumbers the human population. You'll find a marine park that wraps around the entire island, ensuring that the sea life is protected.

Bonaire is one of the best places in the Caribbean to dive and snorkel — and one of the best places in the world to do nothing. The seawater is exceptionally clear — visibility is about 150 ft/45 m. Out of the water, this is a sleepy, somewhat barren island with few diversions.

The island is mostly flat and dry. In addition to its excellent diving, there is a casino, good deep-sea fishing, some tennis courts and duty-free shopping. But it's really an island for those who want to do very little in the way of sightseeing.

The island's small but beautiful capital, Kralendijk (Coral Dike), is a center for diving and snorkeling (diving is also done at dozens of points along the island's west coast and off Klein Bonaire, an atoll just offshore from Kralendijk). The city is very small, but it has a nice waterfront with historical buildings and a fish market. Excursions can easily be made to see old slave huts, salt flats (whose colors change according to what algae is predominant) and huge flocks of flamingos at the Goto Meer, a flamingo sanctuary on the north end (nesting time is May–June).

Nature lovers will want to spend at least a day exploring Washington/Slagbaai National Park. Take the short drive through the park and be sure to stop at Salina Mathijs, a salt flat that attracts flamingos during the rainy season; Mangel Wajaca, a remote reef where you can find turtles, octopuses and triggerfish; and Mount Brandaris, Bonaire's highest peak (at 784 ft/239 m). The entire coastline (and the water itself, to a depth of 197 ft/60 m) is considered to be part of Bonaire Marine Park. Lac Bay is one of the best-known windsurfing sites on Earth. A reef breaks the big waves, creating a great place for beginners inside the reef and a great challenge for pros outside it.

Curacao

As befits its Dutch heritage, Curacao is dependable and solid rather than flashy or spectacular. Its diving may not

De Olde Molen (authentic Dutch windmill on Aruba)

be as good as neighboring Bonaire's and its beaches are rocky, but it has fun nightlife, sun, one of the Caribbean's biggest cities (Willemstad, whose Dutch colonial architecture gives the city an uncommon atmosphere), good scuba diving/snorkeling, varied accommodations, fine restaurants and a lot of nature areas. There are far more visitors from Europe than from North America.

Willemstad   You can best explore the island's Dutch heritage in the rows of pastel-colored, red-roofed townhouses found in downtown Willemstad, the capital city (pop. 94,000). The city is divided into two parts: Punda (Old World Dutch ambiance and great shopping) and Otrobanda ("the other side") — also good shopping, but a more contemporary flavor. We suggest a walking tour of the town to observe the architecture. A highlight of any Curacao stay is a visit to the floating market in downtown Willemstad, where Venezuelan merchants sell a wide variety of food. Willemstad also has many excellent restaurants.

Island Attractions   A great way to orient yourself and take in a number of sights outside Willemstad is to take a full-day Jeep Safari tour. The tour covers an area of salt pans, a plantation, a national park and caves, and even leaves time for swimming and snorkeling at Boca Santu Pretu Beach. On your own, explore some of the man-made attractions and natural wonders. History buffs will enjoy 18th-century Ft. Amsterdam, as well as Mikve Israel Emmanuel Synagogue, the oldest temple in continuous use in the New World. Natural attractions include several interesting caves and the Christoffel National Park. This garden and wildlife preserve is centered on towering Mt. Christoffel (its peak of 1,230 ft/375 m affords a panoramic view of the entire island).

Aruba, Bonaire and Curacao

Review Questions

1. During what part of the year is Aruba's off-season? How do rates compare with those in high season?

2. More than its scenery, what distinguishes Aruba from other Caribbean destinations?

3. What kind of attractions does Aruba's capital, Oranjestad, offer? How far away from Oranjestad are most of the casinos?

4. What out-of-the-ordinary shopping experience can a tourist have in Schooner Harbor?

5. For what activities is Bonaire one of the best places in the Caribbean?

6. For what activity is Lac Bay one of the best-known sites in the world? Why can beginners and pros both take advantage of it?

7. On Curacao, what does a full-day Jeep Safari tour cover?

8. What gives Willemstad an uncommon atmosphere for the Caribbean? How do the two parts of the city, Punda and Otrobanda, compare?

9. For what is Kralendijk a center? What can be seen in this small city?

10. What two countries send the most tourists to Aruba?

Aruba, Bonaire and Curacao

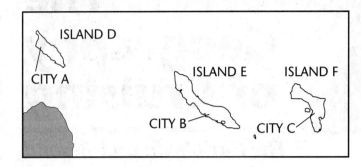

ISLAND D

CITY A

ISLAND E

ISLAND F

CITY B

CITY C

Map Skills Exercise

Match the tourist destination listed below with the corresponding letter on the map. You can use each letter only once.

1. _____ Bonaire

2. _____ Aruba

3. _____ Curacao

4. _____ Oranjestad

5. _____ Willemstad

Selling Exercise

A couple in their twenties is staying a few weeks in Venezuela. They would like to spend a weekend during that time in the ABC islands (Aruba, Bonaire and Curacao). Where in the ABC islands would you suggest they go? What would you suggest they see and do there?

The Geography of Cruising

The Caribbean and Beyond

Cruise Lines and Ships

You do have to be knowledgeable about the various cruise lines and ships. Matching a passenger with the right vessel as well as with the best itinerary is key to the overall success of a cruise experience — and to keep a client as a client. Some considerations:

- *Ship size.* Modern cruise ships range from small yachtlike sailing ships and expedition vessels that carry fewer than 100 passengers to megaliners that carry more than 2,500 people. As you can imagine, the cruise experience varies accordingly.

- *Cabin size and location.* Some passengers want cabins comparable to luxurious hotel suites, complete with verandas; others are more concerned about saving money than where they'll sleep, and figure most of their time will be spent elsewhere anyway. If you know your clients' preferences, they won't return from their cruises disappointed — and they'll likely return to your agency.

- *Ambience/Amenities.* Ships (and ship lines) have distinctive personalities. Some are more formal, offering passengers a sophisticated, white-glove atmosphere and doting personal service. Others bill themselves as "party" ships, lighting their discos with neon and blasting lively music through the ship. Still other ships forgo fancy interiors, offering instead such amenities as onboard naturalists who are knowledgeable about the flora and fauna of the ship's ports of call.

Cruising is different from other forms of leisure travel. You get to hop from island to island — but you take your hotel along with you. You see a variety of exotic (and not-so-exotic) cultures, while back on board ship you enjoy good food served in elegant surroundings, almost nonstop entertainment and, best of all, attentive service. Every year some 4.5 million people choose to go on vacation by cruise ship. They think it's the best way to see the world and minimize the hassles of travel.

As important as the convenience is, however, the destinations are paramount. While a cruise line will maintain that its *ships* sells the cruise, surveys of passengers reveal that where the ship stops is far more important. For that reason, it's critical that travel counselors understand the geography of cruising — where the cruise ships stop and when, and what the various cruising regions and port cities offer in the way of sightseeing, shopping, water sports, attractions, nightlife and culture.

Cruise passengers spend such a short time in each port — usually less than 12 hours. So detailed, up-to-date information about each port is a must. Where are the best beaches? Are any of the historical sites worth visiting? Which shops have the best bargains? What can passengers do on their own? Or is a ship-sponsored shore excursion the best way to see the port?

Ports of Call

Cruise ships visit more than 500 destinations each year. And some of the sights don't even require a shore visit — from the bow of a cruise ship you can marvel at the icebergs of Antarctica, view magnificent Egyptian temples, watch humpback whales breach in the aquamarine waters of Hawaii and glimpse the church spires of Europe's historic cities.

Once in port, the choices are myriad — you can browse the duty-free shops along the cobblestone streets of Charlotte Amalie in St. Thomas, inspect the century-old Russian log houses in Alaska's coastal towns, lounge on the white-sand beaches of the Greek Islands and explore the rain forests of Costa Rica.

Cruises vary in length from a weekend jaunt to the Bahamas to an around-the-world cruise that could stretch into months. The most common cruises are seven to 14 days. Some consist of a loop — Alaskan Inside Passage cruises, for example, begin and end in Vancouver, British Columbia, and include stops in the historic gold-rush towns of Juneau and Skagway. Other cruises are strictly one way — Mexican Riviera cruises may begin in Los Angeles and end in Acapulco (or vice-versa) or continue on through the Panama Canal to Puerto Rico. (You'll likely return by air.)

"Repositioning cruises" are usually longer and take in more sights because, as their name implies, the ships are relocating from one cruise market to another. (When the Alaska cruise season ends, for example, the ships may offer longer cruises from Vancouver to their next cruising area — the Far East or the Caribbean, perhaps.) Still others are billed as "world cruises." These ships may sail from one geographic area to several others before returning home.

Timing is important, too, when considering cruise destinations. High season in the Caribbean is generally Christmas through Easter — when the weather is likely to be cold, snowy or rainy elsewhere in North America. But if you're looking for a bargain on a Caribbean cruise, try the summer or fall — fewer ships are cruising the area then but the weather can be almost as beautiful as it is in the spring. (Be aware that late summer-early fall is hurricane season.) Alaska is a highly seasonal cruise market — you'll find dozens of ships plying the waters of the Last Frontier from mid-May until mid-September. But don't expect to find *any* in December!

Cruising Areas

The Caribbean/Bahamas/ Bermuda

More people board cruise ships bound for the islands of the Caribbean and the mid-Atlantic than for anywhere else in the world. And it's not hard to understand why: the Caribbean islands and their northern neighbors, the Bahamas and Bermuda, offer numerous choices for travelers — lovely beaches, warm and clear water for snorkeling and scuba adventures, duty-free shopping, tropical forests and charming historic cities.

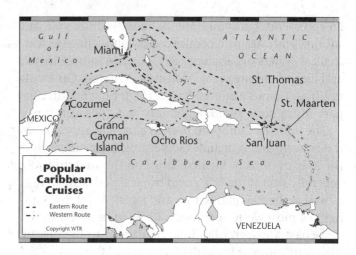

Peak cruising season in the islands is mid-December through mid-April, but there's likely to be at least one ship sailing the Caribbean on any week year round. (Bermuda's high season is a bit later — late spring and summer — because of its northern location.)

The islands reflect the rich history of the British, Spanish, French, Danish, African and Dutch people who settled them, beginning in the 1500s. The pace is generally laid-back, with time for a leisurely beach walk or a tall, cool drink in the shade of a thatched-roof bar on the beach. But an assortment of sporting activities is always available for more energetic and adventurous travelers. You can catch a wave aboard a windsurfer, dive along a coral reef, play a set of tennis or stroke a golf ball onto a luxurious green overlooking the sea.

Cruise ships sailing the Caribbean and nearby waters generally originate from the Florida ports of Miami, Ft. Lauderdale, Port Canaveral and Tampa. Some cruises also begin from New Orleans and Galveston, Texas. In the islands, San Juan in Puerto Rico and Charlotte Amalie in St. Thomas also are common embarkation ports. In addition, it's possible to cruise to Bermuda and beyond aboard ships that sail out of such East Coast ports as New York City and Boston.

Several popular routes in the Caribbean show off the best features of the various island groupings. The most popular route is the Eastern Caribbean. Ships sailing this route generally stop at one or more of the islands of Puerto Rico, St. Martin/St. Maarten, the U.S. Virgin Islands (St. Thomas, St. Croix or St. John) and the Bahamas. The Bahamas and the Eastern Caribbean islands are known for their white-sand beaches, abundant water sports and good duty-free shopping. There are dozens of shore excursion to consider. A city tour of San Juan, Puerto Rico, takes you along the cobblestone streets of the old city to El Morro, the Spanish fortress that has guarded the port city since the 15th century. From

Freeport/Port Lucaya in the Bahama Islands you can snorkel with Atlantic bottlenose dolphins in the clear, shallow waters of Sanctuary Bay. You can sample Dutch and French culture on St. Martin/St. Maarten. On a visit to Virgin Islands National Park on St. John, you can hike past mysterious petroglyphs (ancient rock carvings).

The Western Caribbean route is almost as appealing as the eastern, and it includes something quite different — the Mayan ruins of Mexico. Ships on the western route generally stop at the U.S.'s own tropical island, Key West, as well as the Cayman Islands and Jamaica. But the highlight of most western cruises is likely to be a visit to the east-coast Mexican island of Cozumel or to the nearby mainland cities of Playa del Carmen and Cancun.

In addition to the white sand and blue water that's abundant throughout the Caribbean, Mexico's Yucatan Peninsula has ancient Mayan temples shrouded in jungle, festive cities where the music and the food are as hot as the sun and colorful shops crammed with eclectic goods. A popular shore excursion from Cozumel or Playa del Carmen takes you to the white-walled Mayan city of Tulum, perched on a rocky cliff, for breathtaking views of the sea. Other options include a tour of Cancun's architecturally unusual resorts and a trip to Cozumel's world-famous coral reef to snorkel or dive.

The other islands on the western route offer an assortment of possibilities as well. In George Town in the Cayman Islands you can swim with manta rays and bask in the sun along the Caribbean's longest (seven miles!) beach. Jamaica, one of the Caribbean's biggest islands, has three cruise ports — Montego Bay, Ocho Rios and Port Antonio — and the most varied terrain in the region. You can tour the old great houses on the island's once-vast sugarcane and banana plantations or ride a bamboo raft down a rushing river through the island's jungled interior.

The Southern Caribbean route, which is beginning to rival the other two, offers cruise-ship passengers the chance to visit the lesser-known islands of St. Lucia, Dominica, Martinique and St. Barts, among others. Some southern cruises also include the Dutch islands of Curacao and Aruba and the two-island nation of Trinidad and Tobago. These destinations are a bit more exotic than those closer to the U.S. coast. Visitors can see the towering volcanic peaks of St. Lucia's Pitons, dine on chic French cuisine in St. Barts and go bird-watching in the rain forests of Dominica. If you time your cruise just right, you may even be in port for Trinidad's rousing Carnival. But if a more tranquil Caribbean setting is sought, a deserted beach on nearby Tobago may be the better choice.

Alaska

There's no place quite like Alaska and there's nothing quite like seeing the Last Frontier from the bow of a cruise ship. The geography of the state and British Columbia, to the south, is so spectacular that many people consider a cruise the premier way to see Alaska and Canada's Pacific coast. Without even stepping off the ship you can see milewide rivers of ice tumbling into the sea, pods of killer whales cruising the fjords and rugged islands dense with evergreens.

The big cruise lines typically offer a choice of two routes, both of which take you through the Inside Passage, the protected waterway between the mainland of Alaska and British Columbia and the coastal islands. Trips known as Inside Passage cruises usually begin in Vancouver, British Columbia, and stop in such Southeast Alaska ports as Ketchikan and Juneau, then turn around in Glacier Bay and return to Vancouver. Gulf of Alaska cruises usually run between Vancouver and Seward, Alaska, with connections through Anchorage so passengers can add land excursions that include such remote destinations as Native Alaskan villages inside the Arctic Circle.

Alaska's port cities offer a rich mix of history and breathtaking natural beauty. In Juneau, Alaska's capital,

Popular
**Inside Passage
Cruise**
Copyright Weissmann Travel Reports

baskets of flowers hang from Victorian-style streetlights along narrow avenues packed with interesting shops, museums and parks. Within minutes of town are the world's most accessible (you can drive up to it) glacier, a modern salmon hatchery and rushing streams where you can pan for gold. A tram shuttles visitors 1,760 ft/535 m up the side of a mountain for spectacular views of the city, the Inside Passage and surrounding islands. At night you can sip an Alaskan ale in the Red Dog Saloon, with its swing doors, sawdust floor and gold-rush memorabilia tacked to the walls.

In Sitka, Russian history is what captivates visitors. A city tour takes you through an onion-domed Russian Orthodox cathedral and the Russian Bishop's House and then treats you to a Russian folk dance. If you'd rather commune with nature, you can go to a raptor center, where injured birds of prey are nursed back to health, or take a boat tour to Salisbury Sound to watch sea otters romp in the kelp beds.

In addition, most of the major cruise lines offer a variety of excursions into the wild interior of Alaska. One of the most popular trips is a ride on a narrow-gauge railroad out of Skagway and up the treacherous White Mountain Pass into the Canadian Yukon. Another is a bus-rail trip from Anchorage into Denali National Park to see wildlife and majestic Mt. McKinley (the tallest peak in North America) and Fairbanks, Alaska's second-largest city.

Panama Canal/Western Mexico/Central America

Unlike other places cruise ships go, the Panama Canal isn't so much a destination as an experience. All that most people see of Panama is what's visible from the cruise ship as it squeezes through this slender waterway that links the Pacific and Atlantic oceans. And while the mist-shrouded mountains and dense rain forests are quite spectacular, what's even more captivating are the accounts told by the ship's canal guide of the engineering genius that it took to clear this 50-mi/80-km shortcut.

Most people who traverse the canal do so as part of a 10-day or longer cruise in the Caribbean or along the western coast of Mexico (the trips often begin in San Juan or Acapulco). Canal cruises may include stops in the Mexican ports of Ensenada, Mazatlan, Puerto Vallarta, Los Cabos, Ixtapa/Zihuatanejo and/or Acapulco as well as visits to ports in Guatemala and Costa Rica. Caracas, Venezuela, and Cartagena, Colombia, are sometimes visited as part of longer canal cruises.

The rich cultures of these Latin America cities and countries offer cruise-ship passengers a wide range of choices. Acapulco, for example, is once again a popular resort town, after having been eclipsed by newcomer Cancun. Streets are cleaner, there's less crime on the beaches and fewer peddlers hang out on the street corners. Cruise passengers can watch the famous La Quebrada cliff divers as part of a city tour or visit the lovely homes and gardens that were owned by the '50s movie stars who frequented this swank old city.

In Los Cabos, the choices for cruise passengers center around the water. This area at the tip of Baja Peninsula is one long stretch of white-sand beach lined with resorts. If you'd rather reel in a big one, charter fishing boats are plentiful around Los Cabos, the headquarters for sportfishing in the Sea of Cortes — one of the world's richest fishing areas.

Guatemala's port cities are good jumping off points for tours of the captivating Mayan cities of Tikal and Copan (transportation inland is by airplane and bus). Cruise-ship passengers stopping at Costa Rica's ports can take tours into the interior to see rain forests, volcanoes and exotic wildlife.

New England/ Eastern Canada

The rich hues of fall foliage in New England and Eastern Canada have made the region a favorite vacation site for decades. So it's easy to understand the popularity of recently introduced summer-fall cruises along the northeastern U.S. coast and into the St. Lawrence Seaway. One of the more common routes is between New York City and Montreal, with assorted stops in between in New England and Atlantic Canada cities. In addition to the blaze of autumn color covering the countryside, you'll be able to trace the colonial history of the United States in Boston, tour the million-dollar mansions of Newport, visit a charming fishing village along the rugged coasts of Maine or Nova Scotia and shop for gifts at Montreal's trendy Place Montreal Trust.

Europe/Mediterranean and Baltic Seas

Some of the grandest cities of Europe are located on water. And that fact goes a long way toward explaining

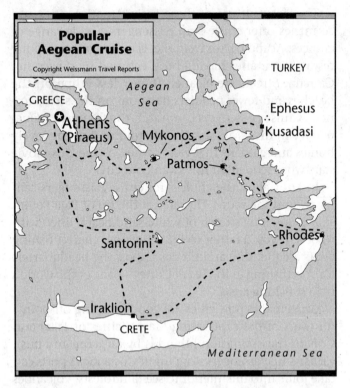

Popular Aegean Cruise

Copyright Weissmann Travel Reports

GREECE
Aegean Sea
TURKEY
Athens (Piraeus)
Mykonos
Ephesus
Kusadasi
Patmos
Santorini
Rhodes
Iraklion
CRETE
Mediterranean Sea

why touring coastal Europe by cruise ship appeals to so many people these days. Among the most popular cruising areas are the Greek islands in the Aegean Sea. Not only will you see sun-drenched beaches, but you can visit Greece's archaeological sites and travel back in time to one of Europe's greatest eras. Ships usually leave from the port of Piraeus near Athens and visit the islands of Crete (largest in the eastern Mediterranean), Mykonos (the island featured in most tourism posters of Greece) and Santorini (its biggest town is perched on the rim of a volcano).

Other Mediterranean cruises offer a host of port cities to choose from in countries such as Spain, Italy, France, Morocco and Tunisia. And there's so much to see on shore excursions, from historical tours of Rome and Vatican City, to shopping sprees in the bazaars in Istanbul, to a romantic gondola ride through the canals of Venice. A northern European cruise takes you to the North Sea or Baltic Sea cities of Amsterdam, Copenhagen, Oslo, St. Petersburg and Stockholm as well as to the spectacular fjords of Norway.

Hawaii/South Pacific/ Southeast Asia

The tranquillity of Maui, the vibrant flowers of Kauai and the excitement of Oahu are all part of a cruise in the Hawaiian Islands. Only one line, American Hawaii

Cruise Lines, currently offers year-round around-the-islands cruises, but it's possible to visit several Hawaiian ports as part of longer cruises that take in parts of the South Pacific. In fact, Honolulu is often the starting point for cruises to the exotic islands of Tahiti, Bora Bora, Fiji and American and Western Samoa.

Stops in Southeast Asia, Australia and New Zealand are sometimes part of longer South Pacific cruises, but separate sailings along the Southeast Asia coast to Thailand and Vietnam are attracting more experienced cruisers. Cruises around Australia and New Zealand also are enticing savvy world travelers.

Antarctica/South America

Still one of the most exotic cruise destinations, Antarctica has seen ship visits increase in recent years. The excitement of Antarctica includes navigating around the region's many icebergs and the chance to see penguins and whales frolic in their native habitats. Cruises to this most remote continent usually begin in Argentina or Chile in South America. Port cities in these countries are welcoming cruise ships in growing numbers.

River Cruises

An increasingly attractive alternative to cruising the high seas is river cruising. In some parts of the world, there is no better way to explore the history and culture of a region. A Mississippi River cruise, for example, introduces passengers to the economic lifeline of the Midwest, with stops to visit Elvis' Graceland in Memphis and the antebellum plantations of Natchez, Mississippi. Europe's heartland can be comfortably appreciated on Danube/Rhine River cruises that take you past rolling hills, castles and vineyards, with stops to tour the palaces of Vienna.

In England and France, numerous canals wind through the countryside and, at a leisurely pace, barges with cabins float tourists along on their waters. Though not designed to cover long distances (most go no more than a few miles per day), the barges offer visitors a great way to see quaint towns, meet local people and relax.

On a Nile River cruise, you can see the grandeur of the ancient Egyptian civilization (and take shore excursions to the Pyramids of Giza and the temples at Luxor). Even more exotic cruises can take you up the Sepik River deep into the primitive jungles of Papua New Guinea or up the Amazon River to a lodge deep within Brazil's rain forest.

The Geography of Cruising

Review Questions

1. What are some sights on a cruise that don't even require a shore visit?

2. What is the duration of the most common cruises? Give an example of a loop cruise. Give an example of a repositioning cruise.

3. Why might a client not want to take a Caribbean cruise in late summer or early fall?

4. List a port where cruises originate in each of the following states or islands: Puerto Rico, Texas, Florida, Massachusetts, the U.S. Virgin Islands and New York State.

5. What is the most popular cruising route in the Caribbean? What are some of the islands that ships generally stop at in this area?

6. What are two attractions on shore excursions in San Juan, Puerto Rico?

7. What is the major kind of attraction that the Western Caribbean route has that the Eastern Caribbean doesn't?

8. What might a cruise passenger tour on the island of Jamaica? What activity in the interior might a visitor do there?

9. What are the two routes that cruise lines typically offer through the Inside Passage?

10. What are some of the islands a ship might visit on a cruise in the Aegean Sea? From what port do ships usually leave to tour this region?

The Geography of Cruising

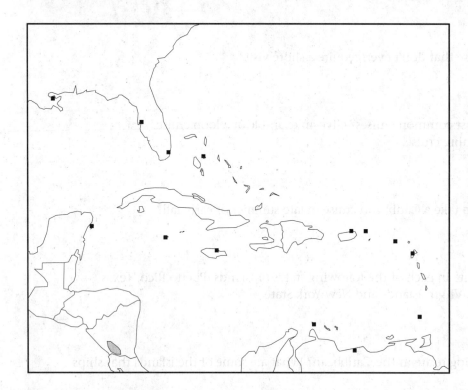

Map Skills Exercise

On the map at left, plot a Western Caribbean, an Eastern Caribbean and a Southern Caribbean cruise. The Western Caribbean cruise should start and end in New Orleans and visit Tampa, Ocho Rios, Grand Cayman and Cozumel. The Eastern Caribbean cruise should start and end in Miami and visit San Juan, St. Thomas, St. Maarten and Nassau. The Southern Caribbean cruise should start and end in San Juan and visit St. Thomas, Guadeloupe, Grenada, Caracas and Aruba.

Selling Exercise

A couple comes into your agency and tells you they have a week for vacation and don't know what to do or where to go. What would you say to persuade them that they should take a cruise to the Caribbean? (Be sure to sell them on the cruise experience as well as the destinations.)

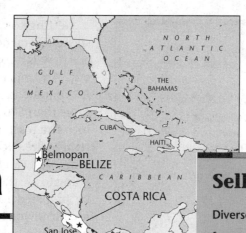

Tourist board 800-343-6332
www.tourism-costarica.com,
ecotur@expeditions.co.cr
; www.expeditions.co.cr

Costa Rica

and Belize

Now that "green" treks are the rage, more and more travelers want to visit Costa Rica's peaceful rain forests (and their rare butterflies, monkeys, birds, turtles and orchids). The government has taken steps to move from mega-developments toward a more sustainable eco-tourism industry. It wants a tourism industry based on small-scale resorts and lodges adjacent to the country's 32 national parks, reserves and refuges (nearly 28% of the land has been protected).

Costa Rica has long refused to conform to stereotypes about developing countries — especially developing countries in Central America. Unlike its neighbors, it enjoys a stable, democratic government (it abolished its military in 1948), adheres to high standards of education and is a relatively prosperous land. It offers a near-perfect blend of recreational and cultural activities.

Costa Rica and Belize are the two hottest destinations in Central America, especially for ecotourism. The countries are several hundred miles apart and are seen by visitors on separate trips. You'll rarely, if ever, package them together.

What to Do There

San Jose   Costa Rica's capital claims to have a perfect, eternal spring climate, and from what we've experienced, that's absolutely on target. The city is set at an elevation of 4,000 ft/1,200 m in a beautiful valley surrounded by tall mountains. Though the center is a bit run down, San Jose is so lively that visitors remember being charmed by the life of the city, its colorful markets and flower-decked parks.

We found the Entomological Museum at the University of Costa Rica fascinating — it houses more than a million butterflies, beetles and other insects. Other noteworthy collections include the National Museum (housed in an old fort — it has fine exhibits detailing Costa Rican history) and the Gold Museum (a fabulous collection of pre-Columbian gold artifacts).

Leave some time for shopping. In the evening or on weekends, just go people watching at the Plaza de la Cultura, where many San

Selling Points

Diverse natural beauty (lowland rain forests and upland cloud forests), black- and white-sand beaches, deep-sea and river fishing, casinos, surfing, white-water rafting, wildlife, bird-watching, volcano climbing, horseback riding, small jungle lodges and resorts, safety, friendly, well-educated people and their culture are the main attractions of Costa Rica.

Most travelers will enjoy Costa Rica. Many of the accommodations outside the cities are geared to the ecotourist, but that doesn't necessarily mean they're rustic. While Costa Rica has some very nice beaches, those interested in snorkeling/diving adventures would do better elsewhere.

Fascinating Facts About Costa Rica

Former President Oscar Arias Sanchez was awarded the Nobel Prize for Peace in 1987 . . . On 14 September, the eve of the national independence day, the entire country comes to a halt at 6 pm to sing the national anthem. It's quite an event . . . In contrast to most other nations in the region, there's little poverty in evidence. . . .

Costa Rica

- ✪ Capital
- ▪ ▫ City/Site
- ▲ National Park
- – – River

Copyright 1997 WTR

Jose residents gather around street musicians and entertainers.

For an interesting day trip out of San Jose, go 50 minutes northeast (on the road to Limon) to the new Rain Forest Aerial Tram. The tram carries 20 six-passenger cars into the canopy environment 120 ft/40 m off the rainforest floor. We advise visitors to make special arrangements to ride the tram at dawn or at dusk when animals tend to be more visible.

A short drive southeast of San Jose (about 35 mi/56 km) is Irazu Volcano, the tallest peak in the Central Cordillera chain. The area around this active 10,000-ft/3,050-m volcano looks positively lunar. About 35 mi/55 km northeast of San Jose is another volcanic option: the Poas Volcano National Park. Poas Volcano (7,000 ft/2,100 m high) is the world's largest active volcanic crater —inside it visitors will find steam, geysers and emerald green Botos Lake.

Other day-trip possibilities include the town of Sarchi, about 40 mi/65 km northwest of San Jose in an area of pineapple, sugar and coffee fields. It's known for its wooden handicrafts and ox cart factory, where gaily painted ox carts are for sale.

Monteverde Cloud Forest Reserve

If the Monteverde Cloud Forest Reserve were Costa Rica's only attraction, nature lovers would still flock to the country. This rain forest on the steep slopes of a mountain range is home to rare and unusual wildlife. Not only do the emerald toucanet and the world's largest population of quetzal birds reside there, but it's also the only known habitat of the golden toad.

Getting to Monteverde can be tough: You have to spend several hours on dreadful roads — so a visit of several days is recommended rather than a quick trip in and out. And once you're there, you may have to wait. Accommodations in the surrounding area can hold more than 500 people, but only 100 visitors are allowed into the reserve at a time. But the hiking trails in the reserve are excellent (though sometimes muddy); the rain forest can be very wet — so take rain gear. If you're going to see the golden toads, plan to visit May-July and be prepared for a long hike up a seemingly vertical incline (if you're not fit, don't even think of going). And be prepared for disappointment, too: The toads are so rare that they are almost never spotted.

Arenal Volcano is another impressive area sight. The best place for viewing Arenal is at the base of the mountain, where a volcano-heated stream flows into a small waterfall and then diverts into a series of mineral baths. At night you can lie in the spa and watch the glowing lava flow down the mountainside.

Other National Parks

In all, there are more than 32 national parks and refuges open to visitors. Here are two other parks that we have found especially interesting:

Braulio Carrillo National Park   This new and largely undeveloped park lies in the mountains west of Limon. Some of its beautiful mountain/forest scenery and waterfalls can be seen from the new San Jose-to-Limon highway. A day trip is available offering a four-hour hike in the park near Barva Volcano.

Tortuguero National Park   A lush, tropical jungle (similar to the area along the Amazon River around Iquitos, Peru), Tortuguero offers the opportunity to see monkeys, sloths and crocodiles. Toured in small outboard boats or dugout canoes, the park is best seen in August, when the green turtle comes ashore at night to nest and lay eggs. Fishing is popular in the area around Tortuguero, especially for tarpon and snook.

Itinerary

An energetic ecotourist's 7-day trip to Coast Rica might look something like this:

Day 1 — Arrive San Jose.

Day 2 — Day trip to Braulio Carrillo National Park and Rain Forest Aerial Tram.

Day 3 — Arenal Volcano.

Day 4 — Monteverde Cloud Forest Reserve.

Day 5 — Monteverde Cloud Forest Reserve.

Day 6 — Return to San Jose.

Day 7 — Depart Costa Rica.

Climate/When to Go

The best time to visit is December-May, when it rains least, but it's really a year-round destination. The inland climate is fairly moderate, and a breeze is almost always blowing, but the coastal tropical areas tend to be hot and steamy. The mountains can be quite cool at night, so take a sweater.

Transportation

Aero Costa Rica, American, Continental and United fly nonstop from the U.S., and many Central American airlines offer flights via their hub cities. Canadian Airlines provides infrequent nonstop service from Canada. Juan Santamaria International Airport (SJO) is 12 mi/19 km from San Jose. Principal cities within Costa Rica are connected by highway, rail (via San Jose) or air. Many of the national parks are accessible by four-wheel-drive vehicle only. We suggest an escorted or hosted tour for first-time visitors.

Accommodations

An increasing number of small-scale (maximum 30-40 units) ecotourism facilities are opening near parks and refuges, as opposed to large, all-inclusive resorts. There are, however, a number of first-class tourist facilities and at least one all-inclusive beachfront resort. Accommodations can be difficult to get December-March, especially at Christmas and Easter, so book well in advance.

Health Advisories

Sanitary conditions in most restaurants outside San Jose are not up to Western standards. Most hot, freshly cooked food should be safe (especially if it's included on a package tour). Except in the better San Jose hotels, assume the water is unsafe. Malaria can be a problem in

Geostats

Official Name: Republic of Costa Rica.

Visa Info: U.S. and Canadian citizens need a passport to enter Costa Rica.

Health Certificates: None required.

Capital: San Jose.

Population: 3,423,000.

Size: 19,700 sq mi/51,022 sq km. Slightly smaller than West Virginia.

Languages: Spanish and English (around Puerto Limon).

Climate: Tropical and semitropical.

Economy: Industry, agriculture.

Government: Republic.

Religion: Catholicism.

Currency: Costa Rican colon (CRC). 100 centimos = 1 CRC. Traveler's checks and credit cards are accepted at most tourist locations. AE, DC, MC, VI.

Time Zone: 1 hour behind EST; - 7 GMT (- 6 GMT from January to March).

Electricity: 110 Volts.

Departure Tax: US$7.

rural areas outside the central highlands. The most serious problems — diarrhea, amoebic dysentery, malaria and typhoid — occur more frequently outside the capital.

What to Buy

Shop for replicas of pre-Columbian jewelry, pottery, coffee, miniature ox carts, necklaces and earrings made of semiprecious stones, wood carvings, leather goods, beautiful embroidery and other local handicrafts. Guayaberas, the ruffled men's shirts, are readily available and are suitable for leisure or business.

What to Eat

In San Jose, there's a wide variety of international cuisine available (including Asian), but try the local specialties: tamales and corvina (sea bass) — don't order mondongo unless you like tripe. Shrimp is also an excellent choice at most places. *Casado* (married) is typical lunch fare and consists of red beans, rice, meat and either yucca or fried banana. *Gallo pinto* is red beans and rice alone. There are all kinds of wonderful tropical fruits, including mangoes, papayas and zapotes (a fruit with an orangelike pulp and the appearance of an avocado).

Travel Tips for the Client

Do be quiet when visiting the natural reserves — noise and crowds tend to scare the animals away...Do bring fast film if you're planning to shoot pictures in the rain forest. About 90 percent of the light gets filtered out at the canopy level and never reaches the jungle floor...Do beware of monkeys. Spider monkeys are known to throw branches at intruders on the ground, and howler monkeys sometimes urinate on them...

Belize

Once frequented mostly by archaeologists and divers, Belize has become a popular destination in the Central

Laughing Bird Caye, Belize

American/Caribbean region in the past few years. The water along its Great Barrier Reef is so clear and so uncrowded that diving there is considered to be among the best in the Western Hemisphere. (If you want to see a diver swoon, mention Belize's Blue Hole.) Ecotourists will be happy to discover that most of the country's interior is unspoiled: It's populated mostly by howler monkeys, tapirs, jaguars and hundreds of species of colorful birds. And the people, most of whom speak English, take such pride in their country that they go out of their way to assist visitors.

As always in developing countries, there is a downside: Roads often are unpaved and services spotty, making travel difficult and, at times, uncomfortable. Poverty is widespread; open sewers flow through the streets of many cities, and crime is on the rise.

The predominantly black culture of Belize more closely resembles those of the Caribbean islands than the cultures of its Hispanic neighbors. The country has been politically stable and free from civil war.

What to Do There

Belize City   Most visitors won't want to spend much time there: It's rough around the edges, with narrow streets crowded with people, widespread poverty, open sewers and increasing crime. If you do chose to visit, look for houses built on stilts (they are built in the Caribbean style). You can visit the small stores and see the 1814 Government House, the Anglican St. John's Cathedral (it's the oldest in Central America), the old Swing Bridge (opened twice a day for river traffic) and the nearby fruit market (colorful, full of unusual fruits and goods). Be sure to dally at the Bliss Institute, look at its art exhibits and talk with the local people. The Belize Zoo is really a kind of wildlife preserve, with more than 100 animals residing in spacious habitats lush with vegetation.

Ambergris Caye   Ambergris is at the northern end of the barrier reef and offers a variety of water sports (including snorkeling, diving and deep-sea fishing), plus narrow palm-fringed white-sand beaches. It's a very informal island (shoes are optional everywhere); go prepared to relax — there really isn't much to do out of the water. San Pedro, the only town on Ambergris, is so small — seven blocks long and three blocks wide — that you can walk everywhere. (Bicycles and golf carts can be rented — but not cars.) Several more secluded, upscale resorts are located to the south

Km 0 25 50
Mi 0 25 50
Copyright 1997 WTR

MEXICO

AMBERGRIS CAYE
San Pedro
Hol Chan
Altun Ha
CAYE CAULKER

Belize City
BLUE HOLE (LIGHTHOUSE REEF)
Belmopan
B A R R I E R   R E E F
Xunantunich
Dangriga
Cockscomb Basin
GLOVER'S REEF
Placencia

Punta Gorda

GUATEMALA

Belize

✪	Capital
■ □	City/Site
▲	National Park
∴	Ruin
— · —	River

Caye Caulker

Caye Caulker is much smaller than Ambergris. It offers a slow-paced atmosphere and extremely informal accommodations (bunkhouses, rooming houses or camping are your choices). Snorkeling and diving along the nearby coral reef are really the only activities of note. The island doesn't have much of a beach; most sunning and swimming is done off the docks.

Placencia

This southern Belize town is located on a peninsula that has the country's loveliest white-sand beaches and plenty of water sports, including tarpon fishing, snorkeling at Laughing Bird Caye and scuba diving. Some of the many area attractions are: rain forests, mountains, excellent bird-watching and the Cockscomb Basin Wildlife Preserve, one of our favorite spots in Belize. The city is not easy to get to (we recommend flying, if possible), but it is a good place to spend several nights because of the variety of activities available — there are even Mayan ruins nearby.

Travel Tips for the Client

Don't wander about in the jungle, even in groups. It is easy to get lost . . . Do take binoculars — the bird population is extraordinary (about 500 species of birds). In the rain forests, try to spot the colorful toucan . . . Don't expect a wide variety of nightlife . . . Do obtain a copy of the Belize Tourism Industry Association's brochure on walking and driving tours. It's most helpful. . . .

and north of town, but you'll need transportation to get to and from San Pedro.

Most of the hotels offer twice-daily trips to sightseeing and snorkeling/dive sites (as well as night dives). There are also glass-bottom boat trips to the Hol Chan Underwater Marine Reserve, an underwater park that can be reached only by boat. The reserve has an amazing assortment of fish — expect to see everything from stingrays and sharks to eels and tiny rainbow-colored fish.

Archaeological Ruins

There are hundreds of Mayan ruins in Belize. The two that are the easiest to get to from Ambergris Caye and Belize City are Altun Ha and Xunantunich. We recommend a tour: We found our guides to be knowledgeable about the sites and well-worth the extra cost. Altun Ha (Water of the Rock), some 30 mi/48 km north of Belize City, contains about 100 mounds and covers nearly 3 sq mi/8 sq km; its Temple of the Sun God is extraordinary. At Xunantunich, 80 mi/129 km southwest of Belize City, you'll see El Castillo (this Classic Mayan temple is the second tallest building in Belize).

Fascinating Facts About Belize

The electric-blue color of the Blue Morpho butterflies makes them easy to spot in the dark-green rain forests of Belize . . . In 1991, Guatemala finally recognized Belize as an independent nation. Guatemala had claimed that Belize was part of its territory on the basis of 500-year-old Spanish decrees. Tensions between the two countries have lessened, but some Guatemalans continue to believe Belize was stolen from them by the British . . . About 30% of Belize is unexplored rain forest . . . 70% of the inland area is forest, containing some 4,000 plant species — including 700 types of trees . . . Because a Chicago TV station broadcasts into Belize, the Chicago White Sox baseball team has a huge following there. . . .

Costa Rica and Belize

Review Questions

1. What will a tourist see in the following attractions in San Jose: Entomological Museum at the University of Costa Rica; National Museum; Gold Museum?

2. What will visitors see inside Poas Volcano?

3. For what is Sarchi known?

4. Where is the only known habitat of the golden toad? What are the best months in which to see it?

5. Tortuguero National Park is similar to what area in South America?

6. What language do most of the people in Belize speak?

7. Why wouldn't a visitor want to spend much time in Belize City?

8. What resort is at the northern end of the barrier reef in Belize? What does it offer?

9. Name two archaeological ruins in Belize. Who built them?

10. What resort town has the loveliest white-sand beaches in Belize?

Costa Rica and Belize

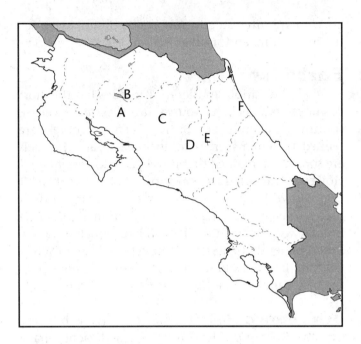
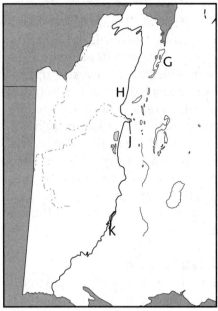

Map Skills Exercise

Match the tourist destination listed below with the corresponding letter on the map. You can use each letter only once.

1. _____ San Jose
2. _____ Monteverde Cloud Forest Reserve
3. _____ Tortuguero National Park
4. _____ Arenal Volcano
5. _____ Irazu Volcano

6. _____ Poas Volcano
7. _____ Altun Ha
8. _____ Placencia
9. _____ Belize City
10. _____ Ambergris Caye

Selling Exercise

Members of the local chapter of the Sierra Club have come to see you. They are interested in ecotourism and want to take a trip to either Belize or Costa Rica. Which country would you recommend to them? Why?

North America Geofile

Anguilla

In the mid-1980s, a few small superdeluxe hotels opened, and suddenly Anguilla (an-GWILL-la) went from a sleepy place to the place to be seen. It became a regular setting for *Lifestyles of the Rich and Famous,* upscale fashion magazines and gossip columns. For the most part, the beautiful people have now headed elsewhere, but they have left behind a small but wonderful selection of hotels, resorts and restaurants in all price ranges. The result is that Anguilla is once again a quiet and peaceful destination. A flat, dry and scrubby island with few trees, Anguilla's beauty lies in the miles of stunning white-sand beaches that rim the island and the clear waters that are perfect for snorkeling.

Antigua and Barbuda

The interior of these sister islands is rather flat, dry and nondescript by Caribbean standards. What sets the two islands (pronounced an-TEE-gah and bar-BEW-dah locally) apart from others in the region, however, are the beaches. These lovely shorelines, which ring both islands with almost pure white sand, began attracting wealthy visitors more than two decades ago — the islands have several exclusive resorts. Today, they attract travelers of all income levels who are interested in sun, scuba diving, deep-sea fishing, sailing and snorkeling.

Barbados

Of all the Caribbean islands, Barbados has the most cosmopolitan feel. Its tourist facilities are modern, sophisticated and very British — many hotels are refined, restaurants serve Continental fare, and the roads are so well maintained that traveling is downright easy. However, the island's popularity has made it a bit crowded with tourists — as well as loud and dirty in places. Travelers seeking a somewhat formal Caribbean holiday with active nightlife will like Barbados. (Some hotels prefer that guests wear jackets to dinner.) While you can dive and snorkel there, the island is not one of the best Caribbean destinations for those sports.

Bridgetown This capital city is a bustling Caribbean seaport. Its lovely white beaches have become a bit too popular lately — on our last visit, we couldn't relax and enjoy ourselves because of the crush and roar of the crowds. We recommend planning your beach time elsewhere on the island. In Bridgetown itself there are plenty of sights to see, including the Careenage (port) area, where a new cruise ship terminal opened in 1994. It has duty-free shops, restaurants and an amusement and gambling arcade. The Barbados Museum shouldn't be missed, it contains prints from the late 1600s, an excellent collection of doll houses, artifacts on the island's history and displays of local artists. We also suggest strolling through Trafalgar Square (with a monument to Lord Nelson predating the one in London), and visiting the house where George Washington is said to have stayed while accompanying his brother, Lawrence, to the island. For nightlife, St. Lawrence Gap and the city center near the Careenage have nightclubs with live music (Caribbean and jazz).

Natural Attractions There are several points of interest for nature lovers, including the Barbados Wildlife Reserve, a mahogany forest that is home to rare green monkeys. We also enjoyed Harrison's Cave (board the tram for an educational ride through the extensive cave system and past streams, waterfalls and tropical foliage). The Flower Forest, a 50-acre/20-hectare park and botanical garden, merits a visit, too.

Travel Tips for the Client

Junk's Hole Beach in Anguilla is a great place to teach children how to snorkel. Hidden away on the eastern side of island, it has calm, shallow waters filled with coral reefs and marine life . . . Don't waste water on Antigua. It lacks ground water, so drinking water is either collected from rainfall or brought in on barges . . . Do expect a wide variety of nightlife on Barbados, ranging from discos to local bands (including steel bands) . . . Don't step on sea urchins, as it can be very painful . . . The majority of Cubans practice some element of Santeria, the homegrown religion that blends African gods and beliefs with Catholic saints. The town of Guanabacoa just east of Havana is a center of the religion and contains an excellent museum of Santeria artifacts . . . Don't walk around Port-of-Spain, Trinidad at night, not even near your hotel. It's simply not safe. . . .

Restored Plantation Homes Try to visit at least one of the restored plantation homes. Those open to the public year round include St. Nicholas Abbey (built in 1660 and thought to be the oldest house on Barbados). Those interested in Barbadian history may want to visit the Morgan Lewis Mill in St. Andrew to get a feeling for sugar-plantation days.

British Virgin Islands

If your idea of the perfect island escape is sailing into a secluded cove with lush mountains as a backdrop, the British Virgin Islands may fit your definition of paradise. With 50 or so islands clustered close together, B.V.I. is one of the most popular yachting spots in the Caribbean. Of course, paradise doesn't come cheap. B.V.I. has traditionally catered to the affluent by building exquisitely private, boutique-style resorts.

Despite the fact that these islands are only a few miles from the U.S. Virgin Islands, they are vastly different in character. There are far fewer people, hotel rooms and tourists on B.V.I., for example. And there's a lot of beautiful scenery to take in — the panorama includes white crescent beaches nestled at the bottom of steep, green mountains and stunning vistas of neighboring islands from the tops of those mountains.

Cayman Islands

The prosperous Cayman Islands — Grand Cayman, Cayman Brac and Little Cayman — were once hideouts for pirates, but are today the "Holiday Inns" of the Caribbean: There are no unpleasant surprises awaiting visitors. Crime is rare. Islanders are friendly, speak English and enjoy the highest standard of living in the Caribbean. Diving and snorkeling opportunities are excellent for beginners as well as experts. And the beaches are wide, sandy and fringed with palm trees.

The largest of the Caymans, Grand Cayman, has the country's capital city, George Town, and the major tourist attractions. George Town is packed with duty-free stores and local souvenir shops that cater to cruise ship passengers. But there are some historic buildings in town as well as an excellent museum, the Cayman Maritime and Treasure Museum. It's full of salvaged treasure (coins, jewelry, etc.) from wrecks off Cayman's shores. Just north of George Town is Seven Mile Beach, one of the best beaches in the Caribbean and the location of most of the island's tourist hotels and condominiums.

Two water-related activities on Grand Cayman stand out: The adventurous will want to visit Stingray City to snorkel with dozens of stingrays. Also, submerged off East End is the 7,500-ton vessel *MV Ridgefield,* which has

The Caribbean

Fascinating Facts About the Caribbean Islands

Anguilla is one of the few former colonies that has asked to reassociate with the United Kingdom . . . In the waters off Barbuda, the graceful spotted eagle-ray, sometimes reaching a width of 6 ft/2 m, may swim right up to you. Don't panic! It's just curious . . . Barbados is still very British. Evidence abounds in the popularity of polo and cricket . . . The Cayman Islands weren't always such a wholesome, family-oriented destination. They were settled in the 17th century by pirates, deserters from the English army and shipwrecked sailors . . . The Carib Indians had separate languages for the women and the men . . . In Haiti, if someone calls you doux doux (pronounced doo-doo), don't be insulted; that's Creole for sweetheart . . . About 65% of the visitors to Martinique are European French . . . The Irish connection is so strong in Montserrat that Irish stew (made with goat meat and called "goat water") is a national dish and the shamrock flag flies at Government House . . . Josephine, the wife of Napoleon and Empress of France, was born on Martinique in 1763 . . . The steel drum, or pan, originated in Trinidad in the late 1930s when resourceful African musicians began beating on instruments made out of cans, pots and car parts during Carnival. Eventually, as oil drums became abundant in this petroleum-rich country, they too were made into musical instruments. Today, steel-drum bands are part of Carnival festivities in Trinidad and around the world . . . The Turks and Caicos once proposed becoming part of Canada (in the 1970s). Many Canadians own property on the islands, and Canada has been one of the most generous donors of aid to the islands. . . .

become an underwater playground for divers. You can also tour the Cayman Turtle Farm.

As to the appeal of the two smaller islands, Little Cayman has some of the best places for snorkeling and diving in the world and Cayman Brac is a great place to go for deep-sea fishing (marlin, bluefin, barracuda) and also for diving and snorkeling.

Cuba

Travelers who go to Cuba will find a beautiful island whose people reflect a blend of Carib Indian, African and Spanish influences. As islands go, it's very large — 780 mi/1,250 km long. The topography ranges from superlative beaches to high, jagged mountain ranges; valleys, lakes and rivers give variety to the land. Industry and agriculture are more intensive on this Communist-run island than on most Caribbean islands. Travelers who must have efficient service at all times or who want a multitude of choices in restaurants, entertainment or shopping will be dissatisfied in Cuba. (There are severe restrictions on U.S. citizens visiting the island.)

Havana   Although the Old Havana section is deteriorating, it still has much of interest. Most of the details on the art-deco buildings lining the narrow cobblestone streets are crumbling, but the Spanish colonial structures are well preserved: be sure to see the Museum of the City of Havana, the Cathedral (on a wonderful plaza) and Castillo de la Fuerza (the second-oldest fortress in the New World). You'll also run across a few Hemingway haunts in that area. Across the harbor from Old Havana are El Morro and La Cabana forts, which are also worth a visit. Central Havana has little of interest to tourists, but Vedado, a modern area, has tourist hotels, nightclubs and the fascinating Columbus Cemetery, where the headstones and monuments are reminiscent of those in New Orleans. Sites relating to the struggles of socialism are spread throughout the city; they include the Museum of the Revolution. At night, take in the glitzy show at the Tropicana Club, seemingly unchanged from pre-Castro days 40 years ago.

Varadero Beach   This magnificent stretch of sand is spread out on a peninsula on the northeastern coast. It's both the best known and most developed of Cuba's resort areas: It offers a variety of hotels, nightclub/cabarets and restaurants. The snorkeling and diving are both good. Varadero is allowed to hold Carnival — it's geared toward tourists. It's among the best Mardi Gras-style celebrations in the Caribbean.

Dominica

Dominica (pronounced dom-in-EE-kah) stands apart from other Caribbean islands, and not just because of its relative lack of resorts and beaches. Its bountiful flora and fauna reflect the fact that tourism developers have chosen to pass the island by for the time being. In fact, if we're lucky, it will stay as little frequented and untouched as it is now: The Dominican forest is the rare oceanic rain forest, alive with very endangered birds and animals, and divers will find irresistible black coral reefs in the depths of the clean waters. This is the perfect place for the wilderness junkie.

Dominican Republic

The government is aggressively trying to upgrade the country's image as a tourist destination. The flashiest addition is the Columbus Lighthouse, which was built as part of the 1992 celebration of the 500th anniversary of the explorer's "discovery" of the New World. While this combination museum/tomb in the capital city, Santo Domingo, is nice enough, we've been more impressed with the country's less heralded improvements: Roads around the country have been paved and widened, and historic areas in the major cities have been renovated. In addition, new construction of hotels, golf courses and other tourist facilities continues at a rapid pace.

Because the country is so large, there's no immediate danger that it will be overrun by tourists or spoiled by development. Prices also remain lower there than on some Caribbean islands. Be aware, however, that the country is still quite poor and relatively inexperienced in tourism. For that reason, travelers interested in a no-hassle beach experience may prefer the smaller, better-known Caribbean countries.

Santo Domingo Besides the Columbus Lighthouse and its museum, other attractions in Santo Domingo include the Cathedral of Santa Maria La Menor, the oldest cathedral in the Americas, and the new open-air National Aquarium, which contains a shark tank and the recreation of a wrecked galleon. Santo Domingo has a lovely Colonial Zone that is gradually being restored. You'll want to traverse its oceanside boulevard which is several miles long and lined with many good restaurants and lively clubs. Annual events in Santo Domingo include Carnival and the Merengue Festival, a music celebration held in July. A three-hour drive east of the city is Casa de Campo, the island's largest, poshest resort. It was designed by Oscar de la Renta.

Puerto Plata On the north coast about a four-hour drive from Santo Domingo, Puerto Plata is a relaxing place. Enjoy the beaches with their dramatic mountain backdrop, deep-sea fishing, diving and golfing. Visit the Amber Museum. (The region, nicknamed the Amber Coast, is the world's largest source of amber.) Movie-goers may recognize the area as the setting for Jurassic Park. Nearby is the resort area of Playa Dorada, a seaside complex with 13 first-class hotels centered around a Robert Trent Jones-designed golf course. Several of the hotels have casinos and discos.

Guadeloupe

When you're in Guadeloupe, you're in both the Caribbean and France. It's a warm cultural combination, but it can confound your expectations: You'll be eating fine food prepared by accomplished chefs trained in France — but you may be disoriented by the liberal use of Caribbean spices. All of this will strike tolerant, curious travelers as just right, especially when you add to the mix the island's natural beauty, from unusual and fabulous beaches to a volcano that is one of the Caribbean's best nature preserves. Relative to the rest of the Caribbean, costs are high.

Grenada

On Grenada, the Isle of Spice, ocean breezes carry scents from cinnamon to cocoa to saffron. In fact, the island produces so much spice — including almost one-third of the world's nutmeg — that until just recently tourism was of secondary importance to its economy. However, tourism has grown steadily in the past few years. This volcanic island has lakes, deep green forests, some 45 golden- or white-sand beaches, rain-forest trails and waterfalls, too many dazzling tropical flowers to count and very friendly people. People who love the outdoors and are looking for a nontouristy destination with gorgeous beaches and mountains will enjoy Grenada.

Haiti

Anyone thinking about visiting Haiti should understand that it's a land whose wounds from intercommunal strife are still very fresh. It is not a destination for anyone looking for a relaxing Caribbean vacation. Those interested in seeing this nation in transition will find lush tropical landscapes, open-air markets and a unique cultural tradition developed by a nation of liberated slaves. The music, the poetic Creole language and voodoo influences enrich this otherwise poverty stricken land (be aware that it's a place of frequent delays, poor roads and power outages — even at luxury hotels). Haiti will appeal only to travelers looking for a Caribbean holiday that offers challenge and adventure. While beaches, water sports and sun-worshipping can be found there, the inconvenience factor is higher than anywhere else in the Caribbean. (On the upside, Haiti's cultural offerings are far more extensive than can be found elsewhere in the region.)

Martinique

Some travelers love Martinique for the same reason others hate it: It's *trés* French. Of course, the lush mountains, miles of sugarcane fields, rain forest and black-sand beaches don't let you forget you're in the tropics. But in Martinique you can buy baguettes, zip around in a Citroen and sunbathe topless. Sixty-five percent of the visitors come from France. But Martinique also maintains a strong Caribbean identity, evidenced in its music, its cuisine and its raucous Carnival. Mount Pelee (a volcano that erupted in 1902, killing 40,000 people) is also a major attraction.

Montserrat

Montserrat reminds us of what the Caribbean used to be like before mass tourism. Few people visit this lush, tiny island, so it retains a tranquil, private atmosphere. Montserrat is not for everyone, however. It doesn't have the spectacular white-sand beaches or crystal-clear turquoise waters found elsewhere in the Caribbean. And there's not much to do in the way of restaurants or nightlife. It is best suited to those who like a relaxing pace of island life and enjoy hiking in lush green mountains. What makes the island very unique is its distinctively Irish flavor. The legacy of early Irish immigrants has given the island the only Irish presence in the Caribbean.

St. Kitts and Nevis

Deciding between St. Kitts and its sister island, Nevis, is too taxing for us. That's why we suggest spending time on both. Although these islands are only about 2 mi/3 km apart, they are quite different geographically and culturally — and delightfully so. Nevis is quaint, sophisticated and peppered with rustic inns; St. Kitts is grander and bolder — you'll find several all-inclusive resorts catering to sports-minded visitors there. (St. Kitts real name is St. Christopher, but it's been called by its nickname for more than 350 years.)

St. Lucia

With all its natural beauty and hiking trails, St. Lucia is a great destination for the environmentally curious who want to visit a Caribbean island — especially if they prefer nontouristy spots. Anyone who loves great beaches amid beautiful scenery and plenty of peace and quiet will be very happy there. With a few notable exceptions, there's not much in the way of nightlife. Anyone going to St. Lucia should be prepared to see signs of poverty.

St. Vincent and the Grenadines

For sheer visual joy, St. Vincent and the Grenadines top our list: they are the most strikingly beautiful islands of the Caribbean. Each of the nation's islands and cays is slightly different in topography and character. Some are completely framed by sandy beaches; some have mountains, while others are fairly flat. However, visitors expecting variety in shopping and nightlife will quickly lose interest in these quiet islands. (The Grenadines consist of approximately 70 various-sized cays and 35 islands. St. Vincent itself is many times larger than all the other cays and islands combined.) We think the spectrum of the Grenadines' beauty is best experienced on a yacht/boat cruise, beginning in St. Vincent and ending in the island-nation of Grenada — many consider these the finest yachting waters in the world.

Trinidad and Tobago

It's no coincidence that the grandest Carnival in the Caribbean is in Trinidad. This island off the coast of Venezuela is an exotic, chaotic fusion of cultures whose people love nothing better than pulsating calypso music and a colorful masquerade. If you like to party, you'll love Trinidad. But while Trinidad swings, its neighbor to the north sways — the rhythm of tiny Tobago is more akin to the gentle rock of a hammock.

Turks and Caicos Islands

The fish and coral that lurk in the water off the Turks and Caicos are magnets for scuba divers from around the world. The islands themselves, however, offer few, if any, draws; Those looking for tropical greenery, highly charged nightlife, historical sites and great restaurants should keep looking.

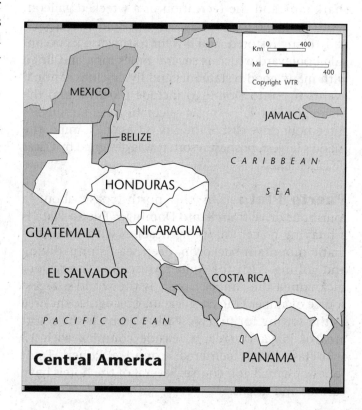

Central America

El Salvador

We are still not ready to recommend a visit to El Salvador, except for the most experienced and adventurous travelers. While the country has lovely beaches, Maya ruins, volcanos and mountains, equally good examples can be found in destinations whose reputation for stability is based on a longer track record. And safer ones, too. Crime has become a serious problem in El Salvador: In the cities, armed gangs rob buses, highjack cars and burglarize businesses. Bandits are present in rural areas. Tourists have been primary targets of late.

Guatemala

In all of Central America, Guatemala has perhaps the most to offer visitors: fascinating Mayan ruins, a rich Spanish-colonial atmosphere, colorful festivals and markets, and spectacular scenery — mountains and jungles and beaches. But it has something else: a history of repressive governments and guerrilla activity. Attacks on visitors, particularly U.S. citizens, have been reported. (The U.S. State Department says all nonessential travel there should be deferred.) But if you're on the adventurous side (or are going with a reputable tour company), you'll find that Guatemala features an attraction that ranks among the finest in the Western Hemisphere: Tikal. In fact, we rate the Mayan ruins at Tikal as one of the three most impressive ruins in the world (the other two are Machu Picchu in Peru and the Valley of the Kings in Egypt).

Honduras

Honduras is a country with beaches and dive sites that rival those anywhere in the Caribbean. The country's Mayan ruins in Copan are considered the best preserved in the world. And Honduras' lush rain forests are home to some of the rarest wildlife on the North American continent. The political situation in the region has stabilized to the point that Honduras can again be considered a vacation destination, but we do offer this caution: Visitors who haven't traveled in underdeveloped countries, or those who are accustomed to high levels of accommodations and services, may find it falls short of their expectations.

Nicaragua

Nicaragua is only for the most adventurous travelers. Infrastructure is poor (many unpaved roads, electricity blackouts in the capital, uncomfortable buses), and civil and social problems still result in strikes, demonstrations and, occasionally, riots. While the country has natural assets that others would envy — a large tropical rain forest, nice beaches, volcanoes, attractive colonial cities — it simply can't offer a reliably pleasant overall experience, as can some of its Central American neighbors.

Panama

Panama is an atypical Central American nation. Its culture shows the influence of many lands, from Jamaica to the nations of eastern Asia—lands from which people came to build the Panama Canal and to work on the country's plantations. In most parts of Panama, tourists are made to feel welcome, but since the U.S.-led removal of Manuel Noriega and his regime, unemployment has skyrocketed, crime has risen and there's some resentment of what is perceived as continued U.S. interference in Panamanian affairs. Visitors to Panama City and Colon might encounter some harassment. In addition to the Canal, attractions include casinos, jungles, shopping, the native Indian culture found on the San Blas Islands, beaches and world-class deep-sea fishing.

Fascinating Facts About Central America

In an effort to avoid incorporation into Mexico in 1823, El Salvador petitioned the United States for statehood. When turned down, it became the first independent country in Central America . . . Train buffs might consider traveling around Guatemala on a chartered steam train that traverses through the rugged mountains as well as the jungle lowlands. Trains Unlimited Tours offers the trip once a year in February . . . The three horizontal stripes of the Honduran flag (blue-white-blue) stand for the Pacific Ocean, the land of the isthmus and the Caribbean Sea. The five stars express the hope that the original five nations of the Central American confederation will unite once again . . . Bianca Jagger (nee Bianca Perez Morena), a vocal human-rights advocate and the former wife of Rolling Stones singer Mick Jagger, was born in Nicaragua and is active in national politics — she's mentioned often as a potential presidential candidate . . . The Panama Canal could just as easily have been the Nicaragua Canal. Proponents of building the project in Panama scuttled the proposal for a more northerly passage when they sent every U.S. congressman letters using Nicaraguan postage. Why? Each stamp featured a range of steaming volcanoes! . . .

North America Geofile

Review Questions

1. What island in the Caribbean is said to have the most cosmopolitan feel? Why is that?

2. What two water-related activities on Grand Cayman stand out?

3. What is the best known and most developed of Cuba's resort areas? What does it offer tourists?

4. What makes Montserrat very unique among Caribbean islands?

5. What islands have a reputation as great places to go yachting?

6. To what island would you send a client who wanted to go to the grandest Carnival in the Caribbean?

7. Among the Central American countries, what nation has perhaps the most to offer visitors? What attractions are there?

8. Which three ruins does Weissmann Travel Reports rate as the most impressive in the world? In what country would you find each of them?

9. What attractions set Antigua and Barbuda apart from other islands in the Caribbean? Describe how these attractions appear.

10. In what country would you find the oldest cathedral in the Americas and the Columbus Lighthouse?

North America Geofile

Map Skills Exercise

Match the tourist destination listed below with the corresponding letter on the map. You can use each letter only once.

1. _____ Panama
2. _____ Guatemala
3. _____ Cuba
4. _____ Dominican Republic
5. _____ Barbados
6. _____ Honduras
7. _____ Cayman Islands
8. _____ British Virgin Islands
9. _____ Guadeloupe
10. _____ Trinidad and Tobago

Unit Review Mexico, the Caribbean,

Bermuda and Central America

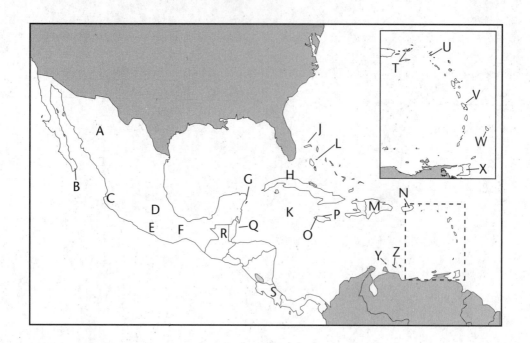

Map Skills Exercise

Match the tourist destination listed below with the corresponding letter on the map.

1. _____ Monteverde Cloud Forest Reserve
2. _____ Ambergris Caye
3. _____ Barbados
4. _____ Cayman Islands
5. _____ Varadero Beach
6. _____ Dominican Republic
7. _____ Martinique
8. _____ Trinidad
9. _____ Tikal
10. _____ Nassau
11. _____ Acapulco
12. _____ Los Cabos
13. _____ Puerto Vallarta

14. _____ Curacao
15. _____ Teotihuacan
16. _____ Copper Canyon
17. _____ Grand Bahama Island
18. _____ Cancun
19. _____ El Yunque
20. _____ U.S. Virgin Islands
21. _____ St. Martin/Sint Maarten
22. _____ Ocho Rios
23. _____ Montego Bay
24. _____ Oranjestad
25. _____ Oaxaca

Unit Review Mexico, the Caribbean,

Bermuda and Central America

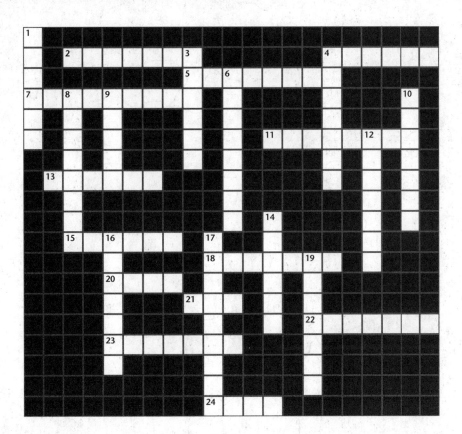

Content Review Crossword Puzzle

Across

2. Islands not far from Florida

4. Its culture is more Caribbean than Hispanic

5. Mexican west coast resort

7. Hot ecotourism destination

11. Bermuda's capital

13. It's the heart of Mexico City

15. Most scenic U.S. Virgin Island

18. San Miguel de _____

20. They built Chichen Itza

21. Phosphorescent _____

22. St. Martin town

23. Cruise ships visit this Mexican resort

24. Dutch island near St. Martin/Sint Maarten

Down

1. No. 1 Mexican tourist destination

3. "The Cave of the Sleeping _____" at Isla Mujeres

4. Great island to dive and snorkel

6. See the cliff divers at La Quebrada there

8. Most developed U.S. Virgin Island

9. Practically a desert island

10. La Forteleza and the Pablo Casals Museum are there

12. Border town

14. The language of Martinique

16. Enjoy Reggae Sunsplash there

17. Mexican colonial town

19. Once owned the U.S. Virgin Islands

Caribbean Sea

NORTH ATLANTIC OCEAN

VENEZUELA

GUYANA

SURINAME

FRENCH GUIANA (FR.)

COLOMBIA

ECUADOR

Quito

EQUATOR

GALAPAGOS ISLANDS (ECUADOR)

BRAZIL

PERU

Lima

SOUTH PACIFIC OCEAN

BOLIVIA

Brasilia

PARAGUAY

CHILE

Santiago

Buenos Aires

SOUTH ATLANTIC OCEAN

URUGUAY

ARGENTINA

South America

✪ Capital

     International Boundary

Km. 0   250   500   1000

Mi   0   250   500   1000

Copyright Weissmann Travel Reports

FALKLAND ISLANDS (U.K.)

SOUTH GEORGIA ISLANDS (U.K.)

South America

SOUTH AMERICA HAS A WIDE RANGE OF GEO-graphic features: glaciers, fjords, jungles, deserts, mountains, rivers, magnificent beaches and lakes. It also has a mix of cultures and languages and a fascinating history. Before the coming of Pizzaro and the Spanish, great Indian civilizations (the last was the Inca) dominated the western part of the continent. In the 1500s, Spain and Portugal divided most of South America between them. Brazil was a Portuguese colony, while most of the rest of the continent was part of Spain's colonial empire.

Any client can find something of interest in South America. The Andes mountain range runs just inland from the Pacific all along the west coast, offering Incan sites and excellent skiing. The Amazon region, which crosses the northern part of the continent and is covered by rain forest, is home to native Indian cultures, as well as unique wild animals and more species of insects than any other single region on Earth. The southern Atlantic coast, from the state of Bahia in Brazil to Argentina's cap-ital, Buenos Aires, is home to lovely beaches and shorelines, beautiful and bustling cities, and some of the most colorful festivals in the world. The southern tip of the continent can be cold, damp, windy and often rather uncomfortable, but it offers a fascinating experience for those who like jagged mountains, rugged sea coasts, cold weather animals and birds, and desolate scenery. The best overall time to visit South America is in February and March, during summer in the southern hemisphere.

On the following pages, you'll find in-depth information about five countries popular among tourists — Brazil, Argentina, Chile, Peru and Ecuador — which together cover about three-quarters of the landmass of South America. The chapters on these countries are followed by the South America and Antarctica Geofile chapter. In that chapter, we take a look at what attracts tourists to the other countries on the mainland of South America as well as to Antarctica and the Falkland Islands.

Brazil

Selling Points

Carnival, beaches, Rio de Janeiro, Iguacu Falls, the Amazon, native and imported cultural attractions, art, colonial towns and exciting nightlife are the foremost attractions of Brazil.

Everyone will love something about Brazil, but the opposite is also true — everyone will hate something about it. To minimize problems, try to stick to the areas and activities that truly match your interests (i.e., if you're not really interested in seeing jungle animals, you probably won't want to put up with the heat, dirt and high humidity that's part and parcel of a jungle excursion).

Fascinating Facts About Brazil

Voters decided in 1993 to reject the reintroduction of monarchy in Brazil. The nation's last emperor was ousted in 1889 . . . Americana, just outside Sao Paulo, is a town founded by Confederate refugees after the U.S. Civil War. The phone book is filled with surnames such as Lee, Jones, etc. Once a year the boys dress up in rebel gray and the girls in long gowns and they hold a formal ball . . . Upon seeing Iguacu Falls, Eleanor Roosevelt reportedly shook her head and said, "Poor Niagara.". . .

There is no better place to be on Earth than Rio during Carnival. The vibrant parades and more-decoration-than-covering costumes are enough to wake the dead and get them dancing. But the more you know of Brazil, the more you'll want to go beyond that glitter.

Equally enticing are the enormous waterfalls of Iguacu, the voodoo-infused city of Salvador and the colonial towns of Ouro Preto and Olinda. If you'd rather explore nature, take a tour of the Amazon Basin or an excursion to the Pantanal, one of the best wildlife preserves in South America. If all you want is sun and sand, you'll find that Rio de Janeiro's Ipanema and Copacabana are just the beginning — Brazil has thousands of miles of beautiful beaches. Rio might draw you to Brazil the first time, but the country's unexplored corners and breadth of attractions will make you want to go back.

Brazil was a Portuguese colony for more than three centuries, and evidence of Portuguese culture abounds in everything from language to food.

What to Do There

Amazon   The Amazon River, second in length only to the Nile, passes through upper Brazil on its journey to the Atlantic Ocean. The Amazon features Brazil at its wettest and wildest, and the cities on the Amazon are among the most fascinating in the country. About 75 mi/121 km inland from the Atlantic is the large port city of Belem. Half-day river-launch cruises to see the jungle, birds, fishermen, dugout canoes, oceangoing vessels, etc., can be arranged for people who aren't going farther up the river, and the city itself has enough of interest to justify a two-day stay. (Its Ver-o-Peso Market features, among the fruit and vegetable vendors, stalls selling crocodile teeth, dried boa constrictors and voodoo charms.)

The other major city on the river tourists visit is Manaus. Manaus, once called the Paris of the Jungle, has fallen on hard times. Part of the center of the city was devastated by a fire, and the city's population has exploded to 1.3 million, overburdening the sanitation and health facilities. Nonetheless, Manaus still serves as a base for tourist excursions exploring the mid-Amazon region. Day trips can be made by riverboat to visit villages built on stilts or to hike through the jungle on foot. Several jungle lodges in the vicinity also offer a wide variety of rain forest programs. The city itself, though rather dirty, is worth exploring. Although Manaus is 1,000 mi/1,609 km inland, huge ocean liners dock there to distribute their cargo throughout the Amazon basin, and it's fascinating to watch them unload. Make a point to see the newly renovated 1892 Opera House, Teatro Amazonas (check to see who's singing; the world's most famous stars have performed there).

Between Belem and Manaus is Amazonia National Park, a huge new national reserve of dense rain forest. As of now, there are only very basic cabins in the park itself (visiting scientists have priority for their use), but there are hotels in the nearby town of Itaituba. During the rainy season (February–April), the rain forest can be toured by boat; during the drier period, hiking trails can be walked.

Iguacu Falls

Brasilia Brasilia, the nation's capital (pop. 1,598,000), was built near the center of the country a little more than 30 years ago, replacing Rio as the capital. A well-planned city on paper, in reality it falls short of its promise. Don't go out of your way to visit Brasilia, but if you do go, one day will be more than ample. Plan just enough time to see some of the more impressive buildings: the Palacio do Congresso (Capitol Building), Palacio do Planalto (presidential mansion and office) and Palacio da Justica (Supreme Court, with artificial cascades). See the National Cathedral, built in the shape of a crown with angels suspended within. A good overall view of the city is available from atop the main television tower. From there you'll see that the city is shaped like an airplane.

Costa Verde The Costa Verde (Green Coast) offers relaxing day and weekend trips from Rio and Sao Paulo. The drive from Rio to the city of Santos is beautiful: small beaches line one side of the road, jungle and mountains the other. Visitors pass cattle ranches and quaint 17th-century towns. Santos itself is Brazil's leading commercial port — both Santos and next-door neighbor Guaruja afford a wide range of nice beaches and boat tours.

East of Santos is the popular beach resort of Ubatuba. Also in this area is the colonial town of Parati (settled in 1650).

Florianopolis Imagine Bavaria by a tropical bay and you'll have some idea of Florianopolis. The scenic spots are on the island part of the city (attractive colonial buildings, 400-year-old forts, baroque churches and the best surfing in Brazil island). Florianopolis' nightlife is active and the bierhalls are popular meeting spots (the city produces some of Brazil's best beer).

Iguacu Falls Located near the junction of Brazil, Argentina and Paraguay, Iguacu Falls (pronounced eeh-gwa-SUE) is a must-see. There are 275 falls in all, stretching 2 mi/4 km from bank to bank and reaching a height of 300 ft/90 m. We suggest flying from Rio, overnighting at the falls, then flying to another destination. That way, you'll have a lot of time at the falls, which look and photograph differently in different light. The adventurous can go by train, road or riverboat; it takes about two days from Rio. A four-minute helicopter ride goes up the river into the falls and over them, then circles and comes down into the falls again before landing.

An easy side trip is to the vast Itaipu Dam built jointly by Brazil and Paraguay. It is the largest hydroelectric works in the world (55 stories high and 5 mi/8 km wide).

Olinda

Olinda has the best-preserved colonial buildings in Brazil. The city's architecture reflects both Portuguese and Dutch heritage (the Dutch invaded and occupied the area in the 17th century). Olinda is usually seen as a day trip from Recife.

Ouro Preto

Unlike many other colonial towns in the country, Ouro Preto is largely unaffected by encroaching modern buildings and skyscrapers. For this reason, it is considered one of the two best-preserved colonial towns of the nation (the other is Olinda). Ouro Preto has cobblestone streets, baroque churches and scenic ruins.

Pantanal

The Pantanal is one of the world's great wildlife reserves. A trip there should be booked through an adventure tour operator. The Pantanal abounds with birdlife (especially waterfowl), and because the terrain is largely open, it's easier to spot some animals there than in the jungles of the Amazon. Fishing is excellent, with more than 350 varieties of fish, some weighing up to 175 lb/80 kg. The reserve has alligators, deer, armadillos and capybaras (the world's largest rodent).

Petropolis

Set in the cool hills north of Rio, this Swiss-style town was the summer retreat for the last emperor of Brazil. Petropolis' main attractions are its Crystal Palace, Gothic cathedral, Museu Imperial (imperial crown and robes — the marble floors are special, too) and the house of Alberto Santos-Dumont. (Brazilians claim Santos-Dumont to be the inventor of the airplane.)

Recife

Called the Venice of Brazil for its canals and bridges, Recife is dirtier than the Italian version (but not by much). Recife has a number of interesting museums, including ones devoted to clay, sugar, trains and subjects such as slavery, archaeology and geography. There are also 17th- and 18th-century churches with beautiful wood carvings and gilded altars. Recife has a fantastic Carnival that rivals those in Rio and Salvador.

Rio De Janeiro

This large city sits on one of the world's most magnificent harbors — arrive by ship, if possible. Upon arrival, almost everyone heads up to the rocky outcropping known as Sugar Loaf Mountain for a spectacular 360-degree view of Rio and Guanabara Bay (a gondola/cable system takes you up and back). The view of Rio at your feet is stupendous, but for an even higher perspective, go up Corcovado Mountain: It's the site of the 130-ft/40-m Christ the Redeemer statue, which overlooks the city. From Corcovado, you'll see that the city is divided by a mountain range into two zones: the southern zone holds most of the city's sights.

Rio, you'll soon find, is not only lovely, it's lively. Cariocas, as Rio natives are called, are fun loving, and it's important to allow time to join in activities where you'll meet the people: Spend a day on one of its famous beaches (Copacabana, Flamengo, Leblon or Ipanema), attend a soccer game at Maracana Stadium (the largest in the world — it holds 200,000 fans!) or plan a night of club hopping. There are several museums in town, covering everything from classical composer Villa-Lobos (his possessions and scores) to the campy Carmen Miranda Museum (the actress' costumes and trademark fruit-basket headdresses).

Every year, during the four days preceding Ash Wednesday, the most chaotic celebration in any city in the world gets under way: Carnival. Everybody is out dancing in the streets. Participants plan (and save up for) their colorful, exquisite costumes for a year, and when the time comes, the streets are filled with a mass of costumed revelers. Carnival is a must — at least once in a lifetime. The best costumes can be seen on Sunday and Monday of Carnival week in the specially constructed Sambadrome. The shows start at 8 pm and continue until 8 am! Buy your tickets well in advance.

Salvador

This striking city, Brazil's longtime colonial capital, lies on beautiful Santos Bay. A strong African influence derives from the slaves brought to work in the sugarcane fields starting more than 400 years ago. Salvador is divided into an upper and lower section, and

Rio de Janeiro

Official Name: Federative Republic of Brazil.

Visa Info: Passport, visa and proof of onward passage and sufficient funds are required of citizens of the U.S. and Canada.

Health Certificates: Yellow-fever certificates required of those arriving from infected areas and endemic zones. The U.S. Centers for Disease Control recommends yellow-fever vaccinations for all persons over nine months of age who travel into rural Brazil.

Capital: Brasilia.

Population: 162,660,000.

Size: 3,290,000 sq mi/8,511,065 sq km.

Language: Portuguese.

Climate: Tropical, with temperate zone in the south.

Economy: Industry, agriculture, tourism.

Government: Republic.

Religion: Roman Catholic, Protestant, Animist.

Currency: Real (RI). 100 centavos = 1 RI. Credit cards and traveler's checks accepted in urban and tourist areas. AE, DI, MC and VI.

Time Zones: In eastern Brazil, 3 hours behind Greenwich mean time; 2 hours ahead of eastern standard time. Daylight saving time is observed Nov–Mar.

Electricity: 110 volts in Rio, Sao Paulo and the South. 127 volts in Salvador and Manaus. 220 volts in Brasilia, Recife and the Northeast.

Departure Tax: US$17.

the enormous Lacerda elevator, which goes from one level to the other, affords outstanding views. Multicolored homes, red-tiled roofs, a great market, twisting and narrow cobblestone streets, great beaches, *terreiros* (voodoo worship houses) and about 300 churches make this an excellent place to stay for a few nights. No tour of the city is complete without seeing the Igreja de Sao Francisco — although relatively plain on the outside (as are most Portuguese churches in Brazil), the inside is covered in gold leaf and is as ornate as it is beautiful. Shopping is good on Rua Alfredo do Brito and exceptional at the Mercado Modelo (good African and Brazilian souvenirs). Pelourinho, one of the oldest areas in

town, has colonial architecture and a pillory (where slaves and prisoners were tortured). The city's culture is celebrated in the Museu da Cidade (Yoruba tribal displays) and the Afro-Brazilian Museum (African displays). Salvador also has a great Carnival celebration, though it's not as flashy as the one in Rio.

Sao Paulo Sao Paulo is the largest city in South America. Don't go expecting to see a beautiful city like Buenos Aires or Rio. While there are lovely neighborhoods, it seems as if everything is made of concrete — even the fire hydrants! The primary reason to go is to sample its wide variety of international restaurants, fabulous shopping and very active nightlife.

The city is centered around the Praca da Se (*praca*, pronounced PRAH-sah, means square). It was near the square's cathedral that the city was founded in 1554 by Jesuit priests. But the sentimental heart of the metropolis, featured in poetry and song, is the intersection of Avenida Sao Joao and Avenida Ipiranga. Nearby is one of the city's loveliest parks, the Praca da Republica, and the tallest building in town (Edificio Italia). Skyscraper-lined Avenida Paulista, once the street where coffee barons lived in splendid residences, is now the commercial center of the city. For an idea of what a millionaire's mansion looked like, visit the McDonald's on Avenida Paulista (the hamburger chain restored one of the last remaining manors for its location).

Ethnic neighborhoods provide the setting for exceptional restaurants and the city's active nightlife. Some of the more interesting areas are Bela Vista and Bixiga (both Italian), Vinte e Cinco de Marco (Arabic), Bom Tiro (Jewish) and Liberdade (Japanese). Liberdade has a colorful street fair on Sunday mornings.

Itinerary

The following is a bare-bones itinerary for first-time visitors to Brazil: You'll enter in Manaus — saving Rio for later will make that city seem all the fresher when compared with other parts of the country.

Day 1 — Arrive Manaus and tour the city.

Day 2 — Day trip on the Amazon River.

Day 3 — Fly to Salvador, afternoon city tour.

Day 4 — Salvador.

Day 5 — Morning flight to Brasilia, city tour, then afternoon flight to Rio.

Day 6 — Rio.

Day 7 — Rio.

Day 8 — Fly to Sao Paulo.

Day 9 — Sao Paulo.

Day 10 — Fly to Iguacu Falls.

Day 11 — Morning flight to Rio or Sao Paulo and depart Brazil.

Climate/When to Go

March–November is the driest and best time to visit. In southern Brazil, the evenings and winter days can be fairly cool, and sweaters or light coats are needed. The Amazon region is always hot and humid, but the best time to see it is July–August.

Transportation

Varig, VASP, American, Delta, Tower Air and United fly nonstop from the U.S. Canadian Airlines International flies nonstop from Canada. Major South American carriers connect through their hub cities.

Sao Paulo's Guarulhos International Airport (GRU) is 15 mi/25 km from the city and Galeao International Airport (GIG), is 15 mi/24 km from Rio de Janeiro. An air shuttle (Air Bridge) flies every half hour from downtown Rio's Santos-Dumont Airport (SDU) to Sao Paulo's Congonhas Airport (CGH). Within Brazil, several local airlines offer flights throughout the country (domestic flights are expensive and the distances large). If you're undertaking extensive travel within Brazil, consider buying Varig or Transbrasil airpasses, which provide discounted travel on domestic routes. Many cruise lines offer extended tours to both the Amazon region and Rio (especially during Carnival). Specialty tour companies offer unique cruises along the Amazon and the coast of Brazil.

Roads between the major southern cities are quite good, but we don't recommend driving north of Salvador. The only decent train is between Rio and Sao Paulo.

Accommodations

Outside the major cities, stay in the best hotel in town — even so, you may find it to be more basic than desired. Along the Amazon, try to book a jungle lodge.

Health Advisories

Things are improving, but sanitary conditions in most restaurants are not up to Western standards, especially outside the larger cities in the south. Avoid local dairy products and assume the tap water is unsafe outside the larger cities of southern Brazil. Vaccines against diseases such as hepatitis, typhoid and polio may be recommended. Malaria is present in northern Brazil and Amazonia. Be aware that Brazil ranks third in known cases of AIDS.

What to Buy

The best buys are shoes, leather goods, coffee, ceramics (including lovely tiles), sculpture, Indian artifacts, *papagaio* (parrot) kites, hammocks, rosewood products and semiprecious and precious stones (amethyst, opal, topaz, citrine, tourmaline, emerald, etc.). Brazilian gold is generally 18K. Don't neglect Brazilian music — samba and *chorinho* are just part of the story. Amazon souvenirs, available in Manaus, include snakeskins, interesting local garb, *balangandas* (to ward off evil spirits) and piranhas (deceased and shellacked).

What to Eat

Try Brazilian cuisine, especially *feijoada* (a delicious mix of rice, black beans, pork, beef and greens). Tropical fruits and fruit juices are wonderful and unlike anything in the temperate zones of the world. Carnivores will love the *churrascarias*, restaurants specializing in delicious grilled meat. The farther north one goes, the less European, the more African and spicier the food is. The country's favorite soft drink is Guarana. Brazilians like their coffee hot, sweet and strong.

Travel Tips for the Client

Crime is a problem in the country's main cities. We recommend that travelers exercise caution . . . Do remember that the language of Brazil is Portuguese, not Spanish . . . Do try to see a soccer game. It's quite a spectacle, with flags waving and tens of thousands dancing, cheering and singing. Brazilians consider themselves the best players in the world (they won the World's Cup in 1994) and take the sport very seriously. . . .

Brazil

Review Questions

1. What region features Brazil at its wettest and wildest? What huge new natural reserve is located there?

2. How would you describe to a client the scenery on the drive from Rio de Janeiro to Santos?

3. Why would a visitor want to spend a lot of time at Iguacu Falls?

4. What are the two best-preserved colonial towns in Brazil?

5. Why can wildlife viewing be easier in the Pantanal than in the Amazon?

6. With which city in Italy is Recife compared? Why?

7. During Carnival in Rio, where would you suggest a client go to see the best costumes?
   On which days of the week?

8. From what does Salvador's strong African influence derive?

9. What is the primary reason for a tourist to go to Sao Paulo?

10. What spectacle will a visitor witness at a Brazilian soccer game?

Brazil

Map Skills Exercise

Match the tourist destination listed below with the corresponding letter on the map. You can use each letter only once.

1. _____ Amazonia National Park
2. _____ Manaus
3. _____ Belem
4. _____ Iguacu Falls
5. _____ Rio de Janeiro
6. _____ Salvador
7. _____ Recife
8. _____ Brasilia
9. _____ Sao Paulo
10. _____ Pantanal

Selling Exercise

The travel editor of a local newspaper asks you to write a 100-word story for the next edition of the paper about your recent trip to Brazil. Be sure to include in the story reasons why visitors planning to travel to Brazil should book through your agency.

Argentina

and Chile

Selling Points

Buenos Aires, Iguazu Falls, cattle ranches, the Andes, historical sites, Tierra del Fuego, beaches, shopping, skiing, nightlife, spectacular scenery, fishing and casinos are Argentina's main attractions. Argentina has something for just about everyone. The only people not to send are those who demand five-star accommodations everywhere they go.

Fascinating Facts About Argentina

There are no liquor laws in Argentina. In theory, bars can stay open 24 hours a day and serve anyone of any age . . . Buenos Aires has the largest number of psychoanalysts per capita of any city in the world . . . Argentines are quick to tell you that their country is on the wrong continent — they despise other Latin Americans (who return the favor) and consider themselves to be misplaced Europeans . . . So many Italians have migrated to Argentina that the Spanish spoken in the country has a slight Italian accent. . . .

When people think of Argentina, they think of dancing the tango in a smoke-filled club, watching Gauchos herding cattle across the pampas . . . and learning of yet another repressive regime. While those elements continue to dominate people's perceptions of Argentina, much more is omitted than included. Argentina is a sophisticated, stylish and cosmopolitan country whose last two administrations broke away from the tradition of governing through intimidation. The nation, like the United States, Canada and Australia, is proud of its immigrant heritage; it has been said that Argentina is a nation of Italians who speak Spanish and think they're British.

The land is as diverse as the population. In the north are subtropical lowlands, but the Andes Mountains rise above much of the length of the nation; rolling, rich soil blankets the central pampas region, giving way to the bleak, windswept Patagonian steppe and Tierra del Fuego in the south. Argentina is one of the most developed countries in Latin American and half the population considers itself middle class. To get a good sense of the soul of Argentina, just sit in a Buenos Aires coffee bar and watch the citizens carry on — walking, talking, conspiring, dreaming and reminiscing.

What to Do There

Bariloche   One of the must-see sights in Argentina is the ski resort of Bariloche. This Andean village looks like it belongs in Switzerland — and like Swiss ski resorts, Bariloche can be quite crowded in high season (though it's a bit run-down in comparison with Swiss resorts). It's easy to see why so many people go — it's in an unbelievably beautiful area. Located on the shores of a lake, Bariloche is surrounded by dense forests and 12,000-ft/3,660-m mountains. Bariloche itself is filled with Swiss chalet-type hotels. Our favorite activities (and everyone else's) can be found on the main street and the slopes — shopping and skiing. Each day you're there, stop in a different chocolate shop. A trip to Bariloche can be combined with an excursion into

Chile through some of the most beautiful, peaceful scenery in South America. Not to be missed!

Buenos Aires

Buenos Aires is a very cosmopolitan capital city — it has areas that remind us of London, Paris or Rome. While its once-immaculate parks, gardens and colonial/ modern architecture have begun to show signs of wear and neglect, much that is beautiful remains, and its hotels, nightlife and restaurants are as stellar as ever.

A first-time visitor to Buenos Aires should begin with an escorted city tour, making sure it includes the main neighborhoods, downtown public buildings, several museums and its extraordinary

Downtown Plaza, Buenos Aires

cemetery. Other things to do and see include the National Museum of Fine Arts (housing both international and Argentine works), at least one of the many cathedrals (possibly the Cathedral of Nuestra Señora de la Mercéd) and a ride down the world's widest avenue, Avenida 9 de Julio. In the heart of the city is the Casa Rosada (Pink House — the office of the president) and the Plaza de Mayo, where the grieving mothers of the *desaparecidos* (the disappeared) continue their vigil every Thursday. (Thousands of opponents of the government disappeared when the military ruled the country in the late 1970s and early 1980s.) Near downtown are the Costanera Sur Natural Park and the English Tower (a replica of Big Ben — there's a large British colony in the city).

After these highlights, it's time for an in-depth exploration of B.A. (as it's often called by the Anglo residents) by foot, bus or horse-drawn carriage. Try the subway; the A Line has charming old cars with wood and leather interiors. You'll find that B.A. is a city of contrasts; tall, modern steel-and-glass skyscrapers sit alongside century-old colonial-style buildings. Perhaps the most colorful neighborhood is the Italian section (La Boca), along the waterfront. The city is famed for its nightlife, especially in the neighborhood of La Boca; bars and clubs where the tango can be enjoyed are plentiful.

The modern art museum is in the district of San Telmo, an area also known for its antique shops and colonial buildings. Stop by or attend a performance at the Colon Theater, B.A.'s opera house. Also go to Recoleta to see the cemetery — look for the ornate mausoleums of the rich and famous. Evita Peron is buried there.

Glaciers National Park

This park, a UNESCO World Heritage site, features some of the most spectacular sights in the country. Perito Moreno Glacier cuts through Lake Argentino, breaking up about once every four or five years when lake water undermines it. This loud spectacle produces many icebergs, but its occurrence cannot be predicted. About 8 mi/13 km outside the town of Calafate are some caves with ancient Indian paintings, though visitors need special permission to view them. The area teems with bird life. In the far north of the park are Mt. Fitzroy and Cerro Torre, popular with climbers and hikers. Calafate is also a good jumping-off point for tours to the Torres del Paine National Park, across the border in Chile.

Iguazu Falls

These spectacular waterfalls can be visited from the Brazilian or Argentine side; either is equally impressive. While the falls are seen more easily from Brazil, the paths, jungle and sunset views are better in Argentina. Iguazu should not be missed: Made up of 275 cascades spanning a distance of 2 mi/3 km and rising up to 300 ft/91 m high, it's one of the most impressive sights in South America.

Mar del Plata

Mar del Plata graces the Argentine Riviera. Beautiful beaches stretch 14 mi/23 km along the Atlantic; the seafood is fabulous and the fishing excellent. Nightlife centers on the world's largest casino (it's mostly roulette — and black tie is de rigueur). The best time to visit is from December to March. Be forewarned that the water can become quite chilly by the end of the summer in the southern hemisphere (March).

Argentina and Chile

⊛ Capital
■ □ City/Site
▲ National Park
----- River

FALKLAND ISLANDS/ISLAS MALVINAS
(UNITED KINGDOM)

| Km | 0 | 200 | 400 |
| Mi | 0 | 200 | 400 |

Copyright Weissmann Travel Reports

set between Puerto Madryn and Viedma, is a marine-life preserve for sea elephants, sea lions, maras (huge rabbits), Magellanic penguins (best seen October–April), rheas (ostrichlike birds) and other animals, as well as whales and migratory birds.

Tierra del Fuego (Land of Fire)

A fascinating region, Tierra del Fuego ranges from barren, desolate landscape raked clean by high winds to beautiful pine and beech forests, beautiful blue lakes and snow-capped mountain peaks (there's good trout fishing, too). The area, shared by Argentina and Chile, is actually on an island at the southern tip of South America. Most people use the town of Ushuaia on the Beagle Channel as a base. Activities include hiking and ferry rides to Isla de los Lobos (sea lions), through the Beagle Channel, to Isla de Pajaros (Bird Island), Martello Island (penguins) and Martial Glacier (you can ski on the glacier — it has a chairlift).

Itinerary

Most week-to-10-day itineraries give three full days in B.A. Lovely as that city is, we think that's a sin — there's much more to see in Argentina. Our minimum itinerary includes the following:

Day 1 — Arrive Buenos Aires.

Day 2 — B.A.

Day 3 — Fly to Iguazu Falls.

Day 4 — Fly to Mar del Plata.

Day 5 — Mar del Plata. Day trip to visit an *estancia* (ranch).

Day 6 — Fly to Bariloche.

Day 7 — Bariloche.

Day 8 — Vicinity around Bariloche.

Day 9 — Depart Argentina, preferably overland to Puerto Montt, Chile.

Climate/When to Go

Climates range from hot and humid in the north to cold and rainy in the south (the seasons are reversed from the northern hemisphere). Buenos Aires' climate is

Patagonia

Beginning in central Argentina and stretching to the Straits of Magellan, Patagonia is a haven for naturalists. Covering 28% of the nation's territory, it's filled with unique animals and flora, windswept barren land, lakes and unspoiled nature. Because it lacks accommodations and travel facilities, we suggest taking an escorted tour if going to the region. Along the Patagonian coast, you may want to stay in Puerto Madryn while visiting the nearby Valdes Peninsula. This fascinating peninsula,

similar to that in Washington, D.C., but with milder winters. Generally, the best time to go is October–April.

Transportation

Few North American carriers provide direct service, but the national airline Aerolineas Argentinas and a few South American airlines join the carriers that do. Ezeiza airport (EZE), for long-distance international traffic, is located 22 mi/35 km from the center of Buenos Aires. Numerous cruise lines include various Argentine ports on South American or around-the-world itineraries. Several national carriers offer air service between major destinations within the country. We feel that first-time visitors should take either an escorted or hosted tour to get an inexpensive overview. During the peak of summer (December–March), specialty cruises depart for Antarctica and the disputed Falkland/Malvinas Islands.

Accommodations

Accommodations range from deluxe, five-star international properties to *estancias* (ranch houses) to below-standard hotels. Some of the quaint inns and rural hotels are more than adequate, fairly inexpensive and fun to stay in, but look at a room before putting any money down — some are filthy. To minimize the potential for problems, stay in as deluxe a property as budget permits in the countryside.

Health Advisories

Competent doctors, dentists and specialists are available in Buenos Aires. There are no particular health risks in Buenos Aires, and no special precautions need be taken there — the tap water is as safe as anywhere else. But it's best to use discretion in rural areas.

What to Buy

Buenos Aires truly offers excellent, high-quality shopping at reasonable prices for leather goods, gems and brand-name products such as Gucci, Dior, etc. Other items to look for include rugs, Gaucho souvenirs, sheepskin products, wines, guitars, art, handicrafts and vicuna products (high-quality wool from a llamalike creature). You also may want to get a pair of Gaucho trousers — *bombachas* — or perhaps a poncho.

Geostats

Official Name: Republic of Argentina.

Visa Info: Passports needed by U.S. and Canadian citizens. Visitors on business require a business visa.

Health Certificates: None required. Contact health authorities for latest information.

Capital: Buenos Aires.

Population: 33,406,000.

Size: 1,065,189 sq mi/2,758,733 sq km. About four times the size of Texas.

Language: Spanish.

Climate: Varied, predominantly temperate, arid in the southeast, subantarctic in the southwest.

Economy: Agriculture, minerals, industry.

Government: Republic.

Religion: Roman Catholicism.

Currency: Argentine peso (ARS). 100 centavos = 1 ARS.

Time Zone: 2 hours ahead of EST. 3 hours behind GMT.

Electricity: 220 volts.

What to Eat

The Argentines have excellent, well-seasoned foods. We like *empanadas, bife de chorizo* (huge two-inch-thick steaks) and other beef (especially ribs), fish, barbecued meats, *puchero de gallina* (a combination of almost everything imaginable), *panqueques* (great crepe-type dessert) and *parrillada* (the national dish, made with assorted cuts of barbecued beef). Try some of the rich desserts and pastries. Italian restaurants tend to be very good. In Latin fashion, mealtimes tend to be much later than is customary for North Americans. Lunch is around 2 pm, with dinner starting at 10 pm.

Travel Tips for the Client

Do change Canadian dollars at the Royal Bank of Canada in Buenos Aires — many other banks won't accept the currency . . . Don't mail things that really matter — the Argentine postal service is reliably unreliable . . . Don't go to major areas without a hotel reservation, as bookings in the resort areas are heavy during their particular seasons. . . .

Chile

Chile is 2,705 mi/4,329 km long (about the distance from San Diego, California, to Charleston, South Carolina), but averages only 100 mi/160 km in width. Desert dominates the north, tundra the south, and the center has many fertile valleys and lovely scenery. (Santiago, the capital, is in the central region.) The nation's coastline is indented by many bays and fjords, while the eastern regions rise into the Andes Mountains. Some people associate all of South America with the Amazon jungle and heat, but there is no jungle in Chile — in fact, much of the land can be freezing cold.

What to Do There

Easter Island   This unique 45-sq-mi/115-sq-km island, 2,200 miles/3,540 km off Chile's coast, is often called the world's largest open-air museum. It's the site of hundreds of *moais,* huge images of gods carved centuries ago from volcanic stone by Polynesian settlers. They set the *moais* all around the island, facing the sea. Easter Island is usually reached via Santiago or Pepeete on the island of Tahiti in French Polynesia.

Glacier Cruise   In our opinion, a cruise through Chile's Inside Passage, the Beagle Channel and around the Cape Horn passage is a wondrous combination of the best of the Alaskan Inside Passage, the Nor-

---

Fascinating Facts About Chile

Chile, along the western coast of South America, is farther east than Miami, Florida . . . The word Chile has no connection with the English word "chilly" — Chile's name is said to have come from the cry of a native bird, heard by Spanish explorers . . . Chile's clear desert air has made it the center of astronomical research in the Southern Hemisphere. Three of the world's largest observatories are in the country. . . .

---

wegian fjords, Antarctica and southern New Zealand. Cruise lines depart from Puerto Montt. Glaciers, unusual fauna and flora, fishing villages, fjords and icebergs combine to dazzle visitors.

Lake District   We recommend seeing this very green, very pretty area in southern Chile on a package tour because both bus and hotel space are often very limited. We like to see the district as a trip from Argentina.

Portillo   This world-famous ski resort offers excellent skiing (both downhill and cross country), ice-skating on Laguna del Inca and splendid mountain views. The ski season is June–September, with August being best. While there, you'll also want to see the Christ of the Andes statue atop a nearby 12,000-ft/3,650-m mountain.

Santiago   The snow-capped Andes provide the backdrop for this large and cosmopolitan capital city. See the Statue of the Virgin atop 1,122-ft/340-m Cerro San Cristobal and observe the city below. Other sights and activities include Santa Lucia Hill (art museum and gardens), Santa Lucia (Spanish fortress and garden — one of the most romantic spots in the city), the Museum of Natural History (exhibiting Easter Island artifacts) and the cathedral (with a painting of the Last Supper). The soul of the city can be found at the Plaza de Armas, especially on a Sunday when families put on their best and head to the plaza to listen to music from the bandstand or watch the street performers that crowd the square. Don't miss a self-guided walking tour of the Bellavista neighborhood, a center for nightlife, art galleries, jewelry shops, theater-cafes and good restaurants.

Vina del Mar   Chile's chief seaside resort offers golf, tennis, very nice hotels, casinos, parks, shopping and good nightlife. Most people go there to lie on the beach (the main season is January–March), but before you swim you ought to know that the ocean is cold, cold, cold!

Travel Tips for the Client

Rainbow trout caught in Chilean lakes can easily weigh 8–14 lb/3–6 kg. The best freshwater fishing is November–March. Some of the world's biggest marlin have been caught off the northern coast . . .Among Chilean specialty tours are those focusing on sheep breeding, wine production, desert flora/fauna, trout fishing and geology . . . Chilean traditional music and dance can be enjoyed in several Santiago nightclubs. . . .

Argentina and Chile

Review Questions

1. In what ways does Bariloche resemble a Swiss ski resort?

2. What should an escorted city tour of Buenos Aires include?

3. Why would a tourist prefer to see Iguazu Falls from the Argentine rather than the Brazilian side?

4. In what region of Argentina is Mar del Plata? What are the best months of the year for a client to visit this city? What season is it in Argentina during these months?

5. Why should you probably recommend that a client take an escorted tour of Patagonia? What are the region's attractions?

6. What does "Tierra del Fuego" mean in English? How might you describe this fascinating region to a client?

7. In Argentina, what are the customary times for lunch and dinner?

8. What is Easter Island the site of?

9. What sights combine to dazzle visitors on a Chilean glacier cruise?

10. What provides the backdrop for the city of Santiago?

Argentina and Chile

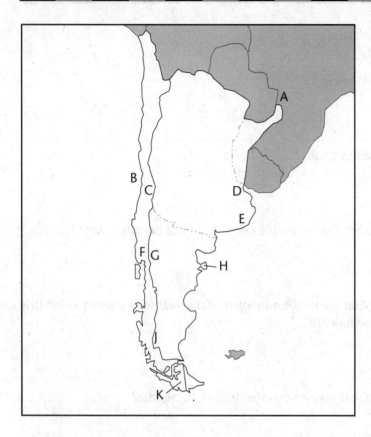

Map Skills Exercise

Match the tourist destination listed below with the corresponding letter on the map. You can use each letter only once.

1. _____ Iguazu Falls
2. _____ Buenos Aires
3. _____ Glaciers National Park
4. _____ Santiago
5. _____ Chile's Lake District
6. _____ Tierra del Fuego
7. _____ Bariloche
8. _____ Mar del Plata
9. _____ Vina del Mar
10. _____ Valdes Peninsula

Selling Exercise

The members of a sports and outdoors club want to visit South America, and they have come to see you for suggestions. You recommend that they tour Argentina and Chile because of the fantastic sports and outdoor opportunities in those countries. Prepare a 10-day itinerary for this group focusing on sports and outdoor experiences.

Peru

and Ecuador

Peru is among the most fascinating destinations in South America, offering tremendous diversity, fascinating history and spectacular sights. The contrast between old and new runs throughout the land: Poncho-clad Indians walk their llamas through modern cities, past Spanish cathedrals built on the foundations of ancient Incan ruins. Coastal deserts give way to the towering Andes, which descend into some of the densest jungle anywhere. And you can stay in a splendid colonial mansion while visiting Machu Picchu, one of the greatest of all ancient ruins.

Physically, Peru is divided into three distinct geographic regions: the extremely arid coastal desert, where most of the major cities are located; the Andean Highlands, where mountain peaks soar above 20,000 ft/6,000 m and whose population is predominantly Indian; and the largely undeveloped Amazon jungle. Some trips to Peru include stopovers in neighboring Ecuador.

What to Do There

Cuzco (Qosqo)   Cuzco (the Inca word means "navel," or center) is the ancient capital of the Incas. Today, as the most-visited city in Peru, Cuzco serves as the center of the tourist trade. In 1534, the Spanish conqueror Pizarro invaded the city and began the long process of pulling down the Inca superstructure and building a new Cuzco on the foundations of the old. The Cathedral Plaza de Armas (which features a solid silver altar) is built on the base of the Inca Viracocha Palace, and the church of Santo Domingo is built over the Temple of the Sun.

Some of the most important sights include ancient Incan ruins such as the Tampumachay ritual bath, the Kenko (amphitheater of sacrifices) and the fortresses of Pucara and Sacsayhuama (whose three ancient central towers — a symbol of empire — were destroyed by the Spaniards). Visit the archaeological museum (excellent display of Incan artifacts) and walk around town — the residents are fascinating.

Note: It is imperative that visitors take it easy the first day or two in Cuzco. Cuzco's high altitude (11,024 ft/3,360 m) can cause altitude sickness.

Selling Points

Machu Picchu, ecotourism jungle adventures, train rides through the Andes, the Nazca Plains, Lake Titicaca, fishing and friendly people are among the chief attractions of Peru.

Send only those travelers with a strong interest in pre-Columbian history or who are looking for a jungle experience. Don't send travelers who require deluxe accommodations and North American or European standards of service or sanitation.

Fascinating Facts About Peru

The great Amazon jungle covers 60 percent of Peru . . . Archaeological exploration of Machu Picchu is not yet complete . . . Millions of years ago, the Amazon drained into the Pacific, through what is now Peru. Eons of continental drift and collision raised the Andes and reversed the course of the mighty river . . . While Spanish is the official language, millions of Peruvians still speak Quechua, the language of the Incas . . . Some of the largest trout in the world come from Lake Titicaca . . . Potatoes and squash were first cultivated in Peru. . . .

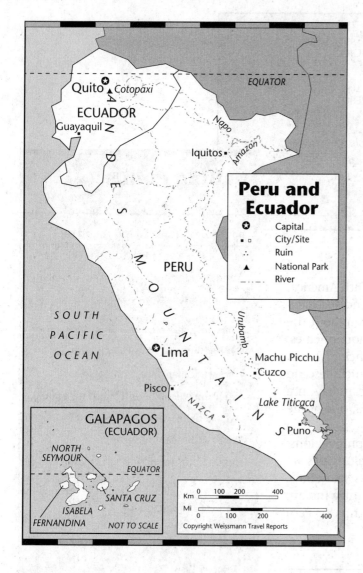

Lake Titicaca Area   Titicaca, the world's highest navigable lake, is a world unto itself — a definite must-see. The classic journey to see Titicaca begins with a 12-hour train ride from Cuzco.

Visit the lake area, then continue on to the city of La Paz in Bolivia. Stop overnight in Puno (known for its colorful fiestas and folk dances), one of the best places in Peru to buy Andean handicrafts (alpaca and vicuna sweaters, rugs, ponchos and tapestries).

Lima   Lima was founded by Francisco Pizarro in 1535. Built on never-developed land, Lima was designed to be a purely Spanish city in a conquered territory. The result turned out to be a rather drab and patched- together place (especially after 450 years of earthquakes).

The highlight of the capital is the outstanding collection of Incan artifacts in the basement vault of the privately owned Museo de Oro del Peru, or Peruvian Gold Museum. As magnificent as the gold collection is, it's sobering to realize that these are merely crumbs — the Spanish melted down or looted the really fine pieces.

Lima boasts 20 more museums, including the Museum of the Inquisition (torture instruments and carved ceiling), the Museo Taurino (bullfighting artifacts, including works by Goya) and the new Museo de la Nacion (National Musuem — tours available in English). Churches to see include the Catedral (Cathedral) on the Plaza de Armas (holding the reputed remains of Pizarro) and the Baroque Church of San Francisco (beautiful hand-carved ceilings and catacombs containing 70,000 skeletons). Nearby is the town of Pacacamac, which has some of the best Incan ruins in the world. The Temple of the Virgins, the Temple of the Sun and the excellent preserved irrigation systems are among its attractions.

Machu Picchu   Machu Picchu, The Lost City of the Incas, at an elevation of 8,000 ft/2,450 m, has the most spectacular setting of any ruin in the world — even those who don't normally like archaeology will be impressed by it. Discovered by Yale University's Hiram Bingham in 1911, Machu Picchu (Old Peak) is a place everyone must see at least once in their lives. The city sits on the spine of a ridge 2,000 ft/610 m above the rushing white waters of the Urubamba River, which makes a U-turn around the base of the site. Capping the end of the ridge is soaring Huaynu Picchu, a peak that offers a challenging climb — and a bird's-eye view of the complex as a reward.

Iquitos   Known as the gateway to the Amazon, Iquitos lies on the banks of the mile-wide Amazon River in the middle of the dense, flat jungle. This city has a fascinating floating market on the river and some interesting shops selling Indian goods. From Iquitos visitors can take escorted tours of one to seven days to the jungle lodges (about an hour away by boat) or the Amazon Biosphere Reserve. The latter, which requires a two-day trip into the interior, is both a tourist attraction and a research center. Jungle lodge tours leaving Iquitos usually include visits to the Jivaro or Yaguas Indians (who use blowguns) or the Chapras headhunters. Some offer crocodile sightseeing tours at night for the brave and/or foolish. Another way to experience the river is on a boat cruise. These vary in length. In addition to the tourist cruises, it's possible (sometimes) to secure accommodations on cargo/passenger boats that go where few tourists go.

Machu Picchu's grassy central court is surrounded by almost 200 houses, palaces and temples built from the precision-fitted stone blocks perfected by the Incas. Especially notable are the Temple of the Sun (the only round building), the Temple of the Three Windows (trapezoidal openings) and the Intihuatana (Hitching Post of the Sun), with its simple, clean lines. Stone and earth terraces (designed for farming and defense) descend down the mountainside around three-quarters of the city — the fourth side is a sheer cliff. To get to Machu Picchu, take the train from Cuzco. You can see the ruins on a day trip from Cuzco, but you'll always regret missing the eerie, misty sunset and an even more magical sunrise over the ruins if you don't spend the night.

Machu Picchu

Nazca Plain

The Nazca Lines on the plains south of Lima can be reached either by air or by a several-hour bus ride. Upon arrival, visitors board a small plane to fly over ruins and stylized designs of people, fish, birds and other, more abstract figures, ranging in size from 100 yd/90 m to several miles/kilometers in length. These enormous drawings were outlined by persons unknown. Since the designs can be seen clearly only from the air, the artists never saw their completed works, unless Erich von Daniken was right (his book, *Chariots of the Gods*, supposes ancient astronauts and landing fields). The lines were most likely made sometime between 900 BC and AD 630.

Itinerary

The eight-day itinerary outlined below is the minimum we recommend for this fascinating country. Because of security problems and the chronic lack of hotel space, we advise against independent travel for the time being.

Day 1 — Arrive Lima.

Day 2 — Day or overnight trip to the Nazca Plain. (If overnighting, extend the entire itinerary one more day.)

Day 3 — In the morning, fly to Cuzco. Rest and adjust to the altitude.

Day 4 — Morning train to Machu Picchu. Overnight.

Day 5 — Morning free, afternoon back to Cuzco.

Day 6 — Fly to Iquitos and transfer to a jungle lodge.

Day 7 — Tour the Amazon River basin.

Day 8 — Fly back to Lima and depart.

Climate/When to Go

There's no one perfect time to see them all, but in February and March the climate is fairly tolerable everywhere. Day temperatures along the coast and the Amazon region will be in the 80s F/28–32 C, with nights in the 60s F/15–22 C. In the mountains, highs will be in the low 60s F/15–22 C, with nights in the low 40s F/5–7 C. The greatest number of foreign tourists visit Peru between July and September, which is also when Peruvians take their vacations. It's best to avoid this time if possible, as prices are high and hotels crowded.

Geostats

Official Name: Republic of Peru.

Visa Info: Passport and proof of onward passage needed by U.S. and Canadian citizens for visit up to 30 days.

Health Certificates: Yellow-fever vaccination certificate required of all over six months of age if arriving from infected area.

Capital: Lima.

Population: 23,729,000.

Size: 496,222 sq mi/1,280,000 sq km. Slightly smaller than Texas, New Mexico and Arizona combined.

Languages: Spanish, Quechua.

Climate: Coastal area, arid and mild; Andes, temperate to frigid; eastern lowlands, tropically warm and humid.

Economy: Industry, agriculture.

Government: Republic.

Religions: Roman Catholicism, Protestantism.

Currency: nuevo sol (PES). 100 centavos = 1 PES.

Time Zone: EST. Five hours behind GMT.

Electricity: 220 volts.

Transportation

Lan Chile, Aero Peru, Aerolineas Argentinas, Varig and Faucett fly from the U.S., and Canadian Airlines International flies from Canada. Jorge Chavez International Airport (LIM), 7 mi/11 km from downtown, serves Lima. (Faucett also flies directly from Miami to Iquitos, for those who want to avoid the chaos of Lima.) Internally, Faucett and Aero Peru crisscross the country. Few cruise lines call in Callao, the port city of Lima. Intercity public buses should be avoided — they're often poorly maintained and moving targets for bandits. The trains are quite good but suffer from an abundance of thieves, especially to/from Cuzco.

Accommodations

Peru lends itself to hosted and escorted tours because of a lack of hotel space. Lima and Cuzco offer excellent first-class hotels, while other cities have adequate, fairly clean and well-managed properties. (When visiting Lima, many visitors stay in nearby Miraflores, where the ambiance is generally calmer and more upscale.)

Health Advisories

Peru's cholera pandemic continues. Caused by poor sanitation, cholera is spread by contaminated water, raw seafood and the unsanitary preparation of food. Most hot, freshly cooked food should be safe (especially if included on a package tour). Assume tap water and ice are unsafe. No matter how tempting it looks, it's best to stay away from the street food. When flying into high altitudes (such as Cuzco) allow a few days for your body to adjust. You may experience altitude sickness (nausea, headaches, insomnia, dizziness, chest pains), which can be serious.

What to Buy

Shop for alpaca and vicuna wool goods and rugs, gold, Incan walking sticks, miniature handmade statues, woven straw items, ponchos, llama rugs, cotton and linen fabrics, blankets, silver, tapestries, wood and leather products, Andean oil paintings, silkscreen prints and pottery. The gold- and silver-filigree work can be excellent.

What to Eat

Native Peruvian dishes are outstanding — but, to be on the safe side, dine in the better hotels and restaurants. Much of the food is highly seasoned (hot), but it's good and hearty. Try the local drinks (except for the wine, which is none too good).

Travel Tips for the Client

Don't allow yourself to be easily distracted by the action around you. Different tactics seem to go in and out of style among thieves, but their main objective is to divert your attention — staging a fight or accident, for example — so they can make their move when you're focused on something else . . . As in many Latin countries, tradition holds that unescorted women are disreputable and thus become the target of unwanted attention and actions. The best defense is to ignore all advances or comments. . . .

Ecuador

This small country packs together scenic and rugged coastline, stunning mountains and steamy jungles (a major tributary of the Amazon has its headwaters in Ecuador), all within a few hours of each other. It is also the home of the "Mecca" of biology: the Galapagos Islands, whose isolated and varied animal populations helped formed Charles Darwin's theory of evolution. Best of all, Ecuadoreans are hospitable and usually provide a warm welcome to visitors.

A unique crab in the Galapagos Islands

What to Do There

Galapagos Islands
Volcanic in origin, these islands are located 600 mi/970 km from the mainland and range from dense rain forest to stark, barren terrain. Travelers should familiarize themselves with what each island has to offer to ensure that they go to the ones they really want to see most. The islands themselves are interesting, but most people go to see rare flora and fauna: tortoises weighing nearly 600 lb/272 kg, marine iguanas, frigate birds, boobies, penguins, sea lions (they like to swim near divers) and big sunflowers. Four days on a cruise ship visiting the islands (usually two islands a day) can show visitors a lot, but those with a strong interest in nature might want to consider an adventure tour — five to seven days in small ships and yachts. The amount of time visitors can spend on the islands is regulated by the government. Prebook before leaving your home country to ensure a spot on the tour that sounds most satisfying (six months ahead is not too early). Many people go to Santa Cruz island, the administrative capital, to get a good overall introduction at the Charles Darwin Research Station. Birds and tortoises abound on Santa Cruz. Among the other major islands are Bartolome (Galapagos penguins on an almost lunar landscape); Fernandina (black volcanic rocks, marine iguanas, pelicans, sea lions, penguins); Floreana (flamingos, sea turtles, green- and white-sand beaches and coral reefs); Isabela (giant tortoises, pelicans, penguins, volcanoes, salt-lake crater); North Seymour (sea lions, blue-footed boobies and frigate birds); and Santiago (fur seals, herons, marine life). Be sure to use a reputable tour group — there are plenty of substandard ships floating around the islands.

Quito
This colonial city high in the Andes was founded in 1534. The architecture is a real treat, from its houses to its markets and plazas. Several cathedral interiors, in particular, are spectacular. Must-sees include the Church of San Francisco (art treasures) and Santo Domingo Church (decorative Moorish ceiling and a statue of the Virgin Mary given to the church by Charles V of Spain). The Central Bank Museum has an exceptional pre-Columbian display, while the Casa de la Cultura displays traditional clothing and musical instruments. The city is nestled in a basin surrounded by mountain peaks; on clear days the snow-covered summit of Mt. Pichincha can be seen. Be sure to spend time on cobblestone La Ronda Street, the oldest in town, and visit El Ejido Park.

For sport and relaxation, there are bullfights and casinos. Plenty of markets dot the area near Quito where Indians go to trade their wares — a good place to buy Ecuadorean crafts. A full-day trip could be made to Cotopaxi National Park where you can see Andean condors, pumas and Cotopaxi, the world's tallest active volcano (19,347 ft/5,897 m).

Travel Tips for the Client

Don't be surprised if you see oil rigs in a jungle clearing. Oil was discovered in the east in 1967 and now accounts for more than two-thirds of the nation's export earnings . . . Don't expect it to be hot along the equator; high altitude keeps things cool . . . Don't forget the departure tax (US$25). . . .

Peru and Ecuador

Review Questions

1. What are the three distinct geographic regions of Peru?

2. Why must visitors take it easy the first day or two in Cuzco?

3. What city is a good starting point for escorted tours to the Amazon jungle? What fascinating attraction does this city offer?

4. A visit to what lake in Peru is a must for every tourist?

5. What would a tourist go to Pachacamac, near Lima, to see?

6. How would you describe the setting of Machu Picchu to a client?

7. Why would you encourage a client to spend the night at Machu Picchu?

8. Why would you advise a client against independent travel in Peru?

9. What volcanic islands are located 600 miles/970 km off the mainland of Ecuador? Why should travelers familiarize themselves with each island before going? Why should they stick with a reputable tour group?

10. On clear days, what can be seen from the city of Quito?

Peru and Ecuador

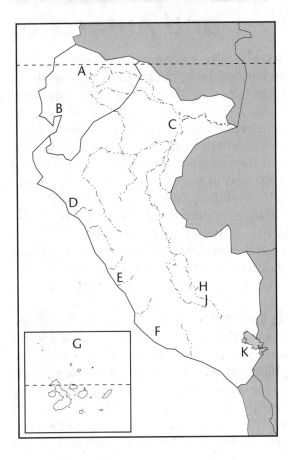

Map Skills Exercise

Match the tourist destination listed below with the corresponding letter on the map. You can use each letter only once.

1. _____ Galapagos
2. _____ Nazca Plain
3. _____ Lake Titicaca
4. _____ Machu Picchu
5. _____ Cuzco
6. _____ Quito
7. _____ Iquitos
8. _____ Lima

Selling Exercise

Your company will have a booth at a travel show whose theme is Exotic Vacation Destinations. At your booth, you will be promoting tours to the Galapagos Islands. You decide to design a poster for the booth that will capture the attention of passersby. Sketch the design for the poster on an 8½" by 11" sheet of paper and include any copy you'd want on the poster in your sketch.

South America Geofile

and Antarctica

Antarctica   Visitors usually see Antarctica on a cruise — sometimes encountering very rough seas — from Argentina or Chile. Once you reach the continent, you'll be rewarded with an incredible view of a world few people have seen: thousands of penguins, elephant seals and icebergs — and even volcanos and a thermal spring! If you are looking for unspoiled wilderness, you can hardly find a better place than this.

Anyone going there should be aware that little of the land mass of Antarctica is actually seen. Mostly, travelers see the islands and coastal areas — and besides, nearly all of Antarctica's land is hidden under thousands of feet of snow and ice. Also, most itineraries are at the mercy of the weather, which can change in a minute; experienced cruise ship operators are usually aware of this and ready to offer alternatives. In the past few years, Antarctica has become very popular, especially with travelers interested in ecotourism.

Bolivia   Bolivia is a country for adventuresome nature lovers who are interested in Latin American culture, who fully understand that they're going to a developing country and who can tolerate high altitudes, inconveniences and schedule delays.

Bolivia spreads across bleak mountains and arid plateaus to a fringe of lush jungle and cloud forests. Over the past few years, local tour groups have proliferated, with many offering hikes along its "Inca Trails," the twisting roads and pathways that knitted the ancient empire together. Other outings glide the remote jungle rivers or cross the nesting grounds of hundreds of species of tropical birds.

Colombia   The beauty of Colombia continues to be obscured by violence. The country seems caught in the tragic drama of narco-terrorists, guerrillas and corrupt politicians battling each other, judges, lawmakers and an innocent populace. The country's charms include mist-shrouded mountains capped with snow, golden-sand beaches and vast green stretches of rain forest. We love the magic of the place. It's probably best to stick to the safer destinations in the country. These include: Bogota (the capital), Barranquilla (known for its Carnival) and Cartagena (most popular resort and cruise destination).

Falklands   The Falklands made the news in the early 1980s after war broke out for control of the islands between Great Britain and Argentina. Most visitors would agree that, once they've arrived, the conflict feels quite distant — the rugged terrain, sloping glaciers and fields of grazing sheep are more likely to inspire reflection than violence. The islanders, for the most part, revel in the desolation and seem content to live in peace and quiet. We found them to be some of the most hospitable people in the world.

The Falklands reminds us of northern Scotland — bleak, isolated scenery and cold weather. They will appeal to travelers planning a vacation to Antarctica or on a South Atlantic cruise who also love nature and can enjoy a somewhat chilly but striking destination.

French Guiana   In the 18th century, when the French were searching for the worst place in the world to dump their prisoners, they chose French Guiana. The heat and humidity were atrocious, insects were everywhere, and the surrounding territory was so unforgiving that inmates preferred harsh prison life to freedom in the jungle. Although the prison on Devil's Island is no longer open, conditions in the country haven't changed that much.

If you're interested in exploring jungle rivers in motorized canoes and staying in South American tribal villages, you can have the cultural experience of a lifetime there. We would stress that this is not mainstream ecotourism: This is adventure.

Guyana   For most tourists, Guyana is an unbearable combination: high crime in the capital, poor transportation in the rural areas, mostly third-rate tourist facilities and hot, muggy weather. For some nature lovers, however, a trip to Guyana is worth the discomfort. The country has perfectly preserved virgin rain forest, spectacular waterfalls and a seemingly infinite variety of birds. Flying over the dramatic Kaieteur Waterfalls in the heart of the rain forest is truly memorable. Although primarily known in North America as the site of the Jonestown tragedy, it's also the country where the hammock was invented. English-speaking Guyana is culturally and politically regarded as part of the Caribbean, not Latin America.

Paraguay

Paraguay   As a travel destination, Paraguay doesn't offer much that can't be found elsewhere in South America, usually in a better version. It is, however, a friendly and unspoiled country. Paraguay's parks offer an impressive diversity (savanna, marshland and subtropical rain forest) that you can have pretty much to yourself. The country will also appeal to those excited by the idea of hearing Guarani Indians sing, watching Nanduti lace being made or taking a riverboat cruise on the off chance of seeing a jaguar or alligator.

Suriname   With only 13 countries in South America, Suriname still doesn't make our Top 10 list. It's not that Suriname has nothing to offer — it's just that the other countries have so much more. Suriname does hold unspoiled rain forests, a fairly relaxed atmosphere and a unique blend of Dutch, African and Amerindian cultures. Suriname will appeal to travelers who want to observe primitive cultures, yet who want to have the option of retreating to modern surroundings.

Uruguay   For the traveler, Uruguay is the poor cousin of Argentina and Brazil. Its gaucho ranches are smaller than Argentina's and its beaches less attractive than Brazil's. While Uruguay is actually a fairly pleasant place, we only recommend it to travelers who have already seen most of the other countries on the continent.

The nation's capital, Montevideo, is a city of beaches, restaurants, cafes, nightclubs and casinos. A pleasant way to start your tour of the capital is to see the entire city from the 11th-story terrace of the Palacio Municipal, located on the main street, Avenida 18 de Julio. See the old Spanish fort, the rose garden in Ordonez Park (more than 850 varieties of roses) and Casa Garibaldi (once the home of Italian freedom fighter Giuseppe Garibaldi).

Venezuela

As a tourist destination, this country has a lot going for it — the world's highest waterfall, miles of beaches, snow-capped mountains, rolling plains, tropical islands, mighty rivers and dense jungles. Venezuela is the most modern, cultured nation on the continent's north coast, thanks to the country's oil wealth. But that wealth is not evenly distributed and great poverty exists.

Angel Falls   The principal natural attraction in Venezuela is Angel Falls. It is the world's highest waterfall (so high that during the dry season the cascade can evaporate into mist before it reaches bottom). Angel Falls plunges 3,212 ft/979 m (15 times farther than Niagara!).

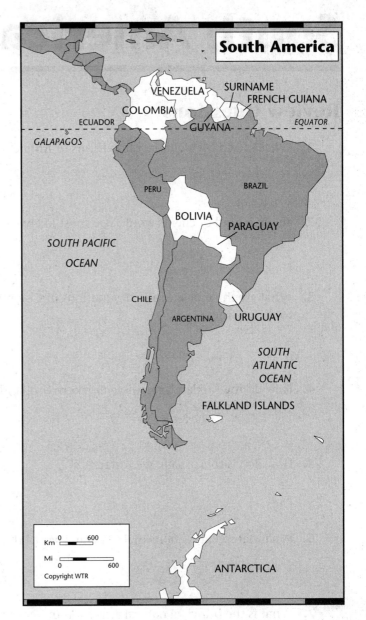

South America

Caracas   The capital and largest city is filled with the image and name of Simon Bolivar, the Great Liberator, who freed much of northern South America from Spanish rule. Visit Plaza Bolivar where you can relax amid the shade trees and squirrels. On the plaza are the Caracas Cathedral (featuring paintings by Rubens and Murillo, and the Bolivar family chapel) and Edificio La Francia (gold and jewelry shops and dealers). North of the plaza is the National Pantheon. (The Pantheon holds the tomb of Bolivar.) After a day of touring, enjoy the nightlife in Alta Mira. Though Caracas is not on the beach, about 12 mi/19 km away is the resort of Macuto, with its excellent beaches and hotels.

South America Geofile

Review Questions

1. What incredible sights reward visitors to Antarctica?

2. To what kind of clients would you most likely recommend Bolivia?

3. What are three of the safer destinations in Colombia? Why is it probably best for a visitor to stick to them?

4. How do the Falklands resemble northern Scotland?

5. How do visitors usually see Antarctica?

6. What natural attractions make Guyana worth the trip for some nature lovers?

7. What is the principal natural attraction in Venezuela? What is the name of a similar attraction in the United States? How do the two compare?

8. The culture of which country in South America is a unique blend of Dutch, African and Amerindian influences?

9. To a traveler, why might Uruguay seem like the poor cousin of Argentina and Brazil?

10. Who was Simon Bolivar? What city is filled with his image and name?

South America Geofile

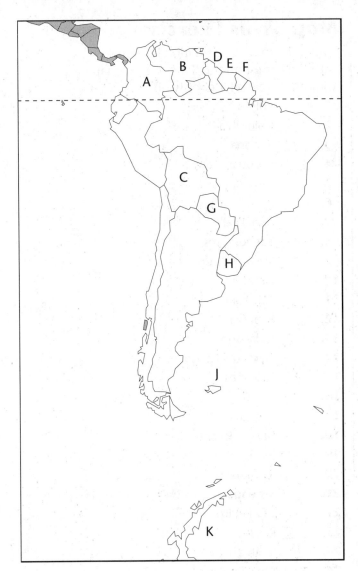

Map Skills Exercise

Match the tourist destination listed below with the corresponding letter on the map. You can use each letter only once.

1. _____ Bolivia
2. _____ Antarctica
3. _____ Venezuela
4. _____ Uruguay
5. _____ Paraguay
6. _____ Guyana
7. _____ French Guiana
8. _____ Colombia
9. _____ Falklands
10. _____ Suriname

Unit Review South America

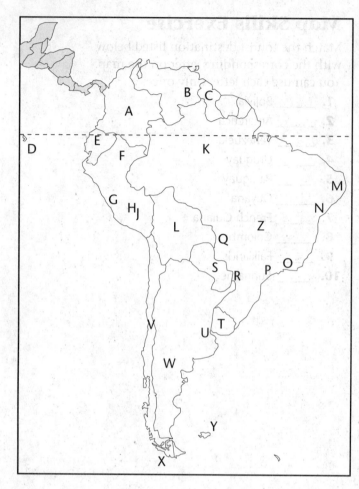

Map Skills Exercise

Match the tourist destination listed below with the corresponding letter on the map. You can use each letter only once.

1. _____ Bolivia
2. _____ Colombia
3. _____ Guyana
4. _____ Uruguay
5. _____ Paraguay
6. _____ Iguacu Falls
7. _____ Angel Falls
8. _____ Buenos Aires
9. _____ Rio de Janeiro
10. _____ Lima
11. _____ Patagonia
12. _____ Pantanal
13. _____ Galapagos
14. _____ Tierra del Fuego
15. _____ Falklands
16. _____ Quito
17. _____ Cuzco
18. _____ Machu Picchu
19. _____ Brasilia
20. _____ Salvador
21. _____ Santiago
22. _____ Sao Paulo
23. _____ Recife
24. _____ Iquitos
25. _____ Amazon River (in Brazil)

Unit Review South America

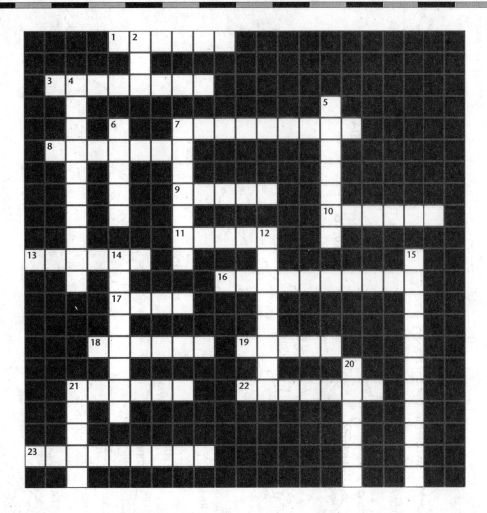

Content Review Crossword Puzzle

Across

1. Tierra del Fuego is one
3. Rio's big celebration
7. Home to huge tortoises
8. Her museum is in Rio
9. Most-visited city in Peru
10. Iquitos is on it
11. Colon Theater is this kind of house
13. His statue is on Corcovado
16. Cruise there from Argentina
17. _____ Titicaca
18. Island with big heads
19. _____ Loaf Mountain
21. Chile and Norway have them
22. Copacabana and Ipanema
23. They're like northern Scotland

Down

2. Do this in Bariloche
4. See these in the Pantanal
5. He's everywhere in Caracas
6. This plain is famous for its lines
7. Argentine cowboys
12. You can get this sickness in Cuzco
14. Strong African influence there
15. The Incas built it
20. Describes northern Chile
21. Iguacu _____

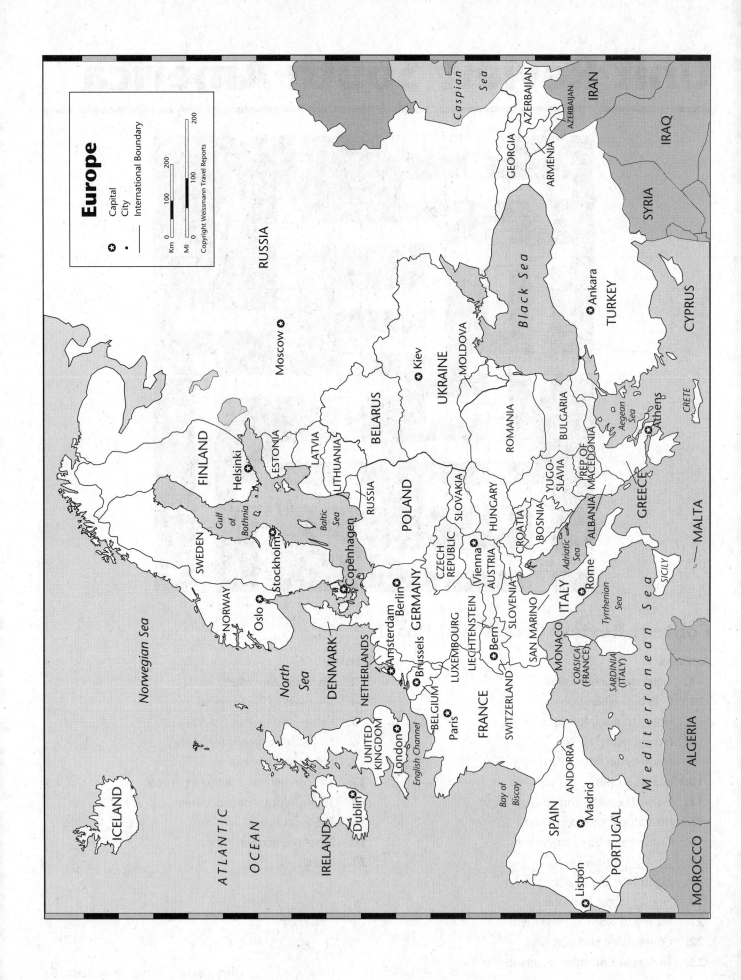

Europe

- ✪ Capital
- · City
- — International Boundary

Km 0   100   200
Mi 0   100   200

Copyright Weissmann Travel Reports

ICELAND

ATLANTIC OCEAN

Norwegian Sea

NORWAY
Oslo ✪

SWEDEN
Stockholm ✪

FINLAND
Helsinki ✪

Gulf of Bothnia

RUSSIA

Moscow ✪

RUSSIA

ESTONIA
LATVIA
LITHUANIA

Baltic Sea

DENMARK
Copenhagen ✪

North Sea

IRELAND
Dublin ✪

UNITED KINGDOM
London ✪

English Channel

NETHERLANDS
Amsterdam ✪

BELGIUM
Brussels ✪

GERMANY
Berlin ✪

LUXEMBOURG

Paris ✪

FRANCE

SWITZERLAND
Bern ✪

LIECHTENSTEIN

CZECH REPUBLIC

Vienna ✪
AUSTRIA

SLOVAKIA

POLAND

BELARUS

UKRAINE
Kiev ✪

MOLDOVA

ROMANIA

HUNGARY

SLOVENIA
CROATIA
BOSNIA
SAN MARINO

Adriatic Sea

MONACO
ITALY
Rome ✪

CORSICA (FRANCE)

SARDINIA (ITALY)

Tyrrhenian Sea

YUGO-SLAVIA

REP. OF MACEDONIA
ALBANIA

BULGARIA

Black Sea

Ankara ·

TURKEY

GEORGIA

AZERBAIJAN
ARMENIA
AZERBAIJAN

IRAN

IRAQ

SYRIA

CYPRUS

GREECE
Athens ✪

Aegean Sea

CRETE

MALTA

SICILY

Mediterranean Sea

Bay of Biscay

SPAIN
Madrid ✪

ANDORRA

PORTUGAL
Lisbon ✪

MOROCCO

ALGERIA

Caspian Sea

RUSSIA

Europe

ALMOST ANYONE WHO WALKS INTO A TRAVEL agency can be made happy with a European destination — the trick is to match clients with the country that will make them the happiest. Those interested in Western civilization, history, arts and culture will be in heaven almost anywhere in Europe, but particularly in Western Europe, where the continent's finest museums can be found (with one exception: Russia's Hermitage, in Eastern Europe, is one of the best museums anywhere in the world). Those interested in folk culture and current events will especially enjoy Eastern Europe.

As a general rule, the northern countries of Western Europe tend to be the cleanest, best organized, most expensive and most efficient (they're on par with, or surpass, North American standards). The southern European countries (including Portugal, Spain, Italy and Greece) tend to be more relaxed and informal, and have a drier, hotter climate.

As a result of the collapse of communism in the early 1990s, Eastern Europe began opening its doors wide to tourism. The sudden interest in Eastern Europe put a tremendous strain on the existing tourist infrastructure there, but conditions have since improved dramatically.

This is especially true in Poland, Hungary, eastern Germany and the Czech Republic. Clients heading to other Eastern European destinations should be advised to be prepared for standards that are lower than what's found in Western Europe.

Europe is a beautiful continent. Most of its countries have at least some mountainous terrain, and the countries where the Alps reach up to the heavens are breathtaking. And whether you're visiting Paris, London or Prague, you're likely to see a picturesque river winding through the city. Beach time is usually scheduled along a Mediterranean shore or on one of the seas along Europe's southern coastline.

Generally speaking, the best time to visit (unless you're going specifically for beaches) is from mid-May to the end of June and mid-September to the end of October. From November to April it's cool to cold, usually drizzly, rainy or snowy — basically, miserable. And summers can be very hot and humid — also miserable — outside of higher elevations.

In the following 11 chapters, we take an in-depth look at the countries and tourist attractions of this exciting continent.

United Kingdom

and Ireland

Selling Points

Historic sites, museums, theater, Stonehenge and other antiquities, London, rural scenery, the Loch Ness monster, formal gardens, walking trails, country estates, canal trips, shopping, friendly people and cultural events are the United Kingdom's main attractions.

There is enough diversity to satisfy 99% of international travelers — everyone will find something to love. The only travelers we wouldn't send are those who can't tolerate cool/damp weather.

Fascinating Facts About the United Kingdom

England is not especially noted for its beaches; the water can be colder than most North Americans are used to . . . The Channel Islands (in the English Channel) were the only part of Great Britain occupied by the Germans in World War II . . . Scotland is and isn't a country, but before the 1707 Act of Union was enacted (some would say imposed), the nation was ruled by its own royalty and the Scottish Parliament . . . Glasgow has the largest area of urban parkland in Europe. . . .

More North Americans go to the United Kingdom than to any other country in Europe. Its relative nearness and a common tongue are probably the main reasons, but the sense of history the country imparts also draws visitors as a fine old leather-bound book attracts a collector of first editions. "Old" in England, Scotland, Wales and Northern Ireland is evaluated on a different scale than on the other side of the Atlantic; it's easy to stay at inns that were built before Columbus landed in the New World. It sometimes seems that every town had a famous event occur there, or has a famous church, monument or museum, or was home to a native-son celebrity who was born, lived or died there.

There are bonds between the United Kingdom and the United States and between the U.K. and Canada that make the country naturally attractive to North Americans. Historic events there during the past 2,000 years have had a tremendous influence on North American law and tradition, and British literature provides the foundation for all contemporary English-language fiction, poetry and theater. Although the U.K. is not as consistently beautiful as neighboring Ireland, it has areas of stunning beauty, particularly in Scotland. Drive through the countryside along roads lined with stone walls, through vibrant green valleys and small, quaint villages. The gardens in the villages are among the loveliest in the world — everyone seems to grow roses. And, last but not least, the U.K. is fun. London, one of the liveliest cities in the world, has great nightlife; the pubs, theater, clubs, music venues and cinemas will provide plenty to do.

What to Do There

Note: Information about Scotland, Wales and Northern Ireland are in their own paragraphs below; all other paragraphs describe English cities. To read about Ireland, see the end of the chapter.

Bath   This town has been famous since Roman times for its mineral baths and hot springs. It also has elegant Georgian architecture, history, beautiful scenery, a beautiful abbey and grand terraces of mellow stone houses. The old Roman baths are the main attraction (the

United Kingdom and Ireland

- ✪ Capital
- ▪ City
- ♜ Castle
- ∴ Ruin
- —— International Boundary
- —·—· River

Km 0   50   100
Mi 0   50   100

Copyright Weissmann Travel Reports

TO SHETLAND ISLANDS

Orkney Islands

OUTER HEBRIDES

INNER HEBRIDES

Dornoch

Inverness
Loch Ness

HIGHLANDS

Aberdeen

Dundee

Oban   *Loch Lomond*   St. Andrews

Bannockburn

North Channel

Dumbarton   Edinburgh
Glasgow

SCOTLAND

Turnberry Pt.   Troon

Lerwick

Shetland Islands

North Sea

NORTH ATLANTIC OCEAN

Giant's Causeway

NORTHERN IRELAND

Belfast

Dumfries   *Hadrian's Wall*   Newcastle
Carlisle

LAKE DISTRICT

THE PENNINES

YORKSHIRE MOORS

ISLE OF MAN

Irish Sea

Blackpool   York

Liverpool   Leeds
Manchester

IRELAND

Galway

Dublin

Shannon

Shannon

Limerick

Chester

Llangollen

Nottingham

ENGLAND   Leicester   Norwich

WALES   Birmingham

Stratford-upon-Avon   Cambridge
Broadway   Ipswich

Waterford

Dingle   Killarney

Blarney   Cork

Laugharne   *COTSWOLDS*   Oxford
Burford

Cardiff   London

Windsor   *River Thames*

Bristol   Avebury   Canterbury
Bath   Stonehenge

DEVON   DORSET   *Strait of Dover*

CORNWALL   *Isle of Wight*

English Channel

FRANCE

Big Ben in London

Canal/Barge Cruises

Numerous canals wind about England and offer an opportunity for a leisurely barge/boat trip. Most of them are in west-central England; some of the departure points are in small towns around Manchester. Perhaps the prettiest and most rural is the recently restored Kennet and Avon Canal, from Bristol to London. A canal trip is a great way to visit quaint towns, meet the local people and relax. The canal season runs mid-March to October.

Canterbury   The 2,000-year-old city of Canterbury boasts the 11th-century cathedral containing Thomas a Becket's tomb (it was the travelers' destination in Chaucer's *The Canterbury Tales*). Also visit the new Canterbury Pilgrims Way museum, which uses audiovisual techniques to bring five of the Canterbury tales to life.

The Cotswolds   This beautiful historic area is one of our favorites: With its small villages of thatched-roof limestone cottages, rolling meadows, grazing sheep and stately manor homes, it looks like what England is supposed to look like. The Cotswolds have an atmosphere unchanged since medieval times.

At least two days are needed to see its charming hamlets. We suggest renting a car and staying in bed-and-breakfasts or inns along the way. The Lygon Arms in Broadway is expensive, but worth it. Ask to stay in the old wing, where Oliver Cromwell and Charles I were once guests.

Hadrian's Wall   Hadrian's Wall, built by the Romans around AD 120 as a barrier to the northern Picts, runs from Carlisle to near Newcastle, essentially dividing England and Scotland. It can be viewed at Carlisle and Housesteads (ancient Vercovicium), among other places.

Lake District   The Lake District, famed as a haven for authors, is also popular with anglers, honeymooners and walkers. In fact, the area has an almost mystical attraction for the British. The district

tour of the Roman Baths Museum and ancient Pump Room is worthwhile).

Cambridge

This picturesque town, built where an ancient bridge crossed the River Cam (Cam-Bridge), is best known for its university, which opened in the 13th century. While on campus, meander among the old stone buildings, stopping at the 16th-century King's College Chapel, Trinity College, the Fitzwilliam Museum and the Museum of Archaeology and Anthropology. Plan to stroll the botanic gardens and, if your timing is good, see a performance by the university's fine choir.

is more than simply beautiful — it has an atmosphere all its own. There's not much to do except relax and enjoy the scenery, or hike, but that's part of the attraction. Many authors and poets, including Beatrix Potter, William Wordsworth and Samuel Taylor Coleridge, were inspired by this land of trees, hills, lakes and England's tallest mountains.

Liverpool This industrial town was Britain's major port city in the days of the empire. Liverpool has the Beatles museum; there's even a two-hour minibus tour that takes in major Beatles sites (such as Penny Lane). Beatlemaniacs will find other shrines honoring the Fab Four.

London By anyone's definition, London is one of the world's great cities, and, in contrast to New York, Rome and other major capitals, it's relatively easy on visitors. The London metropolitan area is fairly large (pop. 7,700,000), but most things of interest are grouped in adjacent compact areas, all within a 3 mi/5 km radius of Covent Garden. While it's possible to "walk" London, you'll find that using the Tube (subway) will add a great deal of flexibility to your day, allowing you to move quickly between sights in central London.

It would take months to see everything of interest; if the city feels overwhelming, attend the "London Experience," a 40-minute film providing a historical background of the city, at the Trocadero complex, and then take a half-day city tour to get oriented.

The city's tourist attractions are sights you've heard about all your life. The Tower of London (dating to 1066), which houses the royal family's crown jewels, is undergoing some major changes. For example, guides in medieval dress have joined the traditional Beefeaters in offering assistance. A three- or four-hour wait to get in isn't unusual during the summer. Huge St. Paul's Cathedral can take hours to wander through if you're in the right mood. The neoclassical British Museum is truly one of the world's greatest — it's home to an incredible range of exhibits, including two Magna Cartas, the Rosetta Stone, the Elgin Marbles (ancient sculptures taken from Athens), Egyptian mummies (keep an eye out for the cats), the Beatles' thoughts on paper and thousands of other fascinating items from around the world.

Newly refurbished Westminster Abbey is where royalty is crowned and some are buried (look for the Poets Corner as well, where Dickens, Ben Jonson and others are interred). Across the street from the abbey is Big Ben, the clock tower atop Parliament. Art lovers will find paradise at the Tate Gallery and the National

Gallery. And finally, if you're visiting in August or September, you can tour Buckingham Palace. Any time of year you can stand outside the palace gates and watch the changing of the guard at 11:30 am every other day (11:00 am on Sundays). Be sure to arrive early for the best views.

Although these attractions may take up all your allotted time, the city and its environs hold several other points of interest. Visitors can pick and choose from the following, time permitting: the two Houses of Parliament; pigeon-filled Trafalgar Square and its towering statue of Lord Nelson; Hyde Park (site of Speaker's Corner, where on Sunday mornings anyone can get up and give a speech on any subject — and find a heckler in the audience); the Old Bailey Courthouse (where judges in powdered wigs stroll the corridors); the Victoria and Albert Museum; the Commonwealth Institute in Kensington (excellent exhibits from Commonwealth countries); and the Tower Bridge. Shoppers will want to walk up Regent Street from Piccadilly Circus to Oxford Circus. Also, stop in at Harrods in Knightsbridge to stroll through the Food Halls — the quality, variety and displays make it one of the top shopping experiences in the world. (Harrods features high tea, beginning in mid-afternoon).

London, once the center of scientific exploration, boasts several museums focusing on natural history and science. Among these are the Museum of Mankind (ethnology), the Science Museum, the Planetarium and the Natural History Museum (with the very popular animated dinosaur exhibit). History is brought to life at the Museum of London; the Imperial War Museum with its "Blitz Experience," recreating London during the 1940 bombing campaign by the Nazis; the London Transport Museum; the Wellington Museum; the Cabinet War Rooms and the National Maritime Museum in Greenwich. (This suburb also boasts the clipper ship Cutty Sark and the Old Royal Observatory, where you can stand on the Prime Meridian — 0 degrees longitude — and set your watch to the official world clock.) For those fascinated with the macabre, there's always the London Dungeon and Madame Tussaud's Wax Museum.

In the evening, a trip to the theater is a must. The center of the "legitimate" theater district is Leicester (pronounced LES-ter) Square (near Covent Garden). Be aware that during the week London rolls up the sidewalks pretty early — it's definitely not a 24-hour city.

Several day trips can be made from London, including excursions to Chartwell (home of Winston Churchill); Runnymede, where the Magna Carta was signed; Windsor Castle (one of the Royal Households);

Geostats

Official Name: United Kingdom of Great Britain and Northern Ireland

Visa Info: Passport only needed by U.S. and Canadian citizens.

Health Certificates: None required.

Capital: London.

Population: 57,965,000

Size: 94,226 sq mi/244,036 sq km. About the size of Oregon.

Language: English.

Climate: Generally mild and temperate; weather subject to frequent changes, but few extremes.

Economy: Industry, services, mineral and petroleum resources.

Government: Constitutional monarchy.

Religions: Church of England, Roman Catholicism, Presbyterianism.

Currency: Pound sterling (GBP). 100 pence = 1 GBP.

Time Zone: 5 hours ahead of EST. the U.K. is on GMT.

Electricity: 220 volts.

and Hampton Court Palace (beautiful tapestries, art and formal gardens).

Northern Ireland Northern Ireland combines a soothing mixture of misty green meadows, soft blue skies and dramatic coastline — it's every bit as enchanting as the rest of the Emerald Isle. If you aren't swayed by its scenic and historic treasures, you'll certainly fall for its lively pubs and friendly people. But Northern Ireland's beauty and charm has long been overshadowed by the "Troubles," the struggle between those who want it to unite with Ireland and those who want it to remain a part of the United Kingdom. Among Northern Ireland's attractions are the museums and architecture found in its capital city, Belfast; beautiful coastal scenery; and Giant's Causeway (40,000 ancient hexagonal basalt columns, whose origins are unknown, leading from a cliff into the ocean).

Oxford Scenic Oxford is home to the oldest university in Britain — the school was founded in 1263. The university is made up of 35 colleges, each with its own traditions, architecture and history. Begin a full day by climbing Carfax Tower to see the view of the entire town. Some of the more interesting places to visit are Magdalen (pronounced MAUD-lin) College, the circular Radcliffe Camera (one of Oxford's many libraries), the excellent botanic gardens and the Tom Tower in Christ Church College. There's also a museum called the Oxford Story that uses audiovisual displays to bring the history of the town and its most famous personalities to life.

Scotland

Scotland, to the north of England, is an extremely attractive tourist destination. True, it can be cold, windy, foggy and drizzly, but these climatic conditions combine to make a vividly green land — Scotland's dramatic terrain is actually enhanced by its dramatic weather. Its history, archaeology, geology, architecture, myth and romance make it a grand place to be; the golfer will be in heaven, the angler won't budge an inch once settled in and the historian, walker and photographer will be dazed with every square inch of the land. Castles, standing stones, Viking ruins, Celtic crosses and medieval churches can be seen at every turn. Scotland's major cities and attractions include:

Edinburgh There are two "towns" in Edinburgh (pronounced ED-in-burr-uh), the New Town and the Old Town, divided by the greenery and floral displays of Princes Street Gardens.

Most travelers will want to start their tour in the Old Town, which is dominated by dramatic Edinburgh Castle. The castle and its treasures (including the Scottish crown jewels) are a must-see. The spacious and orderly New Town, the result of the world's first urban planning project, is no less interesting. Among its treasures is the National Museum of Antiquities, a must for anyone who truly wants to understand Scotland. Excursions can be made from Edinburgh to visit lovely villages as well as massive castles.

Glasgow Once a grimy shipbuilding port, Glasgow today is an exciting center for arts, entertainment, fashion, education, history and science. Though it is Scotland's largest city, Glasgow is compact and easy to see.

The city center is packed with Victorian architecture. Glasgow Cathedral, one of the finest examples of Gothic architecture in Scotland, dates in part to the 12th century. And museums are a major attraction of Glasgow. The Hunterian Museum and Gallery, near

Glasgow University, has much to offer: art, archaeology, geology, ethnology exhibits and the world's largest collection of paintings by James McNeill Whistler. Glasgow has quite a few large theaters and concert halls, as well, including the Scottish Theatre Company and the Scottish Opera.

Glasgow is a good jumping-off point for a number of excursions. During the summer, take a trip down the Clyde River on The Waverley, the world's last seagoing paddle wheeler. North of Glasgow is Loch Lomond (of sentimental song fame). Also in that direction lie the battlefield of Bannockburn and the ancient Scottish capital of Dumbarton.

Golf   Scotland gave golf to the world, and as befits the founding nation of the sport, excellent courses can be played throughout the land. Among the notable courses are St. Andrews (reputed to be the first) and the splendid Dornoch links.

The Highlands   Rich in history and legend, the Highlands, covering most of the northern half of the country, are renowned for their wild beauty. The desolate and untamed splendor is interrupted only by settlements nestled in the bottoms of the fertile straths and glens. Captivating Oban is one of the most attractive seafront towns (it's a good base for touring). South of Oban are Castle Sween, Scotland's oldest keep (secure fortress) and Dunadd Fort, the first capital of the Scots. Loch Ness (of monster fame) is also in the Highlands.

Stonehenge   This circle of megalithic stones on the Salisbury Plain fascinates all who visit. The site itself is thousands of years old; the fence around it is a more recent addition, erected to deter graffiti vandals and tourists who would chip off a souvenir. At the summer solstice, the Most Ancient Order of Druids meets there at dawn for a ceremony. Visitors who want to see the monument close-up should make arrangements far in advance with English Heritage in London.

Stratford-upon-Avon   The hometown of William Shakespeare, Stratford is a must-see. While there, attend a performance at the Royal Shakespeare Theatre and visit all the sites associated with the Bard, including his birthplace, the Guildhall (where he went to school) and Trinity Church (where he's buried).

Wales   Until a time machine is invented, you won't get a better glimpse of the Middle Ages than can be seen in Wales. You can go on a week's tour of the country and

Stonehenge

visit medieval castles each and every day. Some may be on cliffs overlooking rivers, some are set dramatically along a coast, others will be in the center of major urban areas, and yet others are in remote, foggy mountains. Wandering though castles for days on end never seems repetitive — each of these structures reveals a different aspect of Welsh history and character. If you see no other castle, visit the one in the capital, Cardiff.

The medieval red griffin on the Welsh flag is an apt mascot for the country; it harkens back to a time when Wales was an independent land. And though it's now administratively a part of Great Britain, it still clings to the very things that set it apart from England. Wales was the home of poet/playwright Dylan Thomas, and his home and gravesite can be visited in Laugharne.

York   This walled medieval city is a great place to explore, with its stately churches, narrow streets, lovely shops and timbered homes with gabled roofs. Don't miss the 14th-century York Minster (one of the largest medieval cathedrals in Europe) and York Castle Museum (truly one of England's best). The surrounding countryside features the North York Moors and Yorkshire Dales. York is reputed to be the most haunted city in England; tours of spooked locales are given after dark.

Itinerary

If only a week is available for visiting the U.K., plan on spending each night in London, but be sure to make at least two daylong excursions, choosing among the Cotswolds, Stonehenge/Bath, Stratford-upon-Avon and Cambridge. If more time is available, consider taking the following 14-day itinerary of England/Wales (you'll need to rent a car):

Days 1–4 — London.

Day 5 — Stonehenge and Bath (overnight Bath).

Day 6 — Drive through the Cotswolds, overnighting in small village in area.

Day 7 — Start early and drive to (and tour) Oxford in the morning, then on to Stratford-upon-Avon (tour and perhaps see a play in the evening).

Day 8 — Drive to Wales. Overnight there.

Day 9 — Spend the day driving around northern Wales; go on to Liverpool for overnight.

Day 10 — Drive to Lake District.

Day 11 — Lake District — drive, hike, or relax.

Day 12 — Start early and drive to York; tour and overnight.

Day 13 — Drive to Cambridge.

Day 14 — Return to London and depart.

Climate/When to Go

The U.K. has no one season that's across-the-board good. We like May–June and October, when day temperatures are in the 60s–70s F/17–27 C, with nights in the 50s–60s F/10–22 C; but other people prefer July–September, when temperatures are about 10 degrees F/5 C higher. Scotland can, at any time, be windy, misty and chilly (even cold). Always bring a collapsible umbrella and sweaters.

Transportation

The North Atlantic is the busiest international air corridor in the world — nonstop service from many U.S. gateways is provided by any number of carriers. British Airways and Air Canada fly from Canada. Also, London is one of the handful of cities to which you can fly the Concorde (on British Airways) from New York's JFK.

The main London airports are Heathrow (LHR — 50 minutes to London) and Gatwick (LGW — 70 minutes to London). You can also fly to the new terminal at London's third gateway, Stansted Airport (STN). There is also direct service from North America to Glasgow's Prestwick Airport (PIK).

Another way to arrive is by sea — the *Queen Elizabeth II* makes frequent crossings from New York to Southampton. Or, if you're arriving from the Continent, ferries and hydrofoils cross from almost all countries bordering the English Channel or North Sea. The "Chunnel" (Channel Tunnel) opened to rail traffic (with passenger service and a car shuttle) in 1994. The high-speed rail links London with Paris.

If you're planning on driving, bear in mind that driving is on the left, which may take a few days to get used to if you're unaccustomed to it. In London, you'll come to rely on the subway (locally called the "Underground" or "Tube").

Accommodations

Accommodations range from deluxe five-star properties to quaint inns, London flats, B-and-bs, castles, estates and motels. Every visitor should stay in a variety of accommodations to get a better appreciation of the country. London can be costly, but in other cities properties are moderately priced (as well as being clean and well-managed).

Health Advisories

The U.K. has excellent medical and dental facilities. Food and tap water are as safe as in North America.

What to Buy

Shop for crystal, china, antiques, pipes and tobacco, porcelain, silver, teas, pewter, jams, perfumes and potpourri, art, books, woolens and other fabrics and clothing. Watch for Sheffield cutlery in England, whiskey in Scotland, sheepskin items in Wales and linen, tweeds and lace in Northern Ireland.

What to Eat

One either loves British cooking and finds it hearty and filling or hates it and thinks it's bland, greasy or simply incomprehensible. Those who love it head for the nearest fish and chips parlor or a pub serving steak-and-kidney pie. But nobody will starve — in addition to a fine selection of Continental restaurants, there's authentic cuisine from every nation that was once part of the British empire: Middle-Eastern, Caribbean and Nigerian restaurants abound. It seems that every town in the nation has a place that serves excellent Indian food. Among the more traditional British offerings are Cornish pasties (filled with beef, potato and onion), bangers and mash (translation: sausages and mashed potatoes) and shepherd's pie (filled with ground beef or lamb and covered with mashed potatoes).

Travel Tips for the Client

Don't forget to look to the right first when crossing the street or you may not come back . . . Do expect unfamiliar pronunciation of the English language in regions far from London . . . Do consider getting the Great British Heritage Pass — admission to hundreds of attractions . . . Do visit Greenwich with someone you love. You can share a kiss across the Prime Meridian while each of you stands in a different hemisphere! . . .

Ireland

As beautiful as Ireland is, we think the country's main attraction is its people — their hospitality, their marvelous use of the language and their marvelous sense of humor ensure a warm welcome. Enter a pub in Ireland on a rainy day, and you'll find a room full of friends. In between time spent getting to know the Irish, travelers will be enchanted by the emerald-green countryside, scattered with towers, ruins and castles.

What to Do There

Blarney Castle
Blarney castle is home to the Blarney Stone, which is said to give the gift of gab to all who kiss it. Today thousands of tourists take their lives in their hands and lean out over the castle walls to kiss the stone.

Dublin
Dublin is a lively city. It was the "second city of the British Empire" for 200 years, and no expense was spared in its construction and embellishment. As you walk around, notice the brightly colored doors on some of the town houses. Many of the homes are splendid examples of Georgian architecture.

Dublin is also a city of wonderful parks and museums. One of the best outdoor spaces is Phoenix Park, the largest walled park in Europe — with a beautiful and spacious zoo. Indoors, we especially enjoyed seeing the Irish Viking Adventure Center (a recreation of Dublin as it

was 1,000 years ago) and the National Museum of Ireland (Bronze Age displays and a fine collection of Celtic — ancient Irish — gold). And, as the Irish are noted for their great literature and high regard for the arts, it would be a shame to miss the houses of Yeats and Joyce, Ulysses Pub (a must for James Joyce fans) and Bram Stoker's house (he wrote *Dracula*). At night, try to attend a theater performance.

Ring of Kerry
The Ring has long been one of the must-sees of Ireland — which explains all of the tourists. It's a beautiful scenic drive through some of Ireland's most spectacular countryside. Starting in Killarney, you'll skirt the Mountains of Kerry, follow a rugged coastline and pass old monasteries, ruined castles and a third-century fort.

Waterford
This town, founded by Vikings, is the home of the Waterford Crystal Factory. Tour the factory and watch crystal being made.

Travel Tips for the Clients

Do stay at least once in a bed-and-breakfast with an Irish family to get the real flavor of Ireland . . . If you're planning on driving into Northern Ireland, make sure your rental company will allow you to do so . . . Don't initiate conversations about politics or religion — they are both extremely controversial subjects in Ireland. . . .

United Kingdom and Ireland

Review Questions

1. Why do more North Americans go to the United Kingdom than to any other country in Europe?

2. Why has Bath been famous since Roman times? What might you suggest a client tour there?

3. Why is it said that the Cotswolds look like what England is supposed to look like?

4. In London, where are most things of interest to tourists located? What means of transportation allows tourists to move quickly between sights in central London?

5. What should a tourist see to get a good historical background of London?

6. What is Giant's Causeway? Where can a tourist visit it?

7. What does the Hunterian Museum and Gallery offer visitors? In which city in Scotland is it located?

8. What would you visit in Wales to get a glimpse of the Middle Ages?

9. What are the main London airports? How far are they from London? What are their airport codes? What is London's third gateway and airport code?

10. What is the Ring of Kerry?

United Kingdom and Ireland

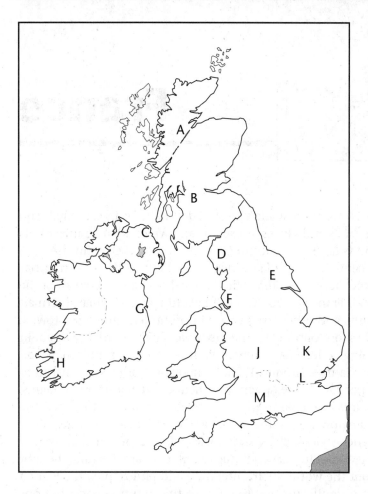

Map Skills Exercise

Match the tourist destination listed below with the corresponding letter on the map. You can use each letter only once.

1. _____ London
2. _____ Dublin
3. _____ Ring of Kerry
4. _____ Stonehenge
5. _____ Lake District
6. _____ Loch Ness
7. _____ Giant's Causeway
8. _____ Stratford-upon-Avon
9. _____ Glasgow
10. _____ York

Selling Exercise

You are a concierge in a major hotel in London. A guest in your hotel asks you to suggest two itineraries for him (including transportation suggestions), one covering key sights in London and the other to attractions outside the city — but not too distant. Develop the two itineraries.

France

United Kingdom & Ireland

Selling Points

Paris, museums, cathedrals, food, skiing, palaces, specialty tours (wine, culinary, hiking, etc.), Versailles, mountain climbing, the Louvre, beaches, the Eiffel Tower, shopping, L'Arc de Triomphe, nightlife, the Champs Elysees, sidewalk cafes, health spas, carnivals, casinos, the Left Bank, Notre Dame, festivals, architecture, walled medieval towns, the Alps, the coasts, scenery, canal trips and French art and culture are the main attractions of France.

Fascinating Facts About France

Nimes claims to be the originator of denim. In fact, the name derives from the French words meaning "from Nimes" . . . True champagne can only come from the champagne region of France. Sparkling wines produced anywhere else — even if they're made according to the *methode champenoise* — are simply sparkling wines . . . Museums, chateaux and other historic monuments operated by the national government are closed on Tuesdays. So visitors need to plan ahead . . . Free weekly fashion shows take place at 10:30 am on Tuesdays at the large Au Printemps department store in Paris (March–October). Get there early to get a decent seat. . . .

France is one of the world's greatest destinations. Its cathedrals and cafes, cities and sauces, museums and wines are magnificent; its towns and villages are charming; and its people, ever so diverse.

Every century has added a new ingredient to the mix that has become the France of today. The Romans, who conquered all of the land we call France by 50 BC, built beautiful arenas, villas, thermal-spring baths and other structures still prominent in French towns. They were soon followed by the medieval religious orders, who built the stunning St. Jean Baptistery in Poitiers and the Trinity Chapel on the Bay of Cannes. Around 1125, flamboyant Gothic styles began to play a major role in the design of cathedrals, such as those in Reims, Chartres and Mont-Saint-Michel. The Renaissance introduced the architecture now seen in the homes and chateaux of the Loire Valley. Today, French styles such as Le Corbusier's Chapel of Ronchamp or the Pompidou Center in Paris continue to influence architectural thought throughout the world. In art, literature and philosophy, the French accent is so significant that to describe the country's contributions would almost be a description of the subjects themselves.

The French call their country *L'Hexagon,* for its roughly six-sided shape. The countryside, relatively flat in the northwest, gives way to gently rolling hills in the north and west and the Massif Central (a plateau) in the center. France is bounded on the south by the Pyrenees Mountains and the Mediterranean Sea; on the east by the Alps and the Rhine River; and on the west by the Atlantic Ocean and the English Channel.

What to Do There

◆ Paris and Vicinity

Paris   We've found very few cities in the world as wonderful as Paris. No visit to France is complete without spending an absolute minimum of four nights there. Given the city's size, we'd recommend a half-day city bus tour to get oriented. Then start your private tour with a visit to the Latin Quarter, on the Left Bank of the Seine River.

English Channel

Calais

BELGIUM

Lille

GERMANY

Guernsey
CHANNEL ISLANDS
(U.K.)

Jersey

Bayeux

Rouen

Chantilly

Reims

LUX.

Caen

Honfleur

Giverny

Paris

NORMANDY

Falaise

Versailles

Marne-la-Valee/
Disneyland

Verdun

Mont-St.-Michel

Chartres

Fontainebleau

Seine R.

Quimper

BRITTANY

Rennes

Nancy

Strasbourg

Carnac

Vannes

Orleans

Angers

Blois

Chambord

Nantes

Tours

Usse

Amboise

Loire R.

Ronchamp

Chinon

Azay-le-Rideau

Dijon

Besancon

Beaune

ATLANTIC

OCEAN

Poitiers

SWITZERLAND

Limoges

Geneva

Vichy

Perouges

Chamonix

Bordeaux

Dordogne R.

Lyon

Garonne R.

Grenoble

ITALY

Rhone R.

Bay of Biscay

Biarritz

BASQUE
REGION

PROVENCE

P
Y
R
E
N
E
E
S

Pau

Lourdes

Toulouse

Nimes

Avignon

Arles

Aix-en-Provence

Nice

Cannes

MONACO

Carcasonne

St. Raphael

St. Tropez

SPAIN

ANDORRA

Marseille

Cote d'Azur

France

⊛ Capital
▪ City
♜ Chateau
— International Boundary
—·— River

Km 0 25 50   100

Mi 0   25   50   100

Copyright Weissmann Travel Reports

CORSICA

Bastia

Ajaccio

Filitosa

MEDITERRANEAN

SEA

A
L
P
S

Notre Dame

The Quarter has an intellectual, international, bohemian character. The heart of the Latin Quarter is Boulevard St. Michel. And Paris' oldest church, St. Germain des Pres, is nearby. Another street that will give you a good feel of The Quarter is Rue Mouffetard. Along this narrow road, full of market stalls every morning, you'll encounter cafes, patisseries (pastry shops) and boulangeries (bakeries). Also on the Left Bank are the Luxembourg Gardens and the Pantheon (housing the remains of French intellectuals, writers and thinkers — Voltaire, Rousseau, Victor Hugo and others).

Travel the Boulevard des Invalides to the gilt-domed Hotel des Invalides, a military museum holding Napoleon's tomb. Just across the street is the Rodin Museum (see *The Thinker* and *The Gates of Hell*), and to the west is Paris' most famous landmark, the Eiffel Tower. Next, go to the Ile de la Cite, the island in the Seine that was the original Paris. The main attraction on the island is the Cathedral of Notre Dame, one of Paris' most historic sights.

To get to the Right Bank, the more commercial area of Paris, take any one of a number of lovely bridges spanning the Seine from the Left Bank. A short walk west along the quai (riverfront street, pronounced *kay*) leads to the elaborate Hotel de Ville (City Hall). Continue up Rue de Renard to one of the world's most novel structures, the Georges Pompidou Center, an outstanding example of 1970s architecture. Inside the building is the Musee National d'Art Moderne, the world's largest contemporary-art museum (from early Picasso to Andy Warhol and beyond). While in the area, visit the site of the Bastille (the prison stormed by angry revolutionary mobs on 14 July 1789, the date celebrated as the start of the French Revolution). The controversial new Paris Opera House (made of glass and steel and called Opera-Bastille) is located there too.

In the center of Paris is the Louvre, once the residence of Louis XIV and now the home of the *Venus de Milo, Mona Lisa* and Whistler's portrait of his mother. This massive museum houses more than 350,000 works of art from ancient times through the 18th century. Don't miss *The Winged Victory of Samothrace* and the Rembrandt section. You simply can't miss the huge plexiglass pyramid — designed by American architect I. M. Pei — in the courtyard; it serves as the main entrance. Adjacent to the Louvre are the Tuileries Gardens, a pleasant resting spot (especially during spring, when flowers are everywhere). The Place de la Concorde is at the opposite end of the gardens from the Louvre. In the center of this square is the 3,300-year-old Egyptian obelisk of Rameses III from the ruins of the temple at Luxor. The Rue du Faubourg St. Honore and its continuation south of Place Vendome, Rue St. Honore, are where designers such as Hermes, Pucci, Gucci and friends have their stores. Continue north along the Avenue de l'Opera to the old opera house, an elaborate building that's still in use — its ceiling was repainted in this century by Marc Chagall. Connecting the Place de la Concorde to the Arc de Triomphe (commemorating the victories of the Revolution and of Napoleon) is the magnificent Boulevard des Champs Elysees (lined with shops, showrooms, sidewalk cafes and cinemas).

To see artists at work, climb the steep hill of Montmartre to the Sacre Coeur Basilica, a beautiful church with a beautiful view of south Paris from its steps. When walking down the hill, stop in the Montmartre Cemetery and look for the graves of Degas, Offenbach and Berlioz, and pause at the tiny vineyard to view the panorama of the city painted by Van Gogh.

Nighttime offerings in Paris are many and varied. We think visitors should spend at least one evening at a cabaret show, such as the Lido and Moulin Rouge (immortalized by artist Toulouse-Lautrec).

Chartres   An easy day trip from Paris, Chartres is the site of one of Europe's best-known cathedrals. Constructed in pure Gothic style (1194–1225), the cathedral is renowned for the quality and brilliance of its stained-glass windows. Chartres sits atop a small hill, so the soaring cathedral can be seen from miles away.

Disneyland Paris   Disneyland Paris opened in 1992 with hopes of duplicating the successes of similar parks in California, Florida and Japan. We recommend visitors from North America not tour it — you could see something just like it closer to home and for a lot less money. If you do go, you'll find the vast majority of the park is just like Disneyland in Anaheim or Disney World: Fantasyland, Frontierland, Adventureland and Main Street, U.S.A. vary little from their U.S. counterparts.

Fontainebleau   Fontainebleau, a palace in a huge forest, is usually seen as a half-day trip from Paris, either by itself or on a full-day trip that also includes Versailles (see separate paragraph). Over the years it has been home to Catherine de Medici, Marie Antoinette and Napoleon. It has spectacular gardens: the English Garden with the Blaud Fontain, Carp Pool and Cascades, and the courtyards and Garden of Diane.

Giverny   Giverny is where Claude Monet, the impressionist painter, planted the gardens he so beautifully depicted in some of his best works. (The paintings are on display at the Orangerie Museum in Paris.) Most people will want to visit Giverny in the spring or summer to see the gardens, which have been replanted to look as they did in Monet's time. Aficionados will thrill at the sight of the Japanese Bridge and the Water Lily Pond. The artist's house and studio have been nicely restored, too.

Loire Valley   The valley of the Loire River has splendid chateaux, rolling countryside and charming villages. Among our favorite chateaux: Usse, home of the Sleeping Beauty legend; Blois, with its King's Garden and dramatic spiral staircase; Amboise, a spectacular castle overlooking the Loire River; Clos Luce, where Leonardo da Vinci lived, died and is buried; Azay-le-Rideau, with splendid gardens — probably the most photographed of all the great houses; and Chambord, a massive, elegant, 440-room castle built by Francis I and surrounded by the National Swan Park and Reserve.

(A slow-paced way to see the Loire and other waterways of France such as the Yonne, Burgundy, Canal du Midi and Canal de la Marne is to take one of the many barge cruises. All are quite nice.)

Reims   Reims is the principal city of the region where champagne is produced (take a guided tour of one of the cellars). But many would agree that the highlight of the city is its magnificent Gothic cathedral. Most of the kings of France were crowned there.

Versailles   The ornate palace and grounds of King Louis XIV (the "Sun King") are a feast for the eyes and fairly resound with history. Within the magnificent halls of Versailles empires were founded, kingdoms collapsed and a World War ended. The palace, known throughout the world as the epitome of extravagance, was built to be big enough to house the king and his court — more than 3,000 people — within a single building. Linger a while in the historic — and huge — Hall of Mirrors (more than 230 ft/70 m long). After viewing the gardens, walk into the surrounding woods to visit the Petit Trianon (home-away-from-home for Queen Marie Antoinette).

◆ Southeastern France

Aix-En-Provence   Aix (pronounced like the letter X) was once a Roman spa, and then the capital of the region of Provence. Today, the town is known for its romantic streets, stately houses and sophisticated atmosphere. Highlights include the renovated atelier (studio) of native-son impressionist painter Paul Cezanne (it now looks the way it did when the artist was alive).

Arles   Set on the banks of the Rhone river, Arles is where Vincent Van Gogh lived and painted. The painting of his bedroom in Arles is among his best-known works. The town has wonderful churches, museums, Roman

Chambord

ruins (theater, baths and forum) and a Roman arena (still in use, 20 centuries after opening day).

Avignon   Avignon is known as the City of Popes. You'll want to visit the Palais des Papes (Papal Palace) constructed in the 14th century when the pontiff's court was transferred from Rome, during the Great Schism. Wander the narrow streets of the city's old town. Start your walk at the Place de l'Horloge. It's full of cafes, restaurants, street vendors and entertainers.

Cannes   Every year, people jam this Riviera city for the internationally renowned Cannes Film Festival. Stroll along La Croisette, the elegant seaside promenade, to the Palm Beach Casino, and visit the Old Harbor. In Le Suquet, the old part of the city, it's fun to just walk around, looking at the lovely flower gardens and shopping on the Rue d'Antibes. Cannes is a place to enjoy the finer, richer things of life.

Grenoble   Site of the 1968 Winter Olympics, Grenoble is an absolutely beautiful Alpine city. It's a fun place just to stroll and relax. Be sure to take the cable car up to the Bastille for the view and tour the distinguished modern-art collection at the Painting and Sculpture Museum. The skiing is excellent during the winter.

Lyon   Lyon is set in the Burgundy region. Get a sweeping view of the city and its waterways from the Basilica of Fourviere, which contains a fine collection of 19th-century Byzantine art. Other attractions are Roman ruins, the *vieux quartier* (old quarter), cobblestone streets and a fabric museum with a collection of some of the world's finest silks.

Marseille   Marseille, the nation's second-most- populous city, is on the Mediterranean coast. This picturesque (though somewhat run-down) industrial port city has laudable examples of ancient and modern architecture. Visit the Notre-Dame-de-la-Garde Cathedral, Museum of the Roman Docks, Puget sculptures at the town hall and fifth-century St. Victor Basilica.

Monaco   This tiny independent principality, about half the size of New York City's Central Park, is usually visited by gamblers, the rich and famous or those who simply want to say they have been there. In Monte Carlo, the main town, try at least one game in the Casino de Monte Carlo. (Observe a formal dress code — jacket and tie are required). While there, visit some of Monaco's beaches, the Oceanographic Museum and Aquarium (its director is Jacques Cousteau), the Princess Grace Rose Garden and the Royal Palace.

Nice   Nice, the most famous of Riviera towns, is popular throughout the year. In summer there are beach activities and a carnival, while in winter there are festivals. Nice has a strong cultural heritage — visit the Opera House; the Chagall, Naval and Matisse museums; and the fine-arts museum, with its Monet, Degas, Renoir and Rodin collections. Take time to stroll down the Promenade des Anglais (along the beach), which passes some very old and exclusive hotels. If you like Renoir, take a side trip to his villa in Cagnes-sur-Mer, which displays some of his paintings and memorabilia.

Nimes   The town of Nimes has an ancient past. Its historic sites include a well-preserved Roman arena, an Augustinian gate, the ruin of Diana's Temple and the Maison Carree (Square House — formerly a Roman temple, now a museum of mosaics and statues). Nimes' ancient arena still serves as the center of bullfighting in France.

Provence   The region of Provence combines historic sites, a warm climate, striking scenery and some of

Geostats

Official Name: French Republic.

Visa Info: Passport only needed by U.S. and Canadian citizens.

Health Certificates: None required.

Capital: Paris.

Population: 56,835,000.

Size: 212,918 sq mi/551,458 sq km. About four-fifths the size of Texas.

Language: French.

Climate: West and North: mild summers and cool winters; South: hot summers and mild winters.

Economy: Industry, agriculture.

Government: Republic.

Religions: Roman Catholic, Protestant, Moslem.

Currency: French franc (FFR). 100 centimes = 1 FFR.

Time Zone: 6 hours ahead of EST. 1 hour ahead of GMT.

the best restaurants in France. Among the wonderful regional specialties are *anchoiade* (anchovy, oil and garlic paste), *daube* (braised meat, poultry, fish or game), *marcassin* (young wild boar) and *panade* (fruit tart). Provence is also prime truffle territory.

Riviera, The   The Riviera, also known as the Cote d'Azur, is famous for its beaches (topless and nude), scenery and moderate climate. We like stopping in at any one of the charming towns along the Riviera (such as St. Raphael). The Riviera has a number of scenic drives; the most spectacular runs from Nice to Monaco.

St. Tropez   This small Riviera town has a poor beach but is quite scenic. St. Tropez has great shopping, an old town and some very interesting museums. Be sure to walk through the winding medieval streets, spend time at a cafe and people-watch. In the summer, St. Tropez is swamped with "beautiful people"; you might even catch a glimpse of Brigitte Bardot (who lives there).

◆ Western France

Biarritz   Biarritz, the major city of the Basque region of southwestern France, is a fishing port and a topflight beach resort that attracts the rich, famous and retired. It also has golf courses, casinos and sophisticated nightlife.

Bordeaux   This elegant city on the banks of the Garonne near the Bay of Biscay is in the heart of the justly famed Bordeaux wine region. Tour the area wineries and sample some of their products. Don't, however, neglect the city of Bordeaux. It has a lively, cosmopolitan air and some of the best examples of 18th-century architecture in the nation.

Brittany   A region of charming seaside towns and villages, Brittany is the European mainland's last bastion of Celtic culture. We like Brittany for its dramatic seascapes, its seafood (France's finest) and its generally tranquil air. Some of the highlights of the region are the mysterious menhirs (stone monoliths) of Carnac; the islands off the coast of Vannes; and the wooden grotesques on the houses in Quimper.

Carcassone   This double-walled fortress town is one of our favorites — floodlit at night, it's a heart-stopping sight. Carcassone offers insights into 15 centuries of turmoil, with sights related to Roman and medieval times. It's best seen on foot.

Mont-Saint-Michel   Mont-Saint-Michel rises like a dream from the coastal flats of the Atlantic. Founded in the 11th century, the citadel sits atop a 258-ft/79-m granite promontory. At high tide, the place becomes an island; at low tide, a sandy causeway links it to the mainland (the tide comes in quite quickly). We recommend seeing it on a tour of Brittany or Normandy.

Normandy   Normandy offers picturesque scenery (rendered on canvas by impressionists), splendid beaches, quaint villages and rich green pastures. And history: It was from Normandy that William the Conqueror launched his invasion of England and it was on Normandy's beaches that the Allies landed in 1944 to begin the liberation of Europe. Although many people go just to see the World War II invasion beaches, there are several nice towns. Bayeux has a beautiful "old town," dominated by an imposing Gothic cathedral. The town's pride and joy is the Bayeux Tapestry, an embroidered rendering of Duke William's conquest of England in 1066. Other interesting towns include Falaise (to see the castle of William the Conqueror) and Honfleur (an often-painted medieval harbor).

Itinerary

In order to get a basic understanding of France, we suggest at least a two week stay:

Day 1 — Arrive Paris.

Days 2–5 — Paris, with at least one day trip to Versailles.

Day 6 — Drive through Normandy and overnight at Mont-Saint-Michel.

Day 7 — Drive to the Loire Valley. Spend the day at chateaux Amboise or Chambord and tour the surrounding area.

Day 8 — Return late to Paris, possibly staying on the southeast side to get an earlier start the next morning.

Day 9 — Depart Paris through the Burgundy region to Lyon.

Day 10 — Drive through Provence (Roman ruins), Avignon to Nimes.

Day 11 — Morning tour of Nimes, continuing on for about three hours to Nice or one of the quaint towns on the Riviera.

Days 12–13 — Riviera.

Day 14 — Depart France.

Climate/When to Go

The best time to visit France is May–October (except August!). Temperatures generally increase as you go south; the extreme south is 10 F/6 C warmer on average. August can be very hot and humid, and it's a more crowded time to travel, since all of France is also on vacation. The months of May and October are probably nicest for touring, but it's often too cool to lie on the beach, even on the Riviera.

Transportation

Nonstop service from the U.S. is provided by Air France, American, Continental, Delta, Northwest, Pakistan International, Tower Air, TWA, United, and USAir; from Canada, service is offered by Air Canada, Air France and Canadian Airlines. Other European and international carriers offer direct or connecting flights from their base cities to Paris, Nice and several smaller French cities. Charles De Gaulle Airport (CDG) is 14 mi/23 km north of Paris, and Orly airport (ORY) is 9 mi/14 km south of the French capital. Air Inter and Air France have frequent domestic flights. Cruise lines often stop in Nice. Excellent rail lines, both internal and international, serve the country. Many of the main lines in France are now high-speed trains, going 185 mph/300 kph. The "Chunnel," which opened with much pomp in 1994, makes it possible to cross by train between France and England. At present the trip on it from Paris to London takes about three hours. The highway system is excellent. The fabulous Paris Metro (subway) system goes to most areas of interest in the city and surrounding areas.

Accommodations

Accommodations range from deluxe hotels and resorts to campgrounds, bed-and-breakfasts, quaint country inns, chateaux, motor homes, spas, apartments, locally run small hotels and Alpine chalets. Most of the smaller properties are clean and well-run.

Health Advisories

France has excellent medical, dental and health facilities. Tap water is safe to drink throughout the country.

What to Buy

Shop for antiques, art, wine, porcelain, Limoges, enamel, original clothing, gloves, mustard, scarves, perfumes, hand-blown glass, cheese, tapestries, cognac and champagne, pottery, striped French Navy T-shirts and Lalique crystal. Monoprix department stores are a discount chain owned by the upscale Galeries Lafayette; Fauchon and Hediard are amazing Paris gourmet-food stores, worth a visit. If at all possible, plan to spend at least half a day at a Paris-area flea market.

What to Eat

French dining is a special treat; you can go into any small cafeteria and have a slice of quiche that tastes as if it were prepared in a fine restaurant. Experiment with various sauces, a French specialty, and be sure to try the coffee (on the strong side), croissants, pastries (generally not as sweet as French pastries in North America), brioches, jams, cheeses (more than 250 kinds), oysters and truffles. The house wines are usually superb and surprisingly inexpensive. Whenever you tire of walking, sit down at the nearest sidewalk cafe. In the south of France, try any dish (especially seafood) made "a la Provencal" — with fresh local herbs, olive oil, garlic and sun-ripened tomatoes.

For the essential (though expensive) Parisian dining experience, you should eat at least one dinner on the Right Bank at the Grand Cafe, Maxim's or Fouquet's, or at the elegant Tour d'Argent.

Travel Tips for the Client

Do make reservations well ahead of time if you want to eat at one of the famous restaurants. Do try to learn and speak some French, no matter how little, as most French people will appreciate the effort (with the possible exception of some Parisians) . . . Don't be surprised that many of the most famous restaurants are closed Sundays . . . Don't be slow getting into or out of the subways! The doors close quickly . . . Do stop and have a lemonade under the plane trees in the Tuileries Gardens near the Louvre. . . .

France

Review Questions

1. What kind of character does the Latin Quarter have?

2. What is the Ile de la Cite? What is its main attraction?

3. From what city is Chartres an easy day trip? For what is the Chartres cathedral renowned?

4. What famous artist is associated with each of the following places: Giverny, Aix-en-Provence, Arles?

5. What scenery and sights does the Loire Valley offer a tourist? What is a slow-paced way to see the sights there?

6. What is Versailles? Where might you suggest a tourist linger there?

7. What kind of people usually visit Monaco? What should a visitor try to do in Monte Carlo?

8. What is the most famous of Riviera towns? What cultural attractions await a visitor there?

9. How might you describe the region of Brittany to a client?

10. Why might you suggest that a traveler avoid France in August?

France

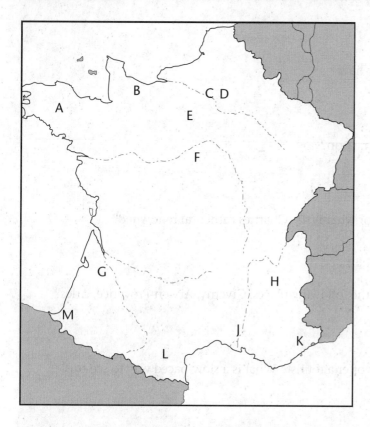

Map Skills Exercise

Match the tourist destination listed below with the corresponding letter on the map. You can use each letter only once.

1. _____ the Louvre
2. _____ Loire Valley
3. _____ Palais des Papes
4. _____ Carcassone
5. _____ Nice
6. _____ Chartres
7. _____ Disneyland Paris
8. _____ Normandy
9. _____ Brittany
10. _____ Grenoble

Selling Exercises

The members of a local high school French club are planning a trip to France, where they want to practice their language skills and experience French culture firsthand. The students have asked you to suggest a two-week itinerary for them that highlights key historical and cultural sights in the country. (Use transparency map #25 to complete this exercise.) On the map, plot an itinerary for the students and suggest key attractions they should visit at each stop along the way.

Italy

We remember being in the train station in Trapani. The station was empty, except for six men and women filling large water bottles at a fountain. They were having an animated discussion, and it was fun to watch them. It just proved what we suspected all along: Italians could have fun doing *anything*, even filling buckets of water.

Of course, those six would probably not have thought of themselves as "Italians." They would have said "Sicilians" — much as others would consider themselves "Romans," "Venetians" or "Florentines" first. As founding statesman Mazzini said, "We have created Italy, but not Italians." Which is the reason, for us, that a trip to Italy is so delightful. It's not just the variety of wine and food and painting and architecture and beaches and ski slopes; it's the people — all gesticulating, all on the edge of some emotion. They are the spice that can turn a trip to Italy into a feast.

A Vision of Cultural Unity

Some say that the people of Italy have civilized Europe twice, once in ancient times and again after the Middle Ages. The Roman Empire, born in what is now Italy, ruled portions of Europe, Africa and Asia for almost 500 years (from 27 BC until AD 476, when the western empire fell). Greek ideals and Roman justice were spread throughout the Mediterranean region by the empire's legions. Today, Rome's legal, cultural and scientific legacies endure everywhere. Places as diverse as Japan, Louisiana and Brazil are ruled by modern versions of Roman law; and the Romance languages (including French, Italian, Portuguese and Spanish), as well as scientific terminology, derive from ancient Latin. At its height, Rome controlled lands from the Irish Sea to the Caspian Sea; Roman ruins can be found across a wide expanse, including portions of Great Britain, Morocco, Turkey and Jordan. Italy rose to the forefront of Western civilization again during the Renaissance, when such notable citizens as Galileo, Michelangelo and Leonardo da Vinci made their contributions to civilization.

Though it gave Europe a vision of cultural unity, Italy itself only achieved political unity in 1870. Before then, Italy was a collection of squabbling kingdoms, dukedoms, city-states and papal states often

Italy

⊛ Capital
■ City
▲ National Park
— International Boundary
-·-·- River

Km 0 — 75 — 150
Mi 0 — 75 — 150

Copyright Weissmann Travel Reports

SWITZERLAND

AUSTRIA

HUNGARY

EASTERN ALPS

CENTRAL ALPS

SLOVENIA

CROATIA

BOSNIA

FRANCE

WESTERN ALPS

Mt. Blanc

Macugnaga
Alagna
Aosta
Gran Paradiso
Varese
Como

TRENTINO-
Bolzano
ALTO ADIGE

Dolomites

Trento

Belluno

Milan

Padova

Trieste

Venice

Turin

Cremona

Po

Asti

Parma

Porto Garibaldi

LIGURIA

Genoa

Bologna

Portofino

Rimini

SAN MARINO

Cattolica

Ventimiglia

APPENNINES

Arno

Florence

Ligurian Sea

Pisa

TUSCANY

Livorno

Siena

Perugia

Adriatic Sea

Elba

Tiber

Corsica
(FRANCE)

VATICAN
CITY
⊛ Rome

Bari

Strait of Otranto

Porto Torres

Olbia

Naples
+Mt. Vesuvius

Brindisi

Sassari

Ischia
Castellamare
Capri

Amalfi
Sorrento

Taranto

Nuoro

SARDINIA

Golfo di
Taranto

Oristano

Tyrrhenian Sea

Cosenza

Ionian Sea

Cagliari

Messina

Reggio di Calabria

Strait of Sicily

Palermo

Cefalu Taormina

Strait of Messina

Trapani

SICILY

Mt. Etna

Acireale

Agrigento

Pantelleria
(ITALY)

MALTA

dominated by outside forces. Although currently unified under the government in Rome, the country is still divided into 20 distinct regions with unique cultures, dialects, foods, historical sites, climates and architecture. In the past 100 years, Italy has gone from monarchy to parliamentary system to fascism to a seemingly unending series of coalition governments — an average of one a year since 1946.

Geographically, Italy resembles a boot (the mainland) about to kick a football (Sicily). One of the most densely populated countries in Europe, it is characterized by mountainous terrain. The Alps form a barrier to the north (blocking bad weather more successfully than they ever did invaders), while the Apennines run the length of the boot. Only in the north, in the Po River valley, is there relatively flat land. No place is very far from the sea: To the east is the Adriatic, to the southeast the Ionian and to the west the Tyrrhenian. Italy can seem surprisingly dry and, in the south especially, a bit dirty and run-down in spots.

What to Do There

The Alps
These mountains offer incredible scenery, great skiing and other winter and summer activities. The Western Alps stretch from the Mediterranean to Switzerland, and include Gran Paradiso National Park, where Mt. Blanc can be seen rising above picturesque villages. The Central Alps run along the Swiss border to Austria — the skiing is excellent in several areas around Sondrio. Don't miss Varese (exquisite scenery and lakes) and the rock carvings in Valcamonica. The Eastern Alps continue along the Austrian and Slovenian borders. This is the Dolomite area, where rose-colored granite and white limestone peaks make the scenery truly spectacular.

Capri
Once an infamous Island of Sin, Capri (reached by ferry/hydrofoil from Naples and Sorrento) is now simply a very nice place to visit. For centuries, it was a retreat of sorts; pirates hid their loot there, and Emperor Tiberius held orgies on the island. Don't expect lush tropical scenery; this is a rocky island of Old World charm, gorgeous grottoes and silver- and rose-colored cliffs plunging straight into clear blue water. Capri boasts superb restaurants, good shopping, water sports, churches, castles and wonderful streets to wander. The people (called *Capresi*) are friendly and helpful. The island can be seen on a day trip from the mainland, but two nights are preferable.

Piazza della Signoria, Florence

Florence (Firenze)
Florence (pop. 417,000) is the one city few visitors allow enough time to see. It lies in Tuscany, a stunning province of hills and mountains. Among its famous sons are Leonardo da Vinci, Dante, Machiavelli and Michelangelo. Upon arrival, walk to the Piazza del Duomo (Cathedral Square) to see the heart of Florence — the red, white and green marble Duomo (cathedral). Climb the 463 steps to the top — the view of the city and countryside is magnificent. Then on to the sights: The most celebrated art museum in the city is the Uffizi Gallery, which has reopened since it was damaged by a car bomb in 1993 (fortunately, only three paintings were destroyed). The collection includes Italian and European masterworks from the 13th to the 18th centuries — paintings by Botticelli, Titian, Caravaggio, Raphael and Rembrandt, among others. Afterward, cross the Arno on the Ponte Vecchio (Old Bridge), which has spanned the river since 1345. The bridge still has shops and rooms jutting out over the sides — a common feature in the Middle Ages, although few examples remain today. Allow at least a half-day each to visit the Palatine Gallery (17th-century art) and the Museum of the History of Science (which houses Galileo's telescope, compass and middle finger). Leave plenty of time just to stroll the city. We prefer Florence either in April–May or in September–October; it's much less crowded, and the climate is nearly perfect.

Lake District
Very near the Swiss border, the Lake District includes Lake Como, Lake Orta and Lake

Maggiore. It's truly exquisite; we suggest no fewer than three nights in the area. In the town of Como, on Lake Como, visit the Torre del Comune monument, the Gothic-Renaissance cathedral and the 13th-century Broletto (once the city hall). Nestled between Lake Maggiore and the Alps, Stresa, the largest town in the district, may appear slightly on the run-down side, but the restaurants/cafes, shopping, parks, palm trees, pretty flowers and general ambiance more than compensate.

Milan (Milano)
Milan (pop. 1,464,000) has a brisk pace and cosmopolitan air. Plan three days to visit this center of business, fashion, design and manufacturing. But don't arrive thinking that all is sleek modernity — one highlight of the city is Leonardo da Vinci's painting *The Last Supper*, housed in the Church of Santa Maria delle Grazie. Be sure to see Il Duomo (the fabulous Gothic cathedral), the Brera Museum (*Madonna and Child* and *Pieta* by Bellini), the superlative La Scala opera house (and the opera, if you can) and the Museum of Science and Technology (an entire wing is devoted to Leonardo's inventions and designs). Shoppers can spend to their heart's content in boutiques owned by Gucci, Fendi, Valentino, Ferre, Armani, Ferragamo and others.

Naples (Napoli)
Although it's still a fairly dirty port city, Naples impresses with its beautiful bay and its backdrop — Mt. Vesuvius, the volcano. Naples (pop. 1,203,000) gave the world Pulcinella (ancestor of Punch and Judy), the Great Caruso and pizza! We recommend stops at the 16th-century Church of San Giacomo degli Spagnoli and several museums — the National Archaeological Museum (Roman murals, coins and pottery), the Museo Nazionale di San Martino (sculpture, glass, etc.), the Museo Nazionale della Ceramica (pottery) and the Museo and Galleria di Capodimonte (works of the Renaissance and Baroque masters).

Pompeii
On the southern outskirts of Naples lies Mt. Vesuvius, the 4,189-ft/1,277-m volcano whose eruption in AD 79 covered Pompeii and nearby Herculaneum with tufa stone and volcanic mud. The cities remained covered until the 18th century, when a farmer discovered Pompeii while digging for a well. The two cities give you a real grasp of what life was like in the Roman Empire — they are exceptionally well preserved. Stroll through the ancient paved streets, stopping at the Forum (central town square), temples, triumphal arches, houses and shops.

Pisa
This town can easily be seen as a day trip from Florence. The 14th-century Romanesque Leaning Tower is, of course, the main attraction (it has 294 stairs). Should time permit, take a taxi to the Church of San Michele degli Scalzi to see the other leaning tower; completed in the 13th century, this seldom-visited tower is worth a look, even though it's not as impressive as the famous one. Pisa (pop. 104,000) is also fun just to walk around: Very compact, it has many narrow streets and a great ambiance.

The Riviera (Liguria)
The Italian Riviera, an extension of the French Riviera, stretches 150 mi/ 250 km from the French border to Livorno in Tuscany. The region is dotted with mountains and villages, small and often secluded beaches (sandy to rocky), a wide range of hotels, enchanting scenery and remarkable culture. Visit several beaches/towns in the area; each is different.

Geostats

Official Name: Italian Republic.

Visa Info: Passport needed by U.S. and Canadian citizens; no visa required if staying less than three months. Reconfirm with carrier before departure.

Health Certificates: No vaccinations are required. Contact health authorities for latest information.

Capital: Rome.

Population: 58,087,000.

Size: 116,303 sq mi/187,166 sq km. Slightly larger than Arizona.

Language: Italian.

Climate: Generally mild Mediterranean.

Economy: Industry, tourism, agriculture, fishing.

Government: Parliamentary democracy.

Religion: Roman Catholicism.

Currency: Lira (LIT).

Time Zone: 6 hours ahead of EST. 1 hour ahead of GMT.

Electricity: 220 volts.

Visitor information: Italian Government Travel Office at 630 Fifth Avenue, New York, NY 10111 (212) 245-4822 or 1 Place Ville Marie, Suite 1914, Montreal, PQ H3B 3M9.

One of the most active towns, Genoa (pop. 715,000), was Columbus' birthplace. Today it's an industrial port city. Though it has piazzas, churches, a medieval inner city and impressive Renaissance buildings, similar sights are more beautiful elsewhere, so we don't recommend adding it to an itinerary unless you're in the area. Portofino, on the other hand, is on one of the most beautiful sections of the Riviera; its attractions include mountains, clear bays, thick evergreen forests, a national park and divine villas.

Rome (Roma)

Exciting, bustling, beautiful Rome (pop. 2,817,000), sprawling among seven hills, is fascinating for both its ancient and modern wonders — four nights there should be required of every human on Earth. This is not to say that everyone will like this city on the Tiber; some people are put off by its untidiness and seeming disorganization. But we feel it's important to see the significant sights.

Most visitors will tell you that the "Eternal City" is best seen by a series of walks. Plan to divide your days concentrating on different aspects of the city, i.e., ancient Rome, the Via del Corso and shopping, the areas outside the city walls and the Vatican.

Among the sights to see: the National Museum (home of the *Discus Thrower*); the Colosseum and other ruins in what was once the center of ancient Rome; numerous catacombs, including the Catacombs of St. Sebastian (take a conducted tour; in the tunnels you'll see antiquities, an underground cemetery and shelves of skulls); the Spanish Steps (we especially like them in spring, when they are ablaze with azaleas); the restored Trevi Fountain (be sure to toss a coin over your shoulder if you want to return to Rome — toss a second coin if you want to make a wish); the Pantheon (Rome's best-preserved ancient building); the Piazza Venezia (where you'll find Mussolini's balcony, the Tomb of the Unknown Soldier and the worst traffic jams in Europe); and literally hundreds of churches (be sure to see the main basilicas, but also stop to see Michelangelo's *Moses* at the Church of St. Peter in Chains). Most piazzas (plazas where several streets intersect) are themselves interesting; the Piazza Navona, for instance, has the Fountain of the Four Rivers by Bernini in its center, and the Piazza del Popolo has an obelisk looted from Egypt in ancient times.

Other Rome sites include the Borghese Gardens (a large park with villas, museums and a zoo), the scenic Appian Way and the Roman walls, baths and circus. The area known as Trastevere is great for walks and quiet sidewalk cafes.

Be sure to return to see the ancient ruins at night, when they're lighted; they take on an even more impressive air (though some lighting is only seasonal). Trevi Fountain, the Spanish Steps and Piazza della Rotonda (in front of the Pantheon) are nighttime gathering places where you'll find young people playing the guitar, singing, talking and laughing.

San Marino

The Most Serene Republic of San Marino claims to be the world's smallest and Europe's oldest republic. Completely surrounded by Italy, San Marino is located inland from the Italian coastal city of Rimini. Set on the slopes of the beautiful Mt. Titano (rising 2,500 ft/760 m above sea level), the republic is almost as tall as it is wide, offering impressive mountain and Adriatic views. The country today has one of the highest per-capita incomes in the world, thanks to the discount shops that line its streets. Tourism is its main source of revenue.

In the capital, also named San Marino (pop. 4,600), cars are prohibited in the medieval town center. Even if they weren't, you'd want to explore the city on foot, wandering along winding narrow streets lined with red-roofed stone houses, medieval ramparts and somber fortresses.

The country is so small that, unless a festival is under way, a half-day should be plenty to shop and see the sights. The currency is the Italian lira.

Sardinia

When approaching the island of Sardinia by boat, you'll be impressed by the colors reflected in its rocks — black from basalt, silver from granite, red from porphyry. A very striking island (150 mi/240 km west of Rome in the Tyrrhenian Sea), it's

More Fascinating Facts About Italy

Siena is Britain's Prince Charles' favorite Italian city; he sponsored an architectural foundation there . . . It is said that the Ponte Milvio (Milvian Bridge), in the north of Rome, is where the Emperor Constantine saw a flaming cross in the sky promising victory in the forthcoming battle for the bridge . . . The Vatican is built on the site of the ancient circus (horse-racing circuit) of Nero . . . The opera is in full swing in spring in major Italian cities. One of our favorite productions (for its dramatic setting) takes place among the massive ruins of the Baths of Caracalla in Rome. . . .

St. Peter's Basilica

had great historic strategic importance; every Mediterranean power has controlled it at one time. Sardinia has a multitude of attractions: sandy and rocky beaches (fairly uncrowded), wild horses, nun seals, great fishing (day and night), mountain climbing, Roman ruins, sailing, reef diving, skiing, small outlying islands, grottoes (the best is Grotta Nuova, near Cala Gonone on the east coast) and spectacular, arid scenery. The town of Olbia is the gateway to the Emerald Coast (Costa Smeralda), one of Europe's most important (and expensive) resort areas.

Sicily

Sicily is a mountainous, arid island — an extension of the Apennine Mountains, separated from the mainland by the Straits of Messina. Many powers have occupied the island: Phoenicians, Greeks, Romans, Arabs and, of course, the Mafia. Historical sites related to those powers are part of the island's attraction. (A Mafia tour visits sites of various "Family" activities and the graves of infamous godfathers and victims.) But there are many other reasons to visit Sicily: water sports, beaches of rock and sand (including black sand), natural beauty, good food and friendly people.

In the center of the north coast is Palermo, the ancient capital and the island's largest city (pop. 731,000); it's a blend of Arab and Norman history and culture. The southern coast has a milder climate, so there's swimming most of the year. And on the east coast is Mt. Etna (10,902 ft/ 3,323 m), an active volcano — although it can erupt at any time, such incidents aren't common. There's good

winter skiing with great ocean views from the mountain.

Siena

This picturesque, well-preserved medieval town (pop. 58,000) lies in the Tuscany wine region. A bitter competitor with Florence for much of its history, Siena is a treasure trove of art, pageantry and architecture. Visit the wonderful black-and-white Gothic cathedral and the Palazzo Publico (for its impressive frescoes). You can climb the Torre del Mangia for a nice view of the city. If you're there at the beginning of July or in the middle of August, take in the world-famous Palio horse race. Bright costumes, crowds, parades and the horse races themselves make for an interesting spectacle.

The Sorrento Peninsula

About 20 mi/ 32 km south of Naples, this area is one of the most romantic and beautiful in Italy. The peninsula (especially the Amalfi Coastal Drive) is spectacular. Begin in Castellammare (in the northern end) and continue to Minori, on the southeast coast (or vice versa). It's only 40 mi/65 km, but en route you'll find secluded beaches, reefs, citrus groves, cliffs, clear blue water, exquisite scenery, excellent restaurants and a hair-raising, narrow cliff road along the sea. Some of the nicer towns along the way are Sorrento (a gardened resort where you catch the ferry to Capri), Amalfi (visit the impressive Paradise Cloister and Gothic Arsenal), and Atrani (fairly deserted; see the Santa Maria Maddalena Church).

Vatican City

Although Vatican City (pop. 1,000), home of Catholicism, is administratively independent, it's completely surrounded by the city of Rome. The first building to see is St. Peter's Basilica (Michelangelo designed its dome, and his *Pieta* is exhibited there). Plan at least three hours in St. Peter's; after walking around inside, go to the top of the dome for the view (if the sky isn't too hazy) and to the grotto (where St. Peter and other popes are interred). Vatican sights include the Apostolic buildings, beautiful gardens and the museums, which house a fantastic collection of art, maps and other possessions of the Church. Also in the complex is the Sistine Chapel, whose ceiling, painted by Michelangelo, has undergone a controversial restoration, which revealed colors much brighter than previously shown. Because the buildings (except for the basilica) are open only 9 am–

1:30 pm, plan to see the Vatican over a period of two mornings, saving the basilica for a time when the other buildings are closed. No overnights are permitted; no passport is needed to enter. The Italian lira is the currency.

Venice (Venezia)

Venice (pop. 321,000), on the northeastern coast, is divided by 177 canals (crossed by 400 bridges). It presents a paradox: It's picturesque and romantic, but also dirty and relatively run-down, and the people can be downright rude. Regardless, Venice shouldn't be missed — it's unique in the world.

Attractions include St. Mark's Square and its 11th-century church (with its radiant gold altarpiece), the Doges' Palace, the Campanile and the Bridge of Sighs. Shop for Venetian glass (and watch it being made), explore churches and leave time to talk to the residents. The Lido area, across the Grand Canal from Venice, offers fine beaches, crystal factories and a good view of the city. Cars are not allowed inside Venice, which makes a delightful change for those coming from traffic-jammed areas. You can hire gondolas, or get around the city on the *vaporetti* (boats that serve as the city's transit system). They are cheap and fun to use. If you can get a room, Carnival (in February) is one of the most fascinating times to visit Venice. Decked out in historical costumes, intriguing black masks and aristocratic capes, Venetians celebrate at balls or in the streets.

Itinerary

For first-time visitors, we recommend an escorted/hosted tour. The itinerary below is much more rushed than we would prefer; it's set up for people who don't have much time. A day or two of padding wouldn't hurt at all.

Day 1 — Arrive Milan. Tour city if time permits.

Day 2 — Spend the morning in Milan, then depart for Venice.

Day 3 — Venice.

Days 4–5 — Florence.

Day 6 — Drive via Siena to Rome.

Days 7–8 — Rome.

Day 9 — Depart Italy.

If time permits, include the following:

Day 9 — Depart for the Sorrento Peninsula. Overnight in a town there.

Day 10 — Tour area around Amalfi Drive or see Vesuvius/Pompeii.

Day 11 — Capri day trip.

Day 12 — Return to Rome.

Day 13 — Depart Italy.

Climate/When to Go

We prefer going from mid-April to mid-June or mid-September to the end of October, when the days will generally be in the 70s–80s F/20–32 C, with nights in the 50s–60s F/10–20 C. July, August and the first half of September are generally quite hot (high 90s F/34–37 C), humid and very crowded with tourists. The winters in the north are chilly — 50s F/10–15 C or colder in the day and much colder at night (often below freezing). In the south, winters are milder, but it can be too cool to lie on the beach or too drizzly to tour happily. Take a sweater for evenings year-round.

Transportation

Alitalia and North American carriers serve Italy with direct flights from the U.S. and Canada; most European airlines connect through their base cities. Several internal airlines join major cities with frequent flights. Numerous cruise lines include Italian ports on their Mediterranean, European and around-the-world itineraries. Ferries link several Mediterranean countries and Italian islands on a frequent basis. Excellent European and internal rail service connects most cities (if you're traveling only in Italy, consider a two-week Italian rail pass as an alternative to the more costly Eurail Pass). Escorted/hosted tours, buses, taxis and self- and chauffeur-driven cars can be used to see Italy.

Accommodations

Accommodations range from deluxe international resorts to dumps. They include fabulous local inns, tiny pensions, bed-and-breakfasts, campgrounds, motels, ski resorts and excellent small hotels. There are five categories of hotels/accommodations: luxury and first-, second-, third- and fourth-class. We recommend staying in properties that impart as much historic ambiance as the traveler can afford. The good ones are expensive, but the locations, setting, architecture and/or service usually make them worth it.

Health Advisories

Health standards are usually high, but if you eat raw oysters, there's a danger of hepatitis. Tap water should be okay in major cities. Hospitals, doctors and dentists are available in most cities. Inquire at your embassy or consulate for a list of English-speaking physicians.

What to Buy

Shop for leather goods (in Florence and Milan), antiques, silks, wood carvings, embroidery, silver and gold jewelry, violins, objects of marble and alabaster, glass (Venice/Lido), knitwear and designer sportswear. Also fun to buy are ingenious kitchen utensils/accessories. Aromatic liqueurs, especially amaretto, can be found in any of hundreds of formulas. In Vatican City, look over the postage stamps and a wide variety of religious products (including relics — among the items for sale are lockets containing small pieces of Pope John XXIII's clothing).

What to Eat

Most visitors need little introduction to Italian cuisine; all we can say is that however much you like it at home, you'll probably like it even more in Italy. Always eat the regional specialties being offered in restaurants; seasonings, style and presentation are very different in different parts of Italy. Among the local dishes to taste are *risotto* (Milan), *polenta* (fried cornmeal mush, often with cheese — Venice), buffalo mozzarella cheese (Rome), fresh fruit and pastries (Sicily) and, of course, pasta. Many restaurants also offer international cuisine, but when in Rome . . .

There are three categories of restaurants: From most expensive to least, the classes are *ristorante*, *trattoria* (a bit more like home cooking) and *osteria*. Eat a meal in each category — just because it's cheap doesn't mean it's bad, and each has its own atmosphere.

Travel Tips for the Client

Don't be surprised by the excessive hotel taxes, additional charges and requests for payment for extras such as air conditioning. Sometimes these taxes/service charges are included in room rates; check upon arrival . . . Don't be surprised by Italy's two-hour lunch break (generally, 1:30–3:30 pm) . . . Don't forget to take your receipt with you when you leave a restaurant — if you don't have it, you can legally be charged for your meal again . . . Do keep your currency-exchange forms if you plan to change money back to another currency . . . Don't plan on finding public rest rooms everywhere, and when you do, you'll probably have to pay to use them. Bring change in 500-lira coins . . . Do plan on doing a lot of walking . . . Don't forget, as European observer Flora Lewis writes, that in Italy there are rules for everything, but nothing goes by the rules. . . .

Tipping: Do expect a 10%–15% gratuity to be added to your restaurant bill (they also expect you to leave more). Tip the taxi driver at least 500 lire or 15% of the fare, whichever is greater.

Note: Purse- and jewelry-snatching and pickpocketing are serious problems in urban areas. All we can suggest is this: Leave jewelry at home, use the hotel's safe, wear a money belt and be careful with passports and other valuables. Be especially alert at major tourist attractions and railway stations.

Italy

Review Questions

1. Why are the people of Italy said to have civilized Europe twice?

2. What is the Duomo in Florence?

3. Which city in Italy is the center of business, fashion, design and manufacturing?

4. What is on view at the Catacombs of St. Sebastian?

5. Why would you encourage a client to see Rome's ancient ruins at night?

6. What impresses tourists who approach Sardinia by boat?

7. What is the main tourist attraction in Pisa?

8. Where would a tourist see Michelangelo's *Pieta* and the Sistine Chapel?

9. What are *vaporetti?*

10. What are the two best times of the year to visit Italy?

Italy

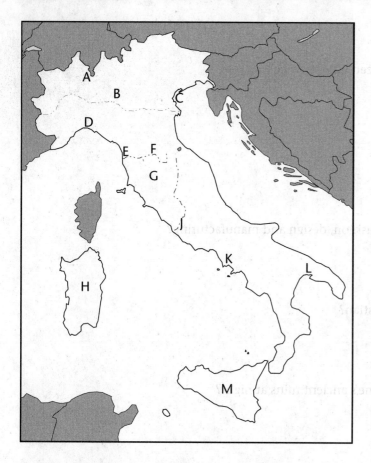

Map Skills Exercise

Match the tourist destination listed below with the corresponding letter on the map. You can use each letter only once.

1. _____ Florence
2. _____ Lake District
3. _____ Milan
4. _____ Pompeii
5. _____ Rome
6. _____ Sardinia
7. _____ Pisa
8. _____ Sicily
9. _____ Siena
10. _____ Venice

Selling Exercise

As a professional travel counselor, you realize that clients often have concerns about traveling to certain countries. You have a client coming to see you at 3 pm who wants to visit Italy. Anticipate three concerns that he or she might have about visiting Italy and discuss what you would say to the client about these concerns.

Spain
and Portugal

Fifteen years ago, Spain was considered a place to vacation on the cheap. Much of the nation had an informal, almost low-rent feel, and it was a real bargain compared with neighboring France. But no more. Today Spain is very much a mainstream, modern European country — and prices have risen accordingly. Much of the change makes a visit there more convenient and comfortable than ever before. Visitors who are returning will arrive at larger airports, ride faster trains, cruise down newly built superhighways and stay at resorts that were just a twinkle in a developer's eye in the 1980s. Fortunately, what will never change is the Spaniards' love of good food and drink and their clear, pure enjoyment of life.

Spain's contribution to Western culture and civilization is hard to overstate and continues to the present day. Among Spain's brilliant artists and writers are El Greco, Velazquez, Goya, Picasso, Miro and Cervantes. In music, Casals, Segovia and Domingo have few peers.

Though Spain's history was shaped by many forces — the Phoenicians, Romans and Germanic tribes all had a strong hand in influencing the people of the Iberian peninsula — the greatest artistic and intellectual ferment in Spain was under the Moors, the Islamic conquerors who ruled the land for more than half a millennium, starting around AD 700. Universities, a unique style of architecture and an age of rare religious toleration were all fostered by the North Africans. The Moors were finally overcome in 1492, the year of Columbus' discovery of the New World. The next century saw the peak of Spain's power and influence throughout the world. Visitors today will see historical and archaeological sites from all stages of the nation's past, including the years when it was part of the Roman Empire, conquered by Germanic tribes, overrun by the Moors, and experienced its golden age—when Spain was the most powerful and wealthy nation in Europe.

Geographically, Spain is Europe's second most mountainous country (only Switzerland has a higher terrain). The country can roughly be divided into three climatic zones: rainy and green in the north, along the Bay of Biscay (resembling the U.S. Pacific Northwest); sunny and semi-arid along the Mediterranean (resembling Southern California); and relatively flat and arid in the Central Plains, with temperature extremes (much like the U.S. Midwest).

Selling Points

Historical sites, some of the finest art in the world, the Alhambra Palace, shopping, cultural events, beaches, museums, caves, windsurfing, castles, skiing, water sports, fishing and good food have long been Spain's main attractions. Golf and tennis are gaining in popularity. From its art museums to its beaches, Spain's appeal is so broad that it's truly a country with something for everyone.

Fascinating Facts About Spain

The port city of Mao on Menorca in the Balaeric Islands is the birthplace of mayonnaise . . . Madrid became the capital in 1561, when Philip II moved his court from Toledo, to be closer to his beloved El Escorial . . . There is more land devoted to vineyards in Spain than anywhere else . . . Catalans are quick to point out that their language, Catalan, is more akin to French than to Spanish . . . The royal family usually summers on Mallorca . . . Motril, on one end of the Costa del Sol, has so many sugarcane refineries that the Spaniards call it Little Cuba. . . .

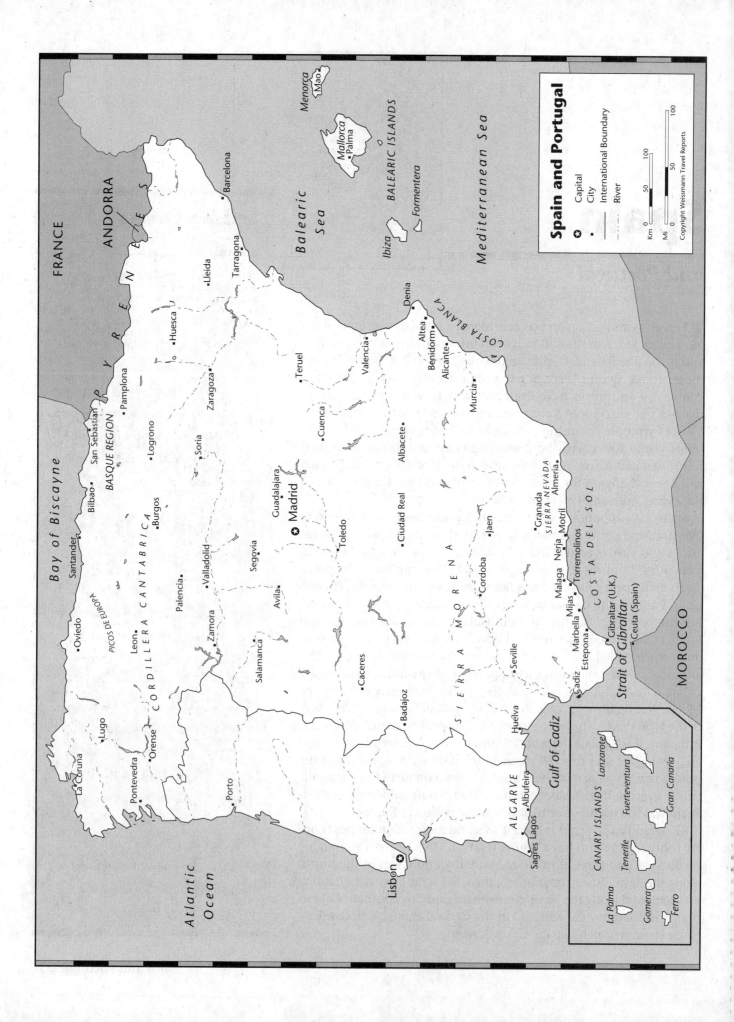

Spain and Portugal

Capital
City
International Boundary
River

Km 0   50   100
Mi 0   50   100

Copyright Weissmann Travel Reports

FRANCE

ANDORRA

P Y R E N E E S

Bay of Biscayne

San Sebastian
BASQUE REGION
Santander
Oviedo
Bilbao
PICOS DE EUROPA
CORDILLERA CANTABRICA
Leon
Lugo
La Coruna
Pontevedra
Orense

Atlantic
Ocean

Pamplona
Logrono
Burgos
Soria
Palencia
Valladolid
Zamora
Salamanca

Huesca
Zaragoza

Lleida
Tarragona

Barcelona

Balearic
Sea

Menorca
Mao

Mallorca
Palma

BALEARIC ISLANDS

Ibiza

Formentera

Mediterranean Sea

Teruel

Cuenca

Segovia
Avila

Guadalajara
Madrid

Toledo

Ciudad Real

Albacete

Valencia

Denia

Altea
Benidorm
Alicante

COSTA BLANCA

Murcia

Caceres
Badajoz

S I E R R A   M O R E N A

Cordoba

Jaen

Granada
SIERRA NEVADA
Almeria
Motril

Nerja

Porto

Huelva

Seville

Estepona
Cadiz
Marbella
Mijas

Malaga
Torremolinos

COSTA DEL SOL

Gibraltar (U.K.)
Ceuta (Spain)

Strait of Gibraltar

Gulf of Cadiz

ALGARVE
Albufeira
Lagos
Sagres

Lisbon

MOROCCO

CANARY ISLANDS

Lanzarote

Fuerteventura

Gran Canaria

Tenerife

La Palma

Gomera

Ferro

What to Do There

Balearic Islands

The Balearic Islands (Mallorca, Ibiza, Formentera, Menorca) sit in the western Mediterranean, about a 45-minute flight from Barcelona. The Greeks, Romans and Moors all controlled the islands before they became part of Spain in the 1300s, and remains from each civilization are still evident. There's excellent shopping, a mild climate (similar to that of Southern California), great food and dazzling scenery. All of these islands are favorites for Northern Europeans on package tours, so don't be surprised if you hear as much Dutch, German or English there as you do Spanish. Mallorca, the largest, is also the most developed. There's plenty to see and do, though the beaches aren't as nice as can be found elsewhere in Spain. Ibiza is more laid-back and has good beaches; it has become increasingly popular with foreign tourists, among them the "lager louts" who see their vacation as a time to stay drunk. Formentera, reached by ferry from Ibiza, is small, attractive and quiet, with no high-rise tourist developments marring the landscape. Its appeal will be very limited, since most people going to the Balearics want a fun, active beach holiday. The same holds true for Menorca, which has good, sandy beaches but is a bit too quiet for most people.

Barcelona

Barcelona is a charming port on the shores of the Mediterranean. The city offers so much to see and do that it is a wonderful vacation all by itself. This prosperous and bilingual (Spanish and Catalan) metropolis vies with Madrid as an intellectual, art and design center: Its museums, theaters, art galleries and nightlife are all of the best quality.

If you haven't been there in a while, you might not recognize parts of the city. In preparation for the 1992 Olympics, Barcelona underwent a major overhaul — older sites were carefully renovated and new sites were seemingly built overnight. Some of the major rebuilding took place around the port (a new marina and a wider beach) and Olympic areas (an entire neighborhood was constructed for the games). Amidst all of the bustle even the Palau Nacional was extensively renovated and reopened as a wonderful new museum of ancient and art-nouveau treasures.

The best place to people watch, stroll or simply relax is Las Ramblas, a pedestrian street with dozens of outdoor cafes. Nearby is Placa Real (bars and restaurants). After seeing these sights, stroll the narrow, winding streets of the medieval Gothic quarter. Or head for the old Barceloneta section on the waterfront: Always slightly run-down and scruffy looking, this working-class area is now lined with paella restaurants.

The art and museum lover would be content to spend the rest of eternity in Barcelona. Visit the Picasso Museum (which includes drawings the artist made when he was five!), the Miro Museum and La Sagrada Familia, the magnificent, surreal church designed by Catalan architectural genius Antoni Gaudi. While still unfinished, it's like no other church you'll ever see: Its design is a combination of a dragon's cave and a castle made from whipped cream. Ride the train to Tibidabo, the mountain overlooking the city, for a sweeping view of the city and a great amusement park.

Basque Region

The Basque region is a fabulous, picturesque area, at the same time rough, cultured and unique. It even has its own very complex language, which is like no other language in the world. Visit Bilbao, San Sebastian and other regional towns. In Bilbao, see the 14th-century Gothic Church of Santiago and Ensanche Park. Museum-goers will enjoy the Museum of Archaeology and Ethnology (Roman, prehistoric and Iberian exhibits) and the Museum of Fine Arts (works of Goya, Diaz and others). San Sebastian, another major town of the region, is beautiful, expensive and very fashionable. The town sits on three hills ringing a crescent bay. The beaches are packed with sunbathers in the summer, and the town takes on a wonderful, festive atmosphere. For a break from the beach, wander the old town, which is filled with bars and restaurants (be sure to try the excellent Basque cuisine). And in the town of Pamplona, each July, the brave, macho and drunk take to the streets for the

Fiesta, Pamplona

annual running of the bulls. They try to stay just ahead of the horns of angry bulls being driven from a corral to a bullring outside of town.

Canary Islands
These islands, 60 mi/96 km west of the African nation of Mauritania, boast a fair, springlike climate year-round. They feature fairly good beaches of white, gold and black sand, casinos, golf, tennis and fishing. Three nights is about right for any of the following islands: Fuerteventura (seclusion, great diving and white-sand beaches); Gomera (good snorkeling, sunbathing, scuba diving, volcanic craters, historic sites related to Columbus, deserts with camels, lush scenery, a pleasant climate, laid-back atmosphere, fairly good nightlife, casinos and shopping); Gran Canaria (the most visited island — there's golfing, yachting, shopping, casinos and great beaches, and Las Palmas, the principal city on the islands, is there); Lanzarote (developing quickly — it now sees 850,000 visitors annually — it features white-, black- and

gold-sand beaches, and 300 volcanoes); and Tenerife (a popular island with beaches, mountains, shopping, banana plantations and a good carnival celebration).

Costa Blanca
This stretch of beach on the southeast Mediterranean shore features popular resort towns like Alicante, Benidorm, Altea and Denia. Benidorm is the center of the action: Less than 40 years ago, it was a sleepy little village with beautiful beaches, but today, it can be compared with Miami Beach or Waikiki. High-rises are everywhere, and all the bars, restaurants and shops cater to tourists. Those seeking a party atmosphere in a beach resort will love Benidorm, while those seeking a calmer beach vacation with old-style Spanish culture should look elsewhere.

Costa del Sol
This famous coastal area stretches 106 mi/170 km along the Mediterranean from Motril (east of Malaga) to Gibraltar, featuring some of the finest beaches in Spain. (Some say that it's been overrun by Northern Europeans on package tours.) In addition to the beaches, there are new golf courses and tennis clubs. The region also spreads inland to include some splendid lakes. Many of the quaint fishing and agricultural villages have become somewhat touristy, but they still have cobblestone streets, flowers on every windowsill and whitewashed houses surrounding the town squares. Costa del Sol is also known for flamenco dancing, caves and fishing. A week could easily be spent in the region visiting the area's towns and villages: Malaga (a pleasant large city with great scenery but beaches in town are polluted); Marbella (whitewashed buildings, shopping, good nightlife, acceptable beaches, strong Arab influence); Estepona (a few miles south of Marbella, it features a yacht harbor and lots of nightlife); Mijas (picturesque, with a distinctly Arab feel); Nerja (nice beaches, caves, isolated coves); and Torremolinos (the first Costa del Sol village to be developed, it's showing its age a bit, but is very popular, with lots of nightlife).

Gibraltar
This British colony (pop. 31,000), grafted onto a steep, rocky Spanish hillside, merits at least a half-day's visit. The Rock, which has been English since 1704, is only 2 mi/5 km long, but it has several attractions, among them St. Michael's Cave, the Gibraltar Museum (historical displays from the Stone Age to the present) and a 12th-century Moorish castle. Climb or take the cable car to the top of the Rock to see the view from Europa Point (at the halfway station, meet the Barbary apes, Europe's only noncaged or "wild" apes).

Granada Probably the main reason to go to Granada is to visit the magnificent 13th-century Moorish Alhambra Palace. The building is simply not to be missed — plan to spend the better part of a day touring it. While you're in town visit the Albaicin (the Moorish section), the Generalife Gardens and the Royal Chapel (the tombs of Ferdinand and Isabella are in the magnificent cathedral).

Madrid Many of the things to see and do in Madrid lie within areas that can be seen on foot. Among these is Calle and Plaza Mayor (medieval Madrid), which is lined by beautiful buildings and the city's oldest church, San Nicolas de los Servitas. Go shopping at Calle Serrano and the Gran Via. Visit the Victory Arch, the Palacio Real (the royal palace, with its own art treasures and crown jewels), the Rastro Flea Market, and the Plaza de las Cibeles and Puerta del Sol (the last two are major intersections, with fountains, monuments and shops).

Madrid is a museum-goer's paradise — reserve at least a day for art museums alone. Madrid has 15 important museums and dozens of galleries. Actually, days could be spent in the halls of its largest museum, the Prado (closed Mondays). This museum is one of the world's greatest. Housed in an 18th-century building, it features the works of Rubens, Goya, El Greco, Bosch (including his masterpiece, *The Garden of Earthly Delights*), Velazquez, Titian, Murillo, Durer and many others, plus collections of coins, enamel and gold. The Prado cannot be seen in one visit — if possible make several short trips. Madrid's newest art museum is the Museo Nacional Centro de Arte Reina Sofia (primarily contemporary art), which features Picasso's antiwar (and anti-Franco) masterpiece, *Guernica*. The Palacio de Villahermosa, also recently opened, is just across from the Prado and houses the fabulous Von Thyssen collection (more than 800 pieces of the highest quality, ranging from Renaissance works to American pop art). There's more artwork at the Lazaro Galdiano Museum (a wide variety of European paintings, ceramics and marble sculpture) and the aforementioned Royal Palace (porcelain and tapestries). Madrid's Tiflological Museum is one of the few art museums in the world designed expressly for the blind. There's also the Museum of America, with exhibits of art and artifacts from Spain's former colonies.

It's quite possible to get "museumed out" in Madrid; if this happens, sit down at a *terraza* (outdoor cafe) and watch the world go by, or visit one of the many beautiful parks and lakes in the city. One of the nicest parks we've seen anywhere is Retiro Park, near the Prado. Note

The Alcazar, Seville

the Victorian greenhouse and the Crystal Palace, with its small lake and swans lazily swimming about. For a panoramic view of Madrid, take the elevator to the bar on the 26th floor of the Edificio de Espana, which faces the Plaza de Espana. Those who love traditional performing arts will want to go to the Teatro Real for Spanish light opera, known as zarzuela. You can also find good flamenco shows in several nightclubs.

Madrid is a city that never seems to close down — bars and restaurants are open very late. Dinner doesn't usually begin until after 10 pm, and then revelers head off to their favorite disco, show, jazz club or late-night cafe to play until dawn. For a concentrated area of late-night activity, head to Huertas Street after midnight.

Plan a trip outside Madrid to see El Escorial, built as a summer retreat by Philip II (the king who sent the Armada against England). El Escorial boasts one of Europe's finest tapestry collections. It also houses sculptures and paintings by Spanish and Italian masters and the tombs of Spain's kings for the last 500 years.

Seville During the Spanish colonial period, Seville was the most important city in Spain (when it had a monopoly on trade with the Americas). The city's spectacular cathedral is one of the world's largest in the Gothic style. Try to see it at night, when it's lighted. During the day, visit Torre de Oro (Gold Tower), the Giralda (a minaret with a belfry) and the old Santa Cruz Jewish Quarter with its twisting medieval streets. Don't neglect the Park of Maria Luisa, the Alcazar (royal residence of Spain's former Muslim rulers) or the 15th-century House of Pilate. The city of the *Barber of Seville* has a relatively new opera house, El Teatro de la Maestranza. Seville also boasts the Christopher Columbus Mausoleum (though some say he's buried in the Dominican Republic). The city is justly famous for two of its festivals: Semana Santa (Holy Week), which takes place the week before Easter, and La Feria (The Festival) the last week in April. Semana Santa is an amazing week of elaborate parades with traditional floats and somber music (but the bars and restaurants are still crowded). In our opinion it is one of the world's greatest parades. La Feria is a wonderful city fair, featuring plenty of food, fun and flamenco.

Toledo
Toledo was the capital of Roman Spain. It's also where El Greco lived and painted. It's a great city to stroll through, as the strong Moorish, Jewish and Christian influences are still evident in the narrow winding streets.

Don't miss El Greco's home (now a museum), the Alcazar (Moorish fortress) and the Museum of Santa Cruz (there are beautiful tapestries inside, but also note the bullet holes on the outside walls — they're from the Spanish Civil War). Toledo is especially beautiful at night, when the tour groups are gone and the narrow streets are lit by wrought-iron lanterns. Visitors often see Toledo on a day's excursion from Madrid.

Itinerary

If you have only one week available for touring Spain, the following itinerary could be used for a broad overview of the country.

Day 1 — Arrive Madrid.

Day 2 — Madrid.

Day 3 — Drive to Toledo.

Day 4 — Drive to Granada.

Day 5 — Drive to Seville.

Day 6 — Seville.

Day 7 — Depart Spain.

If you have any additional time, make traveling to Barcelona a top priority.

Climate/When to Go

The months April–June and September–October are the best times to visit. July and August are usually very hot, and winter, though generally mild, can be rainy, foggy and windy. We think winter, even on the Costa del Sol, is on the cool side — much too cool to sunbathe and swim.

Transportation

Iberia, American Airlines, Continental, Delta and TWA offer nonstop flights from the U.S. Iberia and Air Canada fly from Canada. Nearly every European carrier serves Spain via its hub city. Barajas Airport (MAD) is 10 mi/16 km from Madrid. Spain has 18 international airports, so it may be more convenient to fly into a city other than Madrid. Several cruise and local ferry lines include stops in Barcelona, Cadiz, Algeciras, Malaga and the Balearic and Canary islands.

There's excellent domestic and international rail service, including high-speed trains. Roads are good, and gas prices (though expensive by North American standards) are not as high as in neighboring France. The only downside is the traffic — it can be horrible, especially in and around Madrid. Many of the larger cities have local buses; most of these are very crowded and inconvenient for tourists. Taxis are usually metered, but at airports the drivers usually don't use the meter (tariffs are fixed according to destination). Madrid and Barcelona both have extensive subway systems.

Accommodations

Accommodations range from the best to the basic. They include deluxe international hotels, resorts, *paradores* (converted monasteries or castles), pensions, hostels, apartments, wayside inns, campgrounds (often within or just outside city limits) and budget hotels. Pensions and some of the modest accommodations are sometimes located in old, atmospheric apartments.

Budget travelers can stay in working monasteries for US$7–12 per day (note that some don't allow women).

Health Advisories

Spain has modern medical and dental facilities. Take all prescription and nonprescription drugs you'll need for your trip — your brand names might be unfamiliar to some pharmacies in Spain. In general, you can eat the food and drink the tap water throughout the country.

What to Buy

Spain is no longer the bargain it used to be. Nevertheless, the country offers unique handcrafted items: contemporary and antique paintings and sculpture, knotted rugs, guitars, ornate handmade shawls, decorative pottery, handmade furniture and ornamental combs and fans. Other items found in Spain are *Lladro* (Spanish porcelain), copper products, steelware, leather goods (purses, shoes, wallets), North African goods from Morocco and Algeria, and Spanish antiques.

What to Eat

We think Spanish cooking is reason enough for a trip to Spain. Each region has a distinctive style. Galicia (in the northwest) is known for its wonderful seafood (octopus is our particular favorite); Basque Country for its *bacalao* (a preserved salt cod that tastes better than it sounds); Castile (central Spain) for its cheese, grilled meats and *conchinillo* (roast suckling pig); Andalucia (southern Spain) for gazpacho (a delicious chilled tomato soup) and tapas (more about these below); Catalonia (region that includes Barcelona) for grilled rabbit, *romesco* (a sweet pepper sauce traditionally eaten with grilled spring onions) and paella (a delicious saffron-flavored rice dish with pimiento, peas, fish and shellfish).

One of the best ways to sample Spanish cooking is at a tapas bar. Tapas are small plates of just about anything: cheese, olives, squid, smoked shrimp, sausage, fried potatoes in a paprika sauce (patas bravas) and marinated vegetables, just to name a few. Order enough little plates, and you will have a meal. Of course, no meal is complete without a bottle of good Spanish wine.

Travel Tips for the Client

Don't complain about cigarette smoke in bars — you'll either be laughed at or shown the door. And don't expect to find no-smoking sections in restaurants, either. There is no such thing in Spain . . . Do carry some small change — you'll need it to use the public bathrooms . . . Do try to see the fastest ball game in the world, pelota (jai alai), played mainly in the Basque country. . . .

Tipping: Round up the bill in restuarants. Taxi drivers expect a tip of 10% on fares.

Portugal

The Europeans who descend on out-of-the-way Portugal will testify that the trip is worth the effort. It's a sun-drenched country with fine wine and good food, and though tourism has boomed along the coast, there are many areas where a visitor is still treated as someone special. Old-World European culture, beaches, deep-sea fishing, archaeology, history, golf, scenery, tennis, festivals, castles and friendly people are among Portugal's main attractions.

What to Do There

Algarve Portugal's southernmost province, Algarve, offers some of the finest beaches and recreational facilities in Europe. Its white-sand beaches are clean, the architecture is unique, and the fishing, water sports and golfing are great. To add to the charm, the

Fascinating Facts About Portugal

Algarve gets its name from the Moorish term Al-Gharb (The West). The province once marked the westernmost point of Moorish expansion in the Middle Ages . . . Carmen Miranda, famous as a Brazilian singer and actress, was born in Portugal . . . The country has some of the best golf courses in mainland Europe . . . Half the total number of hotel beds in the country are in the Algarve. . . .

weather is usually comfortable, the people friendly, the gambling exciting and the food excellent! There's even horseback riding. For all these reasons, Algarve is very popular among European travelers (some think it is too popular and crowded). Among the towns you'll want to visit are Albufeira (Moorish architecture and good beaches and nightlife, plus a bull ring); Lagos (wander the narrow streets of the walled city and visit with the people, many of whom still wear traditional clothing); and Sagres (the place from which Portuguese navigators set out to explore and chart the world).

Lisbon

This capital city is the cultural and artistic heart of Portugal. Compact Lisbon is easy to get around, with fine bus, trolley and subway lines. The atmosphere is rich, with wonderful old buildings, Europe's longest suspension bridge and fine museums.

Set aside a day to walk through the old parts of the city. The restored Baixa area affords pleasant strolling and shopping. The Alfama section has excellent fado music and a very Moorish atmosphere. One of the few sections to survive the famous 1755 earthquake, Alfama is much older looking than the rest of the city. Other attractions in the older areas of Lisbon include the botanical gardens, cathedral (Arab mosque design) and Carmo Convent Museum.

Spend a half-day in Belem, a suburb of Lisbon, where Vasco da Gama set sail on the first European voyage to the Orient. The early-16th-century Tower of Belem, a fortress at the mouth of the harbor, is very impressive. The beaches around Lisbon are sandy, though the murky waters are far from ideal for swimming (note that there are no beaches in Lisbon itself).

Travel Tips for the Client

Don't assume that the Portugese speak Spanish. The Portuguese have their own language and are proud of it . . . Do be careful when ordering vintage ports in restaurants. A well-heeled German couple told us that after enthusiastically trying the old ports in a good seafood restaurant, they wound up with a US$600 tab! . . . Do try to hear some fado music in the Bairro Alto section of Lisbon. The black-clad fado dancer moves to a rhythm similar to that of the blues. . . .

Spain and Portugal

Review Questions

1. What are Spain's three climatic zones and in what parts of the country will you find them? What areas in the United States do they resemble?

2. What two Spanish cities vie with each other as intellectual, art and design centers? (HINT: The country's capital is one of the two.)

3. Why is Barcelona's La Sagarda Familia like no other church a tourist will ever see?

4. What attracts tourists to Pamplona each July?

5. Where are the Canary Islands? What will a visitor find to do and see on Gran Canaria, the most visited of the Canary Islands?

6. What can a tourist see in the Prado? On which day of the week is it closed?

7. Describe Semana Santa and La Feria. In which city do they take place?

8. What famous artist lived and painted in Toledo? Why is Toledo especially beautiful at night?

9. What are tapas?

10. Why is Algarve, Portugal's southernmost province, so popular among European travelers?

Spain and Portugal

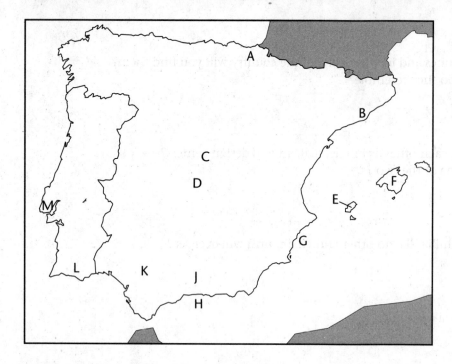

Map Skills Exercise

Match the tourist destination listed below with the corresponding letter on the map. You can use each letter only once.

1. _____ the Prado
2. _____ Ibiza
3. _____ Basque region
4. _____ Alhambra Palace
5. _____ Christopher Columbus Mausoleum
6. _____ Lisbon
7. _____ Mallorca
8. _____ Costa del Sol
9. _____ Barcelona
10. _____ Costa Blanca

Selling Exercise

A client is having difficulty selecting her next vacation spot. She is considering a visit to Spain or Portugal and needs your assistance in deciding which would be best for her. The client is interested in visiting a major city with museums and historical attractions and would also like to spend time at the beach. Prepare a chart showing what each country has to offer. Based on the information in your chart, what country would you suggest she visit? Why?

Germany

Germany is still dealing with all the unexpected problems that arose from the reunification of East and West in 1989. Happily, from a tourist's point of view, much of that work is over: In particular, eastern German cities are now cleaner, easier to visit, and have more hotels and restaurants than before.

Division and reunification has long fit the pattern of the nation's history: Germany has continually experienced periods of conquest, occupation and reorganization. In the first century AD, Germanic tribes fought to hold back Roman armies. Later, the Huns and other peoples from the east ravaged German towns. During this period, Christianity began to take hold over the entire region, culminating in the crowning of Charlemagne as Holy Roman Emperor in 800. But the strong authority of local princes kept Germany from truly uniting as a nation until the rise of Prussian power and the formation of the German empire in the 1870s. World War II, of course, resulted in yet another division of Germany, with the eastern sector under the control of Communists. Today, even with all its problems, reunified Germany is the clear economic powerhouse of Europe.

What to Do There

Bavaria   For most travelers, this mountainous region of southern Germany is the most quintessentially German. Bavaria is the land of lederhosen, wood-carvers, mugs of dark bock beer and streets lined by houses painted with colorful frescoes. One of the biggest attractions is Munich's yearly Oktoberfest. Several days could be spent just driving around, stopping wherever you come across something interesting. The main cities/towns with tourist attractions in Bavaria are Berchtesgaden, Coberg, Fussen, Garmisch-Partenkirchen, Munich and Oberammergau.

Berlin   This once and future capital of Germany is a focus of the excitement that has followed the end of the Cold War. Simply put, it should not be missed. Berlin has always been on the cutting edge of something, and today it's construction. Cranes now line the area like mushrooms, and large office and apartment projects are popping up

Selling Points

History, Berlin, forests, casinos, bratwurst, river cruises, lakes, architecture, art, beer, camping, skiing, hiking, health spas, castles, churches, ballet, opera, concerts, Alpine scenery, farmland, wine, shopping and Munich are the main attractions.

Germany will appeal to travelers who are interested in forest scenery, spas and historical and cultural attractions as well as the flavor of German life.

Fascinating Facts About Germany

The British royal family is actually an offshoot of the German House of Saxe-Coburg-Gotha. In 1917, due to the passions of World War I, British King George V changed the dynastic name to Windsor . . . The 200-mi-/322-km-long Castle Road running between Nuremberg and Mannheim is filled with old homes and castles . . . Enthusiasts of the Bauhaus style of architecture will want to visit Dessau, where the movement was important from 1925 to 1932 . . . There are about 300 spas in Germany. If a town has the word "bad" in it, it means it has a spa . . .

North Sea

NETHERLANDS

BEL.

LUX.

FRANCE

SWITZERLAND

POLAND

AUSTRIA

LOWER SAXONY

THURINGIA

SAXONY

BAVARIA

BLACK FOREST

SWABIAN MOUNTAINS

ERZ GEBIRGE

SPREEWALD

Trave
Elbe
Weser
Havel
Saale
Elbe
Saale
Main
Regnitz
Moselle
Rhine
Rhine
Neckar
Altmuhl
Danube
Danube
Ilz
Inn
Zugspitze

Hamburg
Bremen
● Berlin
Potsdam
Dusseldorf
Muhlhausen
Leipzig
Meissen
Dresden
Cologne
Aachen
Bonn
Eisenach
Weimar
Suhl
Meiningen
Wiesbaden ■Frankfurt am Main
Bayreuth
Wurzburg
Tauberbischofsheim
Bad Mergentheim
Rottingen
Weikersheim
Nuremberg
Heidelberg
Rothenburg
Feuchtwangen
Dinkelsbuhl
Nordlingen
Stuttgart
Harburg
Tubingen
Augsburg
Dachau
Muhldorf
Gutach
Triburg
Munich
Freiburg
Furtwangen
Chiemsee
Hinterzarten
Titisee
Schongau
Berchtesgaden
Bodensee
Fussen
Oberammergau
←Kehlstein
Lake Constance
Garmisch-Partenkirchen
Konigssee
Passau

Germany

● Capital
■ □ City/Site
— International Boundary
River
Canal

Km 0   25   50
Mi 0   25   50

Copyright Weissmann Travel Reports

with managed fury. Even the famous Reichstag is being thoroughly redesigned to make way for the unified government (in 1995, performance artist Christo wrapped it).

Berlin was almost completely rebuilt after the destruction of World War II. While it lacks the romantic feel of other European capitals, it certainly has a jarring sense of the modern. The Kaiser Wilhelm Church, in the center of town, is a good example: The church was all but destroyed in World War II, and the ruined spire was left standing as a monument to the destruction of the war. Next to it, a modern bell tower with stained-glass windows was constructed — a startling contrast.

With the infamous Berlin Wall gone, the city is bisected by what looks like a drained canal — an ugly gash is all that is left of the border that once separated East from West. Most of the wall has been carted off, but a stretch still stands at Muhlstrasse near the train station. Near this area is the impressive Brandenburg Gate, the prewar symbol of Berlin and the site of the first breaches of the Berlin Wall in November 1989.

Of course there is more to Berlin than just an opportunity to ponder the turmoil of 20th-century Europe.

Berlin has evolved into a showcase city of Western Europe. The Kurfurstendamm, one of Europe's great shopping streets, brims with excitement and elegance. The Kurfurstendamm is also a center of Berlin nightlife, and the street remains busy into the wee hours of the morning. Nearby is the fascinating Egyptian (Aegyptysches) Museum, which houses the famous 3,000-year-old bust of Nefertiti, and across the street from it is Schloss Charlottenburg, Frederick the Great's favorite palace and one of the few Baroque/rococo structures to have survived the war (even it had to be thoroughly restored). There are several nice churches, gardens and parks in Berlin (fully one-third of western Berlin's land area is devoted to parks), as well as one of the largest zoos in the world (pandas are among the exhibits) and the Museum Dahlem, which displays works by Rembrandt, Raphael, Vermeer, Velazquez, Botticelli and other European masters. If you're interested in history, you may also want to visit Schoeneberger City Hall, site of Kennedy's "Ich bin ein Berliner" speech, and the Olympic Stadium, site of the 1936 Olympics (and Jesse Owens' victories). Architectural

Berlin at night

Gothic cathedral of Cologne

enthusiasts won't want to miss the Bauhaus-Archiv, which traces the history of that famous design movement.

Prior to World War II, some of the most important parts of Berlin were in the eastern half. The liveliest parts of present-day eastern Berlin are along the Boulevard Unter den Linden and around Alexander Square. Unter den Linden was the city's most fashionable street until the war reduced it to rubble; many buildings have since been carefully restored.

Other sights in eastern Berlin include Academy Square (two domed churches), the Pergamon Museum (an amazing collection of antiquities, including Babylon's Ishtar Gate), the Bode Museum (Egyptian artifacts, Byzantine and European art) and the Museum of German History.

A full-day trip could be made to the western suburb of Potsdam. The city was relatively undamaged during the war, and the architecture of the large houses in its residential areas provides a welcome relief from Berlin's grey uniformity. The city's primary attraction is the Park and Palace of Sanssouci, the ornate summer home of

Frederick the Great. It's done up in high rococo style and every room is completely different. The palace is a monument to excess.

Black Forest   The Black Forest region is a blanket of beautiful, rolling dark pine forest and small lakes. Dubbed the Home of the German Soul, its landscape rises to about 4,000 ft/1,200 m and drops off steeply into valleys. This is the area where cuckoo clocks are made and Old World wood carving is done; older homes in this area are very picturesque.

Cologne (Koln)   This beautiful city is the home of a stunning 13th-century Gothic cathedral. The twin-spired structure is supported by 56 pillars and highlighted by magnificent stained-glass windows. Art lovers won't want to miss the museum complex between the Rhine and the cathedral. It contains paintings from Dutch and German masters (14th–16th century) and modern art in a beautiful setting. If you have time, visit the Roman-Germanic Museum (third-century mosaics). Cologne's a scenic city with plazas, shopping and nightlife. A boat leaving Cologne follows the Rhine to Strasbourg, France (lots of castles, vineyards, hills, etc.).

Dresden   Utterly devastated in fire-bomb raids at the end of World War II, Dresden has been rebuilt and is once again a charming city. Be sure to visit Semper Opera House and the Albertinum Gallery with its famous Green Vault, one of Europe's most amazing treasuries. Also visit the Kreuzkirche (home of a famous boys' choir) and Zwinger Palace (which has the second largest collection of porcelain in the world).

Frankfurt am Main (Frankfurt)   It's unfortunate that most international flights to Germany arrive in Frankfurt, because it's really one of the least interesting large cities in the country. (One possible reason a traveler might spend some time there is that it's the most important center for trade shows and conferences in the country.)

The downtown pedestrian mall has some interesting shops, colorful fruit stands and great bakeries. Among the buildings of historical significance are Katherinenkirche (where Goethe was christened), the Hauptwache (a coffeehouse built in 1730) and the Opera House. We recommend using the town of Wiesbaden, an old-fashioned resort on the Rhine River, as your base, rather than staying in Frankfurt.

Hamburg

The port city of Hamburg, with more than 40 mi/65 km of canals and 2,500 bridges, has an independent, entrepreneurial spirit. Though commerce is Hamburg's strength, it has its share of cultural attractions, as befits a town that was once the home of Johannes Brahms. Be sure to visit the unique Rathaus (city hall, supported by dozens of pillars — it's really a grand building). Hamburg is also a fun city — make time to enjoy some of the beer halls, explore the St. Pauli district and visit the various parks. Stroll through Hamburg's famous fish market (which sells much more than fish). The Reeperbahn is an amusement/entertainment area: Parts of it are family-oriented (video arcades, etc.), but parts are definitely for adults only.

Heidelberg

Heidelberg on the Neckar River is set among lovely hills. Its famous 600-year-old university (the oldest in Germany) has several Renaissance towers and turrets at the base of a hill near Heidelberg Castle. The best way to enjoy the town is to stroll along the Haupstrasse in the old section, to mingle with the local crowds and to sit at one of the many student cafes or beer halls. Also visit the Heidelberg Castle, which changes colors with the different angles of the sun. View the city from the Karl-Theodor Bridge and tour the Kurpfaelzisches Museum (Roman artifacts).

Leipzig

This beautiful, not-to-be-missed city has a long-standing musical heritage. Not only is it the home of the Thomaner Choir — one of the finest in the world — but it's also the site of St. Thomas Church, where Bach worked for 27 years and was buried. Next door is the Bach Museum, opened in 1985. Goethe fans should dine at Auerbachs Keller restaurant, mentioned in *Faust*. The city also has several fine museums, including ones focusing on Egyptology, arts and crafts, natural science, sports and musical instruments (almost 3,000 on display).

Munich

This wonderfully charming southern city located near the Alps is the capital of Bavaria and the home of the world-famous Oktoberfest. Despite its name, Oktoberfest starts in late September and spills into the first week of October — dancing, oompah bands and food dominate. Go prepared not only to drink, but also to eat: You'll have your fill of sausage, that's for sure, but experiment a bit — whole oxen, for instance, are cooked on giant spits. While the food is good, fest-goers never let it detract from the main focus of the festival: beer. The pre-Lenten celebration of Fasching is equally popular.

Munich is an important cultural center, with opera, theater, ballet and concert seasons. It also has museums on every imaginable subject. Some interesting ones are the German Theater Museum, the Residenz (Egyptian Art and the crown jewels) and the Museum of Erotic Art. The Deutsches Museum is the largest science and industry museum in Europe. The Alte Pinakothek and Neue Pinakothek (art museums) house extensive collections of European paintings. The Englische Garten, a riverside park, is a nice place to relax and watch the citizens of Munich take their walks or tan in the sun. The town itself is easy to get around, thanks to an excellent subway and bus system.

Do spend a day driving around the countryside. Munich also has the airport closest to the German Alps (skiing and quaint Bavarian towns). Dachau is both a town and the site of the first Nazi concentration camp. The camp site can be visited 10 mi/16 km from Munich.

The Romantic Road

A beautiful, historic 217-mi/350-km drive, from Wurzburg in the north (Marienburg Fortress) to Fussen in the south (near Fussen is Neuschwanstein, built by mad King Ludwig —Walt Disney used it as a model for Disneyland's Sleeping Beauty castle). The Romantic Road should be driven at a slow, relaxed pace. The road passes through Tauberbischofsheim (medieval town), Bad Mergentheim (spa), Weikersheim (former palace), Rottingen, Feuchtwangen, Dinkelsbuhl, Nordlingen, Harburg

Parade in Bavaria

Geostats

Official Name: Federal Republic of Germany.

Visa Information: Passport needed for U.S. and Canadian citizens.

Health Certificates: None required.

Capitals: While Berlin is the official capital of Germany, the government offices remain in Bonn.

Population: 81,338,000.

Size: 137,800 sq mi/357,863 sq km. About the size of Arkansas and Idaho combined.

Language: German.

Climate: Temperate.

Economy: Industry, mining, agriculture.

Government: Federal republic.

Religions: Protestant, Roman Catholic.

Currency: Deutschemarks (DMK). 100 pfennigs = 1 DMK. Traveler's checks and credit cards are widely accepted. AE, DC, MC, VI.

Time Zone: 6 hours ahead of eastern standard time; 1 hour ahead of Greenwich mean time.

Electricity: 220 volts.

(impressive castle), Schongau (700-year-old city), Augsburg and Rothenburg (nearly perfect medieval city). We suggest taking at least three days to travel through this area.

Thuringian Forest

This beautiful recreational area on the former West/East German border is ideal for hiking, relaxing and taking a vacation from your vacation. Medieval buildings, castles on the Saale River, old monasteries, churches, the Slate Mountains and beautiful hills and valleys characterize this region. Among the important cities there are Muhlausen, with its medieval architecture, and Suhl, where guns with artistic engravings are manufactured.

Itinerary

Even a 15-day tour such as this one gives only an overview of Germany's highlights — at least a month would be needed to begin to feel you know the country.

Day 1 — Arrive Frankfurt. Overnight in nearby Wiesbaden.

Day 2 — Depart for Heidelberg. Tour city and continue on to Wurzburg. Overnight Wurzburg.

Day 3 — Morning tour of Wurzburg and begin drive southward along the Romantic Road. Overnight Rothenburg or another town along the way.

Day 4 — Continue along the Romantic Road, visiting as many of the little towns and villages as time permits. Overnight in Munich.

Day 5 — Tour Munich in morning and drive south in mid-afternoon through the Bavarian towns of Fussen or Oberammergau. Check into a hotel in one of these cities and use it as a base for exploring the region.

Day 6 — See as much in the surrounding area as possible — perhaps visit Neuschwanstein Castle.

Day 7 — Drive to Dresden. Tour city if time permits. Overnight Dresden.

Day 8 — Dresden. Visit nearby Meissen to see the famous porcelain factory, if time permits. Overnight Dresden.

Day 9 — Drive to Berlin and overnight there.

Days 10–11 — Berlin.

Day 12 — Drive to Potsdam to see the Palace of Sans Souci. Return to Berlin for the overnight or drive to Leipzig.

Day 13 — Leipzig.

Day 14 — Drive as far as possible today in the direction of Frankfurt.

Day 15 — Depart from Frankfurt.

Climate/When to Go

June–September is the best time to tour Germany, when the days are warm and nights are cool (definitely take a jacket, especially to Bavaria). April, May and October can also be good, particularly if you're interested in museums.

Transportation

Lufthansa, LTU, PIA, Singapore and most major U.S. airlines fly from the U.S. to Germany. Lufthansa, Air Canada and Canadian Airlines International fly daily from Canada. European airlines offer connecting flights to major German cities. Major international airports include Frankfurt (FRA — 6 mi/10 km from city center), Hamburg (HAM — 8 mi/13 km from city center), Munich (MUC — 29 mi/46 km from city center) and Berlin's three: Tegel (TXL — 5 mi/8 km from downtown Berlin), Tempelhof (THF — 7 mi/11 km from city center) and Schoenefeld (SXF — 12 mi/19 km from city center). Lufthansa offers domestic service throughout the country.

Various cruise lines stop in Hamburg; the KD German Rhine Line offers excellent cruises of two to five days along the Rhine (from the Netherlands to Switzerland). The most scenic part is between St. Goar and Rudesheim on the Cologne-Strasbourg stretch: It features castles, vineyards and hills. There are also river cruises on the Weser, Moselle, Elbe, Danube and Main. Intra-European trains connect with cities throughout Germany, and the domestic rail system is excellent. Germany's IC (Intercity) trains leave every hour between all major cities and travel at speeds of up to 120 mph/194 kph.

Escorted and hosted tours, buses, taxis, bicycles (from most railroad stations) and rental cars are excellent ways to see the country. The autobahns (freeways) and other roads in western Germany are excellent. The major roads in eastern Germany are adequate, but the secondary ones leave much to be desired.

The average speed on the western German autobahns (where there's no speed limit) is 80 mph/128 kph, but many people drive faster. We think independent travelers should take advantage of the efficient trains to avoid the challenges of the autobahn.

Accommodations

Accommodations range from deluxe, world-class properties to quaint inns, hotels, bed-and-breakfasts, hostels, castles, ski chalets, health spas and campgrounds. There is a tremendous disparity between hotels in the east and the west, but generally speaking, hotels in eastern Germany are still nice and clean.

Health Advisories

Western Germany has excellent medical and dental facilities throughout, even in small towns. It's safe to drink the tap water and eat the food. In eastern Germany, medical and dental facilities are adequate, but air and water pollution are more of a problem than in the west; we stick with bottled water.

What to Buy

In western Germany, shop for cuckoo clocks, Hummel figurines, thermometers, sunglasses, wood carvings, leather goods, cameras, optical equipment (such as binoculars), china, musical instruments, porcelain, electronic goods, stainless steelware, antiques, unique toys and dolls, wines, cheese, Danish glassware and local handicrafts. In eastern Germany, shop for wood carvings, tiles (Leipzig), porcelain (especially in Dresden and the Thuringian Forest region), Russian and Eastern European phonograph records, Soviet Army uniform articles, pottery and some local handicrafts (such as wooden nutcrackers).

What to Eat

Dishes tend to be hearty, and include cold meats, veal, pork chops, cheese, wurst (sausage), breads, dumplings served with meat and lots of gravy, *Wiener schnitzel* (breaded veal cutlets), *Konigsberger klops* (pork and veal with capers), *apfelstrudel,* Rhine salmon and sauerkraut. You can find a good pretzel just about anywhere. There's more fish in the north; meals tend to be heavier in the south. Some of the best, most authentic and least expensive food in Germany is in the country inns. Also try the excellent German wines and beers.

Travel Tips for the Client

Try a late afternoon *Cafe und Kuchen* (Coffee and Cake), and take two or three hours at dinner. Germans think dinner shouldn't be hurried . . . Don't make international calls from your hotel (you'll be socked with a tremendous surcharge). Phone from the post office instead. The least expensive way to phone is to get a calling card before leaving home and place calls home through your phone company's international operator . . . The town of Oberammergau, south of Munich, is world famous as the home of a Passion play, performed every ten years. If you are going to be in the Munich area during May–September in the first year of a decade, arrange to see the play. . . .

Germany

Review Questions

1. For most travelers, why is Bavaria the most quintessentially German region?

2. What is the Kurfurstendamm? What is it like there at night?

3. What is the primary attraction in Potsdam? Describe it.

4. Cologne is home to what stunning attraction? How would you describe it?

5. In what city do most international flights arrive in Germany? For what is it Germany's most important center?

6. What is the best way for a tourist to enjoy the town of Heidelberg?

7. What German city has a long-standing musical heritage and is home to the Thomaner Choir? What famous composer worked and is buried in St. Thomas Church there?

8. What city is home to the world-famous Oktoberfest? When does this festival take place?

9 For what will a tourist find the Thuringian Forest ideal?

10. What are the differences between western and eastern Germany in terms of accommodations and health advisories?

Germany

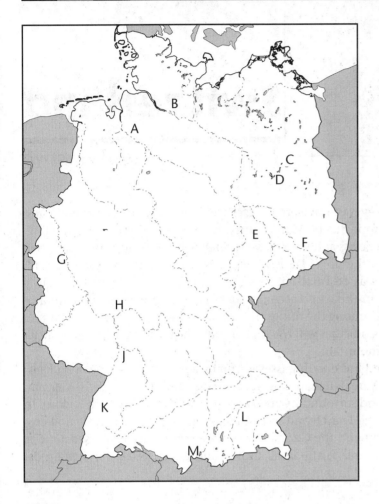

Map Skills Exercise

Match the tourist destination listed below with the corresponding letter on the map. You can use each letter only once.

1. _____ Palace of Sanssouci
2. _____ Dresden
3. _____ Cologne cathedral
4. _____ Frankfurt am Main
5. _____ Reeperbahn
6. _____ Kurfurstendamm
7. _____ Black Forest
8. _____ Heidelberg
9. _____ Neuschwanstein
10. _____ Oktoberfest

Selling Exercise

Two college students want to tour Germany by rail. (The German rail system is very extensive and connects most major cities.) The students have come to you to find out about the rail system and about routes and significant tourist sites along the way. They're particularly interested in attending Oktoberfest. Plan a rail trip through Germany for the students that includes eight stops, including a few days at Oktoberfest.

Switzerland
and Austria

In the eyes of travelers, Switzerland has always risen above the rest of Europe. In the 19th century, it was the place to go for the English upper class and writers (Mary Shelley was on vacation there when she wrote the novel *Frankenstein*). Today the country remains a leading overseas destination. Its stunning countryside, first-class skiing and best-in-the-world accommodations guarantee a memorable vacation. And among the things that are stunning are the prices — at times your expenditures will rise higher than the Matterhorn, the country's highest mountain.

Switzerland encompasses four cultures: French (Geneva and surrounding area), Italian (Lugano and surrounding area), Swiss-German (Zurich and surrounding area) and Romansh (southeastern region). In general, the French and Italian areas tend to be more lively and cosmopolitan and the German area more conservative and sedate. The Romansh area is the least known and developed — and the most "authentic," in our view.

What to Do There

Bern Switzerland's capital city is beautiful. Climb to the top of the cathedral for a sweeping view of the city. The thick-walled stone houses in the Old Town are brightened by boxes of geraniums on the balconies; providing sharp contrast are majestic green-domed government buildings that hang on a high bluff overlooking the Aare River.

Bern is best known for its Bear Pits, where six or so bears spend their days cadging carrots from tourists. The city's name derives from the German word for bear, and you'll see these animals prominently portrayed on the municipal flag and coat of arms.

Visit the 12th-century Clock Tower and see its hourly show of mechanical figures (be sure to get there four minutes before the hour). The Postal Museum can boast the world's largest collection of stamps. For good shopping head to the Arcades, which has elegant boutiques, art galleries, fur and jewelry salons and, of course, Swiss chocolates, watches and knives.

Clock Tower, Bern

Bernese Oberland/the Heidi Area

Chalets in the mountains, yodelers, ski lodges and horse-drawn sleighs are typical images of Switzerland, and there are two adjacent Swiss areas where these images come to life: the Bernese Oberland and the Heidi Area near Chur in eastern Switzerland. You'll probably come across Alp horn blowers, beautiful hilly pastures, waterfalls, glaciers and detailed woodcarvings on houses and bridges. Heidi's home (Heidihof) is in Maienfeld, just a few miles north of the town of Chur, the oldest town in Switzerland. In the Bernese Oberland region, Interlaken is an excellent place to use as a base for short tours. The only downside to Interlaken is that it's very touristy in the summer. Nonetheless, there's a good reason that so many tourists go there: Concerts, equestrian events, tennis, hiking excursions, water sports and the surrounding beautiful countryside are all available then.

Geneva
Geneva is a very French city on Lake Geneva in the far western part of the country. It's clean and charming, but unless time is not a factor, there are more interesting parts of the country to see. If you go, visit the Old Quarter, St. Pierre Cathedral, the headquarters for various international organizations and Le Jet d'Eau (a big fountain in the lake). Then walk along the quaint streets to shop and observe the architecture. Day trips include a ferry ride on Lake Geneva.

Lausanne/Ouchy
Lausanne and its port city, Ouchy (pronounced ou-SHEE), are on the northern bank of Lake Geneva. They can be seen either as a day trip from Geneva or (better yet) in a two-night stay. The older part of the city is fun to stroll; be sure to see the port area, the 13th-century tower, the exquisite Gothic cathedral and the 14th-century Chateau St. Maire. The Art Brut Museum has interesting and inventive works done by unconventional artists (some of whom were eventually institutionalized). Lausanne is also the home of the International Olympic Committee Headquarters, which has a museum tracing the history of the Olympics.

Some ancient villages in the surrounding hills are worth visiting. Just across the lake is the spa/resort Royal Club Evian in Evian, France, where Evian water is bottled. You can also take a long day trip to Chamonix, France, to see Mt. Blanc (the tallest mountain in Europe).

Lucerne
Lucerne is one of Switzerland's most charming medieval cities. We think it's best seen on foot. To begin your tour, cross the 14th-century Chapel Bridge (rebuilt after a fire in 1993). The bridge is covered, and there are wonderful paintings of Lucerne's history on the ceiling. In town, visit the Jesuit church and the Lion of Lucerne, a dramatic rock sculpture of a dying lion that is a monument to the Swiss Guards who fought and died protecting Louis XVI during the French Revolution. The Old Town is a must, especially Weinmarkt; take special

The Matterhorn

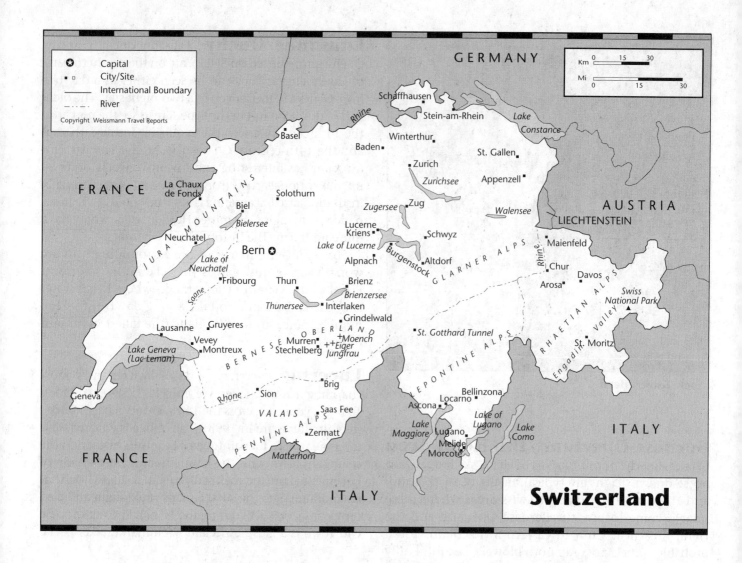

Switzerland

Legend:
- ✪ Capital
- ■ □ City/Site
- International Boundary
- River

Copyright Weissmann Travel Reports

note of the painted facades of the buildings. Just a couple of miles from the town center (along the lake) is the Swiss Transport Museum, one of the best of its kind in the world. There are many trains on display. If you'd rather stay outdoors, rent a rowboat or paddleboat and cruise on the lake among the swans. Also be sure to take the trip via cable car from Kriens to Mt. Pilatus, a huge mountain adjacent to the city, for lunch and a great view.

Lugano   It's been said that Lugano has the "gaiety and romance of Italy, encased in a Swiss precision watch." Its culture, language and food are Italian, yet its accommodations are spotlessly Swiss. It's situated on beautiful Lake Lugano. You can take the cogwheel train up Mt. Bre for a breathtaking view. Lugano's Villa Favorita is said to contain part of the second most valuable private art collection in the world (after Queen Elizabeth's). Lugano now rivals Montreux as a jazz mecca, with a yearly spring festival that lures big names.

Montreux and Vevey   Elegant Montreux, with its large Old World-style hotels and relaxing atmosphere, is in a resort area on the eastern end of Lake Geneva. It and nearby Vevey offer beaches, summer water sports (including windsurfing) and an entertainment complex that includes a casino. Montreux hosts a world-famous jazz festival every July.

Day trips can be made to visit the Nestle chocolate factory in Broc and the Chateau of Chillon on Lake Geneva (Switzerland's best-known castle.)

St. Moritz   This resort in the southeast is famous for being a retreat for the wealthy. Be prepared for outrageous prices and a rather cold attitude exhibited by the residents. Nonetheless, St. Moritz offers beautiful chalets, truly spectacular shopping, mountain views, skiing and relaxation. The soothing properties of the St. Moritz spa were extolled by Roman soldiers in the time of Christ, and the praises haven't yet stopped.

Valais Area This area is home to some of the most dramatic Alpine scenery in the country, including the town of Zermatt — one of the best-known ski resorts in the world. The Matterhorn, Eiger and Mt. Blanc can all be seen (on clear days) on a trip via bus and cable car along the Pillon Pass. Other sights include a fresco that illustrates the story of William Tell.

Zurich Although Zurich has the soul of a business city, it does have a nice setting on the water. Visit the Swiss National Museum (historical displays) and Kunsthaus (fine arts museum), eat in at least one of the famous guild restaurants and visit the well-preserved Old Town. The city's most prestigious shopping can be found on the elegant Bahnhofstrasse. Relax in one of the many outdoor cafes that line the streets.

Itinerary

The one-week itinerary below can be taken in either direction. It's designed to let a traveler see as much as possible without being exhausted.

Day 1 — Arrive Zurich.

Day 2 — Tour Zurich and then proceed to Lucerne.

Day 3 — Lucerne.

Day 4 — Drive or take the train to Interlaken.

Day 5 — Tour Interlaken and sights nearby in the Bernese Oberland region.

Day 6 — Montreux.

Day 7 — Go to Geneva, leaving early enough to allow at least half a day there to tour the city. Overnight Geneva.

Day 8 — Depart Geneva.

Climate/When to Go

Switzerland isn't as cold as most people think. Spring, summer and autumn are all quite comfortable. Lugano and the surrounding area experience temperatures similar to those in Los Angeles (they even have palm trees).

Geostats

Official Name: Swiss Confederation.

Visa Information: Passports required of U.S. and Canadian citizens.

Health Certificates: None required.

Capital: Bern.

Population: 6,860,000.

Size: 15,941 sq mi/41,288 sq km. About twice the size of New Jersey.

Languages: German, French, Italian, Romansh (Latin-based language), English.

Climate: Temperate, varying with altitude and season.

Economy: Industry, services.

Government: Federal state.

Religions: Roman Catholic, Protestant.

Currency: Swiss franc (SFR). 100 centimes = 1 SFR. Traveler's checks are accepted at tourist locations. Credit cards are widely accepted. AE, DC, MC and VI.

Time Zone: 6 hours ahead of eastern standard time; 1 hour ahead of Greenwich mean time.

Electricity: 220 volts.

Transportation

Swissair, American and United offer nonstop service from the United States. Air Canada and Swissair offer direct service from Canada. Other European airlines also fly to Switzerland via their hub cities (flights are available to airports in Geneva, Zurich and Basel). Zurich Airport (ZRH) is 7 mi/11 km from town, and Geneva Airport (GVA) is 10 mi/16 km from that city. Excellent and frequent rail service is available to and within Switzerland. If you're planning to visit different areas of Switzerland, consider buying the Swiss Pass. Bicycles are available for rent at many train stations.

Accommodations

Accommodations range from deluxe international five-star properties to chalets, quaint inns, B-and-Bs, hostels, motels, campgrounds and manors. You'll find them to be well kept and clean with highly professional staffs. After all, the Swiss set the benchmark for European hotels and hospitality, and students gather from all over the world to attend the great hotel schools in Lausanne.

Health Advisories

Excellent hospitals as well as dental and other health-care facilities are available throughout the country. If you're flying into high altitudes, take it easy on your first few days to adjust. Note that altitude sickness can have serious forms.

What to Buy

Shop for pottery, watches, crystal, embroidered items, wood carvings, clocks (including cuckoos), Swiss army knives, Swiss liquors, lace, textiles, folklore souvenirs such as music boxes, Swiss-dressed dolls, cowbells, cheese, antiques, stainless-steel cutlery, ski equipment and clothing, leather goods, shoes and chocolates.

What to Eat

Swiss food is not known for its subtlety — it's a meat-potatoes-and-cheese country — but the Swiss do make nice sauces for vegetables and great desserts. As might be expected, there's a French influence in the west, Italian in the south and German in the north and east. Try the chocolates!

Travel Tips for the Client

Do try to take one of the scenic trains, such as the Montreux-Bernese Oberland or the Glacier Express (between St. Moritz and Zermatt) . . . Don't be surprised by the charge of about US$25 highway tax if you enter Switzerland in a car rented in another country. It's their sensible substitute for tolls. . . .

Austria

With Germany to the north and Italy to the south, Austria is a mix of the Romantic and the Germanic. Although many people enjoy the country most for its physical beauty — the Alps and the Danube River Valley — we love the sense of history it imparts. When we walk, for instance, through the narrow, winding streets of Salzburg, past buildings from the 13th century, we can easily imagine ourselves back in medieval times.

Once the leading nation in Central Europe, Austria was the home of the Habsburgs, the continent's most influential and longest-lasting dynasty. They retained power for 700 years (1218–1918). The country was also the music center of Europe during the 18th century and the focus of literature and science in the 19th and early 20th. Mozart, Haydn, Strauss, Kafka and Freud are but a few of the luminaries of the imperial era.

At the end of World War I, the vast empire broke up and Austria became the small German-speaking country we know today. While Vienna is no longer the capital of a diverse multi-ethnic empire, the city still retains its international flair.

What to Do There

Innsbruck This 800-year-old town, twice the site of the Winter Olympics, is the capital of gorgeous Tirol (also spelled Tyrol) state. Set at the base of the spectacular Alps, Innsbruck is a fairly compact city (with an old quarter reminiscent of the Middle Ages). You'll need to do a good amount of walking to appreciate the city fully. Begin sightseeing on Marien- Theresien Strasse, where you can see the views of the Nordkette mountain range, Triumphal

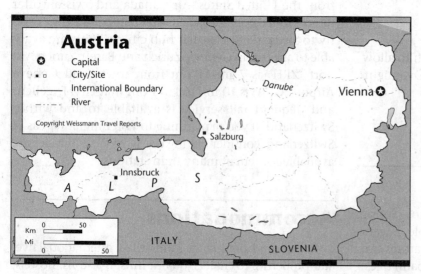

Arch (built in 1765 to commemorate the marriage of the future emperor Leopold II) and St. Anne's Column (erected in 1706). Tour the 18th-century Hofburg (former imperial palace) and the unintentionally humorous Hofkirche, or "Court Church" (with 28 oversized bronze statues of royal relatives — don't miss the statue of the Emperor Rudolf). The city's casino is located in the Scandic Crown hotel. Excursions can be made to the top of Patscherkofel Mountain (a beautiful view); take the bus to the village of Igls and then a cable car to the peak.

Salzburg

Salzburg has a southern-European feel. It's a compact town, easy to get around on foot. Top attractions include the Mirabell Palace (with its Angel Staircase — and gardens which were featured in *The Sound of Music*), Hohensalzburg (a white castle overlooking the city), the superbly carved horse pond with frescoes in Sigmundsplatz and of course the obligatory Sound of Music tour (a fun, kitschy tour with reenactments of the movie's highlights). Fans of Mozart will want to visit the Mozarteum (where he composed *The Magic Flute*) and his Birth House.

On the outskirts of the city is one of Salzburg's top attractions, Hellbrunn Castle. Its water gardens are great fun, especially for kids. Within a short drive of the city in any direction are mountains, gardens and beautiful lakes. Some of Salzburg's annual festivals include Mozart Week (January) and the Salzburg Festival (summer). The city truly comes alive during these times.

Vienna

Austria's splendid capital, Vienna is a smorgasbord of Baroque with a dash of art nouveau. Circling the old town (the Innerstadt) is the pompous revivalist architecture of the Ringstrasse, Vienna's main boulevard. These buildings range from the charming Opera House to the overdone Natural History Museum. Nestled throughout the city are the graceful art-nouveau buildings that are remnants of the artistic and intellectual flowering that took place in Vienna at the turn of the century. Of course, the buildings and the city's history are only a backdrop for the daily culture that can still be found in the concert halls, opera houses and cafes that fill the city.

Tour Vienna and get oriented; we like taking the horse-drawn carriages. If you'd prefer a more elevated impression of the city, go up to the top of the Donauturm (Danube Tower). In the evening take in one of the main attractions (for some of which you'll need tickets),

> ## Fascinating Facts About Austria
>
> Between the New Year and Ash Wednesday, Vienna hosts more than 700 balls, many requiring white tie/evening gown. The dance? The waltz, of course . . . Vienna is also the birthplace of Jugendstil, the Austrian art-nouveau movement. Gustav Klimt and Egon Schiele are two of the best-known Jugendstil painters . . . The Vienna Boys Choir, established by Emperor Maximilian I, dates from 1498 . . . Adolf Hitler was born in the town of Braunau. There is no mention of him in the local museum, however . . . The song *Silent Night* was written in the village of Oberndorf, near Salzburg. . . .

including the Vienna State Opera, the Vienna Boys Choir and the Spanish Riding School (with its famous Lipizzaner stallions).

The pulse of the city can be found along the Ringstrasse. As you walk around the area, be sure to take a break at a sidewalk cafe and have one of the superb pastries. After a coffee, you might want take a walk past the Gothic Rathaus (city hall) or stop by one of the world-class museums along the Ringstrasse. You'll also want to visit the Innenstadt (the old town), now a pedestrian zone where many of the city's main attractions are located. Another corner of the old city is home to the Hofburg Palace, where you'll find the Imperial Treasuries (Habsburg Crown Jewels).

We thoroughly enjoyed seeing the homes of famous Viennese: Sigmund Freud, Johann Strauss, Jr., Beethoven and Mozart. If you feel like taking a short excursion out of the city, consider having a picnic in the Vienna Woods or visiting the Schonbrunn Palace — the Habsburg summer home.

Travel Tips for the Client

Don't expect Austrians to have seen *The Sound of Music*. The film was a flop in that country, and most Austrians have only heard about it from tourists . . . Do say hello ("Gruss Gott" or "Guten Tag") when entering a shop or restaurant — social pleasantries are the norm in Austria . . . Do try local wines and beers — they're among the best in the world. . . .

Switzerland and Austria

Review Questions

1. What four cultures does Switzerland encompass? In what area of the country is each found?

2. For what is Bern best known?

3. What typical images of Switzerland will come to life for a tourist in Bernese Oberland and the Heidi Area?

4. What charming medieval city is home to the restored Chapel Bridge? What will a visitor see on the bridge's ceiling?

5. For what is St. Moritz famous? For what should a visitor to St. Moritz be prepared?

6. To what is the Valais area home?

7. Where are Lausanne and its port city, Ouchy, located? What attractions should a tourist be sure to see in the older part of the city?

8. Many tourist attractions in Austria are connected with the dynasty that ruled the country for centuries. What is the name of that dynasty? For what was Austria the center in Europe during the 18th century?

9. What main evening attractions requiring tickets might you recommend to a visitor to Vienna?

10. Where can a visitor find the pulse of Vienna? What are the area's attractions?

Switzerland and Austria

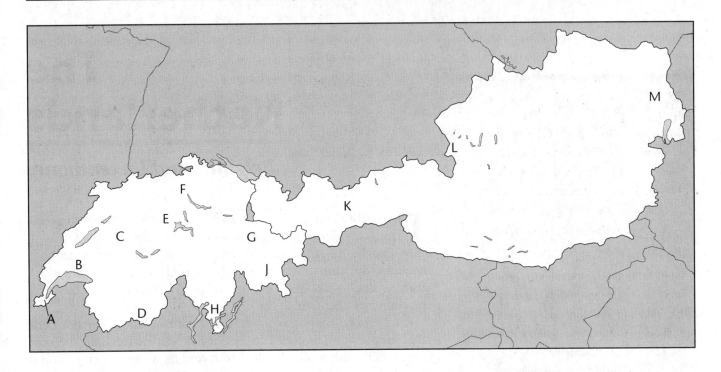

Map Skills Exercise

Match the tourist destination listed below with the corresponding letter
on the map. You can use each letter only once.

1. _____ Geneva
2. _____ the Ringstrasse
3. _____ Switzerland's capital
4. _____ Mozart's birth house
5. _____ The Matterhorn

6. _____ Lugano
7. _____ Lausanne
8. _____ St. Moritz
9. _____ Zurich
10. _____ Lucerne

Selling Exercise

A company in your country wants to set up a branch office in Switzerland or Austria. It plans to send a representative to these two nations to search for a possible location for the office. The representative will have time to visit only two cities and the president of the company would like you to recommend the two. What cities would suggest? Why?

The Netherlands

Belgium and Luxembourg

The Netherlands seems to make a place for everyone and everything. So many of the attractions are what we think of as typically Dutch: dikes, canals, fields of tulips, creaking windmills, incredible museums and genuinely friendly citizens. Yet, Amsterdam's steamier side — both prostitution and drug use are legal — illustrates the country's openness to the diversity of life.

The Netherlands has a long history as one of Europe's major trade and transportation centers. The present-day Netherlands didn't become a formidable power until the late 16th century, when Dutch explorers brought back valuable commodities from around the world and greatly increased the nation's wealth. Buoyed by its wealth and status, the country experienced a Golden Age (1580–1740), producing such painters as Rembrandt, Jan Vermeer and Frans Hals. Its status as a major power began to erode in the late 18th century and finally came to an end when the French, under Napoleon, conquered it in 1795. But it wasn't until the 20th century that it gave up its colonial empire, surrendering its last colony, Suriname (in South America), in 1975.

Water defines life in the Netherlands. Because so much of the country is below sea level (20% is built on reclaimed land), Dutch life depends on 1,500 mi/2,400 km of dikes. To the Dutch, dikes are as much a symbol of the Netherlands as is the windmill.

What to Do There

Amsterdam   At times, this beautiful city seems to be a living 17th-century museum. It has charming architecture from that period in a relatively compact area — it's an excellent city to tour on foot. But the people are very modern in outlook, and Amsterdam at night is alive with the sounds of contemporary music.

We like to begin our tour in Dam Square. There you'll find the Koninklijk Paleis, a former royal palace built in the Baroque style. Also on the Dam are a World War II National Monument, the 15th-century Nieuwe Kerk (now a space for art exhibitions) and the city's largest department store, De Bijenkorf. If you're standing in front of the royal palace, the two narrow streets to the right and left of it are pedestrian shopping streets with many trendy clothing shops. Other sights include the 150-year-old Artis Zoo; the 17th-century Portuguese Synagogue (built by Sephardic Jews expelled from Spain); and the Schreierstoren, or "Tower of Tears" — the name refers to tears shed by sailors' wives as they watched their husbands sail away. A must-see is Anne Frank's house — if you haven't already read it, begin *The Diary of Anne Frank* on the plane en route.

Other points of interest include the old hippie hangout Vondel Park, the diamond workshops (many can be toured), the floating flower market near the Munt tower and the American Hotel, where the World War I spy Mata Hari held her wedding reception in 1894 (it's noted today for its Jugendstil, or art nouveau, style of architecture). Beer drinkers will want to visit the Heineken Brewery (the lines can be long, so go early).

Amsterdam has several excellent museums, and two of the best are next to each other. The Van Gogh Museum is important for anyone even slightly curious about the man and his work. At first, many of the more than 200 paintings and 400 drawings, while good, will seem awfully similar — and then you'll turn a corner and find what is obviously a masterpiece. The juxtaposition is educational. On the same square is the 250-room Rijksmuseum, which contains one of the best Rembrandt collections in the world. Walking into the room that houses the huge painting known as *The Night Watch* is like walking into a shrine — it's awe-inspiring. Spend some time with Rembrandt's self-portraits, too, to see how many different ways he saw himself.

Take a boat cruise (there are more than 100 mi/160 km of canals). A typical cruise will pass 17th-century homes in exclusive neighborhoods as well as houseboats, the Amsterdam dry docks, a selection of the city's narrow buildings (some only one window wide) and the "Skinny Bridge" (a narrow drawbridge built to allow two sisters to cross and have tea together every afternoon). Taking a canal cruise at night is a treat (there's even a wine-and-cheese candlelight cruise). Most of the fancy merchant homes and bridges are illuminated, so the effect is altogether different from a daytime trip.

Amsterdam's red-light district is, oddly enough, a tourist attraction, drawing even those who aren't interested in spending money there. The open-minded Dutch have a neighborhood where women sit in shop windows, casting "come hither" looks at anyone who appears interested. Unlike such areas in other countries, the streets are relatively safe. Prostitution is legal and government-controlled, and there are plenty of police around.

A canal in Amsterdam

It's best to rent a car in Amsterdam to tour the rest of the country. You can set your own pace and see what you want. The Netherlands is relatively small, so most of the cities can be visited on day trips and you can return to Amsterdam in the evening.

Delft The "City of Tiles" has quaint shops, restaurants, windmills, canals and, of course, the famous Delftware pottery. The Huis Lambert van Meerten Museum (Delft tiles) and the Royal Army and Weapon Museum merit stops. So does the De Koninklijke Porcelyne Fles (ceramics factory), which has been in business since 1653 — you can see their museum and working areas.

De Zaanse Schans (Zaanse Schans)

On the banks of the river Schans, De Zaanse Schans is a collection of old Dutch houses assembled from the surrounding (now industrialized) region. The town's main attraction is its open-air Windmill Museum. Each windmill is different: Some were used for pumping water, others for grinding corn and wheat or even for running saws or smithies.

Windmills

Haarlem   This 900-year-old town has beautiful medieval houses, a 13th-century city hall, great tulips and the Teylers Museum (science, technology and Dutch art). If that's not enough, continue with the Nieuwe Kerk, the Frans Hals Museum (Dutch Masters) and St. Bavo Church, locally noted for its 5,000-pipe organ.

The Hague   The official governmental seat (but not the official capital) of the country, The Hague is a beautiful city of parks, trees, government buildings and gardens. See the exterior of the home of the royal family, Huis ten Bos (House of Orange — closed to the public) and the uplifting Peace Palace, home of the International Court of Justice. Visit Westbroek Park (thousands of roses) and the Binnenhof, the center of the Netherlands' political life. Among the government buildings is the 13th-century Gothic Hall of Knights. We also enjoyed window-shopping at the many antique shops. And if you're looking for museums, then you're in the right place. Among the best are the Puppet Museum, Gemeente Municipal Museum (mostly modern art) and 17th-century Mauritshuis Museum (an impressive collection of Rembrandts and other Dutch Masters).

Keukenhof   The Kitchen Garden (as Keukenhof translates) boasts a spectacular 65-acre/25-hectare array of more than 6,000,000 tulips and other flowering plants. Ten mi/16 km of paths wander through some of the most beautiful gardens in the world. Pick out a plant, and when it has finished blooming, the bulb will be mailed to you. The gardens are open from 8 am to 6:30 pm daily from late March to late May.

Rotterdam   Rotterdam's most notable tourist attraction is the 605-ft-/184-m-tall Euromast Space Tower (take the revolving, sit-down elevator to the top). The harbor, one of the busiest in the world, is a draw in itself — and don't miss the nearby maritime museum. Another collection worth seeing is the Dutch, Italian and French art displayed at the Boymans-van-Beuningen Museum.

Volendam   Set aside half a day for Volendam, one of the most picturesque fishing villages in the country. Walk the dike, eat herring and observe people wearing the area's traditional clothing: Women in typical dress, with aprons and big white-winged hats, stroll alongside men who look as if they just walked off a Dutch Boy paint can (black woolen pants flared at the bottom, wooden shoes and round caps).

Itinerary

The Netherlands is small — its length can be driven in one day. Nonetheless, there's a lot to see, and we recommend a minimum of eight days there.

Day 1 — Arrive Amsterdam.

Day 2 — Amsterdam.

Day 3 — Take a day trip.

Day 4 — Take another day trip.

Day 5 — Drive to The Hague via Delft.

Day 6 — The Hague.

Day 7 — Return to Amsterdam.

Day 8 — Depart the Netherlands.

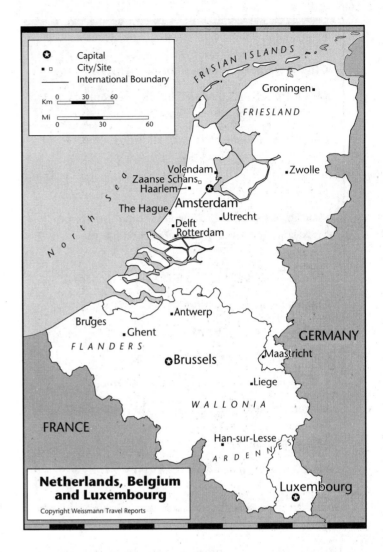

Climate/When to Go

The best time to go is from mid-May to early October, when the day temperatures are generally in the 70s–80s F/20–31 C, with nights in the 50s–60s F/10–20 C (although it can rain quite a bit then — take a folding umbrella!). The winters are long, damp, cold and generally unsuitable for touring. The tulip season runs from April to mid-May.

Transportation

KLM, Martinair Holland and major U.S. and European carriers fly from the U.S., while KLM and Air Canada provide service from Canada. Amsterdam's Schiphol Airport (AMS), is located 9 mi/15 km southwest of town. Several cruise lines include the Netherlands on their world and North Sea itineraries. Excellent ferry service connects the Netherlands with Great Britain, and rail service reaches the rest of Europe. Escorted/hosted and fly-drive tours, bicycles, trains, motorcycles, campers and caravans (small house trailers) are available to see the country. Taxis, buses and/or trams are available in Amsterdam and larger towns. There are several Netherlands Rail passes and rail package tours (primarily in Amsterdam and Rotterdam). The trains are comfortable and one of the best ways to see the country.

Accommodations

Accommodations range from deluxe international hotels and resorts to bed-and-breakfasts, boarding-houses, bungalows, castles, quaint inns, barges, hostels, farm lodging and campgrounds. We generally prefer staying in the smaller local hotels. They're quite interesting and clean, and they add a personal touch to the service.

Health Advisories

The Netherlands has excellent hospitals, and most towns have clinics, doctors and nurses. Dental care is readily available. You can eat and drink confidently in restaurants, as sanitation standards are quite high.

What to Buy

Shop for Delft blue and other porcelain, diamonds, wooden shoes, licorice, cheese, Indonesian batiks, decorative tiles and local items. Look for antiques at

Antiekmarkt de Looier, a large indoor market in Amsterdam. Schiphol Airport has one of the largest duty-free shopping centers in the world (you can buy cheese and tulip bulbs there if you missed earlier opportunities).

What to Eat

The Netherlands has a wide variety of local cuisine and international restaurants, ranging from French and Indonesian all the way to McDonald's. (Note: Indonesia was one of The Netherlands' colonies.) There are excellent seafood and fish dishes (especially herring and oysters), marvelous cheeses and delicious pea soup (usually served in winter). Be sure to go to an Indonesian restaurant offering rijsttafel, a banquet that can include up to 16 courses piled on a rice base (the dishes will include spicy meats, vegetables/fruit and sweet and sour sauces).

Ask at restaurants if they offer a tourist menu, which usually offers modest prices.

Travel Tips for the Client

Do rent ice skates in the winter — and follow the crowds . . . Don't take a camera if you tour Amsterdam's red light district — the women have been known to throw photographers into canals, camera and all . . . Don't buy any tulip bulbs unless there's a customs declaration form included that will allow them to be imported into your home country . . . Do rent a bicycle for a nice day of touring — they are available from most train stations or bicycle shops, and bicycle paths are everywhere. . . .

Belgium

In addition to its great restaurants, pubs and chocolatiers, Belgium is a patchwork of small farms and picturesque rivers and lakes, dotted with ancient cathedrals and some wonderful museums with wonderful art. The northern region, called Flanders, is more densely populated than the South; the landlocked southern region, Wallonia, is more rural and includes the forests of the Ardennes.

The country's history has contributed to its rich diversity: The Romans, Celts, Spanish, Austrians, French and Dutch all occupied Belgium at one time or another, and each culture left its mark.

Fascinating Facts About Belgium

Napoleon didn't meet his Waterloo at Waterloo. The battlefield was actually 3 mi/5 km south, at La Belle Alliance, but then "where Napoleon met his La Belle Alliance" doesn't have quite the same ring . . . Charles V, Emperor of the Holy Roman Empire, King of Spain and ruler of most of Europe in his time, was born in Ghent . . . There are more than 2,100 chocolate shops in the country . . .

What to Do There

Antwerp The home of the 17th-century painter Peter Paul Rubens and the world's diamond capital, Antwerp is a joy to visit. The wide squares and the narrow cobbled streets of the old town are perfect for wandering — they're lined with shops and cafes, which make the walk even more pleasant. The city is still shining from the facelift it received after it was designated the Cultural Capital of Europe in 1993. The Cathedral of Our Lady (which holds Rubens' humbling *Descent from the Cross*) was scrubbed and restored. Besides these new attractions, old favorites still remain: Chief among them is the Rubens House and studio. Antwerp is also one of the world's largest diamond centers. Demonstrations of diamond cutting and displays can be viewed at Diamond Land.

Bruges We really think this "Venice of the North" is a must-see. It is one of the best preserved medieval cities in Europe. Bruges is known for its beautiful walks, scenic canals, ancient squares and some of the best lace in Belgium.

Brussels Beer, waffles and festivals — if this is what you're looking for, you'll find them in abundance when you visit the country's capital city. The center of Brussels on the north side is made up of broad boulevards and stately buildings. By comparison, the south side is a maze of narrow, medieval lanes surrounding the ornate 12th-century Grand Place. Grand Place is one of the most perfectly preserved of all market squares in Europe. After you have seen the square, continue walking down one of the narrow side streets, which are lined with quaint shops, beer halls, cafes and beautiful architecture. Try to see the famous Manneken-Pis Fountain (the 17th-century bronze statue of a boy urinating). Brussels also has some wonderful museums.

Visit the odd-looking Atomium, a 335-ft-/102-m-high perfect replica of an iron molecule enlarged 165 billion times, in Exhibition Park, where the 1958 World's Fair was held. The opposite architectural tack is taken in the adjoining "Mini Europe," where miniatures of 350 famous structures (Big Ben, the Eiffel Tower, etc.) are on display.

Travel Tips for the Client

Do watch out for trams (streetcars) in larger cities. They come at you from unexpected directions and can even appear from underground . . . Do visit at least one of the fascinating caves in Belgium. One of our favorites,

More Fascinating Facts About Belgium

In casinos, the official language is French . . . Highway signs list names of towns in French, Flemish or both, and sometimes the names are quite different — for instance, Mons (French) and Bergen (Flemish) are the same town, as are Lille (French) and Rijsel (Flemish) . . . Often thought of as a "low" country, Belgium also has a number of ski resorts (seven in Ardennes alone) as well as a world-class skier (World Cup champion Marc Girardelli) . . . There are two stories about the origin of Manneken-Pis Fountain: 1) When the Spanish attacked the city, they set fire to the archives in City Hall, and the mayor's son bravely put out the fire the only way he knew how; and 2) a nobleman whose son had disappeared promised he would make a statue of the boy in whatever pose he was in when found (the statue is a tribute to the bad timing of his rescuer) . . . Belgium claims to have had both the first guilds (trade unions) and the first incorporated company . . . Flemish master Van Eyck painted egg white between layers of color, which is why his paintings are more vivid today than Rembrandt's . . . One of Belgium's largest annual festivals — the Procession of the Holy Blood — takes place in Bruges on Ascension Day. The procession celebrates the entrance into the city of a vial said to contain a drop of the blood of Jesus. Ever since the event began in 1150, the day has been celebrated with a parade of biblical tableaux. . . .

Han-Sur-Lesse, has an underground boat tour along subterranean rivers.

Luxembourg

This country is a tiny gem. It's simply beautiful, with wooded, rolling hills, gentle rivers and quaint villages. The northern part has the best scenery, particularly in the heavily forested area of the Ardennes (the southern area is more industrial). Castles, wine-tasting, brewery tours, hiking, camping, mountains, forests, lakes, friendly people and well-groomed Luxembourg City are the main attractions. Send visitors who are outdoor-oriented and who like European history.

The Netherlands, Belgium and Luxembourg

Review Questions

1. What will a visitor find in the 250-room Rijksmuseum?

2. In Amsterdam, what sights will a typical boat cruise pass?

3. What is odd about Amsterdam's red-light district? How does it differ from such districts in other countries?

4. What is the best way to tour the Netherlands outside Amsterdam? Why?

5. What city is the official governmental seat of the Netherlands? How would you describe it for a client?

6. What spectacular attraction will a visitor see in Keukenhof? When is that attraction open to the public?

7. In Volendam, what can a visitor observe women and men wearing?

8. What is *rijsttafel*? Where would a visitor find it?

9. Describe the following tourist attractions in Brussels: the Grand Place, the Mannekin-Pis Fountain, and the Atomium.

10. In Luxembourg, what is the Ardennes?

The Netherlands, Belgium and Luxembourg

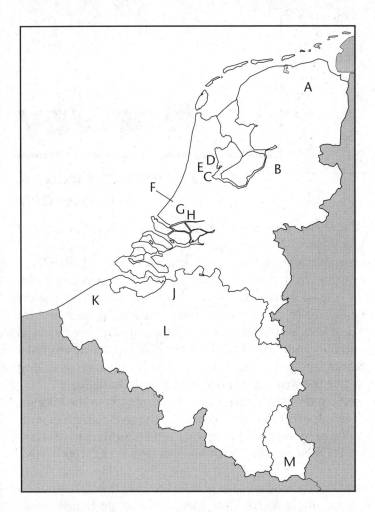

Map Skills Exercise

Match the tourist destination listed below with the corresponding letter on the map. You can use each letter only once.

1. _____ Luxembourg
2. _____ Rijksmuseum
3. _____ Brussels
4. _____ Venice of the North
5. _____ Windmill Museum
6. _____ The Hague
7. _____ picturesque fishing village
8. _____ City of Tiles
9. _____ world's diamond capital
10. _____ Rotterdam

Selling Exercise

(This is a role-playing exercise. Students should work in pairs.)

One student should play the role of a client and the other, an agent for the BENELUX Tourist Office, representing tourism to Belgium, the Netherlands and Luxembourg. The student who is playing the client should write down five questions he or she might ask the agent about traveling to these countries. The student who is playing the agent should respond orally to the questions as best he or she can. Repeat the exercise, but this time reverse roles.

Norway

Denmark, Finland and Sweden

People know more about Norway now than ever before, thanks to the 1994 Winter Olympics. But what they saw on television told them only part of a beautiful story — Norway was, after all, blanketed with snow during the games. We rank it as one of the loveliest countries in the world — year round — and the prime travel destination in Scandinavia. Partly that's because of its variety. The serene rural landscapes near Voss are nothing like the jagged fjords along the western coast, and the countryside near Stalheim could not be more unlike the stark, barren land around Alta. Most of the population lives along the coast, where the weather is moderated by the Gulf Stream.

The country's national identity is hard to separate from the Vikings, who set out by sea centuries ago to conquer the world and met with a surprising degree of success. The explorer Leif Ericsson may well have been the first European to visit North America (around AD 1000 — five

Contemporary Norwegians are a gentler breed — they take pride in the accomplishments of such countrymen as playwright Henrik Ibsen, artist Edvard Munch and composer Edvard Grieg. Their standard of living is among the highest in the world, in part because the country is almost self-sufficient in its energy needs (95% of its energy is supplied by hydroelectricity, and it's a petroleum-exporting country, thanks to its North Sea oil reserves). Among other achievements of modern Norwegian society is a deep-down appreciation of the equality of women — both in theory and in practice.

The other nations of Scandinavia are linked to Norway by culture and geography. Visitors to Norway often travel to or from nearby Denmark and Sweden — and sometimes Finland, which is farther away. The island nation of Iceland, populated centuries ago by settlers from mainland Scandinavia, is far out in the Atlantic. It is rarely packaged with a trip to Norway. (*See the Europe Geofile for information on Iceland.*)

What to Do There

Bergen   Founded in 1070, Bergen (pop. 211,000) is one of the most attractive cities in Norway, and it demands a three-night stay to see everything. Visit the Bryggen area (very old medieval section with interesting shops), the Hanseatic Museum (exhibits about fjords), the Mariakirke (a 12th-century church), Edvard Grieg's statue in City Park, and the 13th-century Bergenhus Fortress. Spend some time just walking around, looking at the city's architecture in general. Also, take a trip on the Floyen, a cable car with a spectacular view. At the top of the ride is a national park with excellent hiking trails.

Check with the tourist board to see when the Bergen Festival will be held (usually May and/or June, lasting for two weeks). This would be an excellent time to visit the city, as many arts, music and other cultural events are scheduled.

Just outside of Bergen in the town of Hop is the home of composer Edvard Grieg — it contains his mementos and original furnishings. Not far away, on a jagged cliff that drops straight into the sea, is his grave.

Sognefjord

Fjords
The main reason to go to Norway is to see the fjords (long, narrow arms of the sea bordered by dramatic high mountains). Our favorite way to see them is to take the 12-day boat trip on the Norwegian national coastal steamers from Bergen north to Kirkenes and back again. Most of the stops are repeated on the way back, but at different times of day; on the trip north, the boats pull up to many of the towns in the middle of the night. Excellent guided tours of the towns can be arranged aboard the ship, and some tours leave the ship at one port, go overland to see interesting sights, then meet the ship at the next port of call.

Make sure any cruise out of Bergen (even just a day cruise) visits Sognefjord — it's the world's longest and deepest. Geirangerfjord, also north of Bergen, is breathtaking. Hardangerfjord, just south of Bergen, inspired Edvard Grieg to write "To the Spring." If you're driving to it, you'll cross the Tokagjelet Gorge, so allow extra time to stop and take a few pictures. Trollfjord, the most beautiful of them all, is reached on the fourth day of the coastal-steamer trip. Only about a mile long, this fjord in the Lofoten Islands has an awe-inspiring approach: The ship squeezes into a strait between two towering mountains; then it turns, and just when you think it will crash into the side, the narrowest possible waterway appears, and there's the fjord. The huge mountains seem almost within reach from the deck of the ship,

and a half-dozen waterfalls spray down from both sides — truly stupendous.

Flam
The preferred way to reach Flam, which is set on Sognefjord, is by train: The rail line drops 2,850 ft/875 m in elevation during the trip. The train makes repeated stops for spectacular waterfall and mountain vistas. Staying the night in Flam requires advance booking — there's only one hotel.

Lillehammer
Long nestled in happy obscurity, this town geared up for a huge influx of visitors for the Olympics and won everybody's heart. Aside from ski runs — more than 250 miles of trails—skating rinks and Olympic villages, Lillehammer has the Maihaugen Open Air Museum. It's one of our favorite museums anywhere. You can spend hours browsing just the old workshops —there's one for practically every occupation. Set on the shores of Late Mjosa, Lillehammer is easy to reach by train from Oslo.

Oslo
At least three nights should be reserved for Oslo (pop. 456,000), Norway's modern, sophisticated capital. Several hours can be spent strolling along Karl Johansgate (the city's main avenue), which is what a lot of Norwegians do — don't be surprised if they're very tan and wearing chic, Italian clothes. Stop at the Edvard Munch Museum, which houses some of the best work of Norway's greatest painter — don't overlook the exhibits in the basement. Some of his masterpieces are on display at the National

Norway, Denmark, Finland and Sweden

✪ Capital
▪ City
── International Boundary
–·– River

Km 0 25 50 100
Mi 0 25 50 100
Copyright Weissmann Travel Reports

North Cape
Hammerfest
Alta
Kirkenes
RUSSIA
L A P L A N D
Lofoten Is.
Trollfjord
Kiruna
Bodo
ARCTIC CIRCLE
Norwegian Sea
Arjeplog
Lulea
Oulu
SWEDEN
FINLAND
Kuopio
Joensuu
Trondheim
Hell
Sundsvall
LAKE DISTRICT
Savonlinna
Punkaharju
Geiranger
Stryn
NORWAY
Gulf of Bothnia
Tampere
Hameenlinna
Sognefjord
Stalheim
Lillehammer
Aura
Voss
Flam
Myrdal
Geilo
Turku
Bergen
Gavle
Helsinki
Hardangerfjord
Oslo
L. Malaren
Stockholm
ESTONIA
RUSSIA
Lyngor
Gota Canal
Gotland
North Sea
Goteborg
LATVIA
Aalborg
Oland
JUTLAND
Aarhus
Billund
Baltic Sea
LITHUANIA
DENMARK
Copenhagen
GERMANY
RUSSIA
POLAND

Gallery, too. (His most famous painting, *The Scream,* was kidnapped during the 1994 Olympics; it was later returned unharmed.) Two of the best museums in Oslo are on the grounds of Akershus Castle — the Resistance Museum, displaying a thorough presentation of Norway's partisan actions in World War II, and the Armed Forces Museum, which includes a vast collection of equipment and displays from Viking days through NATO.

Set aside at least half a day for the Bygdoy Peninsula, reached by ferry from Oslo. There you'll find several museums housing some remarkable oceangoing vessels. *Kon Tiki* (Thor Heyerdahl's raft, made from balsa logs, on which he sailed from Peru to Polynesia) and the *Fram* (the ship used by Roald Amundsen in 1911 on the first expedition to the South Pole) are on display. Visitors are permitted to walk the decks and crawl through the holds. But more amazing — to us, anyway — are the remarkably well-preserved 1,000-year-old Viking burial ships. They're so sleek they look modern. They may change your mind about the "warlike" Vikings. Bygdoy Peninsula also has a Folkemuseum — a collection of ancient Norwegian buildings on 35 acres/14 hectares, where nearly every facet of Norwegian life is on display. Look for the completely reassembled study of playwright Henrik Ibsen.

Ski Areas

Norway has some of the best — and most popular — ski terrain in the world, with the peak time being February and March. Much skiing is cross-country, which is highly suitable for beginners, but there are plenty of downhill trails for the more skilled. Ski jumping is popular, too. Consider the resorts at Geilo and Voss, as well as Lillehammer, which begins to gear up for its season in December. About two hours from Geirangerfjord is the town of Stryn, which is very popular for summer skiing.

Trondheim

Trondheim (pop. 137,000) dates back to AD 996 (it was the Viking capital). At least three nights are needed to really soak it all in. Among the sights are the Wharf District, the Market Place, the Stiftsgarden (the official residence of the Norwegian royal family when they're in town) and the Ringve Museum of Music History (which houses one of the most impressive collections of musical instruments in the world). Should you have the time, drive a few miles east to visit the town of Hell (just to say you've been to Hell and back).

Itinerary

Most people visit Norway only for a week, which allows them to take a short cruise and spend a few days in Oslo or Bergen. Some visitors may want to take the train all the way to Bodo above the Arctic Circle to see the midnight sun. Twelve days to two weeks is really ideal, however, to include the following:

Days 1–2 — Oslo.

Day 3 — Bergen Scenic Railway (about six hours) to Voss.

Day 4 — "Norway in a Nutshell" tour, which includes a ferry ride to Flam and a train to Bergen. Overnight there.

Day 5 — Bergen.

Day 6 — Begin six-day fjord cruise.

Days 7–12 — Six-day fjord cruise.

Day 13 — Depart Norway.

Climate/When to Go

June–September are the prime tourist months, unless you're going to ski or you have a really high tolerance for snow and ice. Day temperatures are in the high 60s F/15–22 C then, with nights in the 50s F/10–15 C. The midnight sun is best seen from early May until the end of July (in the North Cape area, you can see it until the end of July). Keep in mind that, the farther north you travel, the days get longer but they also get colder.

Transportation

Not many North American carriers fly to Norway from North America, but several European carriers fly via their respective capital cities. SAS, the airline of the Scandinavian nations, has the most scheduled flights into Oslo. In Oslo, Gardemoen Airport is 36 mi/58 km from downtown, while Fornebu Airport is only 6 mi/9 km. Ships and car ferries, some operating only May–October, connect Norway to other Scandinavian nations and the rest of Europe. There is excellent rail service from Europe and the rest of Scandinavia. Planes, trains, steamers, buses and rental cars and bicycles are available internally. Try to take the day train ride (about six hours) from Oslo to Bergen via Voss, simply to see some beautiful scenery (the train is called the Bergen Scenic Railway).

Accommodations

Hotel standards in Norway are high — even country inns and guest houses maintain surprisingly good service and amenities at relatively low prices ("relatively low" because nothing in Norway is cheap!). The boats that cruise the fjords have adequate accommodations: The rooms in the new large ships feel somewhat impersonal, but the cabins in the older ships are somewhat cramped.

Health Advisories

Excellent medical and dental facilities are found in the larger cities, with clinics and doctors in smaller ones. Take a sufficient supply of prescription medicine along with you, as Norwegian pharmacies cannot honor prescriptions written out of the country. Medicine is socialized — and inexpensive — in Norway. Water and food are safe everywhere. Ticks carrying encephalitis inhabit the forest near Bergen during summer — ask locally about precautions.

Geostats

Official Name: Kingdom of Norway.

Visa Information: Passports only required of U.S. and Canadian citizens for stay up to 90 days in the Nordic countries of Denmark, Finland, Iceland, Norway and Sweden. Reconfirm documentation requirements with carrier before departure.

Health Certificates: None required. Contact health authorities for latest information.

Capital: Oslo.

Population: 4,331,000.

Size: 150,000 sq mi/389,000 sq km. Slightly larger than New Mexico.

Languages: Norwegian, Sami (spoken by Lapps).

Climate: Temperate along the coast, colder interior.

Economy: Industry, services.

Government: Constitutional monarchy.

Religion: Evangelical Lutheran (state church).

Currency: Norwegian kroner (NKR). 100 ore = 1 NKR. Traveler's checks and credit cards are accepted at tourist locations. AE, DC, MC, VI.

Time Zone: 6 hours ahead of eastern standard time; 1 hour ahead of Greenwich mean time.

Electricity: 220 volts.

What to Buy

Shop for pewter, porcelain, cut glass, textiles, furniture (especially furniture made from pine), ceramics, ski equipment, beautiful hunting knives, wonderfully designed toys, wood carvings and woolens (*fabulous* sweaters — you can get some of the best deals from women selling sweaters out of their cars near train stations or at dockside). Also, don't forget smoked salmon, which can be packed for traveling.

What to Eat

Norwegian food is good, but it might seem unexciting or even bland to those who like their food well-seasoned. Seafood, various meats (including reindeer steak), vegetables and delicious desserts are easy to find. Herring is served every way imaginable — don't be surprised to find five variations at a breakfast buffet. Salmon season is in the spring and summer. A treat for those with Viking appetites is *smalahove* — boiled sheep's head. Of course, if the Norwegian specialties don't suit you, you can find nearly every variety of restaurant food.

Travel Tips for the Client

Do read about Viking history before you arrive —it'll increase your appreciation of much of what you see . . . Do try to make time to see the rural areas . . . Do take plenty of film along with you, as buying it in Norway is three to five times more expensive than elsewhere.

Tipping: Throughout Scandinavia, tipping is not customary. Instead, a 15% service charge is added to restaurant and hotel bills.

Denmark

Denmark may be old in appearance, but the people are young in attitude. This land of Hans Christian

Andersen — only a ferry ride across the North Sea from Norway — is dotted with medieval churches, Renaissance castles and old fishing villages. But the Danes live very much in the present — nightlife is lively and continues until the morning. Most Danes speak English and seem to make it a point to talk to travelers.

There's something in Denmark for almost everyone. The only ones not to send are those looking for warm beaches or deluxe resorts featuring golf, tennis, etc.

What to Do There

Aalborg   Aalborg, in the part of Denmark known as Jutland, is 1,000 years old. Among its attractions are the North Jutland Museum of Art, sand dunes, Aalborghus Castle, Budolfi Cathedral and beautiful beaches. And excellent shopping. Of special interest is Lindholm Hoje — Denmark's largest Viking burial ground. Some of the 682 graves, which date from the ninth century, are marked by stones in the shape of ships.

Aarhus   Denmark's second-largest city, Aarhus lies midway between Copenhagen and Aalborg. A pleasant town to walk through, it has a cathedral, a music hall, Marselisborg Forest, a palace and the 200-year-old Prehistoric Museum of Moesgard. Behind the museum is a trail winding past several historic sites through fields and forest to a sandy beach. Aarhus has a lively music and entertainment scene.

Billund   Take your children to Billund to see LEGOLAND Park — a large "town" with scenes from all around the world built from more than 38 million LEGO plastic bricks. Everything from African animals to Mt. Rushmore has been recreated in LEGOLAND (open May to mid-September). Also in Billund is Titania's Palace, built by Sir Neville Wilkinson for his daughter to house the fairies from the family garden. It has a nice toy and doll collection.

Copenhagen (Kobenhavn)   This city of canals, rivers and parks is one of our favorite European capitals. Copenhagen is a bit spread out and not easy to walk at one go — we suggest visiting a single area at a time. We like to start out at the red brick Raadhuset, or Town Hall, and its square. There's a tourist information booth, and almost every main sight of the city is within 20 minutes' walking distance. To get oriented, first walk the mile-/1.6-km-long Stroget (pronounced *STROY-e*), the pedestrian shopping street around which many restaurants and sights are clustered. Then see the city from one of the canal tours. Another nice way to get a view of the city is to climb the Round Tower (a 17th-century astronomical tower; instead of stairs, a huge spiral walkway winds its way to the top). Following that, visit the National Museum (Viking artifacts), the Old Fish Market, Christiansborg Castle and the Stock Exchange building (don't miss the Fishwife Statue just opposite). Next, go across the canal in Christianshavn to visit Our Saviors Church, with its wonderful view of the entire city.

One of Copenhagen's most famous attractions is Tivoli Gardens, which combines an amusement park with a food festival and an international concert series. Colored lights adorn the fairy-tale pavilions and stately trees, and fireworks splash across the night sky. We like the old wooden roller coaster and the pantomime show.

The area around Amalienborg Palace (the royal family lives there) has some nice sights as well. Rosenborg Castle is one of our favorites (see the crown jewels). Not far away, in the harbor, is the Little Mermaid statue — it's not very big, but it will remind you of the fairy tales you heard as a child. Near the canal the Hans Christian Andersen Cultural Centre offers puppet shows, art exhibits, concerts and lectures. Lovers of the sea will want to visit the restored Nyhavn sailors' section of town, which includes a museum of tall ships, great seafood restaurants and tattoo parlors. Organized castle tours of the Copenhagen area are interesting and may include Kronborg (Hamlet's Elsinore Castle).

Travel Tips for the Client

Do take plenty of traveler's checks — credit cards are accepted only in the major hotels, shops and restaurants . . . Do take a coat and tie; they're required in many restaurants after 6 pm . . . Be punctual if you're meeting with business associates, and call ahead if you are likely to be delayed . . . Do stand up before shaking hands with someone. . . .

Finland

Though one of the least-visited countries in Europe, Finland is certainly one of the loveliest. The lake areas in this country are among the most scenic places in Europe. And the country has a unique blend of traditional culture and modern arts. The summer calendar is chock-full of folk festivals, while winter offers skiing and seemingly endless vistas of magical, snow-covered forests.

Send those who like outdoor activities, wide-open spaces, beautiful lakes, unspoiled nature, charming villages and good food. Don't send those who are looking for a wide variety of nightlife or an inexpensive vacation.

What to Do There

Helsinki (Helsingfors)   The Pearl of the Baltic, this clean city (pop. 492,000) on Finland's southern coast has wide boulevards and a beautiful blue harbor. Unfortunately, most of the architecture is rather modern because of numerous fires in the past. But in the historic center, around Senate Square, you can still see delightful neoclassical architecture in the government buildings and a cathedral. There are several great museums in the city; a list of the best would include the Art Museum of the Ateneum, the Seurasaari Open-Air Museum (on a small island, it displays the country's homes and farmhouses) and the National Museum. When you've tired of museums, tour the Temppeliaukio Church (the Rock Church — carved from solid granite), walk around the walls of 18th-century Suomenlinna Fortress and linger in the harbor area (be sure to take a harbor cruise!). Leave time to see the bustling Kauppatori Market Square on the wharf. While there, be on the lookout for the Havis Amanda Fountain, rising out of the waves — Helsinki residents regard it as their symbol.

Lake District   Finland's lake district is promoted as Europe's most beautiful, and we think the tourist board is right on target. It offers boating and canoeing, fishing, hiking in forests, camping and saunas. If you're there in summer, take the *MS Kristina Brahe* lake cruise.

Tampere   This modern industrial city (adjacent to the Tammerkoski Rapids) is the country's second largest. There are several impressive structures in the city, among them Kaleva Church, the main library and the Byzantine-style Eastern Orthodox church. Check for performances at the open-air Pyynikki Theater (June–August). Children will love the Sarkanniemi Recreation Center (with a children's zoo, planetarium and aquarium). Since Tampere is in the western Lake District, it's an ideal place to board steamers for cruises of the area.

Turku   This large port city at the mouth of the River Aura was founded 750 years ago and, for a time, was the Finnish capital. Visit the open-air Luostarinmaki Handicrafts Museum and the marketplace, walk through the 18th-century wooden quarter, spend at least an hour at 13th-century Turku Castle, stop at 15th-century Turku Cathedral, listen to the music of Jean Sibelius in the Sibelius Museum and see the impressive modern Concert Hall. August is an especially lively month in Turku, filled with festivals.

Travel Tips for the Client

Do take flowers for the hostess if you're invited to a Finnish home. If you find yourself the honored guest at a party, don't touch the wine at dinner until after a toast is made at the beginning of the meal. You will be expected to make a toast of thanks to the host and hostess as soon as the dessert wine or dessert has been served . . . Do shake hands when meeting Finns, including children. . . .

Sweden

We used to tell people that the best of Sweden could be found in its largest city, Stockholm, but now we've begun to add that nobody should miss the vast expanse of forests, lakes and meadow that typify the Swedish countryside.

Although many areas of Sweden are beautiful, travelers should be aware that none of the scenery is as dramatic as that which can be found next door, in Norway. Don't send those who are looking for a wide variety of nightlife (Stockholm is the only place where nightlife as we know it exists).

What to Do There

Gota Canal   Often referred to as the Blue Ribbon Canal, the 300-mi-/483-km-long Gota Canal links Stockholm and Goteborg via rivers and lakes. It is primarily used for pleasure cruising (May–August). Turn-of-the-century steamers pass through a total of 65 locks on the journey. Though many people take only a portion of the cruise, we recommend the whole trip, with overnights on board ship. It's a slow-moving, relaxing cruise past historic sites, spectacular mountains, villages, farmland and valleys.

Goteborg (Gothenburg) A western seaport, Goteborg (pronounced *YET-eh-ber*) is Sweden's second-largest city (pop. 432,000). It's very industrial, but also quite beautiful. Goteborg has many parks, art galleries and fountains (Poseidon, in the center of a major avenue, is the most famous).

Lapland Lapland covers the northern third of Sweden and much of northern Finland and Norway. It is home to one of the oldest civilizations in Europe. Museums in Lulea and Arjeplog in Sweden have excellent displays about the life and history of the Samis (the traditional name of the people formerly known as Laplanders), but contemporary Sami culture is also fascinating. Reindeer, for instance, are of utmost importance to the Samis — they provide food for the society and play a prominent role in literature and myths.

Lapland

Lapland itself is not as barren as most people think; it has forests, winding rivers and mountains, making it an excellent vacation area. The summer sun is up after midnight (from early June to early July); a good place to experience the midnight sun is Kiruna. Winter, which is unrelentingly dark and often very cold and damp, does offer the aurora borealis (Northern Lights) in partial compensation. The best way to tour Lapland is by car, but there is adequate rail and bus service connecting the major towns. We recommend going to Lapland in July and August; avoid June and September, when the mosquitoes are horrible.

Stockholm Founded in the 13th century, Stockholm is a striking city. Its unique location — where the Baltic meets Lake Malaren — forced city designers to build on 14 islands and several islets (*skerries*); ferries ply the waters between them. The city is adorned with beautiful architecture, and almost a third of its land area is devoted to parks. Start your tour by visiting the Gamla Stan (Old Town), with its narrow streets and quaint shops. Be sure to see the sculpture of St. George and the dragon at Stockholm Cathedral, the 600-room Royal Palace, Riddarholmskyrkan (tomb of Swedish royalty) and the Vasa Museum, which houses an impressive 17th-century warship that sank on its

maiden voyage in 1628. Just go strolling. Take a boat along the harbor to see the islands and the scenery in general — this is one of our favorite things to do in Stockholm. Surprisingly, despite the city's size and busy harbor, you can swim at its beaches in the summer. And for those who enjoy ice skating, every Wednesday, Saturday and Sunday during winter expeditions go as far out on the frozen Baltic Sea as safety allows.

Travel Tips for the Client

Do learn the local customs, in case you're invited into a Swede's home. For example, stay on a formal, last-name basis unless you're invited to do otherwise and never touch your drink at a gathering until the host announces *Skoal* (to your health) . . . Do check out the Stockholm Card, which entitles the bearer to discounts to many attractions plus free unlimited public transportation . . . Don't drive after drinking—while it's good advice anywhere, driving while intoxicated is a very serious offense in Sweden (even one beer can put you over the limit). . . .

Norway, Denmark, Finland and Sweden

Review Questions

1. What is the main reason for a tourist to visit Norway?

2. Tourists to Norway will want to visit sites connected with the lives of Edvard Munch, Henrik Ibsen and Edvard Grieg. Who are they?

3. What are the two best months of the year for skiing in Norway?

4. Describe Sognefjord and Trollfjord.

5. Identify and describe the remarkable oceangoing vessels you could see in a visit to the Bygdoy Peninsula.

6. In what country is Billund? What is the principal attraction there?

7. In what city would you find Tivoli Gardens? What are its attractions?

8. In what country would you visit Europe's most beautiful lake district?

9. Where is Lapland?

10. Where did city designers build Stockholm?

Norway, Denmark, Finland and Sweden

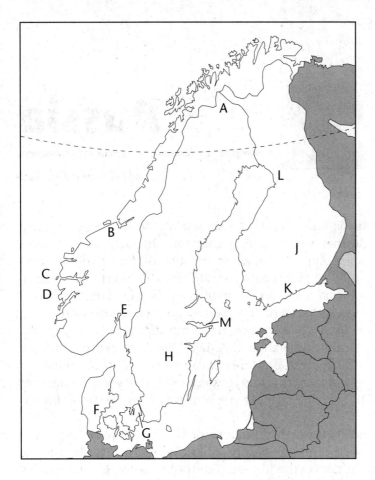

Map Skills Exercise

Match the tourist destination listed below with the corresponding letter on the map. You can use each letter only once.

1. _____ Stockholm
2. _____ Copenhagen
3. _____ Sognefjord
4. _____ the Lake District
5. _____ Gota Canal
6. _____ Oslo
7. _____ Trondheim
8. _____ Bergen
9. _____ Lapland
10. _____ Helsinki

Selling Exercise

You are working for a cruise-ship line that wants to enter the Scandinavian market. Your boss asks you to design an itinerary that a cruise ship might follow in Scandinavia. Write a report to your boss with your suggestions and tell what passengers might do and see at each stop you suggest. Include a map of your suggested route with your report. (Use transparency map #31 for this exercise.)

Russia

and Ukraine

Alas, Russia is not as safe to visit as it was back in the days when Big Brother was watching everyone. In fact, many visitors become so preoccupied with worry about petty crime that they can't relax and enjoy what this nation has to offer. It's wise to take precautions against pickpockets and petty thieving, but don't be overly paranoid or cancel a trip out of fear that the nation is out of control.

A trip to Russia won't be easy. In this time of change, travelers will have to be flexible, tolerant and patient. They'll sometimes find the country to be an unpleasant mix of capitalism and communism — bad service, inflated costs and mysterious surcharges on restaurant and hotel bills. It will seem like everyone wants to take part in the latest hustle.

The difficulty is worth it, though, for Russia is simply a fascinating place — from the imperial beauty of Moscow and St. Petersburg to the bleak romanticism of the Siberian countryside. Best of all, the country is now wide open to the outside world, and travelers can visit nooks and crannies that have been closed for almost 80 years.

Russia spans 11 time zones and offers attractions of mind-boggling diversity. Its land ranges from the highest mountains in Europe to some of the lowest spots in the world, and from Arctic tundra to seemingly endless plains. Its cities are home to some of the finest art and architecture in the world, and its countryside is untamed and beautiful.

What to Do There

Moscow   The best way to introduce yourself to the capital of Russia is to head straight for Red Square, in the very center of Moscow. There you'll find two of the most enduring symbols of Russia: onion-domed St. Basil's Cathedral (stunning interior) and the Kremlin, the centuries-old seat of Russian rulers. There are many exhibits on display at the Kremlin at any one time. It is worth it to pay the extra charge to see the stunning treasures of the czars (Peter the Great's throne, Catherine the Great's carriage and others). Also in Red Square is Lenin's tomb. See it (and him, preserved under glass) while you can;

Russian authorities plan to bury the revolutionary. After seeing Red Square, orient yourself to the rest of the city by taking a half-day bus tour or a riverboat tour.

On Tverskaya Street, just off Red Square, you'll find a mix of Russian and foreign stores and shops (among them Christian Dior and even Pizza Hut). Tverskaya leads to Pushkin Square, one of the liveliest in Moscow. Don't miss a ride on the Moscow subway (Metro), a marvel of efficiency and design. A new tourist destination is the White House, seat of the Russian parliament —it was in front of this building that Boris Yeltsin climbed atop a tank and roared his speech of defiance during the coup attempt. Nearby are the headquarters of the KGB and Moscow University (this Stalinist-style building is one of the largest buildings in the world).

Art lovers will enjoy the Tretyakov Museum (Russian and Soviet art) and the magnificent Pushkin Museum, which has one of the world's largest collections of works by leading painters, graphic artists and sculptors.

We also enjoyed seeing the All-Russian Exhibition Center; the pavilions and fountains are beautiful. At the entrance to the exhibition is a dazzling monument to Sputnik, the first man-made object to orbit the globe. In the evening, the Moscow Circus, the Bolshoi and concerts at the Moscow Conservatory on Gertsen Street are the best bets. Several nearby medieval towns (with onion-domed churches) can be visited on day or overnight trips.

Novgorod

This city, located between St. Petersburg and Moscow, is more than 1,000 years old. At one time it competed with Moscow for domination of Old Russia. Today, it's primarily modern and industrial, but still retains a well-preserved kremlin and old city center. See St. Sofia Cathedral (begun in 1045) with its six domes, and the city's other ancient churches. Just outside of Novgorod is the Vitoslavlitsy Museum of Wooden Architecture, which has a collection of 22 wooden structures, all built without nails.

St. Petersburg (Leningrad)

Located on the banks of the swift-flowing Neva, St. Petersburg is the most beautiful city in Russia. Although it's lovely at any time of year, we really enjoy visiting in late June, during the famed White Nights, when the sun never seems to set and the city never sleeps.

It was designed and built by Peter the Great as Russia's "Window on the West" in the early 1700s. The first stop should be the Hermitage, a museum that ranks with the Louvre, Prado, British Museum and Metropolitan Museum of Art; allow at least half a day to just look at the room decorations, but days and days if you really want to see the museum's incredible collection (which includes works by Leonardo da Vinci, Titian, El Greco, Rembrandt, Picasso, Van Gogh and just about every other of the world's great artists). The bulk of the Hermitage collection is housed in the Winter Palace, the former home of the czars and one of the focal points of the 1917 revolution. Afterward, stroll the Nevsky Prospekt, the city's main street for shopping and restaurants, and visit St. Isaac's Cathedral (which has a wonderful view of the city from its tower).

Another place to see is the Peter and Paul Fortress, on the Neva near the Palace Bridge and downtown; it was one of the first buildings constructed in the city. The fortress has been home to many unwilling guests, including the novelist Feodor Dostoyevsky (*The Brothers Karamazov*). In its dungeons Peter the Great killed his son and Catherine the Great buried her enemies alive.

If at all possible, book tickets (in advance) to see the St. Petersburg Circus, which offers some unusual and exciting acts. Nearby excursions include Russia's first naval base at Kronstadt (there's a lovely church there as well) and several royal palaces (see next page).

Siberia

TO NORTH POLE

URALS

S I B E R I A

KAMCHATKA

Sea of
Okhotsk

Lake Baikal

KURIL ISLANDS

KAZAKHSTAN

Km   0   500 1000
Mi   0   500   1000
Copyright WTR

MONGOLIA   CHINA   JAPAN

St. Petersburg – Area Palaces

Handsome palaces such as Petrodvorets, Pushkin and Pavlovsk surround St. Petersburg. Petrodvorets is a lovely 18th-century palace with marvelous fountains and sculptures and a beautiful interior. Pushkin is the home of the Catherine Palace. This is truly a must for those who appreciate parquet floors. It has gold-painted rooms and what must be the largest lapis lazuli tabletop in the world. The 18th-century Pavlovsk Palace is known for its fountains, gilded statues and artificial ponds.

Siberia and the Far East

Siberia stretches across northern Russia between the Ural Mountains and the Pacific Ocean. The name conjures up images of bleak, snowy wilderness, but that terrain is only part of the picture. Siberia also contains the world's largest forest, its deepest lake (Lake Baikal) and cultures that are somewhat reminiscent of Native Americans. Horseback riding, hunting, river cruises and hiking are some of the activities in the region. Several major cruise lines have begun trips from Alaska to Siberia that include land excursions in Siberia. More exotic excursions include tours of the volcanoes of the Kamchatka Peninsula and the Kuril Islands and cruises to the North Pole via Murmansk. A visit to Siberia is a true frontier experience — travelers should be willing to put up with some discomfort on their odyssey through the region.

Suzdal

Suzdal is one of the oldest towns in Russia, dating from 1024. It's full of onion-domed churches and other examples of traditional Russian structures. Its Museum of Wooden Architecture and Peasant Life has a varied and interesting collection of buildings. Suzdal is one of those places that actually might be better to see

in the winter when the landscape is covered in snow and the Russian Winter Folk Festival takes place (25 December–5 January).

Volga River

The Volga, Europe's longest river, winds through the western section of Russia and offers boat passengers a unique perspective of the industrial urban and scenic rural parts of this vast country. The river has its beginnings south of St. Petersburg and ends in the Caspian Sea. Most river tours last about seven days. While not recommended for first-time visitors (there is so much more to do and see in Russia), the voyages can be interesting for those wanting a deeper appreciation of the country.

Itinerary

We think most first-timers will be happiest seeing Russia on some type of escorted tour. Previous experience traveling in developing countries is almost a prerequisite to independent travel in Russia. The itinerary below is constructed to give a first-time visitor, who has seven nights, a tour of Moscow and St. Petersburg.

Days 1–3 — Moscow.

Day 4 — Moscow. Night train to St. Petersburg.

Days 5–6 — St. Petersburg.

Day 7— Day trip to one of the three palaces near St. Petersburg.

Day 8 — Depart Russia.

If you have more time, add an overnight trip to Suzdal from Moscow or a trip to Novgorod from St. Petersburg or both.

Climate/When to Go

In general, the best time to visit is May–September, when the day temperatures are in the 70s–90s F/23–35 C, with nights in the 50s–70s F/10–23 C. Spring and early fall, however, are unpredictable; snow flurries and temperatures in the mid-20s F/–5 C are possible in May and September. Be sure to take waterproof boots or shoes for spring or fall visits — there's a lot of mud. Winter offers a romantic view of Russia, a chance to

The Hermitage, St. Petersburg

wear the fur hat you buy and to go ice-skating in Moscow's Gorky Park.

Transportation

Aeroflot, once the only Soviet carrier, has been broken up into several entities that use ex-Aeroflot equipment and crews. Along with the breakup has come an alarming drop in safety and maintenance standards, to the point where the U.S. State Department no longer allows U.S. government officials to travel on Russian domestic flights. Until things improve measurably, we recommend you fly to the country on a recognized international carrier and do all of your domestic travel on trains, if time permits. Carriers currently flying year-round from the U.S. to Russia are Aeroflot and Delta; Aeroflot also flies from Canada. Most major European airlines also offer service to Russia from their respective hub cities. Sheremetyevo International Airport (SVO) is located 16 mi/26 km northwest of Moscow. Pulkovo Airport (LED) is 11 mi/18 km south of St. Petersburg. Taxi drivers at the airports in Moscow and St. Petersburg are notorious for overcharging foreign visitors. If possible, arrange for someone to meet you at the airport. Decent train service is available internally. Second-class isn't as comfortable (or as private) as first-class, but it does offer a better chance to meet Russians. We only recommend the Trans-Siberian Railway — which runs from Moscow to Vladivostok — for those who don't mind spending a long time on a train (the trip takes at least nine days) and schedule stopovers to break up the trip. Various cruises and ferry services are available from Northern Europe and along several Russian rivers. Subways are available in St. Petersburg and Moscow.

Accommodations

Accommodations range from very deluxe to basic. Hotels are usually quite clean, comfortable and more than adequate. New to the country are deluxe hotels that truly meet international standards, generally run in conjunction with foreign management. Among the best bargains are the dachas outside of Moscow.

Health Advisories

Medical care is not up to Western standards. Doctors and nurses — who are among the country's worst-paid professionals — have threatened strikes, and some common

Geostats

Official Name: Russian Federation.

Visa Info: Passport and visa are required. Visas must be obtained before departure and require a Russian sponsor (either a tour company, hotel or individual). Visitors staying more than three days must register their visa through their sponsor (it's a good idea to bring a photocopy of your passport, as this might take several days). Check the dates on visa before travel. Reconfirm with carrier before departure.

Health Certificates: No vaccinations are required.

Capital: Moscow.

Population: 149,614,000.

Size: 6,592,812 sq mi/17,074,724 sq km. More than twice the size of the U.S.

Languages: Russian, regional languages.

Climate: Varied; generally long, cold winters and short summers.

Economy: Industry, mining, agriculture.

Government: Republic, with presidential decrees.

Religions: Russian Orthodox, Moslem.

Currency: Ruble (ROU). Because of inflation, kopeks are no longer in use. Traveler's checks may be exchanged at banks. Credit cards are accepted by establishment catering to foreigners. AE, DI and VI.

Time Zone: From 8 to 18 hours ahead of EST (Moscow and St. Petersburg are 8); +3 to +13 GMT.

Electricity: 220 volts.

medications are regularly in short supply. The U.S. Centers for Disease Control recommends cholera, diphtheria and typhoid-fever vaccinations. Avoid fresh salads, and don't drink the tap water (the Russians don't drink it either). Food served at first-class hotels is generally considered safe.

What to Buy

Shop for fur caps, caviar, vodka, wall plaques and tiles, wood and metal sculptures, hand-painted lacquerware, and balalaikas and other musical instruments. Don't do all your shopping in the large tourist shops; while they are the best source for high-quality items, good souvenirs can also be purchased less expensively on the street or in smaller shops. In Moscow, shop the Arbat, a kitschy pedestrian mall lined with hawkers of *matrioshkas* (nesting dolls), scarves, T-shirts, Soviet Army memorabilia and *palekh* boxes. Serious shoppers should spend a Saturday or Sunday morning at Moscow's Izmailovski Stadium, a giant open-air flea market with arts and crafts, souvenirs and antiques. Only buy caviar from an official store, and be sure to keep your receipts — if you don't customs officers might slap you with a 600% export tariff!

What to Eat

Russian cuisine is hearty. Be aware that the cuisine is not one of the country's attractions. Russians like meat and potatoes, and they seem to eat for nourishment rather than enjoyment. Their breads and ice creams, however, are excellent, and pastries taste similar to those found in Europe. The recent past has brought a restaurant boom to the bigger cities.

Travel Tips for the Client

Do bring U.S. dollars. They are the second currency of Russia. You can change them freely anywhere, without any identification . . . Do arrange for airport-hotel transfers ahead of arrival, so you will not have to worry about being ripped off by a cab (they ask exorbitant prices) . . . Do take toilet paper/tissues and carry some with you. Hotels will have toilet paper, but few public rest rooms will. . . .

Ukraine

Tourism development in the country is in its infancy, so anyone going to Ukraine should be aware that glitches and delays are inevitable. The key to enjoying a trip there is to be flexible, tolerant and patient. The main attractions include cathedrals, Black Sea beaches and resorts, art, historical sites and Kiev.

What to Do There

Kiev   Kiev is one of the oldest Slavic cities and an ancient crossroads of trade. Now the political capital of Ukraine, it is perhaps more important as a magnificent monument to the Russian Orthodox Church. The city has seen many churches and monasteries. The chief religious site in town is the golden-domed St. Sophia Cathedral. Along the right bank of the Dneiper River is the Pecherskaya Lavra Monastery (Monastery of the Caves) and its associated catacombs.

Begin your tour of the city with a view from atop Volodymyr Hill, followed by a walk along the scenic Kreshchatik, the main street with fine shops and restaurants. The two museums we enjoyed the most were the Museum of Western and Oriental Art (ivory, fabrics, china and more) and the Folk Architecture Museum (reconstructions of typical Ukrainian buildings), but don't leave the city without seeing the museum that commemorates the Chernobyl disaster.

A sobering, moving experience is a visit to nearby Babi Yar, where invading Nazi troops massacred more than 100,000 Ukrainian Jews during World War II. A stark monument now marks the mass graves.

Yalta   Steep mountain peaks serve as a lovely backdrop for Yalta, our favorite Ukrainian city. This Black Sea resort seems to be a combination of Carmel, California, the French Riviera and Greece. It has exemplary places to stay, museums and beaches. Be sure to see Livadia, the former Tsarist vacation home (palace, really) used for the World War II conference of Stalin, Churchill and Roosevelt.

Along the Black Sea, we enjoy traveling via ferry or hydrofoil to several resort towns. Alupka and Miskhor are our favorites. Special trips can be arranged to

Fascinating Facts About Ukraine

The Russian and Ukrainian languages have about 70% of words in common . . . Twelve cities were given the title of "Hero City of the Soviet Union" for the courage and tenacity of their defenders in World War II. Three Hero Cities are in Ukraine: Kiev, Odessa and Sevastopol . . . Kiev's Independence Square is the location for the Ukrainian version of London's Hyde Park Speakers' Corner. Drop by to see unlimited free speech (and unlimited heckling) in action . . . Kiev boasts the world's deepest subway (it doubles as a fallout shelter) . . . Cossack cavalry troops, fierce fighters and symbolic of Ukraine's independent nature, were used in combat as recently as World War II (they were quite successful in winter operations, when temperatures of -40 F/ -40 C froze all mechanized equipment) . . . Ukraine's flag, a horizontal stripe of light blue set above a stripe of wheat yellow, symbolizes the richness of its agriculture under an endless sky . . . Slavs use a patronymic (modification of their father's first name) as their middle name, and use both names in all situations. A male named Alexander, with a father named Volodymyr, is called Alexander Volodymyrovitch . . . One consequence of the Yalta conference was that Ukraine got full membership in the United Nations (the U.S.S.R. took three seats in all). What goes around, comes around: The Ukrainian delegation used its seat to justify the nation's independence in 1991. . . .

Sevastopol, a lovely port best known for being near the site of the "Charge of the Light Brigade" at Balaklava. Another excursion goes to Bakhchisarai, a city of minarets and mosques — it was once the capital of the Crimean Khanate. While there, see the magnificent palace of Khan Mengli-Girel and the Fountain of Tears.

Travel Tips for the Client

Don't be surprised if your traveler's checks and credit cards are not accepted in Ukraine. These days it's a cash-and-carry economy . . . Don't say the Ukraine, say Ukraine. The definite article implies that it is still a province linked to Russia, while the name alone means it's independent . . . Do see a traditional Ukrainian dance concert. The energetic style is bound to give you a lift. . . .

Russia and Ukraine

Review Questions

1. What does "kremlin" mean? What was the function of a kremlin in ages past?

2. Where will a visitor get the best introduction to Moscow? What two enduring symbols of Russia are found there?

3. Why is St. Petersburg an especially enjoyable place to visit in late June?

4. What is the Hermitage? What are some of the attractions there?

5. In addition to bleak, snowy wilderness, what does Siberia contain?

6. Why would you recommend that a client avoid Russian domestic flights?

7. In Moscow, what is the Arbat?

8. What are the main tourist attractions in Ukraine?

9. Near what city is Babi Yar? What happened there?

10. What resort on the Black Sea seems to be a combination of Carmel, California, the French Riviera and Greece? What leaders met there during World War II? What is Livadia, in which they met?

Russia and Ukraine

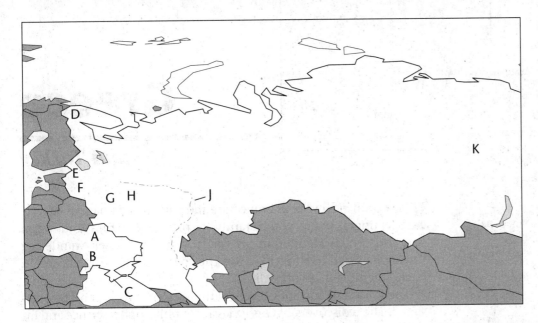

Map Skills Exercise

Match the tourist destination listed below with the corresponding letter on the map. You can use each letter only once.

1. _____ Kiev
2. _____ Yalta
3. _____ Siberia
4. _____ St. Petersburg
5. _____ Novgorod
6. _____ Volga River
7. _____ Moscow
8. _____ Suzdal

Selling Exercise

A business client is traveling to Russia and Ukraine and will be visiting Moscow, St. Petersburg and Kiev. He asks you what he should see and do in each of these cities during his leisure time and how he should travel between them. Prepare a note to him with your suggestions.

Greece
and Turkey

RUSSIA
POLAND
UKRAINE
★Ankara
TURKEY
Athens
GREECE
IRAN
LIBYA
EGYPT

Selling Points

Beaches, historic sites, modern and ancient culture, striking scenery, spas, lots of islands, cave exploration, fun-loving people, casinos, yachting and shopping are among the main attractions of Greece.

Nearly everyone will love Greece; it's a relatively inexpensive destination with diverse attractions. The country will especially appeal to travelers who love history, philosophy, sailing, beaches and quaint villages. Don't expect lush tropical scenery around the beaches (Greece is quite arid).

Fascinating Facts About Greece

The ancient Greeks, before the invention of soap, used to soak in water and then daub themselves with olive oil. The oil (and accumulated grime) was then scraped off with a curved implement . . . There are nude and topless beaches throughout Greece. They probably have nothing to do with the fact that ancient Olympic athletes competed in the nude . . . Domenicos Theotokopoulos — the artist El Greco — lived in Crete. . . .

Few countries evoke as immediate and enticing an image as Greece. Hearing its name, you instantly see pictures of white sand, warm sun and crystal Mediterranean water. You see yourself wandering through a small fishing village on the coast and, looking up, see an ancient temple, high on a cliff.

The impact of ancient Greece on the Western World can't be overstated. The rediscovery of Greek classics of philosophy, science and literature in the 14th and 15th centuries had a profound influence on the development of Western thought, and the effects of those revelations are still with us today.

Though its recorded history goes back thousands of years, modern-day Greece was shaped largely in the past several centuries. It's the story of the conquest in the 15th century by the Ottoman Turks and the struggle that followed to drive them out, lasting into the early years of this century. It's the story of the occupation by the Nazis during World War II. Then in the 1970s, the monarchy was abolished and finally democracy — a concept that was born 2,000 years ago in Greece — was restored.

It's important for first-time visitors to know that, although many of the temples and archaeological sites are well preserved or have been restored, others are in near-total ruin. Initially, travelers should stick to the best-known sites. (A visit to nearby Turkey is sometimes included with a trip to Greece.)

What to Do There

Athens   A visit to 3,000-year-old Athens, the capital of Greece, can be a dream come true — or a nightmare. Usually, it's a little of both. On the one hand, the city is surrounded by beautiful hills; on the other, the peaks can be obscured by terrible pollution. At times the horn-honking and bustle of downtown will drive you crazy — then suddenly you'll find yourself in the Plaka area, strolling cobblestone streets lined with colorful houses, gardens, quaint shops and small *tavernas*.

The Acropolis — the hill upon which the Parthenon and other important structures stand — is the first place you should visit. Its attractions are not all on top of the hill, so take time to appreciate the ruins you'll pass along the way. In fact, before starting up, take a look at the amphitheaters and the Odeon of Herod Atticus (the Athens Festival is held there during the summer). As you climb, pause to look at the various views of the city. Among the structures to investigate on the Acropolis are the small Ionian temple of Athena Niki (also called the Temple of the Wingless Victory), the Erechtheion Temple, the Theatre of Dionysus and the Parthenon (fifth century BC).

Other interesting things to see and do in Athens include taking a trip to the top of the Hill of Philopappou (Hill of the Muses) for a great view of the city and seeing the skirted soldiers (called *Evzones*) perform a changing-of-the-guard ceremony at the Tomb of the Unknown Soldier. Afterward, relax at the Zappion, a beautiful garden with shaded benches. Also see the Temple of Olympian Zeus and Hadrian's Arch (next to each other, just a few blocks from the Acropolis), the first-century-BC Tower of Winds, the Roman Forum and the not-to-be-missed National Archaeological Museum. Upscale shopping can be found in the Constitution (Syntagma) Square/Kolonaki area, and there's a flea market at Monastiraki (especially good on Sunday mornings).

There are several spots near Athens that can be visited as either full- or half-day trips; if time permits, however, overnighting is better. These excursions include the Peloponnesian Peninsula (Epidaurus, Corinth, Mycenae), Delphi and Marathon. Many visitors to Athens take a full-day cruise or hydrofoil/boat/hovercraft out of the port of Piraeus to Poros, Hydra and Aegina, three of the most popular Saronic Gulf Islands.

Corfu
Corfu, off the western coast of Greece in the Ionian Sea, is one of the most beautiful Greek islands. It has rich scenery, numerous cypress and olive groves, gorgeous water (ranging in tone from blue to green), rugged mountains, splendid hidden coves and miles of sandy beaches. Highlights include taking a boat ride into the green and blue grottoes, visiting the monastery and wandering the narrow alleys of the main town, Kerkyra. Walk through the Venetian quarter (much of Greece was once controlled by the Italian city-state of Venice), shop for silver, visit the casino in the gaudy Achillion Palace (built in honor of Achilles, hero of Homer's *Iliad*) or just sit in one of numerous outdoor cafes.

Other popular islands in the Ionian Sea include Cephalonia (water sports, beaches), Levkas (picturesque and untouristy, with quaint villages and nice beaches) and Ithaca (home of legendary hero Odysseus, relaxation, snorkeling, pleasant small villages).

The Parthenon, Athens

Crete
Crete is dry and mountainous, with several fairly sandy, pretty beaches and many historical sites. The capital, Iraklion, can be very noisy and crowded during the summer — we recommend using one of the smaller towns as a base. While in the capital, visit the archaeological museum. It has one of the world's best displays of Minoan artifacts (including incredible mosaics and a strangely inscribed disc from Festos). Also see the Venetian-built fortress along the port.

Three mi/5 km from town is Knossos, once the capital of the ancient Minoan civilization, and now the site of the reconstructed King Minos' Palace. (Minoan civilization on Crete flourished and declined many hundreds of years before the golden age of Athens.) On the western part of the island is Europe's longest gorge, Samaria Gorge (great for hiking). Crete is also the place to go for water sports, including windsurfing, snorkeling and waterskiing.

Cyclades Islands
In the Cyclades, one of the larger island groups, the most interesting islands are Ios (outstanding beaches and plenty of all-night bars and dance clubs catering to the young), Santorini (Fira, its capital, is perched on the rim of an active volcano) and Delos (Temple of Apollo). Perhaps most famous is Mykonos, which looks as if it's straight off tourism posters, with beautiful water, whitewashed houses, sandy beaches (some nude), winding streets, windmills, great restaurants, water sports, colorful domed churches, many gay tourists, lively *tavernas* and very good shopping.

Delphi
Home of the ancient Oracle, Delphi was known in mythology as the Navel of the Earth. Among the treasures there are the Temple of Apollo (where the Oracle was) and the Arcade of the Athenians (columns in

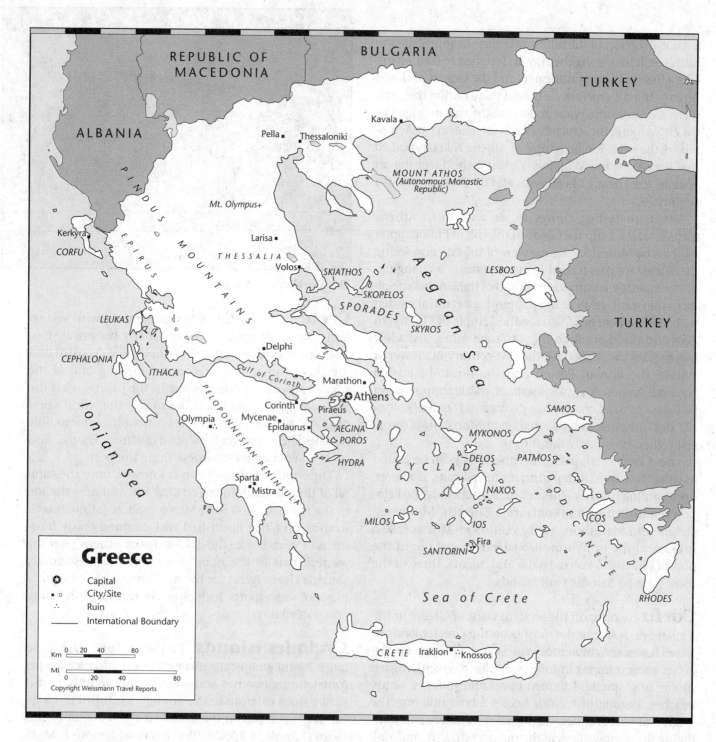

Greece

- ✪ Capital
- ▪ □ City/Site
- ∴ Ruin
- — International Boundary

Km 0 20 40   80
Mi 0 20   40   80

Copyright Weissmann Travel Reports

varying degrees of ruin). Other sites include the Sacred Way and the Treasury of the Athenians. You'll also take in a panoramic view of the Gulf of Itea and the surrounding area from the site. The town's museum is one of the best in Greece; it houses the famous bronze Charioteer.

Dodecanese Islands

This island group in the eastern Aegean, near the coast of Turkey, includes Cos (buildings/ruins, nice beaches, natural beauty, relatively few tourists and birthplace of Hippocrates — the

father of medicine) and Rhodes (very popular with lively nightlife, excellent beaches, flowers, hills, historic sites; the Colossus of Rhodes, a 100-ft/30-m statue of the god Helios — one of the Seven Wonders of the Ancient World — once stood there).

Marathon

This site makes an absorbing half-day trip from Athens — it's the battleground where the Greeks defeated a much larger Persian army. It was also the starting point for the original long-distance run: The story is that a runner raced off to Athens to proclaim victory — and dropped dead as soon as he had delivered his message. Sights include a burial mound and a good museum.

Peloponnesian Peninsula
This is a large peninsula, southwest of Athens and home to many famous sites in Greek history, including Corinth, Mycenae, Sparta and Olympia. Some people tour the peninsula by car out of Athens. Only 40 mi/65 km west of Athens, Corinth may be your first stop. Here you'll see the ruins of the ancient Greek city, including the Temple of Apollo. Corinth is also famous in the Bible — it's one of the towns in which St. Paul preached. Other places to visit on the peninsula include Mycenae (ruins there are much older than those in Athens; sights include the tomb of the legendary Agamemnon, Greek hero of the Trojan War); Epidaurus (one of the best preserved amphitheaters, now used for open-air Greek dramas); Sparta (not much remains of the ancient city that was the chief rival of Athens); Mistra (fine relics from the Byzantine age); and Olympia (site of the first Olympic games; structures here include the Temple of Zeus).

Saronic Islands
The main islands in the Saronic Gulf are Hydra, Poros and Aegina. They can be seen as boat trips from Piraeus. On Aegina, the largest of these islands, you can visit the Temple of Aphea Athena — it's one of the best-preserved temples in Greece. Our favorite of these islands is Poros, known for its wine and unique architecture.

Sporades Islands (The Sprinkled Isles)
The three Sporades Islands, in the western Aegean Sea near the Greek mainland, will be of interest to those who have lots of time (with the exception of Skiathos, they're usually visited by yacht). The islands are Skiathos (rock climbing, ruins, churches, beaches), Skopelos (ruins, sandy beaches, churches) and Skyros (ruins, interesting homes).

Thessaloniki
Thessaloniki is Greece's second-largest city. The drive there from Athens, an enjoyable six or seven hours, passes striking mountain scenery. The port city has several attractions. First, allow several hours to see the archaeological museum, which contains displays of items found in 1977 in the tomb of Philip II, Alexander the Great's father. Also plan to see the White (or Bloody) Tower (a not-to-be-missed mausoleum — it's the oldest and most important monument in town) and the Arch of Galerius (triumphal arch built in the fourth century AD to celebrate Roman victories over the Parthians). Day or overnight trips can be taken to Mt. Athos (monasteries of several faiths) and Pella (once capital of Macedonia, and the birthplace of Alexander the Great).

Geostats

Official Name: Hellenic Republic.

Visa Info: Passport only needed by U.S. and Canadian citizens for tourist or business visits of up to three months.

Health Certificates: Yellow-fever certificate required if you're arriving from an infected area.

Capital: Athens.

Population: 10,100,000.

Size: 50,962 sq mi/131,992 sq km. About the size of Alabama.

Language: Greek.

Climate: Temperate.

Economy: Industry, agriculture.

Government: Presidential parliamentary republic.

Religion: Greek Orthodox.

Currency: Drachma (DRA). Traveler's checks can be easily exchanged. Credit cards are widely accepted. AE, DC, MC, VI.

Time Zone: 7 hours ahead of EST; +2 GMT.

Electricity: 220 volts.

Itinerary

The absolute minimum stay in Greece is one week, although we strongly recommend at least two. For those with tight schedules, cruises are a good way to see the islands. Here's a one-week itinerary that includes a cruise:

Day 1 — Arrive Athens.

Day 2 — Athens.

Day 3 — Athens (possible day trip to Marathon).

Day 4 — Day trip to Delphi. Return to Athens.

Day 5 — Board boat for three-day cruise of islands.

Day 6 — Cruise.

Day 7 — Cruise.

Day 8 — Return to, and depart from, Athens.

Climate/When to Go

Our favorite time to visit is from mid-May to mid-June and from mid-September to the latter part of October, when the temperatures are mild. The latter part of June to the first part of September is hot (and crowded with tourists). In the winter, it's usually too cold to swim or lie on the beach.

Transportation

Delta, TWA and Olympic Airways offer nonstop service from the U.S. Several European carriers provide single-carrier service to Athens. Olympic Airways also offers nonstop service from Canada, as well as relatively inexpensive domestic flights. Athens' Hellinikon Airport (ATH) is 6 mi/10 km from the capital. There is direct rail service from most European countries, although you'll have to travel around the former Yugoslavia). Bus service is also available. Cruise lines offer three-day and longer itineraries through the islands (Sun Lines is geared to the North American tourist slightly more than others). If at all possible, choose a cruise that also stops in Istanbul, Turkey — for the contrast. Local ferries (most leaving from Piraeus) provide cheap travel throughout the islands.

Accommodations

Accommodations range from deluxe international resort properties to basic, locally run small hotels, spas, campgrounds, flats (apartments), villas, private homes and hostels. If you camp, stay only in designated areas. Budget travelers will want to find a room in a small hotel in the Plaka area of Athens, but these hotels may be noisy. In general, you get what you pay for.

Health Advisories

Generally, Western health standards apply. Even so, we stick with prepackaged or boiled drinks. In rural areas, use discretion when choosing restaurants. Good hospitals can be found in larger cities.

What to Buy

Shop for handicrafts, wines, rugs, pottery, lace, embroidery, icons and jewelry. Syntagma and Kolonaki are good areas in Athens for general high-quality shopping. Piraeus is usually less expensive than Athens. Don't be afraid to haggle over prices — it's the norm there.

What to Eat

People tend to love or hate Greek food. The spicing is unusual, and lamb, olive oil and fish are common ingredients (usually sopped up with a lot of bread). There's more to Greek food, however, than gyros: If you've only eaten Greek food in North America, you're in for a treat in Greece. Local specialties include tsatsiki (garlic-yogurt spread), melitzanosalata (eggplant salad), souvlakia (lamb kebabs marinated in garlic), revithia soupa (chick pea soup), chtapodi (octopus salad) and tiropitakia (cheese pie). Don't leave Greece without trying baklava and other pastries made from filo dough, nuts and honey. Greek wines are usually quite good.

Travel Tips for the Client

Do read about the history and mythology of Greece before you go. If you can conjure up the images of those long-gone heros, you are much more likely to enjoy the multitude of ruins found throughout the country . . . Do learn the Greek alphabet; it will help you find your way around . . . It's best to stay away from conversations regarding Turkey, especially if you plan to say something nice about that country. Emotions have run high over Greece's eastern neighbor . . . Do be careful when driving in Greece; the country has one of the highest highway death rates in Europe. . . .

Turkey

Turkey is a great dusty bazaar that offers something to everyone. It has majestic cathedrals from the Byzantine era (5th to 15th centuries); luxurious palaces and mosques from Ottoman times (13th to 20th centuries); the classical ruins of Ephesus, Troy and Pergamon; and the warm sun and beautiful beaches of the Black and the Mediterranean Seas. It also has one of the world's great cities, Istanbul. Here's a look at key tourist destinations: Istanbul, Ephesus and some of the more important Mediterranean resort cities.

What to Do There

Antalya   This Mediterranean town is one of the country's top attractions. Not only is it on a beautiful crescent bay, but dramatic cliffs and the Toros Mountains also contribute one of the most beautiful backdrops on the Mediterranean. Visitors can take a break from the sea and sand to visit Hittite, Greek and Roman ruins right in town.

Bodrum (Halicarnassus)   Spread out on two crescent-shaped bays, this resort has an artsy feel. Recently, it has become a magnet for the jet set, while at the same time maintaining an intimate air. It has a modern marina (it's an important yacht-chartering center), an old waterfront and winding streets. It's a good spot to stay while visiting the Mausoleum of Halicarnassus (one of the Seven Wonders of the Ancient World) and the Castle of St. Peter, a Crusader fortification housing the excellent Museum of Underwater Archaeology. The highlight of the museum: artifacts from the oldest shipwreck ever discovered.

Ephesus   Of all the ruins in Turkey, the grandest and best restored are at Ephesus. This prominent ancient capital was founded in the 10th century BC by ancient Greeks. Biblical scholars may know the town as the inspiration for St. Paul's Epistle to the Ephesians. German archaeologists still digging at the site have reconstructed much of it, including the Temple of Hadrian, the 24,000-seat Great Amphitheater (still used for open-air concerts) and the Temple of Artemis (one of the Seven Wonders of the Ancient World). Cruise passengers can visit Ephesus from the nearby ports of Izmir and Kusadasi.

Hagia Sophia, Istanbul

Istanbul (Previously known as Constantinople, and Byzantium before that.) In this city, capital of vast empires and home of spectacular attractions, a few sights stand out as absolute must-sees. One is the symbol of Istanbul, the lovely Blue Mosque, a massive and rounded structure contrasting beautifully with the airy, vertical spires of its minarets. The nearby Hagia Sophia was once the world's largest church, before St. Peter's in Rome was built — its interior mosaics and spaces are stunning. (After the Ottoman conquest of Constantinople in 1453 AD, the cathedral was turned into a mosque, but it is now a museum.) Another unique attraction is the 19th-century baroque Dolmabahce Palace, which runs along the Bosporus Strait, and ranks among the world's most ostentatious and overdone palaces. Marble, gold, carpets and crystal are all laid on thick. Other highlights are the Museum of Ancient Oriental Art, the Archeology Museum, the city's famed covered bazaar (it's so big that it even has its own post office!) and Topkapi Palace, home of the sultans of the Ottoman Empire. Istanbul is a city that's fascinating to experience just sitting at sidewalk cafes.

Travel Tips for the Client

Do not bargain unless you intend to buy — its considered extremely rude to not buy something after agreeing upon a price. Do bargain hard. If you are trying to buy a rug, you should offer 50%–60% of the asking price . . . Do take toilet paper, a towel and soap with you, especially if you're traveling in eastern or rural Turkey . . . Do be very careful to stay within the law while in Turkey (i.e., avoid drugs, even if it seems safe to use them). Turkish prisons are notorious, and no leniency is shown to tourists. . . .

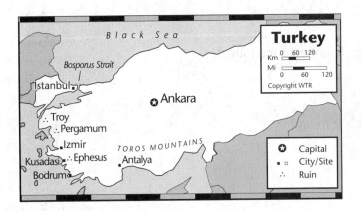

Greece and Turkey

Review Questions

1. What would a tourist see from the top of the Hill of Philopappou (Hill of Muses)?

2. What is the Acropolis?

3. What do the highlights of a visit to Corfu include?

4. Knossos was the ancient capital of what civilization? On what island is it located?

5. Why is Marathon famous in history? From what city would you most likely take a half-day trip to visit Marathon?

6. How long is the drive from Athens to Thessaloniki, and what would you pass along the way? What attraction in Thessaloniki is the most important monument in town?

7. Why would you suggest that a tourist read about the history and mythology of Greece before going?

8. What have German archaeologists digging at Ephesus reconstructed?

9. What is the symbol of Istanbul? How would you describe it for a tourist?

10. What was Hagia Sophia in times past and what is it today?

Greece and Turkey

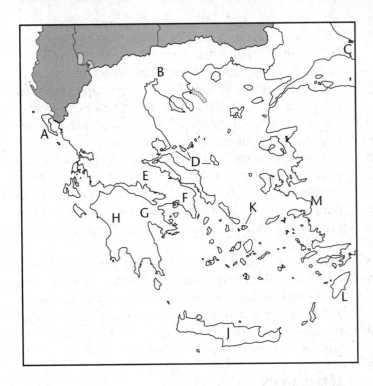

Map Skills Exercise

Match the tourist destination listed below with the corresponding letter on the map. You can use each letter only once.

1. _____ Corfu
2. _____ Istanbul
3. _____ Mykonos
4. _____ Athens
5. _____ Crete
6. _____ Rhodes
7. _____ Mycenae
8. _____ Thessaloniki
9. _____ Sporades
10. _____ Ephesus

Selling Exercise

A client has come to your office and asked you to put together a dream itinerary for a trip to Greece and Turkey. Money is no object. She wants to spend three weeks there, including at least one week on a dream cruise. Prepare the itinerary for her listing key attractions she'll want to see and activities she can enjoy at each stop. Then plot the itinerary on a map. Be sure to plot the dream cruise on the map, too. (Use transparency map #33 for this exercise.)

Europe Geofile

Central Europe

Czech Republic

In one of Europe's newest nations, the best of "Old Europe" survives. The Czech Republic — the western portion of partitioned Czechoslovakia — features marvelous medieval town centers and architectural treasures that rival those found anywhere on the continent. It's one of the few Eastern European nations to have avoided destruction during both World Wars. The result is that a visit to one of its cities can feel like a stroll through a lovely open-air museum. We expect tourism in the Czech Republic to continue to expand as fast as the infrastructure can support it.

Prague   Prague is, we think, one of the most beautiful cities in the world. Built on seven hills, this capital contains beautiful architecture, ranging from Romanesque and Gothic to Renaissance and Baroque. It's often called "the city of 100 spires" because of its many churches, and it also features numerous parks and lots of trees. For younger travelers, Prague is very much the place to be in Europe. Many foreigners, including a number of American entrepreneurs, have moved in, attracted by the city's beauty, commercial opportunity and low overhead.

Large portions of the central city can be seen on foot. Begin your tour by visiting the 14th-century Charles

Central Europe

Bridge and Prague Castle. The bridge, with its interesting collection of religious statues and excellent view of the castle, is a major cultural and architectural monument, like the Ponte Vecchio in Florence. The bridge, reserved for pedestrians, is alive with street vendors, promenaders, lovers and tourists. Prague Castle is the former home of the Bohemian (Czech) royalty.

On the next day, either begin with a visit to the historic Jewish ghetto or walk to Old Town Square to see a huge monument to Jan Hus, the martyred Protestant reformer, and the great collection of well-preserved historic buildings and churches that line the square.

Spas   The Czech Republic is famous for its spas. There are 58 spas throughout the country that claim to help relieve various ailments and diseases relating to circulatory, glandular, nervous, muscular, skin, mental and respiratory conditions and arthritis. Among the best-known and most popular are Karlovy Vary and Marianske Lazne.

Hungary

Hungary is the home of good food (goulashes, fish stews, cherry soup, crepes drizzled with chocolate, to name a few) and one of Europe's most striking capitals — Budapest. We think it provides Westerners with the smoothest introduction to Eastern Europe. Even inexperienced travelers will find it an easy place to visit.

Hungary consists mostly of plains, with hills and low mountains confined to the western and northern portions of the country. The Danube River runs through the middle of the country. Huge Lake Balaton is to the west, while rich agricultural land dominates the east. Ethnically, Hungarians are different from most Europeans — their language, for instance, is related only to Finnish and Estonian.

Budapest   Known as the "Queen of the Danube," this 1,000-year-old city is truly one of the world's most beautiful. It combines modern, Neoclassical, Baroque, art nouveau and other architectural styles with the grandeur of the flowing Danube, which meanders through the city.

Begin your visit in the Castle District of Buda (Budapest is really two cities, Buda and Pest — Pest is as flat as Kansas and Buda is as hilly as San Francisco). There you'll find antique stores, shops, pretty homes, taverns, museums (including an excellent music museum), restaurants and many of Budapest's prime attractions in a relatively compact area. Two must-sees are in the area: the reconstructed Royal Palace and Matthias Church. Matthias Church represents the very soul of the city. You can't miss its colorful, multispired roof, and you'll find the church is just as stunning inside.

Attractions on the Pest side include the National Museum, the glittering Opera House, the newly renovated Market Hall and the Jewish Museum. While in Pest, head to the lavish Cafe Gerbeaud, one of the city's most ornate coffee and pastry shops.

There is usually a lot to choose from in the evening: classical concerts, an opera or operetta, folk dancing, nightclubs or discos. Be sure to visit one of the city's centuries-old Turkish bathhouses — they're great! Because of Budapest's central location, day trips can be taken to almost anywhere in the nation.

Poland

The Poles are working to find their place in a post-Communist world. Their earnest questioning will add intensity to any visit and allow travelers a glimpse at a country in the making. But visitors shouldn't ignore longstanding sights out of Poland's history — from beautiful medieval castles to the stark structures of Nazi concentration camps. Poland will appeal to travelers of Polish heritage who want to visit their ancestral homeland or those who have already visited Eastern Europe and want to gain a broader understanding of the region. Though Poles are outgoing and friendly, visitors who don't speak Polish or German may find it difficult to connect with them — few speak English.

Krakow   Krakow is almost everybody's favorite Polish city — this 1,000-year-old former capital is the only large urban area in the nation that escaped World War II without serious damage. Coupled with Krakow's physical beauty is its standing as the country's cultural center.

In the center of Krakow is the largest medieval square in all of Europe, Old Market Square. It's lined with historic buildings, and in the center of the square are two important structures: the 13th-century Cloth Hall, now home to souvenir and crafts stalls, and the Town Hall Tower, which hosts a summertime tavern in the cellar (a vast improvement over its original use as a torture chamber). Within walking distance of the square are the Gothic 14th-century buildings of Jagiellonian University (its museum houses Copernicus' instruments). Stroll along nearby Kanonicza Street — it is one of Poland's loveliest streets.

Allow for a half-day excursion to Oswiecim to see Auschwitz, the horrifiying Nazi extermination camp. Another half a day could be spent seeing the Wieliczka Salt Mines, which run about 90 mi/150 km underground. You can also use Krakow as a base to visit Wadowice (birthplace of Pope John Paul II) and Czestochowa (home of the holiest religious relic in Poland, the Black Madonna).

Warsaw   Warsaw, though 700 years old, was almost completely leveled in World War II. And the rebuilt city isn't the most attractive capital in Europe. Notable exceptions to the bland architecture can be found in its restored old buildings, which were lovingly reconstructed using old paintings, drawings and blueprints that were hidden away at the beginning of the war. The centerpiece of the Old Town is the Royal Castle, which amazingly has been returned to its original splendor. Extending out from the Old Town is the Royal Way: Historic attractions along this route include palaces and churches (especially the Church of the Holy Cross, where Chopin's heart is entombed). Also along this street are interesting stores and coffeehouses and Warsaw University. Other attractions in Warsaw include the Marie Curie Museum, the Chopin Museum, the Warsaw Ghetto Monument and the Museum of Struggle and Martyrdom (which commemorates Poland's often painful history). The top of the Palace of Science and Culture used to offer the best view of the city; today, the Warsaw Marriott, now the tallest building, rises above it.

Slovakia

Though currently in a slump, the Slovakian tourism industry hopes that word of its quaint villages, skiing, mountainous scenery and natural wonders will one day bring large numbers of tourists to its borders. Formerly the eastern portion of Czechoslovakia, Slovakia is working out the details of becoming an independent nation. And when the country reaches a more settled point in its development, we suspect that its tourism industry will soar to new heights. In addition to its ski areas, the country's attributes include picturesque valleys and streams, caves, castles, wine cellars, health spas and historic sites.

The Baltic Countries and Belarus

Belarus

Belarus appears to be one of the more stable of the former Soviet Republics. Nonetheless, Belarus has little to

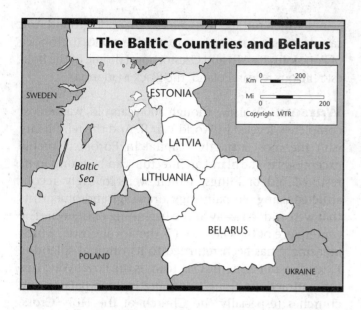

The Baltic Countries and Belarus

offer leisure travelers. The country was repeatedly destroyed in wars, and its towns retain few old structures. There is really very little that's unique in Belarus. The only people to send are those who plan to visit relatives or who are searching for their roots.

Estonia

While other former communist countries have moved cautiously toward the West, Estonia has come running and hasn't looked back. It is the most "Westernized" of the three Baltic states: Visit Tallinn, the capital, and you'll find well-stocked shops and bars patronized by Finns and Swedes taking advantage of low prices. You'll also find that the shops and restaurants have lost their "Soviet" feeling — in other words, you won't wait an eternity to get the attention of a surly shopkeeper or an unfriendly waiter. The main attractions of Estonia are Gothic architecture, historic sites, Baltic culture and scenic islands and countryside.

Latvia

The main attractions of Latvia include the capital Riga, Baroque, Gothic and art nouveau architecture and the countryside. Spend some time in Riga and you'll find good nightlife with an international flair — it's the most cosmopolitan city in the Baltics. But Riga is only part of the adventure. Other charms lie hidden in the green countryside. Geographically, Latvia is characterized by rolling plains, gentle hills, forests, beautiful valleys and more than 5,000 lakes (formed during the last Ice Age).

Lithuania

The main attractions in this intensely Catholic nation are historic and cultural sites, wooden folk sculptures and the cities of Vilnius and Kaunas. In addition, Lithuanians are some of the friendliest people in the Baltics. It's also more agricultural than the other Baltic nations and tends to run at a slower pace. Don't send clients there who must have deluxe accommodations throughout their stay or who are looking for exciting nightlife.

The Balkans

Albania

It used to be said that only madmen, journalists and diplomats went to Albania. That no longer is true — for better or worse, tourists can now venture to the "Land of the Eagle," once the most Stalinist and isolated of the old Communist countries. Though it has been open to outsiders for a few years now, it's still far from being user-friendly. The capital, Tirana, has only a few hotels and the infrastructure for tourism is, to put it kindly, inadequate. Send only those well-traveled few who are motivated by curiosity and want to see a European country where time seems to have stood still for decades. But remember that Greece has better examples of similar Adriatic attractions.

Bosnia and Herzegovina

As this country endures a terrible civil war, all that is certain is that at the end of the '90s, Bosnia and Herzegovina will not be the same nation it was at the beginning of the decade. Among the possibilities for the future are bloody anarchy, a partitioning of the land or an uneasy U.N. or NATO occupation. Until things have settled, no one should travel to the area. When conditions stabilize, the nation's attractions will include fortresses, mosques, Roman ruins, Byzantine-style basilicas, churches, amphitheaters and other monuments reflecting the land's mixed heritage.

Bulgaria

This is one of the most underrated nations in Europe. As it struggles for a new identity in post-Communist Eastern Europe, it hasn't yet discovered how to capitalize on its natural beauty (two mountain ranges), cultural treasures (monasteries that are themselves works of art) and recreational opportunities (skiing, water sports, mineral health spas). Visitors who do make it to Bulgaria find that it has a decent tourist infrastructure in place: The roads and accommodations are more than adequate.

Travelers sent there independently should be slightly on the adventurous side — there's no particular danger, but few Bulgarians speak English (you can always send the timid on tours). Warn clients that there's not a wide variety of food.

Croatia

Croatia is a wonderful travel destination if you have a flexible schedule and don't mind visiting a country that is embroiled in regional conflicts. The Adriatic coast is simply gorgeous: lazy blue water, dry rocky coastline, charming villages and one of the world's great treasures, the ancient city of Dubrovnik. It's no surprise, however, that few travelers are flocking to this former Yugoslavian republic. Most would rather not spend their vacation so close to a war zone, no matter how attractive. On our last visit, the tourist spots along the coast were practically empty, but the natural beauty, the ancient sights and the wonderful seafood were still there. The people were very friendly, thankful to see any tourist back in their country. They would joke, laugh and, only after some time, turn melancholy and talk about the war.

Macedonia

Macedonia's location has given it a turbulent history: Greeks, Romans and Turks have been among the many who have coveted the national territory. Today Macedonia is an independent nation that's worth seeing for its pretty countryside as well as for its historical importance. Seated on a high plateau, Macedonia offers picturesque cities and beautiful lakes and gorges. Its main attractions include Roman ruins, medieval monasteries, Turkish architecture, historic sites, fascinating culture, friendly people and low prices. If you're in Skopje, the capital city, see the 15th-century Daud Pasha Turkish baths, the largest baths in the region. For a nice view of the city, climb to Fort Kale, a ruined castle.

Moldova

Moldova's attractions center on its primarily agrarian countryside, a composite of green rolling hills, picturesque roadside wells, rich river valleys, whitewashed villages and fruitful vineyards and orchards. What draws tourists to Moldova are its cathedrals, art, historic sites and bucolic settings. (Note: Moldova was a province of Romania for many years and its culture and language are Romanian.) Moldova is a destination for the flexible, open-minded traveler who has experienced traveling in Eastern Europe and wants to see more. Don't send those who must have deluxe accommodations throughout their stay, active nightlife or infallible service.

Romania

We think Romania is the most alluring country in Eastern Europe. Its attractions — the Carpathian Mountains, ancient monasteries covered inside and out with frescoes, beaches along the Black Sea, Transylvania (home of literature's Count Dracula) — all evoke an air of mystery that catches travelers like a web. The country retains a side of Europe that has all but disappeared: rural roads filled with horse carts, gorgeous mountain trails empty of tourists, people who greet visitors with curiosity instead of cynicism. In short, it's a visit to the Old Country, where fable and folktale still live.

While the country offers many attractions, it's not hassle-free. Food choices are limited, selections for shopping have not improved as much as in other former Eastern Bloc countries, and accommodations remain under par. And don't plan to spend much time in Bucharest, the depressing capital; the cities in Transylvania are much more interesting.

Slovenia

Slovenia seems to be a charmed country. While some of the other former Yugoslav republics have slipped into warfare and genocide, this tiny country has walked away relatively unscathed. And it has taken a little bit of everything with it: mountains and lakes, castles and alpine forests, caves, pastures, beaches and islands. While the country may not be as impressive as Austria, it is certainly less crowded and less expensive. We think it is a wonderful destination, if you are in the region.

Yugoslavia

The Federal Republic of Yugoslavia, consisting solely of the republics of Serbia and Montenegro, is currently embroiled in the Bosnia and Herzegovina civil war. Until the situation is resolved, travel in or out of the country is difficult at best, dangerous at worst. When the situation calms, both Serbia and Montenegro should see a revival in tourism; the nation features spectacular coastal and mountain scenery, fascinating culture, historic sites, marvelous churches and monasteries and lovely lakes and rivers.

The Caucasus Nations

Armenia

Armenia is best avoided at the present time due to its economic turmoil and the tense situation with neighboring Azerbaijan. As soon as the conflict is resolved and Armenia's economy stabilizes, we would recommend sending only those adventurous travelers who are looking for something truly different and who enjoy roughing it. The nation offers stark natural beauty, historic cities and ancient monasteries in scenic mountaintop settings.

Azerbaijan

In the ancient language of the land, Azer means "fire," and no other name seems quite as appropriate. Once the land of fire worshippers, Azerbaijan is now scourged by the fires of war. Facing both civil war and conflict with Armenia, Azerbaijan is simply not a tourist destination at this time. When calm returns, those who

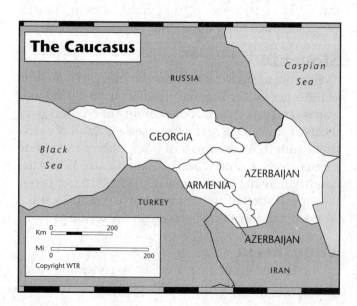

do make the journey there will be awed by the nation's mountainous terrain and beautiful Caspian Sea coast and will enjoy a visit to its spas and cave settlements.

Georgia

In the United States, the state of Georgia epitomizes the grace and gentility of the Old South. The Republic of Georgia in the Caucasus Mountains, however, reminds us more of the American Wild West: Law and order has yet to come to this land, which has been split by ethnic fighting and plagued by organized crime. During the Soviet years, Georgia was the top destination in the region, offering magnificent monasteries, a beautiful seacoast, historic sites, scenic mountains and renowned food and drink. While the sights are still there, the bitter internal conflicts have made the country too unstable for casual tourism for the foreseeable future.

Island Nations

Cyprus

Cyprus blends beaches and mountainous scenery with a wealth of historic attractions—it was on Cyprus that Cicero philosophized, Othello agonized, St. Paul was berated and Aphrodite, created. Its modern history has left some marks as well: the island is politically divided among Greek Cypriots in the south, Turkish Cypriots in the north, and a U.N. buffer zone between them. Most visitors enter the nation on the Greek side and take day trips north (if you enter from the north, you won't be allowed into the south). Send those already in the Mideast who want to spend time on a beach. Don't send those who have already seen the Greek islands or the Turkish coast — they'll probably be unimpressed with Cyprus.

Iceland

Extremes mix in this island nation: Bathers splash in hot springs surrounded by snow; volcanoes smolder near icecaps; and water pours hundreds of feet down a waterfall, only to be shot back into the air by one of the country's geysers. These extremes are caused by Iceland's location — it straddles the turbulent mid-Atlantic ridge just below the Arctic Circle. The combination of frozen environment and geothermic activity is truly a wonder to see. Equally awe-inspiring are the lush green mountains along the fjords. The only drawback is the price — Iceland is one of the world's most expensive countries.

Malta

This nation in the Mediterranean, south of Sicily, includes three major islands: Malta, Gozo and Comino. All are surrounded by clear blue water and have jagged, rocky coastlines with low inland hills. History, water sports/diving, horse racing, casinos, caves, ancient ruins, interesting local culture and good food are Malta's main attractions. The terrain is fairly dry and barren, and there are better beach destinations in southern Europe. If travelers aren't going to be interested in Malta's archaeological ruins, they probably shouldn't bother going.

Mini States

Andorra

Some people think of the country of Andorra, in the Pyrenees Mountains between France and Spain, as the world's largest outlet mall. Visit Andorra la Vella, the capital, and you'll find a collection of small shops selling electronics and wristwatches to frantic Europeans — the shoppers seem to ricochet from store to store in search of tax-free bargains. Visitors can be so put off that they'll just pass through as fast as the traffic jam will allow. But there is more to Andorra than shopping. Like the rest of the Pyrenees, Andorra offers good skiing, hiking and fishing. If you're in the neighborhood you may want to visit just to say you've been there, but don't go out of your way.

Liechtenstein

Squeezed between Austria and Switzerland, it seems more like a small Alpine city surrounded by countryside than an entire country. Most travelers barely give it a thought, and those who visit usually just pause for lunch when traveling from Zurich to Innsbruck. That's a shame, for Liechtenstein has more than its size would indicate. It offers a combination of relaxed sophistication and beautiful scenery — mountains, valleys and vineyards provide the backdrop for almost every scene. Finance and banking draw many Europeans, while skiing, hiking and scenery attract North Americans.

Monaco: *(See France)*

San Marino: *(See Italy)*

Europe Geofile

Review Questions

1. How is Prague's Charles Bridge like Florence's Ponte Vecchio? With what is the Charles Bridge alive?

2. What two cities actually make up the city known as the "Queen of the Danube"? How does the geography of the two cities differ?

3. What city, former capital of the country, is said to be everybody's favorite city in Poland? Describe the city square, including the two important structures in the center of the square.

4. What Baltic country is intensely Catholic? What are the primary attractions there?

5. What are the main tourist attractions in Latvia?

6. What kinds of attractions has Bulgaria yet to capitalize on?

7. To what country would you send a tourist looking to see Transylvania, home of literature's Count Dracula? What other attractions does the country offer?

8. During the Soviet years, Georgia was the top destination in the Caucasus region. Now, however, Georgia can be compared to the American Wild West. Why?

9. Iceland's location straddling the turbulent mid-Atlantic ridge just below the Arctic Circle causes all kinds of geophysically extreme conditions. Describe the "extremes" a tourist might see in Iceland.

10. Why are many Europeans drawn to Liechtenstein? What attracts North Americans there?

Europe Geofile

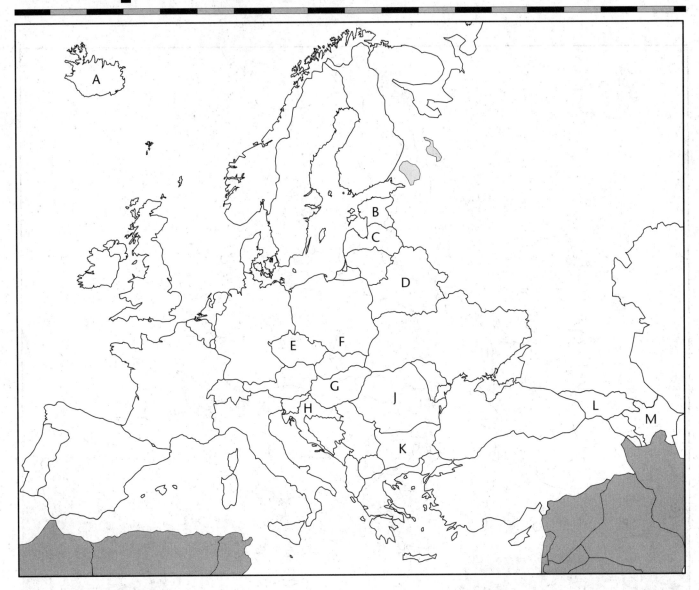

Map Skills Exercise

Match the tourist destination listed below with the corresponding letter on the map.
You can use each letter only once.

1. _____ the "hot" city for younger travelers
2. _____ volcanoes smolder here near icecaps
3. _____ gorgeous Adriatic coast
4. _____ Bulgaria
5. _____ Belarus

6. _____ has most cosmopolitan city in Baltics
7. _____ Auschwitz is here
8. _____ Queen of the Danube
9. _____ Transylvania is in this country
10. _____ was once top destination in Caucasus

Unit Review Europe

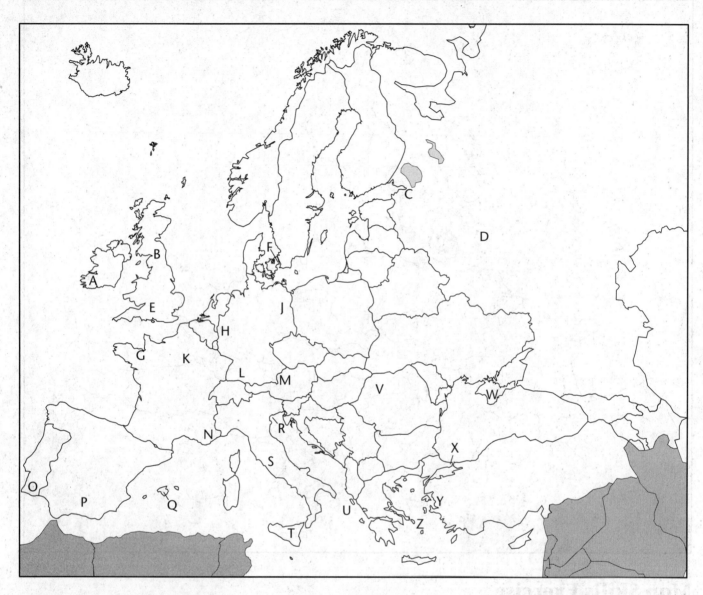

Map Skills Exercise

Match the tourist destination listed below with the corresponding letter on the map.
You can use each letter only once.

1. _____ Versailles
2. _____ St. Basil's Cathedral
3. _____ Transylvania
4. _____ Corfu
5. _____ Vatican City
6. _____ Algarve
7. _____ Mont-St.-Michel

8. _____ Cologne cathedral
9. _____ Hadrian's Wall
10. _____ St. Petersburg
11. _____ Mozarteum
12. _____ Grand Canal
13. _____ Sicily
14. _____ Mallorca

15. _____ Little Mermaid statue
16. _____ Brandenburg Gate
17. _____ Yalta
18. _____ Hagia Sophia
19. _____ Riviera
20. _____ Ephesus

21. _____ Neuschwan-stein
22. _____ Ring of Kerry
23. _____ Stonehenge
24. _____ Mykonos
25. _____ The Alhambra

Unit Review Europe

Content Review Crossword Puzzle

Across

3. Ranks with the Louvre and British Museum
7. The sultans lived in it
9. Famous Rembrandt
11. Home of *Mona Lisa* and *Venus de Milo*
12. Sport from Scotland
15. Visit its Highlands
17. They run in Pamplona
20. It's an outlet mall
22. They're in Switzerland, Italy and France, too
23. Poland's neighbor, destroyed in wars
24. Features works of Goya, El Greco and Velasquez

Down

1. See the summer sun at midnight there
2. Brandenburg Gate's home town
4. Oktoberfest
5. Main boulevard in Vienna
6. Her house is in Amsterdam
8. One of Seven Wonders stood there
10. Cruise through them in Norway
12. French Swiss town
13. Atomium and Mannekin-Pis Fountain there
14. Chateaux galore valley
16. He's under glass in Red Square
18. Museum with Elgin Marbles and Rosetta Stone
19. Opera house in Italy
21. The Parthenon is there

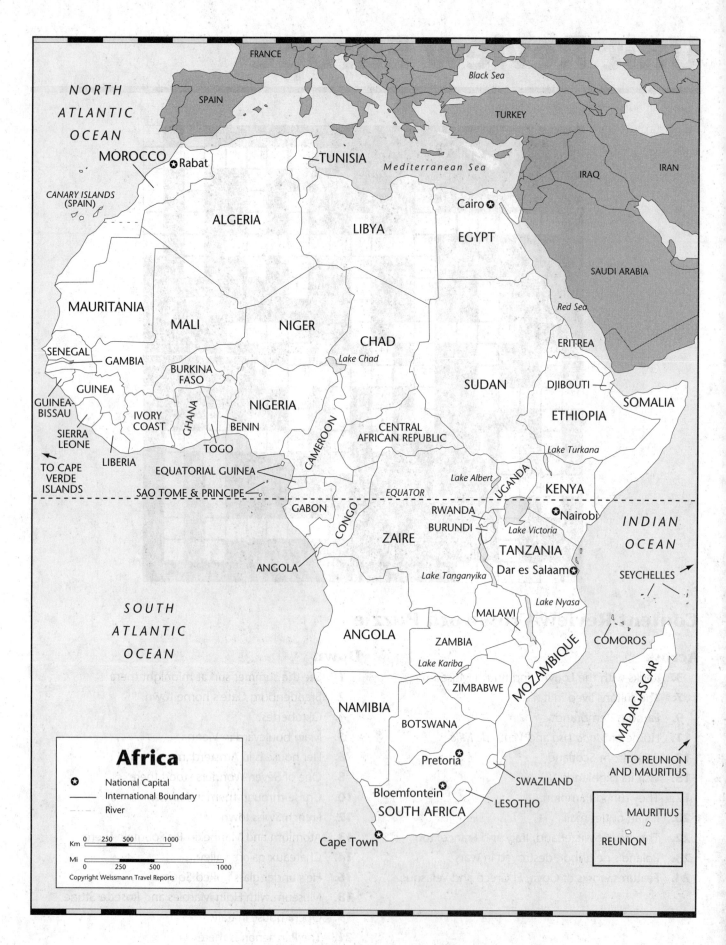

Africa

FABULOUS WILDLIFE EXPERIENCES, ISOLATED beaches, tribal culture, colorful markets, the true home of world beat music—Africa is phenomenal. It's more than three times the size of the United States or Canada, and it contains a tremendous variety of terrains and climates. The Sahara Desert dominates much of North Africa. But you'll still find green areas along the Mediterranean Sea and on the banks of the Nile River. As you travel south of the Sahara you'll discover rain forests in the central part of the continent—it is this jungle terrain that most people associate with Africa. However, unless clients are interested in seeing mountain gorillas, the rain forest is not the place to go to view animals (the thick forest makes most animals virtually impossible to see). On the other hand, the beautiful savanna grasslands of Kenya and Tanzania provide ideal conditions and a relatively comfortable climate for game viewing. Similar terrain exists in Zambia, Zimbabwe, Botswana and South Africa, and these countries, too, are great places for a safari. South Africa also has the continent's most comfortable temperatures.

Africa appeals to romantic, adventurous clients, but it's important to make sure that you send them to a country that won't turn their dreams into nightmares. Most of the countries are not really geared for tourism and don't offer many tourist attractions. Many people interested in Africa will want to see the continent over the course of several trips, so send them first to countries that can provide some of the comforts they're used to: Kenya, Zimbabwe, Botswana or South Africa are good candidates if the clients are interested in seeing animals; Egypt and Morocco will appeal to anyone interested in antiquities or desert life.

On the whole, the best month to visit any given location in Africa is October, but each region has its own very best time. As a general rule of thumb, when it's winter in North America and Europe stay north of the Equator and when it's summer on those continents tour south of the Equator.

On the following pages you'll find in-depth profiles of the most popular tourist destinations on the continent: Egypt, Kenya and Tanzania, Morocco and South Africa. We look at the other African countries, grouped by region, in the Africa Geofile chapter.

Egypt

Selling Points

The Pyramids and the Sphinx, the Valleys of the Kings and Queens, Cairo, ancient temples, museums, churches, casinos, Nile cruises, spas, desert culture and scuba diving are Egypt's main attractions. Nearly everyone will enjoy seeing the country's sights.

We recommend that first-time visitors consider taking an escorted tour. Travelers should be aware that there are areas of Egypt that are quite poor and some places where standards of sanitation are not high.

Visitors may be bothered by the heat (even during winter) or find the amount of walking necessary to see the various temples to be a physical strain. However, if a tour is properly paced for the age of the traveler, there shouldn't be problems.

Fascinating Facts About Egypt

Some of the most common English phrases you'll hear in Egypt are "cheap price," "special offer" and "good deal for you" . . . Many nightclubs offer a buffet and a floor show with dance troupes or belly dancers (also called Arab dancers) as entertainment. We think one of the best shows is at the Cairo Sheraton. . . .

Egypt's attractions are in its mysteries. There are no earthly parallels to the atmosphere of an ancient royal tomb or the temples that cling to the banks of the Nile. There really are no modern equivalents to the Pyramids and the Sphinx — and many of their secrets remain locked away. There are also the mysteries glimpsed in the eyes of Nubian villagers gathered around a fire or the mysteries heard in the sentimental songs of the streets of Cairo. Egypt is an alluring place, a one-of-a-kind travel destination.

Today's traveler must also view Egypt in a modern context, of course. It is an Islamic country at the crossroads of political activity. Violent actions by fundamentalist groups, some targeted at tourists, have brought this point home all too clearly. The government of Egypt is committed to keeping the nation safe, but the situation is, by nature, difficult to control. As in all modern Islamic states, the situation will intensify and relax in cycles for years to come.

An Ancient Nation

Menes, the first Pharaoh, united Upper and Lower Egypt in 3050 BC, starting an empire whose legacy is unmatched in recorded history. Elaborate tombs were designed, magnificent pyramids constructed, and a vast pantheon of gods was honored in huge temples. Hieroglyphs were carved in stone, detailing everything from the lives of the gods to the lives of the lowest slaves. The Nile was harnessed for irrigation. By any standard, this society was very successful and long-lived.

But it eventually fell to outside powers. The most lasting impression was made by Arab invaders, who conquered Egypt around AD 640. In more recent centuries, the country was an inviting prize to the Ottoman Turks, the French and finally the British. Egypt won full independence in 1953. The following year, Gamel Abdel Nasser came to power and ruled with popular support for nearly 20 years. His vice president, Anwar Sadat, succeeded him. Sadat gained the first Arab victory over Israel in 1973, paving the way for a peace treaty. His efforts for peace came with a high price: He was assassinated in 1981. The government today struggles to maintain a delicate balance among the religious, military and popular forces.

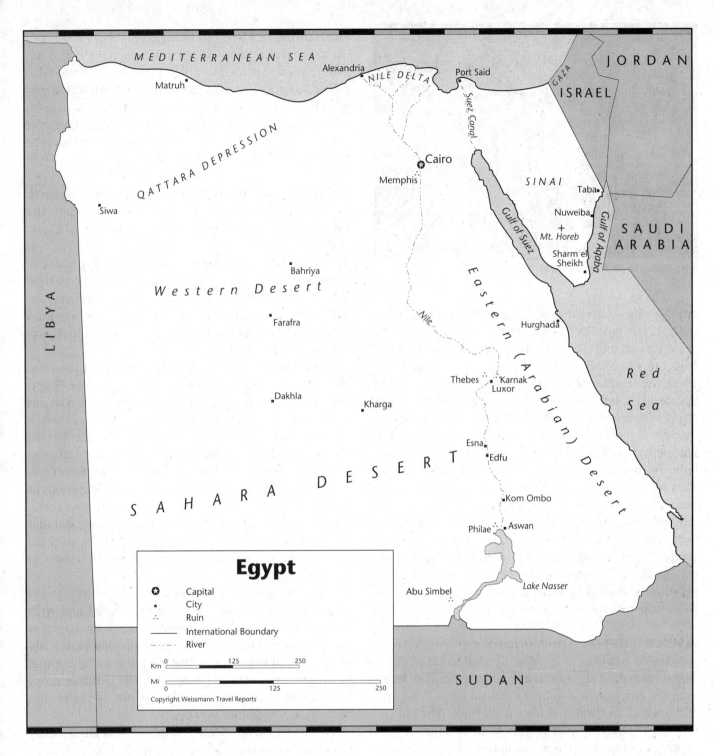

Egypt

- ✪ Capital
- ▪ City
- ∴ Ruin
- —— International Boundary
- —·—·— River

```
Km  0        125        250
Mi  0        125        250
```

Copyright Weissmann Travel Reports

Geographically, Egypt is dominated by sand and water. Nearly all of Egypt is desert, but the small part that isn't — the valley of the Nile River — is vital to the nation (95% of the population lives within a few miles of the Nile's banks). Most tours of Egypt, whether by cruise ship, via train, on a bus or in a private car, never stray too far from the river's shores. Egypt has more people than any other country in the Arab world and, among African nations, is second in population only to Nigeria. Egypt is struggling with enormous demographic and economic challenges.

What to Do There

Abu Simbel   The 3,200-year-old temple at Abu Simbel is not only one of the best preserved and most magnificent temples in the country; it's also a marvel of

The temple at Abu Simbel

engineering — actually, two engineering feats: Originally, it was built by 25,000 workers over a span of 25 years; its four huge statues of Pharaoh Ramses II face the Nile. But when the Aswan High Dam was completed in 1960, the temple was in danger of being submerged in the new lake behind the dam. A massive international effort spearheaded by UNESCO raised the money to move the temple, stone by stone, to higher ground. Before that could be done, however, a mountain similar to the one it was taken out of had to be constructed. This second engineering project took five years. The temple is usually seen as a full-day trip by bus or a half-day trip by air from Aswan (there's free bus transportation from the airport). Allow about two hours to tour the temple. Most people return to Aswan the same day, though there is an adequate hotel, the Nefertari, nearby for those who want to overnight. We suggest overnighting, as the best light on the temple is at sunrise.

Alexandria

The Mediterranean port city of Alexandria has been economically vital to Egypt since ancient times. In spite of its age and importance, however, the city has little to offer tourists except European architecture and walks along the seafront. The Greco-Roman Museum displays items from the time when Egypt was ruled by ancient Macedonians and Romans, positively modern by Egyptian standards (300 BC–AD 300). A causeway leads from the city to the island of Pharos, once the site of the Lighthouse (one of the Seven Wonders of the Ancient World).

Aswan

Aswan is a fairly modern, clean city at the end of the rail line in Upper (southern) Egypt. The main attractions are outside the city itself. Two islands in the Nile, Elephantine and Kitchener's, merit a visit.

Elephantine has two old villages that have managed (so far) to retain their authentic atmosphere. It also has a museum and ruined temples. Kitchener's Island (also called Botanical Island) has tombs and attractive gardens. Also from Aswan you can take a tour (or bargain with a taxi driver) to see the Aswan High Dam (the dam is not so thrilling, but it's brought such change to the country that it should be seen).

Cairo

Cairo has two kinds of attractions: those in the capital itself and those in the suburb of Giza — the Pyramids and the Sphinx. Both are worth a lot of a traveler's time.

First the city: Cairo has 12,000,000 people, pollution, decaying beauty, traffic jams and world-famous treasures. It's hot and noisy, but also exciting and alive. And while some areas are dirty, they aren't any worse than parts of New York City. Like New York, Cairo itself acts as a stimulant.

The prime attraction for tourists seeking to gain a better understanding of Egypt's rich history is the Egyptian Museum. Among its major attractions are a dozen mummies, which, after being in storage for many years, are now displayed in oxygen-free cases. The contents of the tomb of Tutankhamen (King Tut) are still the most popular attraction, but don't overlook the excellent collection of artifacts from the Greek and Roman periods of Egyptian history. (We recommend two half-days there; if your time is limited, ask for directions to the room that contains representative samples of the best the museum has to offer — it'll help you decide where you want to spend your time.)

The other absolute must-see in the city is the Khan-el Khalili Bazaar, a maze of winding streets filled with shops and stalls and carts. In many ways, the bazaar is truly *the* heart of Cairo. You could easily spend a day taking it all in. If you're planning on doing any shopping, be prepared to bargain shamelessly. The perfume shops are particularly memorable. They're run by clerks who can mix any fragrance you desire.

We also enjoyed seeing some of the city's many mosques — especially the Mohammed Ali, or Alabaster, Mosque — which are wonderful examples of Islamic art and architecture, but also help to illustrate the importance of Islam in modern-day Egypt. Other Cairo attractions include the Museum of Islamic Art, casinos (in the Cairo Marriott, Cairo Sheraton and Nile Hilton) and a museum detailing the making of papyrus. Don't miss the Coptic quarter (several million Egyptians are Coptic Christians); it has a very different feel from the rest of the city.

The Sphinx

On to the suburbs: The Great Pyramids and the Sphinx are in Giza, on the outskirts of Cairo. Though most photos make it appear that the structures are out in the desert, they're at the edge of town — you can take a city bus there. Plan at least half a day on the site, and at the very least, go inside the 5,000-year-old Great (Cheops) Pyramid, the biggest one. You'll descend 100 steps into the center; it gets better the deeper down you go. Almost 2.5 million blocks of stone were used in the construction of the Great Pyramid, and the precision and ability of the builders still amaze engineers today.

Just off to the side is the Sphinx. The monumental half-lion, half-man has presented a mystery to scholars and scientists for centuries. No one knows exactly when or why it was built. There seems to be constant scaffolding around it, as repairs are more and more frequent these days (the deterioration is due to air pollution and a rising water table). Don't miss the impressive sound-and-light show performed in front of the Sphinx each night (check to see which language is playing before you head out there).

Another trip out of Cairo will take you to Saqqara, site of the Step Pyramid of Zoser and a number of interesting tombs (a doctor's tomb has depictions of surgical operations). Saqqara's structures are much older than the Giza pyramids, and the artwork in the underground tombs is more impressive than what's seen in the Cheops Pyramid. Also nearby are the ruins of Memphis, once the largest and most important city of ancient Egypt. It has an imposing statue of Ramses II, but hardly anything else remains.

Luxor   Luxor is the most important destination for any visitor to Egypt. The primary attractions are not in the city itself, but across the Nile in the Valley of the Kings and the Valley of the Queens — final resting places of ancient Egyptian royalty. The first indication that you're nearing the valleys is the presence of two enormous seated statues, seemingly isolated in what is now a farmer's field. Known as the Colossi of Memnon, they're the only remains of a temple of Amenhotep III. The tombs, which lie beyond this site, are spread out over quite a large area. Though the treasures that once filled them are long gone, the tombs themselves are very impressive works of art, and each is unique. The colors on the walls have barely faded, and the sculpted bas-relief figures are exceedingly well crafted. One tomb of particular interest is that of the noble Ramose (it displays one of the few examples of the worship of Aten, a short-lived deity). To appreciate the complex fully, spend at least two days or you'll feel rushed (start each day early, before the sun and crowds become oppressive; tickets go on sale at 6 am). If you're in good physical shape, one of the nicest ways to see the sites is to rent a bicycle from your hotel. That way you can explore at your own pace, and you'll be able to ride to some of the digs that are still in progress in the area. (Stay out of the sun during the hottest part of the day, though — dehydration is a serious danger.) Be aware that, at any given time, some of the tombs may be closed for renovation.

One of the best-known tombs is the tiny chamber of young Tutankhamen. Unlike most of the others, it was discovered with its treasures intact.

Back on the east side of the Nile are the Temple of Luxor and the massive Temple of Karnak, two incredibly impressive structures filled with statues, colonnades and ornate wall murals (visit the Temple of Luxor first; it's more compact and easier to take in).

Nile Cruises
A Nile cruise is simply a must for any visitor to Egypt. The cruises range from a five-day trip from Aswan to Luxor on a simple *felucca* (sailboat) to a two-week luxury cruise from Cairo to Aswan. Most ships cruise between Luxor and Aswan; some go all the way from Cairo to Aswan, though it's a long trip between Cairo and Luxor and there's not much to see (you'll want a boat with a swimming pool to help while away the hours). If the cruise embarks in Luxor but does not allow time to see area sights, be sure to get there at least two days early for sightseeing.

Red Sea Resorts
Resorts along the Red Sea, Gulf of Suez and Gulf of Aqaba offer diving, snorkeling, fishing and beautiful desert scenery. One of the best established resort areas is around Hurghada, a 4- or 5-hour drive/1-hour flight from Cairo (or a 3-hour drive from Luxor). It has a beautiful crescent-shaped bay, rugged mountains, great beaches and an offshore coral reef (60 ft/17 m below the surface). The tourist areas on the Sinai Peninsula are every bit as impressive. Sharm el Sheikh (300 mi/480 km southeast of Cairo, is a year-round resort offering excellent accommodations, windsurfing, sailing, fishing and scuba diving. Taba, on the Israeli frontier, offers water sports, tennis and nightclubs, and Nuweiba (on the Gulf of Aqaba) has air-conditioned bungalows, superb sand beaches and water sports.

The Sinai Desert
Located east of the Suez Canal, the Sinai is much more beautiful than the Western Desert, which covers most of Egypt. The Sinai terrain is rugged and rocky, with dunes reaching right up to the Mediterranean. Air and land tours can be arranged from Cairo, and overland trips leave from the Israeli resort town of Eilat. Attractions include Mt. Horeb (believed to be Mt. Sinai, where Moses received the Ten Commandments) and, at its base, the 6th-century St. Catherine's Monastery. The monastery, which houses 20 monks, contains a large library of early-Christian documents and manuscripts, nice gardens and a room full of skulls. (It is closed Friday and Sunday.) Travelers can visit Gaza and the Gaza Strip, but because of the political situation, we don't recommend it at this time.

Itinerary

First-time visitors should probably see Egypt on a hosted/escorted tour, unless they're adventurous, flexible and experienced in traveling in developing countries. Most attractions are along the Nile, which makes Nile cruises so attractive. Visitors who are not taking a cruise should follow this minimum itinerary:

Day 1 — Arrive Cairo.

Day 2 — Cairo (tour Giza and Saqqara).

Day 3 — Cairo.

Day 4 — Fly or take train to Luxor.

Day 5 — Luxor and the Valleys of the Kings and Queens.

Day 6 — Fly to Aswan or travel south by road, stopping to see temples in Edfu and Kom Ombo. Overnight in Aswan.

Day 7 — Aswan. (If you flew to Aswan on Day 6, skip Day 7.)

Day 8 — Round-trip flight to Abu Simbel from Aswan and fly to Cairo for overnight.

Day 9 — Depart Egypt.

A night in Alexandria can be added after Cairo and/or a car (with driver) can be hired for an eight-day drive down the Nile from Cairo to Aswan to see major temples en route. The adventurous who have lots of time can follow the route on buses and trains.

Climate/When to Go

There are basically two seasons in Egypt: a relatively cool season (65–85 F/22–30 C) that lasts November–March (and is by far the better touring season) and a hot season (70–104 F/23–40 C) from April–October. The coastal area has fewer extremes, usually staying 55–85 F/14–30 C year round. It's quite dry: The average humidity stays in the range of 7–20 percent year round. Unlike other destinations, it's simply not worthwhile to go off-season. The crowds are thinner, but it's so hot you won't want to move (the smells and insects can get to you, as well). In the spring, sand and dust storms called *khamsin* blow in, which can reduce visibility (even in Cairo) to less than 100 ft/30 m.

Transportation

Egyptair and other carriers offer direct service from the U.S. to Egypt (European airlines require a connection at their hub cities). There is no direct service from Canada, though a number of European carriers offer connections. Egyptair and Air Sinai also fly internally (Cairo, Alexandria, Aswan, Luxor, Hurghada, the Sinai and Abu Simbel). Cairo International Airport is 15 mi/24 km from Cairo (about 45 minutes to the center of the city). Cruises stop in Egyptian ports, and it's possible to travel overland from Israel. If you're traveling by train, reserve space in an air-conditioned car. Adventurous travelers might want to ride second class (seats) during the day, but shouldn't expect much sleep if they're taking it at night — the seats are uncomfortable, and the lights (and people's radios) are left on 24 hours. If you're buying tickets in Cairo and are having trouble getting reservations for the time you want to travel, the "tourist police" may be able to assist.

Local buses connect most cities but are crowded and uncomfortable. The larger cities have taxis (it's customary to share them with others), which can be hired for a day's sightseeing; always agree on the price before getting in. Medium-sized towns may have horse-drawn taxis, and ox carts and donkeys may be all that are available in small villages. Cairo has subways, trolleys, buses (so crowded that if you get on, you may never get off) and leisurely paced river taxis. Don't try to drive in the cities — it can be a nightmare.

Geostats

Official Name: Arab Republic of Egypt.

Visa Information: Passports and visas needed by U.S. and Canadian citizens. Air passengers may obtain a renewable 30-day visa upon arrival. Others must obtain a visa in advance. All must register with local police within seven days of arrival. Proof of sufficient funds, onward passage and documents required. Reconfirm documentation requirements with carrier before departure.

Health Certificates: Yellow-fever certificate required if coming from an infected area or endemic zone. Cholera-vaccination certificate also required if coming from infected area. Proof of AIDS test required for all staying longer than 30 days. Contact health authorities for latest information.

Capital: Cairo.

Population: 61,948,000.

Size: 386,650 sq mi/1,001,250 sq km. About the size of Texas, Oklahoma and Arkansas combined.

Language: Arabic.

Climate: Hot dry summer, moderate winters.

Economy: Agriculture.

Government: Republic.

Religions: Islamic, Christian.

Currency: Egyptian pound (EGL). 100 piastres = 1 EGL. Traveler's checks and credit cards are accepted. AE, DC, MC, VI.

Time Zone: 7 hours ahead of eastern standard time; two hours ahead of Greenwich mean time.

Electricity: 220 volts.

Accommodations

Accommodations range from deluxe world-class resorts and hotels to smelly dives. It's important to have written confirmation of hotel space prior to arrival. Be aware that if you stay out near the pyramids in Giza, you'll be isolated from the shopping and activities of downtown Cairo.

Health Advisories

Before you go, ask your doctor about any necessary immunizations or the need for malaria suppressants, and take plenty of insect repellent along. Don't forget to take a pair of comfortable, broken-in walking shoes.

Once you're there, avoid local dairy products and assume the water is unsafe (stick with prepackaged or boiled drinks). Other than fresh springwater at the source, don't even *step* into freshwater (including the Nile and irrigation ditches). A dangerous parasite, bilharzia, may be present. Keep away from stray animals, as rabies is a problem, especially outside Cairo. Make sure you're drinking enough fluids — dehydration can be serious.

What to Buy

Among the interesting souvenirs that Egypt offers are mother-of-pearl inlaid wood, jewelry, brassware and leather goods (though some of the cheaper items may not be adequately cured). Other items include carpets, alabaster and soapstone carvings, paintings on papyrus, Egyptian clothing, perfumes and reproductions of antiquities. For the reproductions, the Egyptian Museum is a good source. Elsewhere, if an item is presented to you as an antique, it's probably a fake (and if it isn't, it can't be exported). In fact, be very careful when buying something that may *appear* to authorities to be of historical importance — the police have detained tourists for days while determining the inauthenticity of well-made reproductions. Bargaining is acceptable almost everywhere; the key is to try to keep the price low without being arrogant or insulting.

What to Eat

The nation's history includes occupations by the French, British and Turks, and its cuisine was influenced by all of them as well as by regional neighbors (though Egyptians tend to use more cumin and coriander than is found in most Arab cooking). Meat is usually grilled beef, poultry or mutton. The coarse *foul* bean and spicy vegetables are often served on the side. Pita bread (also known as Arab or Syrian bread) is common, but differs in taste from that in nearby countries. *Shwarma*, a sandwich similar to a gyro, is good fast food, but make sure the meat hasn't been sitting out for too long. Also try *feteara*, an oven-baked pancake filled with coconut and jam, and *moolokhya*, a green soup. We also recommend trying a dish called *kochari*. It's a combination of rice, lentils, chick peas, spices and onions.

Travel Tips for the Client

Do carry bottled water with you, especially if you're touring remote sites. Dehydration in the desert is no joke . . . If you're a woman, don't travel alone outside the main tourist areas. And do expect to be the target of unwanted attention at some point in your visit. (Many Egyptian men get mistaken ideas from Western movies — in some cases, it's their only source of information about foreign women.) Your best defense is to dress modestly, ignore all comments and avoid eye contact . . . Do register with the police within seven days of arrival (hotels will usually do it, for a small fee) . . . Avoid public displays of affection between the sexes (although it's perfectly acceptable for men to hold hands) . . . Do be sensitive about what you say regarding Egyptian politics, economics and law. They were developed on Islamic principles, and to criticize them is to criticize the word of God . . . Don't eat, drink or smoke in public during Ramadan, the Islamic holy month . . . Do be sure to ask people if they mind having photos taken before snapping away. They may ask for money, as is their right. And while we're on the subject, don't photograph anything military or remotely connected to the government . . . Don't pass food (even in a container) with your left hand. . . .

Tipping: *Baksheesh* is a word every visitor hears within an hour of arrival. It means "share" and is usually a justified request for a tip for services rendered (waiters, taxi drivers, porters, doorkeepers, etc.). Keep a supply of small change or small notes ready. But there is a gray area where a request for *baksheesh* is a request for a bribe to get something done that you might feel shouldn't require additional remuneration. Such bribes aren't considered to be seriously wrong in Egyptian culture. Decide for yourself whether you feel the request is justifiable. It's not considered rude to turn down such requests. In general, tip 10% to restaurant staff and taxi drivers.

Egypt

Review Questions

1. Most tours of Egypt never stray far from what waterway?

2. Why was the temple of Abu Simbel moved in the 1960s?

3. What is the most popular attraction at the Egyptian Museum in Cairo?

4. What are the principal tourist attractions at Giza, on the outskirts of Cairo?

5. What attractions would a tourist find at Saqqara?

6. Why would a tourist want to visit the Khan-el Khalili?

7. Why is Luxor considered the most important destination for any visitor to Egypt?

8. What is Taba?

9. Why would a tourist want to journey to Mt. Horeb?

10. Why wouldn't travelers want to go to Egypt in the off-season?

Egypt

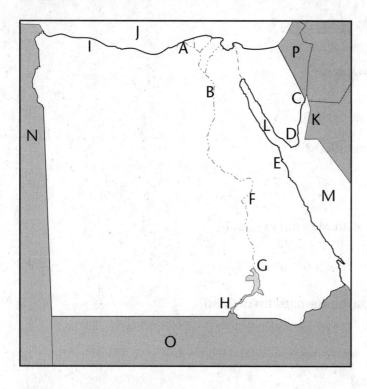

Map Skills Exercise

Match the tourist destination listed below with the corresponding letter on the map. You can use each letter only once.

1. _____ The Sphinx
2. _____ Aswan
3. _____ Temple of Abu Simbel
4. _____ Luxor
5. _____ Hurghada resort
6. _____ Alexandria
7. _____ Taba
8. _____ Israel
9. _____ Mediterranean Sea
10. _____ Red Sea

Selling Exercise

The tour company for which you work wants you to create a newspaper ad for a tour package to Egypt. The tour will last two weeks. Create the ad and in it persuade readers that Egypt is a fascinating destination and that the prices and services of your tour are unsurpassed.

Morocco

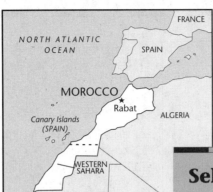

Though Morocco is just a short hop across the Strait of Gibraltar from Europe, it feels a world away. Its culture is a blend of African, Arab and Berber cultures and shows some European influences. (The Berbers were the native people of Morocco, conquered by the Arabs in the 7th century.)

Morocco, Africa's most popular tourist destination, offers fine Atlantic and Mediterranean beaches, wondrous cities, Roman antiquities, resort facilities, mountain villages and towering sand dunes. It is also one of the most photogenic countries in the world — the winding alleys of the city of Fez and the traditional rural villages provide wonderful photo opportunities.

In earlier times, Morocco was part of the Roman and Arab empires. In the first decade of the 20th century, it became a French protectorate, regaining its independence in 1956.

What to Do There

Agadir   A resort southwest of Casablanca on a long, wide, beautiful beach of white sand, Agadir offers most sea sports and excellent beachside hotels (with extensive facilities for tennis, volleyball, riding, etc.). Go there for the warm winter weather. The town has wonderful restaurants, shopping and nightlife. Visit the fortresslike 16th-century casbah on top of the hill (primarily for the view of the town and water). For a change of pace, rent a camel for a ride along the beach or take part in an organized *diffas,* a Berber meal usually accompanied by a traditional dance performance.

Casablanca   Well known because of the Humphrey Bogart film of the same name, Casablanca is a large, modern coastal city inhabited since before the 12th century (the city shows Portuguese, Spanish, French and English influence). Despite its romantic image, it's bound to disappoint most people. It's basically a big commercial and industrial city, and its market pales in comparison with those of Fez or Marrakesh. Sights include the old market, the Royal Palace, the Great Mosque and the elaborate Mosque Hassan II (reputed to be the biggest in the world).

Selling Points

Colorful markets, Marrakesh, antiquities, beautiful architecture, shopping, beaches, diverse scenery, religious shrines, great food, golfing, skiing, water sports, mountains, casinos and desert culture are Morocco's attractions.

Morocco will appeal to the somewhat adventurous and experienced traveler who wants to see an exotic culture and lie on nice beaches. Don't travel there if you're offended by areas that are sometimes dirty and smelly or are overwhelmed by manifest poverty or aggressive local vendors and their commission men.

Fascinating Facts About Morocco

Morocco was the first country to recognize the independence of the United States. The treaty signed by George Washington and the King of Morocco is still in effect . . . Skiing is possible in Morocco between December and April. Trekking is also becoming very popular in the Moroccan Atlas, a beautiful chain of mountains that extends for more than 400 miles/644 km. . . .

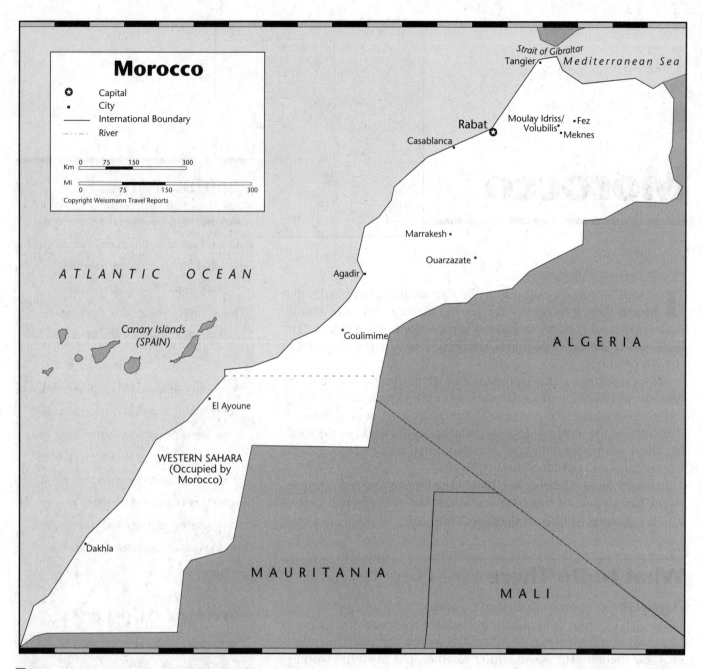

Morocco

Legend:
- ⊕ Capital
- ▪ City
- —— International Boundary
- —·—·— River

Km 0 75 150 300
Mi 0 75 150 300

Copyright Weissmann Travel Reports

Strait of Gibraltar

Tangier

Mediterranean Sea

Rabat

Moulay Idriss/ Volubilis · Fez
· Meknes

Casablanca

ATLANTIC OCEAN

Marrakesh ·

Ouarzazate ·

Agadir ·

Canary Islands (SPAIN)

Goulimime ·

ALGERIA

El Ayoune ·

WESTERN SAHARA (Occupied by Morocco)

Dakhla ·

MAURITANIA

MALI

Fez Three separate towns comprise Fez: the two ancient walled areas — Fez el Bali (the old town) and Fez el Jedid (the new town) — and the more modern, French-built Ville Nouvelle. The contrast between the sections makes the old areas seem all the more fascinating. You truly feel as if you're stepping into the past when you enter the walled sections.

The walled cities are, in fact, the main attraction of Fez. Several days could be spent wandering the narrow, winding alleys of Fez el Bali and admiring the exceptional architecture. The amazing architecture begins with the very gates themselves; once inside the walls, watch for the Medersa Attarine, Medersa Cherratine and Medersa Seffarine, three beautiful old buildings. Explore

the universities, wander by the pits where fabric is dyed and walk past the tanning yards (but beware the odors!). Also in the area are several beautiful mosques and the Boujeloud Gardens. Just outside the walls are two good museums — Borj Nord (exhibiting weapons) and Dar Batha (Moroccan arts) — and the Royal Palace. The pleasant Ville Nouvelle has a European feel, with wide boulevards and sidewalk cafes.

Goulimime Situated at the edge of the Sahara, where desert nomads and sedentary populations meet, this town is where you'll see the Blue People (dye in their clothes tints their skin) ride into town on camels to buy supplies. Unfortunately, tourists often outnumber the local population on market days, but the spectacle can still be fun. You'll also want to shop in the market and, if you haven't already tried it, ride a camel (once is enough for most people).

Marrakesh Known as the "Red City" (actually, it's more pink), Marrakesh was the capital of the Moorish (one of the peoples of Morocco) empire and an academic center of the medieval world. The empire spanned the enormous area from Spain to East Africa. Originally built in AD 1070, the city has gracious wide avenues (in the modern town), lovely palm gardens and several impressive buildings.

Djemaa el Fna (Court of Marvels) is an experience in itself. It is a market scene straight out of the movies, with snake charmers, musicians, acrobats and storytellers. Visit the market by day, but also return at night when it's filled with gaslit restaurant stalls. It feels great to dine on Moroccan fare in the open air, sitting alongside local citizens wearing colorful djellabas (gownlike garments). On other days, visit the impressive Koutoubia minaret (250 ft/77 m tall), the Ben Youssef Medersa (magnificent 16th-century Islamic college), and if time permits, include the Saadian Dynasty tombs, the ruined 16th-century El Badi Palace, the Dar Si Said Museum and the colorful Thursday camel market. You might also consider the museum and gardens donated by fashion designer Yves St. Laurent. We recommend that you spend as much time as possible in the markets and the bazaar north of Djemaa el Fna square — one of the most interesting in Morocco. Be prepared for some rather high-pressure sales tactics.

Day trips out of Marrakesh are as fascinating and varied as the city itself. Excursions include trips to Oukaimeden, a winter resort, with the highest ski lift in Africa and spectacular views.

Meknes Spend at least one night in the old town of this 17th-century imperial city. While there, visit the Bab Mansour Gateway, the Museum of Moroccan Arts (in the Bab Djamai) and the Tomb of Moulay Ismail (one of the great tyrants in history, nicknamed "The Bloodthirsty"). Also in town are the old prisons for Christian slaves.

You can take day trips to two nearby towns. Moulay Idriss, founded in the 8th century, is a holy city for pilgrims. In Volubilis you'll find the well-preserved ruins of the 2,000-year-old Roman city, home of Antony and Cleopatra's daughter, Sylene. The mosaic floors here are among the finest in existence.

Man at prayer

Rabat Here in Morocco's capital, watch the changing of the Royal Guard at the Royal Palace (Friday mornings), walk the narrow streets of the casbah and visit the 12th-century Tower of Hassan (containing the green, gold and white Mausoleum of King Muhammad V). Near Rabat are several interesting towns that should be visited, if time permits. Chief among these are Bouknadel and its Jardins Exotiques (fascinating gardens) and Chellah, which has interesting museums, a 17th-century fortress and Roman ruins.

Tangier Tangier, the closest major African city to Europe, was once known as the "Pearl of the Mediterranean;" today it's a mostly unattractive and depressed area. It's not as interesting as Fez or Marrakesh. But for those who see Morocco only on a day trip from Spain, we recommend taking the hydrofoil to Tangier. Tangier is in a nice setting of hills, and beaches wrap around a large part of the city; the streets are narrow and winding; and there's a fair casbah/market.

Traveler's advisory: In Tangier, beware of pickpockets preying on tourists. Take a money belt or use another

Craft shop

secure means of carrying cash and passport. Also, the street boys in Tangiers pester travelers from the time they step off the ferry until they leave town. While they're not dangerous, the boys are a constant annoyance.

Itinerary

Here's a nine-day itinerary that shows tourists a good deal of the country.

Day 1 — Arrive Casablanca. Go to Rabat.

Day 2 — Morning tour of Rabat. Afternoon drive to Meknes.

Day 3 — Excursion to Volubilis. Tour Meknes. Overnight Meknes.

Day 4 — Drive to Fez.

Day 5 — Fez.

Day 6 — Drive to Marrakesh.

Day 7 — Marrakesh.

Day 8 — Depending upon departure, either spend the rest of the day in Marrakesh or drive to Casablanca.

Day 9 — Depart Morocco.

Climate/When to Go

October–December and March–May are really Morocco's seasons, when temperatures average in the low 70s F/24 C (January and February can be cool and rainy — bad beach weather). The summer shouldn't be ruled out; although the average summer temperature in Marrakesh and Fez can be around 100 F/38 C, the coastal cities (Casablanca, Rabat and Tangier) remain comfortable (low 80s F/ 27–29 C), if somewhat humid.

Transportation

Royal Air Maroc offers nonstop service to Casablanca from New York and Montreal and offers internal air service. Several European carriers offer single-airline service through their respective hubs. Royal Air Maroc also serves major European capitals. Muhammad V Airport (CMN) is 19 mi/31 km from Casablanca and Rabat's Sale Airport (RBA) is 5 mi/12 km from town. A hydrofoil connects Tangier with Gibraltar in Europe. New air-conditioned trains (all but the adventurous will want to ride first-class) connect major cities (the famed Marrakesh Express runs between Marrakesh and Casablanca). Buses connect most cities (those to smaller towns can be very uncomfortable and crowded). The highway system is fairly good, and self-drive or chauffeured cars are available for out-of-town trips. Stick with taxis in the cities and make sure you negotiate a satisfactory price before getting in.

Accommodations

Accommodations include deluxe and Club Med-type resorts, first-class hotels, apartments, budget hotels, youth hostels and campgrounds. In general, we would recommend the best lodging that you can afford, in order to reduce potential problems.

Health Advisories

There is a very limited risk of malaria in some rural areas, so consult your doctor about taking malaria suppressants. Take along all prescription medicine and insect repellent needed for the trip. French-trained doctors can be found in most sizable cities. Don't swim in desert streams; they may contain bilharzia, a potentially fatal parasite.

Sanitary conditions in most restaurants in Morocco are not up to Western standards. Most hot, freshly cooked food should be safe (especially if it is included on a package tour), but peel fresh fruit and raw vegetables, make sure meat is cooked thoroughly, avoid local dairy products and assume the water is unsafe (stick with prepackaged or boiled drinks).

What to Buy

Morocco appears to be filled with bargains, but look closely before buying. Good buys in wool carpets and leather goods can be found, but most of what is sold is of poor quality. Other items available include gems, fossils from the Sahara, wood carvings, pottery, beaten brass, silk, hand-embroidered clothing, copperware, silver and gold. Bargaining is the rule in the market. Offer a quarter to half of the price quoted (less, with carpets) and take it from there. Be patient and polite, but insistent. A Moroccan proverb says, "One hour of bargaining is worth 100 hours of work."

Note: At all costs, avoid young men wanting to be your guide. They're most likely out to take your money. Pay with cash whenever possible; credit cards can be overcharged. It is also better to take goods home with you than to have them shipped. Stores sometimes substitute cheap goods for purchased items when they ship overseas.

What to Eat

Moroccan cuisine is one of the finest in the world. Even if you're traveling on a budget, splurge one night for a feast in a deluxe restaurant. Be sure *bastilla* is on the menu, and don't be put off just because it contains pigeon! Also look for *harira*, the traditional peasant garbanzo-and-noodle soup (it's spicy). We really like *touajen* (a meat or chicken stew) or *hout* (a fish stew), *mchoui* (roast mutton) and *djaja mahamara* (chicken

stuffed with almonds, raisins and couscous). Couscous, a semolina staple, is available with most meals if you ask for it. Meals are eaten with the right hand; don't even pass food with the left hand. Tradition holds that you should be seated on floor cushions. In tourist areas, Western-style eating utensils are available. Almond and filo pastries are excellent, as are almond milk shakes and fresh-squeezed orange juice. Try the sweet mint tea — it's served in a clear glass crammed with mint leaves.

Travel Tips for the Client

Do ask permission before taking pictures of anyone, and be sure to offer a tip in appreciation (a few coins). Some of the more photogenic scenes include the water sellers, trained monkeys, snake charmers and "dentists" with trays of teeth in front of them indicating their level of experience . . . Do guard your possessions closely . . . Although drugs such as hashish seem widely available, drug laws are taken very seriously. There are too many travelers already rotting in Moroccan prisons. Don't do anything that could land you among them . . . Don't assume you can just enter a mosque. Ask first . . . Do tip 10% in restaurants and cafes. . . .

Morocco

Review Questions

1. As Africa's most popular tourist destination, what does Morocco offer?

2. What Moroccan resort is located southwest of Casablanca on the Atlantic Ocean? Describe its attractions.

3. Despite its romantic image, why is Casablanca bound to disappoint most people?

4. Compare and contrast the walled towns that comprise Fez with Ville Nouvelle.

5. When was Marrakesh built? What role did it play in the medieval world?

6. How does Djemaa el Fna resemble a market scene straight out of the movies? What is it called in English?

7. What will a traveler find in Volubilis?

8. What is the closest major African city to Europe? What advisory should travelers heed there?

9. Why should tourists in Morocco pay with cash rather than credit cards? Why should they take goods that they've bought in Morocco with them, rather than shipping the goods to their home countries?

10. According to tradition, where do diners in Morocco sit?

Morocco

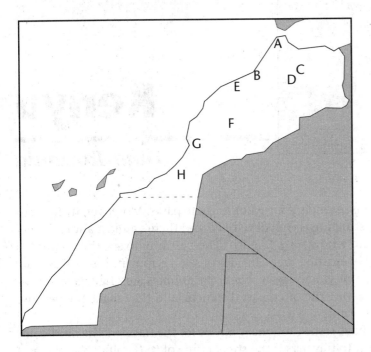

Map Skills Exercise

Match the tourist destination listed below with the corresponding letter on the map. You can use each letter only once.

1. _____ Casablanca
2. _____ Agadir
3. _____ Rabat
4. _____ Fez
5. _____ Meknes
6. _____ Goulimime
7. _____ Marrakesh
8. _____ Tangier

Selling Exercise

A couple wants to take a unique vacation that combines sports (skiing and golfing), relaxing on a beach and exploring a different culture. You suggest they visit Morocco. Prepare an 8-day tour of Morocco for the couple. Include two days of skiing, one of golf, three days visiting one or two Moroccan cities and two days at the beach. Then, plot the tour on a map (use transparency map #36 for this exercise).

Kenya

and Tanzania

Selling Points

Game reserves, beaches, tribal culture, gambling, history, shopping, varied scenery and golfing are Kenya's chief attractions.

Anyone who enjoys the thrill of viewing animals in the wild will adore Kenya. Beach lovers will enjoy the coast, and anyone interested in African culture will find the rural areas more accessible than those of most countries on the continent.

Fascinating Facts About Kenya

In 1952, Princess Elizabeth ascended to Treetops Lodge in Aberdare National Park. The next morning, Queen Elizabeth II walked down the stairs — she learned in the night that her father had died . . . At Mayers Ranch, near Nairobi, you can see young Masai warriors perform dances . . . A portion of Tsavo West National Park is known as "Maneaters": When the Nairobi-Mombasa rail link was being completed, it ran through the center of the park, and from time to time, a worker would be found half-eaten (or not found at all). . . .

Kenya is legendary for wildlife game parks. Moreover, its tourism infrastructure is well developed and there's almost always someone around who speaks English. The best way to see the country is by hosted or escorted tour. The idea of safari is romantic as well as practical: The tour guides know where the animals are, they have experience navigating the often vast distances, and they make the best use of precious time.

We do have some cautionary advice for the traveler: The most common threat to travelers is the street crime of the capital, Nairobi, and the crime that plagues some of the Indian Ocean beach resort areas. Don't, under any circumstances, walk around alone in Nairobi or other larger cities at night — that's an open invitation to be robbed. Also, stay clear of political demonstrations. The country is wrestling with the direction the government will take, and emotions are running high.

What to Do There

Game Reserves

Most visitors go to Kenya to see the game reserves. There are many parks, and each has different animals, terrain, climate and accommodations with varying degrees of comfort. On a typical day at a game reserve, guests rise early (about 6 am), eat breakfast and head out for animal viewing. They return around 11 am for a very long lunch (and sun by the pool), then head out again around 3 pm for more animal viewing. At about 7:30 pm, dinner is served, followed by an evening program or night safari. The methods for viewing animals vary. Minivans carrying six to eight passengers are common. The best companies guarantee a window seat. Other companies either rotate the window seats, or simply let passengers sort it out themselves. Planes, hot-air balloons and private or chauffeured cars are interesting — and popular — adjuncts to the main minivan game viewing. It's much safer and more practical to see the game parks on an escorted/hosted tour than to see them independently.

Choosing which parks to see (and how to see them) is important;

each offers something the others lack. If we had to limit ourselves to three parks, they'd be Masai Mara, Amboseli and Tsavo West, all south of Nairobi. Those who have the time and budget should also include stays at Treetops Lodge (near Aberdare National Park) and the Mt. Kenya Safari Club and Game Ranch (near Mt. Kenya National Park). The following are descriptions of what some key parks have to offer:

Aberdare National Park   This park has a diverse topography that includes waterfalls, rain forests and highlands. There are two country club-type hotels, Aberdare Country Club and Outspan Hotel. Both have a British-colonial ambiance, and each is associated with a tree hotel (the Ark and Treetops, respectively). Guests at both properties normally spend one night at the country club-type facility (where they can see tribal dances) and a night at the associated tree hotel. From the observation decks of the tree hotels, various animals (including warthogs, leopards, birds, monkeys, elephants and, rarely, bongo antelopes) can be seen in their natural surroundings. The area is lit at night, when animals are most active. Most people find the tree hotels among their most memorable experiences.

Amboseli National Park   Amboseli features a semiarid landscape in the shadow of 19,567-ft/ 5,964-m Mt. Kilimanjaro, in neighboring Tanzania. Mt. Kilimanjaro and the dry landscape provide one of the most dramatic settings in the country — the mountain makes a great backdrop for animal photography. (For the best animal viewing, it's a toss-up between this park and Masai Mara.) Poachers have just about wiped out Amboseli's rhino population, but the park does have one of the few elephant herds in East Africa that is not decreasing in number. Also on view there are large herds of buffalo and wildebeests (an occasional cheetah is seen as well). The Amboseli Serena is the premier accommodation there; guest rooms remind us of New Mexican adobes and are decorated with primitive paintings.

Masai Mara National Park   Bordering Tanzania's Serengeti National Park, Masai Mara offers a wide variety of game. In one day alone, we saw lions, hippos, crocodiles, six kinds of antelope, giraffes, wildebeests, warthogs, baboons, hyenas, jackals, zebras, cape buffalo, civet cats and dozens of birds, including eagles, cranes and storks. Every year, millions of wildebeests and zebras migrate into the park in search of water. The timing of this phenomenon varies, depending on the rains: We saw it one time in June and, in another year, in August (it can

occur as late as October). The park is large and can be toured in a variety of ways: four-wheel-drive vehicle, small aircraft and hot-air balloon. Keekorok and Mara Serena are our favorite lodges, but don't overlook the tented camps, which can be quite luxurious (especially Governors Camp). The park's newest lodge, Olkurruk Mara Lodge, is dramatically situated on an escarpment overlooking the Mara plains (the gorgeous landscape that provided the backdrop for much of the film *Out of Africa*).

Mt. Kenya National Park   The park consists of three terrains: forest, alpine and rocky peak. Mt. Kenya, more than 17,000 ft/5,200 m high, comprises 12 glaciers and several peaks; the section above 10,500 ft/3,200 m is designated as the game park. Animals living there include lions, elephants, antelope and leopards. The principal hotel is the Mt. Kenya Safari Club and Game Ranch. The club is a formal place — men must wear a coat and tie for dinner.

Giraffes and zebras, Masai Mara National Park

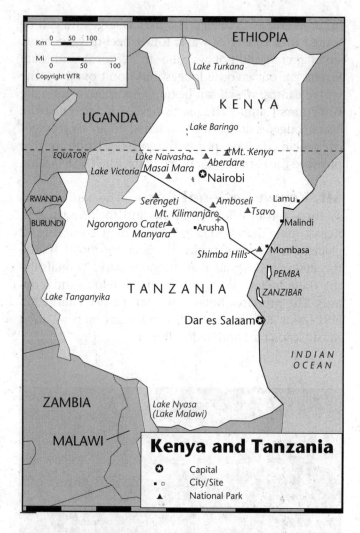

Kenya and Tanzania

- ✪ Capital
- ■ □ City/Site
- ▲ National Park

Tsavo West National Park Tsavo West covers 1,500 sq mi/3,900 sq km and is filled with crocodiles, elephants, baboons, antelope, giraffes and hippos; it, like the Amboseli Park, lies within sight of Mt. Kilimanjaro. The terrain is arid/scrub, dotted with baobab trees (some live up to 1,000 years) and red termite mounds (5 ft/2 m tall). Red dust also covers the elephants in the park, who end up looking more orange than gray. At Mzima Springs, tourists can view animals from a glass-paneled underwater observation tank, although the springs' many hippos seem to avoid the tank. This attraction is really worth the stop, if not for the hippos then for the large variety of colorful butterflies that are attracted by the springs. There are two Hiltons in Tsavo West that share a private game park.

Lakes There are numerous lakes throughout Kenya that host rare and spectacular birds. Many of the animals that populate the game reserves can also be seen around the lakes. Among those that can be visited

are: Lake Naivasha (the waters are loaded with hippos and birds, and there's fishing); Lake Turkana (cormorants and sacred ibises); Lake Baringo (tinted brown by soil erosion, lots of hippos and 450 species of birds—camel rides are a possibility); Lake Victoria (the world's second-largest lake and the main source of water for the Nile River, it ranks fairly low as a tourist destination because the smaller lakes are generally more rewarding to visit).

Lamu One of our favorite spots in Kenya is the island/city of Lamu. Lamu is a Moslem settlement that seems to be living about 500 years in the past: There are no cars — only donkey carts and dirt roads. The women dress in black, the men in white, and they speak an ancient Arabic dialect. They ply the waters in Arab dhows, square-sailed boats whose design has not changed in centuries. The down side of this turn-back-the-clock atmosphere is the turn-back-the-clock sanitation levels — it's somewhat smelly and dirty (you'll notice the open sewers). There are few real sights, but as you walk around you'll notice 29 mosques and nicely carved doors on some buildings. The only things recognizable as tourist attractions are the local historical museum, Peponi Beach (which we would rate as only tolerable) and (for some) the Donkey Sanctuary, a rest home for weary pack animals. Lamu's real strength, however, is its unique look and feel. Accommodations there are rather limited and fairly basic, and hotels are usually closed during Ramadan (Muslim holy month).

Malindi Kenya is fortunate to have an abundance of protected coral reefs and beaches. Malindi, on what's called the Coral Coast, provides a very nice introduction to the area — there's surfing, snorkeling, deep-sea fishing and other water sports. The Malindi Marine National Park is protected and has fine beaches, clear water and very colorful fish; swimming and snorkeling are also available. The town itself has handsome post-colonial homes, trees and flowers; we enjoyed wandering its narrow streets.

Mombasa Mombasa has been a trading center for centuries — Persians, Turks, Indians, Portuguese and the British have all left their mark. Ancient mosques, forts, museums and temples abound. The narrow roads and markets give parts of the city a North African feel; some cafes even play Arab music and feature belly dancing. Visit 16th-century Ft. Jesus (now a museum) at the southern entrance to the harbor and the nearby Ivory Room, which displays various ivories confiscated from poachers. Shop there for the brightly colored *kangas* that local women wear and wood carvings. A real must in Mombasa is the dhow trip from Kenya Marineland, an all-day trip that includes sailing on a dhow with onboard entertainment (acrobats, fire eating, limbo, fashion show).

Nairobi

Nairobi, Kenya's mile-high capital, is only 90 mi/145 km south of the Equator. Founded by the British little more than 100 years ago, the city now has a population of more than 1,500,000. We find Nairobi to be surprisingly pleasant for a large, modern commercial center; the downtown area seems to sparkle. While there, be sure to visit the City Market; on one end, residents shop for tropical fruits, vegetables and meat (it's one of the cleanest large markets in Africa); on the other end, tourists go from merchant to merchant looking at local handicrafts (the fancier stores are on Kenyatta Boulevard). Among the city's attractions are the National Museum (ethnographic, paleontological and ornithological displays), the Arboretum (excellent collection of East African flora), the university (to see the architecture of the buildings) and the superb Kenya Railway Museum. There are casinos at the Safari Park Hotel and the Inter-Continental Hotel.

Since the release of the film *Out of Africa*, there's been a lot of interest in the lives of Karen Blixen (author Isak Dinesen) and Denys Finch Hatton. A half-day trip can be taken to her house in what is now suburban Nairobi (the Karen Blixen Museum) and to the grave of Hatton.

Itinerary

We think the following 15-day itinerary is ideal for a tourist.

Day 1 — Arrive Nairobi.

Day 2 — Nairobi.

Day 3 — Depart for Mt. Kenya Safari Club.

Day 4 — Mt. Kenya Safari Club.

Day 5 — Depart in the morning for Treetops.

Day 6 — Depart (very early if you're driving) for Masai Mara National Park.

Days 7–8 — Masai Mara.

Day 9 — Depart for Amboseli National Park.

Day 10 — Amboseli.

Day 11 — Depart for Tsavo West National Park.

Day 12 — Tsavo West.

Day 13 — Depart for Mombasa.

Day 14 — Mombasa.

Day 15 — Depart Kenya.

Geostats

Official Name: Republic of Kenya.

Visa Info: Visas needed by U.S. citizens; none needed by Canadians.

Health Certificates: Yellow-fever vaccination certificate needed if you're arriving from an infected area.

Capital: Nairobi.

Population: 29,062,000.

Size: 224,960 sq mi/582,646 sq km. Slightly smaller than Texas.

Languages: Swahili, English.

Climate: Tropical to arid.

Economy: Agriculture, industry, services.

Government: Republic.

Religions: Indigenous, Muslim, Protestant, Roman Catholic.

Currency: Kenya shilling (KES). 100 cents = 1 KES. Traveler's checks are accepted in most tourist areas. Credit cards are widely accepted. AE, DC, MC, VI.

Time Zone: 8 hours ahead of EST; +3 GMT.

Electricity: 220 Volts.

Departure Tax: US$20. Please note that tax must be paid in foreign currency.

Climate/When to Go

Kenya is basically a year-round destination — the only months to watch out for are April and May (which can be quite wet). Although Kenya spans the Equator, most of it is situated at 4,000 ft/1,200 m or more, which tends to mitigate the heat. In higher elevations, it can be about 10 F/5 C cooler.

Transportation

There are no direct flights to Kenya from the U.S. or Canada, although most European carriers offer connecting flights via their hub cities. Kenya Airways flies from many European and African capitals and to most major areas within the country (light charter aircraft are also very popular). Jomo Kenyatta Airport (NBO) is 11 mi/17 km southeast of Nairobi. We strongly recommend that first timers take an escorted/hosted tour; even experienced, independent travelers will get more out of a visit with a guide than they could on their own. There is limited train service; the most famous line connects Mombasa and Nairobi. Cars may be rented (traffic moves on the left), but be aware that Kenya has one of the highest road fatality rates in the world due to bad roads, bad vehicles and bad driving. Limited bus service is available. Privately owned minibuses, called *matatus,* are inexpensive, but their safety record is so abysmal we don't recommend them. Taxis are plentiful in urban areas, and shared taxis are a common (and inexpensive) way to travel between cities. If you have the time, ride a dhow, an old Kenyan sailing ship, up the East African coast.

Accommodations

Accommodations range from deluxe, world-class properties to local inns, full-service tent camps, game-park lodges, beach resorts and campgrounds. It should be noted that at most tree hotels, only the suites have private bathrooms, and rooms can be quite tiny.

Health Advisories

Adequate hospital and outpatient treatment is available in Nairobi and Mombasa. The Flying Doctors Society will fly into a reserve/park to treat or evacuate patients. Except in the game lodges or better hotels and restaurants in Nairobi and Mombasa, sanitary conditions are not up to Western standards. Most hot, freshly cooked food should be safe (especially if it's included on a package tour), but peel fresh fruit and raw vegetables, make sure meat is cooked thoroughly and avoid local dairy products. Outside of Nairobi, assume the tap water is unsafe. Malaria is endemic in all areas except Nairobi and locations above 8,200 ft/2,500 m. Take all prescription medicine needed for the trip.

What to Buy

Bargaining is the rule, though some of the deluxe stores have set prices. Shop for local handicrafts and art, elegant elongated wood carvings of animals and people (many done by the Kamba tribe), Kikuyu or Masai baskets, shields, spears, Masai and Kikuyu beadwork, Masai dolls, handwoven fabrics, ebony carvings, batik wall hangings, tapestries, gold, antique coins, Tsavorite and Tanzanite gemstones and soapstone. Clothes — everything from the colorful *kanga* fabric-wraps to saris to safari outfits — are good buys. We found Nairobi to have a great selection of handicrafts from all over Africa. Mombasa offers a good selection of wood carvings and *kanga* fabrics.

What to Eat

In larger cities there's a wide variety of international cuisine, including Chinese, French, Italian and Indian. Wild game is served in some reserves and at the Carnivore Restaurant in Nairobi. The fruit in Kenya is heavenly. Local dishes include *sambusas* (deep-fried pastry filled with mince meat) and *mandazi* (a semisweet flat bread similar to a doughnut).

Travel Tips for the Client

Don't change money on the black market. The illegal money changers are often quick-change artists, and the police will arrest you if they even suspect you're changing money illicitly . . . Though most people know to keep away from lions and other animals that might eat them, they should also steer clear of the vegetarians. Elephants, buffalo, rhinos and hippos are not especially gentle creatures. Even a zebra can give a lethal kick . . . Light, cotton long-sleeve shirts and long pants are best for safaris. . . .

Tanzania

Home of Africa's highest mountain, Mt. Kilimanjaro, this East African nation offers travelers some of the best wildlife-viewing opportunities and largest reserves in the world. However, tourism simply has never achieved a very high priority within Tanzania. Tourist facilities are inconsistent — lodges that were good last year may have deteriorated since, while others have improved. While we

Fascinating Facts About Tanzania

Most of Tanzania was once a German colony (1886–1918). When the borders were being drawn in East Africa between the British colony (now Kenya) and the German colony (now Tanzania), Kaiser Wilhelm of Germany asked his grandmother, Queen Victoria of Great Britain, if his colony could keep Mt. Kilimanjaro. She had the borders changed so he could . . . As a result of Germany's defeat in World War I, the British gained control of the German part of Tanzania . . . The rather lowly rock hyrax, found in the Serengeti and other parks, looks rather like a large hamster. Who would have thought that its closest biological cousin is the elephant! . . . National parks make up one-fourth of the country . . . Africa's deepest lake and tallest mountain can be found in Tanzania. Lake Tanganyika reaches a depth of 4,710 ft/1,436 m and Mt. Kilimanjaro towers at 19,342 ft/5,895 m. The second-largest freshwater body in the world — Lake Victoria — also borders the country . . . In times past, people in Tanzania and Kenya, who had never seen snow, believed that the top of Mt. Kilimanjaro was covered with salt . . . The late rock star Freddy Mercury, leader of the group Queen, was born in Zanzibar (his father was a colonial officer in the British government). The American actor Danny Glover was also born in Tanzania. . . .

Lodge at Ngorongoro Crater

inexperienced climbers can climb Kilimanjaro.

Ngorongoro Crater   This extinct volcano offers, in our opinion, the finest game viewing in Africa. Its combination of abundant game (including rare species such as black rhinos and cheetahs) and awesome scenery will impress even a seasoned safari passenger. The completely intact rim of the crater, rising 2,000 ft/610 m above the floor, is 12 mi/19 km across. With the passage of time, the floor of the crater has become grassland, with a lake in the middle, and it has a high concentration of hippos, elephants, lions, jackals, wildebeests, hyenas, zebras, Cape buffalo and other animals (including a large flock of flamingos).

Serengeti National Park   The Serengeti is an excellent place to observe animal migrations. During the migrations, the wildebeest move first, and then the zebras; lions, hyenas and scavenger birds follow and eat up the sick or weary. A total of more than 3 million animals are on the move. (Avoid late June–October, when most of the animals will probably already have moved north into adjacent Masai Mara Game Reserve in Kenya.)

feel that those traveling with reputable tour operators out of Kenya on a combined Kenya/Tanzania itinerary will find that Tanzania's rewards still outweigh its shortcomings, only the adventurous will want to tackle it independently.

What to Do There

Mount Kilimanjaro   "Kili" is truly one of the most impressive sights in Africa. It can be seen from various points in northern Tanzania, and even as far away as Tsavo and Amboseli Parks in Kenya. Part of its spectacular appeal is that Kilimanjaro is not part of a mountain range. A dormant volcano of 19,342 ft/5,895 m, Kilimanjaro rises dramatically from a relatively flat plain and is the world's highest freestanding mountain. Try to see it prior to 10 am, before clouds cover the snow-capped peak. Because of its relatively gentle slope, even

Travel Tips for the Client

Don't be surprised if you're treated with hostility — perhaps even strip-searched — at land border crossings . . . Do buy plenty of film before your trip as it may be hard to find and/or very expensive . . . Don't wear shorts in towns, though they're now accepted at the game parks . . . Do tip waiters and taxi drivers 10% if a service charge is not included. . . .

Kenya and Tanzania

Review Questions

1. Why might you recommend a hosted or escorted safari to a client going to Kenya?

2. Describe a typical day at a game reserve in Kenya.

3. Which two national parks in Kenya provide the best animal viewing?

4. Although Lake Victoria is the world's second-largest lake and the main source of water for the Nile River, it ranks fairly low as a tourist destination. Why?

5. What gives parts of Mombasa a North African feel?

6. Why does Lamu seem to be living about 500 years in the past?

7. How might you describe the two ends of Nairobi's City Market to a client?

8. Kenya is basically a year-round destination. What are the only months to watch out for? Why?

9. Why should a tourist try to see Mt. Kilimanjaro before 10 am? *cloud cover*

10. What will impress even a seasoned safari passenger about Ngorongoro Crater? *game viewing & scenery*

Kenya and Tanzania

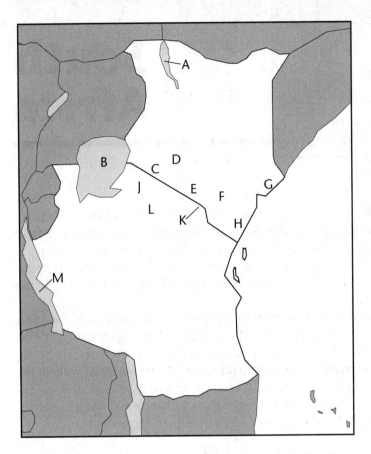

Map Skills Exercise

Match the tourist destination listed below with the corresponding letter on the map. You can use each letter only once.

1. _____ Nairobi
2. _____ Masai Mara National Park
3. _____ Mombasa
4. _____ Amboseli Game Reserve
5. __L__ Ngorongoro Crater
6. __B__ Lake Victoria
7. __K__ Mt. Kilimanjaro
8. __J__ Serengeti National Park
9. _____ Lamu
10. _____ Tsavo National Park

Selling Exercise

A local business organization has invited you to speak at a luncheon about safaris to Kenya and Tanzania. The association would like to know which game reserves and parks members should consider visiting and what they can expect to see and do in each. Prepare a short address to the members that will excite them about taking a safari and make them want to buy safari packages from your agency.

South Africa

South Africa has made an amazing transformation. Seemingly overnight, the country has gone from being the world's stronghold of racial segregation to becoming a shining example of multiracial tolerance. Today, there is a remarkable spirit of cooperation in South Africa among people of all races, and we can only sit in wonder at the pace of change.

The one thing that hasn't changed — fortunately — is the sheer beauty of the country. South Africa packs a wide range of natural attractions within its borders: the vineyards and rocky coast near Cape Town; the rich farmland of the eastern provinces; the snowcapped peaks of the Drakensberg Range; and the green hills and wide beaches of KwaZulu-Natal. The country also has more than 300 game and nature reserves, which help to make it one of Africa's premiere travel destinations.

Traveler's Advisory: Tourists can be targets of street crime in the cities, primarily in Johannesburg and Durban, where muggings occur in the central business district even during the day. Carjackings have become a problem, so it is always a good idea to lock your doors when driving, and be alert when stopping at intersections for a red light.

What to Do There

Cape Town   Perched on the southern tip of the country and continent, Cape Town is South Africa's most cosmopolitan city. It's dominated by the picture-perfect Table Mountain (3,000 ft/915 m), which can be reached by cable car—sunset on the mountain is truly a wonderful sight. View Point on Signal Hill offers another fine view of the city.

Your first stop should be downtown's Malay Quarter, which dates from the colony's founding in 1652. Visit Koopmans de Wet House, which has an excellent collection of Dutch colonial furniture and antiques. Then take in a bit of culture and history at one of Cape Town's many museums. The best is the South African Museum, which has displays on the country's various indigenous cultures. Another city attraction is the Jewish Museum (in South Africa's oldest synagogue). Don't spend all your time in museums: The density and diversity of

Cape Town

flora in the Cape of Good Hope is a botanist's dream. Some lovely plants can be seen and smelled at the Kirstenbosch Botanic Gardens. The gardens have a gorgeous display of wildflowers, including a scent garden for the blind. We recommend trying to get a hotel in the district called Sea Point—it offers magnificent views of crashing ocean waves in one direction and Signal Hill in the other.

Several excursions can be taken from town. Be sure to include a drive to Cape Point — the tip of the Cape of Good Hope — to see the windswept, rocky outcrop where the chilly Atlantic meets the warm Indian Ocean. Allow time to gawk at ostriches, antelopes and baboons. You may also want to take a one-day tour of wineries in Stellenbosch or the state-owned winery at Groot Constantia.

Durban Capital of KwaZulu-Natal and an exciting city on the Indian Ocean, Durban has wide beaches, excellent surfing and a strong East-Indian flavor. Plan to see the Fitzsimmons Snake Park (live snakes), ride in a rickshaw, enjoy the restaurants (particularly Indian), visit the Sea World Aquarium and stop by Durban's city hall.

Some of South Africa's incredible diversity can be sampled at the Juma Mosque (largest in the Southern Hemi-

sphere), the African Arts Centre (collection of items made by the Zulu — South Africa's largest black ethnic group) and Hindu temples (there are two that can be visited). Shoppers will enjoy the Indian market on Victoria Street. (Note that many Hindus and Muslims came to South Africa from India during the time that both were British colonies.)

There are numerous beach resorts south of Durban that are great places to relax. North of Durban, in the area referred to as Zululand, visit two of the oldest wildlife sanctuaries on the continent, Hluhluwe and Umfolozi. The game reserves are home to white and black rhinos, hippos, elephants, lions and other wildlife. Another popular attraction near Durban is the Land of 1,000 Hills, where Zulu dances are performed for tourists. There is a re-created Zulu village, too.

Garden Route This scenic road — on the way from Cape Town to Port Elizabeth — is known for its beautiful wildflowers, forests and mountainous coastline. It takes three days to drive, but five days would be much better so you can stop and smell the roses. The route should go through Mossel Bay (the Portuguese explorer Dias landed there in 1488),

South Africa

- ✪ National Capital
- ▪ □ City/Site
- ▲ National Park or Preserve
- —— International Boundary
- ----- River

Km 0 50 100 200

Mi 0 50 100 200

Copyright Weissmann Travel Reports

GARDEN ROUTE

Mossel Bay · Knysna · Robberg · Storms River · Tsitsikamma

INDIAN OCEAN

Oudtshoorn (center of the ostrich trade, it also has a nice suspension bridge and colorful caves), Knysna (artists' colony), Tsitsikamma Forest National Park and Tsitsikamma Coastal National Park (nature trails, giant trees and caves), Robberg and Goukamma (two nature preserves).

Johannesburg

Johannesburg is the country's largest city. It's very modern by African standards, but it holds relatively few attractions for tourists. Besides, crime is bad and getting worse.

Sights in Johannesburg include the new Museum Africa, which offers an honest and self-critical look at the nation's sometimes troubled past, and the Market Theater Complex, which houses theaters and a Saturday flea market. Negotiate with a taxi driver to give you an impromptu tour through Johannesburg's best neighborhoods — he'll take you past some large and impressive

White rhino

Kimberley We believe that the best way to see the town of Kimberley is to fly in from Johannesburg in the morning, tour the mines, then board the Blue Train to Cape Town about 7 pm that night (you must buy tickets months in advance if you're traveling in high season). In Kimberley, allow at least two hours at the Diamond Mine and Museum to see the mine called the Big Hole, examples of rough-to-finished diamonds and an outdoor town museum.

Kruger National Park This park is one of the world's great wildlife reserves. Kruger has the "big five" animals — rhino, buffalo, lion, leopard and elephant — as well as plenty of others. Make reservations as early as possible, especially if you are visiting during high season or on a holiday. Hikers can trek (with rangers) on seven guided wilderness trails (two or three nights in length). In the nearby scenic Drakensberg Mountains, there are interesting Bushman paintings in caves and rock shelters.

Pretoria The country's administrative capital, Pretoria is less than an hour's drive northeast of Johannesburg. Important sights include former president Paul Kruger's house, the historical museum Melrose House (for its antiques), the Pierneef Museum (collections of the artist Pierneef), the Open Air Museum (cultural history), the South African Mint (collection of world coins) and the Voortrekker Monument, commemorating the battle of Blood River, where descendants of the early Dutch settlers routed the Zulus. The monument is surrounded by a *laager* (defensive circle or encampment) of 64 life-size ox wagons. The National Zoological Gardens is one of the largest in the world with more than 3,500 animal species (the adjoining aquarium is outstanding, too). The city's gardens, parks and jacaranda-tree-lined streets (ablaze with color in October) are unforgettable. Another must-see is the Premier Diamond Mine in Cullinan where the world's largest diamond was found. Papatso to the north has a traditional Zulu kraal adorned with paintings — well worth a half-day visit. If you're staying longer, visit the Cheetah Farm near De Wildt (phone ahead to get permission) and the nearby Crocodile Research and Breeding Farm. Both can be seen from Johannesburg, as well.

Sabi Sand The largest of the private game reserves, Sabi Sand is adjacent to Kruger and includes the Mala Mala

mansions hidden behind imposing security (home security is big business in South Africa). Yeoville is a funky, integrated neighborhood. History buffs will be interested in the Smuts Library at the racially integrated University of the Witwatersrand, where South African statesman Jan Smuts' book collection is preserved. Tours are easily arranged in Johannesburg for those interested in visiting the black suburb of Soweto. Also consider visiting Oriental Plaza, where most of the ethnic Indian population lives.

Excursions include a half-day trip to see the fossils at Sterkfontein Caves. Gold Reef City (the old Johannesburg Gold Mine) is more like a theme park than a mine tour: It features a museum, rides on a vintage steam train and African tribal dancers. There are several working gold mines to visit near Johannesburg. However, prior permission is needed—write months in advance. (Satour will help arrange such visits.) There are also several game reserves and breeding stations within a half-day drive. If you're going to be in Johannesburg on a Sunday, consider a visit to the Heia Safari Ranch where tribal dancers

Reserve, Sabi-Sabi Reserve and Londolozi Reserve (each with its own private game lodges). On a typical day, guests rise early (before 6 am), eat breakfast and head out for animal viewing. They return around 11 for a leisurely lunch and sun by the pool, then head out again around 2 for another look at the animals. At about 6, dinner is served, followed by an evening program or night safari. In these private reserves, guests tour in open four-wheel-drive vehicles with knowledgeable trackers and guides, get very close to the animals and view animals at night.

Sun City

Sun City is South Africa's answer to Las Vegas. Casinos abound, but the resort's most outrageous sight is the Lost City complex, an enormous hotel/amusement park whose opulence borders on the absurd.

Geostats

Official Name: Republic of South Africa.

Visa Info: Passport needed but visas not required for citizens of the United States, Canada, Australia and the United Kingdom.

Health Certificates: Yellow-fever certificate needed if arriving from an infected country.

Capitals: Pretoria and Cape Town both serve as the government seats, each for six months out of the year.

Population: 46,287,000 (75% black, 13% white, 9% colored, 3% Asian).

Size: 472,259 sq mi/1,221,043 sq km. About twice the size of Texas.

Languages: Afrikaans, English, Zulu, others.

Climate: Moderate.

Economy: Mining, manufacturing, agriculture.

Government: Executive.

Religions: Christian, animist.

Currency: The rand (R). 100 cents = 1 R. Credit cards and traveler's checks widely accepted. AE, DI, MC and VI.

Time Zone: 7 hours ahead of Eastern Standard Time; +2 Greenwich Mean Time.

Electricity: 220 volts.

The resort is located in the middle of the Pilansberg Game Reserve whose wildlife includes giraffes and black and white rhinos.

Itinerary

We recommend that most first-time visitors take an escorted/hosted tour. This 14-day itinerary is the absolute minimum needed to see the key areas of the country.

Day 1 — Arrive Johannesburg.

Days 2–3 — Johannesburg.

Days 4–5 — Pretoria.

Days 6–8 — Visit Kruger or other game area.

Day 9 — Return to Johannesburg.

Day 10 — Early flight to Kimberley. Tour mines, then board the Blue Train to Cape Town, arriving the next morning.

Days 11–13 — Cape Town area.

Day 14 — Depart South Africa.

Climate/When to Go

The climate is mild throughout South Africa. There's really not a bad time to visit, but October is our favorite month — it's spring there. Those who go to South Africa specifically for animal viewing may want to go during its winter — grass is short, and the animals tend to gather around watering holes.

Transportation

South African Airways and American Airlines offer nonstop fights from the U.S., while American offers single-airline service from Canada. Many European carriers fly nonstop to South Africa via their hub cities. South African Airways and Qantas fly direct from Australia. Jan Smuts Airport (JNB) is 14 mi/22 km from Johannesburg and 28 mi/45 km from Pretoria. Cape Town International (CPT) is 14 mi/22 km from that city. Internal air service is provided by SAA, and smaller local and regional companies (several have joined together to form Air Link). Several cruise lines ply the waters between Europe or South America and South Africa or make stops on around-the-world itineraries.

There is extensive, inexpensive, reliable rail service connecting all major and many smaller cities. The luxury *Blue Train* begins in Victoria Falls and runs through Pretoria, Johannesburg and all the way to Cape Town. *Rovos Rail* offers a number of luxurious, "Orient Express"-style rail tours on refurbished passenger cars and steam engines. Tours range from an overnight trip between Durban and Pretoria to a four-day tour of the Eastern Transvaal. Some passengers are reporting the experience exceeds that of the more well-known *Blue Train*.

The escorted and independent trips provided by Satour vary in length from one to seven days. They can be combined with others for extensive touring. Excellent bus service operates between major cities and to Namibia, Botswana and Zimbabwe.

Accommodations

Accommodations range from campsites, farmhouses, trailers, youth hostels and guest houses to five-star resort properties. Prices are relatively low, and clean accommodations are easily found. The deluxe Mt. Nelson Hotel — called Nellie by locals — is a Cape Town favorite.

Health Advisories

If you're visiting game parks, you may want to consult your doctor about taking malaria suppressants. This is, however, one of the few countries in Africa where you can drink the water in major cities and eat salads or unpeeled fresh vegetables and assume Western sanitation standards are followed. Don't, however, swim in any lake or river without checking first. Many are infested with a parasite called bilharzia, which can destroy liver tissue and eventually kill you.

What to Buy

Semiprecious stones are very reasonable, as are African beadwork, wood carvings, gold and diamond products, snakeskin items, leather goods, shields, masks and copperware. South Africa is a great place to buy art from all over Africa.

What to Eat

Try some lamb, beef and seafood dishes. There are many Chinese, French, Portuguese and Indian restaurants, as well as those serving South African cuisine. In the local restaurants, try *bredie* (braised and stewed mutton and vegetables), saltwater crayfish (like lobsters, but without the claws) and *bobotie* (a curried meat dish). The private game reserves offer wild-game meat in their restaurants (gazelle and wild boar are good, though the latter can be tough). *Braai* is a South African barbecue usually featuring a spicy sausage called *boerwors*. South African wines are both excellent and inexpensive.

Travel Tips for the Client

Don't be afraid to ask about security when making hotel reservations and when checking into your hotel. Because of the security situation, some Johannesburg hotels now require that everyone — including guests — who enters be asked for identification . . . Don't be surprised by the inexpensive prices for hotels, meals and locally produced products . . . Do tour a working gold mine . . . Don't swim at any beach where others aren't swimming. Sharks cruise the waters, and some beaches aren't protected by shark nets . . . Do take a coat and tie, as some restaurants require them during the evening . . . Do consider adding a trip to one of the nearby countries — especially Zimbabwe, Botswana and Namibia. All three have excellent game parks and attractions (*see Geofile chapter for more details on these countries*). . . .

South Africa

Review Questions

1. What amazing transformation has South Africa recently undergone?

2. Why should a traveler drive to Cape Point?

3. What can a tourist see in the Land of 1,000 Hills near Durban?

4. Oudtshoorn, Knysna and Tsitsikamma Forest National Park are all stops along what scenic road?

5. What is probably the best way to see Kimberley?

6. What are the "big five" game park animals?

7. What does the Voortrekker Monument commemorate? In what city can a tourist see it?

8. How would you describe a typical day at Sabi Sand to a client?

9. Sun City is said to be South Africa's answer to what U.S. city? What are the attractions in and around Sun City?

10. Why should a traveler check first before swimming in any lake or river in South Africa?

South Africa

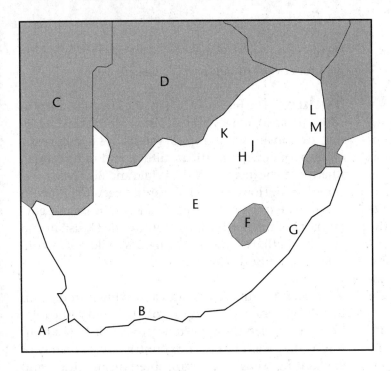

Map Skills Exercise

Match the tourist destination listed below with the corresponding letter on the map. You can use each letter only once.

1. _____ Kruger National Park
2. _____ Cape Town
3. _____ Garden Route
4. _____ Botswana
5. _____ Durban
6. _____ Kimberley
7. _____ Johannesburg
8. _____ Pretoria
9. _____ Sun City
10. _____ Sabi Sand

Selling Exercise

A group of adventurous nature lovers is interested in a tour to South Africa. They have asked you to prepare an itinerary that includes two major cities and two must-see national parks where the ecotourists can take photographs. Plan a 10-day itinerary for the group and include details of what they can do and see on each day.

North Africa

Algeria   Since the military canceled elections (which it would have lost) in January 1992, the country has been racked by guerrilla fighting, which has claimed the lives of more than 20,000 people, including a number of foreigners. Given the risks, we cannot recommend that anyone travel to Algeria at this time. We wish we could: Algeria is the best place to enjoy the Sahara Desert. The face of the Sahara changes almost daily, from sand to rock, from yellowish-pink to black. And thanks to a comparatively good transportation system, desert tours have not been as difficult to undertake in Algeria as in other countries.

The cities in the northern part of the country are quite a contrast to the desert — they're almost European in character — and the only sand you'll find in them is along the beaches on the Mediterranean coast.

Libya   Libya is a land of green coastlines, vast desert wastelands and some good-sized peaks, and although it's a huge country, the overwhelming majority of its people live along the coast. Libya has many interesting archaeological ruins (Greek, Roman and other) and historic sites, but its eccentric foreign policy has alienated much of the Western world, and few people express a desire to visit there.

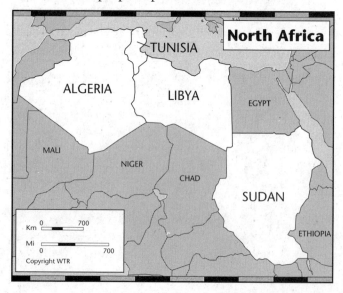

Note: It's currently next to impossible for U.S. citizens to get tourist visas to Libya.

Sudan   The terrain of Sudan, the largest country in Africa (in area), ranges from desert to scrublands, savannas, swamplands and tropical forests. It's a fascinating country of desert and tribal culture, and in its capital, Khartoum, the merging of the White and Blue Nile rivers can be seen. However, a civil war has been fought with varying intensity for the past decade, as the Islamic government of the north tries to control the Christian and animist south. For the time being, it should not be considered a tourist destination.

Tunisia   Tunisia provides a relaxing introduction to North Africa. Its developed coastline and rustic interior give travelers the opportunity to decide how adventurous they want to be. The country offers an array of enchanting sites — from subterranean cities and well-preserved Roman ruins to desert oases and exotic Kairouan (which produces the country's best carpets).

Many tourist sites are connected with the Carthaginian, Roman and Arab civilizations. In the eighth century BC, merchants from Asia founded the city of Carthage in what is today Tunisia; Carthage became one of the great powers of the ancient world. Rome conquered it in 146 BC and ruled the area for centuries. The next great conqueror left the most lasting impression — the Arabs in around 700 AD. The ruins of Carthage are just a short trip east of the capital city of Tunis; the best Roman ruins in the country are found southwest of Tunis at Dougga. In the medieval town of Monastir, visitors can tour the impressive 8th-century red-stone Ribat Monastery/ Fortress, a former refuge for Muslim defenders.

In you're going to Tunisia for sun and surf, consider the beach resorts of Sousse or Jerba Island. Jerba is extremely popular with Northern Europeans. You may want to start your visit to the country in the city of Tunis. Be sure to see the Great Mosque there, stroll the Avenue Bourguiba (modeled on the Champs Elysees in Paris) and visit the National Museum of the Bardo (excellent collection of mosaics).

East Africa

Burundi   The two main ethnic groups in Burundi, the Tutsi and the Hutu, have been struggling for domination for centuries. Because of the political situation between the groups, we strongly advise you not to send clients there at this time. If the country does return to calm, a tourist would want to see its mountainous scenery, forests and valleys and perhaps experience its hot springs. In that case send only those who already plan to be in the area.

Djibouti   Djibouti (pronounced ji-BOO-tee) is a small country at the juncture of the Gulf of Aden and the Red Sea, on the "horn" of northeast Africa. Although it has some beaches and offers duty-free shopping, it's not much of a tourist destination. Anyone who goes there had better love dry, desolate scenery and need few conveniences.

Eritrea   Eritrea (ear-uh-TREE-uh) has finally emerged as a nation, after a 33-year struggle for independence from Ethiopia. Currently, the country is only for those well-traveled souls who are interested in northeastern African culture and in the development of a new nation. Eritrea's chief attractions include its unique culture — its population is half Muslim and half Christian and it was once an Italian colony — beaches and ancient markets.

Ethiopia   After 30 years of sporadic civil war and starvation, Ethiopia has finally settled into peace. Travelers can once again visit this marvelous land of carved churches, ancient markets and shrines and the most ancient human skull and skeleton ever found. The oldest independent nation in Africa, Ethiopia remained in isolation for centuries, which led to the development of a fascinating culture. Ethiopia was converted to Christianity in the 4th century and is considered to be one of the oldest Christian countries. Some of its most important attractions are connected with its Christian heritage and include the famous churches at Lalibela. In this town in the 12th century, eleven churches were created, each carved out of a solid piece of red rock. A trip to Ethiopia is only for the experienced traveler.

Rwanda   Not so long ago, Rwanda was best known for its mountain gorillas, who starred in the

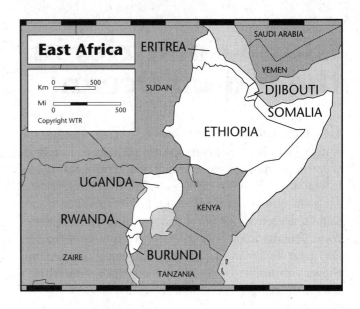

book (and film) *Gorillas in the Mist.* Unfortunately, today the country is better known for the genocidal civil war that erupted in 1993. Given the instability and the uncertainty of the new government, we recommend delaying all travel to Rwanda for the foreseeable future.

Somalia   Somalia, in spite of its rich and ancient history, is today one of the last places on earth most travelers would consider going to because of its ongoing civil strife. War, pestilence and famine continue to be a threat. Even before the problems began, Somalia offered little attraction to visitors — it's a very dry country, without the beauty that makes the Sahara so attractive.

Uganda   Winston Churchill once called Uganda "The Pearl of East Africa." And after decades of tarnish, the world is once again catching glimpses of its luster. The country has become a model of stability in its troubled and beautiful region. Tourist facilities have also improved over the last few years, enabling travelers to once again visit the country's stunning collection of green rolling hills, snowcapped mountains, beautiful rivers and massive lakes.

Uganda will appeal to adventurous travelers who are interested in wildlife and lush African scenery. The highlight to any trip there is a chance to see mountain gorillas in their natural habitat. (Given the turmoil in Rwanda and Zaire, it is currently the only country where you can safely view these fascinating creatures.) Don't go expecting deluxe accommodations or everything to go according to schedule.

Island Countries in the Indian Ocean

Comoros Comoros, between Madagascar and the African mainland, is an archipelago containing four large volcanic islands and several small ones. The blending and interaction of several cultures—African, European and Arab—is one of Comoros' major attractions as is Mount Kartala, an active volcano with a stunning, picture-perfect cone. The islands are beautiful, with white-sand beaches and great diving and snorkeling. The pace is relaxed, but the environment is slightly on the dirty side. There's always the danger of political instability.

Madagascar The island nation off Africa's southeast coast seems to be a monument to diversity. Its populated by a fascinating mixture of Polynesians, Asians, Africans and Europeans; the nation also boasts coastal port cities, rich fertile valleys and 9,000-ft/2,743-m mountains. It also has one of the most varied collections of animal and plant life in the world, some of which are unique to the island. Spectacular scenery, coral reefs, great beaches (for snorkeling/diving) and the opportunity to see unusual varieties of lemurs (which look something like a cross between a fox and a monkey) are the main draws.

Mauritius Mauritius (pronounced more-RISH-us) is known as the most cosmopolitan island in the sun because of its mix of many, many nationalities. The terrain consists of an impressive coastline rimmed with beaches, interesting gorges and volcanic mountains. The surrounding water features excellent deep-sea fishing, coral reefs and 50 submerged shipwrecks. There are few political problems. Nonetheless, it's not for everyone. The surroundings are less than immaculate, the beaches are often strewn with seaweed and few things are going to be within an easy walk — or even drive — from a client's hotel. Mauritius makes a pleasant stopover on a trip to India or Australia.

Reunion This island, an overseas department of France, is truly magnificent. It hosts pristine white beaches, sugarcane fields, volcanoes, beautiful mountain trails, deep gorges, natural amphitheaters (formed by collapsed volcanos), waterfalls (up to ½ mi/1 km high), spectacular flora and unusual bird life. Known as the Perfume Island, Reunion lies far off the southeast coast of Africa in the Indian Ocean. But pretty as it is, it

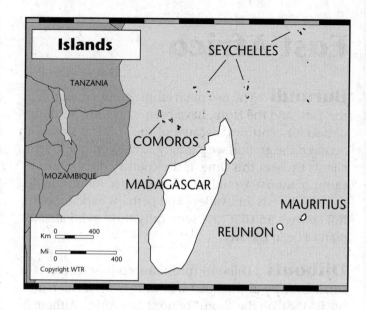

may not live up to every expectation. Although its beaches and the scenery around them are gorgeous, don't send anyone all that way with the idea of having a great beach vacation. The water itself is the island's shortcoming — there's no lagoon available for water sports, and in many places, there's simply too much coral for swimming, yet the water's too shallow for snorkeling/diving over the coral. Reunion's natural beauty and hiking opportunities, however, are quite good enough to justify a visit.

Seychelles The Seychelles are one of our favorite spots on earth — these islands are nothing short of tropical paradise. Composed of more than 100 islands, the country lies about 1,000 mi/1,600 km east of Kenya; each of its islands is unique in character and physical makeup. Among the enticements are white coral beaches, tropical plant life, green-clad hills and warm ocean currents (for snorkeling, surfing, waterskiing and wind sailing). Note, however, that the Seychelles are a very expensive destination.

Southern Africa

Botswana With its dazzling array of diverse ecosystems, Botswana is one of our favorite countries in Africa. For the sophisticated traveler, it is the best African country in which to enjoy game viewing. Because Botswana's economy is buoyed by mineral wealth, it isn't overanxious to flood the country with tourists. Rather, it has placed a higher priority on sound wildlife

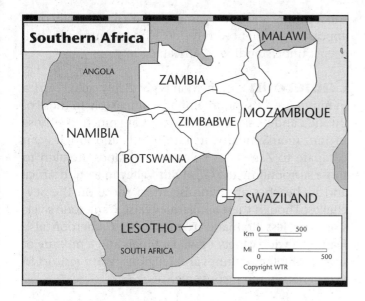

Southern Africa

ANGOLA
MALAWI
ZAMBIA
MOZAMBIQUE
ZIMBABWE
NAMIBIA
BOTSWANA
SWAZILAND
LESOTHO
SOUTH AFRICA

Km 0 500
Mi 0 500
Copyright WTR

management than on tourism promotion. In particular, Chobe National Park and the Moremi Reserve offer fantastic opportunities for game viewing. The vast majority of the country is covered by desert, but even this portion of the land is fascinating. Victoria Falls, while not actually bordering Botswana, is very near its northeast corner. All in all, Botswana is costlier than more traditional game-viewing regions, and it's not the best country to experience African culture, but for nature lovers who can afford it, it's worth every penny.

Lesotho
Lesotho (pronounced le-SOO-too) is totally surrounded by (and economically dependent upon) South Africa. It's truly self-ruling, however. Lesotho is a beautiful country — 90% of the land sits among tall mountains. Camping, hiking trails and good shopping for tribal crafts are among Lesotho's chief attractions. Few people go to Lesotho unless they're already going to South Africa. Those interested primarily in game parks will probably want to pass it by, while for outdoor types, the mountain scenery is the draw.

Malawi
Not many people venture to this country that sits between the popular game-park regions of eastern and southern Africa. Although Malawi's game areas pale in comparison, it wouldn't hurt to send clients there who are already in the region and who would enjoy time in a relaxing, cool mountain retreat and/or lounging on the beaches of Lake Malawi (the third-largest lake in Africa). It also offers a wide variety of beautiful scenery, especially along the Great Rift Valley.

Mozambique
The story of Mozambique, past and present, is depressing. On one hand, its countryside is beautiful and its culture is a unique blend of African and Portuguese influences. Its cities feature Baroque churches and colonial fortresses, and throughout the country are Portuguese-style farmhouses. Game reserves, tropical islands, magnificent beaches, deep-sea fishing and clear water scuba diving give Mozambique the potential to be one of Africa's most inviting destinations. But political conditions and natural disasters have made it one of the least inviting. Civil war, droughts and famine have plagued the populace, and poaching in the game parks has gone virtually unchecked (almost all the parks are now closed).

Namibia
Namibia is a country of shifting, multi-hued sand dunes, exotic plants, huge herds of animals and a shoreline so forbidding that early seamen dubbed it the "Skeleton Coast." (Dense fog caused many ships to run aground there.) The country's Namib Desert along the Atlantic Ocean is one of the driest regions on Earth.

Namibia will appeal to well-seasoned travelers who have already been to countries such as South Africa and Kenya and want to see more of the continent's wildlife. Like Kenya, Namibia's chief attractions are its parks. Its best reserve is Ethosha National Park, a combination of dried lake (salt pan) and grasslands, dense brush and open plains. Ethosha is home to elephant, giraffe, zebra, leopard, cheetah, lion, rhino and 3,000 species of birds.

You may want to begin your tour of Namibia in Windhoek, the capital. It's a small, clean city that the Germans made their administrative center when the country was a German colony. Some parts of the town still have a distinctive German feel; there's even an Octoberfest celebration.

Swaziland
Tiny Swaziland, almost encircled by South Africa, contains nearly every type of African landscape, from mountains to grasslands and river valleys to gorges. It's not uncommon to see Swazi warriors, women and medicine men walking along the streets wearing colorful traditional dress. Most visitors go to Swaziland for its casinos, but we think the country's main attraction lies in its natural beauty (mountains, tropical forests and plains) and the culture of its residents. Swaziland is usually seen in conjunction with a trip to South Africa.

Zambia
Zambia is a great destination for someone who has gotten a taste of the continent's excitement in Kenya or South Africa and is ready to try something a bit more adventurous and rough around the edges. The capital, Lusaka, isn't particularly friendly, and wildlife

management is not as sophisticated as in some other African countries. But Zambia offers — quite literally — a walk on the wild side: You can take a multiday trek through South Luangwa National Park, one of the least-tamed terrains in Africa.

Zambia has many of the same attractions as neighboring Zimbabwe: good animal reserves, views of Victoria Falls and rafting on the Zambezi River. All things considered, we prefer Zimbabwe — Harare is more attractive than Lusaka, and Zimbabwe has the Great Zimbabwe ruins — but views of Victoria Falls are nicer in Zambia and the parks are much less crowded.

Zimbabwe
Zimbabwe has come into its own in the '90s. It's a great game-viewing destination, but more than that, it has become a country with a solid tourism infrastructure and an atmosphere that makes visitors feel welcome and wanted. Zimbabwe can be a fantastic African destination for both first-time and experienced travelers. Of the game areas, Hwange has the most to offer. The other major game area, Matusadona/Mana Pools, has fewer animals, but its location on water adds interest. Victoria Falls (in Zambia) borders Zimbabwe as well, and the Great Zimbabwe archaeological ruins are the oldest permanent structures in sub-Saharan Africa. When sending clients to Zimbabwe, bear in mind that it is very much a developing country; they should expect inconveniences beyond what would occur in a more developed country.

West Africa

Benin
Benin is Africa on a manageable scale. The birthplace of voodoo, Benin has a fascinating history, great music and unusual "water villages." There are also excellent beaches, but the coastal area is extremely hot, humid and rainy. Tribal culture, game reserves and town markets are the other attractions. In many ways, Benin provides visitors with the flavor of West Africa.

Burkina Faso
This poverty-stricken landlocked nation is characterized by three ecological zones. In the north is the semiarid Sahel, where among its short grasses, the herding of animals is traditional. In the middle region is the Sudanian savanna, characterized by tall grass, scattered trees and termite mounds that resemble mammoth sand castles. The humid south is covered by forests and savanna. Although this region has fascinating

tribal culture and a few game reserves, it will really only appeal to experienced travelers who are interested in a deeper understanding of African society.

Cameroon
Cameroon is justifiably called "Africa in miniature." Its mountains are comparable to those of Rwanda and its savanna grasslands are much like those in Tanzania. Similarly, its rain forests and jungles can compare to Zaire's, its volcanic highlands are akin to those surrounding the Great Rift Valley in eastern Africa and its beaches are reminiscent of those on the Seychelles. Though these similarities exist, Cameroon's versions are less dramatic in each case. Cameroon also features a wide variety of wild animals and a mixture of several different cultures and religions. Warn visitors to expect delays and inconveniences.

Cape Verde Islands
This archipelago about 400 mi/644 km west of Senegal comprises 15 physically different islands. They range from flat to mountainous. Less humid than many tropical islands, they're somewhat stark and barren. Formerly a Portuguese colony, the islands are rich in history and culture, and offer a wide variety of water-related activities (scuba diving, windsurfing, etc.). Europeans who want to get away from it all have noticed the Cape Verdes and it's only a matter of time before North Americans will too.

Chad
A relatively barren, isolated and strife-torn country in north-central Africa, Chad offers little to the traveler but unmitigated tragedy. Its Saharan culture, deserts and Lake Chad are its main attractions, but due to the problems associated with a long civil war, it's best to avoid the country for the time being.

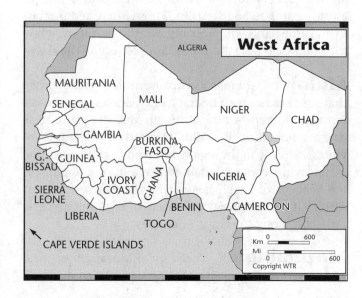

The Gambia   The Gambia is a small country surrounded by Senegal on three sides. Within its borders is Juffure, the village made famous by Alex Haley's *Roots* that has become a mecca for African Americans. In spite of its size, Gambia has a surprising number of other attractions: excellent beaches, decent tourist facilities, historic sites and friendly people. Generally speaking, Gambia is seen in conjunction with a visit to Senegal.

Ghana   Although Ghana is a land of physical diversity — from thick forests to beaches lined with palm trees — it's perhaps most fascinating for its political and social development. Though its people are holding strongly to traditional beliefs, the nation is also in the process of modernization, and the process is bittersweet for many. Ghanaians are friendly and better educated than citizens in many developing countries, and there are several tribes that invite visitors to observe their ceremonies, customs and festivals. All things considered, however, don't send someone who is merely looking for an introduction to West African culture — this isn't the place for beginners.

Guinea   Guinea has physical beauty to spare: tree-covered uplands, steaming mangrove swamps, pleasant beaches, picturesque mountains and spouting waterfalls. It's a friendly, scenic country, but it doesn't really offer much in the way of tourist-type attractions — those who are hoping to find the romantic image of Africa there will be disappointed. Send only those who are well traveled in developing countries and who happen to be in the area.

Guinea-Bissau   This rainy, hot, humid and very lush country includes several islands off the Atlantic Coast. Among its attractions are its beaches, rarely seen saltwater hippos, birds and tribal culture. It's really a country to be visited by those who are primarily interested in saying they have been everywhere.

Ivory Coast (Cote d'Ivoire)   Though the Ivory Coast is seldom visited by North Americans, Europeans have discovered it, and thanks to their continuing patronage, the nation has developed one of the best tourist infrastructures in West Africa. The Ivory Coast is a study in contrasts: Some of the man-made structures are as impressive as the country's natural wonders, impenetrable forests adjoin cultivated fields and the continent's wildest animals can be found within a few miles of bustling city life. The country is one of the more prosperous in tropical Africa and is somewhat costly.

Among the best places to visit are the cities of Abidjan and Yamoussoukro and Comoe National Park. Abidjan is a large, clean, fairly modern city — it seems almost European in many respects. Its attractions include a casino, good shopping, numerous nightclubs — even indoor ice-skating. The cosmopolitan mix of citizens wearing the latest in Paris fashions or the most traditional African garb makes it a great people-watching city. But even though many parts of it feel European, other aspects leave no doubt in your mind that you're in Africa. Make a point to see the huge market in the Treichville area, where merchants sell goods made by the country's 60 ethnic groups. Another attraction to see is the African art collection at the National Museum.

Yamoussoukro is the capital city of the Ivory Coast. The chief attraction here is the now famous basilica, Notre Dame de la Paix (Our Lady of Peace). The basilica cost over $750 million to build and has magnificent stained-glass windows. It's one of the largest churches in the world. Then, for a change of pace go north and visit Comoe National Park — it's the finest nature reserve in the country.

Liberia   Liberia is still plagued by civil war. For the time being, it should not be considered a tourist destination. Although the U.S. did not have a colony in Africa, Liberia came closest to being one. Its capital, Monrovia (named after U.S. President James Monroe) was settled in 1822 by freed slaves, and the nations have kept in close touch. It doesn't really offer much in the way of tourism — its beaches are beautiful, but there's not much in the way of waterfront accommodations.

Mali   If you've always wanted to say you've been to Timbuktu and back, you're obliged to visit Mali. But Timbuktu, that remotest of remote cities, is the least of Mali's attractions. Mali contains within its borders the cultural and geographical separation between tropical rain forests and the Sahara Desert, and the result is an interesting, diversified and colorful population. Fascinating tribal life, absorbing markets and camel rides in the desert are only part of Mali's offerings. The country, however, is not without its problems, among them a susceptibility to famine and drought. The beauty of Mali is tinged with sadness, but we feel that if only one country in West Africa is visited, Mali should be near the top of the list. Anyone sent there should be adventurous and be able to tolerate inconveniences and dirty conditions.

Mauritania   Mauritania's colorful tribes, beautiful deserted beaches and haunting Sahara scenery have made it a fascinating destination for adventurous travelers. It, like neighboring Mali, is a nation of great cultural significance — it bridges an area where Black and Arab Africa meet. Unfortunately, it's currently undergoing some serious civil disturbances, so be sure to check travel advisories before sending anyone there.

Niger

Economically poor but culturally rich, landlocked Niger is almost entirely blanketed by the Saheil, a semiarid region along the southern edge of the Sahara. There are grasslands in the more populous southwest region (90% of the population lives within 100 mi/161 km of the southern border), but the Saheil is the main draw for us. We particularly like Niger because of its special blend of tribal cultures and because it's primarily a country of villages — there are only four cities with populations of more than 20,000. Niger is only for the flexible, tolerant traveler who is experienced in touring developing countries.

Nigeria

Nigeria is by far the most populous country in Africa: one-fourth of the people of sub-Saharan Africa live there. The country is a mad mix of Western development (autos, motorcycles and electronic gadgets) and African tradition. Among the serious problems Nigeria faces are overpopulation and a standard of living that slips whenever oil prices go down. Because Nigeria has a well-known name, you may have inexperienced clients who think it is a good choice as a first-time African destination. It isn't. Send only travelers who have toured Africa extensively and want to see all that the continent has to offer. Nigerians are very hospitable, and there are interesting examples of tribal culture and art, but there are more interesting sights in less stressful environments. Many areas are noisy, dirty, polluted, crowded and relatively expensive (if one wants to remain healthy). The cities of Lagos and Ibadan have very high crime rates, particularly for armed robbery. If you do send clients to Nigeria without giving them all these warnings, they'll haunt you for the rest of your life.

For those who do want to go, make sure they visit Kano, our favorite city in the country, and Oshogbo, the country's creative arts center. Kano is a 1,000-year-old Moslem center in the north with many cultural and historical attractions. Be sure your clients see the walls of the Old City, the massive Kurmi Market, the Central Mosque (open only to Muslims) and the Emir's Palace. The town of Oshogbo, northeast of Lagos, is filled with world-class artists producing original masks, tapestries, batiks and sculptures — a good place to pick up some souvenirs. Outside of town is the Sacred Forest, a wooded area filled with shrines to the gods of the Yoruba people. We recommend hiring a guide who knows the stories behind the shrines when touring the area.

Senegal

Senegal blends the modern and traditional in a way that seems to blur distinctions between the two. Its capital, Dakar, was built to be the showplace of French colonial Africa, with wide boulevards and avenues, yet it has always had a very rough-around-the-edges feel to it. This dichotomy is also seen in the country's modern art museum, where visitors may notice that there's a striking resemblance between the contemporary works and the tribal art for sale in the markets in rural villages. We would not necessarily recommend Senegal to first-time visitors to Africa — there are many countries with better game parks — but those on a return visit to Africa will find that it's a great place to learn more about African culture, flora and fauna. It offers a fascinating mix of traditional village life, modern cities, friendly people, well-wrought crafts and good food. The country is best appreciated, perhaps, when visited with other West African nations. Even though Senegal reveals a lot about the region, what's found in nearby countries will round out the picture. Check advisories if you visit, since it's currently experiencing both civil problems and feuds with its neighbors.

Sierra Leone

This nation in southwest West Africa has little to distinguish itself from its neighbors. There are a wide variety of terrains and cultures represented, and it has adequate beaches and fair game reserves, but little to draw travelers to it in particular. It's a destination only for the well traveled who have a specific interest in British-influenced West African culture.

Togo

Not too long ago, Togo was a wonderful place to explore, but it has fallen on hard times recently. In its favor, the nation offers most of the sights and sounds of West Africa in one place — friendly people, varied cultures, exotic foods and modern infrastructure. Sadly, however, political turmoil has shaken Togo's stability, and a return to tranquillity is not forecast any time soon.

Central Africa

Angola

While Angola is now relatively peaceful, it is still an unlikely tourist destination: The civil war that it has endured for decades has left a mess that will take years to overcome. If indeed peace does take root, and the country's infrastructure is rebuilt, Angola's natural beauty will once again be available for travelers.

Among its foremost attractions are its jungle and

desert scenery, beaches, tours of its diamond mines, and buildings and mosaic sidewalks from the period in which it was a Portuguese colony.

Central African Republic

This nation is not high on many people's lists of countries to tour. It's landlocked, very poor and surrounded by troubled neighbors. It's mostly seen in transit on overland tours of Africa by people traveling on business or visiting relatives. Waterfalls, jungles, tribal art and tribal cultures are the main interests in the Central African Republic. However, better examples of most of its attractions can be seen in other countries.

Congo

When you put things into perspective, the Congo has a lot to offer adventurous travelers. True, its cities aren't as developed and its forests aren't as extensive as those in neighboring countries, but neither are its problems as intractable. We'd much rather be sipping our drink at a pleasant riverside cafe in Brazzaville, its capital, looking across the Congo River at the skyscrapers of Kinshasa in Zaire, than to be on the opposite bank, worried about the chaotic Zairian political situation. The country's main attractions are Central African tribal culture, a dense jungle (complete with wild rivers and stunning waterfalls) and game viewing (albeit limited).

Equatorial Guinea

This tiny but pretty country of lush tropical forests and colonial cities includes the island of Bioko and Rio Muni, 125 mi/202 km away on the African mainland. It also incorporates nice beaches, volcanic mountains and scenery. Unfortunately, Equatorial Guinea issues very few tourist visas — don't bother suggesting this country to clients who are simply interested in visiting Africa.

Gabon

Gabon, bisected by the Equator, looks like what most people expect Africa to look like: its dense forests and jungles, veined by rivers, would make a good setting for any movie set in sub-Saharan Africa. This is the country where Dr. Albert Schweitzer worked, and there are many sites related to him. We like Gabon as well for its white-sand beaches and for its typical African

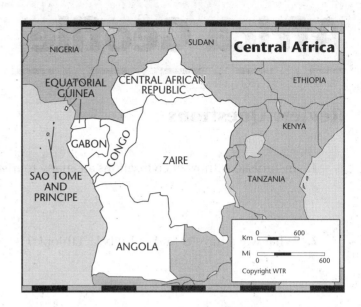

atmosphere. Nonetheless, anyone thinking of going should know it's somewhat expensive and that high heat, humidity, mosquitos and less-than-attentive service are the norm.

Sao Tome and Principe

Sao Tome and Principe are what we imagine the Caribbean islands to have been like 200 years ago: magnificent beaches, great snorkeling, lush tropical scenery, interesting bird life and very few tourists. Some may feel disappointed because accommodations tend to be basic and there's not much in the way of nightlife and shopping. Others will be just as glad that development is being held off.

Zaire

Located in the heart of Africa, this huge land retains the flavor of the continent known to early Western explorers: It features steamy equatorial rain forests, wide jungle rivers, snowcapped mountains, Pygmy villages, active volcanoes, savanna grasslands and a wide variety of wild animals. But the sense that the nation is out-of-control forms as soon as a traveler arrives: It's almost impossible to make it to one's hotel without being accosted for bribes and threatened with physical harm at a variety of stages. Violence against foreigners is now common. We do not recommend traveling to Zaire now or in the foreseeable future.

Africa Geofile

Review Questions

1. In Tunisia, with what civilizations are many tourist sites connected?

2. What will a traveler find in Lalibela, Ethiopia?

3. To what kind of travelers will Uganda appeal? What is the highlight of a trip there?

4. What about Reunion justifies a visit? In what way is water the island's shortcoming?

5. As a tourist destination, how is Namibia like Kenya?

6. For what activity is Zimbabwe a great destination? In what way has Zimbabwe come into its own in the '90s?

7. What attractions might draw a tourist to Abidjan? What is the chief attraction in Yamoussoukro?

8. If a client tells you that he or she wants to visit Timbuktu, to what country will you send the person?

9. What factors contribute to making Nigeria a poor tourist destination?

10. What features make Gabon look like what most people expect Africa to look like?

Africa Geofile

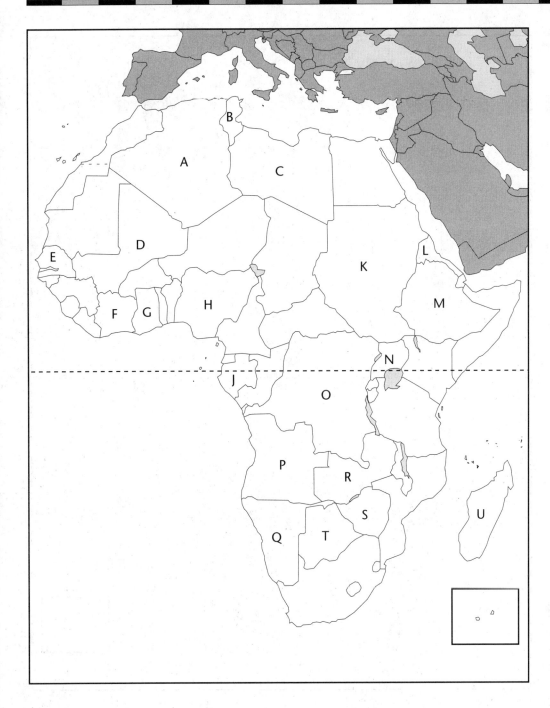

Map Skills Exercise

Match the tourist destination listed below with the corresponding letter on the map. You can use each letter only once.

1. _____ Ethiopia
2. _____ Mali
3. _____ Algeria
4. _____ Ivory Coast
5. _____ Nigeria
6. _____ Botswana
7. _____ Madagascar
8. _____ Uganda
9. _____ Angola
10. _____ Eritrea
11. _____ Tunisia
12. _____ Ghana
13. _____ Namibia
14. _____ Zambia
15. _____ Sudan
16. _____ Zimbabwe
17. _____ Gabon
18. _____ Senegal
19. _____ Zaire
20. _____ Libya

Unit Review Africa

Map Skills Exercise

Match the tourist destination listed below with the corresponding letter on the map. You can use each letter only once.

1. _____ Cape Town
2. _____ Cairo
3. _____ Mt. Kilimanjaro
4. _____ Zaire
5. _____ Madagascar
6. _____ Timbuktu
7. _____ Luxor
8. _____ Rabat
9. _____ Marrakesh
10. _____ Etosha National Park
11. _____ Johannesberg
12. _____ Zambia
13. _____ Cameroon
14. _____ Kano
15. _____ Abu Simbel
16. _____ Carthage
17. _____ Lalibela
18. _____ Ngorongoro Crater
19. _____ Kruger National Park
20. _____ Notre Dame de la Paix
21. _____ Masai Mara
22. _____ Great Zimbabwe ruins
23. _____ Garden Route
24. _____ Uganda
25. _____ Botswana

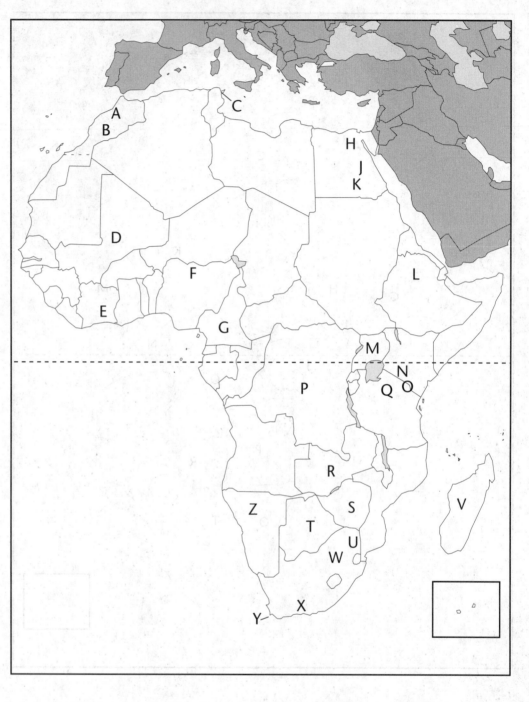

Unit Review Africa

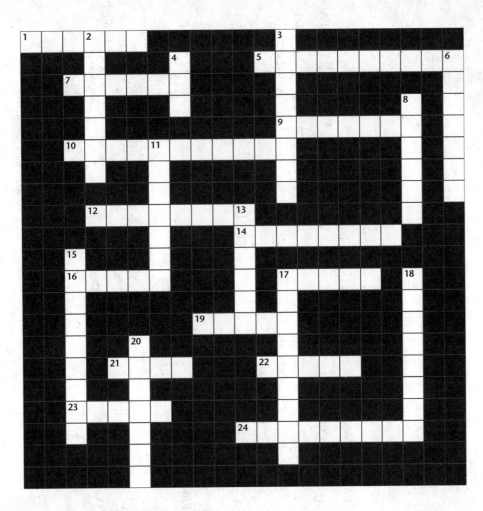

Content Review Crossword Puzzle

Across

1. Abu Simbel has a magnificent one.
5. Moroccans say one hour of it is worth 100 hours of work.
7. Do this on a felucca.
9. Day trip from Spain.
10. You can see it from both Kenya and Tanzania.
12. Carved in solid rock in Lalibela.
14. Site of the Voortrekker Monument.
16. Treetops in Kenya is one.
17. Tour these in Kimberley.
19. Across the Nile from the Valley of the Kings.
21. Major black ethnic group in South Africa.
22. Victoria _____.
23. Ancestors of many in South Africa came from this country.
24. Game park in Kenya.

Down

2. Cheops built one.
3. See it from Table Mountain.
4. The old town, the new town and Ville Nouvelle.
6. Once controlled Namibia.
8. Ngorongoro _____.
11. Wildebeest do this.
13. It's in Giza.
15. Runs between Kimberley and Cape Town.
17. Djemaa el Fna (Court of Marvels) is there.
18. The Ivory Coast has one of the largest.
20. Ruins of Carthage are in this country.

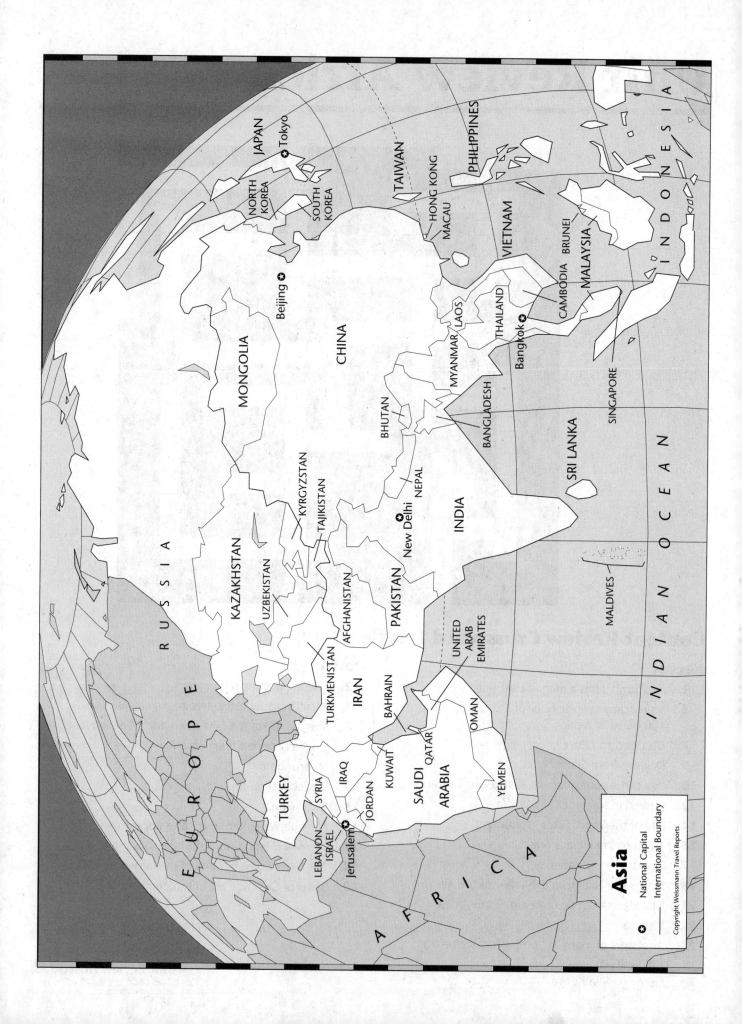

Asia

ASIA IS THE LARGEST CONTINENT, STRETCH-ing from Egypt in Africa on the west to within a few miles of the United States in the east. It's a continent of fantastic landscapes and fabulous cities. There you'll find the vast desert sands of Arabia; the Himalaya mountain range—the highest on Earth; the mind-calming beaches of Bali; and the bustling streets of Hong Kong.

To look at Asia, we often divide the huge continent into regions: East Asia (in the past called the Orient), Southeast Asia, South Asia, Central Asia and the Middle East. (The Middle East is made up of the nations of Southwest Asia and some of the countries of North Africa.)

Its two eastern regions (East Asia and Southeast Asia) lie across the vast Pacific Ocean from the Americas. The two regions are booming economically and tourism is growing rapidly. The most heavily populated country in the world, China, is in this part of the world, as are such other popular tourist destinations as Japan, Thailand, Hong Kong and Singapore. And other countries of these two regions, including Vietnam, are attracting a growing number of tourists. (More U.S. citizens are traveling there since restrictions against selling travel to Vietnam,

imposed by the U.S. government, were lifted in 1993.)

In the central part of the continent, you'll find two more regions, Central Asia and South Asia. Islam has played a major role in the history of both, although most people in South Asia are Hindu. Central Asia consists of Afghanistan and the new republics that were once part of the Soviet Union, including Uzbekistan and Kazakhstan. India is by far the largest country in South Asia and also the chief tourist destination in the entire central part of the continent.

The Asian part of the Middle East begins at the Suez Canal in Egypt and stretches eastward to the borders of Pakistan. For the most part, this is a sparsely populated area that includes vast deserts. Israel, a land holy to Christians, Jews and Muslims, is by far the most popular tourist destination in the area for Europeans and North Americans, though there are wonderful ruins and antiquities in many other Middle Eastern nations, too.

On the following pages, you'll find in-depth profiles of the major tourist countries of Asia. The Asia Geofile chapter has descriptions of all of the other countries on this huge continent.

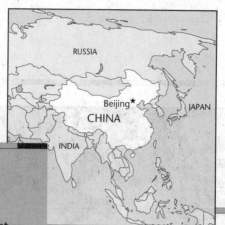

RUSSIA

Beijing★
CHINA

JAPAN

INDIA

China

A trip to China is filled with quirks that seem designed to baffle foreigners. Restaurants tell you they are out of food — but continue to serve Chinese patrons. Your planned trip to some out-of-the-way place is canceled without warning. Service personnel take offense when you interrupt their personal conversations. The country will sometimes seem like a large, slow-moving object determined to discover the limits of your patience. But then you'll find yourself atop the Great Wall, or in a large riverboat suddenly dwarfed by the stark cliffs of a Yangtze River Gorge. All the hassles and stress are more than compensated for by these rewards. If you can overcome its challenges, you'll find China a complex and exhilarating country — one you could visit an endless number of times.

China's history spans more than 5,000 years — it's the birthplace of Confucius and Mao, moveable type and spaghetti, astronomy and gunpowder. Visitors who haven't been to China since the government crackdown in 1989 may be shocked to find that, while free speech has been muzzled, experimentation with a market economy is proceeding full steam. Whereas there was little vehicular traffic ten years ago, traffic jams have become a way of life in Beijing and other large cities. Colonel Sanders, M&Ms, Salem cigarettes and other standard-bearers of Western culture have made solid inroads. The ubiquitous blue, grey and green uniforms of the people have been replaced by the colors and fashions of the West. Service in better hotels is modeled on that found in the better hotels of Europe and Asia (although often something's lost in the translation).

In area, China is the third-largest country in the world (it's bigger than all of Europe). About two-thirds of China is covered by hills or mountains (the west is more mountainous than the east).

What to Do There

Beijing (Peking)   There are many fascinating sights in and near Beijing, but before visiting the attractions, spend an hour or two walking the streets. Get off the main boulevards and wander through the mazelike alleys where most residents live, or perhaps stroll down

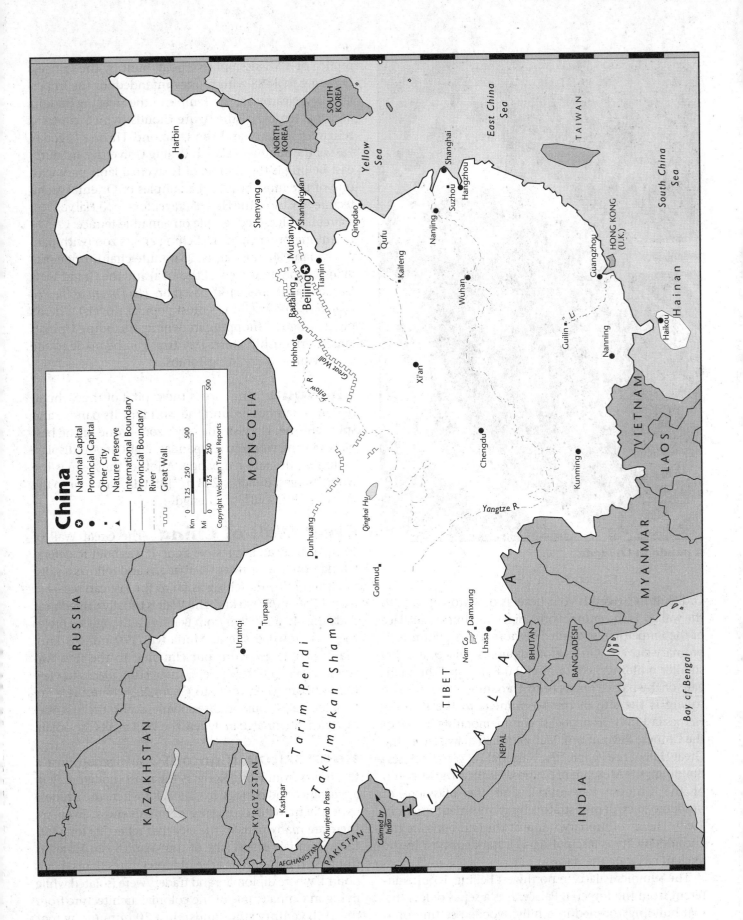

China

National Capital
Provincial Capital
Other City
Nature Preserve
International Boundary
Provincial Boundary
River
Great Wall

Km 0 125 250 500
Mi 0 125 250 500

RUSSIA

KAZAKHSTAN

KYRGYZSTAN

AFGHANISTAN

PAKISTAN

Khunjerab Pass

Kashgar

Urumqi

Turpan

Tarim Pendi

Taklimakan Shamo

MONGOLIA

Dunhuang

Golmud

Qinghai Hu

TIBET

Claimed by India

H I M A L A Y A

NEPAL

BHUTAN

BANGLADESH

INDIA

Bay of Bengal

MYANMAR

LAOS

VIETNAM

Nam Co
Damxung
Lhasa

Chengdu

Kunming

Xi'an

Yangtze R.

Yellow R.

Great Wall

Hohhot

Beijing
Tianjin
Badaling
Mutianyu
Shanhaiguan

Harbin

Shenyang

NORTH KOREA

SOUTH KOREA

Yellow Sea

Qingdao

Qufu

Kaifeng

Nanjing

Suzhou

Shanghai

Hangzhou

Wuhan

East China Sea

TAIWAN

South China Sea

Guilin

Guangzhou

HONG KONG (U.K.)

Nanning

Haikou

Hainan

A panda in Chengdu

replica of a Mississippi riverboat, built by the Princess Dowager in 1888 with money intended for the Imperial Navy. Nearby are the Temple of the Sleeping Buddha and the Temple of the Azure Clouds (which contains religious statuary and the Diamond Throne Pagoda). East of the Summer Palace is Beijing University. In southeast Beijing is the Temple of Heaven, a large park with one of the most beautiful examples of Oriental architecture in China: the Hall of Prayer for Good Harvest. It's a circular, blue-tiled temple on a marble terrace.

Among other sights in Beijing are its zoo (with pandas), Xiang Shan Park (its 20-minute chairlift ride provides a panoramic view of the area) and the Grand View Garden (a "theme park" based on *The Dream of the Red Chamber,* one of China's most popular novels). There's plenty of good shopping in Beijing, including China's largest Friendship Store. Day trips can be made to the Great Wall and the Ming Tombs.

Chengdu
This city is the capital of the Sichuan region — famous around the world for its pandas and spicy cuisine. Do visit the city's zoo — one of the best places in the world to see pandas, eight are on display, including the rare red panda. Another must-see is the world's largest Buddha (233 ft/71 m tall), carved into the face of a cliff, south of Chengdu.

Great Wall of China
The Great Wall of China is truly an impressive sight. It was built to defend China from the northern barbarians and follows a ridge of barren hills, stretching as far as the eye can see — at least 3,750 mi/6,000 km. The Wall is usually visited near Badaling (47 mi/75 km from Beijing), although we prefer the less crowded site at Mutianyu (170 mi/273 km). Many people get worn out climbing to the first two watchtowers (it's very steep). Interesting places to view the Wall are 1) en route to Chengdu, where there are "double walls" (built in case enemies scaled the first one) or 2) near Shanhaiguan, where the Wall meets the ocean.

Guangzhou (Canton)
Guangzhou, just a few hours from Hong Kong, is the most modern city in appearance and outlook in China. It's where the Chinese experiment with economic permissiveness. Even so, there are many parts of the city that reflect its long history. Shamian Island (site of the White Swan Hotel) is fun to stroll around. It's the old foreign residents' compound, where diplomats and traders were isolated while living in China (some of the colonial architecture from the 19th century still stands). Just 20 minutes by foot from the White Swan is the Qingping Free Market, a dra-

Old Culture Street. If your hotel is downtown, walk to the walled 14th-century Forbidden City (Imperial Palace of the Emperors), so named because it was off limits to ordinary citizens. On its grounds are six palaces and 800 smaller buildings, containing 9,000 rooms. The main gate of the palace opens onto Tiananmen Square. The square is the site of the Monument to the People's Heroes (a 118-ft/36-m obelisk commemorating heroes of the Chinese Revolution); Mao Zedong's mausoleum; the Great Hall of the People (the National People's Congress Building); the Museum of Chinese History; the Museum of the Chinese Revolution; and the massacre of prodemocracy demonstrators by government forces in 1989. The revolutionary statue at the end opposite the Forbidden City is fascinating — a stark contrast to the ancient city gate that faces it.

The Summer Palace, in northwest Beijing, is quite different from the Imperial Palace: It is a series of less-formal buildings nestled in a hilly, wooded setting on a splendid lake. Among its unusual attractions is a marble

matic contrast to the modern hotel. This is where many of the Chinese shop for food, but Westerners should be prepared for what they'll see — snakes being skinned alive and many live animals not generally considered food back home (monkeys, cats, and a species of anteater called pangolin).

Near the end of the market is Guangzhou Cultural Park. There, after 7 pm, you can enjoy Chinese operas in the round, acrobat and puppet shows, art exhibits and roller-skating. Other things to see and do include a boat trip on the Pearl River and a visit to the Guangzhou Zoo (the second-largest in China; it, too, has pandas). The city has commendable shopping, especially around Zhong-shan Five-Road and Beijing Road.

Guilin
If any Chinese city has wholeheartedly embraced tourism, it's Guilin, the home base for cruises on the picturesque Li River. Because it has spectacular scenery just a short flight from Hong Kong, Guilin has been flooded with tourists since the opening of China. The flat-bottom boats ply a misty, shallow river, which is flanked on both shores by dramatic outcroppings of limestone. Most cruises last a day, with lunch included.

Hangzhou
Visit Hangzhou to see scenic West Lake. It's like a landscape painting come to life. Lingyin Temple, west of town, is one of the few easily accessible spots in China where Buddhist rock carvings can still be seen (they used to be quite widespread, but most were destroyed during the Cultural Revolution of the 1960s). Try to visit the temple in the afternoon, when the sun's rays are distinct as they stream in amid incense smoke and graceful statues of gods. A cable car runs between the temple and North Peak, offering a fine view of the lake. In town, tour the Hangzhou Silk Factory.

Shanghai
Shanghai is the country's most populous and sophisticated city. Try to be in Huangpu Park at sunrise when, it seems, half the city's residents silently, in unison, perform the meditation/dance tai chi chuan. In the nearby downtown district, poke your head in any store that looks interesting; some are highly specialized, such as one containing theater props and costumes. The Shanghai Municipal Museum is probably the best historical art museum in the country. Other sights and activities in Shanghai include the Huangpu River boat trip, the Shanghai Zoo (pandas), the Shanghai Arts and Handicrafts Research Institute, the summer Yu Yuan Market (oldest and largest in the city) and the former residence of Dr. Sun Yat-sen, republican China's first president. Spend some time walking the streets in the older part of town, and try to get tickets to see an evening performance of the Shanghai Acrobats.

Note: Air pollution is a serious problem in Shanghai. Travelers with respiratory problems should avoid the city.

Silk Road
The Chinese began using this famous trade route through western China in the 2nd century BC, and today tourists can follow in their steps. Use of the route reached its peak during the Tang Dynasty (AD 618–907), then declined dramatically with the opening of sea lanes to the West. The main route began in Xi'an and ended in the Middle East. Those following the Silk Road today don't need to be as adventurous as travelers 1,000 years ago, but it helps to be flexible and not to be overly concerned with creature comforts.

Suzhou (Soochow)
One of the cities on the Grand Canal, Suzhou is often seen as a day trip from Shanghai (it's two hours by train). The city features more

Busy street scene in Shanghai

than a dozen Chinese gardens dating from the 11th century. Each is intended to represent an idealized model of the natural world (rocks = mountains, ponds = oceans, shrubs = forests). Don't miss the Lion Garden!

Tibet

Until the early 1950s, Tibet was semiindependent. Today the country is fully under Chinese control. Demonstrations calling for independence from China lead to the sporadic closing of the area and the cancellation of tours. Most of Tibet's monasteries have been destroyed by the occupying Chinese authorities — much of what you'll see is relatively new reconstruction. Interesting as it is, however, Tibet is not Shangri-la. It's a rather dirty place.

Lhasa, the capital, sits at an elevation of 12,000 ft/3,660 m. A good introduction to Lhasa is the Barkhor Bazaar, where hours can be spent just people watching. In the midst of the bazaar is the fabulous Jokhang, holiest of Tibetan Buddhist temples. It's filled by a steady stream of pilgrims who have come to pay respect to their gods, represented in the temple by an incredible array of devotional art.

Visible from almost any point in Lhasa is the Potala Palace. Once the winter residence of the Dalai Lama (Tibet's religious leader who has been in exile in India since 1959), it's one of the world's architectural wonders — the entire building, consisting of thousands of rooms, was created without the use of a single nail.

Xi'an (Sian)

Xi'an (pronounced SHE-on) is home to several important treasures. Foremost is the Qin Army Vault Museum, home to the army of 2,200-year-old terra-cotta soldiers unearthed 24 mi/40 km east of town. More than 8,000 life-size ceramic soldiers, chariots and horses were buried there to protect the tomb of the first emperor of China. What especially impressed us is that each of the soldiers is different. They're based on warriors of the time, and all segments of Chinese society are represented. The statues remain where they were uncovered, protected by a large hangarlike hall. Individual soldiers can be studied more closely in a museum exhibit housed in an adjacent building.

Tours to see the terra-cotta troops often include stops at the tumulus (ancient grave mound) of an emperor. The unexcavated tomb lies below and is thought to contain fantastic riches (among the treasures rumored to be buried there are gold ducks floating on a river of mercury beneath a sky laden with pearl stars). The most interesting side trip is to the Banpo Museum (6 mi/10 km from town), built around the actual site of a 6,000-year-old Neolithic village.

In Xi'an itself, look for the Great Mosque. Used by

Some of the 2,200-year-old terra-cotta soldiers in Xi'an

Xi'an's surprisingly large Muslim population, its buildings look mostly Oriental, but with obvious Arabic influence. The Big Wild Goose Pagoda, built in AD 625, is one of China's most famous; it has a great view from the top.

Yangtze River Cruise

This cruise is great relaxation, but unless you desperately need rest, it should not last longer than three nights. The scenery is pretty but, in our opinion, not as spectacular as the one-day Li River boat ride from Guilin. If time is at all a consideration, skip the Yangtze, but don't miss the Li! The Yangtze Gorges are the highlight of the trip. The cruise passes through three gorges. With cliffs rising 1,000 ft/320 m from the river, Wushan (20 mi/32 km long) is the most impressive of the three. Unfortunately, these sights will soon exist only in memories — the government has begun building a dam that will reduce the splendor of the most dramatic gorge views.

Itinerary

We recommend a minimum of two weeks stay in China. We also advise departing China via Hong Kong and spending a few days there to ease back into Western culture. The following itinerary is a good introduction to China.

Day 1 — Arrive Shanghai.

Day 2 — Shanghai.

Day 3 — Tour Suzhou.

Day 4 — Return to Shanghai by train.

Day 5 — Early flight to Beijing.

Day 6 — Beijing.

Day 7 — Beijing (one day in Beijing should include the Great Wall).

Day 8 — Fly to Xi'an.

Day 9 — Xi'an.

Day 10 — Fly to Guilin.

Day 11 — Guilin.

Day 12 — Fly to Guangzhou.

Day 13 — Guangzhou.

Day 14 — Depart China.

Climate/When to Go

We prefer seeing China during September–October, with April–May a close second. Heat and humidity make the summer less attractive, but on the other hand, there are fewer foreign tourists and prices can be a bit lower.

China's climate is as extreme as that in the U.S., with hot summers in most parts of the country, bitter winters in the north and comfortable winters in the south. Spring rains can make southern cities (especially Guilin and Guangzhou) dreadfully humid; the Yangtze River cruise is especially unpleasant in midsummer. Sandstorms can be a problem in the north (including Beijing) in spring and autumn. Tibet can be quite cold, even in the autumn and late spring.

Transportation

Air China, Northwest, China Eastern Airlines, Japan Airlines and United provide service to Beijing from the U.S. Only Air China flies from Canada. Another popular route is to take Cathay Pacific into Hong Kong, and then enter China from there. Capital International Airport (PEK) is 19 mi/30 km northeast of Beijing. Hongqiao Airport (SHA) is 8 mi/13 km from Shanghai. Cruises touring Asia also stop in Shanghai, and passenger ships arrive from Hong Kong. Entry is possible overland from Hong Kong (by train or bus), Macau (by bus), Pakistan (by road), Russia (by train via Mongolia and the Trans-Siberian Express) and Nepal (by road and air to Tibet). Some domestic flights don't offer first-class service, and alcohol is never served. The service can be lousy.

Trains with steam locomotives run throughout China, and if at all possible, try to schedule at least one overnight train ride (perhaps between Beijing and Xi'an).

Intercity buses are often horribly uncomfortable (most Chinese are a lot smaller than most tourists) and are recommended only for the experienced or unusually tolerant traveler. Taxis are available in the larger cities, and there's now such a surplus of them that you can hail them from the street. Unfortunately, taxi drivers don't always calculate fares honestly — it may be better to settle on a fare before getting in. Only Beijing has a subway system, and it's rather limited. You can't yet rent a self-drive car in China. Cars with drivers are available in some larger cities.

Accommodations

Rooms are always in surplus, and there are bargains to be found. Tourist hotels offer a variety of Western amenities (everything from putting greens and bowling alleys to business centers and fitness rooms). It's possible to make direct reservations with good hotels in China that are owned by Western hotel chains. In many cities, there are only a few hotels that are allowed to register foreign guests. These hotels can be very primitive at times, so it is a good idea to bring your own blanket and pillowcases to ensure cleanliness. Most package tours offer the choice of "good" or "deluxe" rooms.

The hotels throughout the country range from very good to very simple dorm rooms. In areas such as Inner Mongolia and Tibet, accommodations can be simple government-run rooming houses. It's even possible to arrange (locally) an overnight in a Tibetan yak-hair tent or Mongolian yurt. Many hotels have scheduled times for hot water, so you may have to rearrange your day if you want to take a shower.

Health Advisories

Many visitors develop respiratory problems because of polluted air, high altitude, cold weather and the stress that comes with travel. Currently, immunization against polio, tetanus, typhoid, cholera and hepatitis A and B (especially if you're going to Shanghai) may be recommended, though not required — consult your physician. Also ask your doctor about malaria suppressants.

What to Buy

It's a good idea to visit the government-run Friendship Store in any city to see what's available locally, to look at good examples of the products and to determine what the high end of the price range is. Armed with this information, visit the private or provincial stores, craft shops and local department stores. If you don't see anything as good, go back to the Friendship Store. (Generally speaking, the quality and selection of souvenirs has improved dramatically in the past few years.) The Beijing Friendship Store has several floors (and even sells pianos), while the Shanghai Antique Friendship Store has the best selection of older items we've come across. The best deals are found at stores attached to craft factories. Shop for carpets, wood-block prints, porcelain, glass items, silk, cinnabar lacquer, hand-painted snuff bottles, stone and jade carvings, books, Mao buttons, reproductions of old art (including sculptures), jewelry, patent medicines, musical instruments, silk, embroidered linens, T-shirts, paintings and acupuncture and calligraphy paraphernalia. Don't buy any ivory — you won't be able to import it back home.

What to Eat

Complaints about the food are common. It's not that the food is bad — quite the contrary — it's just that eating three Chinese meals a day for 21 days in a row is too much for most Westerners. The only thing worse, in our opinion, is eating Chinese-prepared Western meals (other than in the best hotels, few Chinese chefs have mastered Occidental cooking). The variety of Chinese cuisines can be thrilling. Try to attend a full-scale Chinese multicourse banquet. When in Beijing, you must try Peking duck; in Tibet, try yak meat or yak cheese. Try to eat one dim sum meal, which allows you to select small portions of several dishes.

There are a few precautions to observe while eating in China: Chew your rice carefully, as it often has grit in it; chew meat such as chicken carefully (bones are often cut up into the food rather than removed); and brace yourself to see those bones being spit out by the Chinese onto tablecloths or the floor — spitting is acceptable.

Travel Tips for the Client

Don't eat cheese in public, as many Chinese consider dairy products disgusting . . . Do learn to count to 10 in Chinese. This will be helpful when shopping because Western hand signals for numbers are completely different from theirs (e.g., forefinger and thumb outstretched mean "eight") . . . Don't try to order chop suey, chow mein or fortune cookies. These dishes are unknown in China . . . Don't go to China without first doing some reading about the country and culture . . . Do learn to use chopsticks before going, or take a fork with you . . . Spitting and blowing your nose onto the ground (without a handkerchief) are accepted in public, so prepare yourself. . . .

China

Review Questions

1. Why is the Imperial Palace of the Emperors in Beijing known as the Forbidden City?

2. Why was the Great Wall of China built?

3. Aside from its spicy cuisine, for what is the Sichuan region famous around the world?

4. Guilin provides a home base for cruises on what picturesque river?

5. What can visitors see at Lingyan Temple, west of Hangzhou?

6. What are seemingly half of Shanghai's residents doing in Huangpu Park at sunrise?

7. What famous trade route through western China can tourists of today follow?

8. What is the Jokhang? What is it filled by?

9. Why were 8,000 terra-cotta soldiers, chariots and horses buried in Xi'an 2,200 years ago?

10. What kinds of medical problems might a visitor to China experience? Why?

China

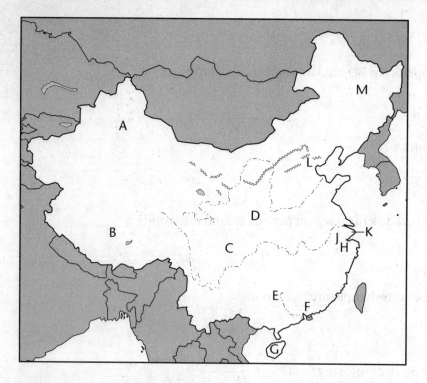

Map Skills Exercise

Match the tourist destination listed below with the corresponding letter on the map. You can use each letter only once.

1. _____ Beijing
2. _____ Tibet
3. _____ Xi'an
4. _____ Guangzhou
5. _____ Chengdu
6. _____ Guilin
7. _____ Shanghai
8. _____ Suzhou
9. _____ Hangzhou

Selling Exercise

(Use Transparency Map #40: China for this exercise.) A client asks you to plot on a map the client's two-week leisure trip to China. She will be visiting five cities: Beijing, Chengdu, Hangzhou, Shanghai and Xi'an. Indicate her arrival airport in China and her departure airport from China on the map (use airport codes), draw in the routes the client will be taking between cities and list recommended attractions, on the map, she should visit in each city.

Hong Kong
Kong

and Macau

A t midnight on 30 June 1997, the British Crown Colony of Hong Kong once again became a part of China. Exactly how this hotbed of capitalism will fit into the Communist system is still a puzzle. Initially, the Chinese stated that they would be happy to leave Hong Kong alone, saying it would have special status. In the last few years, however, China has added an element of uncertainty about the transition, letting it be known that it's grooming Shanghai to become its primary capital of commerce. Many Hong Kong residents anticipate the worst and have emigrated to third countries. Even if China chooses to keep Hong Kong as an entrepreneurial business center, Communist control is certain to change the nature of the colony. We think travelers who want to see Hong Kong as a freewheeling center of enterprise should visit right away.

The British first gained a foothold in Hong Kong in the 1840s, after their victory over the Chinese in the First Opium War. The war had come about because the Chinese wanted to stop the opium trade to their citizens and the British, who were making a lot of money on the trade, wanted it to continue. In British hands, the colony gained an important place as a center of commerce. It also has served as the main avenue for trade between China and the rest of the world. Integration of Hong Kong into China will likely end in a fascinating combination of two very different approaches to market economies. The transition may not be easy, especially for Hong Kong merchants.

Hong Kong is centered around Victoria Harbor, a naturally sheltered deepwater port. The colony consists of numerous islands (including Hong Kong Island) and several hundred square miles of territory on the mainland that is mostly rocky, mountainous terrain. Visitors to Hong Kong often make a side trip to the nearby Portuguese colony of Macau.

What to Do There

Aberdeen   Aberdeen, on Hong Kong Island, is best known for its harbor, where a small portion of the population still lives on boats. Floating restaurants are the main attraction. There are two gigantic ship restaurants, where the typical experience often includes only

Selling Points

Shopping, food, Chinese culture, beaches, nightlife, harbor activity and religious shrines are Hong Kong's chief attractions.

Fascinating Facts About Hong Kong

Ride a rickshaw while you still can. The government is closing down this colonial tradition — it issued the last rickshaw license in 1984 . . . Just across the border at Shenzhen, inside mainland China, is a new attraction called Splendid China. Major structures of China, from Tibet to Beijing, are all on display — in miniature . . .

Even if you're not staying in the Regent, Peninsula or Shangri-La Hotels, enjoy afternoon tea (or drinks) in their lobbies. The view over the harbor and onto Hong Kong Island from the Regent Hotel is one of the most spectacular in the colony . . . Taking the Star Ferry between Kowloon and Hong Kong Island will be one of your fondest memories of Hong Kong. Stand at the railing and watch the activity in Hong Kong Harbor, where sampans mingle with oceangoing freighters. . . .

adequate food, surly service and a bill written in Chinese. Most of the harbor boat tours pause near Ap Lei Chau Island to watch ships being built.

After touring the harbor, head to Ocean Park, outside Aberdeen, to watch trained dolphins and killer whales and to tour an aquarium containing more than 400 species of fish (there's also a roller coaster and a huge aviary with more than 2,000 birds). Adjoining Ocean Park is "The Middle Kingdom," a theme park that recreates the architecture/atmosphere of 13 Chinese dynasties spanning 5,000 years.

Central and Surrounding Districts

Strung along Victoria Harbor, northern Hong Kong Island is both the city's head, heart and pocketbook. This area contains the government and finance centers, as well as the last remnants of old Hong Kong. You'll notice the contrasts immediately: The city's last remaining rickshaw drivers wait to carry you past some space-age skyscrapers.

Stop at the Hong Kong Tourist Association (HKTA) to buy its walking-tour pamphlets. These inexpensive guides will help you get your bearings and find the more interesting, off-the-beaten-track neighborhoods and streets. Several interesting old streets can be found in the area known as Western District. HKTA will also tell you where to find the shopping areas, among them Causeway Bay (Chinese and Japanese department stores), Hollywood Road (a great place for antiques), Cat Street (once a thieves market, now a shopping alley, built on a hill), Egg Street (totally devoted to the processing and selling of eggs — pickled, 100-year-old, salted, fresh, etc.), Landmark Shopping Center (elegant boutiques) and Cloth Alley (the generic name for the alleys with stalls selling cloth and clothing).

After a day's shopping, take the tram to The Peak (Victoria Peak), 1,305 ft/398 m above sea level. Try to arrive about an hour before sunset so you'll have time to walk around this exclusive neighborhood high above the city. Then, after dark, you'll see a view that is spectacular. The entire harbor reflects the bright lights of Kowloon and the Central District. (At the observation point you can have a photo taken of yourself dressed in a traditional Chinese outfit.)

Floating restaurant in Hong Kong

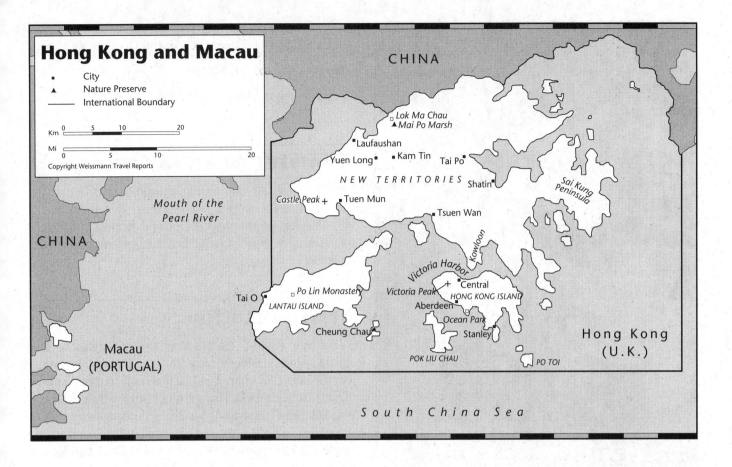

Kowloon   Most travelers visiting Hong Kong stay in Kowloon (Nine Dragons), a peninsula that juts out into Victoria Harbor from the mainland. Many of the best hotels are on or near the Golden Mile, a stretch of Nathan Road within walking distance of hundreds of stores. A few blocks off the Golden Mile are four large, air-conditioned malls. Prices in the malls tend to be higher than in the small shops lining the streets outside. To us, the enclosed shopping centers just don't have the electric feel of Hong Kong. We prefer places like the Sam Shui Po outdoor food market. Other markets include the Jade Market, the Ladies Market (Tung Choi Street) and the Temple Street Market (the last is most active at night). All are outdoors, all cater primarily to residents, and tourists tend to go there to observe rather than for shopping.

Kowloon does have things to do that are unrelated to shopping: Activities include strolling up the Promenade (which runs along Victoria Harbor), visiting the Tin Hau (Taoist sea goddess) Temple and walking along Bird Street (also called Hong Lok Street), where devoted owners feed live grasshoppers to their pets with chopsticks. For an overview on the history of Hong Kong, stop by the Museum of History. To step even farther back in time, stop by the Sung Dynasty Village, a detailed reproduction

of a Sung Dynasty (960–1279) settlement, enlivened by the performances of actors in costume.

Lantau Island   This island's main attraction is the Po Lin (Precious Lotus) Monastery, a beautiful Buddhist temple. The monks there run a restaurant serving vegetarian meals to visitors, and you can overnight at their guest house (though it's not as cheap as other nearby basic accommodations). The monastery recently put the finishing touches on the largest statue of Buddha in Asia — the 273-ton, 112-ft-/34-m-tall statue took more than 10 years to build.

New Territories   The mainland areas to the north of Kowloon are known collectively as the New Territories. Visit Castle Peak, with relaxing beaches, a Buddhist monastery and very good restaurants. While in the area, see the Mai Po Marshes (which house a nature and wildlife reserve), the 17th-century village of Kam Tin (complete with wall and moat) and the Lok Ma Chau vantage point, from which you can see mainland China. Ching Chung Koon Temple is in Tuen Mun, and there's an excellent fish market at Lau Fau Shan. In the New Territories you'll also find the modestly named Temple of 10,000 Buddhas (it actually has 13,000 Buddhas).

Bargaining in one of Hong Kong's markets

Itinerary

If you're seeing Hong Kong as part of a longer Asian itinerary that includes China or Thailand, then you'll find three days sufficient to shop, enjoy the nightlife and watch the sunset from the Peak. If you have time to spend a week in Hong Kong, then the following itinerary will show you the colony in depth:

Day 1 — Arrive Hong Kong.

Day 2 — Shop in Kowloon, then end the day on The Peak.

Day 3 — Morning tour/shopping in Central District. Afternoon tour of Aberdeen, dinner on a floating restaurant.

Day 4 — Ferry to Lantau Island. Either overnight (perhaps at the monastery) or return to Hong Kong/Kowloon hotel.

Day 5 — Ferry back to Hong Kong Island if you stayed

overnight on Lantau. Take a walking tour of a neighborhood near the Central District or sightsee.

Day 6 — Day trip to Macau.

Day 7 — Depart Hong Kong.

Climate/When to Go

We prefer late September to mid-March, when the temperatures are cooler, with October-December best of all. The rest of the year is hot and humid. Typhoons occasionally pop up from July to September, but not every year.

Transportation

Cathay Pacific, Delta, Northwest, Singapore and United offer nonstop service from the U.S., while Cathay Pacific and Canadian Airlines International offer direct flights from Canada. Hong Kong's international airport, Kai Tak (HKG) is 4 mi/7 km from the Star Ferry Pier in Kowloon (it will seem like you are landing right in the middle of downtown). A new airport, Chek Lap Kok, is being built on a landfill off the coast of Lantau Island and is scheduled for completion in 1997.

Hong Kong is a port of call on several cruise lines, and the colony is connected to Macau by jetfoil, high-speed ferry and catamaran; and to China by train, boat and hydrofoil. Buses (comfortable but sometimes crowded) ply the roads on Lantau, Hong Kong Island, Kowloon and the New Territories. Ferries connect the islands to Hong Kong (or occasionally Kowloon). The Star Ferry (founded in 1880) is our favorite way to cross the harbor between Kowloon and Central — you get a ringside seat to harbor activity.

A tram system operates in parts of Central; a subway runs beneath Kowloon and the northern part of Hong Kong Island; and taxis are available everywhere. Rental cars are available, but they aren't recommended unless chauffeured. Bicycles are also available for rent, and there are at least 50 mi/80 km of paths set aside exclusively for pedestrians and cyclists. A railway runs up to the Peak on Hong Kong Island. Take the bus on the way down for a better view of the city's richest neighborhood.

Consider taking the Antique Trams Tours survey of Hong Kong Island — it's done on original Hong Kong trams. Harbor cruises, some passing the spot where the once-great oceanliner the Queen Elizabeth burned and sank, yield yet another perspective of Hong Kong.

Accommodations

Accommodations range from five-star deluxe to dives. Since there are plenty of good hotels, first decide where you want to be (there are excellent properties in Kowloon and on Hong Kong Island). The conventional wisdom is to stay on the island for business, on Kowloon for pleasure. With the colony's excellent transportation facilities, however, we really don't think it makes much difference which side you choose. Hong Kong may well have has more highly rated and award-winning deluxe hotels than any other city in the world.

Health Advisories

In general, medical facilities and hospitals are excellent. British equivalents of medications are available, as are Chinese herbal remedies and acupuncture. Malaria is not present in town, but does occur in rural areas near the Chinese border.

Be especially careful when eating seafood in outlying areas or from street stalls (hepatitis has been transmitted by improperly prepared seafood). Check with your doctor about the advisability of getting a gamma-globulin shot before departure. We recommend that you stick with prepackaged or boiled drinks.

What to Buy

You can buy virtually any consumer item in Hong Kong. And while it's not the shopper's mecca it used to be, there are bargains to be had. You need to do a little preparation. Know exactly what you want before you leave home, and you should take note of what it costs at home. When you get to Hong Kong, don't buy unless the item is far enough below the sale price to justify shipping.

Before handing over any money, make sure that everything works and that all pieces are included. If the item is a brand-name product, make sure that the manufacturer's warranty cards are all there, and that serial numbers on the box match those on the product. Hong Kong merchants are not obligated by law to return or exchange items once purchased.

Prices vary greatly from store to store, so shop around. Bargaining can be done in smaller shops in the main tourist areas. (To give you some idea of costs, the Hong Kong Tourist Association publishes recommended retail prices for a wide variety of goods in a number of free pamphlets.) Cash will usually get you a

better price than credit cards. Stores displaying the Hong Kong Tourist Association sticker are generally considered to subscribe to higher ethics and be of greater reliability than those that don't.

Among the better buys in Hong Kong are cameras, camcorders, stereos, televisions, computer games, tape recorders, binoculars, computers, glasses and contact lenses (take your prescription from home), typewriters, gems (if you know what you're doing), silks, perfume, watches and jewelry, ceramics, Asian art, leather goods, antiques, carpets and clothing (including beautifully tailored suits). Small souvenirs include chopsticks, tea, cinnabar boxes, and kung fu and acupuncture paraphernalia. Make sure that computers and all other electronic goods operate on 110 volts, not 220.

What to Eat

Hong Kong has nearly every type of food available. It's important to understand that Chinese cooking in

Geostats

Official Name: Hong Kong.

Visa Information: Passport and onward ticket required of U.S. and Canadian citizens.

Health Certificates: None required. Contact health authorities for latest information.

Capital: Administrative offices in Victoria.

Population: 5,993,000.

Size: 411 sq mi/1,064 sq km.

Languages: Cantonese, English.

Climate: Tropical, but with defined seasons.

Economy: Industry, trade.

Government: British Crown Colony territory until July 1997.

Religions: Buddhist, Christian.

Currency: Hong Kong dollar (HKD). 100 cents = HU$1. Traveler's checks and credit cards are widely accepted. AE, DC, MC and VI.

Time Zone: 12 hours ahead of eastern standard time; 8 hours ahead of Greenwich mean time.

Electricity: 220 volts.

Departure Tax: HKD 50.

Hong Kong is often different from Chinese food served in the West. It's not uncommon to find the chicken's head, feet and sundry vitals floating in the soup, or to be served an entire fish, complete with eyeballs and scales. Be sure to try dim sum, a breakfast or lunch of small dishes. Waiters or waitresses push carts loaded with bamboo steaming baskets or plates with food. To order, just wave them over and point to what you want (don't feel you need to fill up from one cart — another will be by with something different). Some of our favorite dim sum dishes are shrimp dumplings and steamed barbecue pork bun. More adventuresome eaters may want to try mango pancakes or beef stomach.

Travel Tips for the Client

As in most Asian countries, business discussions are best left until a certain amount of familiarity has been established with your counterpart. Hard-driving, get-right-to-the-point tactics usually backfire . . . Don't change all your money at the airport upon arrival. The rates are better in town. . . .

Do carry a bilingual map with you. It's a misconception that most residents speak English . . . Don't be surprised by people spitting all the time . . . If you get up early, take a walk around. The stores won't be open, but even in the business district you'll pass dozens of Hong Kong residents silently performing tai chi chuan, the Chinese dance/meditation/martial art . . . Tip about 10% in restaurants in addition to the normal 10% service charge. . . .

Macau

The Portuguese territory of Macau is a perfect antidote to the frenzy of Hong Kong. In Macau, everyone slows down. The colony has a much more European flavor than Hong Kong (40 mi/64 km away by sea). The layout of the territory's boulevards and the open plazas remind travelers of Lisbon. Macau gets its revenues from casinos, commerce, light industry and tourism. On weekends and holidays, Macau is filled to capacity with Hong Kong Chinese, who go for the gambling and the slower, more relaxed pace of life. In December 1999, it will come under the control of the People's Republic of China (two years after Hong Kong).

What to Do There

Macau The colony's most famous landmark is the Church of Sao Paulo (circa 1600) — all that remains is the facade (the rest of the church was destroyed by fire in 1835). Up a set of stairs from the church at the Citadel of Sao Paulo do Monte, you can still see the cannon that helped repel the Dutch invasion of 1622; the view of the city and countryside is fantastic (you can see into China).

Once you're back in the city, visit the Temple of Kun Iam — we think it's the nicest religious shrine in Macau (and better than the ones in Hong Kong). We especially liked the lion statues at the gate, the miniature tree that has grown into the shape of the Chinese character for long life, and the statue with the round, bulging eyes (it's supposed to be Marco Polo). The Leal Senado (Loyal Senate) building is perhaps the best example of Portuguese architecture in the colony, and is worth a walk-by. If time permits, tour the maritime museum. Also, take a walk down the Praia Grande to see some of the older buildings, including Government House and the Macau Governor's Residence (built in 1849). At night, the main entertainment revolves around casinos, jai alai and greyhound racing.

Travel Tips for the Client

If you're arriving from Hong Kong, don't worry about changing money. The Hong Kong dollar is accepted everywhere . . . There are nine casinos in Macau: One offers only Chinese games of chance. We think it's the most interesting . . . In Macau, shop for gold jewelry, antiques, watches, cameras, porcelain, pottery and clothing. . . .

Hong Kong and Macau

Review Questions

1. Why was 30 June 1997 an important date in Hong Kong's history?

2. Why can Aberdeen be called a floating city?

3. What should a visitor buy from the Hong Kong Tourist Association? Why?

4. What is the main attraction for tourists at Hollywood Road, Cat Street, Egg Street, and Cloth Alley?

5. Why should a tourist remain at The Peak after dark?

6. What is the name of the peninsula that juts out into the Victoria Harbor from the mainland and is the home of Hong Kong's best hotels?

7. What did the monastery on Lantau Island finish building recently?

8. What is the collective name of the mainland areas to the north of Kowloon?

9. Before shopping for bargains in Hong Kong, how should a traveler prepare at home?

10. On weekends and holidays, why is Macau filled to capacity with Hong Kong Chinese?

Hong Kong and Macau

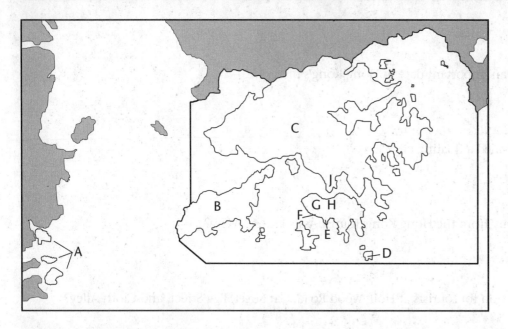

Map Skills Exercise

Match the tourist destination listed below with the corresponding letter on the map. You can use each letter only once.

1. _____ Macau
2. _____ Kowloon
3. _____ Central
4. _____ Victoria Peak
5. _____ Lantau Island

Selling Exercises

A cruise to East Asia has been booked for your clients that includes a two-day stopover in Hong Kong. As your clients would like to take advantage of the two-day stay, they ask your advice as to what five key attractions they should see in Hong Kong and Macau as well as recommendations for shopping and sampling the local cuisine. Prepare a shore excursion itinerary for your clients and include shopping and dining suggestions.

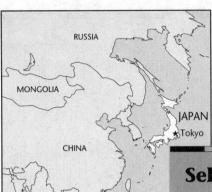

Japan

H igh prices are keeping most travelers from visiting this wonderful destination. (You know a country is expensive when a regular cup of coffee costs US$4.) Still, there are a number of things you can do to keep your trip within a reasonable budget. A Japan Rail Pass provides savings on train travel throughout Japan, including some trips within Tokyo and Kyoto, while daily or weekly subway passes can help trim travel costs within cities.

Accommodations are also pricey, but the Japanese Tourist Board offers a list of less expensive hotels for budget travelers. Another major cost is food, but if you are willing to eat in noodle shops you can get a good meal at an affordable price. And fortunately, some of the most interesting sights in the country are free.

Historians place the date of the founding of Japan around AD 500, with Nara and Kyoto as early capitals. During the next 300 years, the country was greatly influenced by China, borrowing Chinese forms of Buddhism, government and written language, but then changing them to make them Japan's own. At the same time, the shoguns (military leaders) built a feudal system that lasted into the 19th century. During the late 19th century, Japan was transformed from a backward isolationist country to one of the world's leading powers. In the first half of the 20th century it conquered Korea and seized the province of Manchuria from China. Japanese expansion was finally stopped during World War II by the United States and its allies. After the war, Japan began what can only be described as an economic miracle: The country was transformed from an exhausted, occupied nation into an economic powerhouse in just a few decades. It's now a driving force in the world economy.

Japan consists of four major islands (Hokkaido, Honshu, Shikoku and Kyushu) and thousands of smaller ones. Two-thirds of the country is covered by mountains.

What to Do There

Hiroshima   When the first atomic bomb exploded over Hiroshima on 6 August 1945 the city became an immediate symbol for the horrors of war. Today, Hiroshima has several moving reminders

Selling Points

Mt. Fuji, gardens, shopping, cherry blossoms, cultural attractions (from palaces, historic sites and temples to sumo wrestling and Kabuki theater), bullet trains, beaches, fishing, war (and peace) memorials and religious shrines are among the chief attractions of Japan.

Japan is a wonderful, fascinating and, unless you're very careful, an incredibly expensive destination. Do not go if you are on a tight budget or are uncomfortable among dense crowds or in confining spaces. Be aware that you'll have to do a lot of walking to explore most attractions.

Fascinating Facts About Japan

Visitors to Japan, especially those going on business, will generate respect for themselves (and avoid possible embarrassment) if they will learn a few Japanese customs. Always keep in mind that Japanese society is much more formal and hierarchical than in the West. Never call Japanese by their first names, especially in business circles. Handshakes are becoming more and more common, but if a hand is not extended toward you, be prepared to bow.

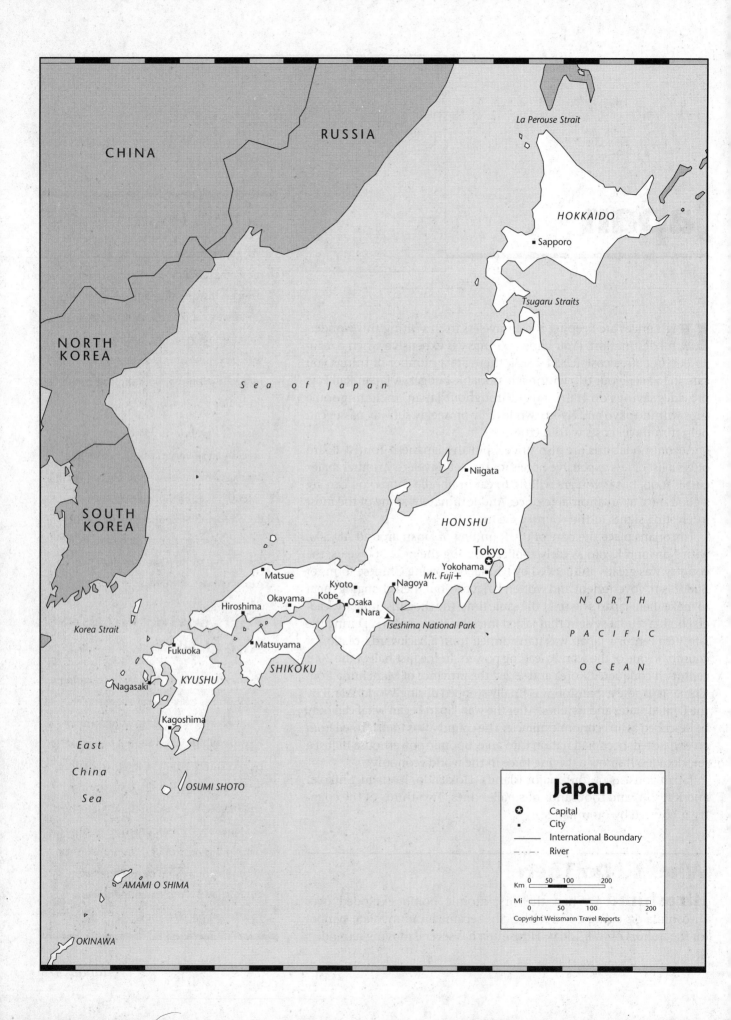

CHINA

RUSSIA

La Perouse Strait

HOKKAIDO

■ Sapporo

NORTH
KOREA

Tsugaru Straits

Sea of Japan

SOUTH
KOREA

■ Niigata

HONSHU

Tokyo
★

Yokohama ■
Mt. Fuji +

■ Matsue

Kyoto
Kobe ■
Okayama ■
Osaka
Hiroshima ■   ■ Nara
Nagoya ■

Korea Strait

Fukuoka ■

■ Matsuyama

SHIKOKU

▲
Iseshima National Park

NORTH

PACIFIC

OCEAN

KYUSHU

Nagasaki ■

Kagoshima ■

East

China

Sea

OSUMI SHOTO

Japan

★ Capital
■ City
— International Boundary
-··-·· River

Km 0 50 100   200

Mi 0   50   100   200

Copyright Weissmann Travel Reports

AMAMI O SHIMA

OKINAWA

of that day of utter devastation. Peace Park, the Cenotaph for the Victims and the Atomic Bomb Memorial should all be visited. Only a short distance from Hiroshima is the most famous bridge in Japan, the Kintai-kyo. Built in 1673, the Brocade Sash Bridge is composed of five gracefully arched spans.

Kyoto

If you can visit only one city in Japan, Kyoto is the one. This ancient city was the capital of Japan for more than a thousand years. Begin your visit at the Nanzen Temple, which has a pretty view of the city. From there, stroll down the Philosopher's Walk (a footpath along a canal lined with cherry trees) to the Ginkakuji (called the Silver Pavilion, though the plan to cover it in silver was never carried out). Ginkakuji has a pretty garden with a stylized version of Mt. Fuji crafted from sand. Its counterpart, Kinkakuju (the Golden Pavilion), is much more impressive — this beautiful, three-story structure is covered in gold foil. Don't miss the 17th-century Nijo Castle, which has beautiful gardens and an ornate interior. The castle also has a wonderfully Japanese security system: the floor boards were designed to make the sound of a nightingale when walked upon. Another wonder is the Sanjusangendo, a hall built in 1266 that's famous for its 1,000-handed statue of Kannon, the sometimes goddess, sometimes god, of compassion.

The city's most sublime garden is the Zen Garden of Emptiness in the Ryoanji (Temple of the Peaceful Dragon). The garden consists of 15 rocks scattered artfully on a bed of raked pebbles (the rocks are arranged so that one rock is always hidden from view). The Imperial Palace is also in the city, but requires advance permission from the Japanese Tourist Office to visit. Also head to the Traditional and Japanese Arts Theater, which presents authentic demonstrations of flower arranging, court music, and the tea ceremony. We especially liked the National Museum, which exhibits ancient porcelains, swords and kimonos.

Mt. Fuji

Mt. Fuji

This familiar snow-capped symbol of Japan is 12,388 ft/3,774 m high. Five trails lead to the summit; each hike takes nine hours. (If you're not sure you can climb the whole length, you can cheat a bit and start out on a bus that brings you to the fifth rest stop.) The season for climbing is the beginning of July until the end of August.

Nara

The first capital of Japan, Nara (pop. 349,000) makes an interesting day trip from Kyoto. The ancient architecture of Nara is well worth seeing, especially the Todai Temple. The temple qualifies for two Guinness Book of World Records mentions: Its Buddha is the largest bronze in the world and its main building is the world's largest wooden building. Another delight is Kusuga Shrine, which has thousands of paper lanterns.

Osaka

Osaka is the third-largest city in Japan. The city is a major commercial center and a lot of its energy revolves around buying and selling. To get a feeling of Osaka, head to the Shinsaibashi area south of downtown. One interesting place you'll find here is the America Mura, a 12-block area of U.S.-oriented youth-culture clothing and music stores. There is a two-story painting of Marilyn Monroe's face, a skyscraper with a Statue of Liberty on top and a store called South Bronx that sells gangsta rap clothing.

The Ginza in Tokyo

There is also a traditional side to Osaka. The city is an important center of Bunraku, the traditional Japanese puppet theater. The puppets are amazingly realistic and require three men to manipulate. Other sites include the Osaka Castle and the Shin-kabuki-za (New Kabuki Theater). Also near Osaka is the city of Kobe, devastated by a major earthquake in 1994.

Tokyo

Tokyo (pop. 11,936,000) is like a group of cities rather than just one. The most commonly visited areas are: Akihabara (for shopping — discount electronics, in particular), Asakusa (temples), Ginza (high-end shopping), Marunouchi (Imperial Palace), Roppongi (nightlife), Shibuyaku (shrines and trendy shopping), Shinjuku (shopping amidst skyscrapers) and Ueno (beautiful park, museums and temples).

In Ginza, some of the stores are attractions unto themselves, showcasing items such as typical wedding-kimono ensembles and scheduling everything from fashion shows to tea ceremonies. If nothing else, stop in and look at the displays at the Sony Building (don't miss the high-density-TV viewing room). Ginza is most active between noon and 6 pm on Sundays.

Less well known, but of more interest to most travelers, is the Ueno district, which holds some of the city's best sights. Start at Ueno Park — inside its beautiful grounds are the Tokyo National Museum (the world's largest collection of Japanese art), the National Museum of Western Art (great French impressionist collection) and the Shitamachi History Museum (fascinating depiction of the daily life of Japan's lower class). Try to visit in April, when the cherry trees are laden with blossoms.

Another must-see is the Meiji Shrine and Treasure Museum. Located in Yoyogi Park, Meiji is Japan's most impressive Shinto (the native Japanese religion) shrine. Weekends are the best time to visit the park. You'll see brides having their pictures taken in elegant kimonos, free concerts, and groups of Japanese kids dressed up like Elvis or punk rockers.

In the heart of the city is the Marunouchi area, home of the Emperor's Imperial Palace. The palace itself is only open two days a year (2 Jan and 23 Dec), but the gardens are open year round.

In contrast to Ueno is Shinjuku, the district with the city's tallest skyscrapers and most futuristic atmosphere. It's home to the trendiest shopping areas and operates as an entertainment district at night. The best entertainment can be found on weekends at the main square — there's a giant TV screen, hordes of musicians, miles of neon, an assortment of hucksters and enough people watching to last a lifetime. You can find everything from 24-hour baseball batting cages to the city's red-light district.

Another very modern shopping district is just south of Ueno: the Akihabara Electric City. This is the largest concentration of electronics shops in the world. Then there's the Roppongi district, jam-packed with nightclubs, some of which specifically target English-speaking clientele. For more traditional entertainment, try to get tickets for a Kabuki (Japanese theater) performance. We recommend renting the headphones for performances, which provide English translations.

Finally, plan to ride a Tokyo train or subway at least once, even if there's no destination in mind (get on and off quickly — the doors close automatically, regardless of whether someone's in the way).

We don't recommend visiting the Tokyo Disneyland; there's not much there that you won't find in Disney parks in the U.S. or Europe at lower prices. Instead, see if you can interest the kids in a visit to Wild Blue Yokohama, a huge indoor beach.

Geostats

Official Name: Japan.

Visa Information: Passport and proof of onward passage and sufficient funds needed by U.S. and Canadian citizens for stay of 90 days or less.

Health Certificates: None required. Contact health authorities for latest information.

Capital: Tokyo.

Population: 125,506,000.

Size: 145,856 sq mi/377,765 sq km. Slightly smaller than California.

Language: Japanese.

Climate: Temperate to cold.

Economy: Trade, industry, services.

Government: Parliamentary democracy.

Religions: Shinto, Buddhist, Christian.

Currency: Yen (JYE). Traveler's checks and credit cards accepted.

Time Zone: 13 hours ahead of eastern standard time; 9 hours behind Greenwich mean time.

Electricity: 100 volts.

Departure Tax: 2000 yen.

Itinerary

The seven-night itinerary below includes the bare minimum that a first-time visitor to Japan must see and do.

Day 1 — Arrive Tokyo.

Day 2 — Tokyo.

Day 3 — Tokyo.

Day 4 — Bullet train to Kyoto.

Day 5 — Kyoto.

Day 6 — Day trip to Hiroshima. Overnight Kyoto.

Day 7 — Day trip to Nara. Overnight Kyoto.

Day 8 — Depart Japan from Osaka.

Climate/When to Go

The temperature varies widely over the country on any given day. In general, the best times to visit are in October and April, when the foliage is changing and the temperatures are mild during the day and cool at night. May, June and July are the rainiest months, and June, July and August are hotter and more humid. Winter months can become quite cold — parts of Japan are on the same latitude as Siberia — and the areas that aren't terribly cold will most likely be drizzly and dreary.

Transportation

Japan Airlines, VARIG, Korean Air, Delta, United Airlines, Northwest, All Nippon Airlines, Malaysia Airlines and Singapore Airlines offer direct flights to Japan from the U.S. Canadian Airlines and Japan Airlines fly from Canada. All Nippon and Japan Airlines offer frequent connections between major Japanese cities. There are two airports serving Tokyo: Haneda (HND), 11 mi/18 km from city center, is infinitely more convenient than Narita (NRT), 41 mi/66 km from Tokyo. Be sure to take a guidebook to get into Tokyo, or have someone meet you at the airport who knows the transportation system. If you know what you're doing and do it right, it takes about an hour to get from Narita to Tokyo. Don't take a cab unless you're willing to pay at least US$250.

Once in Tokyo, there is excellent rail service to points throughout the country, including some new double-decker first-class and dining cars on the bullet trains (Shinkansen). The tiers of classes and services offered for trains can be baffling, so we recommend buying a Japan Rail Pass before you leave home to prevent confusion and to save time and money. The Tokyo-Osaka run takes two hours while regular trains take six. Countrywide buses are reasonably priced, and there are also very good coastal steamships sailing between many cities.

You can get around via escorted tours or rented car (with or without driver), but it's not advisable to drive yourself on your first visit. Not only does traffic move on the left, but traffic laws differ from those elsewhere. We recommend escorted or hosted tours for first-time visitors. Subways can be used to get around in cities. They're color coded and very easy to use.

Accommodations

Accommodations range from very deluxe international to country family inns and pensions. Most fall into one of two categories: the business hotels (designed with Westerners in mind — the toilets will look familiar) and the traditional Japanese-style hotels, called minshuku and ryokans. The traditional hotels are truly fascinating: Minshuku are family-owned bed-and-breakfast-type properties, ranging in price from inexpensive to moderately priced. Ryokans are larger hotels ranging from inexpensive to expensive. Little English is spoken in either. If claustrophobia is not a problem, keep an eye out for the special hotels whose "rooms" are rows of cubbyholes set in a wall, complete with phone and TV.

Note for Business Travelers: Keep in mind that where you stay will be interpreted as a reflection of your company's stature and success. Staying in a cheap hotel can have serious business consequences when dealing with the status-conscious Japanese, especially if your competitors are in upscale accommodations.

Health Advisories

Medical practices differ from those in the West somewhat, but conditions are up to Western standards. Proof of sufficient funds may be required before you are treated in Japanese hospitals or clinics. Water is safe to drink, and restaurants maintain standards equivalent to those in the West.

Note: Clean out your medicine bag before you travel to

The Tea Ceremony

Japan. A surprising number of over-the-counter cold medicines (such as Vicks Inhalers and Sudafed) contain small amounts of amphetamines or amphetamine-like drugs, which makes them illegal in Japan.

What to Buy

Shop for pearls, lacquerware, silks, pottery, furniture, jewelry, furs, cloisonne, paper lanterns, dolls, imari porcelain, shells and red coral, cameras, china, crystal, art, local handicrafts, weavings, silkscreens and fabric. A word or two about lacquerware: A lot of the shiki (black) lacquerware comes from the Kuroe district; today, you'll find that modern designs (in/out trays, for example) are at least as plentiful as the more traditional boxes and trays. Look carefully before you buy — these days, most lacquerware has a plastic, rather than wood, base. Avoid buying electronic goods, since these are frequently more expensive than those same products sold in North America or Europe. Pearls and silks can also be rather expensive, so familiarize yourself with sale prices of these items prior to leaving home.

What to Eat

As would be expected, the sushi (raw fish, rice, seaweed and vegetables) is excellent. Other specialties are Kobe beefsteak (very expensive), sukiyaki, salt- and freshwater fish (often served whole), miso soup and a wide variety of vegetables. Try teriyaki, *gyoza* (dumplings) and *ochawan mushi* (a kind of egg custard) in the winter. Tofu is common, and in fancy restaurants it may be served in different shapes and colors (order *tofu dengaku* to see a good variety). Those on a budget may want to have a quick and delicious meal at a noodle shop, Japan's primary fast-food outlet. Japan is a good country for vegetarians to visit, and it also boasts excellent Chinese food. We recommend (discreetly) looking at the dishes on the other tables and (discreetly) pointing out to the waiter what looks good to you. There are also many Continental restaurants in most cities as well as McDonald's, Pizza Hut and other fast-food imports.

More Fascinating Facts About Japan

Business people always exchange business cards — the protocol is to present your card (be sure to have bilingual cards made) to your counterpart with both hands, then accept his or her card with both hands, look at it closely, give a slight bow, and put it away carefully, preferably in a card holder. Remember that spouses are not welcome at business meetings or dinners . . .

Should you have the occasion to use a traditional Japanese bath, soap and rinse before you step into the bath tub and don't pull the plug after you are done (the same water is used for the next person) . . . A small gift is always appropriate when visiting Japanese in their homes . . . Sumo wrestling is Japan's national sport . . . Only major stores take credit cards. Small ones won't even take traveler's checks in yen . . . Many Japanese read and write English better than they speak and comprehend it. So try writing out your messages . . . Since nearly all restaurants provide only chopsticks, either learn to use them or carry a collapsible fork and spoon. . . .

Travel Tips for the Client

Do see a baseball game or a Japanese movie. Reserved tickets are sold for both . . . Do be aware that you will have to remove your shoes quite often when visiting many of Japan's attractions . . . Don't, under any circumstances, walk into a temple wearing shoes . . . Do try to learn some basic Japanese, including "thank you" (arigato), "good morning" (ohiyo), "good day" (konnichi wa) and "goodbye" (sayonara) . . . .

Do take tissues everywhere. Often you won't find any paper in the bathrooms. And take cloth hankies, as the bathrooms don't always have paper towels and restaurants don't provide napkins . . . Don't blow your nose in public; delicately dab at it with a neatly folded hanky, if you must . . . Do be aware that there can be severe criminal punishments for even minor crimes, including traffic accidents . . . Don't tip, as it's considered rude. . . .

Japan

Review Questions

1. What are Hokkaido, Honshu, Shikoku and Kyushu?

2. What historic event happened over Hiroshima on 6 August 1945?

3. In what ancient city can a visitor see Kinkakuju, Nijo Castle, and the Zen Garden of Emptiness?

4. What is the familiar snow-capped symbol of Japan?

5. What will a visitor find in the area of Osaka known as America Mura?

6. Why can some stores in Ginza be considered attractions unto themselves?

7. What is Japan's national sport?

8. Why wouldn't you recommend the Tokyo Disneyland to an American or European client?

9. What should a business traveler in Japan keep in mind about his or her accommodations?

10. Why would a traveler in Japan want to eat at a noodle shop?

Japan

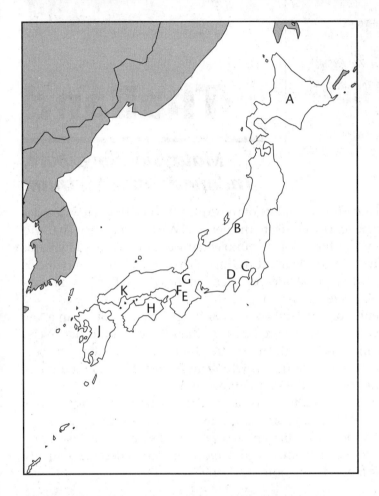

Map Skills Exercise

Match the tourist destination listed below with the corresponding letter on the map. You can use each letter only once.

1. _____ Tokyo
2. _____ Mt. Fuji
3. _____ Kyoto
4. _____ Osaka
5. _____ Nara
6. _____ Hiroshima
7. _____ Hokkaido
8. _____ Kyushu

Selling Exercises

A sales trip to Japan has been booked for one of your business travelers. The client will be staying in the Shinjuku area of Tokyo for four days while conducting business. This will be the first time this traveler has been to Japan and the person is asking for business tips. Based on what you learned in the chapter, list five business tips you might suggest.

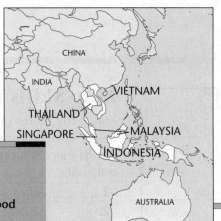

Thailand

Malaysia, Singapore, Indonesia and Vietnam

Thailand offers the allure of the exotic, tempered by a few decades of experience catering to the needs of Western travelers. Thailand is the only Southeast Asian country that was not colonized by Europeans. The ruins throughout northern Thailand are the remnants of kingdoms whose royal lineages extend to the current king, a very popular and respected monarch.

The center of Thailand consists of flat plains no more than a few feet above sea level, watered by the Chao Phraya and other rivers. There are mountains in the north stretching southward along the border with Myanmar (Burma), high plains in the east, and mountains and jungle covering the southern peninsula.

Other countries in the region are also fascinating destinations. Trips to nearby Malaysia and Singapore are often packaged with a visit to Thailand. Indonesia, a bit farther away, may be best visited on a separate trip, while Vietnam, closed to most tourists for decades, is finally becoming a hot destination.

What to Do There

Bangkok Thailand's capital city is large (pop. 5,876,000), modern and progressive, but it doesn't intimidate visitors — the buildings aren't too tall, the people are usually polite, the sidewalks aren't overly crowded, and it has one of the lowest crime rates (against tourists, at least) in the world. However, it does have more than its share of traffic jams, noise and pollution. You'll find that you can often get to places faster by walking than by taking a taxi or bus. We recommend that you use the water taxis whenever possible.

Bangkok's temples, despite being in the center of a thriving modern metropolis, are some of the finest and most ornate in all of Asia. The most spectacular are in the same complex: the Grand Palace and the Temple of the Emerald Buddha (Wat Phra Keo). These sights, with their fantastic roof lines and spires, are bright, extravagant and richly ornamented. Wat Arun (Temple of the Dawn) is on the other side of the Chao Phraya River and should also be visited; classic Thai dancers are sometimes there (be prepared to pay them

Temple of the Emerald Buddha

a fee for posing). Another good place to see dancers in traditional dress is at the small Erawan Shrine at the corner of Ratcha-Damri Road and Sumkumvit. Very popular with locals and camera-toting foreigners, the shrine is a nice place to enjoy the music and dance. Another important temple is that of the Reclining Buddha, which boasts the largest (152 ft/46 m long) Buddha in Thailand. Walk its whole length — the mother-of-pearl feet are sensational. Be sure also to tour the *klongs* (canals). The floating market that once bobbed on the *klongs* has now moved to shore and is rather touristy. Other canals, however, where the people live, are interesting.

Other sights in Bangkok include the National Museum (a great introduction to the country's history and artifacts); the Red Cross Snake Farm (to watch venomous snakes being milked); the Weekend Market near Chatuchack Park (there's a little bit of everything, including neat arrangements of giant dead roaches for sale in the food section); and Chinatown.

Jim Thompson's House brings alive the era of an American who was almost solely responsible for reintroducing Thailand's silk-weaving industry; his home is a tribute to Thai art and architecture. Vimanmek Mansion, the world's largest golden teakwood building, is filled with priceless antiques and paintings. Also, visit the Royal Barges, which are housed on Klong Bangkok Noi across from the Thonburi Railway station. They're magnificent boats used by the king and for special occasions.

Much is made of Patpong, the red-light district. Not much goes on there that doesn't occur in other countries, but rightly or wrongly, people feel safe on the streets in the area.

There are several day trips from Bangkok that should be considered, among them the royal ruins at Ayutthaya and the Thai Cultural Village (performances of traditional dance and music). Ayutthaya was the capital of Thailand during the period 1350–1767. It has a well-preserved complex of temple and palace ruins.

Chiang Mai

Chiang Mai is Thailand's second most cosmopolitan city, after Bangkok. It is located in the hilly Golden Triangle, where much of the world's opium is grown. Chiang Mai itself is quite pleasant: It has most of Bangkok's amenities (including excellent food and accommodations) without the quicker pace, traffic jams and pollution. Most people use the town as a jumping-off point for exploring the region.

Chiang Mai is an ancient city and the moat around the original town is still intact. There are several old and interesting *wats* (temples), among them Wat Suan Dawk (with an adjoining handicraft shop), Wat Chiang Man. See the Elephant Training School on the Chiang Rai-Lampang road near Lampang. For another driving excursion, go to Phuping Palace (the royal family's winter residence).

Chiang Mai-Area Treks

A popular activity for energetic travelers is to explore the Golden Triangle, a region around Chiang Mai. The area is remote, so the most practical way to see it is to walk, or trek. The organized treks into the surrounding tribal hill country usually last four nights, stopping in a different village each night. An elephant ride and river rafting are now often included in the price.

There are several risks, however. Among the horror stories we've heard from trekkers were that they were robbed by armed bandits. Our five-day sojourn into the hill country was the highlight of our trip to Thailand, but please choose your trekking group with great care.

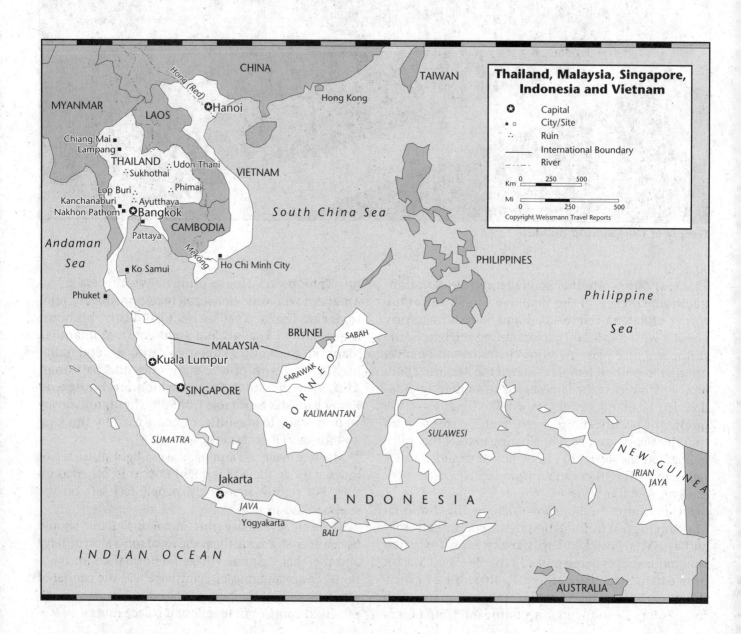

Islands   There are a number of resort islands off the coast of Thailand. One is Phuket (pronounced poo-KET), which is large and highly developed. It's located 570 mi/917 km south of Bangkok. The island features a tropical beach (Patong Beach), excellent accommodations and food, snorkeling and other water activities and sightseeing. Visitors can tour rubber plantations, batik factories and a crocodile farm. Another important island is Ko Samui, which has recently undergone intensive development but is still very pleasant.

Kanchanaburi   The attraction here is the nearby bridge over the River Kwai. Many Allied prisoners of war perished during World War II building the infamous Death Railway that ran over the bridge. Visit the nearby museum, which chronicles life in the POW camps and the history of the jungle railroad's construction (there is even a simulated Allied bombardment). Also take a walk through the immaculately maintained Allied War Cemetery, where you'll find the graves of more than 8,000 POWs who died working on the bridge and railway for the Japanese Army. It's a very moving experience. Also, take a side trip to Nakhon Pathom to see the largest Buddhist monument in Thailand.

Pattaya   On the Gulf of Thailand, this resort was developed in 1968 and has since become a major Southeast Asia tourist beach. Pattaya attracts more visitors than any other destination in Thailand, save Bangkok. Because of sewage runoff, the main beach along the strip is periodically unsuitable for swimming; outlying beach areas are still okay for swimming and other water sports. What is euphemistically called bachelor nightlife is the main attraction for some visitors (primarily Northern Europeans). We recommend avoiding Pattaya — there are many other beach areas that are much nicer. If you do decide to go there, take the glass-bottom boat to see the coral off the nearby island of Ko Laan.

Ruins   The ruins of northern and northeastern Thailand are exceptional. Many are in cities that were once capitals, and the remains are unusually well preserved. Since they were built in various time periods, each is unique, and it's possible to visit them all and not worry about being bored. You can make a loop north and northeast from Bangkok and see all of the important ruins in about five days using a rented car with driver (or in a week if you're taking trains and buses). The route would be Bangkok-Ayutthaya-Lop Buri-Sukhothai-Udon Thani-Phimai-Bangkok. Sukhothai, Thailand's first capital, has the most interesting and varied ruins in the country.

Itinerary

The itinerary below will give first-time visitors a good feel for the country:

Day 1 — Arrive Bangkok.

Day 2 — Bangkok.

Geostats

Official Name: Kingdom of Thailand.

Visa Information: Passports and proof of onward passage and sufficient funds are required of U.S. and Canadian citizens who are staying up to 30 days and entering via the major airports. Visas required for longer stays, entry at other airports or for overland entry. Persons with AIDS will be denied entry.

Health Certificates: Yellow-fever certificate required of any traveler arriving from an infected area or endemic zone.

Capital: Bangkok.

Population: 60,271,000.

Size : 198,500 sq mi/514,115 sq km. About 3/4 the size of Texas.

Languages: Thai, dialects.

Climate: Tropical monsoon.

Economy: Agriculture, industry, tourism.

Government: Constitutional monarchy.

Religion: Buddhist.

Currency: Baht (BHT). 100 satang = 1 BHT. Traveler's checks and credit cards are widely accepted. AE, DC, MC and VI.

Time Zone: 12 hours ahead of eastern standard time; 7 hours ahead of Greenwich mean time.

Electricity: 220 volts.

Departure Tax: BHT200 for international departures; BHTD30 for domestic travel.

Day 3 — Day trip to Sukhotai. Overnight Bangkok.

Day 4 — Go to Phuket or Ko Samui.

Day 5 — Another day on whichever island is chosen.

Day 6 — Travel to Chiang Mai (may require overnight in Bangkok).

Day 7 — Chiang Mai.

Day 8 — Chiang Mai.

Day 9 — Chiang Mai.

Day 10 — Return to Bangkok and depart Thailand.

Climate/When to Go

The weather in Thailand is always hot and humid, although the northern highlands are generally 10 degrees F/5 C cooler. The best time to go is November-February. March-May is very hot. Avoid mid-May through October, when it's humid and rainy (the streets of Bangkok flood easily).

Transportation

Thai International Airways, United, Delta and Northwest offer frequent flights from the U.S., and Canadian Airlines International and Thai International fly from Canada. The International Airport (BKK) is 18 mi/29 km from Bangkok. It's also possible to arrive overland (by train or bus) from Malaysia and Laos. Thai Airways connects larger cities internally. Train service is adequate (the stations are exceptionally well maintained). Rails go north to Chiang Mai (sleeping cars and air-conditioning available on some routes). Express bus service between Bangkok and other cities is excellent. Transport on Bangkok's river is by launch, motorized longboats or river taxis (which make scheduled stops near major attractions). If you rent a car, get a driver, too — it doesn't cost that much more, and it's worth the money. Roads are generally good. Traffic moves on the left.

Accommodations

Accommodations include deluxe hotels and resorts, guest houses, thatched-roof huts on beaches and very basic lodging in small villages. Bangkok boasts a number of world-class deluxe hotels. As a general rule in Thailand, try to get a room that doesn't face the main street, as those on the street tend to catch a lot of noise.

Health Advisories

Outside of Bangkok, Chiang Mai and major beach resorts, sanitary conditions in most restaurants are not up to Western standards. Assume the water is unsafe. Malaria is present in some of the border areas (although not in Bangkok or other tourist places). Skin infections are common; even the smallest wound should be disinfected and covered with a bandage. Most common prescription medicines are available.

If you're on a trek in the Golden Triangle, you'll likely be offered a chance to smoke opium. We strongly advise against it. Be aware that nausea is a common side effect. In the case of intimate encounters, take precautions (AIDS is a serious problem in Thailand).

More Fascinating Facts About Thailand

Anna and the King of Siam took place in Bangkok, but don't praise the book (or *The King and I,* the play and movie based on it) to Thais; they find it to be an offensive and condescending portrayal of one of their greatest kings . . .

One phrase you'll hear often is *mai penh rai.* It means "it's nothing" and is used the way "no problem" is in English. . . .

What to Buy

Shop for lacquerware, celadon (greenish in color) pottery, painted umbrellas, silks, tribal weavings and handicrafts, temple rubbings, custom-made shoes and clothing, bronze, silver, sapphires and rubies, pillows, temple bells, sand paintings and carved water buffalo bells. You may not export Buddha images. Bargaining is common in markets and with street vendors, though not in shops. Those Rolex watches and Lacoste shirts sold on street corners are, of course, not genuine.

Preparing Thai desserts

What to Eat

Thai food is our favorite Asian cuisine. The variety of vegetable and meat dishes is astonishing, and the presentation at better restaurants is a work of art, so pause to take a look at the vegetable and fruit carvings before popping them in your mouth. Pork, poultry and some beef are used; seafood is outstanding. Try *tom yum koong,* a spicy shrimp soup. We like the street food, which is generally safe to eat in Bangkok. Try the barbecued chicken legs, omelettes, sweet crepes, and sticky rice and taro rolled up in a leaf (don't eat the leaf!). Thailand is a paradise for tropical fruits — and tropical fruit lovers. There are more than 20 kinds of banana. Definitely try rambutan (*ngau* in Thai). It tastes like a sweet lemon.

Travel Tips for the Client

Don't go shirtless or in shorts, and don't wear beach attire anywhere except on the beach . . . Don't touch the heads of Thais (not even children!) . . . Do visit a celadon-pottery factory. As the glaze cools and cracks, the air is filled with hundreds of musical pings . . . Do be careful of the con games in Bangkok; some even include Westerners posing as tourists . . . Tip waiters 10%. . . .

Malaysia

Malaysia has almost as much to offer as Thailand: great beaches and resorts, modern shopping, unique tribal cultures and fantastic displays of nature (from butterflies and sea turtles to orangutans and elephants) — with a bit less traffic. Prices are surprisingly low.

The country comprises two main regions: the southern part of the Malay Peninsula and the northern coast of Borneo (the provinces of Sarawak and Sabah). In both areas, coastal lowlands give way to mountainous interiors. Tropical vegetation abounds. Malaysia is one of the most prosperous Southeast Asian countries.

What to Do There

Kuala Lumpur   Malaysia's capital city sits in a valley surrounded by jagged hills. Chief among the attractions are the Parliament House, the Jame Mosque and the National Zoo and Aquarium (animals in lush, natural surroundings — it's one of the finest in Asia). We also like touring the National Museum (natural history and Malay cultural displays). The Central Market, once the city's fish, vegetable and food market, is now a huge center with restaurants and good shopping for quality brand-name and handicraft items.

Travel Tips for the Client

Use only your right hand when touching food. The other hand is reserved for unclean things . . . Don't bring up the topic of ethnic relations in Malaysia; it is a very sensitive subject . . . Don't even think about buying or transporting illegal drugs — there's a mandatory death penalty for trafficking.

Singapore

Actually a city-state, Singapore is one of the economic success stories of Asia. In a relatively short time, it has been transformed from a backward, swampy place with no natural resources into one of Asia's capitalist powerhouses. The city-state is a good destination for those who enjoy shopping or want to spend some time in a big, modern city during a visit to some less developed regions of Southeast Asia. Things to buy there include cameras, watches, Thai silks, batiks (try Arab Street), wood carvings, porcelain, leather and suede goods, Chinese antiques, electronics, gems and Persian carpets. The population is predominantly ethnic-Chinese, but also includes many people of Malay, Indian and European descent.

What to Do There

Singapore City
Try a cruise to get a feel for the busiest harbor in the world. Then it's fun to spend some time walking around, especially in the ethnic neighborhoods. Chinatown is the cultural soul of the city. Wander its streets and visit the Fuk Tak Ch'i Temple — featuring a god of wealth. Add to the atmosphere by riding in a tricycle rickshaw. Then visit Little India and Arab Street. The gold-domed Sultan Mosque is the heart of Arab Street. The area is especially interesting to visit around Ramadan, the Muslim month of daytime fasting, when the streets are filled nightly with food stalls. Don't miss the Colonial District with vestiges of times of British rule. The newly restored Empress Place is a museum in former colonial buildings. For shopping, head to Orchard Road where you'll find the big stores and nice shops.

Travel Tips for the Client

Don't miss the various religious temples, including Hindu, Moslem, Taoist and Buddhist . . . Drug laws are taken very seriously here, particularly those regarding narcotics. Penalties range from whippings with a cane and a prison sentence to death . . . Most buildings in Singapore are nonsmoking . . . Fines are aplenty. So don't litter (fine S$625), don't forget to flush a public toilet (S$94) and don't eat or drink on the subway (S$314), etc. . . .

Indonesia

Indonesia, at one time part of the Dutch colonial empire, stretches across the waters between Asia and Australia. Of its thousands of islands, only six are considered major: Bali, Java, Sulawesi, Sumatra, Irian Jaya (on New Guinea) and Kalimantan (part of the island of Borneo).

Muslim mosques and Hindu temples, puppet shows, the gorgeous beaches of Bali, the giant lizards of Komodo and live volcanoes scattered throughout the islands are all part of the Indonesian experience. Combined with the friendly people — 350 ethnic groups, speaking 250 languages — the sights and sounds of Indonesia make it one of East Asia's most compelling vacation spots.

What to Do There

Bali
This island is, without a doubt, the most popular stop in Indonesia. Bali's unique Hindu culture, volcanoes, rhythmic and flowing dances, rice paddies, indescribably beautiful jungle and mountain scenery, friendly people and spectacular beaches — combined with world-class hotels and food — make it one of the most interesting islands you'll find anywhere on earth. The best way to see the "real" Bali is to hire a car and driver and head inland.

Jakarta
Jakarta, Indonesia's capital, is a crowded and polluted city. It's best to tour it quickly and get out as soon as possible. Jakarta's sights include Merdeka Square, a batik factory (allow at least an hour), Old Batavia (also called Kota, it has colonial Dutch buildings), the old Dutch East India Company fortress and the port at Sunda Kelapa. Recreational sites include the Jakarta Zoo (see a Komodo dragon there) and the Bogor Botanical Garden and Orchid House (truly one of the most spectacular gardens in the world). South of town, Taman Mini-Indonesia Indah is a cultural park with 27 pavilions re-creating architecture and customs from around the country.

Yogyakarta
Yogyakarta is Java's cultural capital. It can be reached by air, train, bus or car from Jakarta. Among the sights are the Sultan's Palace, a museum (modern Indonesian paintings), Kalasan Temple and the Kota Gede silverworks. Yogyakarta is a good place to buy

Fascinating Facts About Indonesia

There are still 5,000 elephants in the country, mostly in Sumatra . . . 34% of the world's active volcanoes are located in Indonesia . . . The island of Java is one of the most densely populated places in the world, with 1,500 people per square mile/577 people per square kilometer. . . .

batik. See the shadow puppets and the three-dimensional wooden puppets plays if you can. Try to include a trip to Borobudur, an elaborate 1,000- year-old Buddhist temple complex (promoted as the world's largest).

Travel Tips for the Client

Don't ever drink the water from the tap, regardless of what the hotel tells you . . . Don't sign traveler's checks unless the cashier watches you sign. Indonesian banks may refuse to cash your check if they weren't watching every stroke of the pen . . . Do travel light. It's easier, and chances are that you'll find many interesting souvenirs to fill your suitcase. . . .

Vietnam

Ravaged by war and politically isolated from much of the world, Vietnam had been closed to travelers for more than a decade. A lot has changed in the mid-'90s, and as it opens up, Vietnam promises to become one of Southeast Asia's great tourist destinations. The main attractions for Westerners are Vietnam War sites, cultural and religious attractions, beautiful scenery and beaches. Much of the country is mountainous and covered by rain forests. Two great rivers flow through Vietnam and empty into the South China Sea: the Red River in the north, and the Mekong in the south.

What to Do There

Hanoi   Vietnam's capital city, from its narrow, winding Old Town streets, to its grand tree-lined boulevards and French colonial architecture, is not without charm. It's filled with a variety of shops and outdoor markets (and their sights and smells). Ancient Hanoi can be explored through the architecture and exhibits of the Temple of Literature, founded in 1070 in homage to Confucius. A more modern "temple" is the Ho Chi Minh Mausoleum, honoring the father of Vietnamese independence; his home and a museum documenting his life are nearby. For a North Vietnamese viewpoint of the Vietnam war, see the Army Museum, on Dien Bien Phu Street.

Fascinating Facts About Vietnam

Two new mammal species have recently been discovered in the mountainous regions of Vietnam: The sao-la, a kind of small ox with straight, daggerlike horns and the muntjak, a giant deer . . . At the 1919 peace conference ending World War I, Ho Chi Minh, the future Communist leader of Vietnam, tried to enlist the aid of U.S. President Woodrow Wilson against colonial France. . . .

Ho Chi Minh City   Ho Chi Minh City (formerly Saigon, when it was capital of South Vietnam) remains in many ways the economic capital of Vietnam—and it's booming with new hotels and businesses opening daily. The city has changed since the Vietnam War, but the basilica (a kind of Roman Catholic Church), markets, the Rex Hotel, the French-built governor's palace and the blocks of colonial houses are still there. We like to wander in the streets of this busy city, amid the thousands of shops and stalls selling everything from coconuts to VCRs. See the floating market on the Rach Ben Nghe River and, if you can't sleep, the 24-hour vegetable market on Nguyen Trai Street.

But the city isn't all shopping and markets. The Emperor of Jade Pagoda houses gilded figures and paper mache statues of Buddhist and Taoist divinities. For those interested in history and propaganda, the War Crimes Exhibition offers a display of military equipment and photographs of bloody battles. (Be aware that some U.S. citizens may find some of its contents offensive.)

Travel Tips for the Client

Do have your film hand checked at the airport. Vietnam's ancient X-ray machines can do damage . . . Do be cautious if dealing with the map-selling street urchins. Some of them are skilled pickpockets . . . Don't, under any circumstances, be tempted to deal in the black market . . . Do keep your hands straight down by your sides when walking through Ho Chi Minh's mausoleum in Hanoi. If they're behind your back or your elbow is bent at all, soldiers will unceremoniously straighten them for you. . . .

Thailand, Malaysia, Singapore, Indonesia and Vietnam

Review Questions

1. How would you describe Bangkok's Grand Palace and Temple of the Emerald Buddha to a client?

2. How is Chiang Mai like Bangkok? How is it different?

3. What is a *wat*?

4. What is the most practical way for a traveler to see the hilly region around Chiang Mai?

5. What are three unusual industries a visitor can tour on Phuket?

6. What exceptional, important kind of sights would a traveler see on a loop north and northeast from Bangkok?

7. What should a tourist who orders *tom yum koong* be prepared to eat?

8. Why is Singapore considered an economic success story of Asia?

9. Bali, Java, Sulawesi and Sumatra are all islands of which nation?

10. For Westerners, what are Vietnam's main attractions?

Thailand, Malaysia, Singapore, Indonesia and Vietnam

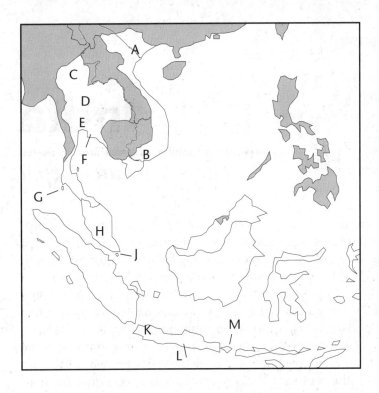

Map Skills Exercise

Match the tourist destination listed below with the corresponding letter on the map. You can use each letter only once.

1. _____ Bangkok
2. _____ Pattaya
3. _____ Phuket
4. _____ Chiang Mai
5. _____ Singapore
6. _____ Bali
7. _____ Hanoi
8. _____ Kuala Lumpur
9. _____ Jakarta
10. _____ Ho Chi Minh City

Selling Exercise

Clients who are preparing for a trip to Thailand will be coming into your travel agency and would like you to speak with them about attractions in that country. After doing some research, you select five wonderful attractions that are must-sees, because they capture the richness and enchantment of Thailand. List the five attractions you'd suggest and briefly describe what you'd tell your clients about each of them.

India

and Nepal

India refuses to let anyone merely observe. The country's sights, sounds and smells get inside all visitors, almost from the moment they step off the plane. If they arrive at night, between the airport and the hotel they'll pass hundreds of people sleeping on the sidewalks. If they arrive during the day, their bus or taxi will join a mind-boggling swirl of bicycles, motorcycles, cars, an occasional cow, hand-pushed carts, pedestrians, ox carts and (in Calcutta) human-powered rickshaws. The mass of humanity that populates India requires that visitors be patient, flexible and tolerant — traits that Indians themselves have cultivated over the centuries. India is a country that is at once fascinating and frustrating, beautiful and squalid, draining yet enriching.

A bonus for Western visitors to India is that many residents speak English (and they enjoy talking with travelers). It doesn't take long for visitors to find themselves in conversations about politics, religion, work, Indian history and dreams for the future. We can't think of another culture that is so different yet so accessible.

A Rich History

India is an ancient civilization, and almost all of its attractions are bound up in its history. The Hindu temples that can be found on almost every street corner were built to honor gods that were worshiped thousands of years before Christ was born (Hinduism, the world's oldest surviving religion, and Buddhism, established in the 6th century BC, both came out of India). The Taj Mahal is not only a monument inspired by love, but also an art treasure from the Mughal period (1526-1738), when Islam was the religion of the ruling class. And the formal architecture of New Delhi's parliament buildings is a legacy of the British Raj (1818-1947), the colonial period when Britain ruled India. After the British left in 1947, the ensuing battles between Hindus and Moslems culminated in the partition of India into predominantly Hindu India and Moslem Pakistan. Although the two nations have fought a number of wars since then, there is some prospect for a peaceful future.

A fascinating side trip from India — and an exciting destination in itself — is the mountain country of Nepal, a long-mysterious kingdom on India's northern border.

Selling Points

The Taj Mahal, religious shrines, the Himalaya, tigers, magnificent architecture, beaches, spiritual pilgrimages, caves, excellent food, great works of art, diversified scenery and culture, shopping, golfing and houseboat vacations are among the foremost attractions of India.

Send naturally curious, adventurous travelers who can tolerate heat. Don't send anyone without telling them that they will in all likelihood be exposed to poverty.

Although India is much easier to see independently than many developing countries, we believe that most people will be happiest on an escorted tour for their first visit. It must be stressed that any itinerary, even on package tours, is subject to modification after arrival.

Fascinating Facts About India

Near the Hanging Gardens in the upper-class Malabar Hills section of Bombay are the Towers of Silence of the Parsee faith, where the dead are left to be eaten by vultures . . . A word about beggars: Begging has a legitimate place in Indian society. Even poor people give to beggars or charity to earn religious merit. . . .

What to Do There

Agra   This city is best known for being the site of the Taj Mahal. The Taj is, of course, the single most important sight a visitor to India can see. If time permits, schedule at least two days in Agra so you can visit the Taj twice — each time you approach the white building, it stirs your emotions anew. (Plan on spending a minimum of an hour and a half on each visit; note that the building is no longer accessible at night.) Three other sights in the area should not be missed: Agra Fort, built under the Mughal emperor Akbar in 1565, contains several palaces and a white-marble mosque; Itmad-ud-Daulah's tomb, which is a marble forerunner to the Taj; and, 25 mi/40 km outside of town, Fatehpur Sikri, an extremely well-preserved 16th-century city that was once the capital of the Mughal empire (abandoned 15 years after it was built, it remains deserted to this day). The newer parts of Agra are unexceptional, but if you follow the road out of the main gate of the Taj you'll end up in old Agra, which has a lively market.

Bombay   Bombay is India's most cosmopolitan city. Its main attraction is Elephanta Island, which is 6 mi/10 km (about an hour by boat) out in the Arabian Sea. It has 1,200-year-old rock-cut Hindu temples. Outside of the monsoon season, daily boat tours depart from the early-20th-century Gateway of India (an arch on the waterfront near the Taj Hotel). After seeing the island, walk along Marine Drive (beside the sea), called the Queen's Necklace because of its sparkling night lights. Other city attractions include the Prince of Wales Museum, which has separate wings for natural history, art and archaeology; the Jehangir Art Gallery (contemporary Indian art); the Jhaveri Bazaar (where you bargain in relative comfort, on piles of pillows); the Chor Bazaar (thieves market where you can buy almost anything); and the Gandhi Memorial/ Museum (in honor of Mohandas Gandhi, the man who led the drive to free India from British rule).

Calcutta   India's largest city (pop. 11,000,000 and growing) is fascinating and awful. For many people, 24 hours in Calcutta is all they can take; the poverty, slums and filth are enough to make this a once-only destination for some. But there are also enough beautiful things in Calcutta to justify a three-night stay. Among the sights are the Marble Palace mansion (paintings and statues), the temple of the Jain religion and the Dakshineswar Hindu temple (12 shrines to the god Shiva).

The Taj Mahal

Climb the Octherlony Monument (218 steps up to a spectacular view of the city). A visit to Mother Teresa's Ashram Home of Children is a moving — and sobering — experience.

Delhi/New Delhi   Though officially two separate cities, for all intents and purposes Delhi and New Delhi are really two sections of one city. New Delhi, the capital of India, has clean, modern areas with broad, tree-lined boulevards, but old Delhi's quarters, considerably less clean, have changed little over the past 100 years. The combined city contains temples of all the ancient religions, as well as museums and monuments honoring the heroes of the modern Indian republic.

There's lots to see and do. Among the most impressive of the city's sights is the Red Fort, built under Shah Jahan (who also constructed the Taj Mahal). It is more palace than fort. Nearby is the old and busy Chandni Chowk Bazaar — a great place for wandering and looking. The Qutab Minar Complex, another great example of Indian architecture, has a five-story 13th-century Tower of Victory made of sandstone and marble. Jama Masjid (Friday Mosque) is a beautiful, huge, onion-domed 17th-century mosque complex surrounded by an interesting flea market.

Game Parks   India's game parks offer as much adventure, mystery and beauty as their African counterparts and contain many similar animals: hyenas, jackals, wild dogs, antelope, buffalo, elephants, monkeys, crocodiles and a splendid assortment of large and colorful birds. As a bonus, there are species not found

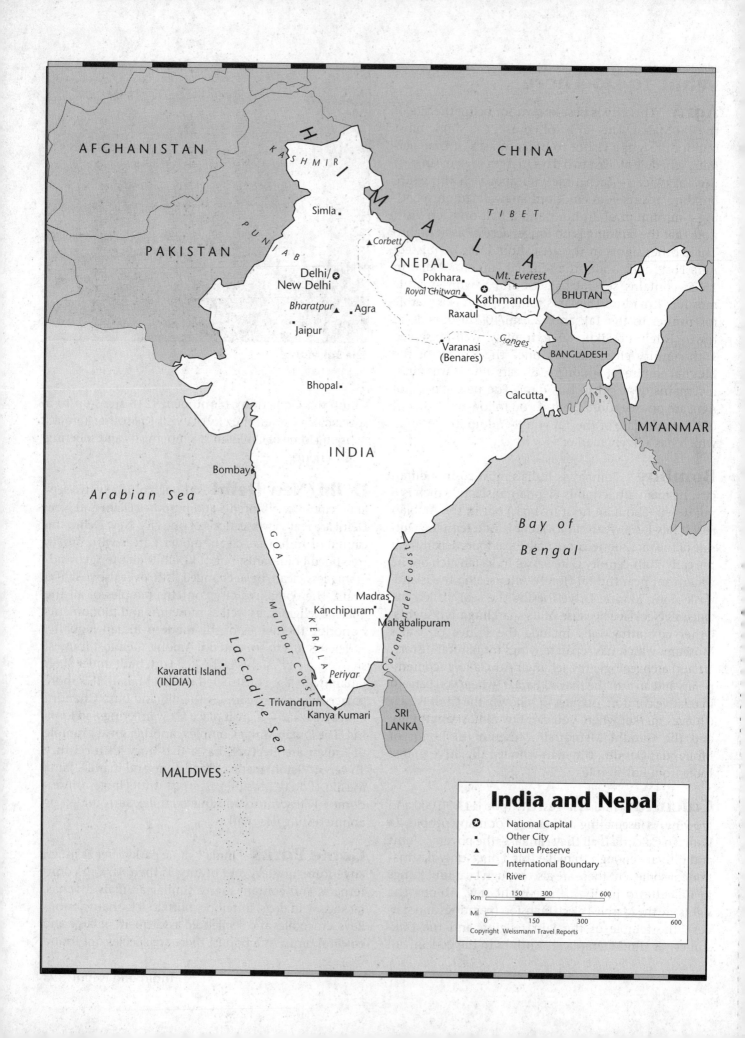

AFGHANISTAN

CHINA

KASHMIR

PUNJAB

Simla

▲ Corbett

TIBET

NEPAL

PAKISTAN

Delhi/ ✪
New Delhi

Pokhara

Mt. Everest

BHUTAN

Royal Chitwan

Bharatpur ▲ Agra

Kathmandu ✪

Jaipur

Raxaul

Ganges

BANGLADESH

Varanasi
(Benares)

Bhopal ▪

Calcutta ▪

MYANMAR

INDIA

Bombay ▪

Arabian Sea

Bay of
Bengal

GOA

Madras

Malabar Coast

Kanchipuram ▪

Mahabalipuram

KERALA

Coromandel Coast

Kavaratti Island
(INDIA)

Periyar ▲

Laccadive Sea

Trivandrum

Kanya Kumari

SRI
LANKA

MALDIVES

India and Nepal

✪   National Capital

▪   Other City

▲   Nature Preserve

——   International Boundary

—·—·—   River

Km 0   150   300   600

Mi 0   150   300   600

Copyright Weissmann Travel Reports

in Africa (most notably, bears and tigers). The park fees are generally lower, and many parks are easily reached by public transportation. However, patience is required of a visitor to Indian parks: You're unlikely to see vast herds of animals. Bharatpur (Keoladeo Ghana), one of the most important bird sanctuaries in the world, lies just an hour's drive from the Taj Mahal. Winter (October–January) is the park's best season. At Corbett, which is easily accessible from Delhi, visitors taking park-sponsored elephant rides are likely to see tigers, herds of elephants and several varieties of deer. If they're lucky, they'll see leopards and sloth bears. November–May is the best season. Periyar, in the southwestern state of Kerala, is the best elephant sanctuary in India. It's set on a large lake (most viewing is done from a boat). Occasionally, tigers are seen. October–April is our favorite season to visit.

A tiger in one of India's game parks

Goa
Goa used to be a Portuguese colony on India's west coast. It became part of India in 1961. It still shows a strong Portuguese influence in its plazas and architecture (note the cathedrals). The region is best known for its 65 mi/105 km of palm-lined beaches.

Jaipur
Jaipur is called The Pink City because of its unusual rose-colored sandstone architecture. It has more than a few magnificent buildings erected by local maharajahs. The early-18th-century Jantar Mantar is the largest and best preserved of the five observatories built by the astronomer prince Jai Singh II. The other must-see attractions are the city palace and museum, formerly a beautiful royal residence; the Palace of the Winds, whose facade is adorned with elaborate, perforated screens — it's one of the most photographed monuments in India; and Albert Hall, a museum housing metal ware, ivory carvings and other works of art. Not far out of town is the 18th-century Amber Palace and Fort. The palace is, in our opinion, the finest and best preserved in the country.

Kashmir
The part of India known as Kashmir is in the northwest. It provides breathtaking views of the Himalaya and great trekking. Be sure to visit Srinigar, a beautiful city whose main attraction is the houseboats on the lake — more house than boat, they are anchored to the shore. Visitors need to be aware that Kashmir continues to experience considerable religious and political tension; sometimes, it breaks out in violence.

Madras
The fourth-largest Indian city, Madras, is ancient. Located in the cradle of Indian Christianity, the city is where the first missionaries arrived nearly 1,900 years ago — there are some *very* old churches. Visit the Cathedral of San Thome, the Moorish-style Chepauk Palace, the lighthouse (for its view — be prepared for a strenuous climb), the central flower market, Ft. St. George (17th-century fort with a moat — within the walls is the oldest Anglican church in India), the Moore Market and the very fine Marina Beach. Among the interesting Hindu temples in Madras are Tirukalikundram, Kapaleeswarar, Mallikarjuna and Chennakesava. There are several must-see temples/ruins outside Madras, such as the ruined temples at Mahabalipuram and Kancheepuram.

Varanasi (Benares)
Varanasi is guaranteed to stun. This city of 900,000 is the holiest site in India, and thousands of Hindu pilgrims bathe in the Ganges River to gain religious merit. Thousands more go simply to die and have their ashes thrown into the holy waters. You must be emotionally prepared, because the waters contain not only ashes, but corpses in various stages of decomposition. If you're braced to see this, you'll want to venture down to the boats and onto the water at dawn to see an amazing and spiritually uplifting sight. Scores of people enter the water from one of 70 *ghats* (riverside platforms with steps) to purify themselves

before the rising sun. Don't even think of entering the water, however—it may be spiritually pure, but it's one of the most polluted rivers in the world. Providing a backdrop for this sight are 2,000 temples and shrines. The holiest, Vishvanatha, is closed to non-Hindus, but the Durga Temple can be visited. It teems with monkeys (hold onto your valuables!). There's also a wonderful temple devoted to the Ramayana, a Hindu tale of love and adventure. Take a walking tour of the Islamic section (Muslims make up a quarter of the population). The streets are filled with Arabic music and veiled women, and it's there that Varanasi silk is dyed, dried and woven.

Itinerary

To try to see all of India and get to know the country's diverse cultures, scenery and cuisines would take at least a year; most people try to do it in a few weeks. (It can be exhausting rather than enjoyable.) We offer here an "All-India" itinerary that first-time visitors should consider; much of the travel is by plane. If they're taking an escorted tour, they should make sure the tour includes as many of these stops as possible. They can also, without much difficulty, add time in neighboring Nepal.

Day 1 — Arrive Delhi.

Day 2 — Delhi.

Day 3 — Fly/drive to Agra.

Day 4 — Agra.

Day 5 — Travel to Jaipur.

Day 6 — Jaipur.

Day 7 — Early flight to Varanasi. See non-river sights.

Day 8 — Dawn tour of Ganges riverfront. Fly to Madras.

Day 9 — Madras.

Day 10 — Fly to Bombay.

Day 11 — Bombay.

Day 12 — Depart India.

Climate/When to Go

For most of the country, November–March is (by far) the best time to visit, with temperatures ranging from 40–60 F/5–15 C in the north to 65–85 F/19–30 C in the south. March–June is dry and very, very hot (85–110 F/30–44 C), and July–October is monsoon time (20–80

Geostats

Official Name: Republic of India.

Visa Info: Passports, visas, proof of onward passage and sufficient funds required of U.S. and Canadian citizens. (Passport must be valid for at least six months after arrival.) Reconfirm documentation requirements with carrier before departure.

Health Certificates: Yellow-fever certificates are required if you are arriving from a country, any part of which is infected, or from other countries on the Indian government's list (check with the Indian embassy). Contact health authorities for latest information.

Capital: New Delhi.

Population: 936,566,000.

Size: 1,268,8840 sq mi/3,287,263 sq km. About twice the size of Alaska.

Languages: Hindi, English, 14 other official languages.

Climate: Temperate to subtropical monsoon.

Economy: Industry, agriculture, manufacturing.

Government: Federal republic.

Religions: Hindu, Islamic, Christian, others.

Currency: Rupee (INR). 100 paisas = 1 INR (the paisa is rarely used). Traveler's checks are accepted in tourist areas. Credit cards are not commonly accepted. AE, DC, MC and VI.

Time Zone: 10.5 hours ahead of eastern standard time; 5.5 hours ahead of Greenwich mean time.

Electricity: 220 volts.

Departure Tax: INR300.

in/50–203 cm of rain will fall in one season). The best time to visit the mountain areas is April–November. Obviously, India is less crowded with tourists during the off-seasons, but spring/summer can be so hot that it's really not possible to stay outdoors for long periods of time. Another problem is that in the rainy period the monsoon washes away many roads in game parks and the rural areas. If you're going to India during the spring or summer, you'll want to stick with the hill stations (60–70 F/15–21 C).

Transportation

Air India and Delta fly direct from the U.S., and Air India offers service from Canada. Most international European carriers travel via connections in their hub cities. Indian Airlines and Air India fly internally. Bombay Airport (BOM) is 23 mi/36 km from town (an airport bus service is available — there's also a separate domestic airport, so be sure your driver knows which one you want); the Indira Gandhi International Airport (DEL) is 9 mi/15 km outside New Delhi; Dum Dum Airport (CCU) is 17 mi/27 km from Calcutta; and Meenambarkkam Airport (MAA) is 10 mi/16 km outside of Madras.

Unless your time is very tight, plan at least one train trip. There are specialty tours on train carriages restored to British colonial conditions (the "Palace on Wheels" is the most popular), but even lesser trains can be fun. Purchase an Indrail Pass (we recommend the first-class pass) to save time getting tickets. Most overnight trains have bedding that can be rented at the departure station and turned in at the arrival station. Usually available for first class only (and reserved in advance), it can make berths quite comfortable.

Buses connect most cities, and they vary greatly in comfort. Tourist buses or video coaches (showing tapes of Hindi-language movies) are tolerable. Local buses are cramped and generally awful. Taxis are available in most cities, but auto rickshaws are cheaper (although less safe). Calcutta has human-pulled rickshaws. It is possible to rent cars, but don't do so without getting a driver. If getting around sounds like a big hassle, you're right — it is. If you want to avoid the hassle, take an escorted tour.

Accommodations

Accommodations range from world-class deluxe properties to game-reserve lodges, palaces, campgrounds, locally run adequate hotels and way-below-basic guest houses. The adventurous might want to stay in simple accommodations, but it's a good idea to inspect the rooms before accepting them. In smaller towns, all that may be available are very rustic guest houses. If you're traveling to rural areas, buy a colorful piece of cloth to toss over the bed before sleeping on it—some guest houses don't change their sheets between guests. If you're staying in a hotel with a pool, be sure to inquire about swimming hours. Often men and women are required to swim at separate times.

Health Advisories

Sanitary conditions in many restaurants in India are not up to Western standards. Most hot, freshly cooked food should be safe (especially if it's served on a package tour), but peel fresh fruit and raw vegetables, make sure meat is cooked thoroughly, avoid local dairy products and assume that tap water is unsafe (stick with boiled drinks). Beware of vendors selling soft drinks that are not normally available in India (whatever's in those bottles, it's not what it says on the label). Don't accept ice in your drinks, except from the absolutely finest hotels—the water that went into the ice might not be good. If you need medical attention while in India, see a doctor who was trained in the West or who has a diploma from a major Indian university. Skin infections are common; even the smallest wound should be disinfected and covered with a bandage. Before you go, see your doctor about obtaining malaria suppressants. Take along insect repellent, as well as all prescription medicine needed for the trip.

More Fascinating Facts About India

Almost everywhere you go, people will approach you to try to sell you something or to offer you a "good deal"—a taxi driver may offer to be your guide for a day or to give you a free ride to your hotel. Of course, nothing is free. The "free" ride to the hotel may boost your hotel bill by 40% (his commission for taking you there), and the free tour will undoubtedly include several souvenir shops, where a commission will also figure into any price you pay . . . Banks are open about four hours a day. They usually have long lines, and require that you stand in at least two lines for every transaction, so be prepared. . . .

What to Buy

Sandalwood items, fabrics (including silks), papier-mache, brassware, wood carvings, clothing, religious paraphernalia, paintings and prints, dhurri rugs, oriental carpets, marble-inlay boxes, dolls, musical instruments, silver, jute products, tea, bamboo products, fossils and crystals are among the good buys. It's true (as you'll be told by gem dealers) that you can buy gems to take home for profit, but you can also get burned—only attempt it if you know a lot about gems. Most often, bargaining is the name of the game in shops. Depending on the product, you may want to offer one-third to two-thirds of the initial asking price and take it from there. When buying name-brand items, be careful—copycats abound.

What to Eat

There's more to Indian food than curry sauce — the nation has more than 15 different regional cuisines (curries are favored in the south). Even those afraid of spicy food will love the mild chicken tandoori or Kashmiri-style dishes. *Pakoras* (fried vegetable fritters) also provide an easy introduction to Indian cookery. *Samosas* are breaded, fried vegetable triangles. *Dal,* an Indian lentil soup, can be found everywhere. *Dum aloo* is a wonderfully spicy potato dish found in the north. The breads are superlative — there's none better than naan, but do try *papadum,* a wafer-thin lentil-flour bread, at least once. For dessert, try *kheer* (rice pudding). Fruit *lassis* are a yogurt-based drink that can be very refreshing. We generally advise against eating from street stalls. Indian food is eaten with the fingers of the right hand only. In addition to Indian foods, Western and Chinese restaurants abound.

Travel Tips for the Client

Don't accept damaged or torn local currency notes, as they may not be accepted by others . . . Don't take photos at the burning ghat where cremations take place in Varanasi . . . Do be thorough when filling out your Tourist Baggage Report Form when you land. Otherwise, your camera, jewelry, binoculars, etc., may be heavily taxed when you leave. Likewise, report theft of any of these items to the police, or you'll be taxed upon departure as if you sold them . . . Do dress conservatively at Indian beaches (women). Much of Indian society is very conservative, and normal Western beach attire may send a strong, though unintended, signal. Attacks on foreign women have occurred . . . Do take off your shoes when entering temples or mosques . . . Do be careful when walking city streets. Pedestrians are expected to watch out for vehicles, not vice versa . . . Staring is not the social taboo in India that it is in most Western countries . . . Always carry toilet paper with you . . . Do keep an especially close eye on your bags when on trains. We've (twice!) lost bags before the train even pulled out. . . .

Tipping: Do tip 10% in better restaurants that haven't added a service charge to the bill. Small change will be appreciated in modest restaurants. Tip taxi drivers by rounding off the fare (more only if you get exceptional service).

Nepal

Nepal's capital city of Kathmandu, once a byword for the mysterious and exotic East, is no longer so isolated and different. Modern-day problems — air pollution and overcrowding — were evident on our last few visits. Once you leave Kathmandu and head into the mountains on a trek, there are no faxes, phones or even highways. And the mountains are why Nepal remains one of our favorite destinations. One of the main sights is Mt. Everest, the highest mountain in the world (29,028 ft/8,848 m). There are other reasons to go to Nepal, of course: The cities are an incredible mixture of the old and new, the game parks are superb, and not enough can be said about the

An Indian dancer

Nepalese people. There's something about the way they look at the world that makes them secure about their place in it, yet open to outside cultures and ideas.

Nepal — sandwiched between India and Tibet — will appeal to open-minded, flexible travelers who want to see a unique and truly exotic place. Don't send those who are reluctant to be exposed to poverty or to unsanitary conditions, who are intolerant of delays and cultures very different from their own or who have difficulty at high altitudes.

What to Do There

Kathmandu   The capital of Nepal is unlike any other city in the world, its main attraction being its atmosphere. Everywhere you look there's something of interest. The highest concentration of attractions is within the area of Durbar Square. Among the most impressive structures: the 16th-century pagoda-style Taleju Temple, the old Royal Palace, the Kumari Bahal or (Temple of the Living Goddess). Be sure to see the erotic carvings on Jagnath Temple, and the Shiva-Parvati Temple, where statues of the gods stand in an ornately carved window and look down on the action in the square. Just off the square is Freak Street (it was a hangout for Western hippies during the 1960s and 1970s). The neighborhood of Thamel is somewhat of a "tourist ghetto," but it offers a wide range of cuisines and souvenir shopping.

Day trips can be taken to Nagorkot (to see Mt. Everest far in the distance), Pashupatinath (one of the most famous Hindu temples in the world), Swayambhunath (a temple high atop a hill that has great views and dozens of resident monkeys) and Bhaktapur (the 55-Window Palace and Nyatapola are musts).

Pokhara   Pokhara, the center of the second major tourist area in Nepal, is about 45 minutes by plane northwest of Kathmandu. There's not much in the town of Pokhara itself, so visitors stay at a resort area on the banks of Lake Phewa. You can rent a rowboat and paddle out to a temple located on one of the lake's islands. Most tourists don't plan on staying in Pokhara for more than one or two days. The area is the starting point for treks into the Himalaya. If you're not planning a full trek, a day trip can be made to Sarangkot, a small village about a two-hour walk into the mountains. Your view of the mountains from there will be far superior to what you can see in town.

Royal Chitwan National Park

This, the third major tourist area in Nepal, lies in the southern lowlands. It's a world apart from the mountain region, as it's hot, humid and, in many areas, quite lush. Royal Chitwan is home to tigers, leopards, rhinos, crocodiles, monkeys and magnificent birds. Most visitors stay at one of the Tiger Tops accommodations. They're quite comfortable. They offer elephant rides and provide bait for tigers to improve viewing opportunities. White-water raft trips end at Tiger Tops.

Trekking   Trekking is possible throughout the mountainous area that is open to visitors. Permits can be obtained with a minimum of fuss. Treks can be taken with an escorted group or arranged independently, though independent treks should only be considered by experienced, adventurous travelers. Most escorted treks employ local guides, as well as porters to carry everyone's belongings, set up tents and cook meals. It's important to know that treks are not mountain climbing or wilderness hiking. Trekkers walk on paths fairly heavily traveled by Nepalese. Neither is a trek a race: The whole idea is to stop and look at the views every time you turn a corner. The treks vary in difficulty and length (from one to four weeks). Most visitors walk about five hours (7–8 mi/10–12 km) a day—a lot of up and down at high altitudes. Tour organizers usually rate the difficulty of various treks. We recommend treks in the Annapurna range, out of Pokhara, for first-time trekkers.

Travel Tips for the Client

Do get a multiple-entry Indian visa if you are seeing Nepal in conjunction with a tour of India and wish to return to India . . . Do ask permission before taking photos in temples, and don't wear anything made of leather into a Hindu temple . . . There are a number of cultural practices and taboos you should know: Always walk clockwise around stupas (religious spires). Never step over other people's feet (or any other part of their body). Don't offer food to a Nepalese after tasting it. Never use your left hand to eat or handle food, to shake hands, etc., but always present or accept items with both hands. Don't touch Nepalese dressed all in white; they're in mourning. Don't pat children on the head or sit with your feet pointing at someone (especially toward a monk or lama); both practices are considered insulting). . . .

India and Nepal

Review Questions

1. What is the single most important attraction for a visitor to India?

2. What city in India is the most cosmopolitan?

3. Why might you suggest that a tourist stay only one day in Calcutta?

4. What tourist attractions are common to both India and Africa?

5. Why is Madras important in the history of Indian Christianity?

6. What do Hindu pilgrims in Varanasi (Benares) do to gain religious merit?

7. Why should a traveler to India generally decline drinks with ice?

8. What mountain in Nepal is one of the country's main tourist attractions?

9. Where would a tourist see the highest concentration of attractions in Kathmandu?

10. What is a common way for visitors to tour the mountainous areas of Nepal?

India and Nepal

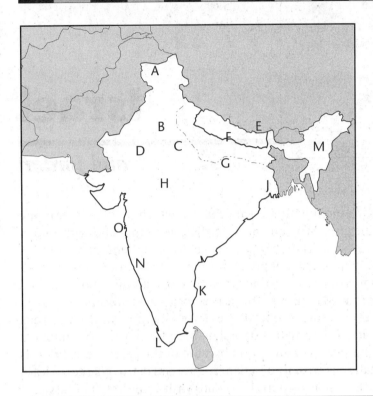

Map Skills Exercise

Match the tourist destination listed below with the corresponding letter on the map. You can use each letter only once.

1. _____ New Delhi
2. _____ Taj Mahal
3. _____ Kashmir
4. _____ Bombay
5. _____ Calcutta
6. _____ Varanasi
7. _____ Mt. Everest
8. _____ Royal Chitwan National Park
9. _____ Goa
10. _____ Madras

Selling Exercise

Your agency is promoting a trip to India and you have been asked to prepare a short slide show to present to a group of people interested in a tour. In order to organize your thoughts, you prepare for the presentation by first selecting five slides of India that will capture the essence, the heart and soul of the country. Describe the five images you would select and write down the narration you would provide as each image appears on the screen.

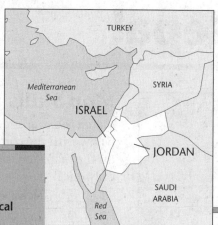

Israel
and Jordan

Selling Points

Religious shrines, beaches, historical sites on top of historical sites, spas, nature reserves, fascinating cultures, diving, museums and great food are among the main attractions of Israel.

Almost everyone will learn a great deal — about the world and about themselves — during a visit to Israel. But don't send those who will be so preoccupied with safety questions that they won't be able to relax.

Fascinating Facts About Israel

The grave of Oskar Schindler, the Polish industrialist who saved more than 1,000 Jews during the Holocaust, can be found at Mt. Zion. His grave has become a popular site since Steven Spielberg's film *Schindler's List* was released . . . Native-born Israelis are known as *sabras,* from the Hebrew for the cactus fruit—tough on the outside and soft inside . . . The Dome of the Rock is where Muhammad is said to have ascended into heaven on a white horse. The mosque has a cabinet displaying a hair from the beard of the Prophet — it is said that if you stick your hand in the cabinet and make a wish, it will come true. . . .

The agreement with the Palestinians (which includes autonomy for the Gaza Strip and areas of the West Bank) and with Jordan has given Israel (and the region) a chance at long-term peace and stability. Many fundamental problems remain to be ironed out (including the status of Jerusalem), and a number of extremists on both sides seem determined to disrupt the peace process. Despite random bombings and events such as the killing of Israeli Prime Minister Yitzhak Rabin, Israeli, Palestinian and Jordanian leaders appear committed to seeing the process through. And because of the peace treaty, visitors to Israel can now cross into Jordan (see the end of this chapter to learn about key tourist attractions in Jordan) with a minimum of fuss.

Israel has a great emotional and spiritual effect on every visitor. Some are touched by its magnificent religious shrines; others are impressed by the tenacity of a nation that, against all odds, made the desert bloom. The land of Israel is the site of some of the holiest shrines in three major religions: Christianity, Islam and Judaism. In fact, there are so many sites of religious importance spread throughout Israel that the Bible could well be the best guidebook for the nation.

What to Do There

Bethlehem   Bethlehem is believed to be the birthplace of Jesus Christ and is the site of the Church of the Nativity. The original church was built in 325 by Helena, mother of the Roman Emperor Constantine, over a grotto that's thought to be the exact spot where Christ was born (the manger where the Magi viewed the child was close by — a chapel marks the spot). The present structure dates from a 6th-century rebuilding and a 12th-century Crusader repair. In December 1995, the Israeli army evacuated the city and it came under Palestinian control.

Eilat   Eilat is a resort town in southern Israel on the Gulf of Aqaba. The town provides visitors with an opportunity for snorkeling, beach time or just a break from touring. You don't need to be a scuba diver to appreciate its coral reefs; they begin only a few yards from shore, so

Israel and Jordan

- ✪ National Capital
- ■ ▫ City/Site
- ∴ Ruin
- ▲ National Park or Preserve
- —— International Boundary
- —·—· River

Km 0 20 40

Mi 0 20 40

Copyright Weissmann Travel Reports

MEDITERRANEAN SEA

SYRIA

GOLAN HEIGHTS

GALILEE

Acre
Haifa
Zefat
Tiberias
Sea of Galilee
Nazareth
Megiddo
Beit Shean

Tel Aviv

WEST BANK

Jordan

✪ Amman

Jericho
Jerusalem ✪
Bethlehem

JUDAEAN DESERT

Ein Gedi ▲
Masada
Dead Sea

Karak

Beersheva

Shivta
Sde Boker

Avdat

Mitzpeh Ramon

NEGEV DESERT

Petra

EGYPT

Timna Valley ▲

Eilat
Aqaba

LEBANON
SYRIA
IRAQ

Jerusalem ✪
✪ Amman
ISRAEL
JORDAN
EGYPT
SAUDI ARABIA
Gulf of Aqaba

even novice snorkelers can wade in and start looking around. We think the diving is among the most spectacular anywhere. And if you don't want to get your feet wet, you need only visit the nature reserve on Coral Beach, where the Israelis have placed an underwater observatory. The observatory, a four-story tower set atop a reef, allows spectacular views of marine life. Eilat is also a rest stop, in the spring and summer, for more than 425 species of migrating birds. Eilat is just a few minutes' drive from both Egypt and Jordan. Plans have been made to extend the resort's shoreline promenade to Taba in Egypt and Aqaba in Jordan. From Eilat you can also take escorted excursions into the Sinai Desert of Egypt.

Galilee

The hilly region around the Sea of Galilee is quite different from the flat desert that covers much of Israel. An area that looks almost lush in winter, Galilee is the site of several important events and attractions, including Jesus' Miracle of the Loaves and Fishes, which took place on the banks of the "sea" — the church there

Church of the Holy Sepulchre

Jerusalem

If Israel had only Jerusalem, it would be worth the expense and energy to get there from any point on earth. A great way to start your visit is to enter through the Damascus Gate, and at the fork in the road, go right. This is the most colorful entrance to the city's old market. Our advice: Wander. Enter any store that appeals to you and bargain with the proprietor (offer one-third the price quoted, then play it by ear from there).

As you shop and stroll, you'll eventually "discover" some of the most magnificent holy shrines in the world. If you don't stumble upon them, ask for directions to the Mosque of Omar (also known as the Dome of the Rock, one of the holiest sites in Islam); the Church of the Holy Sepulchre (marking the site of the crucifixion, burial and resurrection of Christ) and the Western (Wailing) Wall, once part of King Solomon's Temple. Another great walk is the Via Dolorosa, the original Stations of the Cross.

There are scores of other interesting sights in and around the old city, and even a few beneath the town: King David's Tomb and King Solomon's Quarry (the latter is also called the Caves of Zedekiah). The Room of the Last Supper is now a very plain chamber attached to a yeshiva (a school to train rabbis). There are also two deeply moving museums: The Chamber of Martyrs (Yad Vashem), a memorial to the victims of Nazism; and the Armenian Museum, which gives a fascinating look at the turbulent history of the Armenian people. Outside the walls is a beautiful Franciscan church on the slope of the Mount of Olives; the church is built around the rock in the Garden of Gethsemane and features a gorgeous mosaic floor.

The Me'a She'arim quarter of Jerusalem (just outside the Old City walls) is populated by strictly observant Jews, and a visit to it is like walking the streets of a shtetl or Eastern European ghetto of the mid-1800s. Please respect the community's request that women dress modestly (skirts and covered shoulders) and that conspicuous photography be avoided. Don't miss a visit to the Israel Museum (actually a complex of museums), where you can see artifacts collected from innumerable digs throughout the centuries, but whose highlight is surely the Dead Sea Scrolls.

Judean Desert

This desert bordering the Dead Sea has several points of interest. The Ein Gedi Nature Reserve, one of the most beautiful spots in the country, is a lush green finger cutting through the dry desolate land. In April the desert blooms, and seems carpeted with wildflowers. After hiking a trail, cool off by jumping into the Dead Sea. The heavy mineral content will assure that you won't sink, but don't get any water in your eyes — it can sting something fierce! The room-

has a marvelous mosaic floor. Be sure to visit nearby Tiberias (site of a Crusader castle, hot springs and rabbis' tombs) for a few hours, and order St. Peter's fish, netted in the Sea of Galilee, for lunch. Also nearby is the Mount of the Beatitudes, where Jesus preached the Sermon on the Mount. On the loop around the sea, pause at the entrance or exit of the Jordan River. If you see people being baptized, more likely than not they'll be American fundamentalists. Because of its rugged terrain, the Galilee has recently been developed as a site for adventure tours: cliff rappelling, rock climbing and river kayaking and rafting.

Haifa

This city, built on a hill overlooking the Mediterranean, is reminiscent of San Francisco in some respects. Although Haifa suffers from a bad reputation because of its large industrial areas, we like the city. In town are the Baha'i Temple and Gardens (the world center of the Baha'i faith), the National Maritime Museum and some art museums. Visit Elijah's cave, held sacred by Christians, Jews and Muslim alike.

sized "icebergs" you see floating about are chunks of nearly pure salt, formed by evaporating water. Also in the desert is Masada, a mountain where 900 Jews kept 10,000 Roman soldiers at bay for more than a year.

Tel Aviv   In Tel Aviv, sidewalk cafes provide a decidedly European flavor, and shopping at the enclosed Dizengoff Center is pleasant. Cultural opportunities beckon: Be sure to visit the Tel Aviv Museum, with its small but impressive collection of art. If at all possible, attend a performance of the world-class Israeli Philharmonic at Mann Auditorium. Also tour the Diaspora Museum for insight into the history of the dispersed Jewish people and their cultures. Evening brings heavy nightclub and disco activity. If you're looking for something different after hours, go to Old Jaffa, a restored historical area that includes exclusive shopping, restaurants and night clubs. During the day, swim at the Tel Aviv beaches.

Hassidic Jew prays at Wailing Wall

Itinerary

One week is an absolute minimum itinerary for seeing Israel. Here's what we suggest you see.

Day 1 — Arrive Tel Aviv.

Day 2 — Tel Aviv.

Day 3 — Drive to the Sea of Galilee. Overnight there.

Day 4 — Drive to Jerusalem.

Day 5 — Jerusalem.

Day 6 — Day trip to Bethlehem or Masada. Overnight Jerusalem.

Day 7 — Return to Tel Aviv.

Day 8 — Depart Israel.

Climate/When to Go

Our favorite times to go are April–May and September–October. The Negev Desert forms the southern two-thirds of the country, and summer in the Negev can be too hot to enjoy (temperatures over 100 F/37 C). It's possible to see desert sights in the summer if sightseeing is done early in the day. In the more densely populated northern third of the country, summer temperatures are generally in the 80s F/28–32 C during the day and 60s F/16–22 C at night. It can get quite wet and cold during the winter, with day temperatures in the 50s F/10–16 C and nights in the 30–40s/0–15 C (you might even see a white Christmas in Jerusalem or Bethlehem).

Dome of the Rock

Transportation

El Al Israel, Tower Air and Trans World Airlines fly nonstop from the United States. Air Canada provides nonstop service from Canada. Several European airlines offer single-carrier service via their hub cities. Ben Gurion Airport (TLV) is 12 mi/19 km east of Tel Aviv. Frequent air service by the domestic airline Arkia connects the major areas within Israel. Most visitors travel by *sherut* (shared taxis) or rental car. The U.S. State Department, however, recommends avoiding buses and bus stops because of a number of terrorist bus bombings. Israel has limited train service. Those crossing to Jordan via the Allenby Bridge are still required to have visas and bridge-crossing permits.

Geostats

Official Name: State of Israel.

Visa Info: Canadian and U.S. citizens need passports and proof of sufficient funds and onward passage. Have Israeli officials put the entry stamp on separate sheet of paper if you plan to visit Arab countries other than Egypt, Morocco or Jordan.

Health Certificates: None required. Contact health authorities for latest information.

Capital: Jerusalem, but the U.S. and some other countries maintain embassies in Tel Aviv.

Population: 4,770,000.

Size: 7,850 sq mi/20,325 sq km. About the size of New Jersey.

Languages: Hebrew, Arabic, English.

Climate: Temperate, except in the desert.

Economy: Agriculture, trade.

Government: Parliamentary democracy.

Religions: Judaism, Islam, Christianity.

Currency: Shekel (ILS). 100 agorots = 1 ILS.

Time Zone: 7 hours ahead of EST, 2 hours ahead of GMT.

Electricity: 220 volts.

Accommodations

Accommodations range from deluxe hotels and resorts to B-and-Bs and Jerusalem hospices. Moderately priced local accommodations are clean and comfortable. The King David in Jerusalem is a world-renowned classic — sit in the lobby one evening and soak in the atmosphere. Many American hotel chains are located on Hayarkon Street in Tel-Aviv; most of them have nice views of the Mediterranean.

Health Advisories

Israel meets Western standards of sanitation, and no special precautions need to be taken. The water and food are safe to consume, and medical facilities, while not quite up to U.S. levels, are more than adequate. The government requires that at least one pharmacy in each neighborhood be open or on call at all times.

What to Buy

Shop for brass and copper ware (including coffee sets), furs, silver jewelry, diamonds, glasswork, artwork, leather coats, painted tiles, embroidery, religious items, bottled Dead Sea mud and antiques. A good place for souvenirs is Ben Yehuda street in Tel Aviv. Many shops close for a "siesta" after lunch and reopen in the late afternoon.

What to Eat

There's a wide range of restaurants offering fare from Continental to East Asian, Russian and Ethiopian. There's even a "1st-century" Roman restaurant in Jerusalem, Cardo Culinaria, serving only food of that era — before tomatoes, potatoes and sugar were known in the Old World. While fast-food franchises are there in force, you'd be foolish to pass up the more traditional fast food: Falafel (a pocket sandwich of fried chick peas and herbs served with salad in pita bread) is a treat, as is *shwarma* (also known as *doner kebab* — it's similar to gyros). Hummus (a blend of chick peas, sesame seed paste, lemon and olive oil) should also be sampled.

Travel Tips for the Client

Don't arrive late for a flight. You will need at least two hours for predeparture screening and yet more time to check in (Israeli airport security is probably the tightest in the world) . . . Do carry your passport with you at all times . . . Do take the city tours or other excursions offered by the major Israeli touring companies (Egged Tours and Dan Tours). Israeli guides are very knowledgeable and are strictly regulated by the Israeli Ministry of Tourism . . . Don't drive through the Me'a She'arim Orthodox Jewish section of Jerusalem after sunset on Friday or on Saturdays before sunset — it would break the rules of their Sabbath and they have been known to throw stones . . . Don't enter a mosque wearing shoes . . . Do take appropriately modest clothing for visiting religious shrines. . . .

Jordan

Jordan lies in the heart of the Middle East and all its problems. Though most of the country is covered by desert, the nation also has mountains, beaches, and fertile river valleys. Send those who love history (political and biblical), architecture, desert climates and scuba diving (Aqaba, near Eilat). For the history buff, Jordan has Roman ruins, Byzantine mosaics and Crusader fortresses, among other attractions. Don't send anyone who is too nervous about the political situation, who isn't prepared for the inconveniences found in developing countries or who hates hot weather.

What to Do There

Amman   Jordan's capital, known as Philadelphia during Roman and Byzantine times, lies just a short drive from the Israeli border. Attend a performance in the 2,000-year-old Roman amphitheater (it holds 6,000) or the new Royal Cultural Center. Also visit the Basman Palace, the city's Folklore Museum, Museum of Popular Traditions and the National Archaeological Museum. Tour the Forum and Citadel Hill to see the few remaining

> ### More Fascinating Facts About Israel
>
> Megiddo is the site of ancient Armageddon, where some believe the final Apocalyptic battle between good and evil will take place . . . The Dead Sea, at 1,296 ft/389 m below sea level, is the lowest point on earth. The body of water is also one of the saltiest, with a 33% mineral content. . . .

Roman ruins (including a temple of Hercules). The hill affords a sweeping view of Amman and is a tranquil escape from Amman's crowded atmosphere. The Jordan National Gallery displays modern Jordanian and Middle Eastern art. Don't miss the huge King Abdullah Mosque, completed in the late 1980s.

Karak   This Crusader castle and museum rates a half-day visit. Built 3,400 ft/1,036 m above sea level, the castle boasts an impressive view, as well as a moat, lookouts and chapel — all in good shape.

Petra   This ancient rose-colored city in the Wadi Musa Canyon should not be missed. The city is unlike any we have seen before. You'll have to leave your car and walk or ride a horse through a narrow gorge to get to it. When the road opens out, an awesome sight is revealed — it's akin to one's first view of the Grand Canyon. This perspective of the magnificent 2,000-year-old city carved from solid red sandstone makes the effort to get there worthwhile. Don't miss the Roman theater, Urn, Corinthian and Palace tombs or the freestanding temple. Located a 45-minute walk away are a monastery and the High Place of Sacrifice. (Bring plenty of water if you're thinking of making this trip.)

Travel Tips for the Client

Do see the Amman folklore performance at the Roman amphitheater . . . Do visit in the spring, when the wildflowers are in bloom . . . In order to show respect for Muslims, don't eat, drink, or smoke in public during daylight hours during the month of Ramadan. . . .

Israel and Jordan

Review Questions

1. Israel is the site of some of the holiest shrines in what three major religions?

2. What is said to have happened at the Dome of the Rock?

3. What resort town in southern Israel provides visitors with opportunities for snorkeling, beach time or a break from touring?

4. What might a visitor see happening at the entrance or exit to the Jordan River?

5. What is the highlight of the Israel Museum?

6. What happened at Masada? Where is it?

7. List three attractions a tourist might want to visit in Haifa.

8. Why should a traveler arrive on time for a flight to Israel?

9. What kind of clients should you send to Jordan?

10. Why can't a visitor drive all the way into Petra?

Israel and Jordan

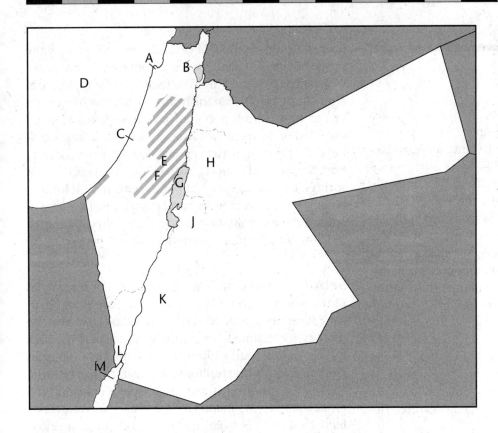

Map Skills Exercise

Match the tourist destination listed below with the corresponding letter on the map. You can use each letter only once.

1. _____ Jerusalem
2. _____ Tel Aviv
3. _____ Bethlehem
4. _____ Dead Sea
5. _____ Amman
6. _____ Eilat
7. _____ Petra
8. _____ Karak
9. _____ Galilee
10. _____ Haifa

Selling Exercise

At your agency's next staff meeting, you will be presenting a brochure that you've created for a tour package to Israel and Jordan. Your market for the tour is members of churches in your community. Fold an 8 1/2" by 11" piece of paper in half and use all four faces to create the brochure.

Asia Geofile

East Asia

North Korea

A visit to Communist North Korea is a bizarre, fascinating and wearing experience. As you tour the cities, you'll feel as if you've walked into an Asian-language translation of the novel *1984*—every aspect of society is controlled by the state. Your guide will be constantly bombarding you with examples of the virtues of North Korean philosophy and politics as he or she boasts endlessly about the nation's accomplishments. North Korea does contain spectacular mountain scenery, as well as Buddhist pagodas and fantastic sculpture and architecture. North Korea will be appreciated by the curious traveler who's interested in East Asian culture or communist societies.

South Korea

The '90s is a fascinating time to visit South Korea. Despite the country's rapid rush into the modern world, its unique heritage remains intact. The country calls itself the Land of the Morning Calm, and its flag features the

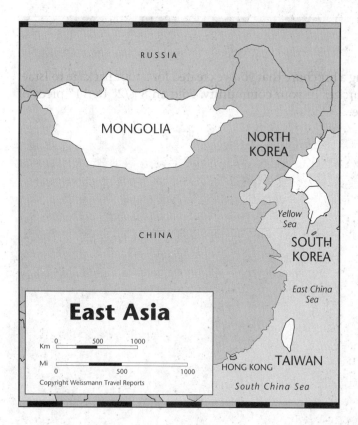

ancient Chinese symbol of yin and yang, representing the union of opposites. Its calmness is contagious; visitors can experience it in the Pulguksa Temple in Kyongju, from atop Mount Namsan in the heart of Seoul or while gazing at the moon from a coastal pavilion. Korea is often included on tours of East Asia, but even as a lone destination, it offers more than enough to fill a two-week vacation. Shrines and temples, palaces, casinos, beaches, hot springs, caves and national parks (both mountain and oceanic) are among the foremost attractions. Take time to enjoy a game of golf, snow skiing, mountain climbing, or trekking, or attend a traditional cultural performance.

Seoul

Korea's capital, Seoul, is one of the largest cities in the world and is set in a pretty valley cut by the Han-gang River. Seoul is divided into an old and new city. The old city, proclaimed the nation's capital in 1392, was walled until the early 1900s. Some of the city's old gates remain. To get a true feel for Seoul, visit the markets that still operate just inside these gates. Seoul is emerging as a prime shopping destination in East Asia — you can get better deals than in Bangkok and its markets are more interesting than those you'll find in Hong Kong or Singapore.

The city has lots more to offer, too. Some old palaces are right in or adjacent to downtown. Toksu Palace, a large parklike area with several fine old structures, stands in the shadows of high-rise hotels on the west side of downtown. Located within Kyongbok Palace, the National Folklore Museum is a must-see. Among the city's other attractions are the National Museum of Korea, the Tong-gunung tombs, the railroad station (1920s Renaissance style), the National Art Gallery, Toksugung Palace (it shows definite Western influence in its architecture) and the Korea House (where you can enjoy demonstrations of traditional lifestyles, as well as entertainment and restaurant facilities). The city has a number of beautiful gardens and parks, which come alive in the spring and summer. For a great view of the city, head to the Seoul Tower, set atop 900-ft/274-m Namsan Mountain.

Mongolia

Mongolia will appeal to people who are truly world travelers, who enjoy history and who want to see something completely different. Because it is a country of nomads, visitors should be wary of trying to design itineraries based around cities, as a Mongolian "city" has

East Asia

Km 0 500 1000

Mi 0 500 1000

Copyright Weissmann Travel Reports

410 Asia Geofile

usually sprung up around a 20th-century mine or factory, with no attractions for the visitor at all. To get a true flavor of the country, all but the most resourceful travelers should take a tour. The main attractions include nomadic culture, camels, the Gobi Desert, Buddhist culture, trekking and wildlife safaris. (It may not get much attention these days, but under the leadership of Genghis Khan and his successors, Mongolia was *the* world power in the 12th and 13th centuries, controlling much of Asia and European Russia.)

Taiwan
One of the best places to see historical China is in Taiwan. When the Nationalist government fled the Communist takeover in 1949, they took a lot of China's history with them, including the imperial collection of Chinese artifacts — they're now in the National Palace Museum in Taipei, the island's capital. Even the Buddhist temples are better preserved than those on the mainland, because they escaped the ravages of China's Cultural Revolution.

The modern and the old haven't exactly blended in Taiwan; they coexist. On one hand, there are hotels in Taipei that can match any in the world for elegance, service and comfort, and business travelers will find a modern communication system in place that's capable of handling their needs without much fuss. But there are also days when you'll feel you're very much in a developing country: You can't drink the tap water, the cities are somewhat dirty and anarchy reigns in the traffic lanes. In addition to Chinese antiquities, the key attractions in Taiwan are its peaceful lakes, shopping, beaches, food, gardens and deep-sea fishing and scuba diving. You may want to drop in here if you're already in the area visiting Japan, Hong Kong or another destination.

Southeast Asia

Brunei Darussalam
This nation, commonly referred to as Brunei (pronounced brew-NIGH), is a very small but extremely wealthy country on the island of Borneo (which it shares with Indonesia and Malaysia). Most visitors go there on business; Brunei doesn't really seek tourist trade, and it's an expensive country to visit. Though we'd never recommend that someone make a special trip there for a vacation, you may want to stop in for a visit if you're already on the island of Borneo if only to see what life is like in one of the wealthiest nations in the world.

Cambodia
Cambodia can't seem to emerge from its long national nightmare. Although the 1992 lifting of the U.S. ban on travel to the country resulted in increased tourism, the nation continues to find difficulty in forging a lasting peace. When normalcy returns, serious adventure travelers will head to Cambodia to tour Angkor Wat, one of the most magnificent complexes of ruins in the world — it's in a class with the Great Pyramids of Egypt and Peru's Machu Picchu.

Laos
Though not a very popular tourist destination, Laos has a lot to offer visitors, especially those who enjoy natural beauty (mountain and jungle scenery) and historic sites. An advantage to traveling there sooner rather than later is that, for the time being, you'll virtually have the country to yourself; it's rare to run into another outsider once you've left the capital. It's easiest to book with a tour company but independent travelers may also obtain visas.

Myanmar
The attractions in Myanmar, also called Burma — including its Buddhist temples (such as Shwedagon Pagoda in the capital city, Yangon) and ruins (like those in Pagan) — are very spectacular sights. Because the government needs hard currency, it is trying to increase tourism and has made some things easier for travelers. Myanmar will appeal to experienced travelers, especially those who love Asian architecture and religion.

Philippines
The Philippines may not have the ancient temples or palaces found in other Southeast Asian countries, but its natural beauty is stunning enough to help you forget. And it's one of the region's best bargains. These 7,000 islands are a good destination

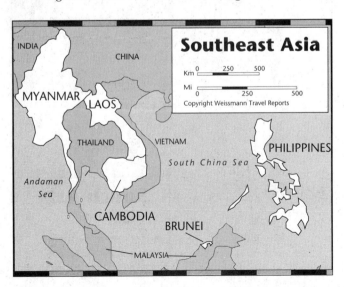

for travelers who have already visited Thailand, Malaysia or Indonesia and want to explore more of Southeast Asia. They'll find an endless, jagged coastline; dramatic waterfalls; ancient rice terraces; beautiful beaches and hypnotic reefs. Additionally, the government has also made valiant efforts, with some success, to stop dishonest taxi drivers, petty street crime and tourist cheats.

South Asia

Bangladesh   Bangladesh is an unlikely tourist destination — it's one of the most troubled countries in the world, facing unrelenting poverty and overpopulation problems, as well as the constant threats of flooding, typhoons and famine. But Bangladesh can offer a memorable experience for adventurous travelers: lush mangrove swamps, great river scenery, beaches, hill stations and the largest tropical rainforest in the region. If you are willing to accept that bad weather and large crowds come with the territory, Bangladesh can be a fas-

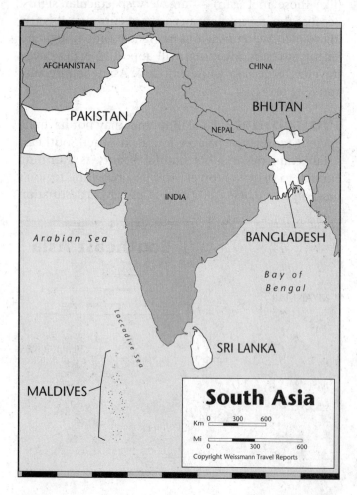

cinating destination. We can also say that the people there are among the friendliest and most generous we've ever met.

Bhutan   Bhutan, an ancient kingdom high in the Himalaya mountains, first opened its doors to Western travelers in 1974 and still severely restricts tourism. In doing so, the country's leaders have managed to both protect the country's culture and maintain relatively high standards for those who do visit. Visitors must pre-arrange the whole trip, and the vast majority go with a tour. The nation's foremost attractions are its beautiful Buddhist *dzongs* (monasteries or fortresses), which are set in dramatic mountain scenery; steep gorges, jungles and game reserves are also part of the draw. Consider sending flexible and somewhat adventurous travelers who are in the region. Don't send anyone who requires deluxe accommodations and a wide variety of food, shopping and nightlife, or who is adversely affected by high altitudes.

Maldives   The Maldives (pronounced MAHL-dives) consists of more than 1,200 coral islands and atolls. Some have towns, and others only hotels or private homes; one holds only the airport, and some are totally undeveloped. All share great fishing and excellent visibility for diving and snorkeling. A visit here is most often tied in with a trip to India or Sri Lanka. Send only those who will enjoy flat, fairly isolated islands, spectacular water, great beaches, snorkeling and scuba diving. Don't send anyone who is looking for exciting nightlife.

Pakistan   An alluring country, Pakistan has inspiring scenery that has attracted travelers for centuries. Unfortunately, many of Pakistan's most interesting areas — in the mountainous north, along the Afghan border — are somewhat dangerous to visit at the present time. However, there are many interesting historical sites and archaeological ruins to be seen throughout the country. Among them are the ruins of Moenjodaro, a birthplace of the Indus Valley Civilization over 4,000 years ago and Lahore, once the capital of the Moghul empire and today one of Pakistan's major cities.

On the surface, Pakistan has many similarities to India (of which it was once a part, and of which it is now an antagonist). Send adventurous clients who won't mind the dry, dusty conditions, transportation delays, less-than-desirable sanitary conditions, poverty and the fact that haggling accompanies nearly every transaction.

Sri Lanka   We can't imagine anyone not liking Sri Lanka (pronounced shree LAHN-kah), one of the most beautiful islands in the world. Gorgeous beaches, high mountains with tea plantations and some of Asia's highest and most impressive waterfalls are just some of its charms. It's culturally rich — you may happen upon one of several festivals — and has excellent wildlife sanctuaries. Unfortunately, civil strife between the Buddhist Sinhalese majority and the Hindu Tamal minority is tearing the country apart, and even though many parts of the nation aren't in the thick of the fighting, the random violence in the capital, Colombo, is enough to scare off most potential visitors.

Central Asia

Afghanistan   Right now, we cannot recommend a visit to any part of Afghanistan. We say this with sadness, because the country has always been intriguing: its colorful history, its rugged scenery comprising mountain ranges (some upwards of 25,000 ft/7,615 m) and vast arid areas, its fascinating markets, its fiercely independent people. But the war that has been raging for years — against the Soviet Union in the '80s and now between seemingly irreconcilable factions within Afghanistan itself — has made it an unsafe place for anyone. Much of the infrastructure has been turned into rubble. Millions of land mines are scattered throughout the country. When peace does come, it will take many, many years to reconstruct the nation.

Kazakhstan   Once you've reached Kazakhstan, you may feel as if you've reached the final outposts of the civilized world. Desolate desert scenery leads to flat, seemingly endless plains, broken only occasionally by isolated cities. Geographically, the nation is large, and encompasses a wide range of stark, yet beautiful, scenery. Travelers who wish to go there should have a broad range of interests and a great deal of flexibility (they won't find prompt service or many deluxe accommodations). The country's current political and economic difficulties have put limitations on supplies and tourist facilities.

Kyrgyzstan   If you are an adventurous trekker and want to get off the beaten track, go to Kyrgyzstan (pronounced cur-GHEE-stan). Hikes in Kyrgyzstan will pass by glacial lakes, pink marble cliffs and dramatic vistas. The country's Tien Shan Mountain Range provides some of the most challenging peaks in the world. You'll also experience, as you trek, a hospitality that has with-

stood the changes sweeping Central Asia. Though it's not easy to get to Kyrgyzstan, anyone who makes it there will be richly rewarded for the effort. The cultural makeup of the country is surprisingly varied. In some places you'll find a robed populace that still uses camels as beasts of burden and lives in houses similar to those found in the Middle East. But even after the fall of the Soviet Union, there is still a significant Russian presence. Please note that because of the possibility of civil disturbances, certain areas have sometimes been closed to visitors.

Tajikistan   Surrounded by the towering ranges of the Himalaya and Hindu Kush Mountains, Tajikistan has been called the "Roof of the World." Perhaps "Earth's Attic" would be more appropriate, since Tajikistan is cluttered with age-old rivalries, borrowed political rhetoric and the broken remnants of the defunct Soviet Union. Tajikistan, the poorest of the ex-Soviet republics, has become mired in civil war. Nonetheless, it holds promise as a tourist destination — to a certain type of tourist. Those who like to travel off the beaten path will find that you can't get much farther off than this. When peace returns, it will attract some adventurous travelers drawn by its scenic vistas, exotic markets and religious sites.

Turkmenistan   There are few sights a tourist would want to see in this arid land and precious little infrastructure to serve visitors. Bleak terrain, severe shortages of food and fuel and the nation's general inaccessibility are the reasons to avoid it as a leisure destination. If clients are too curious to pass it up, warn them that accommodations, services and nightlife will not be up to Western standards. They may, however, find interest in the country's archaeological sites, desert views, carpet factories and the Kara-Kum canal.

Uzbekistan

No country captures the mystery of Central Asia better than Uzbekistan. It is by far the region's most fascinating land: It has several ancient Silk Road cities — Bukhara and Khiva as well as Samarkand, the historic capital of 15th-century savage conqueror Tamerlane. (Tamerlane once had a grisly pyramid built out of 70,000 human skulls.) In Bukhara, Khiva and Samarkand, see sights connected with the history of the Silk Road and with Muslim culture — in Bukhara the Djuma Mosque is the most famous. In Samarkand, you'll want to visit the Registan, an ancient trading center, and see the tomb and palace of Tamerlane himself.

The capital and largest city of Uzbekistan is Tashkent, with a terrific blend of architecture showing Persian, Islamic and Russian influences. Its ancient monuments can't compare with those in Samarkand or Bukhara, but its modern attractions are draws. Check out Teatrainaya Square and the Opera and Ballet Theater.

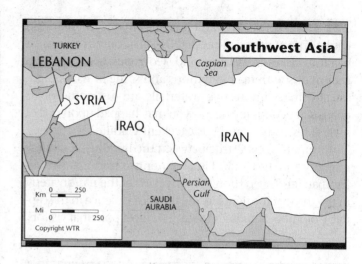

Southwest Asia

Iran

Although few people think of Iran (formerly Persia) as a tourist destination anymore, it really has some wonderful sights. Most of the popular mountain and desert areas are in the north, around the majestic Elburz Mountains. Archaeological ruins and beautiful architecture can be found throughout the country. These include the ruins of Persepolis, capital of the Persian Empire, and the blue-tiled mosques of Isfahan. Because of the internal political situation and strident anti-West feelings (anti-U.S., in particular), Iran is not recommended as a tourist destination at this time. Anyone who does visit must strictly adhere to rules and regulations that will seem very conservative by Western standards — to vary from them in ways that you might think are trivial can have dire consequences.

Iraq

It does not seem so long ago that Iraq (ancient Mesopotamia) was a fantastic tourist destination. Rich in history, culture, archaeology and a unique blend of people and religions, the country was proud of what it had to offer. It was home to the Sumerian, Babylonian and Assyrian civilizations. After the Muslim conquest in the 7th century, the region became a center of Arab learn-

ing and arts. For a time, Baghdad, Iraq's present-day capital, was the most important city in the Moslem world. In the aftermath of continuing battles with U.N. forces in the 1990s, however, both physical and legal barriers to travel there have been erected. At this point, the nation's closing to normal tourism is the least of its problems, but it's a loss felt by any serious traveler.

Lebanon

Until 1975, Beirut was one of the most sophisticated, cosmopolitan capitals of the region and was regarded as the Paris of the Mideast. Lebanon abounds with historical attractions and, in a relatively small area, features diverse terrain: Along the coast is a narrow, flat plain that gives way to mountains, whose tallest peaks are snow-covered in the winter. Despite the country's offerings, we feel that it would be ill advised to visit because of potential dangers from various factions. U.S. passports are not currently valid for Lebanon.

Syria

A few years ago, Syria threw open its doors to visitors; now it is attempting to clean up its image, in hopes that the tourists will start coming in. No doubt because of its reputation for supporting terrorists, the country wasn't attracting the number of travelers that its biblical and historical sites merit. (During its long history, Syria has been occupied by the Babylonians, the Assyrians, the Persians, the Phoenicians, the ancient Israelis, the Macedonians, the Romans, the Crusaders, the Arabs, the Ottoman Turks, the French and others; there are attractions in Syria connected with each of these forces.) Travelers to Syria will find that they have an opportunity to tour without an accompanying horde of tourists. Key attractions include Damascus, its capital and one of the world's longest continuously inhabited cities, Mediterranean beaches, desert scenery and Palmyra — the most important attraction in the country and a key commercial center on the Silk Route to

China in ancient times. The city was also home to Queen Zenobia who gave the Romans such a hard time.

Arabian Peninsula

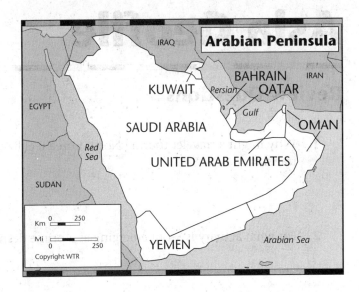

Bahrain   Bahrain is a very old nation of 33 islands in the western Persian Gulf. Though its climate is very hot and humid, it has more modern conveniences than many of its neighbors. That, coupled with its very cosmopolitan atmosphere, makes it a good destination to introduce travelers to the Mideast. While it doesn't have the endless sand dunes of larger countries in the region, there are areas that have a certain Lawrence of Arabia feel. Its markets, camel trains, beaches, ancient culture and shopping opportunities offer plenty to do.

Kuwait   The situation in Kuwait has improved greatly since the Persian Gulf War. The oil fires are out, the hotels rebuilt, and life has more or less returned to normal. But even before the war, Kuwait was never very high on anyone's list of tourist destinations. The Mideast's primary attractions — dramatic desert scenery, ruins from ancient civilizations, shrines relating to Arab and Islamic culture — are in short supply there. The only people who should consider going to the country at this time are those headed there for business. Besides, Kuwait doesn't want casual visitors now or at any time in the near future.

Oman   Oman is opening up in a big way to Western tourists. In fact, the national government aims to have 100,000 foreign tourists a year there within ten years. Oman features striking mountain and desert expanses, ancient forts and beautiful beaches. Its people reflect a mixture of African, Indian and Arab influences. Portuguese forts are all that remain from the period when Portugal controlled the region (1507–1650). The British were dominant from the mid-19th to mid-20th centuries and a thin veneer of British practices and customs still exists.

Qatar   Qatar (pronounced KAH-tar), an oil-rich peninsula and island sheikdom, really doesn't offer much for tourists. It's just as well: Only business travelers or those going to visit friends or relatives are likely to get a visa (visitors must have a Qatari sponsor). Should clients who merely want to sightsee get a visa, make sure they understand that they must follow what may seem like very conservative rules of conduct.

Saudi Arabia   While the country has many visitors, it has few tourists. More than two million Muslim pilgrims visit the cities of Mecca and Medina during the holy month of the pilgrimage (*hajj*). But the country's religious taboos, visa restrictions and lack of interest in developing Western-style tourism make it a poor destination for the typical Western leisure tourist. Business travelers, however, have been making their way through the country for thousands of years. During the caravan days, they carried coffee and frankincense from the markets of Yemen to the homes of Europe; now they purchase petroleum and sell computers and jet fighters. We recommend that only people with business, religious or family reasons travel to the country.

United Arab Emirates   Although most travelers to the United Arab Emirates will be going for business reasons, the country continues to develop its leisure tourism. Visitors will find beaches, Arab culture, desert scenery, water sports, coral reefs, mosques and historical sites. Still, it isn't a great choice for a first-time traveler to the Mideast; too many other countries in the region have much more to offer.

Yemen   Yemen is one of the world's most intriguing destinations. Within its relatively small territory, it contains a wide variety of terrains, climates, historical sites, peoples, cultures, architecture, music, clothing and food. Sana'a, its capital is a beautiful and fascinating city of unique architecture and veiled women — in many ways, it hasn't changed in centuries. Among the attractions a tourist would want to see in the city is the world's first skyscraper — the 2,000-year-old, 20-story Palace of Ghamdan (now, alas, in ruins).

Asia Geofile

Review Questions

1. Why might a traveler touring North Korea feel like he or she has walked into an Asian language translation of *1984*?

2. For what activity is Seoul emerging as a prime destination in East Asia? Why?

3. Why is Taiwan one of the best places to see historical China?

4. In what Southeast Asian country is the complex of ruins known as Angkor Wat?

5. Bhutan is an ancient kingdom located high in which mountains?

6. On the surface, to what country is Pakistan similar?

7. For tourists, which is the most fascinating country in Central Asia?

8. Why is Iran not recommended as a tourist destination at this time?

9. In which Southwest Asian country would you visit Damascus and Palmyra?

10. Why does Saudi Arabia have many visitors but few tourists?

Asia Geofile

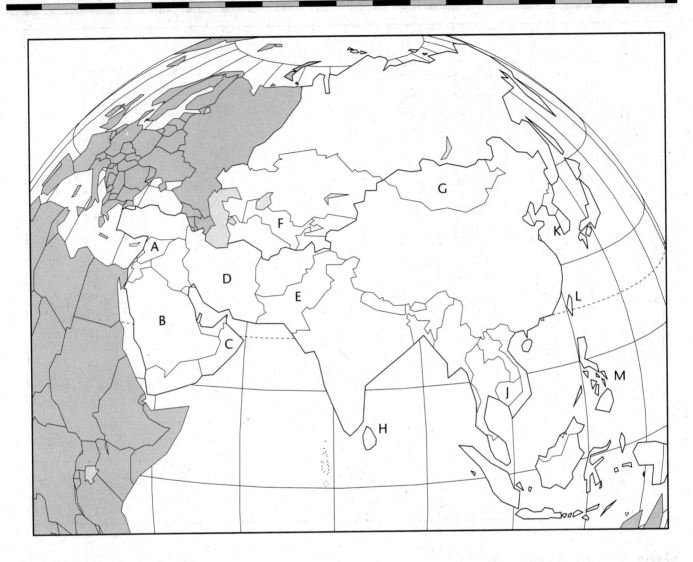

Map Skills Exercise

Match the tourist destination listed below with the corresponding letter on the map.
You can use each letter only once.

1. _____ Mongolia
2. _____ Syria
3. _____ Cambodia
4. _____ Philippines
5. _____ South Korea

6. _____ Taiwan
7. _____ Uzbekistan
8. _____ Saudi Arabia
9. _____ Oman
10. _____ Pakistan

Unit Review Asia

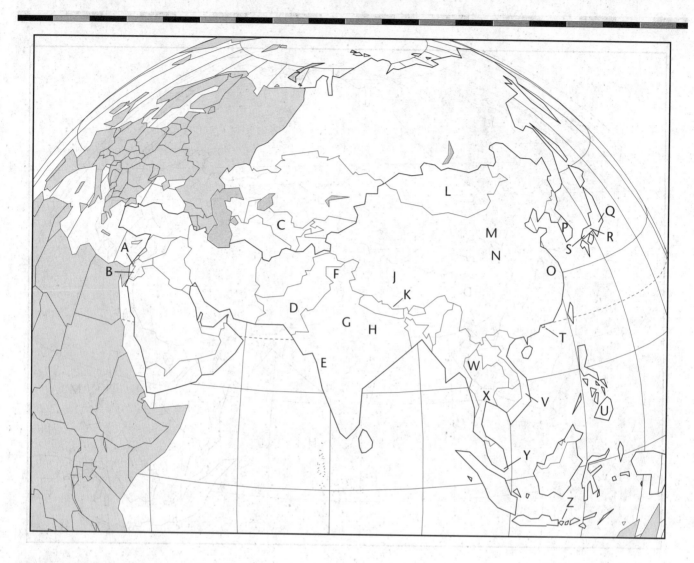

Map Skills Exercise

Match the tourist destination listed below with the corresponding letter on the map.

1. _____ Mt. Fuji
2. _____ Hiroshima
3. _____ Kyoto
4. _____ Petra
5. _____ Bali
6. _____ Moenjodaro ruins
7. _____ Mongolia
8. _____ Elephanta Island
9. _____ Taj Mahal
10. _____ Uzbekistan
11. _____ Kashmir
12. _____ Vietnam

13. _____ Varanasi
14. _____ Mt. Everest
15. _____ Bangkok
16. _____ Singapore
17. _____ Philippines
18. _____ South Korea
19. _____ Jerusalem
20. _____ Great Wall of China
21. _____ Xi'an
22. _____ Chiang Mai
23. _____ Shanghai
24. _____ Hong Kong
25. _____ Tibet

Unit Review Asia

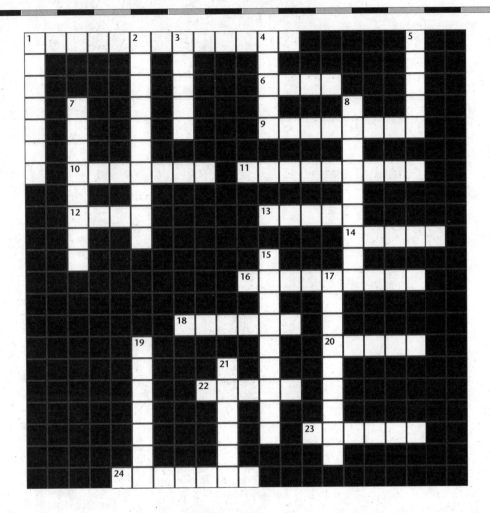

Content Review Crossword Puzzle

Across
1. Was off limits to most people in China
6. Most popular stop in Indonesia
9. India's top attraction
10. Where most travelers to Hong Kong stay
11. Church of the Nativity is there
12. Country of Persepolis ruins
13. Tokyo shopping district
14. Ayutthaya has them
16. Memorial to victims of Nazism
18. Resort island in Thailand
20. Visit Imperial Palace there
22. Easy to journey to from Hong Kong
23. Animals to see in China
24. A main sight in Nepal

Down
1. Something to eat in Israel
2. Amusement park in Japan
3. Gulf of Aqaba resort
4. Potala Palace country
5. See it from Mount Namsan
7. Popular in Nepal
8. In Africa and India
15. His tomb is in Samarkand
17. Key site in Cambodia
19. Has a European flavor
21. Hindu pilgrims bathe in it

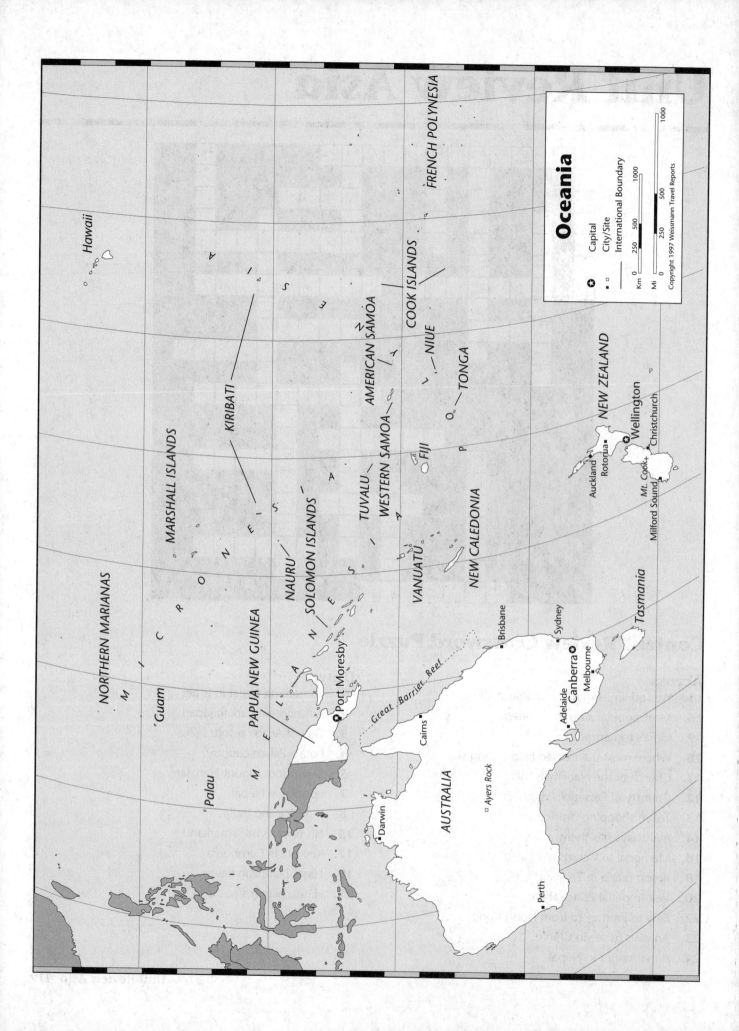

Oceania

Capital ✪
City/Site □
International Boundary ───

Km 0 250 500 1000
Mi 0 250 500 1000

Copyright 1997 Weissmann Travel Reports

Hawaii

FRENCH POLYNESIA

COOK ISLANDS

NIUE

TONGA

AMERICAN SAMOA

WESTERN SAMOA

FIJI

KIRIBATI

MARSHALL ISLANDS

NORTHERN MARIANAS

Guam

Palau

MICRONESIA

NAURU

SOLOMON ISLANDS

PAPUA NEW GUINEA

Port Moresby ✪

MELANESIA

TUVALU

VANUATU

NEW CALEDONIA

POLYNESIA

NEW ZEALAND

Auckland
Rotorua
Wellington ✪
Mt. Cook
Milford Sound
Christchurch

AUSTRALIA

Great Barrier Reef

Ayers Rock

Darwin

Perth

Adelaide

Cairns

Brisbane

Sydney

Canberra ✪

Melbourne

Tasmania

Oceania

THE PACIFIC OCEAN ISLAND NATIONS OF Oceania vary in size from Australia, the sixth largest country in the world, to tiny 8-sq-mi/21-sq-km Nauru. Some are coral atolls that rise just above the water's surface, others have that lush, mountainous look that the word *paradise* was created to describe. The crystal clear lagoons sheltered on some of these islands have snorkeling that's the best in the world; scuba divers and deep-sea anglers won't complain either.

The largest islands, Australia, New Zealand and New Guinea (of which Papua New Guinea accounts for half), have a wide range of activities and attractions that are not water related. Australia and New Zealand are as developed as any country in North America or western Europe, and are understandably the most popular destinations in Oceania (we are not counting Hawaii, which is part of the United States and profiled in North America).

Culturally, the islands of the Pacific are divided into the regions of Polynesia, Micronesia and Melanesia (*see the* Physical Geography *chapter*). While some visitors find the Polynesian culture most interesting, others prefer Melanesia, whose inhabitants have had less contact with Westerners. And still others feel that the waters of Micronesia are enough to lure them from halfway around the world.

When sending a client to one of the smaller islands, it's very important to choose carefully. While the most beautiful of the smaller islands by far outshine anything in the Caribbean, not every island is attractive; in fact, some are even physically unattractive. The water clarity, turbulence and depth, the terrain of the island itself, the degree of development, the climate, the cultural attractions and the availability of entertainment should be taken into consideration. The best time to visit varies from island to island, according to the client's needs.

In this section, we take an in-depth look at the most popular Oceania destinations: Australia, New Zealand, French Polynesia, Fiji and the Cook Islands. The Oceania Geofile, which follows, will help you discover what's unique about each of the other islands in this geographic area.

Australia

Selling Points

The Great Barrier Reef, Aboriginal culture and art, Ayers Rock, kangaroos, Tasmania, koalas, the Queensland rain forest, casinos, Sydney, beaches, opera and the Outback are the country's main attractions.

Almost everyone will love Australia. The only ones who shouldn't go are those who prefer to have their South Pacific vacations on lush and mountainous islands (most of Australia is flat and dry) or who prefer a somewhat formal atmosphere.

Fascinating Facts About Australia

Australians call themselves Aussies (pronounced Ozzies, not Awzies), and say they speak *Strine* (Australian), rather than English . . . Australia has no sales tax . . . Some long-distance buses in Australia play movies for passengers . . . Australia's animals seemed so downright weird to Europeans that the first platypus specimen sent to England was denounced as a hoax. Scientists said the creature was obviously a beaver onto which a duck's bill had been sewn. To see the platypus in the wild, hike into Eungella National Park in Queensland. . . .

It's hard to believe that, just two hundred years ago, people had to be forced to go to Australia. (Of course, it was a British penal colony at the time.) Today, people flock there freely — the country has become a popular destination for travelers from all over the world.

It's easy to understand why. Australia is filled with the unique and the unusual: animals that exist nowhere else, the red-dust emptiness of the Great Outback and the aqua and coral beauty of the Great Barrier Reef. We're especially fond of Australians; they are among the friendliest people we've met.

The first human settlers (ancestors of the Aborigines) arrived in Australia at least 50,000 years ago, passing across land bridges and shallow seas connecting Ice Age Asia to Australia. It wasn't until 1787 that the first English colonists arrived — convicts from overflowing British prisons. More prisoners were transported and free settlers soon followed. Slowly, the continent was explored and settled — in some ways reminiscent of the opening of the West in North America: Settlers in wagons followed pathfinders to make homes in wild country; great cattle stations (similar to ranches) were founded; gold was discovered.

With approximately 3 million sq mi/7 million sq km, Australia is the world's largest island. It is both country and continent. While most of it is barren outback, Australia has a wide range of environment, including tropical rain forests in its northern regions, temperate forests along the east coast and even a few snowy mountains spotting the Great Dividing Range. Off the northeast coast is the world's largest coral reef.

What to Do There

Adelaide   Adelaide is noted for its handsome Victorian and Edwardian buildings and vast stretches of parkland. Key attractions include the Migration Museum, Maritime Museum, Botanical Gardens and the 110-year-old Zoological Gardens. The culture of the Australia's native peoples can be sampled at the South Australian Museum (Aboriginal artifacts) and Tandanya Aboriginal Cultural Institute (museum and performing arts center). If you're looking for nightlife, try the elegant casino housed in what was once an ornate railway station. Day trips can be made to nearby valleys to explore vineyards and sample their products. Another nice day trip is to Hahndorf, a town settled by German immigrants in the 1830s. Today it has small inns, good restaurants and shopping. Farther afield is Kangaroo Island. We like it for its charm and varied wildlife, including sea lions, koalas and kangaroos. We also recommend considering taking a steamboat on the nearby Murray River.

Alice Springs The Alice, as it's known, is a good introduction to Australia's Great Outback. It lies in the center of Australia and in the middle of nowhere. In town, visit The School of the Air and the Frontier Camel Farm. Excursions into the surrounding red desert enable you to see incredible natural wonders, chief among them Ayers Rock (*see separate paragraph*). Other desert attractions are rare and ancient palms and Australian wildlife (including wild camels).

Ayers Rock Ayers Rock is the world's largest monolith and a truly stunning sight. It's a huge rock (1,142 ft/348 m high, 9 mi/13 km around) surrounded by a vast plain that disappears into the horizon. You'll want to see it at both sunset and sunrise, which change the colors of the rock to orange and red and purple (the rest of the day, it's a reddish brown). The rock has religious significance to the Aborigines.

Brisbane We go to Brisbane primarily as a place to stay while taking excursions to enjoy subtropical forests, Aussie wildlife and a taste of Australian country life. Mt. Coottha overlooks the city — go there at night for the view or during the day to visit the botanic gardens (subtropical flora). At the Lone Pine Sanctuary, southwest of town, visitors can hold koala bears and see kangaroos and other Australian fauna close up. The Australian Woolshed offers sheepshearing as well as "ram parades." There are two very different beach resorts nearby. One offers lots of nightlife and the other a quieter atmosphere. While in Brisbane, don't miss the Natural Trust of Queensland's Currumbin Sanctuary noted for huge flocks of brightly colored lorikeets (a type of parrot).

Cairns Tropical Cairns is mainly a jumping-off point for trips to the northern Queensland rain forests, Kuranda and the Great Barrier Reef. Don't plan to surf-and-sun there. Cairns has mangrove mudflats rather than beaches. For a road less traveled, push north to Cape Tribulation, where the rain forest extends all the way to the coastline. And take the half-day Kuranda Barron Gorge Tour (by rail and bus), over the gorge and

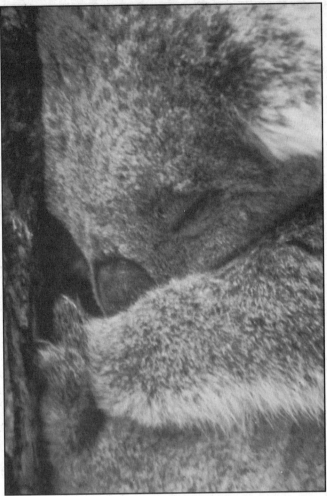
Koala bear

into jungle and mountains. Kuranda itself has a butterfly farm and a great street market on Sundays and Wednesdays (local crafts). Don't miss the Tjapukai Dancers, a world-famous Aboriginal dance troupe.

Canberra Canberra, Australia's capital, is filled with lakes, gardens and, of course, government buildings. Don't miss the dramatic new Parliament House, the lakeside Australian National Gallery, Australian War Memorial and National Botanical Gardens. Canberra is best seen as a fly-in day trip (it is easily reached by air from Sydney and Melbourne). For a change of pace, visit a sheep station in the hills beyond town and enjoy an Australian bush barbecue.

Darwin This port town (pop. 73,000) in the Northern Territory is very isolated from other key tourist attractions. It's a good place to lie on the beach, but make sure the water is safe before swimming (sharks, saltwater crocodiles and deadly jellyfish have been known to swim offshore). Tour the Reptile Farm, War Cemetery,

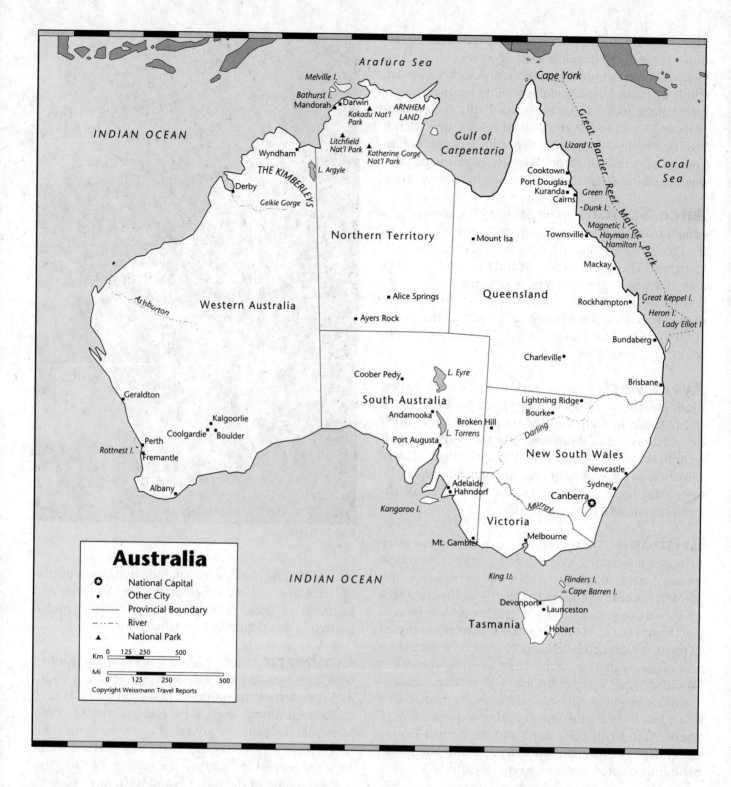

Map legend:

Australia

⊛   National Capital
▪   Other City
    Provincial Boundary
–·–·–   River
▲   National Park

Km   0   125   250   500

Mi   0   125   250   500

Copyright Weissmann Travel Reports

Government House (built in 1869), Chinese Temple and Doctor's Gully (to watch the fish feeding at night).

Great Barrier Reef

One of the world's most magnificent reefs, the Great Barrier extends nearly 1,200 mi/2,000 km along Australia's northeast coast. The reef and its islands provide opportunities to sail, snorkel and dive, ride in glass-bottom boats and semisubmersible submarines. The underwater sightseeing is amazing.

Of the many coral islands that are parts of the reef, only three offer overnight accommodations: Heron, Green and Lady Elliot. Our favorite is Heron Island. We recommend that first-time visitors stay at least two nights. It's an ideal spot for divers, nature lovers and those wanting to get away from it all. Visit Green Island on a day or overnight trip from Cairns. The closest coral island/cay to the mainland, it's great for snorkeling, reef walking, scuba diving and coral viewing.

A number of resorts have also been built on islands that are not part of the reef but are nearby. You can stay on one of them and take day trips (by boat) over to the reef.

Melbourne
This charming city (pop. 3,200,000) on the banks of the Yarra River is often called the San Francisco of the Southern Hemisphere. It has a formal side, but it also has a reputation for being a hip city, one with a passion for theater and sports. Attractions include the Victorian Arts Centre and National Gallery (look for its stained-glass roof), Chinatown and the city zoo (founded in 1857). You might also want to see the Royal Botanic Gardens, Fitzroy Gardens (with Captain Cook's house), the old-time trams and the somewhat morbid but fascinating Old Melbourne Gaol (jail, complete with death masks and other prison memorabilia). Day trips from Melbourne will take you to Phillip Island (beaches, fairy penguins, koalas and fur seals); Healesville Sanctuary (emus, kangaroos, koalas, Tasmanian devils, platypuses and others); Wilson's Promontory National Park (hiking trails, beautiful beaches and an array of wildlife); Port Campbell National Park (captivating coastal scenery and the "Twelve Apostles" islands offshore); and the Oswin Roberts Reserve (koalas and fur seals).

The Outback
The Outback refers to the vast and mostly desolate interior of Australia. It's perhaps best appreciated at one of the three national parks most easily accessible from Darwin. 1) Kakadu National Park is a huge wilderness reserve whose swamps are filled with crocodiles and innumerable species of birds and other wildlife. It has Aboriginal paintings, too. Hire a boat to tour the billabongs (lakes). 2) Rugged Katherine Gorge National Park has 13 sandstone gorges filled with Aboriginal paintings and wildlife (such as emus and dingoes). The gorges are usually seen by boat, but there are also many trails. 3) Litchfield National Park, a national park without hotel facilities, is accessible only to four-wheel- drive vehicles. Day tours there include a tea break in an abandoned tin mine, visits to waterfalls and termite mounds 10 ft/3 m high.

Perth
Similar to San Diego in both climate and scenery, Perth (pop. 1,119,000) is located 1,700 mi/2,735 km from any other large city. Walk along the Swan River and visit at least one of the splendid beaches (some are nude or topless). Drop by the Western Australia Museum (Aboriginal art) and visit the King's Park (undeveloped land with a great view of the city).

Neighboring Fremantle, the port town at the mouth of the Swan River, is where the America's Cup yachts were based. The quaint city's real claim to fame, however, is that it has the world's largest and best collection of 19th-century British colonial architecture.

Sydney
Poised to host the 2000 Summer Olympics, Sydney (pop. 3,596,000) is Australia's largest and best-known city. Begin your stay by purchasing a Sydney Pass, good for three days of bus and ferry travel as well as a round trip to the airport and a ride on the Sydney Explorer Bus, which stops at 20 of the city's most popular tourist attractions. Sydney's symbol is the very

Geostats

Official Name: Commonwealth of Australia.

Visa Info: Visas, onward tickets and sufficient funds needed by U.S. and Canadian residents.

Health Certificates: Yellow-fever certificate needed only if arriving from an affected country. Contact health authorities for latest information.

Capital: Canberra.

Population: 18,043,000.

Size: 2,966,139 sq mi/7,682,300 sq km. About the size of the continental U.S.

Languages: English and Aboriginal languages.

Climate: Relatively dry, ranging from temperate in the south to semitropical in the north.

Economy: Industry, service.

Government: Federal democracy, member of British Commonwealth.

Religions: Anglican, Roman Catholic.

Currency: Australian dollar (AUD). 100 cents = 1 AUD. Credit cards and traveler's checks widely accepted. AE,CB, DC, MC and VI.

Time Zone: Australia has three time zones. The Australian west is 13 hours ahead of EST (+8 GMT), the center 14½ ahead (+9.5) and the east coast 15 hours ahead (+10).

Electricity: 240/250 volts. Many hotels provide 110- volt outlets for small appliances.

Departure Tax: 25 AUD.

recognizable Opera House, which should be visited for its architecture alone. Other attractions include the King's Cross area, the Mint, St. Mary's Cathedral and the Hyde Park area. We enjoyed lunch on a Sydney Harbour cruise and surfing and sunbathing on one of the area's fine beaches. And don't neglect seeing the Art Gallery of New South Wales, the Powerhouse Museum (one of Australia's best — and newest) and the Taronga Zoo (superb for an introduction to koalas, kangaroos and other unique animals). If shopping is what you're after, try Paddington or Darling Harbour. The original settlement of Sydney, the Rocks, has been restored and is well worth a visit. After seeing it, go to the top of Centrepoint Tower for a striking view of the city.

But don't limit yourself to the city proper. One nearby day trip is to the Royal National Park. The park has great surfing, impressive cliffs and interesting wildlife (such as swamp wallabies). About 65 mi/105 km west of Sydney are the Blue Mountains, a beautiful range with hiking trails (starting near the town of Katoomba) and cool weather — allow a full day for this excursion.

There are several other excursions you might also consider. Hunter Valley wine country, for instance, can provide an introduction to Australia's great wines. Some tours last from one to four days, such as those to Lightning Ridge and Broken Hill and Dubbo (country life, sheepshearing).

Tasmania   This island is perhaps best known outside of Australia as the home of the Tasmanian devil. It has long stretches of uninhabited beaches, jagged (and often snow-capped) mountains, slow-moving creeks and rivers, gorges, historical sites, forests and a rugged shoreline. Visit Hobart, the largest city on the island, to walk around and see its early-19th-century homes and buildings. From Hobart, travel to Port Arthur, site of an old penal colony. For 57 years (1830–87) Port Arthur confined nearly 12,000 prisoners. Today, it has a museum displaying captains' logs that list the crimes of their passengers (read Dickens' Oliver Twist prior to arrival!). On your visit, also try to see Russell Falls (a tropical waterfall decked with wild ferns).

Itinerary

Though we'd encourage a longer stay, the absolute minimum for a first-time visitor would be one week. Here are two possible one-week itineraries:

Day 1 — Arrive Sydney.

Day 2 — Sydney.

Day 3 — Sydney.

Day 4 — Canberra. Don't overnight — fly to Melbourne.

Day 5 — Melbourne.

Day 6 — Melbourne.

Day 7 — Depart Australia.

The following itinerary looks at Australia's more rugged side:

Day 1 — Arrive Cairns.

Day 2 — Cairns.

Day 3 — Cairns.

Day 4 — Fly to Alice Springs.

Day 5 — Overland to Ayers Rock.

Day 6 — Fly to Sydney.

Day 7 — Sydney.

Day 8 — Depart Australia.

The ideal two-week itinerary would follow Days 1–5 in the first schedule above, then add the following: two nights in Alice Springs, one night at Ayers Rock, three nights at Cairns and the Great Barrier Reef and two in Brisbane.

Climate/When to Go

The seasons are the opposite of those in the Northern Hemisphere — when it's summer in the north, it's winter south of the equator (Australian winters are fairly mild, but a bit rainy). Our favorite months are October and April, when days are in the 70s F/23–27 C and nights in the 60s F/15–22 C in the southern temperate zone (above the tropic of Capricorn, Australia is considered subtropical to tropical). September–May is all right in most parts of the country, with day temperatures ranging from highs of 70–110 F/23–44 C to lows of 50–85 F/10–30 C. December and January are the hottest months, July and August the coldest (Melbourne and Sydney, in particular, can be rather cold and drizzly then). The Great Barrier Reef is best visited September–December, but can also be seen May–August (it's a bit cooler then; cyclones can disrupt sightseeing plans in January–April).

Transportation

Qantas, Air New Zealand, Northwest, Continental and United fly from the U.S. Canadian Airlines International flies from Vancouver and connects with Qantas or Air New Zealand in Honolulu. International flights from all over the world land in Adelaide, Brisbane, Cairns, Darwin, Melbourne, Perth and Sydney. Sydney's Kingford Smith International Airport (SYD) is 6 mi/10 km northwest of the city. Limited cruise-ship service is also available from North America.

Internally, Ansett, Australian Airlines, East-West and regional carriers provide frequent air service, but are expensive. For the best fares, you should investigate air passes, sold only overseas (check with the individual air carriers). More reasonable alternatives include excellent rail and bus service; foreign visitors can purchase rail and bus passes. The famous Indian Pacific train ride from Sydney to Perth takes 65 hours and is only recommended for those with a great passion for trains. Major bus companies include Australian Coachlines, Greyhound, Pioneer and Bus Australia. Escorted/hosted tours, rental cars, caravans (camping trailers) and boats/cruises (along the Great Barrier Reef) are other means of exploring Australia.

Accommodations

Australia offers every form of accommodation, from deluxe properties to farmhouses. Five-star hotels, B-and-Bs, resorts, campsites, motels and very basic quarters (on remote islands) can all be found. Almost without exception, the accommodations are clean and the proprietors friendly. At Home Down Under is an organization that provides lodging in private homes as an alternative to hotel accommodation.

Health Advisories

When you get there, you'll find that Australian health and sanitation standards are equal to those in North America and Europe. Hospitals accept Blue Cross and Blue Shield. Drugstores carry familiar brand-name medicines.

What to Buy

Shop for boomerangs, gold, sheepskins and wool products, paintings, stuffed koala bears (made from kangaroo fur), local art and Aboriginal handicrafts (didgeridoos and bullroarers), Broome pearls, opals and other gems.

What to Eat

The food shows a definite British influence, tending to the hearty. The emphasis is on good steaks (beef) and chops (lamb), often cooked on a "barbie" (barbecue grill). The national dish, however, is the meat pie, a pastry shaped like a small pie and filled with mysterious meat in a dark gravy. It is best eaten with "sauce" (ketchup).

Visitors can be thankful that the post-World War II wave of immigrants from southern Europe brought with it spices, garlic and a greater menu variety, strongly Mediterranean. Seafood (no longer coated in a heavy batter) is a treat almost everywhere. We liked the crayfish (lobster), prawns, Sydney rock oysters (raw with a touch of lemon and black pepper), Moreton Bay bugs (a type of lobster) and mud crabs. Crocodile, buffalo, kangaroo (usually kangaroo-tail soup) and withchey grubs (large white insects that taste surprisingly like peanut butter) sometimes crop up on Outback-type menus. Beer still reigns as the national beverage, but wine has mounted a strong challenge.

Travel Tips for the Client

Do go to an Aussie pub for conversation, drinks and a meal . . . Do attend a game of "footy" (football with Australian rules) . . . Don't brag endlessly about the U.S. or Canada; it will only reinforce prevalent negative stereotypes . . . Don't forget your sunscreen, especially in Queensland — it's hot, hot, hot . . . Don't be surprised by what they wear (or don't wear) on the beaches. Lady Jane is the nude beach in Sydney . . . Do try Vegemite, a yeast spread that has the same standing that peanut butter has in North American cuisine . . . Do visit a working sheep station. . . .

Tipping: Not required in restaurants or taxis.

Australia

Review Questions

1. Why has Australia become a popular destination for travelers from all over the world?

2. Why should a tourist visit Ayer's Rock at both sunset and sunrise?

3. What can a visitor do at the Lone Pine Sanctuary, southwest of Brisbane?

4. Why shouldn't a tourist plan to surf and sun in Cairns?

5. Where is the Great Barrier Reef? How long is it?

6. What city on the Yarra River has a reputation for being hip?

7. To what does "the Outback" refer?

8. What city will a visitor see from the Centrepoint Tower?

9. How would you describe the natural environment of Tasmania to a client?

10. Which term best characterizes Australian food? Exotic, spicy, vegetarian, or hearty?

Australia

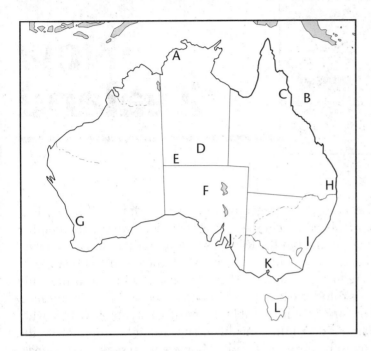

Map Skills Exercise

Match the tourist destination listed below with the corresponding letter on the map. You can use each letter only once.

1. _____ Perth
2. _____ Great Barrier Reef
3. _____ Sydney
4. _____ Tasmania
5. _____ Ayers Rock
6. _____ Melbourne
7. _____ Brisbane
8. _____ Cairns
9. _____ Darwin
10. _____ Alice Springs

Selling Exercise

You have just returned from a two-week familiarization trip to Australia visiting Melbourne, Sydney, Brisbane, Ayers Rock, Alice Springs and Cairns. You are so excited about all that Australia has to offer — from the natural beauty and unusual animals to the sophisticated cities — that you decide to tell your travel-agency clients about your trip. Write a one-page letter that will go out to your clients telling them about this must-see destination.

New Zealand

Selling Points

Great natural beauty, friendly people, Maori culture, Alps-like mountains, beaches, fishing, camping, surfing, skiing, bungy jumping, golfing, mineral baths, tramping (the local term for hiking), sheep and fjords are New Zealand's foremost attractions.

The only thing lacking is snorkeling comparable to that at other South Pacific destinations.

Fascinating Facts About New Zealand

Consider a stay on a sheep farm to capture the flavor of this nation of sheep, where sheep outnumber people 22 to 1 . . . Relative to body size, the kiwi lays the largest egg of any bird — up to 25% of its body weight. Kiwis can lay up to three eggs at a time! . . . Pubs in New Zealand have invented the sport of horizontal bungy-cord jumping. Set a beer at the end of a long bar and go to the other end and strap on a cord. Run as far as you can until you grab the beer — or are snapped back. Do it again. Another pub pastime is wall-splattering, where players wear a Velcro suit and have a leap at a felt-covered wall — the highest "stick" wins. A small trampoline helps one achieve altitude. . . .

New Zealand is so gorgeous, so naturally dramatic — glaciers, fjords, isolated beaches — that we wonder if we should mention . . . bungy jumping. But the Kiwis, as the New Zealanders are known, can take credit for making it a sport. Then there's the jet boat. They can take credit for that, too. There are any number of other truly adventurous things to do in New Zealand — sportfishing, for instance, or skiing or surfing. But probably the most satisfying activity is what New Zealanders do all the time: hike. They call it "tramping." It's the perfect way to meet these friendly people and to soak up the amazing beauty of the place.

New Zealand was originally settled in the 1300s by the Maoris (pronounced *MAU-rees*) — a long tradition of oral history recounts how the settlers arrived in 10 great canoes from an island near Tahiti. For 500 years their lives went untouched by the outside world. They wore spectacular zigzag tattoos, made war among themselves and either enslaved or ate their enemies.

The Dutch explorer Abel van Tasman was the first European to arrive in New Zealand, but he left without claiming it. Captain Cook claimed the islands 130 years later for the British, but it wasn't until the 1830s that *Pakeha*, or white, settlement began in earnest. Conflict between the Maoris and the British settlers finally ended with a live-and-let-live attitude that persists to this day. New Zealand remains an independent member of the British Commonwealth and has declared itself a nuclear-free zone.

The nation consists of two large islands, logically enough called North Island and South Island, and some smaller islands. Both major islands are rather mountainous, with coastal plains. North Island, where most of the people live, has a warmer, more temperate climate. The South is colder, but more spectacular, with fjords, glaciers and hundreds of streams and lakes.

What to Do There

Auckland   Also known as the City of Sails, Auckland is New Zealand's largest (pop. 856,000) and most cosmopolitan city. Auckland, on North Island, has two harbors ringed by 14 extinct volcanoes

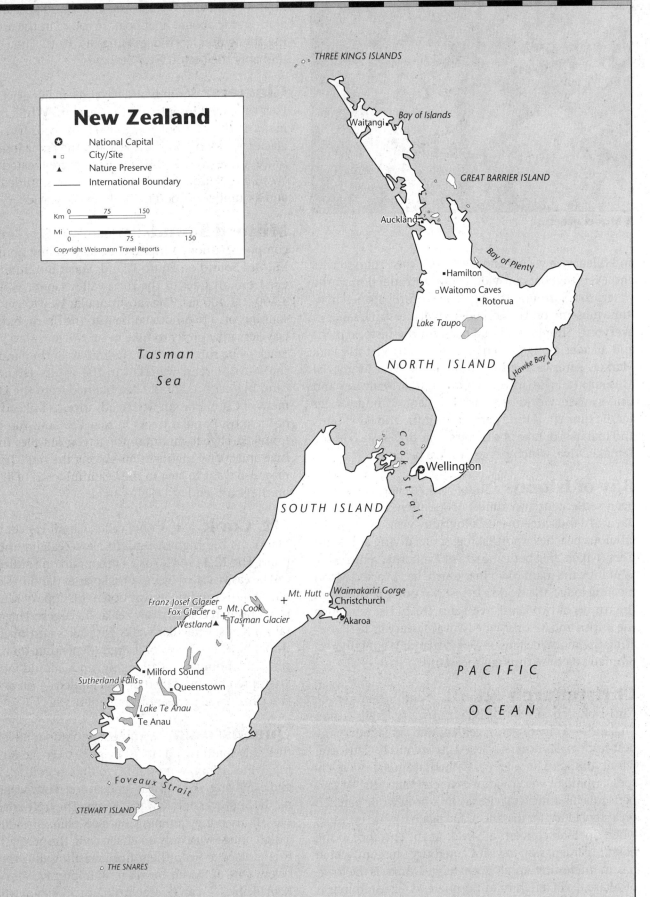

New Zealand

- ✪ National Capital
- ■ ▫ City/Site
- ▲ Nature Preserve
- ─── International Boundary

Km 0 · 75 · 150
Mi 0 · 75 · 150

Copyright Weissmann Travel Reports

THREE KINGS ISLANDS

Bay of Islands
Waitangi

GREAT BARRIER ISLAND

Auckland

Bay of Plenty

■ Hamilton
▫ Waitomo Caves
■ Rotorua

Lake Taupo

NORTH ISLAND

Hawke Bay

Tasman

Sea

Cook Strait

✪ Wellington

SOUTH ISLAND

Mt. Hutt
Waimakariri Gorge
Christchurch

Franz Josef Glacier
Fox Glacier   Mt. Cook
Westland ▲   Tasman Glacier

Akaroa

PACIFIC

OCEAN

■ Milford Sound
Sutherland Falls
■ Queenstown

Lake Te Anau
Te Anau

Foveaux Strait

STEWART ISLAND

▫ THE SNARES

A Maori greeting

and filled with yachts and sailboats. Cruise ships, ferries and even tugboats provide a good introduction to the waters that surround the city. The recently opened maritime museum on Hobson Wharf will please the sailor in everyone. Shoppers should head for the historic malls and arcades along Queen Street or go to Victoria Park Market. Afterward visit the Auckland War Memorial Museum (a great introduction to Maori culture) and Underwater World (the world's largest underwater acrylic tunnel). If time permits, visit the zoo (kiwi birds and tuataras) or take one of the scenic drives, such as the Tamaki Drive, which passes peerless beaches.

Bay of Islands
Site of New Zealand's first European settlement and almost 150 scattered islands, the Bay of Islands area merits a four-day visit. We like the fabulous beaches, sportfishing, scuba diving and kauri trees (which are about the size of California redwoods). Waitangi, the main town in the area, has a carved Maori meeting lodge, the world's largest war canoe (made from the trunks of two kauri trees) and Treaty House, where the British and Maoris signed a peace treaty in 1840, creating the modern state of New Zealand. We highly recommend a cruise through the islands.

Christchurch
Peaceful and picturesque Christ-church, on South Island, is more English than England — a city of parks, gardens and art galleries. The best-known landmark is the Christchurch Cathedral (climb the spire for a view). Cathedral Square is a lively spot at midday, when a local character called the Wizard performs his antics (playing a ram's horn while perched on a stepladder, for instance), and again toward evening, when open-air concerts are held. At the entrance to the botanic garden, stop to visit Canterbury Museum, which has an interesting Antarctica exhibit. Nearby is the town of Akaroa, as French in atmosphere as Christchurch is

English. Also visit Waimakariri Gorge and take an exhilarating ride aboard a jet boat. If you're in the area during the winter, consider skiing Mt. Hutt. The skiing is probably the best in New Zealand.

Glaciers
South Island has three major glaciers: the Fox, the Franz Joseph and the Tasman. While the Tasman (*see the* Mt. Cook *paragraph*) is the country's largest glacier, we found both the Fox and the Franz Josef to be more impressive. These two glaciers are located in the Westland National Park; the park offers guided walks and a number of good trails along the glacier.

Milford Sound
No journey to New Zealand is complete without a trip to the breathtaking fjords near Milford Sound on South Island. Sheer mountain cliffs rise from all sides of the river valley (some as high as 4,500 ft/1,400 m). The most popular way to get to the sound is on a two-hour cruise into the fjords, but hardy travelers may prefer to hike in on the four-day Milford Track — be sure to follow the trail to Sutherland Falls, the fourth-largest waterfall in the world. Hiking and camping permits should be obtained from the Department of Conservation well in advance, as Milford is one of the most popular tracks in New Zealand. You can go from lake edge to mountaintop to glacial valley in a day hike and spend nights in huts along the trail. Travelers may also want to stay in the beautiful town of Te Anau on the south end of Lake Te Anau.

Mt. Cook
Mt. Cook, called Cloud Piercer by the Maoris, is the highest peak in New Zealand and Australia. The 12,345-ft/3,763-m mountain on South Island can be easily scaled by bus or ski planes (landings can be terrifying). Grinding its way down the slope of Mt. Cook is the Tasman Glacier, New Zealand's largest. The mountain offers spectacular walks past lakes and rivers and through fields of snow or flowers (depending on the season). Climbing is challenging and should only be attempted by the skilled or well guided — on average, five climbers die a year on the mountain.

Queenstown
If you enjoy outdoor adventure, then this South Island city is the place to go. Besides fishing, windsurfing, waterskiing, golfing, horseback riding and paraflying, you will find jet-boat and white-water rides on the Shotover and Kawarau Rivers. The truly adventurous can try bungy jumping: Jumpers plunge headfirst off a high bridge with only an elastic cord, the bungy, tied to their ankles to keep them from crashing into the river below. One of Queenstown's most impressive sites — the Remarkables — can be seen from just about anywhere in

Milford Sound

the city. These 6,700-ft/2,000-m mountains are particularly beautiful at sunset and sunrise.

Rotorua

Rotorua, on North Island, sits on top of the most active thermal spots in the country (the town reeks of sulfur). Visit the boiling mud pots and geysers at the Whakarewarewa Thermal Reserve (also known as *Whaka*) or take mineral baths and marinate in mud packs and mineral oils at one of the many spas around town. Rotorua's water organ and art gallery are worth a look; the art gallery building was a turn-of-the-century spa and is a sight in itself. The city is also a center of Maori culture: attend a Maori *hangi* (feast and concert) and tour the Ohinemutu Maori village. Near the main entrance to Whaka is the Maori Arts and Craft Institute, a replica of a traditional Maori village.

Waitomo Caves

For an unforgettable, eerie adventure, visit the three Waitomo Caves south of Hamilton on North Island. The main draw at the caves is what hangs from the ceilings—not the stalactites, but the thousands of luminescent glowworms. Ride the tour boats through the Waitomo Cave or (if you're feeling adventurous) try black-water rafting in the Ruakuri Cave.

Wellington

Wellington, the capital of New Zealand, is rarely visited, and those who do go seldom stay more than a day. It's a pity—for one thing, the North Island city has outstanding architecture. Other attractions include the cable-car ride up Kelburn Hill to visit the magnificent botanical gardens (waterfalls, orchids and roses), the National Museum (good Maori exhibits, art, live exhibitions) and the Old Government Building (one of the oldest wooden structures south of the equator). Wellington earns its nickname, the Windy City, every year, particularly at the beginning of winter, when gale-force winds gust through town. If you've rented a car, drive along breathtaking Marine Drive.

Itinerary

New Zealand lends itself to all forms of travel: escorted, hosted, fly/drive, adventure and specialty. We think the first-time visitor will want to take an escorted tour to get a good overview for the best price. The absolute minimum stay for a first-time visitor in New Zealand would be 8 or 9 days.

Day 1 — Arrive Auckland (if you're coming from anywhere but Australia). Overnight in Auckland.

Day 2 — Visit Waitomo Caves on the way to Rotorua. Overnight in Rotorua.

Day 3 — Rotorua.

Day 4 — Fly to Christchurch. Overnight.

Day 5 — Drive to Mt. Cook. Overnight.

Day 6 — Drive to Queenstown.

Day 7 — Queenstown to Te Anau.

Day 8 — Te Anau. Side trip to Milford Sound.

Day 9 — Return to Queenstown to depart country.

Climate/When to Go

North Island is warmer than South Island by at least 10 degrees F/5 C year round. Auckland always has fairly mild temperatures. During their summer (November–March), the highs are in the 80s F/28–32 C and the lows in the 60s–70s F/15–27 C. In winter (May–October), day temperatures will be in the 50s–60s F/10–22 C, with nights in the 40s–50s F/5–14 C. Our favorite months are mid-September through October, when the flowers and apple trees are in bloom, dotting the greenest-of-green countryside. Take a sweater year round. There's skiing July–September on South Island.

Transportation

Air New Zealand, United, Qantas and Continental fly from the U.S., and Air New Zealand and Canadian Airlines International fly from Canada. We recommend stopovers in Tahiti, Hawaii, Fiji or the Cook Islands to break up this terribly long flight from the U.S. — about 16 hours nonstop. Air New Zealand, Mt. Cook and other local airlines fly between domestic cities. Auckland International Airport (AKL) is 15 mi/26 km south of Auckland. Transport is by taxi and airline or hotel coaches. Several freighters and shipping lines also sail between islands. You can take freighters to New Zealand from the U.S., but that can take a long time (possibly a month). Superb bus service on each island connects major and smaller cities. Kiwi Coach Passes, available both in the U.S./Canada and in New Zealand, allow unlimited bus travel for periods ranging from 8 to 22 days. Escorted and hosted tours, trains, rental cars, campers and bicycles are all popular ways to tour the country.

Accommodations

Accommodations range from deluxe to local inns, lodges, trailers (or caravans) to hostels and campgrounds. New Zealand lends itself to bed-and-breakfasts, primarily because the people are so friendly. It's also possible, through a travel agent or the New Zealand Tourist and Publicity Office, to arrange a stay with someone who shares the traveler's interests or occupation. Around Mt. Cook, plan to stay in Queenstown or smaller towns nearby — there aren't many hotels at the site. Our favorite hotel at Mt. Cook (and everyone else's) is the Hermitage. The Milford Sound Hotel is closest to the fjords and is sold out well in advance; if you can't get in, stay in Te Anau and take a day trip to Milford Sound. For travelers interested in extended tramping, the government provides several categories of huts along the trails

Geostats

Official Name: New Zealand.

Visa Info: Passport needed by U.S. and Canadian citizens for stay up to three months. Onward ticket and visa (if needed) for the next destination as well as sufficient funds for visit required. Reconfirm with carrier before departure.

Health Certificates: None required. Check with health authorities for the latest information.

Capital: Wellington.

Population: 3,344,000.

Size: 103,736 sq mi/269,063 sq km. About the size of Colorado.

Languages: English, Maori.

Climate: Temperate.

Economy: Services, industry, agriculture (exports beef, wool, dairy products).

Government: Parliamentary democracy.

Religions: Anglican, Presbyterian, Roman Catholic.

Currency: New Zealand dollar (NZD). 100 cents = 1 NZD.

Time Zone: 17 hours ahead of EST. 12 hours ahead of GMT.

Electricity: 220 volts.

for overnight stays. They are occupied on a first-come, first-served basis.

Health Advisories

Western health standards are adhered to and good medical facilities are available. There are no special food, health or drink precautions necessary.

What to Buy

Shop for paua-shell jewelry, Maori woodcarvings, recorded music, sheepskin rugs, sweaters, greenstone jewelry and items carved from *kauri*, *rumi* or other native woods.

What to Eat

Most restaurant food is heavily influenced by the British. There are also excellent local foods, such as oysters, venison, kiwi fruit (of course), passion fruit, *kumara* (sweet potatoes, a Maori staple) and a wonderful dessert called a *pavlova* (an incredibly sweet meringue "cake" flavored with passion fruit). Lamb and *hogget* (one-year-old lamb) is delicious. Lately there has been a trend toward more elegant gourmet cuisine, which can be found in the major cities and the more remote luxury lodges. "Entree" on the menu means appetizer, not the main dish (called, clearly enough, "Main").

Travel Tips for the Client

Don't be surprised by all the rain, especially in the many mountainous areas . . . Don't forget that traffic

More Fascinating Facts About New Zealand

In common with many other island nations (especially in the South Pacific), New Zealand has many types of flora and fauna that are found nowhere else on Earth (such as the flightless kiwi and the extremely rare kakapo birds). It also has no snakes and relatively few insects — but do watch out for hungry mosquitoes and sand flies . . . The now-extinct moas would have to have been New Zealand's most exotic bird; some of these ostrich-like creatures reached heights of 14 ft/ 4 m . . . When people say, "*Kia ora*," they're welcoming you . . . Author Douglas Adams called New Zealand's southern region "one of the most astounding pieces of land anywhere on God's earth, and one's first impulse, standing on a clifftop surveying it all, is simply to burst into spontaneous applause" . . . Backpackers should purchase the Backpacker's Pass, which includes coupons for ground transportation throughout the country, including special services for hard-to-reach areas. The pass is available from travel agents in New Zealand. . . .

moves on the left, and watch for signs saying Camera in the left-turn lane. It is illegal to make turns on a red light, and the camera photographs those who do. Fines go as high as NZ$250, although the police tend to be a little more lenient with tourists in rented cars . . . Don't be obnoxious about taking pictures of the Maoris in Rotorua. It *is* their home, and their privacy should be respected . . . Do go to a sheep station and watch sheep shearing, if it's the right time of year. . . .

Tipping: Don't tip, as service charges at restaurants are unheard of. Taxi drivers never expect a tip.

New Zealand

Review Questions

1. Who are the Kiwis?

2. In which city would a tourist see two harbors ringed by 14 extinct volcanoes?

3. Why is the town of Waitangi important in New Zealand's 19th-century history?

4. What does Mt. Hutt offer visitors?

5. What is grinding its way down Mt. Cook?

6. Near what sound are New Zealand's fjords located?

7. Why does it smell so bad in Rotorua?

8. What makes a visit to Waitomo Caves unforgettable and eerie?

9. Why does New Zealand lend itself to bed-and-breakfast accommodations?

10. About how many hours is a nonstop flight from the U.S. to New Zealand?

New Zealand

Map Skills Exercise

Match the tourist destination listed below with the corresponding letter on the map. You can use each letter only once.

1. _____ Bay of Islands
2. _____ Christchurch
3. _____ Wellington
4. _____ Waitomo Caves
5. _____ Mt. Cook
6. _____ Rotorua
7. _____ Milford Sound
8. _____ Auckland
9. _____ Queenstown

Selling Exercises

Your office is hosting an open house featuring Adventure Travel. Each agent is responsible for selecting and promoting a specific destination that will appeal to this target market. You decide to focus on New Zealand with its variety of spectacular sights and recreational activities. Create a flyer that you might hand out to prospective clients that includes a list of things to do as well as an eye-catching picture (just describe the picture you'd use) that symbolizes adventure travel in New Zealand.

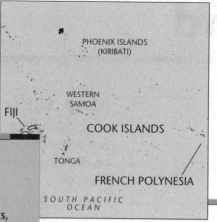

French Polynesia

Fiji and the Cook Islands

A lmost everyone who beholds French Polynesia agrees: Earth's landscape just doesn't get any prettier. The vibrantly green vegetation and dramatic mountains that soar out of the crystal water form the perfect portrait of the South Pacific. Of course, getting there seems to take forever, and some parts of Tahiti are crowded, rundown and dirty. Service often seems lax by Western standards. But don't let those things scare you off. We think you'll find, especially if you go beyond Tahiti, something close to paradise.

The whole island chain is sometimes incorrectly referred to as "Tahiti," but French Polynesia actually consists of 115 islands (though Tahiti is the most populous by far). Many are flat coral atolls, but the most beautiful islands are volcanic mountains, dramatically thrust up from the sea and covered with lush vegetation. The chain is located in the South Pacific, 4,100 mi/6,600 km southwest of Los Angeles, California, and 3,800 mi/6,100 km northeast of Sydney, Australia.

What to Do There

Bora Bora   James Michener described Bora Bora as "the most beautiful island in the world." You'll see why: The clear blue-green water, reefs, jagged volcanic peaks, palm trees and lush vegetation will leave you speechless. The island's airport sits on a coral ring that surrounds the main island, so as soon as you arrive you'll be treated to a 30-minute boat ride across the lagoon. The side of the island facing away from the airport is the prettiest, but none of it is ugly. There's snorkeling, picnicking on the beach, motorbiking — plenty of opportunities for relaxation. You can even make an excursion to watch the feeding of the black-fin reef sharks.

Cruises/Freighters   There are several island-hopping tour boats, which embark from Tahiti for the less-frequented islands. If you have at least three weeks, take the freighter *Aranui* or the cheaper, more basic and less reliable *Taporo V* to the Marquesas Islands (*see separate paragraph*). The *Aranui* sails to the islands in northern French

Polynesia from Papeete about every four weeks, allowing passengers an opportunity to see the islands that have no airports. Few visitors ever get this glimpse of true Polynesia. The deluxe, 148-passenger sail cruiser *Wind Song* travels weekly from Tahiti to Moorea, Bora Bora and other islands.

Huahine

This island has been open to tourists for a relatively short time, and it's consequently more basic and natural than some of the others. Scattered throughout the island are *maraes* (ancient temples) and important archaeological sites. Huahine is our favorite island in the territory: It's just modern enough, just uncrowded enough, just easy enough to get to and just untouristy enough to convince us that old Polynesia still exists.

Marquesas Islands

These islands are geographically among the world's most remote. However, there is a reward for those who persevere and go there: The Marquesas are beautiful and rugged. Waves pound at the base of jagged, volcanic cliffs, and it's often windy, foggy and cool-to-almost-cold. The people live much as they have for centuries. With several flights now arriving in the Marquesas, the islands feel somewhat less remote than before.

The most populous island (1,120 residents) is Hiva Oa. The artist Paul Gauguin spent the last years of his life there and the most visited site on the island is Gauguin's grave, set in a hilltop cemetery.

Moorea

The island of Moorea is quickly reached from Papeete by ferry or plane. It's a terrific place to spend several nights, with its white-sand beaches, turquoise lagoons, coconut palms and volcanic peaks shooting straight into the air from the water. Geared to tourists, Moorea offers a variety of excellent hotels, transportation and restaurants and is quite relaxed, having none of the traffic jams, noise and air pollution of Papeete. You can get around the island by car or moped, and with either, be sure to take the road leading into the interior for the view of Cook's Bay and Opunohu Bay from the Belvedere Lookout. There are also interesting marae ruins and stone archery platforms in the Upunohu Valley at the center of the island.

Raiatea

Raiatea is a tall volcanic island whose central mountains reach heights of 3,350 ft/1,000 m. Include in your visit Uturoa, the largest town on the island, on a market day, when the whole island turns out to shop and trade and greet the commercial freighters

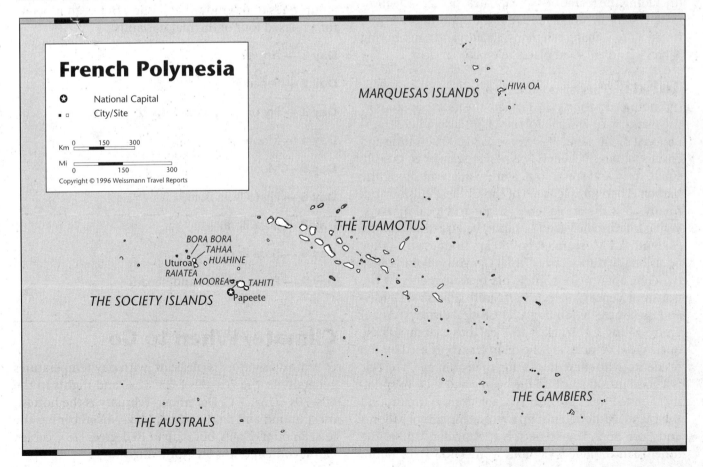

A beach in Tahiti

delivering fresh food and picking up islanders' creations. Rent a bike to ride south along the 50-mi/80-km partially paved road, past the lagoon scenery to see *maraes* (including the Marae of Taputapuatea, perhaps the most sacred *marae* in all Polynesia). If the opportunity arises, watch a fire-walking ceremony. Raiatea and neighboring Tahaa Island are good places to charter a yacht.

Tahiti This island and its principal city, Papeete (pronounced pah-pay-AY-tay), are the most populous in the territory of French Polynesia; it's also where international flights land. Papeete (pop. 30,000), bustling and cosmopolitan by French Polynesian standards, is fairly small, dirty and spread out. Start with a walk along the harbor. Then sample some of the Chinese cuisine and, finally, visit the art galleries, shops and local markets. While touring the island of Tahiti, be sure to stop at the Gauguin Art Museum (30 mi/50 km from town — they occasionally display an original Gauguin), Point Venus (where Captain Cook made his measurements of the transit of Venus), the Harrison Smith Botanical Garden and the Musee de Tahiti (good historical displays). You'll enjoy riding Le Truck, the local bus system. These open-sided vehicles are the main transport used by the residents (who sometimes bring their animals). The ride is a good introduction to the people and their hospitality. Guided tours are also available for the trip around the island. Although not up to the standards of Moorea and Bora Bora, the scenery is spectacular. Unlike the other islands, there is nightlife as we know it on Tahiti.

Itinerary

French Polynesia is really not a place to go if you're in a hurry; it's to be enjoyed at leisure. Here's an itinerary for a relaxed tour of the major islands.

Day 1 — Arrive Papeete.

Day 2 — Papeete.

Day 3 — Fly or (we prefer) ferry to Moorea.

Day 4 — Moorea.

Day 5 — Moorea.

Day 6 — Fly to Bora Bora.

Day 7 — Bora Bora.

Day 8 — Bora Bora.

Day 9 — Fly to Papeete and depart.

Climate/When to Go

Almost any time is pleasant, with day temperatures generally in the 70s–80s F/23–32 C and nights in the 60s–70s F/15–27 C. December–February is the hottest, most humid and rainiest time; May–November has the least amount of rain, but is up to 10 degrees F/5 C cooler. Our favorite months are April–August.

Transportation

Air France, Air New Zealand, Hawaiian Air, Qantas and Air Minerve fly from the U.S. There is no direct service from Canada. Our favorite way to visit the region is on a Polynesian Airlines Polypass. The pass flies you to the South Pacific from Los Angeles or Hawaii and then allows unlimited travel between Tahiti, the Cook Islands, Fiji, Tonga, Noumea and Niue as well as round-trip tickets to Australia and New Zealand. Air Tahiti flies between many of the islands and has an "air pass" program that allows you to make a circuit of the islands at a favorable rate, compared with the cost of regular one-way or round-trip flights. All international flights land at Faaa International Airport (PPT), 4 mi/6 km west of Papeete. Major cruise lines include various islands on their itineraries from the U.S. to Australia/New Zealand, though few offer one-way passage. There's reliable ferry and once- or twice-weekly boat service between many of the islands. Wind Song Cruises offers regular week long itineraries to some of the more popular islands and,

occasionally, extends the sailing to the Marquesas (depending on the level of its bookings). Le Truck on Tahiti is the local bus service; flag it down as it goes by. There is no regular bus service elsewhere. Car, motorbike and bicycle rentals are popular on major islands.

Accommodations

Accommodations range from deluxe (though not high-rise) to trashy. On some islands, the only lodging is in private homes, which is usually quite basic, but clean. To avoid possible hassles, it's advisable to stay in as deluxe a property as possible — but even the "deluxe" hotels vary widely in amenities. Except on Tahiti, most hotel rooms are in thatched-roof bungalows. The price of accommodations in French Polynesia can be compared with the cost of a stay in the Hawaiian Islands.

Health Advisories

On the larger islands, many of the doctors and dentists speak English, but if you get really ill on the outer islands, you'll most likely be flown to Papeete. The tap water should be safe to drink in the major hotels and better restaurants.

What to Buy

Shop for bathing suits and French clothing, colorful local fabrics and clothes, Tahitian artifacts, tikis and other woodcarvings, jewelry (pearl and shell) and local art. Wonderful shops in Papeete have a wide variety of goods (from perfumes to Melanesian masks), but they're expensive.

What to Eat

There are marvelous Chinese, French and Tahitian restaurants, though you'd be foolish not to concentrate on seafood dishes. Local specialties include fish marinated in coconut milk, *fafa* (a pork and chicken casserole with coconut milk) and *aua'a chous* (a cabbage and pork combination). Other common dishes are escargot, curry, rice and fresh tropical fruits. Prices for meals are comparable with those in most large American cities. If at all possible, attend a *tamaaraa* (a feast similar to a luau); the music, dance and activities guarantee a good time.

Geostats

Official Name: French Polynesia.

Visa Info: U.S. and Canadian citizens need passports. Obtain visas for stays of longer than 90 days. Reconfirm with carrier before departure.

Health Certificates: Yellow-fever certificate required if coming from an infected area; contact health authorities for latest information.

Capital: Papeete.

Population: 201,000 (more than half on Tahiti).

Size: Land area is 1,544 sq mi/3,999 sq km (a bit larger than Rhode Island), spread out across an expanse half the size of the U.S.

Languages: French, Tahitian, English.

Climate: Tropical.

Economy: Tourism, coconuts, mother-of-pearl, vanilla beans.

Government: French Overseas Territory.

Religions: Protestant, Catholic.

Currency: Pacific French franc (CFP).

Time Zone: 5 hours behind EST. 10 hours behind GMT.

Travel Tips for the Client

Do take everything you need (from film to sunblock) if you want to escape higher prices . . . Do not go swimming at just any beach you come across. Because of rip tides, sharks and pollution, travelers should only swim at beaches where others are swimming . . . Don't expect room, hotel and restaurant service to meet high standards. They reflect the relaxed way of life of the islands . . . Don't go to French Polynesia if you're not a romantic. For some, the inconvenience, expense and uneven service can block even the beauty of the islands . . . Do book flights there early, as they're often full weeks in advance. . . .

Tipping: Do not tip; it goes against Tahitian notions of hospitality. Do bring T-shirts, caps, etc., to thank residents who have assisted you in various ways.

Fiji

Fiji is a melting pot of Melanesian, Polynesian and Indian cultures. While its scenery isn't as dramatic as that of some Pacific islands, it's attractive for other reasons: Its prices are low and its people are among the friendliest in the Pacific. (Almost half of the islanders are descended from laborers brought from India by the British to work on sugar plantations.)

Located 1,300 miles east of Australia, the Fiji archipelago is made up of thousands of islands. The two largest, Viti Levu and Vanua Levu, are covered with sharp peaks and rock outcroppings. Those looking for beautiful water and slow-paced island life will enjoy Fiji, but they should be aware that other Pacific islands have more lush, tropical scenery. Some of the world's top diving areas (Great White Wall and Rainbow Reef) are located off Taveuni Island.

What to Do There

Cruises   Short cruises (mostly from Nadi and Lautoka) are fun and popular. The Beachcomber Cruise includes swimming, snorkeling and a buffet lunch on a beach on Beachcomber Island. A full-day ride on a glass-bottom boat is available for an extra fee.

Nadi   While the city of Nadi on Viti Levu doesn't really offer much, the beauty of the surrounding region and the offshore islands is reason enough to at least pass through. Cruises depart from Nadi and nearby Lautoka. Just outside of Lautoka is the Garden of the Sleeping Giant, an orchid garden that once belonged to actor Raymond Burr. Either city can be used as a base to explore the sugar plantations, Sabeto Valley (beautiful mountain scenery), and the Sigatoka Valley (an Indian settlement).

Suva   The capital, Suva, is on the southeast coast of the main island of Viti Levu. You'll need a day to see this bustling port city. Climb Tamavua Ridge for a magnificent panoramic view, and stop at the market to shop for local goods. Don't miss Fiji Museum, which contains a wonderful collection of Fijian artifacts as well as relics from the *Bounty,* of *Mutiny on the Bounty* fame. If time permits, walk down Victoria Parade and see the gardens. Suva has good restaurants, duty-free shopping, and plenty of nightlife.

Vanua Levu   The second-largest Fijian island, Vanua Levu offers coconut plantations, striking mountains and bays, tropical foliage and total relaxation. Most visitors head to sleepy little Savusavu and its gorgeous harbor and to nearby beaches for snorkeling and scuba diving.

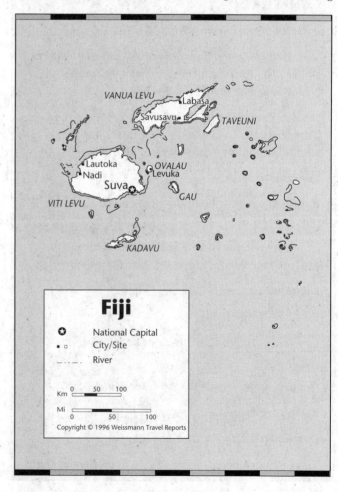

Savusavu now has excellent accommodations. The mountain road between Labasa and Savusavu is spectacular.

Travel Trips for the Client

Do attend a fire-walking ceremony. Fijian fire walking is performed at the hotels for tourists. Though totally commercial, it's still fascinating . . . Do attend a *meke*, where Fijian legends are acted out by costumed dancers . . . Don't waste your time with sword-sellers, young men on the streets who try to sell you poor wood carvings . . . The Pacific Harbour Resort has an excellent 18-hole golf course. Tennis is very popular, and most hotels have courts. . . .

Cook Islands

The Cook Islands are a protectorate of New Zealand, and most islanders speak English. Maoris, who are descendants of the original Polynesians, today make up the majority of the population.

The Cook Islands are a beautiful sampling of the South Pacific, but lately they're becoming more crowded as increasing numbers of tourists arrive. The islands are located about halfway between Hawaii and New Zealand. Gorgeous scenery, deep-sea fishing (primarily off Rarotonga), dances, snorkeling/scuba diving, volcanic peaks, beaches and lagoons are some of the islands' foremost attractions.

What to Do There

Aitutaki Aitutaki is about an hour's flight from Rarotonga, the main island. Aitutaki has a wide lagoon that we rank as one of the loveliest in the world. Be sure to hire a motorbike to explore the island and then snorkel in the lagoon. Or take a catamaran ride. Serious anglers can try their hand at saltwater fly-fishing while golfers will enjoy Aitutaki's golf course. Most visitors see Aitutaki as a day trip from Rarotonga.

Rarotonga Rarotonga, where most visitors stay, is rather small (67 sq mi/108 sq km) and a little crowded. Avarua, the main town, is very compact and easy to see on foot — it's laid out along the harbor. A good way to get oriented to the island is to take a day and bicycle or motorbike around. If you're in good physical condition, hike across the island to see the view from the base of the Needle (Te Rua Manga), a 1,355-ft/413-m volcanic spire. Also visit Ngatangilia Harbor (where the Polynesians left for New Zealand). The rusting hull of the *Yankee,* an old brigantine, lies on a reef there. Other destinations include the Avarua museum and the Philatelic Bureau (stamps). It's also fun to swim at Muri Lagoon. And visit the Araiatiu-Te-Tonga stone sacrificial altars just east of town.

Travel Tips for the Client

Don't be surprised, upon arrival, if someone goes through the plane spraying insecticide. Nothing personal — they're just trying to keep bugs from their fruit trees . . . Do take a collapsible umbrella, as it rains periodically . . . Do bring your own film; it's quite expensive on the islands . . . Don't bargain. It is not considered part of Polynesian culture . . . Protestant fundamentalism is very strong in the islands. One tour conductor was suspended for a year after taking tourists on a Sunday boat outing. . . .

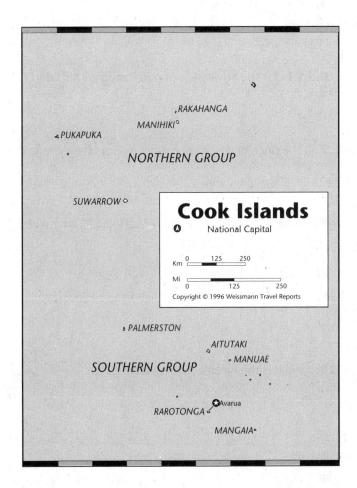

French Polynesia, Fiji and the Cook Islands

Review Questions

1. What island did James Michener say is "the most beautiful . . . in the world"?

2. Why is Huahine among the most basic and natural of islands in French Polynesia?

3. The Upunohu Valley, with ruins and stone archery platforms, is in the center of what island in French Polynesia?

4. What happens in Uturoa, on the island of Raiatea, on market day?

5. What is Le Truck?

6. What is the advantage of purchasing an Air Tahiti "air pass?"

7. The price of accommodations in French Polynesia compares with the price of a stay in the _____ Islands.

8. What kind of attractions are located off Taveuni Island in Fiji?

9. Why do visitors to Vanua Levu head to Savusavu?

10. What is the Needle? Where is it?

French Polynesia, Fiji and the Cook Islands

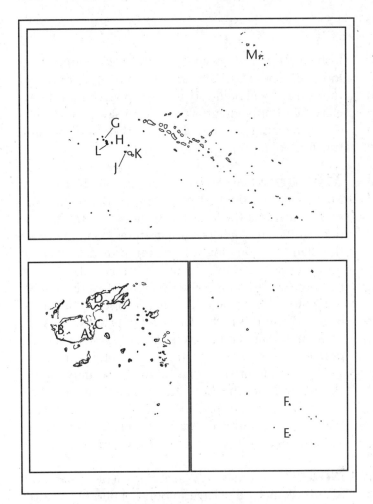

Map Skills Exercise

Match the tourist destination listed below with the corresponding letter on the map. You can use each letter only once.

1. _____ Tahiti
2. _____ Moorea
3. _____ Bora Bora
4. _____ Marquesas Islands
5. _____ Suva
6. _____ Nadi
7. _____ Rarotonga
8. _____ Aitutaki

Selling Exercises

Clients of your travel agency are going to stop by to discuss a trip to the South Pacific. They are considering visiting French Polynesia, Fiji or the Cook Islands and would like to know what there is to do and see in these destinations. Select three selling features for each island group and then briefly describe how each feature would appeal to your clients.

Oceania Geofile

American Samoa   American Samoa is a bit of the U.S. in Polynesia. These five volcanic islands and two coral atolls offer mountainous scenery, beaches and deep-sea fishing. They're more beautiful than nearby Western Samoa but they should only be recommended to clients who want to see a South Pacific island and don't want to forgo North American comforts. Many people who go to Polynesia do so with the intention of immersing themselves in a non-Western culture, and they'll only be irritated by all the reminders of home in American Samoa.

Guam   If you think Guam doesn't much resemble the visions of paradise conjured up by the song Bali Hai, you're right. Compared with the other islands in the Pacific, Guam seems to have been cheated out of its fair share of natural wonders. On the other hand, its new-found prosperity has created an abundance of visitor attractions, and the increased air service and year-round summer have attracted enough additional visitors to justify all the construction. Guam's charm is revealed in flashes in patches of hilly jungles, in a few of its beaches, and in its ragged coastline and rocky cliffs.

Kiribati   The republic of Kiribati (pronounced KIR-ee-bas) stretches across nearly 2,000 mi/3,219 km of the central Pacific Ocean. Although the snorkeling/diving and deep-sea fishing are good to excellent, this chain of islands doesn't have the lush, mountainous scenery that some Pacific nations feature. (Kiribati is made up almost entirely of coral atolls. The highest point barely reaches 6 ft/2 m above sea level.) While there may be better scenery and beaches in other South Pacific locales, we found the Kiribati residents fascinating, especially in villages off the beaten path; they're very friendly, and their culture has not been changed very much by outside influences. The least complicated way to island-hop across the country is by private yacht, but it is possible to see a few of the major islands by using regularly scheduled boat or plane service. The island of Tarawa in Kiribati was the scene of a bitter battle in World War II between the Japanese and the Americans.

Marshall Islands   If you're looking for a paradise of beautiful beaches on crystal clear lagoons with lush, mountainous scenery in the background, keep looking. The Marshalls aren't really developed for tourism and will hold very limited appeal for most travelers. Send only clients who like to say they've been everywhere in the world (and even they won't want to stay for long).

Micronesia   We've met divers who believe that Micronesia has the best dive spots in the world. And we'll vouch that the land-side scenery is nothing short of magnificent. These physical features, combined with the islands' fascinating culture, can provide a wonderful, remote vacation. Several of the islands — most notably Kosrae, Pohnpei and the Chuuk Islands — measure up to anyone's definition of paradise, but it should be noted that this particular brand of paradise does not have all the standard conveniences of Western civilization. (For many, of course, that's part of the attraction.)

The islands offer a wide range of scenery. Some, almost level with the water, are coral atolls, while others feature high volcanic peaks. Beautiful reefs, rugged coastline, stunning waterfalls, crashing waves and lush, tropical jungles are all part of the Micronesian experience.

Nauru   Nauru is truly an ecological nightmare. The island is composed of large amounts of phosphate, a salt used in making fertilizers. And after 86 years of mining, it has been almost hollowed out, leaving little but a wasteland of massive pits and coral spikes. We don't recommend it to anyone, except maybe those with a bizarre interest in mining.

By the year 2000, the phosphate supply will have been exhausted. At one time, plans were made for all the people of Nauru to abandon the island and move elsewhere. Recently, however, many of the residents decided they wanted to stay. But even if tons of topsoil are shipped in, we think Nauru will continue to have limited appeal as a tourist destination.

New Caledonia   New Caledonia is a land of contrasts: The western (leeward) side of this island (250 mi/400 km long and 31 mi/50 km wide) is arid, while the eastern (windward) side features waterfalls, lush fern forests, crystal clear lagoons, palm-tree-lined beaches and scenic, rugged mountain roads. Three islands (Mare,

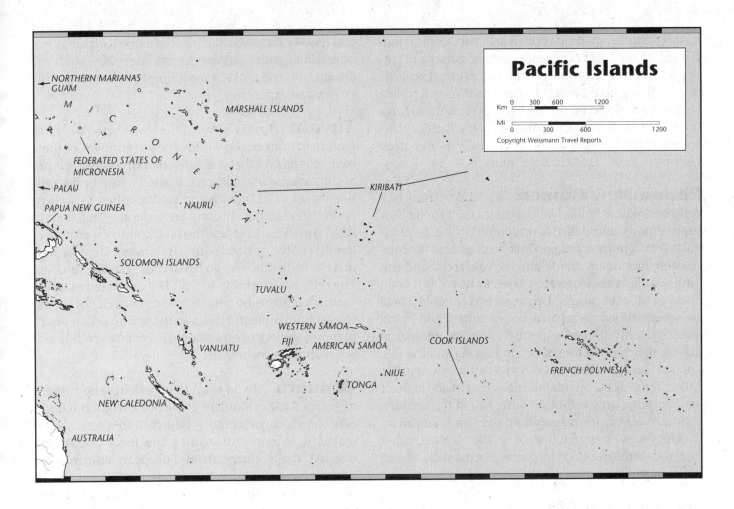

Lifou and Ouvea) lie just off the east coast and two (Ile des Pins and Ile Ouen) off the south coast. All of these are lush, with beautiful, unspoiled beaches that offer a relaxing, if slightly primitive, vacation. New Caledonia experiences occasional civil unrest related to its Melanesian population's desire for independence from France, but things have calmed considerably since the mid-'80s. The islands offer superlative scuba diving (with 150-ft/46-m visibility), limestone caves, spectacular beaches, interesting blends of European and Melanesian cultures and a casino. It's a very informal destination, with mostly basic hotels and all the inconveniences, delays, etc., of developing countries, yet it's somewhat expensive.

Niue

Niue is a pretty little island in the middle of nowhere. Like most dots in the South Pacific, it has clear, clean water, good snorkeling and friendly people. What sets it apart are the jagged limestone cliffs that ring the island. In some places they rise more than 20 ft/6 m above the waves, and their cracks and crevices hold spectacular caves and isolated swimming holes. The foreboding fortress look that the cliffs give the island may be the reason British explorers dubbed it the Savage Rock.

Niue is not a typical South Pacific island. It has no rivers and relatively few beaches; its waters are extremely deep and clear (visibility up to 300 ft/90 m), and it's nearly surrounded by a coral reef. The reef doesn't protect the island's eastern coast, where pounding waves lash at the rocks. On the island's central plateau is a rain forest filled with ebony and other hardwoods.

Northern Marianas

This U.S. Commonwealth comprises several islands that form an arc in the eastern Pacific Ocean north of Guam. The names of two of the 14 major islands, Saipan and Tinian, will be familiar to those who lived through World War II; the battle to liberate Saipan was an important victory for the Allies in the Pacific theater, and it was from Tinian that planes took off to make that fateful journey over Hiroshima. Today, the islands are known not only for historic sites, but also for their beautiful water, snorkeling, diving and windsurfing.

Palau

More than one seasoned traveler has pronounced Palau to be the most beautiful spot in the world, and it's certainly near the top of anyone's list. Gorgeous mountainous scenery, stunning caves, dramatic waterfalls, rocky coastlines, inviting beaches and lush, tropical jungles define the Palau experience. Deep-sea divers, in particular, will be in heaven in Palau as there are excellent reefs, a diving hole 100 ft/30 m deep, a dive wall (called Ngemelis) and several underwater caves. Although it's not as well known as other paradises of the Pacific, plans are on several drawing boards to bring divers and other visitors to these islands in large numbers.

Papua New Guinea
It's hard to think of a destination more unlike North America than Papua New Guinea (pronounced POP-oo-wah noo GIN-ee). Its physical beauty is tropical and primitive, with isolated beaches, volcanic mountains, dense jungles, wild rivers and colorful, exotic birds. Its greatest asset, however, is its rich blend of tribal traditions, languages and cultures. There are several thousand separate communities, and many have had only limited exposure to the technological developments taken for granted in Canada and the U.S. Though Europeans first explored the coastal regions in the 1400s, some of the Highlands tribes have made contact with outsiders only within the latter half of this century. Unfortunately, crime plagues both cities and rural areas. For safety reasons, suggest that clients take escorted, rather than independent or FIT, programs. Bougainville Island, site of much civil unrest, should be avoided.

Solomon Islands
The islands that make up the Solomons consist primarily of lush, tree-covered mountains where hot and humid conditions prevail. The islands' features include good beaches and great diving as well as jungle walks, canoeing, fishing and World War II battle sites. Send only experienced travelers who have been to the eastern South Pacific and want to learn more about island cultures, who like isolation, or who, perhaps, were there during World War II and want to return (one of its islands, Guadalcanal, was the site of a fierce battle).

Tonga
Tonga is no longer off the beaten path. Airlines are offering more flights to the island nation (some fly directly from Los Angeles) or are including it in (relatively) inexpensive tours of Polynesia. This is good news for travelers, because Tonga is unique among Pacific islands. It offers fascinating historical sights, beautiful coral reefs and reasonable prices. Unlike other islands in the Pacific, Tonga was never colonized by a European power. To this day, it is much less developed and less Westernized than its neighbors. Tonga may not offer deluxe resorts or Western-style amenities, but it will appeal to those looking for a simpler, more authentic Polynesian experience.

Tuvalu
Tuvalu is one of the least visited and most remote nations in the world. The government of these nine islands says that it is interested in tourism but not at the expense of traditional island culture or the pristine nature of its lagoons and beaches (there's excellent diving/snorkeling). Visitors are welcome, but only in small numbers: Tuvalu is the only country we know of that has only one hotel within its borders. Of those who make it to Tuvalu, few go beyond the capital, Funafuti. The only practical way to visit the inhabited outlying Tuvalu islands is by private yacht, because local boat service is infrequent. However, those who do get out to them will experience traditional Polynesian culture as it exists almost nowhere else.

Vanuatu
If you want to experience the authentic South Pacific, Vanuatu is the place to go. But don't expect a warm welcome — which is, in a sense, what makes it so authentic. Since the local population wrested the country from European control, the islands have gone back to their traditional life — which did not include a lot of tourists wandering around. Stick to the main islands (Efate, Espiritu Santo and Tanna) and you'll be rewarded with a look at a truly traditional culture, beautiful scenery and the timelessness of the South Pacific.

Western Samoa
We greatly prefer Western Samoa to American Samoa, even though it's larger, more heavily populated and less beautiful. The reason is that we go to Polynesia to enjoy Polynesian culture, and that culture is much more alive in Western Samoa than in American Samoa. The country has clearly been influenced by New Zealand (and, by extension, Great Britain), but its culture is generally felt to be the purest of the Polynesian-based civilizations. There's excellent scuba diving, good beaches, deep-sea fishing, good food and plenty of opportunities for relaxation. Although most people interested in the South Pacific will enjoy Western Samoa even if they've never been to any other island, it's a good place to send those who have already visited Hawaii, Tahiti or Fiji, and who want a better understanding of Polynesian culture.

Oceania Geofile

Review Questions

1. To what kind of clients would you recommend a trip to American Samoa?

2. Why should most travelers not visit the Marshall Islands?

3. Why is Nauru an ecological nightmare?

4. To which Pacific nation do Kosrae, Pohnpei, and the Chuuk Islands belong?

5. What set Niue apart from other South Pacific islands?

6. Why might World War II veterans want to visit the Northern Marianas?

7. What is the greatest asset of Papua New Guinea?

8. Why is Tonga unlike other Pacific islands?

9. Why do the few tourists who make it to Tuvalu rarely go beyond its capital, Funafuti?

10. Since the local population of Vanuatu wrested the country from European control, what has happened on these islands?

Oceania Geofile

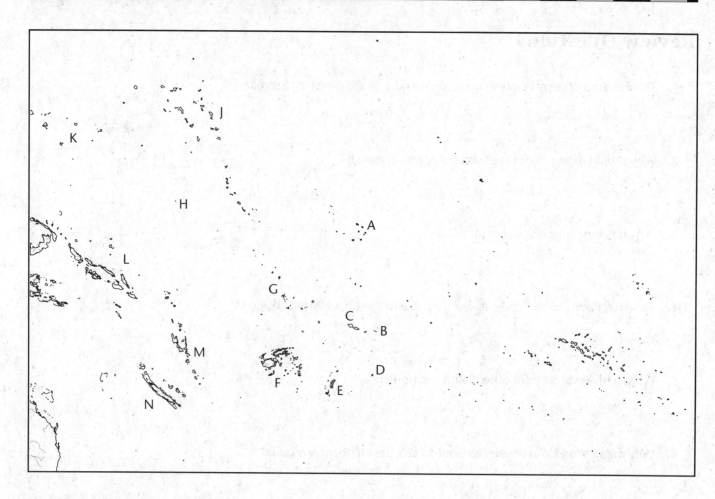

Map Skills Exercise

Match the tourist destination listed below with the corresponding letter on the map.
You can use each letter only once.

1. _____ Tonga
2. _____ Vanuatu
3. _____ Kiribati
4. _____ Western Samoa
5. _____ Nauru

6. _____ New Caledonia
7. _____ Tuvalu
8. _____ Solomon Islands
9. _____ Fiji
10. _____ American Samoa

Unit Review Oceania

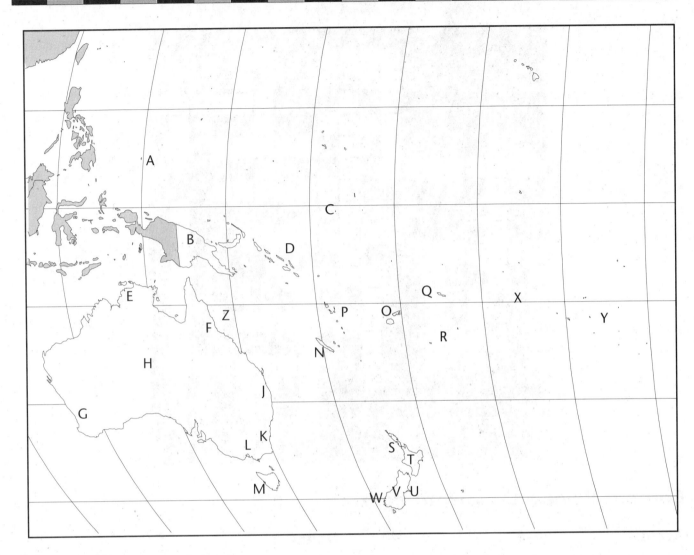

Map Skills Exercise

Match the tourist destination listed below with the corresponding letter on the map.
You can use each letter only once.

1. _____ Ayers Rock
2. _____ Great Barrier Reef
3. _____ Sydney
4. _____ Melbourne
5. _____ Brisbane
6. _____ Auckland
7. _____ Christchurch
8. _____ Mt. Cook
9. _____ Milford Sound
10. _____ Rotorua
11. _____ French Polynesia
12. _____ Cook Islands
13. _____ Fiji

14. _____ Tasmania
15. _____ Cairns
16. _____ Darwin
17. _____ Perth
18. _____ Papua New Guinea
19. _____ New Caledonia
20. _____ Western Samoa
21. _____ Solomon Islands
22. _____ Vanuatu
23. _____ Palau
24. _____ Nauru
25. _____ Tonga

Unit Review Oceania

Content Review Crossword Puzzle

Across

2. Attend a fire-walking ceremony here
4. Principal island in French Polynesia
6. Great Barrier _____
8. Sport in New Zealand
9. Australian animal
10. The interior
12. Most beautiful island, says Michener
13. Jumping-off point
15. Similar to San Diego
18. Moreton Bay bugs
19. Mountains west of Sydney
20. What Australians call themselves

Down

1. Capital of Fiji
2. In Norway and New Zealand
3. San Francisco of the Southern Hemisphere
4. Fly directly there from Los Angeles
5. Do not do this in Tahiti
7. Artist who lived in French Polynesia
11. See them in New Zealand
13. A good way to see Fiji
14. Visit the opera house here
15. Incredibly beautiful
16. Home of the devil
17. Cold month in Australia
21. American and Western

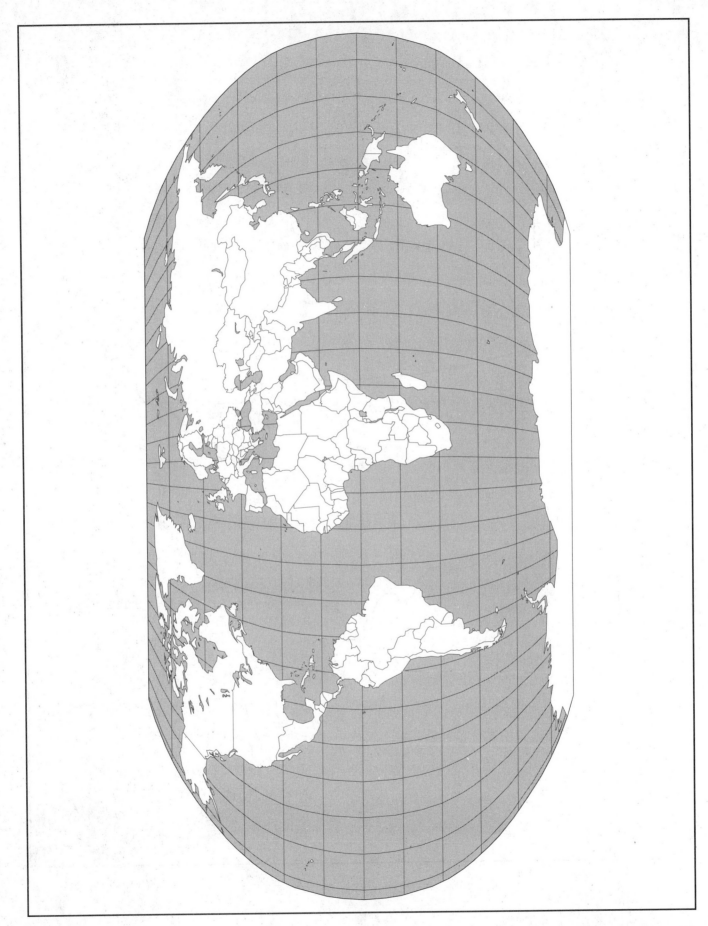

see inset for
Lesser Antilles

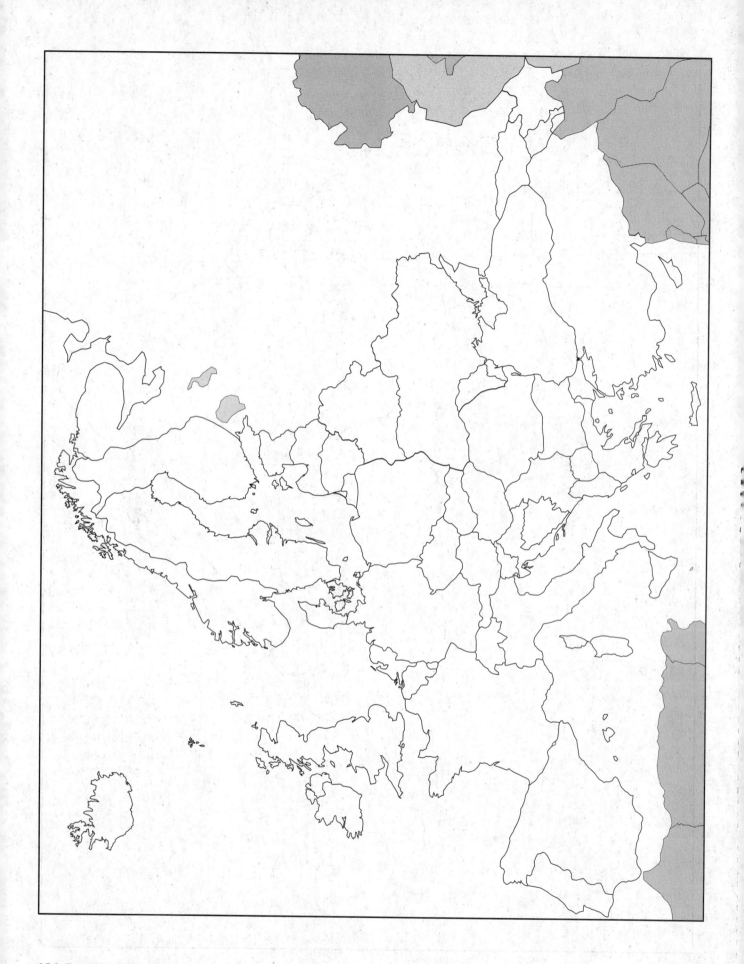

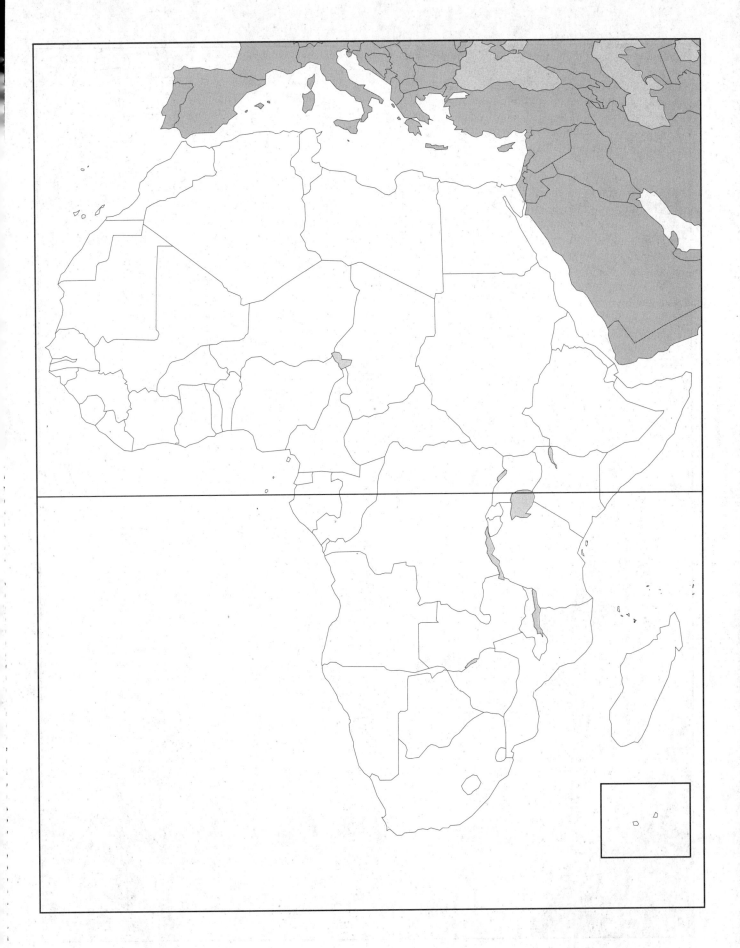

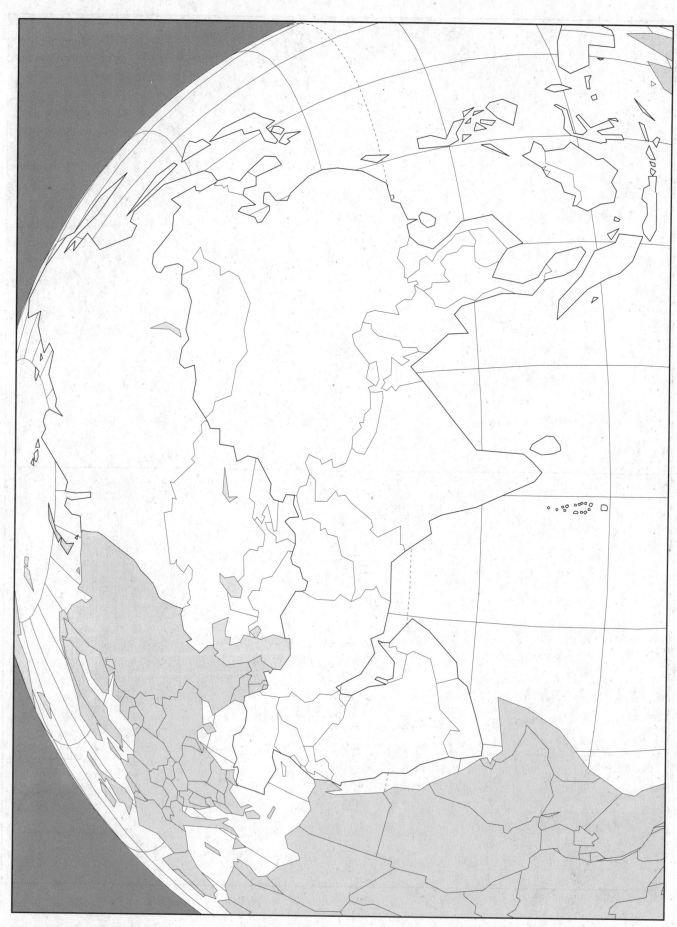

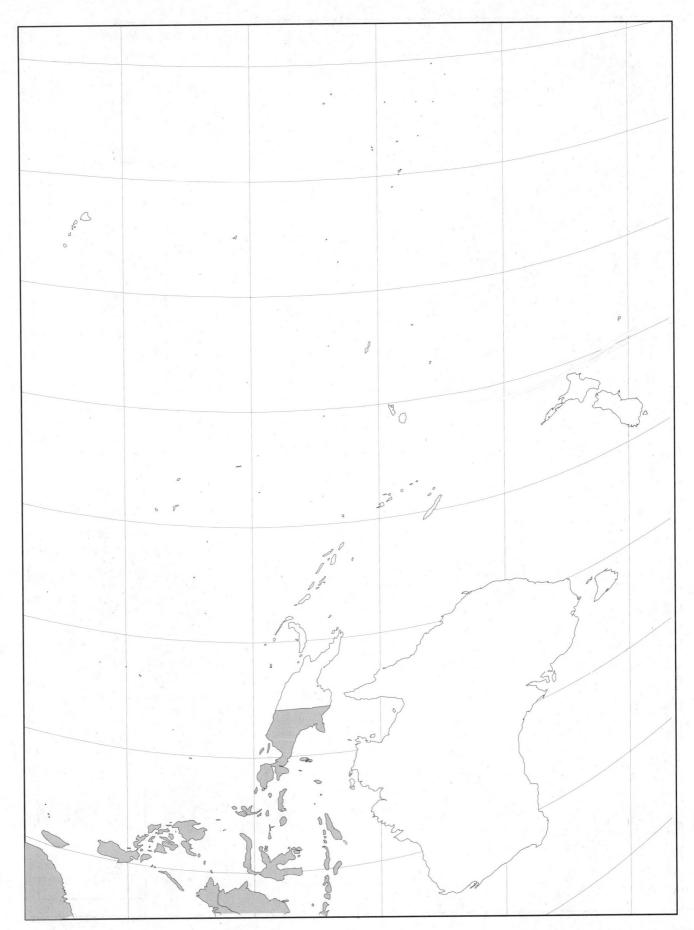

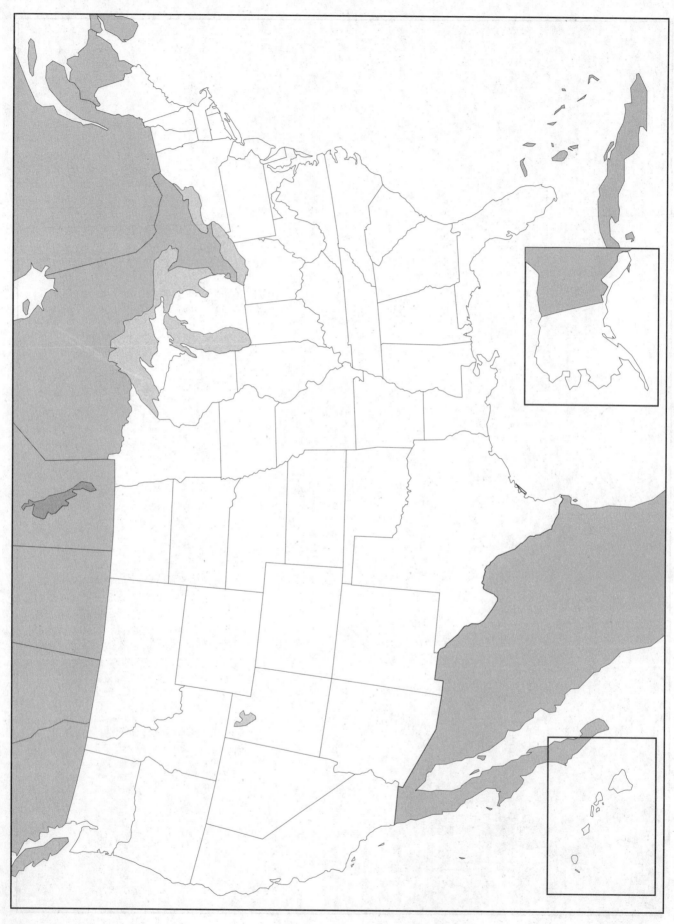

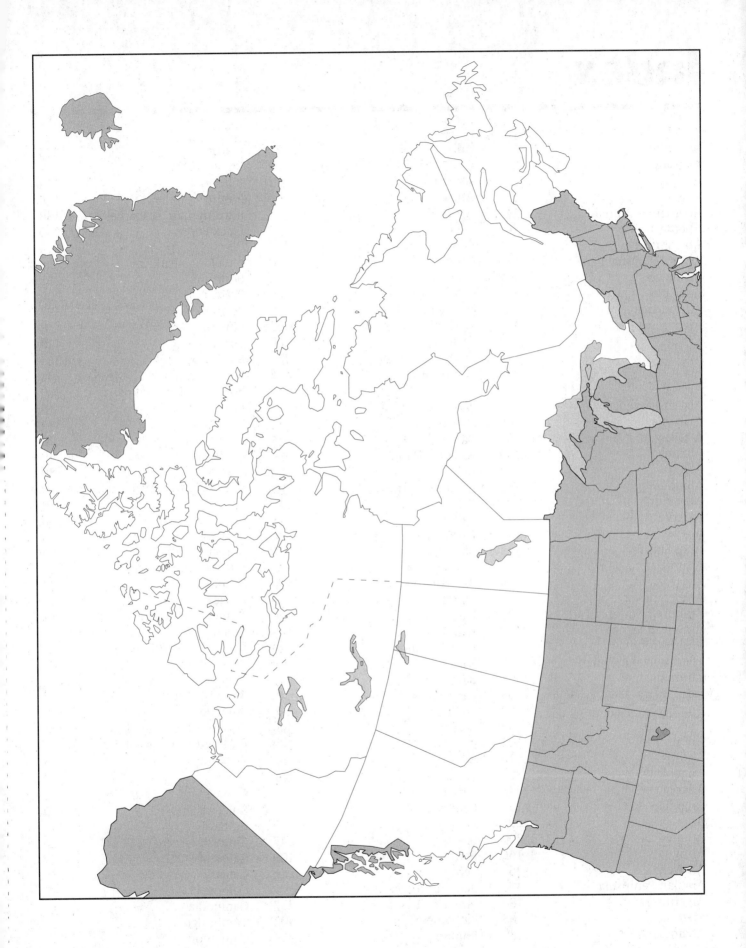

Index

Photo Credits

Aruba Tourism Authority — page 149
Australian Tourist Commission — page 423
Bahamas Tourist Office — page 117
Bermuda Department of Tourism — page 111
British Tourist Authority — page 210
China National Tourist Office — pages 358, 359, 360
Luc-Antoine Couturier — page 79
Drie/Meir — page 87
Egyptian Tourist Office — page 312
French Government Tourist Office — pages 207, 220, 221
Government of India Tourist Authority — pages 393, 395, 398
German Information Center — pages 249, 250, 251
David Gunderson — pages 177, 195
Jo Ann Hardy — pages 309, 331
Banford Harris — pages 162, 313, 355
Hong Kong Tourist Association — pages 366, 368
Israel Ministry of Tourism — pages 404, 405
Italian Government Tourist Board — page 229
Jamaica Tourist Board — page 141
Japan National Tourist Organization — pages 376, 378
Maine Office of Tourism — pages 17, 20
Massachusetts Office of Travel and Tourism — page 18
Mexican Government Tourism Office — page 106
Moroccan Tourist Office — pages 321, 322
Netherlands Board of Tourism — pages 265, 266
New Zealand Tourism Board — pages 432, 433
Norwegian Tourist Board — pages 273, 279
NYS Department of Economic Development — pages 13, 26, 27
Joe Petrocik — page 136
Puerto Rico Tourism Company — pages 97, 124
South Africa Tourism Board — pages 335, 337
Switzerland Tourism — page 257
Tahiti Tourism Board — pages 421, 440
Tourism Authority of Thailand — pages 383, 387
Tourism Halifax — page 74
Tourist Office of Spain — pages 239, 241
U.S. Travel and Tourism Administration — pages 36, 40, 49, 51, 59, 63
Arnie Weissmann and Beth Dupuis — page 327
David Winegar — page 285

Unit Opener Photos

Unit 1 — Arizona Desert
Unit 2 — Brooklyn Bridge and Lower Manhattan
Unit 3 — Beach Scene in Puerto Rico
Unit 4 — High in the Andes Mountains
Unit 5 — The Louvre and I. M. Pei's pyramid
Unit 6 — Kikuyu Villagers in Kenya
Unit 7 — Street Scene in Hanoi
Unit 8 — Children in Tahiti